IDEAS AS WEAPONS

RELATED TITLES FROM POTOMAC BOOKS

Information Operations: Warfare and the Hard Reality of Soft Power
E. Leigh Armistead

Information Warfare: Separating Hype from Reality
E. Leigh Armistead

Asymmetrical Warfare: Today's Challenge to U.S. Military Power
Roger W. Barnett and Stephen J. Cimbala

Undoing Saddam: From Occupation to Sovereignty in Northern Iraq
Wayne H. Bowen

Insurgency and Terrorism: From Revolution to Apocalypse, Second Edition
Bard E. O'Neill

Beating Goliath: Why Insurgencies Win
Jeffrey Record

Nontraditional Warfare: Twenty-First-Century Threats and Responses
William R. Schilling

The War of the Flea: The Classic Study of Guerrilla Warfare
Robert Taber

Chasing Ghosts: Unconventional Warfare in American History
John J. Tierney, Jr.

IDEAS AS WEAPONS

INFLUENCE AND PERCEPTION IN MODERN WARFARE

Edited by G. J. David, Jr., and T. R. McKeldin III

FOREWORD BY
COL H. R. McMASTER, U.S. ARMY

Potomac Books, Inc.
Washington, D.C.

Copyright © 2009 G. J. David, Jr., and T. R. McKeldin III.

The *Marine Corps Gazette* retains copyright for the articles that appear as chapters 15, 36, 40, 41, and 42. Reprinted with the permission of the Marine Corps Association.

Published in the United States by Potomac Books, Inc. All rights reserved. No part of this book may be reproduced in any manner whatsoever without written permission from the publisher, except in the case of brief quotations embodied in critical articles and reviews.

The views expressed in this book are those of the authors alone and do not reflect the official policy or position of any branch of service, the Department of Defense, the Department of State, or the U.S. government.

Library of Congress Cataloging-in-Publication Data
Ideas as weapons : influence and perception in modern warfare / edited by G.J. David, Jr., and T.R. McKeldin III ; foreword by Brigadier General (Promotable) H.R. McMaster, U.S. Army. — 1st ed.
p. cm.
Includes bibliographical references and index.
ISBN 978-1-59797-260-4 (hbk. : alk. paper) — ISBN 978-1-59797-261-1 (pbk. : alk. paper)
1. Information warfare—United States. 2. Counterinsurgency—United States. 3. Psychological warfare—United States. 4. War on Terrorism, 2001– 5. United States—Military policy. I. David, G. J. II. McKeldin, T. R.
U163.I52 2004
355.3'43—dc22
2008024350

Printed in the United States of America on acid-free paper that meets the American National Standards Institute Z39-48 Standard.

Potomac Books, Inc.
22841 Quicksilver Drive
Dulles, Virginia 20166

First Edition

10 9 8 7 6 5 4 3 2 1

CONTENTS

List of Illustrations	ix
Foreword, *COL H. R. McMaster, USA*	xi
Acknowledgments, *Maj G. J. David, Jr., USMC, and*	
LtCol T. R. McKeldin III, USMCR	xiii
U.S. Military Ranks	xv
Introduction, *Maj G. J. David, Jr., USMC, and*	
LtCol T. R. McKeldin III, USMCR	1

Part I: Geopolitical

1. Exploiting Structural Weaknesses in Terrorist Networks: Information Blitzkrieg and Related Strategies, *Calvert W. Jones*	7
2. The Limits of Military Information Strategies, *Philip M. Taylor, Ph.D.*	13
3. Defining the War on Terror, *Col Philip G. Wasielewski, USMCR*	17
4. Information Warfare, *Col Thomas X. Hammes, USMC (Ret.)*	27
5. The Power of Weakness, *William S. Lind*	35
6. Strategic Communication: A Mandate for the United States, *Jeffrey B. Jones*	39
7. Reflections on Psychological Operations: The Imperative of Engaging a Conflicted Population, *Ambassador David Passage*	49
8. New Tools, New Rules: International Law and Information Operations, *Duncan B. Hollis*	59

Part II: Strategic

9. Learning Counterinsurgency: Observations from Soldering in Iraq, *GEN David H. Petraeus, USA*	75
10. Thoughts on Journalism and the Military, *Tom Fenton*	87

11. Strategic Innovation: Integrating National Power to Win in Iraq, *LTC John A. Nagl, USA (Ret.)*   93
12. Maneuvering Against the Mind, *LtCol Frank G. Hoffman, USMCR (Ret.)*   99
13. Clausewitz's Theory of War and Information Operations, *COL William M. Darley, USA*   111
14. Information (in) Operations: More Than Technology, *LtCol James P. West, USMC*   123
15. Winning on the Information Battlefield: Is the Story Getting Out? *LtCol Roger S. Galbraith, USMCR*   133
16. In Defense of Military Public Affairs Doctrine, *CDR J. D. Scanlon, Canadian Forces*   137
17. Waging an Effective Strategic Communications Campaign in the War on Terror, *CAPT Timothy J. Doorey, USN*   145
18. Marketing: An Overlooked Aspect of Information Operations, *CPT Stoney Trent, USA, and CPT James L. Doty III, USA*   163
19. Religion in Information Operations: More Than a "War of Ideas," *Pauletta Otis, Ph.D.*   171
20. Telling the Afghan Military Story . . . Their Way, *LTC Charles W. Ricks, USA (Ret.)*   187
21. Army IO Is PSYOPS: Influencing More with Less, *COL Curtis D. Boyd, USA*   195
22. Estimates, Execution, and Error: Losing the War of Perception in Vietnam, 1960–1973, *Col Eric M. Walters, USMC*   207

Part III: Operational

23. Iraq and a Singular, Enduring Information Failure, *Bing West*   221
24. Between War and Peace: Low-Intensity Conflict Doctrine and the Iraqi Scenario, *Jose L. Delgado*   227
25. Are We Outsmarting Ourselves? *Col Keith Oliver, USMC (Ret.)*   235
26. Marines Are from Mars, Iraqis Are from Venus, *Maj Ben Connable, USMC*   241
27. Clouding the Issue: Intelligence Collection, Analysis, and Dissemination during Operation Iraqi Freedom, *LTC George J. Stroumpos, USA*   251
28. Massing Effects in the Information Domain: A Case Study in Aggressive Information Operations, *LTG Thomas F. Metz, USA, with LTC Mark W. Garrett, USA; LTC James E. Hutton, USA; and LTC Timothy W. Bush, USA*   263

29. Getting Inside the Cultural Context and Achieving Intelligence Success: Strategic Debriefing in the Iraq Survey Group, *Col John A. Wahlquist, USAF (Ret.)* — 275
30. Insights from Colombia's "Prolonged War," *GEN Carlos Alberto Ospina Ovalle, Colombian Army* — 289
31. Winning in the Pacific: The Special Operations Forces' Indirect Approach, *MG David P. Fridovich, USA, and LTC Fred T. Krawchuk, USA* — 297

Part IV: Tactical

32. Tactical Information Operations in West Rashid: An Iraqi National Police Battalion and Its Assigned U.S. Transition Team, *Maj E. Lawson Quinn, USMC* — 307
33. "But How Do I Do It?" Tactical Information Operations and the Planning Process, *Maj Phillip M. Bragg, USMC* — 323
34. Operation Iraqi Freedom II: Information and Influence in South-Central Iraq, *Maj Clint Nussberger, USMC* — 337
35. The Massacre That Wasn't, *Maj Ben Connable, USMC* — 341
36. "Census Operations" and Information Management, *Maj Morgan G. Mann, USMCR* — 351
37. Frustration, *LtCol James McNeive, USMC (Ret.)* — 357
38. Getting Out the Word: Information Operations on the Ground in Iraq, *CPT Kyle Norton, USA* — 363
39. Fighting for Perceptions: Tactical IO in 2004 Iraq, *Maj Jennifer Morris Mayne, USMCR* — 367
40. By Other Means, *Capt Zachary D. Martin, USMC* — 373
41. Patrolling Ar Ramadi, *Cpl Tom Sloan, USMC* — 379
42. The Privatization of Victory, *Sgt Roger D. Huffstetler, Jr., USMC* — 383
43. "Twenty-Eight Articles": Fundamentals of Company-Level Counterinsurgency, *LTC David Kilcullen, Australian Army (Ret.)* — 389

Conclusion: Information in Conflict, *Maj G. J. David, Jr., USMC, and LtCol T. R. McKeldin III, USMCR* — 403
Notes — 407
Index — 439
About the Editors and Contributors — 449

ILLUSTRATIONS

13.1:	A Continuum of Violence in the Universe of Political Conflict	114
13.2:	The Universe of Political Conflict	115
13.3:	A Line of Demarcation between Kinetic- and IO-Domintated Factors	119
19.1:	Ideology to Behaviors	176
21.1:	A Better Way to Do IO Business: PSYOPS and PAO in the Lead	205
26.1:	Iraqi Loyalty Range Fan	246
28.1:	Operation Al-Fajr—Fallujah Insurgent Activities Map	271
28.2:	Fallujah Vignette #3, National Islamic Resistance Operations Center Atrocities	271
32.1:	Situation in West Rashid	308
32.2:	Symbology	311
32.3:	Signs and their Meanings	312–13
32.4:	Safety Announcements	320
33.1:	Concept of: The Combination of All the IQ Tasks	326
33.2:	Example of a Completed IO Task	327
33.3:	IO Synchronization Matrix	330
33.4:	Consequence Management: Gaining and Maintaining the Initiative in the Information Environment	331
33.5:	Planning Template for an Enemy Action That Has Informational Effects	331
33.6:	Planning Template for a Friendly Action That Has Informational Effects	332
35.1:	Impact	343
35.2:	Aftermath	344

FOREWORD

COL H. R. McMaster, USA

In the 1990s, enthralled with potential applications of new communications, information, and precision munitions technologies, many defense analysts argued that U.S. technological competitive advantages had brought about a revolution in military affairs (RMA). Some RMA advocates argued that the aggressive development and application of these technologies would permit U.S. forces to skip a generation of conflict and achieve full-spectrum dominance over potential adversaries well into the future. There would be no peer competitor for U.S. forces until at least 2020. Military concepts such as rapid decisive operations, shock and awe, and network-centric warfare promised rapid, low-cost victories if adversaries had the temerity to challenge vital U.S. interests. Today, the United States and its Coalition partners are engaged in conflicts in Afghanistan and Iraq that advocates of defense transformation never considered—protracted counterinsurgency and state-building efforts that require population security, security-sector reform, reconstruction and economic development, the reconstitution of governmental capacity, and the establishment of the rule of law. The United States and its partners are fighting these wars in the context of a broad struggle against transnational terrorist organizations that threaten the security of all civilized peoples. Since Al Qaeda conducted its September 11, 2001, mass murder attacks, it has become clear that the successful prosecution of contemporary war demands much more than a reliance on U.S. technological superiority.

Although combat in Afghanistan and Iraq continue to require the defeat of the enemy on physical battlegrounds, U.S. commanders have discovered that lasting success over terrorist and insurgent groups requires winning on the battleground of perception. The U.S. Army's *Counterinsurgency* manual puts security of the population at the center of counterinsurgency operations. Terrorist and insurgent groups often combine violence with sophisticated propaganda to gain the support or acquiescence of the population. It is for this reason that the counterinsurgent's and counterterrorist's success against these groups requires efforts to clarify their own intentions while countering enemy disinformation. Ideas are weapons in the information age, and the essays in this volume shed fresh light and understanding on this vital dimension of contemporary conflict.

It seems clear that understanding the multifaceted subject of how to fight on the battleground of perception calls for an interdisciplinary approach. The wide range of terms associated with this aspect of war, such as strategic communications, information operations, public diplomacy, psychological operations, and influence operations, can confound even the most determined student. Taken together, these essays impart clarity by first placing the subject in geopolitical and strategic context and then by examining influence and perception in modern warfare from a wide range of perspectives. Experts and practitioners provide historical, sociological, anthropological, legal, and psychological insights as well as make important observations based on a wide variety of experiences.

If there is an overarching conclusion to draw from these essays, it is that war is not network or technology centric. War has always been and remains people centric. Defeating the determined and brutal enemies that the United States and other nations are facing today places a premium on the study of people and societies rather than on weapons and technology. Delivering the "message of war" requires appropriate deeds as well as the right words. Contemplating the rich material in this book will not only help readers think clearly about what to say, it will help leaders understand better what they must do to fight effectively on the battleground of perception.

ACKNOWLEDGMENTS

Maj G. J. David, Jr., USMC, and LtCol T. R. McKeldin III, USMCR

This compilation would not have been possible without the support of the Marine Corps University Foundation and its President, BGen Tom Draude, USMC (Ret.), who took an active interest in it at inception and maintained that interest throughout the work that followed. While the book is not a Marine Corps University project, the foundation chose to provide sponsorship to what it viewed to be valuable and lent the considerable weight of its moral support to the effort, especially in contacting potential authors. The foundation also helped us contact and work with the editors of military periodicals regarding the possible republication of works from their pages. Finally, Brigadier General Draude provided periodic guidance as to how to proceed, giving the necessary direction to keep us on the right track.

While Commanding General at Fort Leavenworth in 2006, we contacted GEN David Petraeus to ask about the possibility of his writing for this effort. As it turned out, the time at which we contacted him was extremely busy as he was about to be appointed successor to General Casey and assume command of the Multinational Force–Iraq. As a result, he declined to offer a separate piece; instead, he asked the Army's *Military Review* to allow us to republish from its pages his article on his experience in Iraq up to that date. The editorial staff at the *Military Review* went a step further and enabled us, after approval, to republish what works we deemed appropriate to our effort.

The staff of the *Military Review*, including COL William Darley, LTC Arthur Bilodeau, and LTC Steve Boylan, U.S. Army, provided invaluable support in reviewing our requests for republication and also by placing us in contact with authors who had previously written for the journal. It was the actions of the *Military Review* that led us to request the same access from the *Marine Corps Gazette* and the *Joint Forces Quarterly* supported by Brigadier General Draude and the Marine Corps University Foundation.

We must thank Col David "Cow" Gurney, USMC (Ret.), senior editor of the *Joint Forces Quarterly* (*JFQ*), not only for providing a point of contact with whom to discuss the republication of *JFQ* articles, but also as a point of contact for publishers. His contributions were superlative; we greatly appreciate his guidance.

Col John Keenan, USMC (Ret.), editor of the *Marine Corps Gazette*, offered his assistance in republishing articles from the pages of the *Gazette* and with suggestions on other articles of interest that lent depth and scope to our anthology. Further, we need to thank the staff, including Mr. Kerry Knowles and Ms. Kelly Hasselbring, for their help in contacting authors.

The editors undertook this book project while deployed to Iraq and Afghanistan, respectively, in support of Marine Corps and Department of Defense missions. As a result, much of the effort had to be organized and maintained digitally in order to proceed. Mr. Jay F. Stratton, Major, U.S. Air Force Reserve, and a senior employee of the Defense Intelligence Agency, was instrumental for his digital network assistance, providing pop-server addresses so that we could communicate with government networks averse to webmail, and for his sense of humor when dealing with stupid computer questions. He also provided space on his private network server so that we could store and exchange materials independent of a particular terminal so long as we had Internet access. His efforts enabled the book to progress in a reasonable period of time.

Dr. Pauletta Otis, Marine Corps University, assisted both as an author and with advice on presentation that helped our formatting the book into a common, readable scheme. She is among the contributing authors who took an interest beyond her own work, helping us in formatting and placing essays within the manuscript.

There are, of course, many others whom we should name, but for brevity's sake cannot. It suffices to say that the level of support that we have received has been exemplary, especially for a project conceived and executed by independently deployed field grade officers. We ask our readers to please understand that the works contained herein and the efforts given to this project are all those of persons acting as private individual citizens rather than on behalf of the U.S. government, Department of Defense, other government departments, or any specific military service. The views expressed in this book are similarly those of their authors alone and may not be construed as the official position of any U.S. government entity whatsoever.

U.S. MILITARY RANKS

Rank	Army	Air Force	Navy	Marines
Commissioned Officers				
General / O-10	GEN	Gen	ADM	Gen
Lieutenant General / O-9	LTG	Lt Gen	VADM	LtGen
Major General / O-8	MG	Maj Gen	RADM(UH)	MajGen
Brigadier General / O-7	BG	Brig Gen	RADM(LH)	BGen
Colonel / O-6	COL	Col	CAPT	Col
Lieutenant Colonel / O-5	LTC	Lt Col	CDR	LtCol
Major / O-4	MAJ	Maj	LCDR	Maj
Captain / O-3	CPT	Capt	LT	Capt
First Lieutenant	1LT	1Lt	LTJG	1stLt
Second Lieutenant	2LT	2Lt	ENS	2ndLt
Chief Warrant Officers				
Chief Warrant Officer – 5	CW5	N/A	CWO-5	CWO-5
Chief Warrant Officer – 4	CW4	N/A	CWO-4	CWO-4
Chief Warrant Officer – 3	CW3	N/A	CWO-3	CWO-3
Chief Warrant Officer – 2	CW2	N/A	CWO-2	CWO-2
Warrant Officer	WO1	N/A	WO1	WO

INTRODUCTION

Maj G. J. David, Jr., USMC, and LtCol T. R. McKeldin III, USMCR

The United States has struggled to define its approach to what has been termed the "information battlefield" since the dawn of the information era. What will information systems, computer networks, and the advent of digital knowledge to the desktop, the palmtop, and the podcast, the new medium of every soul in every nation overseas, mean to the policy of the United States or other world powers? Some assumed that the passive introduction of American entertainment and educational domination would preclude any need for an active government effort to solidify American preeminence, but the war on terror has violently challenged that supposition. Like many optimistic reactions to new technology, optimism proved premature.

Warfare directed specifically at the information received by republics, or those governments whose systems defined themselves by the will of their citizens, cannot be considered an innovation of the information age. What can be considered new, however, is the means by which such war is promulgated. Ideological demigods now have unprecedented channels by which to disseminate their message to those who are uncertain, sympathetic, or actively engaged in their philosophy. For this reason, the twenty-first century has brought a dawn of tactics, if not of strategy, with which republics must make their reckoning. Republics, those governments that once claimed the hegemony of public will over private ambition and power, now face that same ambition and domineering power in a new form.

From the caves of southeastern Afghanistan to the streets of Baghdad, the *message* predominates the thinking of those who perpetrate horrific acts of violence in the name of ideology, ethno-sectarian banners, and religion (and by the letter of that religion's more obscure law). It is a tactic that seems to be peculiarly adapted to affecting the contemporary world, especially that of the republics. The constitutional monarchy, republic, and empire had constrained violence into the military construct of force-on-force war by the beginning of the twentieth century as the world embarked upon World War I. By mid-century, following World War II, even this constrained notion had wrought such horrific results that these governments and their publics attempted to constrain violence even further and ascend to some hopeful plane beyond. The representative republic has sought to educate and provide for a mass of those who thought for themselves and therefore provided the center of gravity for a consensus of rational opinion on how we all ought to live and behave. This avenue of thinking did not consider that the path down which it headed was antithetical to other parts of humanity. The West sought to "move beyond" undirected violence as a medium for human conversation, not realizing that in so doing it abdicated an argument that was still ongoing.

Republics have not provided a history of unmitigated success. Indeed, that twentieth-century record of extravagant conflict merely to delineate the demarcation between consensus and publicly derived autocracy belies the ability to alter the environment so quickly. Small, but highly motivated, bands of true believers sought greater good through dominance enforced by physical power: the Bolsheviks, the Nazis, the Imperial Japanese and the "East Asia Co-Prosperity Sphere," the latter-day Communists, Maoists, and South American Populists. Some Ba'athists fell into this train of thought, so it should not be altogether surprising that in its death throws, the reaction to the ultimate pendulum swing of Enlightenment should occur where that revolution in thinking never really occurred.

In the latter stages of its ultimate demise, Communism sought to challenge its adversaries by causing the voter to cringe, blink, and turn away. Repeatedly over its final years, the objective of Communism's main tactical efforts was to terrify its Western counterpart into submission rather than to actually produce a substantive alternative. This terror stemmed in part from revealing a battlefield that had always been there (but had only been visible to the Soldiers) through modern information means and in part from reverting to methods considered by many beyond the scope of dignified civilization, whether they had been militarily ubiquitous or not. Moreover, it brought back the moral challenges inherent in the roots of civilization, in the confrontation between the settlement and the nomad, in the reason for having the settlement to begin with: to drive away the need for using violence as the primary means of persuasion, rather than as the ultimate military extreme of politics—what the nineteenth-century European would have termed "savagery." Nineteenth-century Europeans retained a much closer memory of the effects of violence as the only political discourse than did their twentieth-century counterparts for whom violence had been isolated to being an extreme, resorted to only for national survival by the nation-state. They retained a recognition that the original purpose of the nation-state was to keep the specter of violent debate at bay, at least sometimes. Twentieth-century Europeans then grew accustomed to a form of organization in their clashes inherent in the post–World War II philosophies seeking to rarify and supplant armed conflict as the medium for human discussion.

Just as Napoleon Bonaparte's destroyed the stagnant rules of war in late eighteenth-century Western Europe, terrorists now have sought and gained the attention of the world's prosperous nations by rejecting their rules. Though many who enjoy the benefits of the modern nation-state may find this both terrifying and abhorrent, they must also recognize the effectiveness of the method. Far from rejecting technology in and of itself (regardless of what the faithful are told), most terrorists have wholeheartedly bent information and other technologies to their uses, exploiting the anachronistic measures of governments to control them. The most effective means of bringing distracted citizens of wealthy republics to focus is by use of the same measures that brought fear with the wind off the central Asian steppe from time immemorial—violence. Vo Nguyen Giap may have predicated his strategy on its political impact in the United States, but he did so using recognizable conventional means as well as guerrilla war and terrorism. The former two methods proved costly. Given the speed with which horror propagates worldwide today, Osama bin Laden has opted to isolate his efforts into the most effective and yet easily controllable and dispersed of these means—terrorism. Action need not even be directed; so long as thoughtful fanatics strike well, as in Madrid in 2004, the act need merely be claimed.

How will the national republic respond? For the most part, this remains to be seen. Thus far, the United States has proved inept at quickly adapting the vast, dominant, commercial information infrastructure it enjoys to national security purposes. This is in part owing to a healthy suspicion of government direction of news or academics (a suspicion that Soviet propagandists sought unfailingly to provoke, for better or for worse). Moreover, it busily spent the 1990s deconstructing most of the remaining anti-propaganda measures it had put in place to confront the Soviet Union, as did much of the West. Furthermore, in its quest for balance between liberty and equality, the West has gone through a self-absorbed period of intense intra-scrutiny that provides extremely fertile ground for assault by external values. The confidence in the "moral effect" of empires that bestrode the world prior to 1945 vanished in the ruins of world war.

In its periods of lucidity, however, the West recognized its postwar authority to drive the direction of events and was actually able to do so while simultaneously fulfilling its values and allowing self-government. Great Britain met insurgencies in Malaya and Kenya with efforts designed as much to train and woo a population preparing to be independent as to attack armed fighters of an opposed ideology. These issues were occurring as the United States was just adapting to its role on the world stage. Indeed, the American realization of the need for actors in psychological operations and, more recently, information operations is itself an acknowledgment of the need to promulgate the positives, or the values and ideals that are the best efforts of the United States. Struggling with lingering concepts such as colonialism and empire, the United States has yet to form an operational or strategic direction that can effectively advance its notions of values.

At the forefront of this conflict, where the messages are formed and ultimately promulgated, are actors for the nation-state attempting to uphold the rule of law, those who must act in a civil or military capacity, and those who provide some of the conduits with which information is disseminated. The military, Foreign Service, academia, and news media—these institutions form the foundation on which the nation is attempting to act. These are the institutions that must struggle with the messages of war.

This book seeks to illuminate the uses of information in armed conflict by providing the views of those who have been engaged in attempting to do so while juxtaposing against historic context and depth. It spans the spectrum from the sergeant leading men on foot to the political leader establishing the national direction. Observers and actors tend to maintain a perspective with which they are most comfortable or for which their backgrounds or research best prepare them. For this reason, the anthology is divided into four sections: Geopolitical, Strategic, Operational, and Tactical. The geopolitical level of perspective is dominated by world politics, diplomacy, and the elements of national power other than military force. The strategic view, in this case, is confined to those circumstances where violence has begun and the military element of power has become a major contributing factor, even if the issue remains worldwide and the subject may not be isolated into a specific campaign. The operational perspective deals with campaigns to accomplish a specific purpose on the world stage, for example, the Iraq campaign. Finally, the tactical level views the perspective of the individual or of individual clashes within specific campaigns. As the nexus of information conflict is most easily viewed in the world's contemporary violent confrontations, this anthology is heavily weighted toward military personnel who have had to manage these issues firsthand in the most difficult circumstances. These works will show both the strokes of genius and the glaring failures as they play out along the front lines of today's violent clashes.

Armed conflict provides the focus, but the concepts apply beyond such conflict to interactions in the international arena between adversaries, potential or actual. As such, these works gravitate toward those aspects of information in war that are timeless. Though the twenty-first century has radically altered all the means by which the message is disseminated, the message still occupies central importance. What, then, is the message of war?

Part I:
Geopolitical

1

Exploiting Structural Weaknesses in Terrorist Networks: Information Blitzkrieg and Related Strategies

—Calvert W. Jones

Introduction

After losing Afghanistan as a secure state sanctuary, Al Qaeda recovered by adapting into a diffuse global network linking groups inspired and supported, if not controlled, by its remaining leadership. One school of analysts sees Al Qaeda and its associated groups as highly dangerous adversaries because of this evolution: having melted into a broader, looser, and more decentralized structure spanning online and offline space, they may be harder to track and apprehend.[1] Because they are not dependent on a central hierarchical decision-making body, dispersed nodes in the network have more freedom to experiment on their own, exploiting local conditions for attack. Deciding which elements of the network to target is also more difficult without clear hierarchical chains of command; leadership that is captured or killed may quickly shift to other nodes or regenerate in other communities. Technologically agile and free from the rigidity of hierarchy, networked jihadist terrorists may be more flexible, innovative, and fast moving, able to improvise and adapt more rapidly to countermeasures.[2]

Although Al Qaeda's networked evolution is dangerous, it has also created weaknesses in structure that may have been underestimated by this school of thinking. As these terrorists become more reliant on global information and societal infrastructures rather than on a geographically isolated safe haven, their vulnerability to infiltration and manipulation grows. Afghanistan provided Al Qaeda a secure home base with an advanced network of training camps that took years to develop, legitimize in terms of jihad, and market to potential recruits around the world. Indoctrination, training, planning, and decision-making could be carried out in this relatively secure location with minimal risk. Now, expelled from Afghanistan and enmeshed in societies around the world, Al Qaeda–influenced terrorists must depend on a far more varied and uncertain constellation of external support. Without a reliable, widely recognized, and trusted central headquarters for training and networking, aspiring terrorists must seek "legitimate peripheral participation" in global jihad.[3] Legitimate peripheral participation is a model of informal learning that emphasizes how newcomers are socialized into an organization, gradually winning community recognition. It is a useful construct for understanding how globally dispersed jihadists are adapting to the loss of a secure state sanctuary where they could train, organize, and plan more formally.[4]

Exploiting the technologies of globalization, the Al Qaeda terrorist phenomenon has survived without a state sanctuary. But its survival has come at the cost of internal security, professionalism, and coherence of community—casualties of a more diffuse, dispersed structure. As this essay will illustrate, networked evolution has given rise to structural vulnerabilities that can be exploited. The network's porousness may be especially susceptible to culturally and linguistically informed information operations (IO) that raise the costs of legitimate peripheral participation in terrorism.[5]

Manipulating Amateurism

The destruction of Al Qaeda's Afghanistan base has divorced thousands of recruits from an advanced, globally recognized, and well-coordinated center of training camps and jihadist social networking. These scattered militants and those newly interested in jihadist terrorism have no such obvious, central, and accessible place to train, meet like-minded people, and connect with the resources and expertise needed to launch successful attacks. The Afghanistan sanctuary played a key role in converting unskilled recruits into professional terrorists posing a much more significant threat.[6] Classes provided detailed, hands-on training in tactical, operational, organizational, and technical aspects of terrorism, and are not easily replicated in a scattered structure. Where the Afghanistan training camps represented a well-known rite of passage for training and networking, no such universally recognizable and relatively secure clearinghouse exists today.

As a result, the dispersed elements of global jihad and those hoping to join must seek out on their own peripheral opportunities to train and link with resources they need to launch attacks. Post-9/11 attacks demonstrate this weakness. Many have been locally improvised, amateurish efforts with their perpetrators receiving sloppy, haphazard training over weekends. The Casablanca terrorists, for example, were hurriedly trained during weekend camping trips outside Casablanca.[7] Allegedly funded by Al Qaeda, they had aimed to continue the organization's trademark style of coordinated, synchronized attacks by setting off five simultaneous bombs, but their improvised explosives were heavy and unreliable, and only one resulted in mass casualties.[8] One of the attackers may have gotten lost, moreover, and detonated his bomb in front of the wrong target.[9] This is not to say that locally improvised attacks are not dangerous but rather to highlight the state of amateurism implied by scattered terrorist elements that lack an obvious, reliable, institutionalized, and ultimately trusted center for training and networking.

Such uncertainty combined with the amateur's typical need for assistance, resources, and expertise may be exploited. Lacking hierarchical oversight, a central base, and a reliable means to authenticate potential connections and suppliers, the more diffused network of jihadist terrorists post-9/11 may be far more open to infiltration and manipulation than is generally acknowledged. Dispersed and more autonomous, these terrorists and new recruits are likely to be looking outward, uncertainly fishing for the tools, equipment, resources, expertise, and connections that would previously have been available through Afghanistan. This network porousness creates a set of opportunities for counterterrorism information operations that exploit jihadist amateurism. In particular, these operations could set traps by appearing to provide resources, connections, and linkages sought by aspiring but isolated terrorists.

For example, the seven men allegedly planning terrorist attacks against the Sears Tower in Chicago and other buildings in Miami fell into a trap designed to exploit their need for assistance and legitimacy. According to the indictment, the "ringleader," Narseal Batiste, connected with a man claiming links to Al Qaeda.[10] Batiste reportedly requested weapons, vehicles, and $50,000 from the man for an "Islamic Army to wage jihad" and swore allegiance to Al Qaeda. But the man was an FBI informant; the group was monitored and then apprehended. While future aspiring terrorists may learn not to be so gullible, they will still have a need for resources and assistance that can be exploited in this way, especially if they are dispersed around the globe and lack the means to authenticate new connections.

Degrading Online Resources through Information "Blitzkrieg"

Another way of taking advantage of this network's growing structural vulnerabilities is to degrade the Internet as a means of communication for dispersed terrorists hoping to collaborate. Many analysts have drawn attention to Al Qaeda's growing use of the Internet for recruitment, propaganda, planning, and information sharing, an increase that was central to the organization's ability to adapt to the loss of its physical sanctuary.[11] Bomb recipes, training videos, tactical manuals, intelligence on targets, and compilations of "lessons learned" are all available online. Proposed strategies to counter this "cyber-mobilization" include shutting down terrorist-oriented websites and posting alternative sites to undermine jihadist propaganda. Yet shutting down sites is only a temporary remedy, as they can easily be replaced through new hosting services. Attempting to counter Al Qaeda propaganda with alternative sites is also very problematic given that Internet users choose which sites they wish to view and may simply ignore or disparage sources they do not consider credible. Moreover, not much evidence suggests that people are motivated to change their attitudes and intentions based on reading a website outside of the context of their own community.

There is evidence, however, that people are frustrated by online resources that are burdensome to use and potentially untrustworthy. For example, people abandon blogs and message boards that are overrun with bots, trolls, flame wars, irrelevant posts, and other interference. For example, the South-East Asia Earthquake and Tsunami Blog, an informal, ad hoc effort to help volunteers around the world provide disaster recovery assistance, was deluged within a short period of time with fake charity scams, advertisements, and spam.[12] This pollution of the resource was discouraging to contributors who genuinely hoped to use it to aid in disaster recovery and degraded its worth and effectiveness. The interference in this case was mainly motivated by commercial opportunism, but examples exist in which such online resources have been degraded for other reasons. For instance, the Chinese government attempts to suppress dissent and political opposition online through the use of citizen monitoring. Citizen monitors and "moles" participate in chat rooms, message boards, websites, and other online forums to offer pro-Beijing perspectives and keep tabs on possible dissidents who might influence opinion more broadly, threatening the regime.[13] One famous dissident, known online as "Stainless Steel Mouse," was allegedly monitored and apprehended through her online association with one such informant.[14] By stoking the perception of great risk in using online resources, the government has been able to erode communications and trust among peripheral participants who might otherwise come together in opposition.

As networked, dispersed terrorists turn to the Internet to sustain and extend their efforts without a central geographic headquarters, they can be countered through information operations that degrade and undermine online communications in similar ways. Such operations should aim to so pollute the terrorists' online environment of learning, information sharing, social bonding, and coordination as to permanently discredit it, rendering it unreliable, risky, cumbersome, and ultimately useless. "Blitzkrieg" techniques could bombard terrorist-oriented message boards and chat rooms with false, misleading, or simply annoying and voluminous contributions that create chaos and sow distrust. Fake documents purporting to represent expertise gleaned from Iraq and other theaters could be circulated and then discredited. Phishing scams could be launched against users of particular websites to generate further uncertainty and erode trust. While simply shutting down certain websites encourages their appearance elsewhere online, these blitzkrieg strategies may have a more lasting effect on overall trust in the Internet as a resource for terrorists.

Infiltrating Peripheral Support Structures

Finally, the more diffuse, networked structure of jihadist terrorism implies a greater reliance not only on the Internet, but also on societal infrastructures around the world. While the image of terrorists melting into local communities has raised concerns that they will be harder to identify and apprehend, they may actually be far more exposed and vulnerable as a result of this evolution. Relying on external players can be very risky since these players cannot easily be authenticated and may exhibit varying levels of commitment. The more varied and uncertain constellation of support that has allowed a networked Al Qaeda to survive the loss of its physical sanctuary is a major potential vulnerability.

One way for counterterrorism efforts to take advantage of this dependency is to make it easier and more attractive for members of transnational support networks to provide information to authorities. While this is not a novel strategy, it may have been overlooked because of the conventional wisdom that diffuse networks of terrorists are more "invisible" than traditional state adversaries.[15] In fact, their embeddedness in global society creates structural vulnerabilities that can be tapped. For example, the terrorist Ramzi Yousef, loosely connected to Al Qaeda, befriended a student at the Islamic University in Islamabad who later helped authorities apprehend him in 1995.[16] Although the student, Ishtiaque Parker, was drawn to Yousef initially, sharing some of the terrorist's general views and grievances, he did not support terrorist tactics. After Yousef asked him to transport a bomb from Pakistan to the United States, Parker reportedly grew fearful, realizing the seriousness of Yousef's intentions. As a result, he provided information to Pakistani authorities that led to Yousef's capture. The intermingling of terrorists with local communities, as opposed to their concentration in a relatively isolated safe haven, introduces vulnerabilities of this kind that can be better exploited.

Exploiting these structural vulnerabilities effectively, however, may require more cultural nuance and understanding than merely offering a financial reward for betrayal. Indeed, Ishtiaque Parker was reportedly shunned by his community as a traitor after becoming an informant. He was ostracized for what was perceived as willingness to sell out his friends and faith for the $2 million reward offered by the U.S. government. A devout Muslim who had studied to be a cleric, Parker hoped to return to his South African hometown. Yet even the imam of his family's mosque expressed doubt over whether Parker could return given persistent community resentment. Thus, while Al Qaeda's more diffuse structure and consequent reliance on transnational support networks widens the pool of potential informants, informing can carry significant costs.

Taking advantage of structural vulnerabilities may require greater flexibility in efforts to mitigate such costs. Counterterrorism specialists should investigate the possibility of increasing and diversifying opportunities to inform or defect in ways that respect cultural norms, individual preferences, and perceived costs. Friends and family of aspiring terrorists may sense and disapprove of plans for jihadist violence. But they may be unwilling to obstruct it openly, not because they tacitly approve, but because of loyalty and community solidarity. More sensitivity to these situations—including guaranteed anonymity and openness to negotiation—may be required. Less personal, largely functional support structures, such as smuggling rings, drug traffickers, and front companies, whose help is more pragmatic than anything else may be especially inclined to cooperate.

Conclusions

The networked evolution of Al Qaeda has generated weaknesses, therefore, that may be exploited with more dexterity and cultural sensitivity. Information operations can manipulate scattered jihadists by dangling expertise, resources, and connections that are sought with greater uncertainty and even desperation, without recourse to a reliable central base. Such operations can also attempt to degrade the Internet as a means of recovering from the loss of that base through "blitzkrieg" techniques. By overwhelming online resources terrorists are known to use with interference, creating a cacophony of spam and false or misleading contributions, these techniques may erode trust in the Internet as a medium for terrorist use. While terrorists tend to adapt to countermeasures, they can more easily adapt to the shutting down of websites than they can to blitzkrieg techniques that undermine the Internet as a whole for their purposes. A lack of trust in online resources may seriously reduce their room for maneuverability as a geographically dispersed non-state actor. Tapping into the broader, more varied support structures implied by a greater reliance on societies around the world may also limit maneuverability.

A number of security experts have focused less on these general structural weaknesses and more on the internal inconsistencies and conflicts composing global jihad itself, involving a diverse set of actors with local and even divergent interests at heart.[17] David Kilcullen has proposed a promising strategy of "disaggregation" that would capitalize on these internal conflicts, seeking to dismantle the "links that allow the jihad to function as a global entity."[18] Yet it is not only jihadists' links with one another, but also their links to any form of terrorist expertise and assistance online and off that makes them a threat. Indeed, the links between post-9/11 attacks, including Madrid, Casablanca, and London, and the remaining Al Qaeda leadership have been tenuous at best.

Targeting structural weaknesses more broadly as discussed in this chapter may therefore be an important complement to a strategy such as disaggregation. Exploiting the need for expertise and resources by isolated amateurs and reducing their trust in online communications generally may be as productive as interdicting their attempts to link with other jihadists in particular. Their ability to function as a serious threat stems not only from jihadist "aggregation," but also from the ability to access deadly weapons, connections, and expertise from any source, jihadist or not. Raising the costs of accessing these resources by taking advantage of the network's structural vulnerabilities, thwarting "legitimate peripheral participation" in jihadist terrorism, should play a role in any counterterrorism strategy.

2
The Limits of Military Information Strategies

—Philip M. Taylor, Ph.D.

Most of the current military thinking about information operations (IO) and strategic communications is based on the assumption that it is possible to take command and control of the battle space. Because adversaries employ weapons of mass persuasion, especially increasingly sophisticated attempts to manipulate television and the Internet, the natural reaction is to attempt to counter this "propaganda"; to leave it unanswered would be to accept defeat in the battle to win hearts and minds. Immediately, we see a fundamental problem: namely, this is a defensive reaction that produces counteroffensive initiatives. Caught on the back foot, all subsequent efforts are about catch-up, and given the speed at which info-players now operate, this tends to be a permanent condition. This, in turn, has given rise to considerations as to how to respond to such asymmetric warfare. But the very word "respond" is indeed part of the problem, not the solution. From such a base, full-spectrum dominance of today's global infosphere is probably impossible.

Even so, attempts to tackle this problem continue to reflect more on the control-freak mentality of institutional culture in military thinking than the realities of what is required in a global information war on terrorism. Although the record of IO and its components like psychological operations (PSYOPS) is a mixed one, it is possible to conclude that, for the most part, the military is quite effective at military informational strategies at the tactical and operational levels. It is at the strategic level where the real problem lies because that is where the military has to compete with all sorts of factors that are beyond its control, especially in the political domain.

If there is too much of a disconnect between the distinctly unattractive hard power elements and the soft power of a nation's foreign policy, then no amount of skillful marketing or branding can make others want to buy into it if they cannot see that it is in their interests to do so.

This is precisely what has gone wrong with American foreign policy since 9/11 and why the increasing efforts to win the global struggle for hearts and minds in the fight against terrorism have failed to stem the tide of anti-Americanism worldwide. While it would be inappropriate for the military to dictate policy about what should be done, it needs more input into the political decision-making process about what can be done, especially through the deployment of hard power. Many senior commanders have constantly complained about too few men being supplied for Operation Iraqi Freedom—not so much during the combat phase, since the rapid fall of Baghdad in a three-week campaign was a spectacular military success, but in the period that followed when the "liberation" turned into an "occupation"— and having to deal with a serious "insurgency" to which far too little forethought or planning was given.

That said we have to deal with the world as it is, not as it might be. Yet the latter part of that sentence reveals a further problem. U.S. foreign policy as it is currently configured under the Bush doctrine tends to deal with futures based on little understanding of the past. The policy of preemptive war, for example, and the identification of an "axis of evil" of states sponsoring terrorism that might one day supply terrorist organizations with weapons of mass destruction appear to be rooted in fear of the future. Although the Global War on Terrorism has now been re-branded "The Long War," the possibility of an eternal war fills the rest of the world with dread. For how do you end such a "war"? Historically and legally, wars have been defined as armed conflicts between two or more nation-*states*. Waging war against a non-state actor like Al Qaeda cannot be achieved solely with kinetic weapons because, whatever Al Qaeda was or has become, the need now is to wage war against an idea or a concept. The enemy is elusive, vague, and extremely skillful in exploiting Western mistakes such as Guantanamo and Abu Ghraib. How does one negotiate an end to hostilities with such an adversary when Western policy has always been never to negotiate with terrorists? It was a huge mistake to call it a "war" in the first place and it is a mistake to keep on doing so for it is, quite simply, a war without end. And dealing with futures creates self-fulfilling prophecies. For example, if there was no connection between 9/11 and Iraq before Operation Iraqi Freedom, there is now.

This policy has been translated, despite assertions to the contrary in Washington and London, into a "clash of civilizations" by Al Qaeda and its supporters. Early mistakes, like President Bush's use of the word "crusade" or the labeling of the Global War on Terrorism (GWOT) as "Operation Infinite Justice," for example, provide "evidence" for Al Qaeda supporters of the fact that the West is fighting a war against Islam. Any study of public opinion among Arab and Muslim audiences makes disquieting reading. Many believe the American President is a greater threat to world peace than bin Laden is, that the United States is embarked upon a neo-conservative and neo-colonial military campaign to dominate the world's oil supplies (with further evidence stemming from the Bush family's oil connections), and that U.S. support for Israel—and its reaction to the election of Hamas in Palestine—reveals what U.S. foreign policy is actually about. In a world where rumours and hearsay are often more powerful than "facts," or where the "facts" are carefully selected to "prove" the American conspiracy, indigenous paranoia is exploited skillfully by carefully timed bin Laden statements to punctuate a sustained campaign conducted through the Internet and slickly produced CDs and DVDs. In some Muslim countries, "documentaries" have been broadcast that reveal that the World Trade Center and Pentagon were attacked by a CIA-Mossad alliance to provide a pretext for waging war in Afghanistan. Indeed, some argue that the Pentagon was not even hit by a hijacked passenger plane at all because the explosion was caused on the ground. They point out that isn't it odd that none of those recorded cell phone messages from the doomed passengers mentioned the word "Arab." And it is widely believed that 4,000 Jews failed to turn up for work on September 11, 2001, while in Britain after July 7, 2005, some voices were heard that the London bombings could not have been carried out by Muslims and that MI5 had a hand in yet another conspiracy theory.

Accusations of Western selectivity and hypocrisy are reinforced by the works of Americans themselves, from Samuel Huntington to Noam Chomsky and Michael Moore. Further "proof" of American hostility to Muslims is recounted by the treatment of visiting Muslim brothers and sisters by U.S. immigration officials at most U.S. international airports. Long forgotten is the assistance given by U.S. troops to the Muslims of Kuwait, Somalia, Bosnia, and Kosovo. Anti-American levels declined slightly after the 2004–5 tsunami but that was short term. Al Qaeda quickly exploited the chaos of Hurricane Katrina to demonstrate "God's revenge against the city of homosexuals" while many international news reports focused on the slowness of FEMA to help the nation's poorest victims. The 2005 G8 summit's rhetoric of "making poverty history" was quickly seen as yet another propaganda stunt while Darfur and Zimbabwe provided yet more "evidence" of Western hypocrisy and selectivity.

It is, of course, unrealistic to expect the United States or the G8 nations to solve the problems of the world overnight. But if the Long War is to be won, there needs to be a strategy that not only deals kinetically with terrorists but with the long-term causes of why some people become terrorists in the first place. This is indeed a hearts and minds issue, and senior officials in Washington have recognized that it will be a "generational war." But the real challenge for any strategic communications campaign is not for Americans themselves to tell the rest of the world that they have it all wrong. Foreigners don't like to be told what to think by other foreigners. That is why public diplomacy initiatives such as Radio

Sawa or Alhurra TV are unlikely to have a profound impact in changing minds and consequently hearts. The challenge is how to secure the support of governments in Arab and Muslim countries to conduct their own national information campaigns for their own national audiences. And this is where U.S. policy toward Palestine becomes a major strategic hurdle. Unlike the thirty-strong "Coalition of the willing" that was assembled in 1991 to oust Iraq from Kuwait, no Arab or Muslim country was prepared to join the 2003 Coalition to conduct "regime change" against Saddam Hussein. That, in itself, is highly revealing.

Although Secretary Donald Rumsfeld once professed to not know what "soft power" meant, he has belatedly come round to recognizing that the 1999 closure of the United States Information Agency might have been a mistake. Such a realization came after the United States had been involved in the GWOT longer than it had actually been involved in World War II. Joseph Nye's concept of soft power is, however, merely one component of what is required. So much damage has already been done to America's reputation and credibility abroad, that it is going to take years to repair—not least because the "evidence" for past mistakes has been enshrined as "facts" on the Internet. Rapidly responding to misinformation and disinformation, refuting rumors and conspiracy theories as quickly and as convincingly as possible, and filling information vacuums with credible and verifiable interpretations of what is actually happening may all seem obvious short-term necessities. But the Global War on Terrorism cannot be won by America alone. As Richard Holbrooke famously remarked, "How can a man in a cave out-communicate the world's greatest communications nation?" This question, like the one asked after 9/11 about "why do they hate us so much?" revealed a failure to understand a fundamental appreciation grasped so quickly by World War II's information warriors: know your enemy. But if the information war is to be won over the long haul, you also need to know yourself.

3

Defining the War on Terror*

—Col Philip G. Wasielewski, USMCR

On September 11, 2001, America was attacked not by a nation-state but by a non-state group. Now the nation is involved in a war on terror—but what type of war is it? Although America has used military force against non-state groups, such as Pancho Villa's troops in 1916 and Jean LaFitte's pirates in the early nineteenth century, it has never considered such operations a "war."

Defining the type of war we are engaged in also means defining our goals.[1] If the policy goal is the destruction of all terrorist groups with global reach, will the war on terror thus be a series of counterinsurgency campaigns, a war of covert actions, or a series of preventative wars? Properly defining the war on terror follows the Clausewitzian dictum, "The supreme, the most far-reaching act of judgment that the statesman and commander have to make is to establish the kind of war on which they are embarking; neither mistaking it for, nor trying to turn it into, something that is alien to its nature."[2] Who are we fighting, and what is their nature? What kind of war is the "war on terror," and what is its nature? And what are the implications for future U.S. security strategy? This chapter attempts to answer these questions by providing an overview of terrorism. It then delves into the specific threat from Sunni Islamic extremism and describes its ideological basis and goals. Next, it looks at Al Qaeda. Based on these analyses, the chapter concludes with plausible answers to the foregoing questions and possible implications for national security strategy.

* *Reprinted by permission from* Joint Forces Quarterly, *1st Quarter 2007.*

Terrorism: The Idea and the Deed

The Department of Defense (DOD) defines terrorism as the calculated use of unlawful violence or threat of unlawful violence to inculcate fear, which is intended to coerce or to intimidate governments or societies in the pursuit of goals that are generally political, religious, or ideological.[3] This definition is crucial for creating a framework in which to answer questions of what type of war we are fighting and what policy goals it should achieve. The DOD definition makes a direct connection between terrorist acts and specific goals that is important in linking terrorism to policy and therefore giving political context. When one reviews this political context, it becomes clear that terrorism is not a modern phenomenon.

The Travels of Marco Polo tells of the Old Man of the Mountain, who kept a stable of assassins and dispatched them to murder neighboring princes who might be at odds with him, using calculated violence to inculcate fear for political purposes.[4] This centuries-old example shows that politically motivated terrorism may be as old as politics.

Modern terrorism, however, has been a weapon of the weak in their attempt to bring down the strong. The first modern terrorist movement, known as anarchism, arose in the late nineteenth and early twentieth centuries. Anarchism was inspired by a utopian idea that revolted against the inequalities of the early capitalist period. According to Barbara Tuchman, anarchists believed that property was "the monarch of all evil," and if it were eliminated, "no man could again live off the labor of another and human nature would be released to seek its natural level of justice among men."[5] Since owners would not release their property voluntarily, only a revolution could topple the structure and install a "new social order of utter equality and no authority." The only thing wanting for the masses to arise and fulfill this idea was a spark—an act—to show them the way. The anarchist's task was to awaken the masses by propaganda of word and of deed (an attack against a major symbol of the current order that would one day flash the signal for revolt).

During this period, several world leaders were assassinated in the name of the deed. There was no real leadership; rejection of all authority doomed anarchism since the movement opposed the concept of organization it needed to reach its goals. Moreover, there was no leadership hierarchy between the (usually well-born) philosophers of the idea and the (usually poverty-stricken) perpetrators. Social reforms and police action killed the movement by the end of the century. Its energy morphed into trade unionism in the Western democracies while its energy was funneled into Vladimir Lenin's revolution of 1917 in Russia.[6] But the movement established itself as the first worldwide terrorism phenomenon of non-state actors using targeted violence to fulfill political goals.

Many national liberation movements in the post–World War II environment used terrorism as a tactic to gain political goals of independence. Examples include the bombing of the King David Hotel in Palestine by the militant zionist group Irgun with help from the Stern Gang in 1946, the Mau Mau use of terror against European farmers in Kenya in the 1950s, and the deeds of Palestinian and Provisional Irish Republican Army operatives. Other groups, such as the Japanese Red Army and the Italian Red Brigades of the 1970s and 1980s, used terrorism to pursue ideological goals, however ephemeral.

What all these groups—Jewish, Catholic, Muslim, atheist, African, European, Asian, Middle Eastern, nihilist, religious, nationalist, or socialist—had in common was their calculated use of unlawful violence to coerce or intimidate governments or societies in the pursuit of goals that were generally political, religious, or ideological. Terrorism is thus an old tactic that transcends race, creed, and nation and adapts to almost any type of religious, political, or ideological goal.

To understand this phenomenon, we must review the different types of organized terrorism—mainly those used by religious militants, more specifically Al Qaeda. Jessica Stern identifies three organizational models religious militants use: inspirational leaders and their followers, lone-wolf avengers, and commanders and their cadres.

According to Stern, inspirational leaders and their followers use moral suasion rather than cash to influence their followers, appealing to higher-order deficiency needs, including the desire to be part of a community and gain recognition for one's achievements. They inspire "leaderless resisters" and lone-wolf avengers rather than cadres. They run networks, or virtual networks, rather than bureaucracies, and they encourage franchises. Inspirational leaders rarely break the law themselves.[7] Stern cites a violent segment of the anti-abortion movement in the United States, where leaders use websites not only to identify and target doctors but also to inspire others to acts of violence against them. The inspirational leaders' model is also a good description of the nineteenth-century anarchist movement.

Lone-wolf avengers are similar to followers of inspirational leaders, but instead of acting on a higher calling from a leader, they are often directed by internally based pathologies, frustrations, or impulses. Lone wolves often develop their own ideologies, combining personal vendettas with religious or political grievances. The Washington, D.C., area sniper John Allen Mohammed, Unabomber Ted Kaczynski, and Mir Aimal Kansi, who attacked employees of the Central Intelligence Agency outside its headquarters in 1993, are examples. Although these were domestic cases, this model has potential for a future wave of international terrorism.

The model of commanders and their cadres is hierarchical and is found in many terrorist movements. Commanders recruit cadres based on appeals to a higher cause as well as on the more immediate needs of food, shelter, and safety. Rewards and punishments play an important role in the organization. Although many initially join for a higher cause, they may continue their participation for the material benefits, whether they are monetary rewards or a sense of belonging. Lashkar-e Taiba, which recruits young men from the madrassas in Pakistan to fight in Kashmir, is such a group.

Stern describes Al Qaeda as the ultimate terror organization and worthy of a model in itself. In her view, it is hierarchical, with cadres, managers, and commanders. Cadres consist of skilled and unskilled labor. According to Stern, Al Qaeda has changed its organizational style since 9/11 to counteract the loss of its original leadership and now relies on an ever-shifting network of sympathetic groups and individuals, including the Southwest Asian jihadi groups, franchise outfits in Southeast Asia, sleeper cells trained in Afghanistan and dispersed abroad, and freelancers such as Richard Reid, the convicted "shoe bomber."[8]

Al Qaeda is both an organization and a movement. Michael Scheuer suggests that the threat America faces from Osama bin Laden is not the episodic campaign typical of traditional terrorist groups. It is rather a worldwide, religiously inspired, and professionally guided Islamist insurgency against "Christian crusaders and Jews" being waged by groups that bin Laden might control, direct, and inspire.[9]

Sunni Islamic Extremism

Historically speaking, Western dominance in world politics has been a phenomenon of the past two and a half centuries. The change in global positions of power over that time still rumbles seismically throughout much of the Islamic world. Bernard Lewis explains that "in the course of the nineteenth and twentieth centuries, the primacy and therefore the dominance of the West were clear for all to see, invading the Muslim in every aspect of his public and—more painfully—even his private life."[10] There have been many attempts to remedy the imbalance.

Secularism under the model of Mustafa Kemal's modern Turkey was one response, but it was abhorrent to most Muslims. Arab nationalism and socialism under Egypt's charismatic Gamal Abdel Nasser was briefly popular but died in the Six-Day War of 1967. Regarding the attempts of Muslim societies to regain past glory and influence, Lewis notes, "Many remedies have been tried, but none achieved the desired result. Here and there they brought some alleviation, and even—to limited elements of the population—some benefit. But they failed to remedy or even to halt the deteriorating imbalance between Islam and the Western world."

With the failure of secular (and Western) concepts such as democracy, socialism, nationalism, and Communism to bring restoration to the Islamic world, some Muslims began to believe that a return to early Islam—Islam of the sword—could regenerate their society. Like terrorism, this concept had a substantial history of Islamic thought and jurisprudence. Not all Muslims agree with this thinking, but it has had substantial influence on those who fight the modern-day jihad.

For many Muslims, the Golden Age of their faith was the time of the Prophet Mohammed and his four immediate successors, when Islam spread rapidly throughout the Arabian Peninsula and beyond—before the split between Sunni and Shi'a and before early Islamic achievements were destroyed by the invading Mongols. Yet the main theoretical foundations are more recent. Al Qaeda's ideology has its origins in the late nineteenth-century attempts to modernize faith and society in Egypt. These efforts became known as Salafism to honor the supposedly uncorrupted early Muslim predecessors (salafs) of today's Islam.[11] The Salafi strategy is based on two tenets: Islam became decadent because it strayed from the righteous path; and recapturing the glory of the Golden Age requires a return to the authentic faith and practices of the ancient ones, namely, the Prophet Mohammed and his companions.[12]

Jamal ad-Din Al-Afghani (1839–1897) was the modern-day founder of Salafism. He taught in Cairo and believed that a return to the path led by Mohammed and his original followers could create a spiritual revival of the faith. He also believed that with this spiritual renewal of Muslim society, the Muslim world would soon develop the intellectual equipment to redress the West's technological and military advantages.[13]

The next Egyptian spiritual thinker to develop these ideas was the founder of the Muslim Brotherhood, Hassan Al-Banna (1906–1949). He sought to unite and mobilize Muslims against the cultural and political domination of the West. When Banna reached an accommodation with King Farouk, however, the more radical members of the movement began searching for other leadership.

One of these former members of the Muslim Brotherhood was Sayyid Qutb (1906–1966), who developed the theological justification for jihad against other Muslims and the need to remove corrupt Muslim rulers. Before Qutb, one of the most feared concepts in Muslim thinking was fitna, the state of chaos or disunity of two civil wars that tore the Muslim community apart within a half century of the Prophet's death, resulting in the Shi'a-Sunni split. According to most Muslim scholars, even a poor Muslim ruler was better than fitna.

Qutb, however, took a line of reasoning that harked back to the days of the Mongol invasions, when it was believed that the Arabs could not wage jihad against the Mongols because the invaders too had accepted Islam. But a contemporary Muslim scholar, Taqi ad-Din Ahmed ibn Taymiyya (1263–1328), had argued that since the Mongols did not use Islamic sharia law and instead maintained their own tribal laws, they were not really Muslims but apostates and therefore legitimate targets of jihad.

Referring to *jahiliyya*, or the state of barbarism and ignorance that prevailed among the Arabs before Mohammed's revelations, Qutb argued that modern secular Muslim leaders were illegitimate not only because they did not follow sharia but also because they had reverted to jahiliyya. This reasoning was used to justify opposition to Nasser's secular policies. Qutb was jailed for his teachings and hanged for sedition in 1966.

Muhammad Abd Al-Salam Faraj, a theologian for an extremist group in Egypt, spread Qutb's message among those opposed to Nasser's successor, Anwar Sadat, and his peace policy toward Israel. He wrote a manifesto entitled *The Neglected Duty* that called for attacks against secular Muslim rulers and developed a strategy for defeating the near enemy (apostate Muslim regimes that had to be attacked and overthrown) before the far enemy (Israel, the United States, and the West in general).

The modern Salafi philosophy was codified by the mid-1970s, but it needed two events to galvanize it into an organization. The first occurrence was the Soviet war with Afghanistan. The second was the failure of Islamic extremists to overthrow the secular Egyptian government. These events sparked the beginning of Al Qaeda in its present form.

The Soviet invasion of Afghanistan created a broad reaction in the Islamic world. Muslim nation-states supported Western efforts to undermine the incursion both to assist their coreligionists and to protect their geopolitical position from further encroachments. Some Muslim states also used the jihad against the Soviets as a safety valve, sending their own disaffected youths in hopes that they would be more engaged in fighting Communism than finding fault with their own societies. Some Muslims began to believe that a return to early Islam—Islam of the sword—could regenerate their society.

The Afghan commander who invited the first Arab jihadists to fight was Abdul Rasul Sayyaf, an Islamic scholar who studied in Cairo prior to the invasion. To assist the movement of Arabs into Afghanistan, a Palestinian, Sheik Abdallah Azzam, created the Mekhtab al-Khidemat (Service Bureau) to address administrative problems for volunteers and the Bait al-Anser (House of Supporters) to house them. For Azzam, Afghanistan was the first step in a worldwide jihad to recapture lost lands. However, his view of jihad was essentially defensive, arguing for recapture of old Muslim lands but not the conquest of new ones. His assistant was young Osama bin Laden, and the two worked throughout the 1980s supporting the Afghan jihad.

During this time, the efforts of the Egyptian underground movement to over-throw the secular regime of Anwar Sadat and then Hosni Mubarak failed. The movement split into two groups—Egyptian Islamic Jihad under Ayman al-Zawahiri and the Islamic Jihad Group. Al-Zawahiri, a medical doctor, was arrested and later exiled to Saudi Arabia. He then moved to Peshawar, Pakistan, and worked with Azzam and bin Laden, treating wounded mujahideen and supporting their jihad work. With him were many other Egyptian radicals in exile.

When the Soviets withdrew from Afghanistan in 1988, the jihadis began debating what to do next. Azzam dreamed of using his current organization to help Muslims in other oppressed areas, such as Bosnia, Kashmir, and the Philippines, and regain control over their traditional lands. While many Arab mujahideen went home, those who were in exile, such as the Egyptians, could not. Thus, by a process of elimination, the most radical elements remained in Afghanistan and Peshawar.

There were different opinions regarding future actions. The Egyptians believed in Qutb's and Faraj's teachings and wanted to use their Peshawar "base" (Al Qaeda) to overthrow the Mubarak regime. Azzam disagreed with Faraj's teachings, stating that jihad should not be waged against Muslim rulers but only against non-

Muslims who had taken over Muslim lands (first and foremost his native Palestine). Azzam and two of his sons were murdered in Peshawar on November 24, 1989, by a remote-controlled car bomb. Their murder is still unsolved.

With Azzam's death, leadership of Al Qaeda fell to bin Laden and his deputy, al-Zawahiri. They worked with the Afghans to defeat the Najibullah regime but became exasperated with Afghan infighting. When Iraqi forces invaded Kuwait in 1991, bin Laden volunteered his force to Saudi authorities to drive them out. When the Saudis deferred and instead invited Western troops, bin Laden's relationship with the royal family soured. He returned to Afghanistan and moved Al Qaeda headquarters to Sudan, where it could more easily support operations against the Egyptian regime.

The Sudan interlude lasted until 1996. Following a failed assassination attempt against President Mubarak in 1995 that was traced to a bin Laden associate, Sudan received pressure from Egypt and bin Laden left the country.

The Sudanese period, however, had one long-lasting effect on Al Qaeda. It changed its Qutb-Faraj–inspired Salafist philosophy from attacking the near enemy to striking the far enemy. This change was announced in bin Laden's "Declaration of Jihad against the Americans Occupying the Land of Two Holy Sites," released in late 1996 from Al Qaeda's new sanctuary in Afghanistan. This text redefined the principal goal of jihad as Saudi Arabia's liberation from its American protectors.[14] The reasoning behind this change of tactics was reflected in the thinking of Al Qaeda's subcommander, Mamdouh Mahmud Salim, who argued that the main obstacle to the establishment of a Muslim state and the primary danger for the worldwide Islamist movement was the United States, which was seen as moving in on Muslim lands, such as the Arabian Peninsula and East Africa. While some disagreed, believing the focus should stay on the near enemy, subsequent events confirmed the switch from attacking corrupt Muslim regimes to hitting their erstwhile supporter, the United States. This led to a chain of attacks, from the Kenyan and Tanzanian U.S. embassy bombings in 1998 to the attack on the USS *Cole* in 2000 and finally to September 11.

The Al Qaeda Mind

To the popular imagination, the 9/11 hijackers and other Al Qaeda members are mentally disturbed—after all, only a depraved mind would hijack a plane to kill innocents and themselves in such a horrific way or would seek weapons of mass destruction to commit even worse horrors—or they are impoverished, single young men with no hope of a future, unaware of the benefits of modern Western society, who were brainwashed in medieval madrassas since infancy.

According to data on 172 known Al Qaeda terrorists, none of the assumptions is true. A minuscule number showed only a trace of sociopathic aberration. Actually, antisocial personalities would find it difficult to work in such an organizational structure. Nor were many particularly religious in early life; most attended secular schools. Instead of poor, ignorant, single young men with no knowledge of the West, most were middle- to upper-middle-class, highly educated, married, and middle-aged men. Most had traveled to or lived in the West.

What drew most terrorists to the Salafi philosophy was a sense of alienation and loss when they moved into new environments, most often urban and Western (for example, the Hamburg cell), that their earlier belief system could not handle. As Marc Sageman notes in his study: "They were isolated when they moved away from their families and became particularly lonely and emotionally alienated in this new individualistic environment. The lack of spiritualism in a utilitarian society was keenly felt. Underemployed and discriminated against by the local society, they felt a personal sense of grievance and humiliation. They sought a cause that would give them emotional relief, social community, spiritual comfort, and cause for self-sacrifice. Although they did not start out particularly religious, there was a shift in their devotion before they joined the global jihad, which gave them both a cause and comrades."[15]

Once they had selected themselves for involvement, they attempted to join Al Qaeda by finding facilitators with access to the global jihad. These contacts provided hubs that interacted between the top leadership of Al Qaeda and the three main sources of its cadres (Muslims from Southeast Asia, the core Arab states, and the Maghreb). Once access was established, these volunteers attended training camps. Only the most dedicated were invited for further training and then to participate in missions.

By this method, Al Qaeda leadership recruited, vetted, trained, and tested its cadres. The results were seen on September 11, 2001. Instead of crazed lunatics, the enemy was a well-trained and dedicated foe who hated us. What probably surprised Americans most were the lengths some would go to in the name of ideology.

What Must Be Done

The enemy we are fighting is both a terrorist organization and an ideological movement. The original structure has evolved from a hierarchical model to a more adaptable network, functioning via modern communications between its depleted leadership and a pool of cadres facilitated by hubs of organizers in different countries. Coupled with similar Islamic extremist groups, Al Qaeda has a diffuse and loose structure coordinating its anti-American operations in Muslim lands while it still prepares to strike the U.S. homeland again. Its "far enemy" belief structure puts America at the root of all Muslim problems.

The nature of the organization is to attack the far enemy until it is either destroyed or suffers such losses that it will reform and rethink its purpose. The nature of the movement is to foster anger, resentment, and violence against Western civilization and its supporters in the Muslim world, and to seek answers in the past rather than taking an introspective look and developing a viable future to address the real problems found in Muslim society.

Terrorism is a tactic that has been practiced by every race and creed for diverse and incompatible political, religious, or ideological reasons. But one cannot wage war against a tactic. One can wage war, however, against terrorists who are animate and therefore susceptible to force. The war on terror may be global, but it is not universal. Despite the post-9/11 rhetoric of destroying all terrorist groups that have global reach, we cannot destroy the Tamil Tigers and all other terror organizations. That would not only be beyond America's capacity, but it would also fritter away resources from destroying the one group that is specifically dedicated to harming America. To eradicate that most immediate threat, then, the United States must understand Al Qaeda and destroy it as an organization and as a movement.

The nature of the war against Al Qaeda the organization should be aimed at finding and destroying the hubs that connect the leadership in hiding with the pool of candidates wishing to participate in the jihad, further isolating the leadership by stripping it of communications, eventually capturing it, and turning those prisoners against their former comrades as either informers or propaganda spokesmen. In Afghanistan and Iraq, this would take part in the context of our ongoing counterinsurgency campaigns. In the rest of the world, however, this would be an intelligence officer's and policeman's war, sometimes assisted by military special mission groups. This war depends on close cooperation with governments such as Pakistan's, which will wish to avoid appearing to be puppets of the West. Their fears of overt American involvement in their internal affairs preclude most conventional, and even some unconventional, military options.

Destruction of Al Qaeda the movement requires:

- Neutralizing Al Qaeda propaganda and making it irrelevant with the long-term commitment of the diplomatic, informational, intelligence, developmental, educational, and covert action tools of statecraft
- Removing emotional sources of inspiration for those who are searching for a cause for self-sacrifice
- Keeping close contact with religious leaders, encouraging them to counteract the philosophy of Salafi extremism so Muslims can show other Muslims how harmful and bankrupt this ideology is.

To answer Carl von Clausewitz's question as to the type of war we are embarking on, we must consider the war on terror as both an act of force to compel a group to our will and a struggle to convince civilization of the evil of its intentions. The nature of the struggle will be long term and nuanced. Its future military context should be constrained to specific instances that cannot be solved with other applications of American or international statecraft. It is not a conventional war. And although it involves violence, we should avoid turning it into an open war that could benefit the enemy.

What are the implications for future U.S. security strategy? Graham Fuller suggests a three-part strategy for the war on terror.[16] First is the elimination of the Al Qaeda organization and those who support it, such as the Taliban. Second is intensified police and intelligence work to deter and block future attacks. Third and most important is attending to sources of grievances in the Muslim world that constitute the soil for terrorism. This is similar to the National Defense Strategy, which provides succinct policy goals: protecting the homeland, countering ideological support for terrorism, and disrupting and attacking terrorist networks. The National Defense Strategy is also correct in stating that victory will not be on the battlefield alone.[17]

There are three major implications for our future security strategy in regard to the war on terror. First, it is a struggle against both a non-state group and a particular ideology. Pronouncements by senior DOD officials in 2005 trying to define the war on terror as a global struggle against violent extremism were a step in the right direction but were still incomplete. Whatever new catchphrase is used, it must mention the specific Salafi content of the extremism we are fighting, and new strategies of statecraft must work to disconnect this ideology from what sustains it: a sense of alienation brought on by perceived threats to the faith and injustice to Muslim peoples. Therefore, one of the lessons to be learned is to do everything in our power to avoid another war in the Muslim world that could further inflame these perceived threats, however unjustified, while we work to destroy Al Qaeda the organization. Otherwise, a future war, no matter how it will be seen in Western eyes or however necessary it may appear to strategists, will provide the renewal that Al Qaeda the movement needs, which in turn will regenerate the organization.

Second, because of the ideological underpinnings of this struggle, America will have to engage its soft power far more. This is not a struggle against a bearded man in a cave in Waziristan; it is a clash of ideas and beliefs and over who can mobilize more support in a part of the world that is critical to American security.

Third, efforts to transform the Muslim world to end the causes that brought us Al Qaeda the movement must be left to the Muslim world itself and supported through the many tools of U.S. statecraft but not with overt military force. Egypt, Saudi Arabia, and other "near enemies" must reform in their own way, with American assistance and prodding if necessary, but not with American coercion so as to remove the justification for the movement and battle cry that these regimes are American creatures.

We should remember the advice of T. E. Lawrence: "Do not try to do too much with your own hands. Better the Arabs do it tolerably than that you do it perfectly."[18]

4

Information Warfare

—Col Thomas X. Hammes, USMC (Ret.)

The insurgents in Iraq and Afghanistan have demonstrated a clear understanding of the importance of information warfare. Captured documents, prisoner interrogation, and insurgent day-to-day actions indicate that they consider information warfare to be central to their strategy. Of particular note is their discussion that in the information arena, the tactical, operational, and strategic levels of war merge. One of the reasons that they videotape almost every attack is because they understand that while the attack is tactical, the resulting video is a crucial element of their strategic information campaign.

In contrast, the United States still has not developed an effective definition for this essential element of warfare. In fact, the recent release of the new Joint Publication 3-13 *Information Operations* clearly indicates the U.S. military considers information operations to be just one of a list of support elements. It lumps it together with four disciplines focused on the technical aspects of keeping digital information systems working.

This is the central difference between the insurgent's understanding of information operations and the U.S. military's. The insurgents understand that information operations are the central element of insurgency. They also understand that the "OODA loop" (a term coined by Col John Boyd, USAF, based on his experience as a pilot for the cycle of decision making through which a commander observes, orients, decides, and acts repeatedly over time) for information operations needs to keep up with events as they happen. Therefore, while insurgents provide commanders guidance to unify the information themes, they decentralize the actual generation of messages. In contrast, the U.S. military sees information operations as just one of many supporting elements of "real" operations—and it heavily centralizes the approval and release of messages.

Essentially, the insurgents understand that the dominant form of warfare has changed while the United States seems to think these messy conflicts are merely aberrations. In the West, there continues to be a great deal of debate concerning the validity of the four generations of war (4GW) model. In contrast, Al Qaeda and other Islamic websites have stated they will use 4GW to defeat the United States. The Preaching Information Department of the Global Islamic Media Front actually released a document titled "Fourth Generation Warfare Presented by the Global Islamic Media Front."[1]

While 4GW proponents have not agreed on a single definition, for the purposes of this chapter, I will use the following definition. "Fourth Generation war uses all available networks—political, economic, social and military—to convince the enemy's political decision makers that their strategic goals are either unachievable or too costly for the perceived benefit. It is an evolved form of insurgency. Still rooted in the fundamental precept that superior political will, when properly employed can defeat greater economic and military power, 4GW makes use of society's networks to carry on its fight. Unlike previous generations of warfare, it does not attempt to win by defeating the enemy's military forces. Instead, via the networks, it directly attacks the minds of the enemy decision makers to destroy the enemy's political will. Fourth Generation wars are lengthy—measured in decades rather than months or years."

I selected this definition because it places a premium on ideas and the use of information networks to transmit key messages to the various actors involved in the conflict. Those messages are at the heart of this kind of war. The ability to drive your message home to the enemy decision makers is the central concept of 4GW. Modern insurgents do not plan to defeat U.S. military forces. They know they cannot. They plan to break U.S. political will—and have repeated examples of other insurgents doing so over the last thirty years. Only information enters the minds of decision makers; thus, it is central to this form of war.

U.S. Failure to Adapt

Since 2003, the U.S. military has adapted extensively to adjust tactically to the 4GW wars it is fighting in Afghanistan and Iraq. From strategic to the tactical level, American military personnel are rethinking how they fight insurgents. The U.S. military has rewritten doctrine and updated those tactics, techniques, and procedures that have been successful against previous insurgents to face the constantly evolving insurgencies they are now fighting. Across the government, people are looking at ways to make the U.S. government as a whole more effective in counterinsurgency.

Of particular importance is the shift in education from a focus on the techniques of fighting high-tech short wars to the ideas and concepts necessary to fight the protracted, political struggles the U.S. armed forces face today.

Thus it is particularly puzzling that the United States has made so little progress in information operations. On March 13, 2006, the Pentagon released Joint Publication 3-13 *Information Operations.* Despite three years of additional painful experience against insurgents, the document repeats the 2003 road map almost word for word. In its Executive Summary, *Information Operations* states:

"Information is a strategic resource, vital to national security, and military operations depend on information and information systems for many simultaneous and integrated activities.

"Information operations (IO) are described as the integrated employment of electronic warfare (EW), computer network operations (CNO), psychological operations (PSYOPS), military deception (MILDEC), and operations security (OPSEC), in concert with supporting and related capabilities, to influence, disrupt, corrupt, or usurp adversarial human and automated decision making while protecting our own. . . . The principal goal is to achieve and maintain information superiority for the U.S. and its allies."

The Pentagon has completely missed the significance of information in today's warfare. The only element remotely related to influencing perceptions is psychological operations, and it is buried among the technical aspects of information warfare. Clearly the Pentagon remains focused on large-scale conventional war as the primary threat. This seems to be based on the potential catastrophic effects if a near-peer competitor should arise in the next couple of decades. However, that competitor is most likely to use 4GW concepts and techniques rather than the 3GW the Pentagon is preparing for. Thus, the Pentagon's failure to integrate the wars it has been fighting for five years into its new IO doctrine is truly remarkable. Instead, the goal remains information superiority. This is despite the fact that in the three conflicts the United States is currently fighting—Iraq, Afghanistan, and the Global War on Terrorism—it is fighting at a significant information deficit. The new document simply ignores the hard knocks the United States is taking daily and continues to base its future on the assumption that it will have information dominance.

At this point, the U.S. approach to information operations resembles the old joke about modern logistics and the line infantry officer who says, "I don't know what this logistics stuff is, but I want some of it."

We know 4GW operates across the spectrum of political, economic, social, and military fields. Thus, information operations must span the same arena. Further, they must not be packaged with electronic warfare and computer network operations. This simply reinforces the Department of Defense's propensity to seek technical solutions to every problem. Rather, IO must be broken out not just from the limitation of the technical fields but also from the limitations of DOD.

Information operations must be a tool used across the entire spectrum of modern warfare and not seen as primarily a military function.

The White House appeared to understand the broader requirements of what they correctly labeled "strategic communications" when it appointed Karen Hughes, a very trusted Bush adviser, to the position of Undersecretary of State for Public Diplomacy. First, the choice of strategic communications showed an understanding that the war of perceptions is much broader than DOD's narrow definition of information operations. For the balance of this chapter, I will use the term "strategic communications" because it better captures the issue and because the DOD definition has rendered information operations essentially useless for strategic discussion. Reinforcing the importance of the White House's announcement was the appointment of one of the President's closest advisers as the first Undersecretary. It seemed to indicate the critical importance of this element of national power and the requirement to coordinate the effort across the federal government.

Yet even as it announced the position, the White House made it clear it didn't see this as an urgent task. The announcement of the office was made on March 12, 2005. Unfortunately, the same statement announced that Ms. Hughes would not actually start work until sometime in the fall. Clearly strategic information was not an urgent requirement. Her first trip to the Middle East in September 2005 was less than successful, and since then her office essentially dropped out of the news.

How Did the Insurgents Adapt?

In contrast, the insurgents are acutely aware of the requirement to keep their message in front of both their supporters and their opponents. Using a series of more than thirty taped statements since the beginning of 2005, Al Qaeda continues an aggressive worldwide public information campaign. In essence, the United States is losing the public communications battle to an organization that wants to take the world back to the seventh century! The various insurgent groups in Iraq have developed very sophisticated strategic communications campaigns that include TV, radio, CDs, and even cell phone clips. In fact, this has been the pattern for insurgents since Ho Chi Minh.

They understand that the massive, worldwide communications revolution has fundamentally changed not only how people communicate but also how they get their information and form their opinions. Despite the Pentagon's insistence that information technology has transformed war, its impact has been felt much more strongly in the political-social sphere than in the military arena.

While in the military sphere the superb connectivity offered allows faster decision cycles and greater situational awareness on the conventional battlefield, it has yet to provide major dividends in fighting an enemy that chooses to use 4GW techniques rather than earlier forms of war. In contrast, the new communications technologies have literally transformed how our 4GW enemies are using IO to recruit, train, motivate, and direct a widespread web of people with similar ideas. In fact, it is in developing, implanting, and nurturing those ideas that our enemies are making transformational use of cell phones, text messaging, chat rooms, streaming videos, and e-mail. Their ability to use new technology to do so should not surprise us.

Al Qaeda provides an excellent example. Starting with a self-selecting group of unsatisfied males, Al Qaeda provides a closed virtual environment where they can express their dissatisfaction, have their concerns echoed by like-minded people, and then have them reinforced by Al Qaeda's 4G warriors. The very nature of the group excludes any opposing views, so it becomes a self reinforcing, closed loop that confirms and reinforces the radical Islamist teachings of the group. In addition to the online reinforcement of initial beliefs, these websites provide contacts at radical mosques near where the patrons live. These mosques further reinforce both the Al Qaeda view and their isolation from other viewpoints. When a person is ready, he can be proselytized, recruited, and even trained online with streaming video of everything from lectures on religion to how to fire an SA-7 missile.

Al Qaeda and other insurgent groups have used the information pathways to conduct broad-spectrum information operations that contact like-minded zealots across the world. Further, they do it largely out of sight of the security services. The March 11, 2004, bombings in Spain and the July 7, 2005, bombings in England were done by people who had at most minimal contact with any recognizable element of Al Qaeda. Rather they had simply acted on the message Al Qaeda had been promulgating through various paths.

These activities are all based on Al Qaeda's understanding that the population is the correct target of strategic communications. Their strategic communications campaign has created effects from the strategic (continued hostility of a large part of the Muslim community toward the United States) to the tactical level (bombs exploding in countries around the world.)

The Message Must Reflect Our Actions

The key question seems to be "Can a democracy conduct an effective information campaign in the modern world?" I contend that we can. The first step is to understand some key realities of strategic communications.

By far the biggest truth is "What you do speaks so loudly, they cannot hear what you say." We say our message is about freedom and individual rights and then lock our own citizens up for years without trial. We state that we are not fighting a war against Islam. Then we allow LTG William Boykin, who publicly stated that Islam is a false religion, to hold a key position in the war on terror. We invite Jerry Falwell to the White House for a prayer breakfast and photo opportunities just after he broadcast comments that all Muslims will burn in hell. Each action directly undercut our strategic message. Al Qaeda knows this and uses the publicly available film clips of each event to refute our message. Our strategic message must reflect our actions. In today's fully connected world, we cannot say one thing to the world and act in another way for domestic political reasons.

Mission Orders Based on Commander's Intent

From the strategic to the tactical level, the cost of writing, filming, producing, and disseminating messages has dropped to essentially zero. All that is required is the ideas and talent. As we are seeing in Iraq and Afghanistan, the insurgents are superb at exploiting both international and local themes and disseminating them through DVDs, CDs, audiotapes, and cell phones. They even make enough on sales of the products to cover the production costs. Since the insurgencies are also coalitions of the willing, they operate as highly distributed networks that have authority to respond immediately to any opportunity. However, from Indonesia to the Netherlands, the Sunni Islamists have a unifying theme—the commander's intent in effect—provided by Osama bin Laden via audiotapes. Each cell is free to use those themes in locally produced and disseminated messages.

In contrast, the West has essentially ceded the strategic communications battlefield to the Islamist radicals. Other than the truly weak efforts by the White House Office of Communications, the United States has essentially failed to respond to the messages of the Islamists. In fact, no nation in the West even seems to have an effective system to identify the false themes being pushed by the Islamists and then provide a truthful alternative message to counteract the Islamist message. The insurgents are winning the battle of IO because the West has conceded the field to them. While our European allies harp on the United States for failing to talk rather than fight, the Europeans have utterly failed to put out an effective counter message within their own nations. The recent riots in France, the "comic wars" throughout the world, and the bombings and murders conducted by completely independent elements heeding Al Qaeda's message all originated within the radical Islamic populations in Europe.

So how does a bureaucratic Western democracy organize to fight this information battle?

First, we have to think about strategic communications rather than information operations so that we get away from the focus on technology. We need to understand that it is about influencing a number of distinct audiences—the population of the country where the conflict is being fought, the population of the region, potential sympathetic populations worldwide (to neutralize the support for the insurgents), and our own populations (to reinforce our political will).

The problem of what office should be responsible for framing the message is critical. Currently, that responsibility is in the Department of State in the United States. While this is logical, the State Department lacks the manpower, funding, and bureaucratic muscle to force other elements to respond. It will require direct

White House attention to ensure the responsible office has the clout to unify the American message across the U.S. bureaucracy.

Once we are grounded in a broader concept of strategic communications and have an organization to execute the plan, we must develop the cultural and language expertise to work effectively with the targeted audiences. Our national-level decision makers must decide on the key themes to be used by our communications campaign, but the specific messages must be left to the regional and country experts who can frame messages in a culturally appropriate way.

We will have to change our personnel system to reward genuine expertise in both cultural and strategic communications. To be rated as a cultural expert one must have both near-native proficiency in the language and years studying and living in the culture. The U.S. government will have to create SES billets and provide sufficient compensation to attract such people. At the same time, we need to establish long-term scholarships and subsidies to provide a new generation of students with the opportunities to become true experts in their areas.

Frankly, bureaucratic resistance has been and will remain the single biggest obstacle to success in this area. While no single agency wants to be responsible for the message, none wants to give up whatever portion of that message it currently has either. And of course, not one of the agencies is interested in changing its firmly entrenched and sadly antiquated personnel systems to create a system that will attract the type of people needed for this effort. However, this effort must be made.

When we have both the message and the experts, then we can use those experts to determine the channels that are most effective within target societies to reach our audiences. Obviously the interconnected nature of today's information environment means that any message we deliver anywhere in the world will bounce around the world rapidly. Therefore, it is essential that regional and country teams craft their messages in consonance with the guidance provided from the national level. Yet, it is also critical that national decision makers do not attempt to approve each message. The excruciatingly slow bureaucratic process inherent in the U.S. government has crippled our IO efforts in Iraq simply because by the time the message is approved it has been overcome by events on the ground.

Only mission type orders based on a clear intent should be provided from the national level. Draft and release authority must reside at the local level. This will allow us to compete effectively against the insurgent IO campaign by either anticipating or responding quickly to insurgent messages. It will also allow us to coordinate closely with host nation and regional officials to make use of their much greater cultural knowledge and to tie IO themes together. In places like Iraq, this will be particularly challenging given the separate goals of various Shi'a, Sunni, and Kurdish groups. Thus, IO must be closely tied to the overall campaign plan to reflect the strategy through our messages.

In summary, the West has failed in the information arena. To recover, the West must get in the game. First, we have to understand IO is much broader than our current definition. Then we have to find talented people with the language and cultural knowledge to be effective in IO—and establish a system to educate the next generation. Finally, we have to overcome the bureaucratic inertia that inhibits effective people from producing effective IO campaigns for the targeted audiences. Until we do all three, we cannot even begin to succeed.

5

The Power of Weakness

—*William S. Lind*

Central to understanding why states usually lose Fourth Generation wars to non-state opponents who, by all the usual measures, are vastly their inferiors in combat power is the concept of "the power of weakness." This concept is a contribution to the Fourth Generation theory by Martin van Creveld, the Israeli military historian and theorist whose book *The Transformation of War* remains the most important text on the subject more than fifteen years after it was first published.

According to van Creveld, the power of weakness means that when fighting against non-state forces, states that make full use of their overwhelming military superiority will find that doing so works to their defeat. The weaker the non-state element, the more this is the case.

Martin van Creveld explains why this happens with an analogy. If an adult starts viciously beating a small child in a public place, the child can do little but suffer and bleed. But bystanders are horrified by the disparity in strength. They see the adult who is administering the beating as a monster. Soon, they intervene to stop the beating. The adult is not only prevented from continuing his actions, he is arrested and jailed on criminal charges.

Two elements of this analogy are worth drawing out. First, the beating must be visible to a larger public. If no one can see it happening, the adult can beat the child to death if he wants to, though he may pay a subsequent price. Second, the beating must continue over time. The adult can almost certainly get away with giving the child one good whack. For other parties to be motivated to intervene, the disproportionate act must continue. The power of weakness thus can only send its message in a conflict outside observers can see and that lasts long enough for them to observe, orient, decide, and act.

A second analogy may also be helpful: David and Goliath. In almost any Fourth Generation conflict, the state is Goliath and the non-state force is David. The secret to the story of David and Goliath is that Goliath always loses. Why? In the 3,000 or so years the story has been told, how many listeners have identified with Goliath?

To understand the power of weakness by more than analogy, we have to turn to the three levels of war—not the classical three levels of strategic, operational, and tactical but the three levels identified and emphasized by Col John Boyd: the moral, the mental, and the physical. Boyd stressed that the physical level of war—killing people and breaking things—is the weakest, the moral level is the most powerful, and the mental level falls in between.

Second Generation war, the only kind of war the American military knows how to fight, focuses on the physical level: putting firepower on targets. Third Generation war, or maneuver warfare, which is best exemplified by the German blitzkrieg, works primarily at the mental level. It pulls the enemy apart by facing him with unexpected and dangerous situations faster than he can deal with them. Fourth Generation war, like guerrilla warfare, works primarily at the moral level, and it does so mainly through the power of weakness.

When a powerful state military such as the American armed forces faces a physically weak Fourth Generation opponent, it can easily dominate on the physical level. It can take and hold virtually any piece of ground it wants. By pitting aircraft, missiles, tanks, and artillery against a lightly armed enemy, it can inflict far more casualties than it suffers. At the mental level, it can only make itself appear unbeatable and can terrify, if not the opposing fighters, then certainly much of the civilian population. It is in this "sea" that those fighters swim.

But at the moral level, some very different things happen. The Fourth Generation warriors gain great honor by continuing to fight someone much stronger than themselves. This provides them motivation, recruits, and financial support. The terrified civilian population also hates the state armed services that dominate it and tries to get revenge by giving the Fourth Generation fighters the base they require. Neutral parties, including world and home country public opinion, rally to the underdog. Finally, the physically dominant state Army comes to turn inward on itself, demoralized simultaneously by the unfairness its own superiority represents and by its inability to put an end to the resistance. The demoralization often leads it to be even more brutal to the civilian population, exacerbating the moral problem further. In the end, when Goliath looks in the mirror, he too sees a monster.

In Boyd's three levels of war, as in the classical three levels, a higher level trumps a lower. Just as an Army or a country that wins at the tactical and operational levels but loses at the strategic level loses the war (Germany's fate in both world wars), so a state military that wins against a Fourth Generation opponent at the physical and mental levels but loses at the moral level also loses the war. We now see exactly this phenomenon playing itself out in Iraq and in Afghanistan.

It is here that information operations (IO) enter the picture. Often, the state military in a Fourth Generation conflict has at least some glimmer of understanding of its dilemma. It realizes that its own physical superiority works against it, at least in the eyes of the civilian population, locally, at home, and around the world. It seeks to mitigate the problem with IO, ranging from leaflets and broadcasts telling the local populations it is their friend; through civic action projects such as building schools, providing medical clinics, and helping local businesses get started again; to wrapping the whole war in rhetoric about liberation, democracy, and freedom.

Seldom do any of these efforts succeed. The reason they fail is that for state armed services engaged in 4GW, IO is not what you *say* but what you *do*. No matter how many leaflets you print or articles you plant in the local newspaper about your good intentions, if what people see is doors broken down in the middle of the night, prisoners brutalized, and civilians killed in air strikes, you are a monster, Goliath.

If real information operations are what you do, what should a state military do in order to have effective IO? The answer can be given in one word, a word easy to say but very difficult for state armed services (especially Second Generation armed services) to act on. That word is "de-escalation." In almost every situation, from an individual confrontation at a roadblock through the situation in an entire province or country, the state military must seek in every way to de-escalate, to resolve the situation without violence or with an absolute minimum of violence.

How to accomplish this is too much to lay out in a short chapter. It is explained in some detail in the only field manual for Fourth Generation war published to date, the FMFM 1-A, *Fourth Generation War*, which is available on the Defense and the National Interest website (http://www.d-n-i.net/ as of January 31, 2007).

What is important to discuss here is why state militaries have such difficulty de-escalating. From the first day a Soldier or Marine begins his field training, he is taught that if he is not getting the result he wants, he should escalate. He should bring in more troops, employ heavier weapons, call in tanks, artillery, or air strikes. He is taught this to the point where it becomes second nature and his definition of how war is fought. Again, unfortunately, in Fourth Generation wars it leads not to victory but to defeat, even if the engagement is won.

If state militaries are to learn to de-escalate, their training needs to become more like that of the police. A policeman's goal in almost every situation is to de-escalate. Escalation works against the safety and order a policeman exists to protect. It can also easily end with him going to jail.

It is no surprise that in the war in Iraq, a number of Reserve and National Guard units have had more success establishing order than have their regular counterparts. The successful Guard and Reserve units have had many members who are police officers in civilian life. The units have let their cops take the lead in establishing how the unit operates, and they have in turn operated as police rather than as Soldiers or Marines.

While training like police may offer some answers to the dilemma posed by 4GW, it brings other dilemmas of its own. One is that if Soldiers and Marines are taught to de-escalate, how will they act in combat against other regular military forces? In that situation, a reluctance to escalate could quickly prove fatal. Can we in effect equip troops with a "switch" that can be positioned for either combat with other state armed forces or 4GW, with behavior changing to match? This may be asking too much of eighteen-year-olds.

A second dilemma is that the principal tool police use to de-escalate situations is talk. Good police training is largely training in how to talk situations down from violence or a threat of violence to compromise and cooperation. Assuming we are fighting 4GW in a foreign country and not in our own, how many of our troops will speak enough of the local language to talk to anyone? Without an ability to talk to the people, how can they de-escalate difficult situations? How can we even think of information operations without an ability to speak the language?

To believe that this fundamental disconnect between our troops and the local population can be overcome with the usual IO tools, with pamphlets, broadcasts, civic action programs, and the like, is naive. To have any hope of success in Fourth Generation war, we must accept that IO is not what we say but what our troops do, day in and day out, in all their various interactions with the local population.

This is the basic conundrum of Fourth Generation war, one that information operations must face directly: how do we avoid sending the message "We are Goliath," when by every physical measure, we *are* Goliath? Until we can solve that riddle, the power of weakness will continue to defeat us, and most of our own actions, including our IO, will merely make our defeat come all the faster.

6

Strategic Communication: A Mandate for the United States*

—*Jeffrey B. Jones*

In an era where the power of information affects every human being in matters both mundane and transcendent, individual and social, national and international—when images are transmitted instantaneously worldwide, radio programs are translated into hundreds of languages and broadcast to every corner of the earth, and periodicals and the Internet are universal communications media—there is no alternative but to harness information to protect and promote national interests.[1]

The Mandate

As a subset of the national security strategy, there is a need for a national communications strategy coequal with the political strategy overseen by the Department of State, the economic strategy led by the National Security Council Office of International Economic Affairs, and the national military strategy implemented by the Secretary of Defense and the uniformed military. The national communications strategy should provide objectives and guidance for both regional and transnational issues. A mechanism to coordinate all interagency informational efforts at the national level is essential to its success. The forum should meet routinely, not just in times of crisis.

This call for a national communications strategy is not an argument for a propaganda minister, but for better coordination of information efforts among agencies. The information war must be waged during peacetime, crisis, operations

---

* *Reprinted by permission from* Joint Forces Quarterly, *4th Quarter 2005.*

other than war, war itself, and in the post-conflict period. It should shape the informational and intellectual environment long before hostilities. The effort is not restricted to the White House Office of Global Communications or to interagency spokesmen, press officers, information warriors, or technological innovations that are shaping the digitized battlefield; it must include the public diplomacy activities of the Department of State as well as the full spectrum of global activities of the U.S. Agency for International Development (USAID) and other agencies.

In reality, we are talking about strategic communication—the synchronized coordination of statecraft, public affairs, public diplomacy, military information operations, and other activities, reinforced by political, economic, military, and other actions, to advance U.S. foreign policy objectives. To date, the predominant concern has been for reaching domestic audiences through public affairs and dealing with U.S. and Western media and the twenty-four-hour news cycle, with our public diplomacy efforts severely constrained by the disestablishment of the U.S. Information Agency some years ago and the reality that we have had chronic resource insufficiency across the strategic communications' domain. As Joseph Nye points out, to get America's message across, we need assurance, positive actions and examples, persuasion, moral suasion, and other inducements as much as we need deterrence, dissuasion, and coercion.[2]

Using information also requires coordination with the information efforts of allies, friends, and former adversaries. Further, it demands constant multi-agency, multiservice, multidisciplinary, and multidimensional integration as well as orchestration, choreography, and synergy. This chapter deals with the use of information to affect attitudinal and behavioral change (the nonlinear and intellectual fourth dimension) and the mandate for successful communications with the first wave (agrarian), the second wave (industrialized), and what Alvin and Heidi Toffler call the "postindustrial" third wave of societies.[3] The following factors impact today's informational environment:

- Traditional dividing lines between public affairs, public diplomacy, and military information operations are blurred because of immediate access to information. Domestic press announcements are broadcast and monitored globally, and they influence as well as inform. Reports and examples of focused, tactical U.S. psychological operations (PSYOPS)—all truthful but designed expressly to influence foreign attitudes and behavior—are also available in this country on the Internet. Each is important and designed for specific audiences. None is preeminent. Synergy is impossible without coordination. The information activities of other government agencies are distinct, although some of the means may be the same.
- Resources dedicated to the information realm, which some would argue is the most critical element of national power, have been estimated to be insufficient by a factor of ten.

- There is extensive proliferation of animosity, alienation of allies, disappointment of friends, and disillusionment of those who have traditionally looked to a trusted America for hope.
- Technological innovations exist but are insufficiently funded, tapped, or fused. The Joint Staff's information management portal, conceived during operations in Afghanistan, only came to fruition in 2005. Integration with unclassified systems at the State Department remains an unfulfilled requirement.
- Bureaucratic turf battles, misperceptions, and the absence of visible, sustained interagency commitment are detriments to progress.
- Al Qaeda and other parties constitute an active adversary in the propaganda domain. What previously existed in the training camps of Afghanistan is now on the Internet. In 2005, Abu Musab al-Zarqawi's terrorist group released a CD-ROM urging Muslims to battle against Coalition "crusaders" in Iraq, and others have followed. That is not an argument to engage in propaganda; for the United States, truthful information is the best antidote and is exactly what its public affairs, public diplomacy, and information operators seek to provide.
- Policy issues that dominate the "hierarchy of hatred" against the United States, such as the Middle East peace process, remain unresolved. With increased and balanced U.S. pressure on both sides, and sustained engagement, some progress is being made. But as the United Nations' *Arab Human Development Report* recently underscored, we are not the only guilty party, despite accusations to the contrary.
- From the highest levels of government, there is growing overreliance on non–face-to-face communications that do not convey national seriousness of purpose or even interest in allied opinion. Perceptions become reality in the mind.
- Our national ability to use television and the Internet in sophisticated ways to reach the full spectrum of audiences remains woefully inadequate if we are to influence the future.
- There is a mandate to apply the lessons of the past, positive and negative: organizational, technological, planning; education and training; phasing; interagency, joint, and coalition; strategic, operational, and tactical.

The Requirements

At this point, as the Tofflers point out in *War and Anti-War*, there is no overarching knowledge or information strategy at the national level, nor is there a focused and effective mechanism for coordinating dissemination to all prospective audiences around the world—allied, friendly, neutral, potentially hostile, and hostile. While the U.S. Information Agency had the predominant responsibility for public diplomacy until it was disestablished, national assets for communication, information, and education around the globe have degraded, and other actors and key communicators are now involved. There is little evidence of cooperation, coordination, or appreciation for the impact of strategic communications. Thus, there is a need for a permanent mechanism to coordinate as well as implement and monitor all interagency information efforts. Several attempts have been made since 2001, but none have been effectively institutionalized in a national security presidential directive, which is needed to add discipline, guidance, and direction as well as to monitor implementation.

This is a requirement in peacetime as well as during crises, conflicts, and post-conflict operations. Members of such an interagency structure would also work together to implement strategic information plans proposed by the affected geographic combatant commanders to both the Secretary of Defense and Chairman of the Joint Chiefs of Staff. The secretary and chairman would provide these requests for interagency support such as was executed so successfully during Operation Uphold Democracy in Haiti.

At the theater level, each combatant commander has a theater security cooperation plan, which should include senior leader engagement, international military education and training, security assistance, pervasive use of DOD-sponsored regional security studies centers, peacetime PSYOPS programs, and, ideally, a theater information strategy derived from the national communications strategy. All elements of the plan should be designed to help achieve political, economic, and military objectives for the region. Coordination mechanisms include elements of the combatant command staff (operations, intelligence, strategy and plans, public affairs, strategic communications, information operations, PSYOPS, and civil affairs and the Staff Judge Advocate), U.S. embassies (foreign policy, intelligence, State Department public diplomacy affairs, defense attachés, and regionally oriented USAID advisers), and, to the extent possible, allied representatives. Each combatant command should draft a theater information strategy concentrating on proactive, influential, and shaping (rather than reactive) efforts to reduce sources of conflict; assistance to nations in their transition to democratic systems; increasing dialogue by building political, economic, military, medical, commercial, social, and educational bridges; development of collaborative approaches to regional problems; reduction of the motivation and perceived legitimacy of those who possess nuclear weapons and other weapons of mass destruction; and emphasis on the correct role of the military in a democracy, including constructive domestic uses.

These same advisers would meet regularly to coordinate their respective efforts with those at the interagency level, channeled through the DOD-led/J–39 Battle Update Brief apparatus to maximize the informational impact throughout the region and implement the agreed strategy. As a matter of course, strategic communication plans would be integrated into operation, concept, and contingency plans in much the same way as we have incorporated flexible deterrent options. Finally, when problems arise and contingency planning commences, a theater-wide strategic communication-supporting plan must be developed and implemented. Every effort must be made to "informationally" prepare the battle space (Phase 0) to defuse, deter, or contain the conflict. Combatant commanders should submit their requests for interagency consideration in terms of encouraging multinational organizations such as the North Atlantic Treaty Organization, Organization of American States, and Association of Southeast Asian Nations to participate in developing and implementing such an information strategy and to accept an increasing role. The George C. Marshall European Center for Security Studies and regional centers of National Defense University (Africa Center, Near East and South Asia Center, and Center for Hemispheric Defense Studies), which institutionalize the self-help process through sharing the ideas and experiences of Western democracies and their free market economies, could play an invaluable role as well. New centers of this type should be proposed to meet theater needs.

At the tactical level, there are myriad applications for peacetime information use. Conveying information by all means available can enhance one's ability to see, hear, know, disrupt, deny, "outcommunicate," and "outthink" the adversary. In addition, it can encourage dissension, defection, and surrender, thus ending the battle quickly and saving lives. Also at the tactical level, information must be used to help in the all-important multifaceted, multiagency, and probably multinational efforts after the battle. Allies can be invaluable contributors to common goals and objectives as well as provide key conduits to enhance the effectiveness of our informational efforts.

Planning across the Spectrum

In peacetime, strategic communication issues are both regional and transnational. The construct is more encompassing than yesterday's deterrence and dissuasion, although those remain central to national survival and our global interests. Given the U.S. reputation for unilateral action, with little (or at least perceived as insufficient) coordination and inclusion of allies, we need the following to ensure that we have enduring bridges of understanding: an effective and active strategy of reassurance for friends; assurance of our capacity and enduring commitment for potential adversaries; persuasion of friends, allies, adversaries, and neutrals; enhanced perceptions in terms of military and other presence; and two-way education and capacity enhancement programs at all levels. In addition, we need more effective human rights assistance, informational efforts to speed newly free countries on the road to democracy, humanitarian and disaster assistance, refugee and counterdrug operations, and full-spectrum information efforts in support of President George W. Bush's Proliferation Security Initiative.

An unfulfilled task from the administration's first term is the aforementioned need for a national communications strategy to drive the creation of cascading theater information strategies for each region, more comprehensive theater security cooperation plans, better coordination with U.S. embassy Mission Performance Plans, robust information plans implementing each of the regional combating terrorism strategies, better allied capacity-building, and increased means of measuring strategic, operational, and tactical effectiveness. The Department of Defense needs to establish a comprehensive strategy for its role of supporting the State Department in public diplomacy, as well as more rational and responsive product and action approval authority.

In crises, there are again both regional and transnational requirements: tailored, non–order-of-battle intelligence requirements as well as a mandate for enhanced dissuasion, deterrence, deployment enhancement, perceptions of presence, prepositioning, interagency cross-fertilization, and accessing broader coalition assistance and cooperation. As requested but denied in Rwanda, there may be opportunities for information intervention (U.S./allies/UN) to counter the genocidal encouragement from such entities as hostile radio broadcasts. Strategic communication and information planning accelerators are needed as well as enhanced capacity for technological reachback, tempered with the enduring requirement for physical presence to assess ground truth and the resonance of our messages. We need to develop or take better advantage of other conduits for our messages, especially those with proven or likely resonance.

Just as in peacetime, as crises escalate, we must better understand that our actions—political, economic, or military—convey messages more loudly than rhetoric, but that both are important and neither in isolation is a panacea. While there are indeed strategic, operational, and tactical measures of effectiveness, there must be organizational elements dedicated to tracking them and providing feedback to information planners at all levels. A more rational and responsive product/action approval process is needed that prescribes authorities down to the lowest level. Earlier information as well as intelligence preparation of the battle space are required. There must be better analytic, human factor, perceptional, and environmental guidance in terms of what to expect for planners, commanders, and deploying service members. Some sources exist, but simply posting information on the Defense Intelligence Agency website is insufficient. Both push and pull are necessary. There must be attention to identifying full-spectrum intelligence and open-source requirements that are essential to effective understanding as well as communication at all levels.

As crises become more volatile, there must be better pulsing and synchronization of information. There is a need for face-to-face engagement instead of the increasing tendency to rely on demarches delivered by others, telephone calls, cables, and interlocutors that do not convey the same national purpose. Moreover—and this is especially key for forward-deployed combatant commanders—we must more pervasively engage multilateral and international organizations (including nongovernmental organizations that understand who the true influences are in an affected population and have conduits to them), expand our flexible deterrent options, refine interagency requirements in plans, integrate strategic communications planning elements into the standing joint force headquarters, develop documents that identify interagency requirements, and establish standing information coordinating committees to better fuse strategic communications both in theater as well as with Washington.

As combat operations appear imminent, we must finalize information planning with both the interagency community and with allies. Country-specific, regional, and transnational strategic communication requirements should have already been identified and expertise deployed to key information nodes in the region so that planning and relationship-building are completed in advance and refined implementation can occur. Moreover, while planning is indeed done in phases, there must be simultaneous informational and operational planning for the post-conflict period, which can clearly prove more complex, challenging, and of longer duration than force-on-force operations. Feedback loops are essential to ensure resonance and modification of approaches, conduits of influence, products, and actions when appropriate. As during crises, dedicated personnel and systems must be in place to measure the effectiveness of messages and actions, monitor adversarial media, accelerate response times at all levels, and preempt or counteract enemy misinformation and disinformation. We must ensure the capacity for both individual and collective targeting—from sophisticated elites to the illiterate. Databases drawn from all available sources must be assembled months in advance. Targeting guidance must be issued, and tactical as well as theater-wide plans for radio, television, Internet, print, and face-to-face communications must be in place.

Operations in Afghanistan and Iraq have underscored that we must create a greater capacity to capture still and video images and develop improved means to transmit, package, and use them imaginatively. Every effort must be made to more effectively reach out to allies, friends, and neutrals and to prioritize our organizational, joint, interagency, and Coalition efforts. Based on experience, there are requirements for rapid adjustment, dissemination of good news, and phasing away U.S. voices and faces to fade into the background while those of the nation in which the operation is being conducted take the lead. We must understand that we may no longer be the critical or most credible deliverers of the message. In fact, we must do everything we can to assist the nation in articulating what must become its, not our, priorities. Coordinating messages with combat power on every level, we must accelerate the defeat of enemy forces and be prepared for such factors as the desertion, defection, and surrender of enemy forces as well as demonstrations by civilians.

Service members must understand that in today's information environment, as underscored by the actions of a few at the Abu Ghraib prison, their individual deeds can have strategic consequences for either good or ill, affecting not just their immediate surroundings but things as far reaching as alliance trust, confidence, and even continued Coalition participation. Improvement is needed in capturing the positive acts of our own Soldiers, Sailors, Airmen, and Marines; the activities of the U.S. Agency for International Development; the citizens themselves; and other parties across the country. It is essential that the world, as well as regional and U.S. domestic audiences, sees these images of security, collaborative progress, and hope.

In post-conflict operations, interagency coordination on the ground becomes even more critical regionally as well as internationally. Information-coordinating committees become vital for interagency, coalition, and potentially international coordination, cooperation, and synergy. Again, the importance of good news cannot be overemphasized. Nor can constantly assessing resonance and target audiences, disseminating to multiple audiences, dealing with insurgents and former regime elements, not giving untoward legitimacy to low-level "thorns" in the process, and "incentivizing" the populace toward cooperation and providing information. Better care must be taken in preparing the armed forces for the always difficult transition from warfare to positive engagement with a defeated populace. Joint interagency coordination groups, such as those established in Iraq, are key to engagement at the personal level as well as to coordination, providing cogent explanations for coalition activities, responding to questions from key communicators and "influentials," managing funding for projects identified as critical to the quality of life for the common citizen, and transitioning from occupier to partner. The message must be communicated to locals that it is their country and their future and thus their responsibility—with international assistance—to achieve post-conflict stability.

Measures of Effectiveness

At issue is how to establish and institutionalize measures of effectiveness—standards of comparison used to evaluate the progress of an operation—at the strategic, operational, and tactical levels. Lack of established and agreed criteria, failure to fuse intelligence efforts, and shortfalls in dedicated personnel, linguistic oversight, and technological monitoring continue to inhibit data compilation, fusion, and dissemination.

For instance, there is a need to measure the sentiments and actions of:

- The populace (not monolithic in Iraq or Afghanistan—demographics must be understood)
- Elites, whose actions and messages impact audiences and decision makers
- Decision makers (de facto and official).

Regarding media monitoring, we must keep a pulse not only on what is watched but also on its public credibility. In addition, those involved in such efforts must do more than simply document what was broadcast. They must also tell commanders the range of implications as well as propose what might be done about it—and by whom.

Strategically, leading indicators include alliance participation, statements by heads of state and government leaders, policy endorsement, mobilization, votes in the United Nations and other multinational organizations, resource commitments (forces, equipment, funds, civilian police or other trainers, and facilities), regional Friday sermons, intercepts and intelligence cooperation, international and national media coverage, actions and messages from multinational organizations (such as the Gulf Cooperation Council, Organization of Islamic Conference, and Arab League), local alliances, cross-border cooperation, polling, *fatwas*, resonance in academic publications, recall of ambassadors for consultations, and the closing of foreign missions.

Operationally, primary indicators are statements by senior officials and military commanders, statements from religious organizations such as the *hawza*, regional Friday sermons, troop movements and exercises, combat power demonstrations, border and maritime operations, demonstrations or other civil disobedience, national media reporting, enhanced intelligence-gathering, key leader defections and large-scale desertions, self-generated grounding of combat aircraft, self-generated return to garrisons, *fatwas*, national polls, and large unit surrenders.

Tactically, important indicators are individual or unit desertions; defections; surrenders; abandonment of equipment; civilian compliance or noncompliance; local open-source print, radio, and television coverage; Friday prayers; influential imams' statements; *fatwas*; meetings; attendance at established local, regional, or provincial coordination committees; polling; recruitment and retention figures in military/security forces (such as the National Guard, police, Facilities Protection Service, border police, and Army); attacks on Coalition forces and civilians; level of intelligence reported to Coalition forces or hotlines; intercepts; paramilitary cooperation; reestablishment of a secure environment; school attendance or closings; civilian compliance with interim government directives; Internet traffic; willingness of students and others to engage in discussions and participate in focus groups; telephone call-in data; reports from USAID and its British equivalent, the Department for International Development, as well as other nongovernmental organizations; willingness to be hired for Coalition-led infrastructure enhancement projects; focus groups; surveys of elites; open-source photography; and graffiti.

In a time of defense budgets predominantly focused on Iraq and Afghanistan but with other global concerns, evolving overseas basing, sustained forward deployments, and increased instability, it is critical to reinforce perceptions of American commitment through diplomatic engagement and outreach, particularly toward the Muslim world and against Islamic and other extremists. It is vital to underscore the nation's economic and developmental assistance as well as its military capacity and reliability. The way friends, allies, former adversaries, future enemies, and neutrals view our capabilities, as well as our intentions, remains fundamental to strategic and conventional deterrence and to our ability to resolve disputes and prevail in conflict. Today's international security environment requires not only the effective application of emerging technologies to enhance the command and control of the tactical commander, but also the imaginative implementation of information strategies and campaigns at the national and theater levels.

Enhanced cooperation, coordination, and cohesion of information efforts, from the national level to the tactical, bringing to bear all the resources and conduits of influence needed, are essential to meet today's challenges and tomorrow's unknowns. By encouraging long-term change, attacking the sources of conflict, and encouraging openness and dialogue, strategic communicators can contribute significantly to keeping the peace, reinforcing stability, and inhibiting terrorism, the proliferation of weapons of mass destruction, and the flow of drugs. In addition, they can enhance U.S. power projection, accelerate war termination, and help in complex post-conflict stability and reconstruction operations.

Maintaining the peace is better than resolving crises. Containing conflict is better than committing forces. If combat is necessary, shortened conflict with minimal loss of life on both sides and post-conflict stability are the preferred outcomes. Winning the information war is imperative to all these efforts. Thus, strategic communication—the effective integration of statecraft, public affairs, public diplomacy, and military information operations, reinforced by political, economic, and military actions—is required to advance these foreign policy objectives. No single contributor is preeminent. All are required in a synchronized and coherent manner.

7

Reflections on Psychological Operations: The Imperative of Engaging a Conflicted Population

—*Ambassador David Passage*

Events of 2007—with the United States well into the fourth year of Operation Iraqi Freedom and sixth year of U.S. operations in Afghanistan—clearly suggest an urgent need to reexamine what appears to be a significantly changed paradigm in the information operations environment.

The traditional practice of tailoring U.S. PSYOPS messages to what we think people in revolutionary or insurgent circumstances will find persuasive is probably past its prime. PSYOPS practice has been to design messages to articulate and defend official policy, support governments the United States was trying to help, and persuade undecided residents of affected countries that the side the United States supported (their government) was legitimate and deserved popular support and that attacking forces were illegitimate and should be defeated.

Because of the new information "universe" created by a 24/7 news cycle and the emergence of an abundance of alternative sources of information (e.g., radio and TV channels galore, satellite and Internet, the blogosphere, etc.), audiences are no longer dependent on governments for their information. Challenges to the credibility of government-produced news have often found resonance not only among critics but sometimes among supporters of those governments as well.

The task confronting the United States and governments we are associated with is to find ways, in this new information era, of identifying critical issues those governments and their peoples face, clearly and persuasively explain why what we and their governments are trying to do is the best course of action, and try to convince them to actively support and participate in efforts to achieve the desired objectives.

The Criticality of Public Support

It has long been axiomatic in guerrilla warfare that a defending force (such as a government the United States is associated with) will find itself confronted with almost insuperable odds unless it can enlist the *active*—not passive—support of its own citizens in countering an insurgency. In his article "Counterinsurgency Redux," LTC David Kilcullen, one of GEN David Petraeus's counterinsurgency advisers, articulates it simply and concisely: in modern counterinsurgency, the side wins that most successfully mobilizes and energizes its global, regional, and local power base.

Insurgents, to use Mao Tse-tung's imagery, swim in the sea of the people. To the degree that they can enlist the support of the people in achieving their objectives, so much the easier for them. But guerrillas and insurgents can also operate successfully among and within a *passive* population and environment since they can exploit passivity or noninvolvement of the masses of people to mask their activities.

The fact that insurgents get to pick the times and places of their attacks means they can conserve their forces and hoard weaponry and ammunition and other matériel until they are ready to strike—whereas government forces have to protect all the places and all the people all the time. This puts government forces at a nearly insurmountable disadvantage unless they can enlist the active support of their own population, for the primal imperative in trying to defeat a guerrilla insurgency is to acquire actionable intelligence—and that, in turn, requires enlisting citizen participation. It is the local population that is most likely to know where guerrillas or insurgents in their vicinity are and how and where they operate. But noncombatants are unlikely to volunteer this information unless they believe government forces are likely to act on it (and are capable of doing so successfully) and will protect villagers who volunteer such information to them.

Unless the people are willing to support their government and security forces by volunteering actionable intelligence, defending forces will almost inevitably face nearly insuperable odds. One of the most important messages the United States helped spread in El Salvador during that country's internal conflict in the 1980s was that unless and until Juan Valdez and his donkey reached the point that they were willing to trundle down off the volcano and come into the local police station or military *cuartel* and volunteer to the officials therein that they needed to investigate activities in the yellow villa on the left-hand side of the third ravine from the top of the volcano, El Salvador's security forces were unlikely to defeat their insurgency.

The United States never witnessed the degree of popular support in South Vietnam required for the government of that country—which we supported—to win its internal conflict, but let me come back to that a bit further along in this chapter.

What Happens without Public Support?
There is at least one eminently clear take-away from what we have seen in the conflict in Iraq: thus far the *overwhelming* majority of the Iraqi people—Sunnis, Shi'as, Alawites, and others (although not Kurds)—have chosen not to participate in the internal conflict. They're sitting on the fence. The number of people involved in daily attacks against U.S. and other Coalition forces has been quite small—several thousand, possibly as many as 20,000, but no credible estimates suggest numbers much higher than that. It is equally clear, however, that only a few thousand hard-core activists willing, even eager, to give their lives to disrupt or defeat U.S. and Coalition forces and their own government can easily wreak the havoc they seek.

I find it impossible to accept—this I firmly believe—that dozens of vehicles can be prepared every twenty-four hours to serve as mobile explosive devices in a densely packed urban area without a lot of otherwise uninvolved people being aware of it. The continuing calamity of Iraq is that the United States has thus far been unable to persuade the vast majority of the people—who are paying the price for the death and destruction wrought by a relatively small number of people (a substantial percentage of whom are not even Iraqis)—to help identify the bad guys and thus perhaps begin to curb the havoc. This is what our PSYOPS effort needs to focus on.

(Note that I have cast this as "the United States has been unable to persuade…": it is not clear, at least to me, that the current Iraqi government of Prime Minister Nouri al-Maliki shares the U.S. desire to see the death and destruction end. While this chapter is neither a policy analysis nor critique and I am not going to turn it into one, it *is* abundantly clear that the current government of Iraq (GOI) has at the very least often turned a blind eye toward illegal and disruptive activities perpetrated by its own supporters and by those it saw as aligned with its goals. The United States, meanwhile, seeks to quell all such illegal and disruptive activity, whether by opponents or supporters of the GOI.)

The Incapacity of Traditional Deterrence
Herein lies the central dilemma of the insurgencies the United States faces in Iraq and Afghanistan: the traditional historical deterrent, from practically the inception of organized warfare, has been to say, "Guys, stop it! If you don't, we're gonna come after you. We have incontestably superior weapons and intelligence, and we will eventually track you down and take you into custody. If we have to, we'll throw you in jail—perhaps in the United States if you're lucky, or maybe on a desert island someplace. If absolutely necessary, we'll shoot—and if you resist, we'll kill you if we have to."

What happens to that deterrent if their reply is to flip us an obscene gesture and say, "Save your ammo, infidel; we intend to kill ourselves in the process of trying to kill you"? The deterrent collapses; if the threat to kill the enemy, which is our ultimate deterrent, doesn't work or produce the desired effect, it becomes a Hobbesian world of kill-or-be-killed. And that's where the United States is in Iraq today.

The number of those opposing the elected government of Iraq and us is small to the point of being numerically inconsequential. But trivial numbers of people willing, even eager, to die for their cause can outmaneuver and politically defeat vastly larger armies. Exhibit A can be the relatively tiny number of Zionist guerrillas who forced the mighty British Empire (yes, even after the end of World War II) to abandon its plan to create a unified Palestinian state across the River Jordan in 1947 and 1948. If the United States is forced to abandon its objective of a unitary federal Iraqi state following the ouster of Saddam Hussein, it will not be because we were opposed by huge numbers of non-consenting Iraqis; it will be because a handful (relative to a U.S. force of more than 165,000 of its own troops plus an additional 30,000 Coalition forces plus associated Iraqi Army and police forces the United States and others trained) of suicidal insurgents were unmoved by traditional means of deterrence. U.S., allied, and Iraqi forces have been left to twist slowly in the wind by the unwillingness of the large numbers of ordinary Iraqi citizens to support our objectives or their own elected Iraqi government. And the U.S. public and publics in other Coalition countries are reacting accordingly.

So there lies the challenge for a successful PSYOPS campaign. If the only way to deal with insurgents like the ones in Iraq is to find them and kill them all before they can kill defending forces, the United States has to be able to find a successful way to enlist the willing, active participation by all Iraq's citizens—not just Iraq's national security forces. People have to be persuaded to come down off the fence and report clandestine and covert preparations to attack Iraqi, U.S., and Coalition forces. Instead of trying to persuade the people that we're right, we may be more likely to be successful by pointing out what will happen if we and their government fail—and ask if they really want that ugly possibility.

Vietnam: The Failure to Win Popular Support

Many years ago, I was among the military and Foreign Service officers detailed to the Civil Operations and Revolutionary Development Support (CORDS) program, the joint civil-military "pacification" program in South Vietnam, that is in many ways a model for the provincial reconstruction teams the United States is setting up in Afghanistan and Iraq. My office's task at Military Assistance Command, Vietnam (MACV) headquarters was to analyze the effectiveness of the U.S. effort to build security and civil institutions that could protect against internal and external enemies (Viet Cong guerrillas and the North Vietnamese Army [NVA]) and help repair the war-ravaged South Vietnamese economy and society. The CORDS program consisted of both security components and political development and economic reconstruction ones.

The security components included creation of the Peoples' Self-Defense Force (PSDF), a lightly armed village cadre whose principal purpose was to deter Viet

Cong infiltration into villages and hamlets and provide elementary defense against attacks until larger and better-trained and equipped forces from Popular Forces (available to provincial governors), Regional Forces (available to the four corps-level regions), or national-level military forces (Army of the Republic of Vietnam [ARVN], Vietnam Air Force [VNAF], and the South Vietnamese Navy) could respond. The National Police provided nationwide police services, the *Phuong Hoang* program (the "Phoenix" program) targeted the Viet Cong infrastructure, and the *Chieu Hoi* program sought to attract Viet Cong and NVA defectors.

CORDS' economic development and reconstruction programs tackled major elements of social and political well-being required to produce a healthy, democratic state: the election of officials at hamlet, village, province, and national levels; training programs to produce competent national, regional, and local administrators; construction of schools; repairs of dikes, canals, and rice paddies; rebuilding roads and railways; and repair and construction of basic infrastructure such as waterworks, the electrical grid, sewage treatment facilities, and so on. There were also agricultural, educational, medical, and other programs basic to moving the economic life of the country forward—as the United States is trying to do in Iraq and Afghanistan.

CORDS provided the essential programs—both security and reconstruction—that should have enabled the United States and the government of Vietnam to defeat the Viet Cong. After all, similar programs had been used successfully by the United States against the Hukbalahap Rebellion in the Philippines after World War II and by the British during the "Emergency" in Malaya in the early 1950s.

But critical to the success of CORDS was attracting the active support of the South Vietnamese people for their government and armed forces. And this was never really achieved. The enduring reason why the GVN—the side the United States supported—did not prevail in its struggle against the Vietcong (VC) and NVA was that it never had the wholehearted, *active* support of its own people.

Let me take a moment to comment on a much-discussed article in *Armed Forces Journal* (May 2006) by LTC Paul Yingling, entitled "A Failure in Generalship." Yingling suggests that the primary causes of failure in Vietnam were erroneous tactics and strategies for the task at hand plus inadequate forces, and that if U.S. military leaders had gotten it right and insisted on appropriate support from our national political leadership, there might have been a different outcome in Vietnam. He goes on to suggest that the same thing is taking place in Iraq and asserts that if the United States is to prevail in that country, our generals need to change their ways. Any condensation, such as I have just done, of a complex discussion like Lieutenant Colonel Yingling's is, by its very nature, going to be inadequate and I am neither criticizing him or his article, much of which I agree with. My point is simply that his argument leaves out a critically important set of facts and conditions: the nature of the entity—i.e., the GVN then and GOI today—that the United States is trying to support. I do not believe the GVN could have been saved, and I'm not sure I believe a unitary Iraq can be—any more than "Yugoslavia" could have been, despite extraordinary U.S. and European diplomatic efforts, after the death of Josip Broz Tito aka Marshal Tito.

One can argue ad infinitum over the adequacy and appropriateness of tactics, financial and economic support (e.g., congressional restrictions on funding for the South Vietnamese), corruption and incompetence on the part of the GVN and its armed forces, and inadequacy or dishonesty of U.S. military leadership. But, in the end, the critical factor was that the majority of the South Vietnamese people declined to support their own government and armed forces and declined to participate in the effort to save a democratic South Vietnam by coming forth regularly, on a daily basis, with information about the whereabouts of the VC that defending forces could use to go after, capture, or kill an enemy determined to seize power from the GVN. The rice farmers in the fields and villagers in hamlets, towns, and cities simply averted their eyes and went back to planting rice and conducting their business of survival—until the Vietcong and NVA marched in, and then they voted with their feet or with their fear.

During the time I was in South Vietnam (February 1968–August 1969), virtually all of the major military and civilian CORDS pacification programs showed significant progress: the number of elected village governments increased in practically a linear projection; the number of Chieu Hoi defectors grew; the number of villages with PSDF forces increased; the number of Viet Cong infiltrations and assassinations in villages declined; kilometers of roads repaired, dikes reconstructed, hectares of rice under cultivation, schools built, clinics established increased. Virtually every significant indicator for the pacification showed positive gains.

The problem was, there was little or no significant or consistent engagement by "the people" on the side of the government the United States sought to bolster.

Words have meaning and it's important to be clear and precise with language: the United States did not lose in Vietnam, but the Vietnamese government—the side the United States supported—did not, in the end, prevail because it was never able to elicit the active support of its own people. The Vietnamese government did not prevail because of the many and manifest mistakes in both strategy and tactics committed by the United States, the GVN, and our other allies who fought to save South Vietnam from a VC/NVA/North Vietnamese victory, but because it did not have the support of its own people.

To the rice farmers in the fields of South Vietnam, each side was equally unappealing. Both sides conscripted labor, both sides confiscated or stole whatever supplies they wanted or needed, and neither side attracted meaningful participation by "the people" in the government structures and institutions that ruled them. In the end, the rice farmers in the fields simply lowered their heads, seeking to be left alone. That's not a prescription for success in countering an insurgency, and it's very close to being an accurate description of the situation that prevails in critical parts of Iraq today.

The Difference in El Salvador

Ten years after the last helicopter departed the roof of the U.S. embassy in Saigon, the United States, faced with a not dissimilar situation in Central America, sought to help another small, friendly country beset by internal and external foes (the Farabundo Martí National Liberation Front (FMLN) guerrilla movement, aided and trained primarily by Cuba and Nicaragua but with significant—and now Communist—Vietnamese support). Determined to avoid some of the mistakes made in Vietnam, the United States took a different approach in El Salvador.

After discounting all the many other differences between El Salvador and Vietnam, the United States approached revolutionary insurgencies in Central America fundamentally differently in three key ways. First, in El Salvador, the United States made clear that this was their war—not America's. Salvadorans would win their war or they—not the United States—would lose it. Second, we would help "professionalize" (i.e., train) El Salvador's armed forces to fight successfully against the enemy they faced. The United States would help with equipment and other matériel, but ours was a training mission—not an advisory one—and we intended to keep our numbers small—the legendary "55 trainers."

And third, as the price for U.S. assistance, the United States required the Salvadoran government to fundamentally change its attitude and approach toward its own people in order to win their active support and cooperation. The test of the willingness of the people to help their government win the fight against the FMLN would be the degree to which they were willing to actively cooperate with and assist their government and armed forces and provide worthwhile and valid actionable intelligence against the guerrillas.

A parenthetical comment about nomenclature, referring back to the earlier injunction that "words have meaning": What's the difference between "trainer" and "adviser"? If you're training a force, it's clearly their people's fight, not yours. You're training them to the best professional standards you can, but in the end, success is up to them. If, however, you're an adviser, then the outcome of the fight is at least partly a function of the quality of the advice. It's always easy for a host country's force to say, "We could have won that battle but for the lousy advice we got from our foreign advisers who didn't speak our language, didn't understand our culture and institutions, didn't know the terrain and environment as well as we and our enemies do, and were only here for a matter of months—not the years this war is going to take." The United States needs to understand the difference between the role of a trainer and that of an adviser and decide which it wants to be.

The result was a different outcome from that in Vietnam: El Salvador's military accepted the need to transfer political power to a freely and fairly elected constitutional civilian government. When a popular and charismatic center-left politician, José Napoleón Duarte, was elected in 1984, the Salvadoran military— which had, twenty years earlier, deprived him of electoral victory and driven him into exile in Venezuela—became his most determined backers. Duarte pushed needed economic, political, and social reforms through El Salvador's legislative body and built a substantial popular consensus in favor of his government. Support for the FMLN guerrillas, never very strong, began to wane, and by the end of the 1980s, the FMLN chose to negotiate the best deal it could and came down out of the mountains to participate in the political process. Ten years after the United States elected to help El Salvador defeat a homegrown Communist insurgency, the war was won and the U.S. mission was complete.

The Socratic Method

The challenge in Iraq and Afghanistan is, likewise, to mobilize popular support for the governments we back. So long as a major portion of the Iraqi and Afghan people sit on the sidelines, declining to participate in identifying, locating, and tracking down insurgent forces determined to overthrow their governments, it's going to be exceedingly difficult for the U.S.-backed governments in Baghdad and Kabul to prevail. And so, how do we do this?

First, there is no single silver bullet. Training security forces, both police and military, is clearly important. Encouraging national, regional, and local governments to be responsive to their citizens, end corruption, and provide more honest, more reliable, and more practical economic reconstruction and development is also vital. The assistance of international organizations, nongovernmental and private voluntary organizations, can also contribute mightily, so it does not appear to be an effort just by two governments assisted by the United States—which would easily and inevitably be portrayed as the puppeteer manipulating its stooges. Any successful campaign to support the Iraqi and Afghan governments has to enlist the active support and participation of the peoples of Iraq and Afghanistan.

Let me return to the opening paragraphs in this soliloquy: the modern age has reached the point where, given the babble of conflicting, contradicting, and combative messages, populations are decreasingly likely to simply accept what they are told. In the welter of competing messages and mediums, government-sponsored messages are at a particular disadvantage. First, they take too long to create and to obtain necessary coordination and approval for dissemination. Second, their effort to be credible and factually accurate flies in the face of opponents' frequent disdain for truth. Third, they not infrequently end up in the eyes of their beholders—their purported audience—to seem weak and defensive.

Government messages almost invariably "preach." They attempt to persuade a conflictive population, caught between government forces and insurgents, to believe them and accept their premises, and to trust their government and support it, despite all its shortcomings—which may have led to the rise of the insurgency against it in the first place.

"Preaching" is unlikely to win converts or persuade an undecided public to throw its support toward its government, given the cacophony of voices in the public marketplace.

A better approach might be to ask questions rather than provide answers. Instead of asserting the government's determination to prevail, how about casting the government and its opposition as alternatives and ask the people which they support? Do they support continued sectarian killing? Are they willing to help their governments try to end it? Or do they support suicide bombers and the destruction they wreak? Are they willing to help identify the perpetrators, and help uncover the sites where improvised explosive devices (IEDs) are made and cars and trucks packed with explosives? Do they not care when they see repeated attacks on mosques and markets and clinics and hospitals and public places? If they do care, are they prepared to step forward and help their national (or local or provincial or tribal) authorities try to curb such violence? Even though Iraqi and Afghan national governments fall well short of the standards we and their people would like to see of them (and, indeed, of the standards they have set for themselves), they are not beheading people in front of cameras in front of shacks in Diyala or Helmand; they at least try to stay within the laws they represent. It is the insurgents who eschew all morality, Islamic or otherwise. Do the people really prefer this alternative?

People need to come down off the fence—and if they are to do so, it will have to be of their own volition. A successful PSYOPS program needs to put the alternatives to them—not presume to tell them which to choose.

The fundamental message to the people of Iraq and Afghanistan and other countries in conflict needs to be, as the U.S. message was in El Salvador twenty years ago, "This is your country; the kind of country it's going to be is up to you—not the United States or any other foreign country. What kind of country do you want it to be? Are you willing to help restore order, and law, and civility—or are you going to sit quietly while those who seek to destroy what you have do their work?"

A phrase we repeatedly used in El Salvador, at all levels with military and civilian government officials, was "Sin el apoyo de su pueblo, ustedes no pueden vencer; con el apoyo de su pueblo, ustedes no pueden perder" (without the support of your people, you can't win; with the support of your people, you can't lose). The latter might not, in the end and for different reasons, prevail—but the first part is certainly true.

A major theme of the U.S. "message" in Iraq and Afghanistan therefore needs to be: "The United States can help rebuild your electrical system, but only you can protect it; the United States can help build hospitals and schools and bridges and repair roads and get the oil industry working again—but the United States and its Coalition partners can't protect them once built against people determined to destroy them. If reconstruction and development projects are to be protected, Iraqis and Afghans are going to have to actively participate in their protection." They need to more actively support and assist their own governments in bringing an end to the violence and destruction.

Twenty-five hundred years ago, Socrates challenged his colleagues and his students by asking questions—not providing the answers himself but, rather, obliging them to question and reexamine what they were confronted with and what they thought the best answers or solutions might be. It may well be that this approach—rather than preaching a message—is the one most necessary to persuade people to come down off the fence and take sides in countries facing insurgent challenges—to support their own governments if the United States is to do so as well. At the heart of it all is self-interest. Our PSYOPS campaigns need to challenge target audiences to think that through.

8

New Tools, New Rules: International Law and Information Operations

—Duncan B. Hollis

For more than a decade, military thinkers have debated the impact of "information operations" (IO) on armed conflict. Responding to the possibilities (and vulnerabilities) inherent in the Internet's interconnectivity and the worldwide spread of new forms of communication, IO has emerged as a "new category of warfare."[1] According to the U.S. military, IO seeks "to influence, disrupt, corrupt or usurp adversarial human and automated decision making while protecting our own."[2] It employs various methods to achieve these objectives. IO can involve psychological operations (PSYOPS) that utilize both new and old methods of conveying information (e.g., broadcasting satellite radio messages, dropping leaflets from aircraft) with the aim of manipulating the views of foreign governments, organizations, or individuals.[3] Or IO may involve cutting-edge computer network attacks (CNA) that spread viruses to—or hack into—adversary computer systems for the purpose of disabling, degrading, or destroying such systems or the infrastructure they support.[4] The overall goals, however, remain the same: affecting and protecting information and information systems. Nor is the United States alone in these efforts; more than thirty other states, including China, India, and Russia, have reportedly begun to develop similar IO doctrines or capabilities.[5]

As militaries work through what IO can do, they must also wrestle with when and how they can employ it—the question of law's effect on IO. States must address what domestic legal constraints, if any, to place on their militaries' IO. For international law, however, the question is not so much *if* legal rules constrain IO but *whether* the existing rules do so appropriately. IO conceives of information and information systems as both new tools and new objectives for military activities. As such, the existing international legal paradigm operates largely by analogy and, even then, in a patchwork fashion. Most states appear content with this situation, denying any need to develop IO-specific rules. In doing so, however, states are doing themselves and their militaries a great disservice. Even as it applies to IO, the existing system suffers from several, near-fatal conditions: *uncertainty* (military commanders lack a clear picture of how to translate existing rules into the IO environment); *complexity* (i.e., overlapping legal regimes threaten to overwhelm military commanders seeking to apply IO); and *insufficiency* (the existing rules fail to address the basic challenges of modern conflicts with non-state actors). To redress these deficiencies, I propose that states adopt a new set of rules—an international law for information operations (ILIO).

The Existing Regime—International Law by Analogy

In the first treaty prohibiting a weapon of war—the 1868 St. Petersburg Declaration—the parties agreed "the only legitimate object which States should endeavor to accomplish during war is to weaken the military forces of the enemy."[6] IO's object, in contrast, is different. It focuses on affecting the entire adversary (e.g., political elites), not just its military, and those effects need not result from classic applications of kinetic force. Such different goals might justify different rules for IO (or even suggest prohibiting IO insofar as its objectives differ from the St. Petersburg formulation).

But it would be a mistake to justify ILIO on such grounds. In reality, war has always been about the message—deploying force not only to gain territory, but also to send messages influencing enemy (and even allied) decision making. Thucydides' account of the Melian Dialogue portrays Athens's justification for its eventual slaughter of hostile Melian islanders purely in terms of message. Rejecting Melian pleas for neutrality, the Athenians contended:

> [I]t is not so much your hostility that injures us; it is rather the case that, if we were on friendly terms with you, our subjects would regard that as a sign of weakness in us . . . by conquering you we shall increase not only the size but the security of our empire. We rule the sea and you are islanders, and weaker islanders too than the others; it is therefore particularly important that you should not escape.[7]

Nor is "war as message" an entirely Western invention. Sun Tzu gauged the ultimate military objective as lying well beyond the battlefield: "To win one hundred victories in one hundred battles is not the highest excellence; the highest excellence is to subdue the enemy's army without fighting at all."[8] Clausewitz's characterization of warfare belies any claim that IO's goals are somehow new:

> War is not merely an act of policy but a true political instrument, a continuation of political intercourse, carried on with other means . . . [t]he political object is the goal, war is the means of reaching it and means can never be considered in isolation from their purpose.[9]

Even if IO's objectives do not place it beyond the reach of existing international law, perhaps the tools employed in IO do. CNA, for example, provides a new weapon that can be deployed instantaneously and surreptitiously thousands of miles away from its target. Although its effects can certainly equate to those of kinetic force (e.g., the death and destruction that would flow from unleashing a computer virus on a nuclear power plant's operating system), CNA also has the potential to avoid, or at least minimize, such effects (where employed to disable or usurp adversarial information systems temporarily). Such military capacity was never foreseen by, let alone available to, states in developing the existing law of war. As a result, the law of war does not include provisions specifically addressing IO. In such circumstances, perhaps the *Lotus* principle—i.e., what international law does not prohibit, it permits—exempts IO from existing international law.[10]

As with arguments differentiating IO's objectives, however, exceptional arguments about IO methods cannot succeed. The *Lotus* principle was adopted in a specific context where states sought to apply their criminal laws beyond their borders and has never garnered universal application. Indeed, states have explicitly declined to extend *Lotus* to the law of war. Under the Martens Clause, the absence of a treaty provision explicitly prohibiting conduct during armed conflict does not mean that international law permits it.[11] The modern version of the clause, found in Additional Protocol I to the 1949 Geneva Conventions (AP I), indicates in such circumstances "civilians and combatants remain under the protection and authority of the principles of international law derived from established custom, from the principles of humanity and from the dictates of public conscience."[12] In other words, the law of war governs IO even without mentioning it.

Nor does CNA's novelty or other IO technological innovations preclude application of the law of war and restrictions on the use of force. States have readily subjected prior "novel" developments in warfare (e.g., submarines, airpower, chemical and biological weapons) to legal regulation. In its advisory opinion on nuclear weapons, the International Court of Justice had "no doubt as to the applicability" of international law, reasoning that any threat or use of nuclear weapons must comply with "the international law applicable in armed conflict."[13] Moreover, the law of war now explicitly requires its continued application to novel developments. AP I Article 36 records the affirmative duty of states developing or acquiring "a new weapon, means or method of warfare . . . to determine whether its employment would in some or all circumstances be prohibited by this Protocol or by any other rule of international law applicable."[14] Thus, IO cannot escape a law of war analysis.[15]

To say the law of war covers IO does not tell us when and how it applies. States have historically accommodated changes in weapons, tactics, and conflict in one of three ways. First, as AP I Article 36 suggests, states frequently extend existing rules to new types of warfare by analogy, as was the case in analogizing the rules for land warfare to the air. Second, states develop specific rules regulating or prohibiting particular weapons or their deployment, such as the treaties on biological and chemical weapons.[16] Third, states periodically seek to update and revise all of the law of war, usually in reaction to recent experience; the additional protocols to the 1949 Geneva Conventions represent the most recent iteration of that phenomenon.[17] At present, there are no specific rules for IO, nor is there any sign of a more general revision to accommodate IO. Thus, IO falls under the first approach: the law of war governs IO by analogy.

Conventional wisdom suggests that IO can be effectively governed by the analogy approach. In 1998, states were cool to Russia's suggestion that international law prohibits information weapons.[18] The U.S. Department of Defense Office of General Counsel later rejected calls for IO-specific rules as "premature," arguing, for example, that "the process of extrapolation" of the law of war to IO "appears to be reasonably predictable."[19] More generally, in 2003 the International Committee for the Red Cross (ICRC) opined that "the existing legal framework is on the whole adequate to deal with present day international armed conflicts."[20] A majority of military thinkers agree, arguing in favor of an analogy approach or decrying the possibility of IO-specific rules as premature or unrealistic.[21]

The Need for ILIO

A closer examination of the IO law-by-analogy approach reveals substantial flaws in the conventional wisdom. First, even in the context of armed conflict, there are serious "translation" problems with extending the existing rules to IO. Such translation problems produce uncertainty for those asked to employ IO, creating disincentives to engage in IO and conflicting views of what the law requires. Second, the vast majority of IO scholarship has focused solely on regulating IO's application to armed conflicts involving two or more states. But such analyses are clearly insufficient. They ignore the new reality of asymmetrical conflict increasingly pitting states not against each other but against non-state actors. Moreover, any consideration of IO beyond international armed conflict immediately encounters nearly incoherent complexity as IO finds itself subject to multiple legal regimes. Such complexity undoubtedly further clouds the minds of military commanders asked to employ IO. Third, and finally, the current rules operate almost exclusively in a restrictive fashion, limiting when and how states employ IO. The current regime fails to acknowledge, let alone encourage, the functional benefits IO can achieve in both traditional and asymmetrical conflicts.

By adopting ILIO, states could alleviate all of these problems. Military commanders would benefit from a single set of rules, especially if it covered the entire range of circumstances in which militaries might employ IO. At the same time, ILIO offers the possibility of lessening the collateral costs of armed conflicts while improving the relative position of states in their fight against global terror.

TRANSLATION PROBLEMS

Hundreds of rules currently govern when states can use force (the *jus ad bellum*) and how they can use that force in an armed conflict (the *jus in bello*). Some of these rules have little to say about IO specifically (e.g., the protections owed the wounded, sick, or shipwrecked). Others involve principles of general applicability—including those on the use of force, distinction, military necessity, proportionality, and perfidy—that encompass IO. Nevertheless, the gap between kinetic weaponry (including biological and chemical variants) and IO methods can be substantial, creating acute translation problems. Attempt to apply existing basic principles, such as the rules on use of force or civilian distinction, and either no clear rule emerges or the rule ends up operating in contravention of the policies that motivated the rule in the first place.

Prohibition on the Use of Force: The UN Charter prohibits states from the threat or use of force, except when authorized by the UN Security Council or pursuant to the inherent right of self-defense in response to an armed attack.[22] Historically, states defined "force" in terms of the instrument used, including "armed" force within the prohibition but excluding economic and political forms of coercion.[23] Although not without controversy, this distinction reflects an effort to proscribe those acts most likely to interfere with the UN's purposes—maintenance of international peace and security.

The use of force prohibition encounters real difficulty, however, when translated into the IO context. Commentators have "come to widely divergent conclusions," such that no bright line rule exists for when IO constitutes a use of force, let alone an armed attack for self-defense purposes.[24] Three different possibilities remain in play. First, the classic "instrumentality" approach argues IO does not qualify as armed force because it lacks the physical characteristics associated with military coercion.[25] The UN Charter offers some support for this view: Article 41 lists "measures not involving the use of armed force" to include "complete or partial interruption of... telegraphic, radio, and other means of communication." Second, the "target-based" approach suggests IO constitutes a use of force or an armed attack whenever it penetrates "critical national infrastructure" systems.[26] Third, the "consequentiality" approach, favored by the U.S. Department of Defense, focuses on IO's consequences—whenever IO intends to cause effects equivalent to those produced by kinetic force (death or destruction of property), it constitutes a use of force and an armed attack.[27]

The problem, however, goes beyond picking a definitional standard; absent further elaboration, the novelty of IO methods generates confusion regardless of the standard chosen. The instrumentality approach, for example, would not restrict IO against communications systems. But does that mean IO shutting down a civilian air traffic communication system potentially downing airliners and causing significant casualties does not qualify as a use of force or give rise to a right of self-defense? In contrast, the target-based approach might suffer from over-inclusion. IO can produce wide-ranging effects, from merely informational (distributing propaganda) to inconvenient (disrupting systems temporarily via a denial-of-service attack) to potentially dangerous (implanting a Trojan horse doing no immediate harm but with the potential to cause future injury) to immediately destructive (disabling a system permanently via a virus). Does the target's identity as somehow "critical" alone qualify such divergent acts as uses of force or armed attacks? Finally, even as the consequences approach covers IO effects that replicate kinetic force it excludes the very consequences that make IO so novel. Neither kinetic force nor political or economic sanctions can disable an entire stock market or banking system the way IO can—immediately and without casualties or physical destruction. Do we treat IO as outside the charter whenever its effects differ from kinetic force or do we include it under the prohibition where its effects have an immediacy not seen in economic or political coercion?

The Principle of Civilian Distinction: Irrespective of how it commences, once states engage in armed conflict, the jus in bello applies. Among that law's core principles is civilian distinction, requiring that conflicting states "shall at all times distinguish between the civilian population and combatants and between civilian objects and military objectives and accordingly shall direct their operations only against military objectives."[28] Militaries can only "attack" military objectives— "those objects which by their nature, location, purpose or use make an effective contribution to military action and whose total or partial destruction, capture or neutralization, in the circumstances ruling at the time, offers a definite military advantage."[29] All other objects are deemed civilian and off-limits (as are civilians themselves unless they take a direct part in the hostilities).[30] Application of this principle has proved difficult even in traditional international armed conflicts— witness questions about whether Serbian television stations or Baghdad's electrical power system constituted proper military objectives.[31] The IO context, however, exacerbates existing confusion and, indeed, may actually undermine the concept of civilian distinction entirely.

Among IO's most significant challenges to civilian distinction is confusion surrounding (1) what IO triggers the civilian distinction requirement and (2) the dual-use nature of most information infrastructure.[32] Generally, civilian distinction does not protect civilians and their objects from all military operations, only those that qualify as "attacks," defined as "violence against the adversary, whether in offense or in defense."[33] As in the use of force context, much depends on which IO qualifies as an "attack." IO that results in casualties or physical destruction likely qualifies, but other effects remain open to debate (e.g., neutralizing a target, denying service to a system), while others certainly fall outside the definition (e.g.,

PSYOPS, electronic embargoes). The irony of IO is that the less likely a particular IO functions as an attack, the more likely its use against civilians and their objects is permissible. IO's development may actually result in warfare having more impacts on civilians by expanding militaries' ability to target (but not attack) them. In such circumstances, applying existing civilian distinction rules to IO challenges the notion that the law of war should protect civilians and their property as much as possible.[34]

Restricting IO "attacks" to military objectives may equally run afoul of the goal of protecting civilians and their property. The law of war places on states a responsibility to separate "to the maximum extent feasible" civilian populations and objects from the vicinity of military objectives and dangers of military operations.[35] When they do not—i.e., where infrastructure has a "dual use" serving both civilian and military purposes—it qualifies as a military objective subject to attack, even if its primary purpose is not military, but civilian. If that rule holds for IO, then militaries may attack virtually all computer networks. As of the year 2000, 95 percent of all U.S. military traffic moved over civilian telecommunications and computer systems, and the trend is clearly toward greater consolidation of civilian and military technology.[36] The dual-use rule suggests, therefore, that U.S. adversaries may treat all U.S. communication systems as military objectives and attack them by IO or kinetic means.[37] As such, application of the civilian distinction principle to IO not only involves uncertainty, it also suggests increasing tension with the principle's purported goal of restricting military attention on civilians and their property as much as possible during conflict.

Both of these examples illustrate the scope and depth of confusion that IO generates in the context of armed conflict. In both cases—use of force and civilian distinction—the current rules do not translate easily or clearly. Nor are these isolated examples. Similar problems emerge in deciphering how the rules on neutrality extend to IO that will often transit—if not actually affect—neutral states and their infrastructure. Perfidy—prohibiting certain deceptions that lead an enemy to believe it must provide protected status (e.g., feigning surrender or civilian status)—also raises a host of translation questions in the information context.[38]

All told, states are left without any real sense of what they can and cannot do in their IO. This leaves militaries in a quandary—they can apply their own translation of the law of war and use of force prohibitions to IO and trust others will acquiesce. But foreign forces may not acquiesce. Indeed, they may adopt conflicting translations that produce unanticipated uses of IO or kinetic force. Alternatively, militaries may avoid IO's uncertainty and decline to employ it entirely. For example, during the 1999 Kosovo conflict, widely circulated reports described how plans to conduct an IO depleting Serbian leader Slobodan Milosevic's personal financial holdings were never executed.[39] Of course, when militaries have avoided IO that usually means they have relied instead on traditional weaponry, which may actually cost more lives and exact more damage than the more novel IO method avoided.

The lack of clarity has individual effects as well since certain violations of the law of war (e.g., civilian distinction) constitute war crimes. We live in an era of increasing individual legal responsibility at national and international levels. Today, war crimes charges can seize the attention of courts in Belgium or Germany, not to mention the International Criminal Court. Although jurisdictional hurdles may make actual prosecutions of U.S. forces unlikely, that will not stop investigations or even indictments if these institutions interpret some IO as violating the law of war. Moreover, the "CNN factor" makes allegations of war crimes a matter of public discourse, rapidly dispersed through media outlets and information networks worldwide. In this environment, it is not surprising that military commanders may shy away from IO, especially if they do not know which conduct will lead to war crimes allegations. Looking at Kosovo again, the United States apparently refrained from planned CNA against Serbian computer networks for purposes of disrupting military operations and basic civil services in part out of concerns that some CNA would be a war crime.[40]

INSUFFICIENCY AND COMPLEXITY

Current efforts to apply existing international law to IO by analogy have focused almost exclusively on its application to *international* armed conflicts between two or more nation-states.[41] Although such conflicts retain undoubted importance, it is a mistake to force all discussion of IO into the interstate conflict paradigm. Today, the center of gravity has shifted away from such conflicts; future (indeed, current U.S.) conflicts will more likely pit states against non-state actors such as Al Qaeda than the more traditional state-to-state paradigm. Current conditions in Iraq and Afghanistan demonstrate, moreover, that even conflicts between states will frequently devolve into conflicts with non-state actors, whether as insurgents or terrorists. When combined with the novelty and variety of IO, such shifts reveal the insufficiency of existing analysis. IO must be considered as more than something states in conflict do to each other.

Moving beyond international armed conflicts, however, IO faces an even murkier environment, filled with new translation problems and the complexity of multiple legal frameworks. For conflicts that do not occur between states, for example, IO may operate under the rules governing non-international armed conflicts. Of course, much debate already surrounds these rules, such as whether a conflict can exist that is neither international nor non-international in character.[42] Even if a conflict is clearly non-international, all agree the rules are more rudimentary than those operating among states. There is no "non-international" counterpart to the use of force prohibition. Common Article 3 of the Geneva Conventions—which does apply—appears to have little relevance to IO, given its focus on humane treatment for individuals not actively participating in the conflict. Additional Protocol II—which governs classic civil wars—has a few relevant rules, including a prohibition on making civilians the object of attack and protecting certain installations.[43] But Protocol II requires no protection for civilian objects, nor does it prohibit perfidy. The ICRC has recently suggested, not without controversy, that customary international law fills many of these gaps, importing rules similar to those found in AP I such as civilian distinction and rules on deception.[44] Of course, if true, that simply replicates the translation questions for IO that already exist in the international context.

The most important IO questions occur when IO does not rise to the level of an armed attack, since that will be where states and non-state actors will most likely collide. After all, although militaries have devoted extensive time to developing IO capabilities and doctrines, non-state actors can perform IO as well. IO technology remains widely accessible, much less expensive than traditional kinetic weaponry, relatively easy to use, and capable of deployment from virtually anywhere in the world. As such, IO has a particular attraction to non-state actors, including transnational criminal and terrorist elements looking to target public or private interests.

Once IO leaves the law of war paradigm, however, state options to conduct or defend against IO become much more limited. Absent state sponsorship, IO by a non-state actor against a state—whether for criminal or terrorist purposes—does not qualify as an armed attack. Self-defense is not an option when dealing with non-state actors; states are expected to deal with them through domestic law enforcement, not military coercion.[45] Even if a victim state traces CNA to a non-state actor operating in another state's territory (no easy task given the ability to mask CNA's origins and route it through multiple states), it cannot respond directly. To do so would implicate one of the fundamental principles of the international legal order: the principle of nonintervention, which provides a state with the right to be sovereign within its own territory, free from external interference.[46] A state will view another state exercising military or law enforcement powers within its territory as a violation of that sovereignty. So, what should an injured state do? International law contemplates that the injured state would notify the state from whose territory it believes the IO originated and request that state put a stop to it.[47] The requested state is expected to comply with such requests, and only if the requested state is unable or unwilling to do so, can the aggrieved state take countermeasures (or perhaps, à la Afghanistan, exercise a right of self-defense against the requested state).[48]

When a state is considering deploying IO in ways that will not constitute a use of force (assuming it can overcome the translation hurdles to make that assessment), the situation becomes even more complicated. States have more than six different legal regimes to assess in deciding whether and how to proceed. First, as with responding to non-state actor IO, a state considering using IO offensively must consider the principle of nonintervention and whether its IO will improperly affect the territory of another state. States are likely to view injury or physical damage as interfering with their sovereign rights, but not all effects will so qualify. Although states generally treat it as violating their domestic law, espionage—the covert collection of information about other states, often in the other state's territory—does not violate any explicit provisions of international law and states widely engage in it.[49] As a result, the method of IO (i.e., whether it merely collects data as opposed to altering, usurping, or destroying it) may dictate the principle's application.

Second, states need to adjust their IO to take into account their obligations under the various and specialized regimes of international law. For example, since information infrastructures frequently use outer space to relay communications or collect data, space law may affect IO. Under Article IV of the Outer Space Treaty, states have agreed to use the moon, other celestial bodies, and, by extension, space itself "exclusively for peaceful purposes."[50] Although this does not automatically preclude lawful military activity in space, determining the contours of "peaceful purposes" has long been a subject of debate that IO will do nothing to ease. Moreover, Article IX of the Outer Space Treaty imposes a notice and consultation requirement before a state engages in any IO it believes "would cause potentially harmful interference with activities of other States Parties in the peaceful exploration and use of outer space."[51] A similar obligation exists under the Constitution of the International Telecommunications Union (ITU). Article 45(1) requires that all telecommunications stations operate so as not to cause "harmful interference" to other states' radio services or communications.[52] In both situations, states need to consider forgoing IO effects that might constitute harmful interference (e.g., jamming radio broadcasts). In the ITU, however, the prohibition does not apply to military radio stations, which may reopen the door to some otherwise prohibited acts.[53] If for some reason IO transits or involves the sea or civilian airspace, additional legal regimes will constrain IO.[54]

Finally, states contemplating IO must assess how other states' domestic laws come into play. States whose territory is the target of an IO may regulate it under their criminal law based on effects within their territory. States through whose territory IO transits en route to its destination may do the same. Moreover, if a military conducts IO from an overseas base, the law of the host nation can regulate that conduct and form a basis for prosecuting individuals engaged in the IO. Although status of forces agreements (SOFAs) may protect these individuals if acting in their official capacity, that protection often only applies where both sending and receiving states recognize the offense. If IO is only a crime under the receiving state's laws, it retains exclusive jurisdiction. Accordingly, depending on its content, which will vary enormously, foreign law may have significant implications for IO.

Combined, these two problems—the insufficiency of the law for international armed conflict and the multiple, overlapping legal regimes beyond the law of war paradigm—suggest a system that is extraordinarily hard for states and their militaries to navigate. If, as David Kaye suggests, complexity in the law of war itself is already a problem for those who use force, IO only compounds that problem given the array of additional legal rules to consider, interpret, and apply.[55]

Is it reasonable to expect militaries and their lawyers to process all of these legal issues simultaneously, particularly in situations where they may be asked to react immediately? If legal confusion creates an incentive to use traditional military force instead of IO, perhaps the conventional wisdom on the viability of IO law by analogy is simply wrong.

ILIO's Benefits

Devising an international law for IO could rectify many of the deficiencies of the current legal system for IO and provide states with additional functional benefits that do not currently exist. First, ILIO can remedy uncertainty. Drafting new rules provides an opportunity to rectify all those translation problems that plague IO under the laws of war. It could give states and their militaries a clear sense of the rules of engagement in the information age. Nor does ILIO have to supplant the existing system entirely; it can easily preserve basic principles that continue to make sense—such as the rule requiring military necessity in using force—while adjusting others (e.g., civilian distinction, perfidy) to fit the context in which IO occurs.

Why not wait—as the ICRC suggests[56]—and rely on what states actually do in lieu of negotiating an ILIO? For starters, it can take years for state practice to coalesce into binding custom. States will remain confused and wary of IO in the interim. Second, attribution issues may make it difficult to ever discern state practice in IO. IO's strength often lies in its anonymity and secrecy. Victims of IO may not know they have been subjected to it, let alone who is responsible (although constantly changing technology ensures this will not always be the case). Thus, it may not be clear what a state believes the law to be until such time as that state is revealed to have been conducting IO and is consequently forced to justify the operation (assuming the victim state wants to publicize the IO, rather than respond in kind). Ironically, this means states with weaker IO skills may actually set the agenda. In contrast, by discussing ILIO prospectively, states can discuss the rules free from operational security constraints and achieve greater certainty concerning their future conduct, even if done in secret.

The need for greater certainty is particularly acute for the United States. Although it clearly has a comparative advantage in terms of IO technology, the United States is simultaneously the most vulnerable to IO given its society's growing dependence on information and information systems. In such circumstances, U.S. interests should favor ILIO. It presents an opportunity to develop rules that could cement U.S. comparative advantage while mitigating existing vulnerabilities. Of course, other states with less developed IO capabilities are aware of this situation and might be reluctant to endorse ILIO because of it.

But ILIO could include functional benefits, luring even reluctant states to the bargaining table. Currently, the rules applicable to IO by analogy are restrictive, limiting what states can do in the interest of maintaining international peace and security, protecting civilian populations, and prohibiting morally reprehensible conduct. But those interests may not always be served only by restricting IO. If we live in a world where the threat to states is no longer primarily from other states but from non-state actors, do we serve international peace and security by imposing so many restrictions on how states use IO against non-state actors? Similarly, although IO may impose wider impacts on civilian populations, IO also has the capacity to produce less harm overall—or even on an individual basis—than traditional warfare. Such possibilities suggest that we conceive of the ILIO project not simply as refining restrictions on IO, but as actually *enabling* it in circumstances that advance the common interests of states.

For example, rather than seeing ILIO as essentially a question of restricting what states do to one another, ILIO could establish rules enabling states to better meet the challenges posed by non-state actors, particularly those bent on global terror. In the language of economists, ILIO may reduce the transaction costs states face in combating transnational terrorism. The current system—which would prohibit a state from responding to an Al Qaeda IO attack from Pakistan directly or immediately, requiring it instead to ask Pakistan for assistance—is not terribly efficient and may have high costs for that state's safety and security. In its place, ILIO offers an opportunity for states to acknowledge their collective interest in combating non-state actors engaged in terrorism, to treat them as a threat to the state system itself, and devise cooperative mechanisms that increase the efficiency of such efforts. This might involve, for example, states such as Pakistan consenting to suspend the nonintervention principle in certain pre-agreed circumstances and allowing injured states to respond immediately and directly to IO generated from their territory (i.e., to conduct an active defense to CNA). There is already some precedent for this in the maritime context, through the practice of "shiprider" agreements, in which a foreign state agrees that one of its officials may serve aboard a U.S. ship and authorize it to conduct law enforcement activities against ships of that foreign state and even within the foreign state's territorial seas.[57]

At the same time, developing new rules does not mean sacrificing the bedrock rationales for the existing legal system, especially those applicable in international armed conflicts (i.e., to minimize human suffering). To the extent the current law of war relies extensively on the principle of reciprocity (i.e., a state grants—or forgoes—certain treatment toward the adversary on the expectation its own forces will be treated likewise), ILIO can operate as a bargain among the consenting states in much the same way. ILIO's translation of the use of force prohibition would undoubtedly retain the principle's inherent reciprocity: each state agrees to refrain from force, however defined, so long as the other side does so as well. Similarly, to the extent the law of war also has a universalist or moral basis (i.e., states do not engage in certain acts even if done by the adversary because they deem such acts morally reprehensible), nothing precludes ILIO from accommodating that basis as well—IO-tailored rules on perfidy.

Finally, ILIO offers an opportunity for the law of war more generally. It is no secret that the law of war has proven largely inadequate or incapable of addressing non-international armed conflicts. For the most part, states see such conflicts as implicating their sovereignty (or even their very survival) at levels not presented in conflicts with other states. Similarly, when the conflict only involves one state actor versus a non-state actor, the reciprocity rationale for the law of war is largely absent. As a result, states have been reluctant to agree to detailed rules for such conflicts. For ILIO, however, many of the sovereignty concerns are, if not nonexistent, at least diminished. IO will frequently lack any direct territorial impact or its impacts can be temporary and more easily remedied than the casualties and destruction so often witnessed in civil wars. Moreover, the non-state actor threat often transcends the territorial ambitions that dominated the post-colonial era. To the extent actors like Al Qaeda constitute a threat, it is not simply to certain nation-states and their territorial integrity, but to the very concept of a system of secular, equal sovereign states. As such, unlike past non-international conflicts, there is a reciprocity concern here—not a concern of reciprocating restrictions, but reciprocating cooperation to forestall a common threat. ILIO offers an opportunity to do this. It provides states a chance to devise rules in areas that have so far proven difficult to regulate and to elaborate what international law requires in non-international conflicts (and to coordinate rules in cases short of actual conflict).

Conclusion

Conventional wisdom's favored law by analogy approach has clear flaws. Its translation to IO is rife with uncertainty and complexity, which will result in less IO or greater conflict among states, courts, and international institutions about what international law requires of IO. At the same time, a law of war or use of force effort to regulate IO is clearly insufficient where the fight with Al Qaeda, the Taliban, and other insurgents typifies future conflicts far more than old interstate conflicts. The need for ILIO becomes even more apparent as the uncertainty of IO under the law of war is magnified and compounded in trying to discern the array of rules that govern IO outside of an interstate conflict. Such deficiencies in the status quo beg for a new framework. A new framework could not only remedy the existing system's deficiencies, but also offer additional advantages of its own. States may adopt cooperative mechanisms—common tools to address new threats—preserving their strengths in IO technology while shoring up against their individual vulnerabilities to IO.

ILIO's content can (and should) be subject to great debate. Similarly, careful consideration needs to be given to the form ILIO should take. The few suggestions to date have idealized a multilateral treaty that could contain precise and detailed rules on IO; however, a framework convention might be more politically palpable, setting forth general principles for IO while reserving space for more specific sets of rules as states agree on them. Nor is a multilateral treaty necessarily the right format. Why not perfect ILIO first through bilateral or regional arrangements? Or perhaps the starting point should be an experts' code of conduct like the San Remo Manual.[58] Of course, all of this presumes that states and military thinkers appreciate the need to move beyond the law by analogy approach. The first step, therefore, is to recognize the deficiencies of the current system and the need for, not to mention the advantages that would come from, a new set of rules: an ILIO.

Part II: Strategic

9

Learning Counterinsurgency: Observations from Soldiering in Iraq*

—GEN David H. Petraeus, USA

Observations from Soldiering in Iraq

1. "Do not try to do too much with your own hands."
2. Act quickly, because every army of liberation has a half-life.
3. Money is ammunition.
4. Increasing the number of stakeholders is critical to success.
5. Analyze costs and benefits before each operation.
6. Intelligence is the key to success.
7. Everyone must do nation-building.
8. Help build institutions, not just units.
9. Cultural awareness is a force multiplier.
10. Success in a counterinsurgency requires more than just military operations.
11. Ultimate success depends on local leaders.
12. Remember the strategic corporals and strategic lieutenants.
13. There is no substitute for flexible, adaptable leaders.
14. A leader's most important task is to set the right tone.

The U.S. Army has learned a great deal in Iraq and Afghanistan about the conduct of counterinsurgency operations, and we must continue to learn all that we can from our experiences in those countries.

* *This essay appeared in the* Military Review, *January–February 2006, and is reprinted by permission.*

The insurgencies in Iraq and Afghanistan were not, in truth, the wars for which we were best prepared in 2001; however, they are the wars we are fighting, and they clearly are the kind we must master. America's overwhelming conventional military superiority makes it unlikely that future enemies will confront us head on. Rather, they will attack us asymmetrically, avoiding our strengths—firepower, maneuver, technology—and come at our partners and us the way the insurgents do in Iraq and Afghanistan. It is imperative, therefore, that we continue to learn from our experiences in those countries, both to succeed in those endeavors and to prepare for the future.

Soldiers and Observations

Writing down observations and lessons learned is a time-honored tradition of Soldiers. Most of us have done this to varying degrees, and we then reflect on and share what we've jotted down after returning from the latest training exercise, mission, or deployment. Such activities are of obvious importance in helping us learn from our own experiences and from those of others.

In an effort to foster learning as an organization, the Army institutionalized the process of collection, evaluation, and dissemination of observations, insights, and lessons some twenty years ago with the formation of the Center for Army Lessons Learned.[1] In subsequent years, the other military services and the Joint Forces Command followed suit, forming their own lessons learned centers. More recently, the Internet and other knowledge management tools have sped the processes of collection, evaluation, and dissemination enormously. Numerous products have already been issued since the beginning of our operations in Afghanistan and Iraq, and most of us have found these products of considerable value as we've prepared for deployments and reviewed how different units grappled with challenges our elements were about to face.

For all their considerable worth, the institutional structures for capturing lessons are still dependent on Soldiers' thoughts and reflections. And Soldiers have continued to record their own observations, particularly in recent years as we have engaged in so many important operations. Indeed, my own pen and notebook were always handy while soldiering in Iraq. I commanded the 101st Airborne Division during our first year there (during the fight to Baghdad and the division's subsequent operations in Iraq's four northern provinces), and during most of the subsequent eighteen months, I helped with the so-called train and equip mission, conducting an assessment in the spring of 2004 of the Iraqi Security Forces after their poor performance in early April 2004 and then serving as the first commander of the Multinational Security Transition Command-Iraq and the NATO Training Mission-Iraq.

What follows is the distillation of a number of observations jotted down during that time. Some of these observations are specific to soldiering in Iraq, but the rest speak to the broader challenge of conducting counterinsurgency operations in a vastly different culture than our own. I offer fourteen of those observations here in the hope that others will find them of assistance as they prepare to serve in Iraq or Afghanistan or in similar missions in the years ahead.

Fourteen Observations

Observation Number 1 is *"Do not try to do too much with your own hands."* T. E. Lawrence offered this wise counsel in an article published in *The Arab Bulletin* in August 1917. Continuing, he wrote, "Better the Arabs do it tolerably than that you do it perfectly. It is their war, and you are to help them, not win it for them. Actually, also, under the very odd conditions of Arabia, your practical work will not be as good as, perhaps, you think it is. It may take them longer and it may not be as good as you think, but if it is theirs, it will be better."[2]

Lawrence's guidance is as relevant in the twenty-first century as it was in his own time in the Middle East during World War I. Like much good advice, however, it is sometimes easier to put forward than it is to follow. Our Army is blessed with highly motivated Soldiers who pride themselves on being action oriented. We celebrate a "can-do" spirit, believe in taking the initiative, and want to get on with business. Yet, despite the discomfort in trying to follow Lawrence's advice by not doing too much with our own hands, such an approach is absolutely critical to success in a situation like that in Iraq. Indeed, many of our units recognized early on that it was important that we not just perform tasks for the Iraqis, but that we help our Iraqi partners, over time enabling them to accomplish tasks on their own with less and less assistance from us.

Empowering Iraqis to do the job themselves has become the essence of our strategy—and such an approach is particularly applicable in Iraq. Despite suffering for decades under Saddam, Iraq still has considerable human capital with the remnants of an educated middle class, a number of budding entrepreneurs, and many talented leaders. Moreover, the Iraqis know the situation and people far better than we ever can, and unleashing their productivity is essential to rebuilding infrastructure and institutions. Our experience, for example, in helping the Iraqi military reestablish its staff colleges and branch-specific schools has been that, once a good Iraqi leader is established as the head of the school, he can take it from there, albeit with some degree of continued Coalition assistance. The same has been true in many other areas, including in helping establish certain Army units (such as the Iraqi Army's 9th Division [Mechanized], based north of Baghdad at Taji, and the 8th Division, which has units in five provinces south of Baghdad) and police academies (such as the one in Hillah, run completely by Iraqis in 2004–2005). Indeed, our ability to *assist* rather than *do* has evolved considerably since the transition of sovereignty at the end of late June 2004 and even more so since the elections of January 30, 2005. I do not want to downplay the amount of work still to be done or the daunting challenges that lie ahead; rather, I simply want to emphasize the importance of empowering, enabling, and assisting the Iraqis, an approach that figures prominently in our strategy in that country.

Observation Number 2 is that, in a situation like Iraq's, the liberating force must *act quickly, because every army of liberation has a half-life* beyond which it turns into an army of occupation. The length of this half-life is tied to the perceptions of the populace about the impact of the liberating force's activities. From the moment a force enters a country, its leaders must keep this in mind and strive to meet the expectations of the liberated in what becomes a race against the clock.

This race against the clock in Iraq has been complicated by the extremely high expectations of the Iraqi people, their pride in their own abilities, and their reluctant admission that they needed help from Americans, in particular.[3] Recognizing this, those of us on the ground at the outset did all that we could with the resources available early on to help the people, to repair the damage done by military operations and looting, to rebuild infrastructure, and to restore basic services as quickly as possible—in effect, helping extend the half-life of the army of liberation. Even while carrying out such activities, however, we were keenly aware that sooner or later, the people would begin to view us as an army of occupation. Over time, the local citizenry would feel that we were not doing enough or were not moving as quickly as desired, would see us damaging property and hurting innocent civilians in the course of operations, and would resent the inconveniences and intrusion of checkpoints, low helicopter flights, and other military activities. The accumulation of these perceptions, coupled with the natural pride of Iraqis and resentment that their country, so blessed in natural resources, had to rely on outsiders, would eventually result in us being seen less as liberators and more as occupiers. That has been the case to varying degrees in much of Iraq. The obvious implication of this is that such endeavors—especially in situations like those in Iraq—are a race against the clock to achieve as quickly as possible the expectations of those liberated. And, again, those expectations, in the case of Iraqi citizens, have always been very high indeed.[4]

Observation Number 3 is that, in an endeavor like that in Iraq, *money is ammunition*. In fact, depending on the situation, money can be more important than real ammunition—and that has often been the case in Iraq since early April 2003 when Saddam's regime collapsed and the focus rapidly shifted to reconstruction, economic revival, and restoration of basic services. Once money is available, the challenge is to spend it effectively and quickly to rapidly achieve measurable results. This leads to a related observation that the money needs to be provided as soon as possible to the organizations that have the capability and capacity to spend it in such a manner.

Commander's Emergency Reconstruction Program (CERP) funds—funds created by the Coalition Provisional Authority with captured Iraqi money in response to requests from units for funds that could be put to use quickly and with minimal red tape—proved very important in Iraq in the late spring and summer of 2003.

These funds enabled units on the ground to complete thousands of small projects that were, despite their low cost, of enormous importance to local citizens.[5] Village schools, for example, could be repaired and refurbished by less than $10,000 at that time, and units like the 101st Airborne Division carried out hundreds of school repairs alone. Other projects funded by CERP in our area included refurbishment of Mosul University, repairs to the Justice Center, numerous road projects, countless water projects, refurbishment of cement and asphalt factories, repair of a massive irrigation system, support for local elections, digging of dozens of wells, repair of police stations, repair of an oil refinery, purchase of uniforms and equipment for Iraqi forces, construction of small Iraqi Army training and operating bases, repairs to parks and swimming pools, support for youth soccer teams, creation of employment programs, refurbishment of medical facilities, creation of a central Iraqi detention facility, establishment of a small business loan program, and countless other small initiatives that made big differences in the lives of the Iraqis we were trying to help.

The success of the CERP concept led Congress to appropriate additional CERP dollars in the fall of 2003, and additional appropriations have continued ever since. Most commanders would agree that CERP dollars have been of enormous value to the effort in Iraq (and in Afghanistan, to which the concept migrated in 2003 as well).

Beyond being provided money, those organizations with the capacity and capability to put it to use must also be given reasonable flexibility in how they spend at least a portion of the money, so that it can be used to address the inevitable emerging needs. This is particularly important in the case of appropriated funds. The recognition of this need guided our requests for resources for the Iraqi Security Forces' "train and equip" mission, and the result was a substantial amount of flexibility in the 2005 supplemental funding measure that has served that mission very well, especially as our new organization achieved the capability and capacity needed to rapidly put to use the resources allocated to it.[6]

Observation Number 4 reminds us that *increasing the number of stakeholders is critical to success*. This insight emerged several months into our time in Iraq as we began to realize that more important than our winning Iraqi hearts and minds was doing all that we could to ensure that as many Iraqis as possible felt a stake in the success of the new Iraq. I do not want to downplay the importance of winning hearts and minds for the Coalition, as that extends the half-life I described earlier, something that is of obvious desirability. But more important was the idea of Iraqis wanting the new Iraq to succeed. Over time, in fact, we began asking, when considering new initiatives, projects, or programs, whether they would help increase the number of Iraqis who felt they had a stake in the country's success. This guided us well during the time that the 101st Airborne Division was in northern Iraq and again during a variety of initiatives pursued as part of the effort to help Iraq reestablish its security forces. And it is this concept, of course, that undoubtedly is behind the reported efforts of the U.S. Ambassador in Iraq to encourage Shi'a and Kurdish political leaders in Iraq to reach out to Sunni Arab leaders and to encourage them to help the new Iraq succeed.

The essence of Observation Number 5—that we should *analyze costs and benefits of operations before each operation*—is captured in a question we developed over time and used to ask before the conduct of operations: "Will this operation," we asked, "take more bad guys off the street than it creates by the way it is conducted?" If the answer to that question was "No," then we took a very hard look at the operation before proceeding.

In 1986, GEN John Galvin, then Commander in Chief of the U.S. Southern Command (which was supporting the counterinsurgency effort in El Salvador), described the challenge captured in this observation very effectively: "The . . . burden on the military institution is large. Not only must it subdue an armed adversary while attempting to provide security to the civilian population, it must also avoid furthering the insurgents' cause. If, for example, the military's actions in killing fifty guerrillas cause two hundred previously uncommitted citizens to join the insurgent cause, the use of force will have been counterproductive."[7]

To be sure, there are occasions when one should be willing to take more risk relative to this question. One example was the 101st Airborne Division's operation to capture or kill Uday and Qusay Hussein. In that case, we ended up firing well over a dozen antitank missiles into the house they were occupying (knowing that all the family members were safely out of it) after Uday and Qusay refused our call to surrender and wounded three of our Soldiers during two attempts to capture them.[8]

In the main, however, we sought to carry out operations in a way that minimized the chances of creating more enemies than we captured or killed. The idea was to try to end each day with fewer enemies than we had when it started. Thus we preferred targeted operations rather than sweeps, and as soon as possible after completion of an operation, we explained to the citizens in the affected areas what we'd done and why we did it.

This should not be taken to indicate that we were the least bit reluctant about going after the Saddamists, terrorists, or insurgents; in fact, the opposite was the case. In one night in Mosul alone, for example, we hit thirty-five targets simultaneously. We got twenty-three of those we were after, with only one or two shots fired and most of the operations requiring only a knock on a door, vice blowing it down. Such operations obviously depended on a sophisticated intelligence structure, one largely based on human intelligence (HUMINT) sources and very similar to the Joint Interagency Task Forces for Counter-Terrorism that were established in various locations after 9/11.

Observation Number 6 holds that *intelligence is the key to success*. It is, after all, detailed, actionable intelligence that enables "cordon and knock" operations and precludes large sweeps that often prove counterproductive. Developing such intelligence, however, is not easy. Substantial assets at the local (i.e., division or brigade) level are required to develop human intelligence networks and gather sufficiently precise information to allow targeted operations. For us, precise information generally meant a ten-digit grid for the target's location, a photo of the entry point, a reasonable description of the target, and directions to the target's location as well as other information on the neighborhood, the target site, and the target himself. Gathering this information is hard; considerable intelligence and operational assets are required, all of which must be pulled together to focus and deconflict the collection, analytical, and operational efforts. But it is precisely this type of approach that is essential to preventing terrorists and insurgents from putting down roots in an area and starting the process of intimidation and disruption that can result in a catastrophic downward spiral.

Observation Number 7, which springs from the fact that civil affairs are not enough when undertaking huge reconstruction and nation-building efforts, is that *everyone must do nation-building.* This should not be taken to indicate that I have anything but the greatest of respect for our civil affairs personnel—because I hold them in very high regard. I have personally watched them work wonders in Central America, Haiti, the Balkans, and, of course, Iraq. Rather, my point is that when undertaking industrial-strength reconstruction on the scale of that in Iraq, civil affairs forces alone will not suffice; every unit must be involved.

Reopening the University of Mosul brought this home to those of us in the 101st Airborne Division in the spring of 2003. A symbol of considerable national pride, the university had graduated more than 100,000 students since its establishment in 1967. Shortly after the seating of the interim Governor and Province Council in Nineveh Province in early May 2003, the council's members established completion of the school year at the university as among their top priorities. We thus took a quick trip through the university to assess the extent of the damage and to discuss its reopening with the Chancellor. We then huddled with our civil affairs battalion commander to chart a way ahead, but we quickly found that although the talent inherent in the battalion's education team was impressive, its members were relatively junior in rank and its size (numbering less than an infantry squad) was simply not enough to help the Iraqis repair and reopen a heavily looted institution of over seventy-five buildings, some 4,500 staff and faculty, and approximately 30,000 to 35,000 students. The mission, and the education team, therefore, went to one of the two aviation brigades of the 101st Airborne Division, a brigade that clearly did not have "rebuild foreign academic institutions" in its mission essential task list. What the brigade did have, however, was a senior commander and staff, as well as numerous subordinate units with commanders and staffs, who collectively added up to considerable organizational capacity and capability.

Seeing this approach work with Mosul University, we quickly adopted the same approach in virtually every area—assigning a unit or element the responsibility for assisting each of the Iraqi ministries' activities in northern Iraq and also for linking with key Iraqi leaders. For example, our signal battalion incorporated the civil affairs battalion's communications team and worked with the Ministry of Telecommunications' element in northern Iraq. It helped reestablish the local telecommunications structure, including assisting with a deal that brought a satellite downlink to the central switch and linked Mosul with the international phone system, producing a profit for the province (subscribers bore all the costs). Our chaplain and his team linked with the Ministry of Religious Affairs, the engineer battalion with the Ministry of Public Works, the Division Support Command with the Ministry of Youth and Sports, the Corps Support Group with the Ministry of Education, the Military Police Battalion with the Ministry of Interior (Police), our surgeon and his team with the Ministry of Health, our staff judge advocate with Ministry of Justice officials, our fire support element with the Ministry of Oil, and so on. In fact, we lined up a unit or staff section with every ministry element and with all the key leaders and officials in our area of responsibility (AOR), and our subordinate units did the same in theirs. By the time we were done, everyone and every element, not just civil affairs units, were engaged in nation-building.

Observation Number 8, recognition of the need to *help build institutions, not just units,* came from the Coalition's mission of helping Iraq reestablish its security forces. We initially focused primarily on developing combat units—Army and police battalions and brigade headquarters—as well as individual police. While those are what Iraq desperately needed to help in the achievement of security, for the long term there was also a critical need to help rebuild the institutions that support the units and police in the field—the ministries, the admin and logistical support units, the professional military education systems, admin policies and procedures, and the training organizations. Lack of ministry capability and capacity can undermine the development of the battalions, brigades, and divisions, if the ministries, for example, don't pay the Soldiers or police on time, use political rather than professional criteria in picking leaders, or fail to pay contractors as required for services provided. This lesson underscored for us the importance of providing sufficient advisers and mentors to assist with the development of the security ministries and their elements, just as we provided adviser teams with each battalion and each brigade and division headquarters.[9]

Observation Number 9, *cultural awareness is a force multiplier,* reflects our recognition that knowledge of the cultural "terrain" can be as important as, and sometimes even more important than, knowledge of the geographic terrain. This observation acknowledges that the people are, in many respects, the decisive terrain and that we must study that terrain in the same way that we have always studied the geographic terrain.

Working in another culture is enormously difficult if one doesn't understand the ethnic groups, tribes, religious elements, political parties, and other social groupings—and their respective viewpoints; the relationships among the various groups; governmental structures and processes; local and regional history; and local and national leaders. Understanding of such cultural aspects is essential if one is to help the people build stable political, social, and economic institutions. Indeed, this is as much a matter of common sense as operational necessity. Beyond the intellectual need for the specific knowledge about the environment in which one is working, it is also clear that people, in general, are more likely to cooperate if those who have power over them respect the culture that gives them a sense of identity and self-worth.

Many of us did a lot of "discovery learning" about such features of Iraq in the early months of our time there. And those who learned the quickest—and who also mastered some "survival Arabic"—were the most effective in developing productive relationships with local leaders and citizens and achieved the most progress in helping establish security, local governance, economic activity, and basic services. The importance of cultural awareness has been widely recognized in the U.S. Army and the other services, and it is critical that we continue the progress that has been made in this area in our exercises, military schools, doctrine, and so on.[10]

Observation Number 10 is a statement of the obvious, fully recognized by those operating in Iraq, but it is one worth recalling nonetheless. It is that *success in a counterinsurgency requires more than just military operations*. Counterinsurgency strategies must also include, above all, efforts to establish a political environment that helps reduce support for the insurgents and undermines the attraction of whatever ideology they may espouse.[11] In certain Sunni Arab regions of Iraq, establishing such a political environment is likely of greater importance than military operations, since the right political initiatives might undermine the sanctuary and assistance provided to the insurgents. Beyond the political arena, other important factors are economic recovery (which reduces unemployment, a serious challenge in Iraq that leads some out-of-work Iraqis to be guns for hire), education (which opens up employment possibilities and access to information from outside one's normal circles), diplomatic initiatives (in particular, working with neighboring states through which foreign fighters transit), improvement in the provision of basic services, and so on. In fact, the campaign plan developed in 2005 by the Multinational Force-Iraq and the U.S. embassy with Iraqi and Coalition leaders addresses each of these issues.

Observation Number 11, *ultimate success depends on local leaders*, is a natural reflection of Iraqi sovereignty. It acknowledges that success in Iraq is, as time passes, increasingly dependent on Iraqi leaders and at four levels:

- Leaders at the national level working together, reaching across party and sectarian lines to keep the country unified, rejecting short-term expedient solutions such as the use of militias, and pursuing initiatives to give more of a stake in the success of the new Iraq to those who feel left out
- Leaders in the ministries building the capability and capacity necessary to

use the tremendous resources Iraq has efficiently, transparently, honestly, and effectively
- Leaders at the province level resisting temptations to pursue winner-take-all politics and resisting the urge to politicize the local police and other security forces,
- Leaders in the Security Forces staying out of politics, providing courageous, competent leadership to their units; implementing policies that are fair to all members of their forces; and fostering loyalty to their Army or police band of brothers rather than to specific tribes, ethnic groups, political parties, or local militias.

Iraqi leaders are the real key to the new Iraq, and we thus need to continue to do all that we can to enable them.

Observation Number 12 is the admonition to *remember the strategic corporals and strategic lieutenants*, the relatively junior commissioned or noncommissioned officers who often have to make huge decisions, sometimes with life-or-death as well as strategic consequences, in the blink of an eye.

Commanders have two major obligations to these junior leaders: first, to do everything possible to train them before deployment for the various situations they will face, particularly for the most challenging and ambiguous ones; and, second, once deployed, to try to shape situations to minimize the cases in which they have to make those hugely important decisions extremely quickly.

The best example of the latter is what we do to help ensure that, when establishing hasty checkpoints, our strategic corporals are provided sufficient training and adequate means to stop a vehicle speeding toward them without having to put a bullet through the windshield. This is easier said than it is done in the often chaotic situations that arise during a fast-moving operation in such a challenging security environment. But there are some actions we can take to try to ensure that our young leaders have adequate time to make the toughest of calls—decisions that, if not right, again, can have strategic consequences.

Observation Number 13 is that *there is no substitute for flexible, adaptable leaders*. The key to many of our successes in Iraq, in fact, has been leaders—especially young leaders—who have risen to the occasion and taken on tasks for which they'd had little or no training[12] and who have demonstrated enormous initiative, innovativeness, determination, and courage.[13] Such leaders have repeatedly been the essential ingredient in many of the achievements in Iraq. Fostering the development of others like them is critical to the further development of our Army and military.[14]

Observation Number 14 underscores that, especially in counterinsurgency operations, *a leader's most important task is to set the right tone*. This is another statement of the obvious but one that nonetheless needs to be highlighted given its tremendous importance. Setting the right tone and communicating that tone to his or her subordinate leaders and troopers are absolutely critical for every leader at every level, especially in an endeavor like that in Iraq.

If, for example, a commander clearly emphasizes so-called kinetic operations over non-kinetic operations, subordinates will do likewise. As a result, they may thus be less inclined to seize opportunities for the nation-building aspects of the campaign. In fact, even in the 101st Airborne Division, which prided itself on its attention to nation-building, there were a few mid-level commanders early on whose hearts really weren't into performing civil affairs tasks, assisting with reconstruction, developing relationships with local citizens, or helping establish local governance. To use the jargon of Iraq at that time, they didn't "get it." In such cases, the commanders above them quickly established that nation-building activities were not optional and would be pursued with equal enthusiasm to raids and other offensive operations.

Setting the right tone ethically is another hugely important task. If leaders fail to get this right, winking at the mistreatment of detainees or at the manhandling of citizens, for example, the result can be a sense in the unit that "anything goes." Nothing can be more destructive in an element than an "anything goes" mentality.

In truth, regardless of the leader's tone, most units in Iraq have had to deal with cases in which mistakes have been made in these areas, where young leaders in very frustrating situations, often after having suffered tough casualties, took missteps. The key in these situations is for leaders to ensure that appropriate action is taken in the wake of such incidents, that standards are clearly articulated and reinforced, that remedial training is conducted, and that supervision is exercised to try to preclude recurrences.

It is hard to imagine a tougher environment than that in some of the areas in Iraq. Frustration, anger, and resentment can run high in such situations. That recognition underscores, again, the importance of commanders at every level working hard to get the tone right and to communicate it throughout their units.

Implications

These are fourteen observations from soldiering in Iraq for most of the first thirty months of our involvement there. Although I presented them as discrete lessons, many are inextricably related. These observations carry with them a number of implications for our effort in Iraq (and for our Army as well, as I have noted in some of the endnotes).[15]

Success in Iraq—which clearly is important not just for Iraq, but also for the entire Middle East region and for our own country—will require continued military operations and support for the ongoing development of Iraqi Security Forces. Success will also require continued assistance and resources for the development of the emerging political, economic, and social institutions in Iraq—efforts in which Ambassador Zalmay Khalilzad and GEN George Casey and their teams have been engaged with their Iraqi counterparts and have been working very hard.

Last, success will require time, determination, and resilience, keeping in mind that following the elections held in mid-December 2005, several months will likely be required for the new government—the fourth in an eighteen-month period—to be established and functional. The insurgents and extremists did all that they could to derail the preparations for the constitutional referendum in mid-October and the elections in mid-December. Although they were ineffective in each case, they undoubtedly will try to disrupt the establishment of the new government—and the upcoming provincial elections—as well. As GEN John Abizaid and GEN George Casey made clear in their testimony on Capitol Hill in September 2005, however, there is a strategy—developed in close coordination with those in the U.S. embassy in Baghdad and with our interagency, Coalition, and Iraqi partners—that addresses the insurgency, Iraqi Security Forces, and the other relevant areas. And there has been substantial progress in a number of areas. Nonetheless, nothing is ever easy in Iraq, and a great deal of hard work and many challenges clearly lie ahead.[16]

The first six months of 2006 were of enormous importance, with the efforts of Iraqi leaders being especially significant during this period as a new government is seated and the new constitution enters into force. It is essential that we do all that we can to support Iraq's leaders as they endeavor to make the most of the opportunity our Soldiers have given them.

Conclusion

In a 1986 article titled "Uncomfortable Wars: Toward a New Paradigm," GEN John R. Galvin observed that "[a]n officer's effectiveness and chance for success, now and in the future, depend not only on his character, knowledge, and skills, but also, and more than ever before, on his ability to understand the changing environment of conflict."[17] General Galvin's words were relevant then, but they are even more applicable today. Conducting counterinsurgency operations in a vastly different culture is exceedingly complex.

Later, in the same article, General Galvin counseled, "Let us get our young leaders away from the grindstone now and then, and encourage them to reflect on developments outside the fortress-cloister. Only then will they develop into leaders capable of adapting to the changed environment of warfare and able to fashion a new paradigm that addresses all the dimensions of the conflicts that may lie ahead."[18]

Given the current situation, General Galvin's advice again appears very wise indeed. And it is my hope that, as we all take time to lift our noses from the grindstone and look beyond the confines of our current assignments, the observations provided here will help foster useful discussion on our ongoing endeavors and on how we should approach similar conflicts in the future—conflicts that are likely to be the norm, rather than the exception, in the twenty-first century.

10

Thoughts on Journalism and the Military
—Tom Fenton

Journalists and the military look at each other with suspicion these days, but we have something in common. I should know because I have been on both sides of the fence. I was a regular U.S. Navy officer for a decade in the Cold War and since then have worked as a journalist and foreign correspondent. I often joke that "journalism beats working," but you could say the same of both professions. The people who go into them tend to be highly motivated.

We both have an idealistic streak. Most of us are not in it for the money. (Journalism doesn't pay very well unless you reach the top of your profession in network television news.) We both believe we are doing something for mankind. The military is trying to make the world safer by making war. We journalists are trying to make it a better world by giving it the benefit of our version of the truth. Of course, we are both a bit delusional.

But let's assume that Soldiers and journalists are not doing their jobs just for the money. We both believe we are doing it for higher reasons, and that's why we also tend to clash. We have different reasons for being in Iraq, or Afghanistan, or Kosovo. The aim of the military is winning the war and being seen to be winning. Journalists these days tend to question whether there should be a war at all, and they want to poke their noses into how it is being conducted.

Those of us who have seen combat know that making war is like making sausage. What goes on in the kitchen is not a pretty thing. The military public affairs officer would like the war correspondent to describe the beautiful new sausage. The correspondent wants to describe the blood and guts that went into making it.

❖ ❖ ❖

Although journalists and the military have different aims, that does not mean they cannot work together. My colleagues who covered World War II, famous journalists such as Edward R. Murrow and Walter Cronkite, never questioned that the United States was on the right side. They considered themselves to be part of the war effort. They wore uniforms and were given the privileges of an assimilated rank. They understood the necessity for military censorship because they were experienced war correspondents. (I cannot say the same for all the journalists the American news agencies, newspapers, and television threw into the wars in Afghanistan and Iraq. Some of them came from the world of fashion, lifestyle, and celebrity reporting. They were a danger to themselves as well as to the Soldiers who were shepherding them.)

Throughout the years, the relationship between the military and the media evolved with the nature of the wars our country fought. It remained much the same in the Korean War, although the advent of a new medium of reporting added another dimension. CBS television reported an infantry landing while it was under way in August 1950—a security breach that was a harbinger of future tensions between those who wage war and those who report it.

The chummy relationship fell apart a decade and a half later when America waded into the jungle of Vietnam. The military helped defeat its own efforts at information management by taking journalists to the battlefields. An initially unquestioning press corps gradually began to see the gap between the military's upbeat assessment of the way the war was going and the downbeat reality the reporters saw on the battlefield. When CBS News anchor Walter Cronkite, who initially supported the war, proposed an "honorable" withdrawal from Vietnam, President Lyndon Johnson knew he had lost the support of the country. That's a lesson the government never forgot, and it fundamentally changed the way the military and the media have looked at each other since then.

Commercial television cameras were simply shut out of the American mini-invasion of Grenada in 1983. In the first Gulf War, the military could not ban the media, so it assigned them to pools far from the scene of action and fed them a diet of briefings and videos of bull's-eyes on Iraqi bunkers. One of my CBS News colleagues, correspondent Bob Simon, became so frustrated that he set out on his own with his producer and camera team to cover the action. They were captured in the desert by the Iraqis and spent forty days in prison.

In the Second Gulf War, which followed the national trauma of 9/11, the military tried to turn back the clock and enlist the media's help as it had in World War II and the Cold War, before the bond of mutual trust was broken. The Pentagon embedded correspondents and camera teams in combat units and initially reaped a harvest of gung-ho reports. It made for great television as well as great military PR. However, it was not great reporting.

Most of the embedded journalists had no war experience. When the advance on Baghdad paused to allow the baggage train to catch up, they reported that the invasion had bogged down. When the advancing troops met sporadic resistance, the embeds saw it with the myopia of the battlefield and magnified local skirmishes into battles. The American public was given a confused picture, which the Pentagon and the briefers at GEN Tommy Franks's headquarters in Doha, Qatar, tried to spin to their advantage.

From the standpoint of the media, the Doha Coalition Briefing Center was a farce. The military herded hundreds of journalists from all over the world into an air-conditioned warehouse, where initially the only sources of information were wall-mounted television monitors that carried mostly American news programs. A cocky young man from the White House who paraded around in a khaki uniform and seemed to be running the place assured me that we would be given "the big picture." For the first few days, the American military information officers gave us no briefings at all, and we had to glean a few scraps from friendlier British briefers who took us around the corner and gave us what information they could.

When the U.S. briefings finally began, they consisted of snappy target videos that told us very little and vague generalizations about the progress of the invasion that told us less than the Iraqis themselves knew. What we were not given was the big picture. At one point, an American information officer offered me a "story" on trained dolphins that were being used for mine clearance on the Shat-al-Arab waterway. We were being treated like trained seals.

❖ ❖ ❖

It might be useful to set forth a few of my own observations on how to handle war correspondents. You may not agree with all of them, but I offer this from the standpoint of four decades of experience in dozens of wars from the 1967 Six Days' War to the War in Iraq. Call it "a short guide for information officers on the care and feeding of journalists."

1. Most of us are almost as intelligent as you are but not very knowledgeable about military affairs.
2. Except for experienced war correspondents—a rare breed—most of us make numerous mistakes and appreciate any effort by the military to give us technical help in reporting military affairs, especially if it keeps us from making fools of ourselves.
3. Our lack of expertise means that you may be able to manipulate us. I am not advocating that you should try, just pointing out one of our obvious weaknesses.
4. Television correspondents, especially those who are more interested in furthering their careers than in getting the story right, are especially susceptible to manipulation.

5. On the other hand, journalists have highly developed "bullshit meters," and once we find that we have been used, we will never trust you again.
6. It is hard to make a silk purse out of a sow's ear, so it's best not to try. In the long run, honesty and frankness are the best policy in dealing with journalists. If things go wrong, admit it and explain why it happened. We are more likely to believe you in the future when you have a really hard case to sell.
7. Journalists have a herd mentality. We stick together and ask each other what's the lead to the story. We usually feel more comfortable if we are all reporting a story the same way. Our editors do, too.
8. Once we make up our minds about a person or an event, you will have a hard time changing them. Those in the media are no more willing to admit their errors than the military is.
9. Don't promise us more than you can deliver. It is better if we approach an assignment with low expectations and are pleasantly surprised when it turns out to be a real story. That allows us to think we have been especially clever.
10. Don't treat journalist like fools. Or trained seals.

❖ ❖ ❖

Sadly, the initial flush of victory in Baghdad was followed by years of miscalculations and blunders that have undone the hard work of the military and done immense damage to the position of the United States in the world. I do not need to go into the details. A series of books by experienced journalists and experts in military affairs has recounted what went wrong.

At the time that this is being written, almost four years into the Iraq campaign, it is clear that neither the American military information officers who dealt with the media, nor the reporters who covered the war, served our country well. Much of the blame for what amounted to a vast deception must lay with the top echelons of our government, but we are all complicit. The public was led to believe that Iraq would be a piece of cake. Too few journalists questioned the basic assumptions that were used to justify a war we will be paying for in manifold ways for years to come.

In the end, probably nothing that the White House, the Pentagon, and any number of military briefers or jaded journalists could do would have changed the current American perception of the war. The American people are not fools. It may take them a long time to get it, but in the end they usually see things for what they are. They have turned against the war in Iraq because the daily drumbeat of news has convinced them it was fought in the wrong way and for the wrong reasons. Facts have trumped propaganda. The public has finally got it right.

I would like to note that some critics of the American media complain that we never report the good news from Iraq. Iraq has become too dangerous for

Western journalists to report such stories as the opening of a new school. It is nearly impossible now to cover firsthand what daily life is like for an Iraqi family in Baghdad and most other Iraqi cities. If we could do such reports, the picture the American public receives would be even darker.

❖ ❖ ❖

Do America's adversaries in the "war on terror" handle their information programs any better than we do? The answer is clearly yes. They are highly effective with their audience in the Arab and larger Muslim world because it is now predisposed to see America as an enemy. The United States is assumed to be cruel, duplicitous, hungry for oil, and without regard for Muslim lives. With a target audience like that, one does not have to be subtle. The myths I regularly hear in the Muslim world never seem to die. To this date, the "Arab street" is convinced that the attack on the World Trade Center was a Jewish plot. Many Arabs who otherwise seem perfectly reasonable and intelligent take that for a fact.

Many of these misperceptions and outright falsehoods are fed by outrageously slanted reporting in the Muslim media, but some of this is influenced by fact. America's double standards in some of its foreign policy choices are one such factor. Washington threatens Iran because it refuses to stop its illegal nuclear research program, but it quietly supports Israel's nuclear weapons and even lavishes aid on Pakistan, which not only has its own bomb but has sold the technology to several of America's adversaries. President Bush speaks of spreading democracy and encouraging free elections in the Middle East, but when the Palestinians elect a government run by Hamas, Washington's reaction is to try to starve them into throwing out Hamas and reinstalling a government led by the Fatah gang they just rejected.

Al Qaeda and its affiliated groups have an easy job spreading their gospel because they are preaching to the converted. Their videos and Internet messages have a profound impact on the Muslim world, but they have also become highly skillful in manipulating American public opinion. Like the Iraqi insurgents who seek to drive Coalition troops and even international aid organizations out of their country, they learned early in the game that one picture is worth a thousand words. Improvised explosive devices (IEDs) and car bombs in Baghdad eclipse most other perceptions of the American campaign in Iraq. Whether that represents a true picture of the situation is immaterial. The Pentagon can ban pictures of coffins coming home to America, but it cannot keep pictures of the chaos in Baghdad from coming into America's living rooms. They have had the most profound impact of all. The American military has not been defeated in Iraq, but America has lost the war.

❖ ❖ ❖

What can the United States do to improve its image in the world? The government's answer always seems to be that it needs to do a better job at getting its message across. But recent U.S. government attempts at planting stories in the Arab media or running government-sponsored television have been inept and not very effective. The problem is not how America sells its message. The problem is that our actions speak louder than our words, and much of the world, rightly or wrongly, disapproves of our country's actions, especially our recent track record in the Middle East. You only have to look at opinion polls around the world to see how unpopular our government is these days. Anti-American sentiment is higher than I have ever seen in my forty years as a foreign correspondent, even higher than it was at the height of the war in Vietnam. That is not only a challenge for our government. It is a challenge for the American people. The real strength of a true democracy is that it is not the government that has the last word. It is not the media. It is the people. That is why we have free elections.

11

Strategic Innovation: Integrating National Power to Win in Iraq

—*LTC John A. Nagl, USA (Ret.)*

Defeating an insurgency is not primarily a military task. David Galula, the French counterinsurgency expert, estimated that the task was 80 percent political and only 20 percent military.[1] Counterinsurgency is a long, slow process that requires the integration of all elements of national power—military, diplomatic, economic, financial, intelligence, and informational—to accomplish the tasks of creating and supporting legitimate host governments that can then defeat the insurgency that afflicts them.[2]

The national strategy for "Victory in Iraq" lays out a comprehensive interagency plan for achieving ultimate success there, but the challenge of implementing that strategy with instruments of national power not optimized for that task is a pressing one.[3] To cope more effectively with the messy reality that in the twenty-first century many of our enemies will be insurgents, America's national security establishment must create an operational capability to influence the actions of other nations and of subnational groups that struggle with the challenge of radical Islam. It must also improve the way we gather and analyze intelligence from the population. These overdue steps will help us win the war in Iraq and the broader Global War on Terrorism.

Information Operations

Insurgency is ultimately a war of ideas. An insurgency grows based on its ability to convince fighters to risk their lives against a conventionally superior opponent and survives in the face of a stronger enemy only because it is able to convince or coerce the people to provide it with what it needs to fight: weapons, ammunition, food, money, and, most important, concealment and cover among the civilian population. Recognizing this fact, successful counterinsurgents have devoted as much effort to defeating the enemy's propaganda as they have to defeating his fighters. Winning the war of ideas has often been the decisive line of operations in successful counterinsurgency campaigns.

The United States has not done an adequate job of explaining to the American people, to its allies overseas, and, most important, to the people of Iraq and of the broader Islamic world what we are fighting for in Iraq and what we hope to achieve there. Nature abhors a vacuum and insurgents love one; they have filled the airwaves and the Internet with their versions of the truth and have found willing listeners worldwide. In the words of the Secretary of Defense, "Our enemies have skillfully adapted to fighting wars in today's media age, but for the most part we, our country, our government, has not."[4]

Insurgencies are rarely defeated militarily; some degree of political accommodation is essential in convincing all but the most committed insurgents that politics rather than force is a viable way to pursue their objectives. Historically, successful counterinsurgents have defeated their opponents by peeling off the less ideologically committed subelements with promises of political progress toward their ultimate goals. In the case of the Sunni minority in Iraq, political outreach would provide promises of a greater degree of political power than the Sunnis have believed would be granted to a minority population in such an immature democracy. The Shi'a majority must understand that suicide car bombings will end only when the Sunni insurgency has received such political promises. These political understandings are essential for any kind of stability in Iraq.

During the Cold War, which was primarily an economic battle and only secondarily a military one, the United States Information Agency (USIA) did yeoman's work to win hearts and minds behind the Iron Curtain. The global war that we are now fighting against radical Islamic extremists is primarily a war of ideas. A dedicated corps of public affairs professionals funded and equipped to speak to Muslims in their own languages could help win the war of ideas over time by providing vital support to moderate Muslims. A more focused effort in Iraq can help convince the uncommitted but hopeful people of Iraq to provide the information we need to kill and capture those who are now murdering Iraq's future. Ideas are far cheaper than bullets and much more effective in defeating an insurgency.

Enemies of freedom in Iraq kill innocent Muslim men, women, and children on a daily basis with suicide bombs that make a virtue of their randomness. Why are these heinous attacks inflicted on the innocent by our enemies not publicized throughout the Muslim world—indeed, throughout the entire globe? There is no more powerful indication of the difference between the United States and its enemies in Iraq, no greater evidence of what is at stake there for the future of the entire Middle East, than the fact that insurgents intentionally target with suicide bombs the children who gather around American Soldiers in the expectation of candy and school supplies donated by the American people. A country that can turn multimedia political advertisements within twenty-four hours in a presidential campaign should certainly be able to produce black-and-white posters within that same span of time showing the names and faces of Iraqi children slaughtered by terrorist bombers and begging for information to bring their murderers to justice.

Intelligence Derived from a Supportive Population

The prime requirement for a successful military component of a counterinsurgency effort is intelligence derived from a supportive population. While in conventional war the successful army is generally the side that masses firepower at the decisive point in time on the battlefield, a wily insurgent enemy rarely provides his superior conventional foe with a massed target, preferring to hide in "the sea of the people." Massing intelligence collection and analysis resources, rather than firepower, is the key to capturing or killing insurgents.

Armies confronting an insurgency have historically struggled with the transformation from their traditional focus on firepower to slowly and painfully cultivating the intelligence sources necessary to defeat an insurgent enemy. While the U.S. Army and Marine Corps have made significant strides in developing this capability, there is still much work to be done. The tank and infantry battalions on the front lines of counterinsurgency in Iraq were initially designed for a very different form of combat than the one they find themselves fighting today. Organized with an intelligence staff of just a handful of personnel among hundreds of tankers and infantrymen, they are learning that to wage counterinsurgency successfully these ratios must be dramatically revised. Turning every rifleman and tank driver into an intelligence collector and analyst is extraordinarily difficult but necessary to defeat an insurgency.

Chief among the skills required, but currently lacking in all but a few of the Soldiers and Marines in Iraq, is facility in the Arabic language. The ability to talk with and thus gain intelligence from the local population allows the trained Soldier to turn an everyday presence patrol into an opportunity to identify the enemy—the crucial and most difficult step on the road to defeating him. While the ability to talk with the local population is inherent in the ever-increasing number of capable Iraqi units, Americans will be required to serve alongside and within Iraqi units for many years to come. To make them as effective as possible, they need more translators and greater familiarity with Arabic language and Iraqi culture. The recent decision by the U.S. Marine Corps to require that every Marine develop expertise in a foreign area and language is a step in the right direction, one that the Army—and the State Department, CIA, USAID, and even FBI—would be well advised to emulate.

There are technological solutions to the demand for improved language skills in the works, but there is no substitute for the interpersonal nuance that only human interaction in the native language can provide. Dramatic efforts are required to ensure improvements in language capability for every patrol that goes outside the wire and corresponding improvements in the ability to analyze the greater quantities of intelligence that will flow from our Soldiers as a result. Much more can be done to exploit captured insurgents and documents, understand enemy networks, and conduct targeted raids to capture or kill the leadership of the insurgency. The missing nails in the horseshoe are interpreters who understand the local culture and the local insurgency and intelligence analysts who have the patience and cultural understanding to piece together the puzzle.

A Better War

GEN Peter Schoomaker has written that "self-aware, thinking Soldiers and leaders build learning, adaptive teams and organizations. For the twenty-first century, we must have an Army characterized by a culture of innovation and imagination."[5] The Army is showing itself to be a learning organization by taking many of the steps it must accomplish to become more effective in the difficult, dangerous type of war in which we are now engaged. We have much more work to do.

Success in Iraq requires more emphasis on political outreach to the Sunni insurgents, a sharper focus on the advisory effort at the expense of large-scale American units, more interpreters and cultural advisers, and a more coordinated use of all elements of national power to accomplish the United States' objectives in Iraq. Most important would be a vastly expanded effort to fully explain American actions and objectives in Iraq both to the domestic audience in the United States and to our friends and allies overseas—especially the Iraqi people most affected by the conflict. Their actions will ultimately prove decisive in this fight, and we must do more to convince the Kurds, Shi'a, and especially the Sunnis that their best hope for a successful future is a unitary Iraq at peace with its neighbors and secure inside its borders.

Even these course corrections, important as they are, will take time to affect the course of events in Iraq. It will take a comprehensive national effort to ensure that all government agencies place the same emphasis on success in Iraq that has marked the military effort there; redouble efforts to provide sufficient interpreters for every American patrol; improve manning, training, and equipping of the advisory teams on the front lines of our efforts to improve Iraqi police and Army battalions; reshape the intelligence effort in Iraq to provide sufficient, properly trained and educated intelligence collectors and analysts to understand and identify the insurgents; and create and employ an information agency to fight and win the war of ideas in Iraq and beyond. These actions are all long-term investments. Successful counterinsurgency campaigns of the past suggest improvements such as these will enable us to win in Iraq—if we, as a nation, are patient enough to make the investment that a free Iraq deserves and a secure America requires.[6]

The most important lesson of the past is the critical role of national patience and persistence in defeating an insurgency. We are four years into a counterinsurgency campaign that history suggests will take at least a decade to win. This lesson cannot be repeated too often, sobering though it is for a democracy accustomed to quick victories or speedy withdrawals from intractable conflicts: insurgencies are long wars.

We should take comfort in the knowledge that armies rarely prepare correctly for the kind of war they will have to fight in the future and therefore generally have to adapt to the particular demands of the kind of war they are actually tasked to fight. In the words of British military historian and Soldier Sir Michael Howard, "In structuring and preparing an army for war you can be clear that you will not get it precisely right, but the important thing to ensure is that it is not too far wrong, so that you can put it right quickly."[7] In Iraq, the United States Army is learning counterinsurgency quickly, making up for lost time and making great strides in the effort to help the Iraqi people build a free, stable, and secure Iraq. We must not falter in this effort.

12

Maneuvering Against the Mind

—*LtCol Frank G. Hoffman, USMCR (Ret.)*

T. E. Lawrence may have been the first irregular warfare theorist, but he was not the first practitioner to note that the cognitive domain is a major consideration in such conflicts. In the *Seven Pillars of Wisdom* he emphasized the psychological power of ideas.[1] These wars are what Baron Antoine-Henri Jomini had previously termed "wars of opinions." But the salience of the cognitive element of modern conflict is clearly rising to even greater importance. In the future, winning "hearts and minds" may be the most dominant aspect of the battle space. This "new" portion of the battle space is being expanded to a more global scale thanks to the ubiquitous and diffuse nature of modern communication techniques. Marines and other members of the national security community must adapt their application of maneuver warfare to effectively operate in this arena of modern war.

Ideas and grievances are the seeds of most irregular wars, and modern information technology has given anyone with access to a computer the ability to spread a message globally at the speed of light at a fraction of what it used to cost. Given that most so-called small wars are ultimately won or lost in the political and psychological dimension, the importance of communications and information dissemination is vital. The velocity of information flows and the power of imagery can now be readily transmitted almost instantly. This can generate significant support for one's cause throughout the international system or through a network of sympathizers. It can be a "force multiplier" to the side that can employ the information domain to secure and sustain a positional advantage in the moral or psychological dimension.

While the U.S. military has a demonstrated capacity to dominate a situation with its technological supremacy and computer software, its performance in Iraq suggests it remains handicapped by its techno-lust and falls well short of mastering properly understood modern information warfare. At the strategic level, the American government can be accused of unilaterally disarming itself in today's Long War against religious extremism.

The Rising Salience of the Virtual Dimension

The informational component of war, as the Long War clearly reveals, is increasing in impact. Modern 24/7 news cycles and graphic imagery combined with the worldwide networks produce even faster and higher response cycles from audiences around the globe while offering powerful new tools. Advanced methods and lower costs allow many insurgent or terrorist groups to communicate directly to their target audiences. The number of websites devoted to jihadist literature or themes has exploded exponentially since 9/11. As Professor Bruce Hoffman notes, modern irregular warriors have a wider tool kit today and are not limited to

> simply the guns and bombs that they always have used. Now those weapons include the Minicam and videotape; editing suite and attendant production facilities; professionally produced and mass-marketed CD-ROMs and DVDs; and most critically the laptop and desktop computers, CD burners, and e-mail accounts; and Internet and World Wide Web access that have defined the information revolution today.[2]

In addition to being a source of power to antagonists, advanced information technology extends the potential support base of the adversary to a global dimension. This extended support base can provide financial, material, or personnel support to the cause. Of particular relevance to future wars, the availability of modern information technology radically changes the manner by which potential adversaries acquire and disseminate strategic intelligence, garner resources, conduct planning and rehearsals, and even recruit.[3]

Most important, the rapidly diffusing nature of information technology has increased the relevance and focused the power of ideas and imagery. Ideas and grievances are ammunition within insurgencies. Modern information technology has given anyone with access to a computer the ability to fire these rounds and spread a message globally at little or no cost. Given that irregular wars are quintessentially won or lost in what is now sometimes called the "virtual dimension," the importance of communications and information dissemination is a vital factor.[4] The decision to withdraw the Marines from Fallujah in April 2004 highlights the powerful effect of modern communications and near-real-time dissemination to local, regional, and global audiences.[5]

This is not necessarily a new factor; today it's a matter of the diversity of means of transmitting ideas and the speed of the dissemination that influenced events in Iraq. Long ago Marine veterans of irregular wars recognized the impact of modern communications. The Marines' *Small Wars Manual* noted that revolutions could be rapidly fanned by "modern" communications.[6] But in the past, it was only the state and major media outlets that could obtain mass coverage and influence large populations.

Today, many small groups have mastered "armed theater" and promoted "propaganda of the deed" to arouse support and foment discord on a global scale.[7] There are a plethora of outlets now in the Middle East and an exponentially growing number of websites and bloggers promoting radical visions. These outlets constantly bombard the residents of Iraq with pictures, videos, DVDs, and sermons. Ironically, in Iraq and in the Long War, we are facing a fundamentalist movement that is exploiting very modern and Western technologies to reestablish an anti-Western social and political system.

The velocity of information flows and the power of imagery can now be readily transmitted almost in real time anywhere around the globe. This can generate significant support for one's cause in the international system. It can be a force multiplier to the side that can employ the information domain to secure and sustain a positional advantage in the moral or psychological dimension. Given that persuasion and popular opinion can be a center of gravity or a critical vulnerability in the conduct of irregular contests, this development may become crucial to the successful prosecution of irregular wars and become the focal point for transformational efforts within DOD or the U.S. government. While the U.S. military has focused on its technological supremacy and computer software, the adversary has exploited the same technology to influence the most important software—the thinking and emotions of its target audience.

Adapting Classical Theory

Classical counterinsurgency theory stresses the isolation of the guerrilla from the population.[8] Isolation, in the physical sense, is a common security measure during insurgencies and rebellions. Creating a means of physically isolating a threat or at least negating his ability to easily enter and plunder one's own population has been a component of strategy since Emperor Hadrian ordered the construction of the Roman fortification line across Britain. A number of other cases suggest that blockhouses, defensive lines, and outposts have been a regular feature in this mode of war.[9]

But isolation does not have to be limited to only the physical dimension. The counterinsurgent force must physically and psychologically separate the insurgents or opponents from both external and internal sources of support. Here the counter-irregular force must use both military force and information operations to demoralize the active or armed elements, but more important to de-legitimize their underlying ideology or political movement. To use a common medical metaphor, one should begin to "cauterize" around the insurgency to keep it from spreading or acquiring support.[10]

Looking back over a wide range of case studies, the physical and psychological isolation of the insurgent was a key contributor to all successful examples. Isolation cuts off resources and other sources of support from within the host nation or from contiguous territories used as sanctuary. Physical isolation by barrier or other means makes interference with the host government harder, maximizes freedom of action within other domains such as economic development, and limits the ability of the insurgent to intimidate or coerce friendly or neutral indigenous personnel.

Isolation in the ideological or political sense is also critical to both neutralize the insurgent's message or appeal and reduce potential forms of intelligence gathering, recruiting, or funding. The classic experts in irregular warfare, including Lawrence, Mao Tse-tung, and David Galula, have all pointed to the importance of information as a weapon. However, its mastery has proven to be elusive even to modern powers. Galula went on to add, "If there was a field in which we were definitely and infinitely more stupid than our opponents, it was propaganda."[11] This is a poignant comment given the paucity of effective informational activities in Iraq. Today's 24/7 news cycles and graphic imagery produce even faster and higher response cycles from audiences around the globe and offer powerful new "weapons" to those who can master them.[12] It has taken almost four years for the Pentagon's leadership to understand its own limitations in this regard. The former Secretary of Defense himself has acknowledged, "If I were grading I would say we probably deserve a 'D' or a 'D-plus' as a country as to how well we're doing in the battle of ideas that's taking place in the world today."[13]

There are a number of ways to isolate the adversary in the psychological dimension. These strategies seek to undermine the true source of strength of the adversary in complex irregular wars, his ideological base and the attractiveness of his appeal for support, intelligence, or resources. There are a number of indirect approaches within this broader and less kinetic suite of strategies.

The first is subversion. Subversion is a well-worn strategy for counteracting an insurgency and generally involves sowing internal discord or mistrust into the adversary organization. Attacking inconsistencies or shortfalls within the adversary organization's purpose, structure, or achievements is conducted in order to subvert its internal cohesion or undermine its attractiveness to current or future members.[14] A center of gravity for many networks is their internal cohesion or trust. In that many groups have multiple factions, internal leadership struggles, or internal arguments about goals and methods, subversion may be a way of introducing increased friction or higher operating costs on the enemy. Subversion can be accomplished by effective information operations, including leaks, street gossip, or introducing items into broadcast media or even the communications links of the adversary's system.

An advanced but risky form of subversion entails what are called pseudo operations.[15] Pseudo operations have been used in past counterinsurgencies and require the use of indigenous or foreign units to dress, arm, and behave as an insurgent organization. Pseudo operations are not new. Many law enforcement agencies conduct what in police jargon is known as a "sting" operation. They attempt to lure a criminal into committing a crime or providing evidence inadvertently by having police officials or surrogates act as fellow criminals. Pseudo techniques were used successfully by the British in Kenya against the Mau Mau, by the U.S. MACV-SOG (Studies and Observation Group) in Vietnam, and by Rhodesian Selous Scouts. Pseudo-operational techniques may be oriented on gathering intelligence, luring insurgent units into ambushes in their own backyard, or repressing a supporting populace in order to separate an insurgent from his popular base. This latter technique is fraught with risk if the true nature of the unit is ever revealed and could be counterproductive. It is possible to create counterforces in the virtual dimension that undercut the irregular opponent's legitimacy or the credibility of his posting in the cyber world or in the media.

Penetration is another potential approach. Against modern terrorist organizations, the chances of a significant penetration by an individual are unlikely but not impossible. American law enforcement officials were successful in penetrating the American Mafia over time, using both turncoats and its own agents. British intelligence has had success in penetrating the IRA in Northern Ireland from time to time. But modern cells of the Islamic movement are widely distributed and built on group dynamics that make penetration very improbable.[16] But penetration into their thinking and their cyber operations is still possible and may be useful as a means of undercutting the confidence in which they operate in this dimension or as a source of intelligence. Here the technical side of information wars or net wars may retain relevance.[17]

Both subversion and penetration may be extremely effective forms of inciting factionalism within complex organizations such as networked entities conducting Fourth Generation Warfare (4GW). Complex insurgent networks may be hard to penetrate, but they are vulnerable to internal fissures and destructive behavior owing to personal dynamics and the stresses that such groups may be under. Of course, this requires a fairly comprehensive understanding of the network and its internal values, leadership, and behavior. Western military forces and their intelligence organs have not demonstrated any virtuosity in so doing so far.

Reconceptualizing IO

Overall, classical theory can be applied in the information age by simply expanding the basic principles to the particular context in which historically proven precepts are employed. IO in conventional operations involves those actions taken by the military to directly or indirectly affect the enemy's information and information systems.[18] In major combat operations, the focus of IO is on the key decision makers and the decision-making process to degrade, influence, or paralyze their ability to understand the situation or respond effectively. In conventional campaigns, the essence of IO is to influence the enemy decision-making processes while enhancing and protecting our own. But in dealing with an insurgency, a greater preponderance of the decision making involves the perceptions of the civilian population and their collective decision-making process to support the host nation's government.

The overall objective is to compete in the informational battle and win the battle of ideas and the politico-military struggle for power. The IO capabilities and supporting related activities enable or support military operations that create opportunities for decisive battles. These capabilities, when synchronized, counter the opponent and subversive activity while seizing and maintaining the initiative with a steady broadcast or delivery of information. IO certainly applies to nontraditional forms of warfare. As T. E. Lawrence observed, "The printing press is the greatest weapon in the armoury of the modern commander."[19] It may now be the video camera or the DVD copier.

The U.S. military has myopically focused on information warfare and its cousin, net-centric warfare, to enhance traditional, conventional military functions and missed the larger strategic influence of cyber tools. It has conceptualized IO as composed of five major pillars: computer network attack, computer network defense, electronic warfare, deception, and psychological operations. This framework and the way it was introduced in an age of supposed revolutionary change warped its utility for more irregular scenarios. The U.S. military has repeated the most frequent mistake of military innovation, attempting to laminate new technology on top of old processes while underestimating the imagination of our enemies. Recent scholarship has persuasively compared the ongoing cyber-mobilization of Muslims around the world to the French Revolution and the *levée en masse*.[20]

Modern cyber-mobilization benefits from numerous parallels to the French Revolution. These include a democratization of communications, an increase in public access, sharp cost reductions in both production and distribution of media, and an exploitation of images to create and reinforce a mobilizing ideology or narrative. Today's computer- and media-saturated audience has an astonishing array of cyber choices that also have clear analogues to France's rising: blogs are today's revolutionary pamphlets, websites are the new dailies, and list services are today's broadsides.

Like the levée en masse, the evolving character of communications today is altering the patterns of popular mobilization, including both the means of participation and the ends for which wars are fought. It is enabling the recruiting, training, convincing, and motivating of individuals. "Today's mobilization may not be producing masses of soldiers, sweeping across the European continent," a modern *Grand Armée,* but it has produced a globally distributed uprising. This has profound implications for human conflict in this century. Dr. Audrey Cronin perceptively warns, "Western nations will persist in ignoring the fundamental changes in popular mobilization at their peril."[21]

In future scenarios, U.S. forces' must exploit our technical capabilities to block or limit the irregular forces capacity to "maneuver" in this portion of the battle space. Some theorists have talked about a virtual sanctuary. Here traditional counterinsurgency theory comes in play, as denying the insurgent his own bases or form of sanctuary has always been the best approach. Thus, new countermeasures and tactics must preempt today's notion of "virtual sanctuary."

More important, however, the American security community must reconceptualize its understanding of information operations. The current information operations concept and the resulting mix of capabilities are too oriented on computer network attacks and electronic warfare. Such capabilities are not irrelevant in irregular conflict and will increasingly be exploited to better secure our own systems against penetration, as we simultaneously attempt to infiltrate the irregular network's own internal networks. The most relevant source and form of software in irregular warfare, however, is the intricate software of the human brain. Our emphasis must increasingly focus not on the technical means of information dissemination but on the culturally relevant content we are issuing to impact the strategic and operational portions of the battle space. To do this we will need to better integrate, if not totally rethink, our strategic communications, public diplomacy, command information, and public affairs capabilities.

We will also have to expand our thinking in terms of the strategic and operational aspects of information operations (IO). Like Lawrence, we must discriminate between distinct audiences in our rear, our flanks, and the deep battle for public opinion in the international community. Lawrence understood the full range of the psychological element of his war. He noted that he had to "arrange the minds of the enemy, so far as we could reach them, then those other minds of the nation supporting us, then the minds of the enemy nation, and of the neutrals looking on; circle beyond circle."[22] Our efforts will have to serve the same ever-expanding circle and include the American people, who remain both a center of gravity for any significant U.S. interventions as well as a critical vulnerability if we ignore the requirement for public support against a protracted and protean adversary.

Marine Information Operations in Operation Iraqi Freedom (OIF)

Unlike the other services, the Marines did not consider IO to be the complete domain of a specialist community. Senior Marine leaders understood the role of the psychological dimension of their counterinsurgency plans. The role of deploying "a bodyguard of truth" around everything was important to the campaign plan and all subsequent operations. Information operations at a strategic level are "how you dry up the swamp that's festering [in] this plague," Marine LtGen James Mattis said in an interview.[23]

Nor, unlike the office of the Secretary of Defense (OSD) or the Joint Staff, did they perceive that IO was a capability largely tied to information technology or computer network attack. They saw it, naturally, as a supporting arm with all Marines participating (with the exception of the public affairs community). Many Marines see IO broadly defined as a key supporting arm or form of "fires" in any counterinsurgency. Like any supporting arm, the Marines did recognize that the capability had to be integrated into the overall scheme of maneuver and serve the commander's overall intent.

Instead of asserting that only "IO personnel do IO," Marine leaders stressed the importance of every Marine in the role of information dissemination. Because of this, they also believed that a commander's themes need to be pushed down to every man in their area in order to ensure congruence between all actions and all words in support of the commander's intent. Thus, every Marine was to be a rifleman, an intelligence collector, *and* an IO disseminator. The Marines understood that actions would speak louder and with more credibility than just leaflets, broadcasts, and posters. Thus, every patrol and every council meeting were opportunities to influence the population and ensure that the key themes of the American support to Iraq were consistently and frequently communicated. This represents a broader understanding that was very common among Marines in that all activities they conducted, whether it was a town council meeting, building a school, or conducting a patrol, were opportunities to reinforce a message. Senior commanders generally defined this message as their principal IO theme per Marine doctrine.[24]

Such tactical fusion however will not resolve the larger problem of connecting the strategy to strategic IO themes and supporting operational and tactical actions. Regrettably, the processes that the U.S. government has put into effect to manage the strategic level of the informational component of the counterinsurgency never seemed to click. Universally, operational commanders could not identify key strategic themes from Washington or gain any additional support for operational and tactical information activities. Equally frustrating were the long production and product approval cycles for IO products that were completely out of synch with the rapid nature of information processing in modern societies and the need to rapidly counter gossip, misinformation, and outright distortions coming from the insurgents.

Information operations are modern "fires" used to mold perceptions and inform target populations of ongoing efforts that impact their lives and aspirations. The difficulty of achieving effective IO in foreign cultures cannot be underestimated. It requires an acute understanding of the culture and belief systems of a people. Influence cannot be achieved without a thorough understanding of the local culture and an understanding of their own cultural narrative. It also is necessary to be able to counter the narrative being employed by the irregular opponent as well. Psychological operations (PSYOPS) are a critical supporting arm in 4GW. PSYOPS also have a counterpropaganda role to negate an adversary's attempt at influencing local, U.S., and Coalition audiences. Commanders must be alert to this threat, with prepared "counter-battery fires" in the information domain to offset or negate this influence. An effective enemy propaganda campaign can have enormous impact on operations from prompting neutral parties to resist military operations to causing a Coalition partner to withdraw support.

But because the Marine Corps has no organic psychological operations units and no organic equipment for disseminating products or broadcasts, the ability to apply well-designed IO campaigns was limited in OIF. "We spent a lot of time reacting to what the insurgents were putting out," noted one IO officer, "rather than being proactive and better supporting the scheme of maneuver because we had limited resources."[25] Because of the paucity of organic capability, the Marines rely on Army augmentation for this capability, and they were satisfied with the Army's capabilities and performance. Interviews indicated general satisfaction with the ability of Marine staffs to incorporate an information component into their plans and operations.[26] But at least one commander found himself hampered during the transition phase in trying to communicate within a fairly large city to a large and varied population because the assets available to Marines were limited to just loudspeakers and leaflets.[27]

Marines did identify the need for more effective communications with the population at the strategic and operational levels. At the strategic level, they desired a multitargeted information operations plan with such targets as the international community, Coalition members, the U.S. public, Middle Eastern countries, and Muslims. At the operational level, the focus should be on the Iraqi population—those who support the Coalition, those who oppose the Coalition, and particularly those who are still undecided. In this effort it will be necessary to leverage multi-dimensional media—U.S., international, and, in OIF especially, the Iraqi media. Among the concrete information operations identified was the need for a satellite TV outlet that daily shows those who resist as killed and captured, with the goal of portraying resistance against the Coalition as hopeless. Several commentators have expressed a need for a satellite-based Iraqi forum to counter Al Jazeera.

The general consensus indicated from a Marine after-action report is that there were no theater-wide IO plans available to them as they embarked. Marine staffs create ad hoc IO plans, built around their understanding of the importance of the information contest or war of ideas, but the lack of IO-related resources (mass media capabilities) inhibited the scope and effectiveness of these plans. At the same time, Marine commanders realized that mass communication was just one means and that other means, including direct face-to-face talks, town meetings, and discussions with key leaders, had to impart the same messages and themes.

Because they have few if any school-trained information officers, the Marines did find it necessary to create and fill billets at major headquarters and down to the battalion level to fill this role. The role of this IO billet was called "key" to operations in this environment, or critical to the battalion's success. But it should not be regarded as a collateral duty, as it too often has been in OIF to date. It was usually assigned to a fire support or artillery coordinator on some staffs. As with many other unique skills—public affairs, HUMINT, intelligence, and civil affairs—the Marines found that the standard battalion's staff configuration does not lend itself well to the unique demands of day-to-day operations in a contested area like Al Anbar Province. Counterinsurgency operations demand a heavier emphasis on non-kinetic functions such as intelligence, information, and civil military operations. A battalion uses all of these functions in conjunction with kinetic fires in its employment of combined arms.[28] But the battalions often did not have dedicated assets or attachments providing direct support. Some field grade officers bemoaned the lack of attention to this critical tool. "IO at the tactical level in the Marine Corps is not properly staffed," noted one Marine veteran from Iraq. "There are not enough people to do it, it's paid lip service, and it's extremely important."[29]

The Marines recognize the importance of this aspect of conflict, however, and the need to expand their capabilities. The growing importance of IO is reflected in the addition of IO as a potential fourth block to expand the original Three Block War concept.[30]

Munitions of the Mind

Given the importance of perceptions and the salience of the psychological dimension in irregular wars, U.S. capabilities must be sharpened. We must be as effective at deploying munitions of the mind as we are with conventional munitions. Future forces cannot be shortchanged at any level of warfare. The global audience must be reached as well as those within the theater battle space, with consistent themes and targeted messages. Local commanders must have access to mass media outlets or whatever medium that the local populace normally uses to obtain information. This might include civilian radio broadcasting facilities, local TV, newspaper, Internet networks, or simple DVD/CD production capabilities. The key is to communicate to as many people as possible and as quickly as possible in order to influence the situation—with a consistent message and in a culturally effective manner. Furthermore, conceptual distinctions between bureaucracies and existing occupational fields like public affairs and psychological operations need to be rethought. As the journalist Robert Kaplan put it,

> Because the battles in counterinsurgency are small scale and often clandestine . . . it becomes a matter of perceptions and victory is awarded to those who weave the most compelling narrative. Truly, in the world of postmodern, 21st century conflict, civilian and military public affairs officers must become warfighters by another name.[31]

But war fighters will have to become information warriors as well, contesting in the virtual dimension for what Gen. Sir Frank Edward Kitson called the "goal" of any insurgency, "the minds of men."

To conclude, the ideological aspects of irregular warfare will continue to influence the conduct of operations in novel ways. As in Lawrence's day, when "antique arms were the most honored," we too will depend on what he referred to as the "metaphysical weapon" for the means of victory.[32] We will learn to maneuver in both the physical environment and the virtual dimension to achieve a positional advantage in the population's collective mind. We will be as effective and precise with our mental munitions as we are with close air support. As in most irregular and protracted conflicts, the contest for the support of the population is the central or decisive front in the campaign and requires us to recognize that perception may matter more than factual results in the physical battlefield.[33] The "wars of opinion" of Jomini's day are now the wars of ideas and images of the twenty-first century.[34]

13

Clausewitz's Theory of War and Information Operations*

—COL William M. Darley, USA

> The first, the supreme, the most far-reaching act of judgment that the statesman and commander have to make is to establish . . . the kind of war on which they are embarking. . . . This is the first of all strategic questions and the most comprehensive.
>
> —*Carl von Clausewitz,* On War[1]

The debate over information operations (IO) grows more confused because IO continues to be wrongly understood in its relationship to the so-called kinetic elements of military operations. Contrary to entrenched perceptions, IO is not merely a family of related skill sets or capabilities that in all cases augment "kinetic operations." Collectively, they are properly understood as a *specific purpose and emphasis* within an overall plan of action that under some circumstances might be the main effort. The most essential factor for employing IO is therefore the commander's intent with regard to the political objective of a given operation. Viewing IO in any other way precludes recognition of the relationship the "IO purpose" inherently has with other activities of war within the universe of political conflict and consequently distorts thinking with regard to full incorporation and appropriate employment of all tools that might generate a desired information effect. Thus, operational planning that regards IO as mere augmentation to operations by

* *Reprinted by permission from* Joint Forces Quarterly, *1st Quarter 2006.*

application of five narrowly defined "pillars"—currently revised and identified as operations security, psychological operations (PSYOPS), deception, computer network operations, and electronic warfare—is fatally flawed.

Information operations, unlike other battlefield effects, focus on influencing perceptions or attitudes as opposed to destroying things or seizing terrain. During Operation Desert Storm, one of the most powerful IO instruments against Iraqi forces consisted of preannounced B-52 strikes that followed leaflet drops detailing procedures for surrender, with the key IO element being the B-52 itself. Similarly, the purpose for employing a weapon may be either to destroy a specific target or send threats to influence personnel targets, or both. Understood in this way, it is apparent that almost any weapon, tool, or element at the commander's disposal apart from the five pillars may have potential for achieving a specific IO objective.

Part of the difficulty in distinguishing information operations from kinetic operations has resulted from a failure to understand IO within any kind of general theory on the relationship of the dynamics of war, such as between a joint direct attack munition and PSYOPS. Consequently, the lack of intellectual discipline imposed by such a paradigm confuses the roles and relationships of the elements of combat operations and the circumstances in which they are appropriately applied. Application of a theory is thus essential to highlight the distinguishing qualities of IO and their relationship to kinetic operations. This chapter examines IO in the context of Clausewitzian theory and proposes a model that shows the role of IO across the spectrum of conflict.

A Political Instrument

The usefulness of a theory depends on how well it can explain the relationship of elements not formally understood and predict the unknown and as yet unobserved. Clausewitz's theory of war offers surprising predictive insight into the dynamics of IO within the multidomain universe of political conflict and a clearer understanding of the dynamics that dictate the role and situational employment of elements of power to achieve IO objectives. As a reminder, *On War* was an effort to develop a genuine theory of war that described both the characteristics and relationship of various dynamics within armed conflict:

> Theory will have fulfilled its main task when it is used to analyze the constituent elements of war, to distinguish precisely what at first sight seems fused, to explain in full the properties of the means employed and to show their probable effects, to define clearly the nature of the ends in view. . . . Theory then becomes a guide to anyone who wants to learn about war from books; it will light his way, ease his progress, train his judgment, and help him to avoid pitfalls.[2]

In developing his theory, Clausewitz describes war within the context of political conflict, which is broadly dominated by two factors: violence and "moral" (psychological) factors. The relationship these two factors share appears to be the same one that modern doctrine writers and military operators are struggling less successfully to describe with the terms "kinetic operations" and "information operations."

The power of his IO theory results from analyzing the relationship of two basic factors that Clausewitz asserts undergird it: political policy and military force expressed in violence.[3] Political policy is derived from his famous dictum: "War is thus an act of force to compel our enemy to do our will . . . not merely an act of policy but a true political instrument, a continuation of political intercourse, carried on with other means."[4]

The first key extrapolation is that IO—as a subcategory of war operations—is a political activity. This may appear to belabor the obvious; however, this deceptively simple observation highlights the essential and intensely political character of IO as it relates to political conflict in general. It also points out how intertwined IO is with the purely political machinery of what Clausewitz called "policy"— the political process he considered the third basic element of war.

Though IO and kinetic operations share the mutual purpose of achieving political objectives, unless the political nature of IO is clearly established, the dominant military culture tends to regard rhetorical activities associated with persuasion and influence as mere sideshow techniques adopted from civilian life into military operations with limited importance rather than as intrinsic elements of political conflict itself. So what ultimately defines IO as opposed to nonpolitical informational activities—such as advertising or personal engagement with key personalities—is the purpose of application and not the instrument used. In contrast, defining the tools for kinetic operations, such as tanks or combat aircraft, is relatively easy because these have no role in civilian society and are almost never assembled for any other end except coercive political purposes such as war.

The second factor that Clausewitz asserted distinguished mere political contention from war is violence. Moreover, in his theoretical sense, the more purely violent a political contention becomes, the more closely it approximates the abstract concept of an "ideal" state of "total war."[5] This is seen as Clausewitz equates the Platonic abstraction of "ideal war" with "pure violence."

> The thesis, then, must be repeated: war is an act of force, and there is no logical limit to the application of that force. . . . This is the first case of interaction and the first "extreme" we meet with.[6]
>
> War, therefore, is an act of policy. Were it a complete, untrammeled, absolute manifestation of violence (as the pure concept would require), war would of its own independent will usurp the place of policy. . . .[7]
>
> This conception would be ineluctable even if war were total war, the pure element of enmity unleashed.[8]

114 — Ideas as Weapons

In contrast, the less violent a political conflict is, the less reflective it is of a condition that would define it as war:

> The more powerful and inspiring the motives for war . . . the closer will war approach its abstract concept [pure violence], the more important will be the destruction of the enemy, the more closely will the military aims and the political objects of war coincide, and the more military and less political will war appear to be. On the other hand, the less intense the motives, the less will the military element's natural tendency to violence coincide with political directives. As a result, war will be driven further from its natural course, the political object will be more and more at variance with the aim of ideal war and the conflict will seem increasingly political in character.[9]

In depicting graphically the relationship of violence to political objectives at the heart of Clausewitz's theory, a continuum emerges (see figure 13.1). It is the political nature of war as reflected along this continuum, which graduates in intensity of violence from one extreme to another depending on political objectives, that makes Clausewitz's theory valuable for understanding the nature of information operations and their relationship to kinetic operations.

The end of the spectrum approaching total war would mean a condition so violent and frantic that it reaches the point of chaos and surpasses the ability of policymakers to control it. Clausewitz described this condition:

> When whole communities go to war—whole peoples, and especially civilized peoples—the reason always lies in some political situation, and the occasion is always due to some political object. . . . [Were pure violence to usurp the place of policy] it would then drive policy out of office and rule by the laws of its own nature.[10]

FIGURE 13.1: A Continuum of Violence in the Universe of Political Conflict

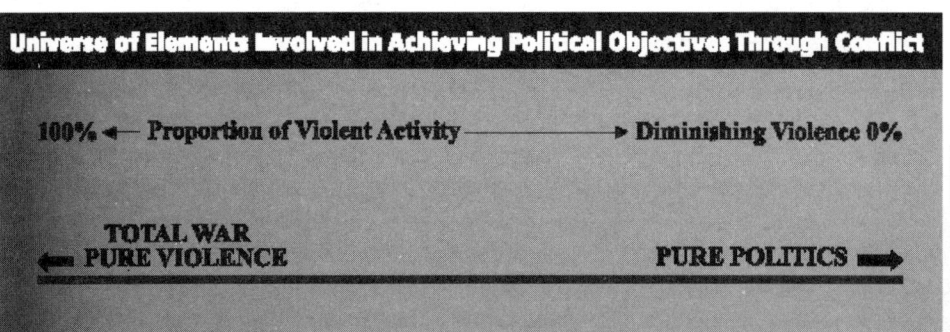

Levels of Violence

If taken to the extreme that the theory predicts, a war of pure violence would be characterized by such unbridled use of kinetic instruments that other instruments of political conflict would be reduced to virtual irrelevance—a level of violence and singleness of purpose with no other object but the total destruction of the adversary and his civilization.

In finding a real-world example, some would argue that wars approaching this level of violence have actually been fought. Some posit World War II with its policies of "genocidal lebensraum" on the one side and "unconditional surrender" on the other.[11] Also, Bernard Brodie asserts that nuclear war approaches Clausewitz's notion of pure enmity and absolute violence.[12]

What would be the role of IO in such a conflict? At the extreme end of the spectrum, information operations—if they existed at all—might include activities associated with computer attack, signals intelligence, deception, or PSYOPS measures. However, there would be little concern for cultivating through political rhetoric (PSYOPS or public diplomacy) some grounds for hope of political reconciliation or post-conflict cooperation, as the political objective would be total destruction of the enemy—a war of annihilation (see figure 13.2).

In contrast, what does the theoretical model of political violence predict at the opposite end of the continuum? In the abstract, the theory predicts a political conflict that would be contested in a manner completely devoid of violence. Such a conflict would be characterized as totally ideological, a political clash decided exclusively by ideas, words, and symbols—in other words, a contest between pure information operations campaigns.

Clausewitz's theory appears to specifically predict contests settled mainly by political rhetoric without violence. He obliquely refers to them while observing

FIGURE 13.2: The Universe of Political Conflict

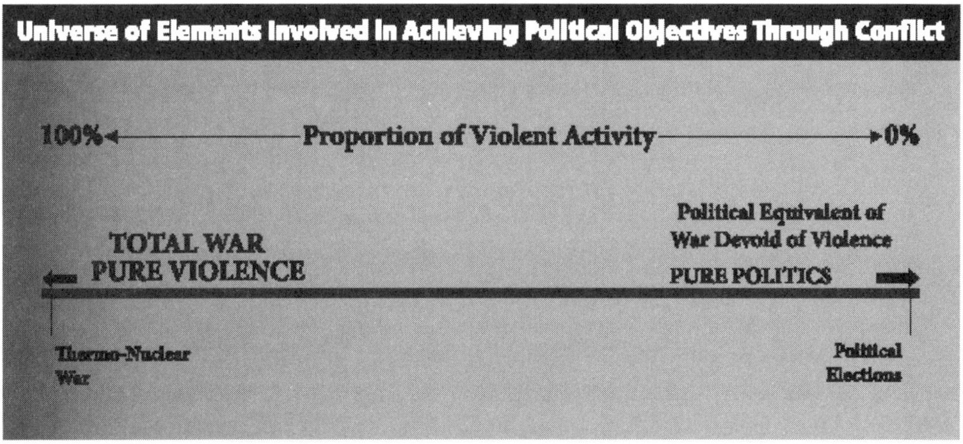

that when a graduated recession of military force and violence accompanies a change in commitment to political objectives, the conflict decreasingly displays the characteristics of war and becomes primarily political:

> [The political object of the war] has been rather overshadowed by the law of extremes, the will to overcome the enemy and make him powerless [by military force and violence]. But as this law begins to lose its force and as this determination wanes, the political aim will reassert itself. . . . Situations can thus exist in which the political object will almost be the sole determinant.[13]

Are there real-world examples of purely political conflicts devoid of violence, as the theory predicts? Practical examples in our own time include elections in stable democratic societies. A nineteenth-century senator from Kansas provides insight into such bloodless struggles:

> The purification of politics is an iridescent dream. Government is force. Politics is a battle for supremacy. Parties are the armies. The decalogue and the golden rule have no place in a political campaign. The object is success. To defeat the antagonist and expel the party in power is the purpose. The Republicans and Democrats are as irreconcilably opposed to each other as were Grant and Lee in the Wilderness. They use ballots instead of guns, but the struggle is as unrelenting and desperate, and the result sought for the same.[14]

Understanding elections as a form of war as deduced from Clausewitz's theory helps explain why elections held in countries without the benefit of mature democratic institutions and a tradition of peaceful handover of power are often accompanied by some measure of violence.

The extremes on the continuum predict something that looks like thermonuclear war at one end, where the persuasive elements associated with IO would have little influence or role, and something like democratic political elections on the other, where IO wholly dominates political conflict.

What the above suggests may initially be surprising: in contrast to total war, which is characterized by pure violence, an information operations conflict without violence should be viewed as "pure politics." In fact, Clausewitz appears to have anticipated a need for a nuanced second definition of politics and has provided an unflattering description to explain the difference between politics as a broad activity within which war operates, as opposed to specific characteristics of politics as the business of diplomatic wrangling and chicanery:

> While policy is apparently effaced in the one kind of war [conflicts tending toward extreme force and violence] and yet is strongly evident in the other,

both kinds are equally political. If the state is thought of as a person, and policy as the product of its brain, then among the contingencies for which the state must be prepared is a war in which every element calls for policy to be eclipsed by violence. Only if politics is regarded not as resulting from a just appreciation of affairs, but—as it conventionally is—as cautious, devious, even dishonest, shying away from force, could the second type of war appear to be more "political" than the first.[15]

Politics as a negotiating activity that characteristically is "cautious, devious, even dishonest, shying away from force" describes the basic nature of information operations fairly accurately. This supports the conclusion that IO in its most extreme form would be a manifestation of "pure politics." Such an observation has far-reaching implications that lead to another surprising conclusion supported by the theory: IO is not only the outward communication of information impacting policy, but also a participant in policy formation itself, shaping the overall political character of the conflict. Information operations are involved in the policy formation process along the entire spectrum of conflict, with an increasingly significant role as conflict approaches the "devoid of violence" extreme. The graduated progression away from violence leads to a situation in which the development and formation of policy and the public expression of policy increasingly become one and the same. The emphasis on daily press briefings by Secretary of Defense Donald Rumsfeld in the early stages of Operation Enduring Freedom, where policy adjustments seemed to be made from the dais in response to news reporting, illustrates this predicted theoretical tendency.

With the two polar extremes established, the next step in developing this theory is to insert types of conflicts along the continuum, categorized by the relative similarity each bears to one extreme or the other. The order reflects a logical sequencing of conflicts according to estimates of the proportional dominance of two factors within each: the intensity of violence relative to clarity and strength and the duration of political objective.

A Vaguely Defined Threshold

Conflicts characterized by high levels of focused violence over lengthy periods, and having broad political purposes, occur near the polar extreme of total war, as, for example, World Wars I and II, owing to the amount of extreme violence each generated relative to the expansiveness and clarity of their political objectives and comparatively long duration (see figure 13.3). In contrast, shorter conflicts involving less violence, and having either less focus or more limited political objectives, tend to occur nearer the center of the continuum and include such conflicts as Operation Just Cause and the Kosovo bombing campaign. Similarly, events with important regional political objectives but with less actual violence and potential for violence, such as elections in Indonesia or the occupation of Bosnia, have been inserted near the devoid-of-violence extreme. A graduated scale of conflicts based on the content of violence in relation to the political objective appears to be specifically what Clausewitz had in mind as he developed his theory:

> A military objective that matches the political object in scale will, if the latter is reduced, be reduced in proportion; this will be all the more so as the political object increases its predominance. Thus it follows that without any inconsistency wars can have all degrees of importance and intensity, ranging from a war of extermination down to simple armed observation.[16]

Admittedly this is a subjective process, but with a range of conflicts inserted in logical order along the continuum, the pattern that emerges confirms that IO-related factors are infused throughout the universe of political conflict and along the entire spectrum of violence associated with it. On further inspection of the pattern emerging, the conflicts that populate the area nearer the total war extreme are characterized by achieving political objectives through actions to control geography—for example, decisively destroying military formations or infrastructure for the ultimate purpose of seizing terrain.

In contrast, the conflicts that populate the devoid-of-violence area focus on obtaining political objectives by influencing the opinions and behavior of specific people or population groups. This suggests that a working definition for kinetic operations is accomplishing political objectives through seizing terrain while information operations amount to achieving political objectives by influencing people. This further suggests that what we understand today as the specialties and disciplines of IO are in orientation and principle what Clausewitz may have had in mind when prescribing measures to deal with the "moral" dimension of war:

> The moral elements are among the most important in war. They constitute the spirit that permeates war as a whole, and at an early stage they establish a close affinity with the will that moves and leads the whole mass of force. . . . The effects of physical and psychological factors form an organic whole, which, unlike a metal alloy, is inseparable by chemical processes. In formulating any rule concerning physical factors, the theorist must bear in mind the part that moral factors may play in it. . . . Hence most of the matters dealt with in this book are composed in equal parts of physical and of moral causes and effects. One might say that the physical seem little more than the wooden hilt, while the moral factors are the precious metal, the real weapon, the finely-honed blade.[17]

Additionally, further consideration of the pattern reveals a curious phenomenon. Conflicts grouped nearer the total war extreme are uniformly kinetic operations clearly claiming the dominant/supported role in relation to IO. However, conflicts

Clausewitz's Theory of War and Information Operations — 119

grouped toward the devoid-of-violence extreme appear to have an equally legitimate claim on being the dominant/supported activity according to the internal logic of their own particular circumstances and place on the continuum of political conflict. This predicts the existence of a vaguely defined threshold somewhere in the middle of the continuum, the crossing of which signals a seminal change in the relationship between information operations and kinetic operations—a line separating areas on the continuum in which either IO or kinetic operations dominate according to their similarity to the characteristics of the nearest "ideal" conflict at the polar extremes.

This dichotomy would predict the need for not only different leadership and management skills, but also units and personnel with different skill sets, training, and equipment for different types of conflicts depending on where they fell on the continuum. Operations grouped nearer the pure violence extreme in figure 13.3 would reflect a requirement for leadership, skill sets, training, and equipment of the kind traditionally associated with operations characterized by great violence

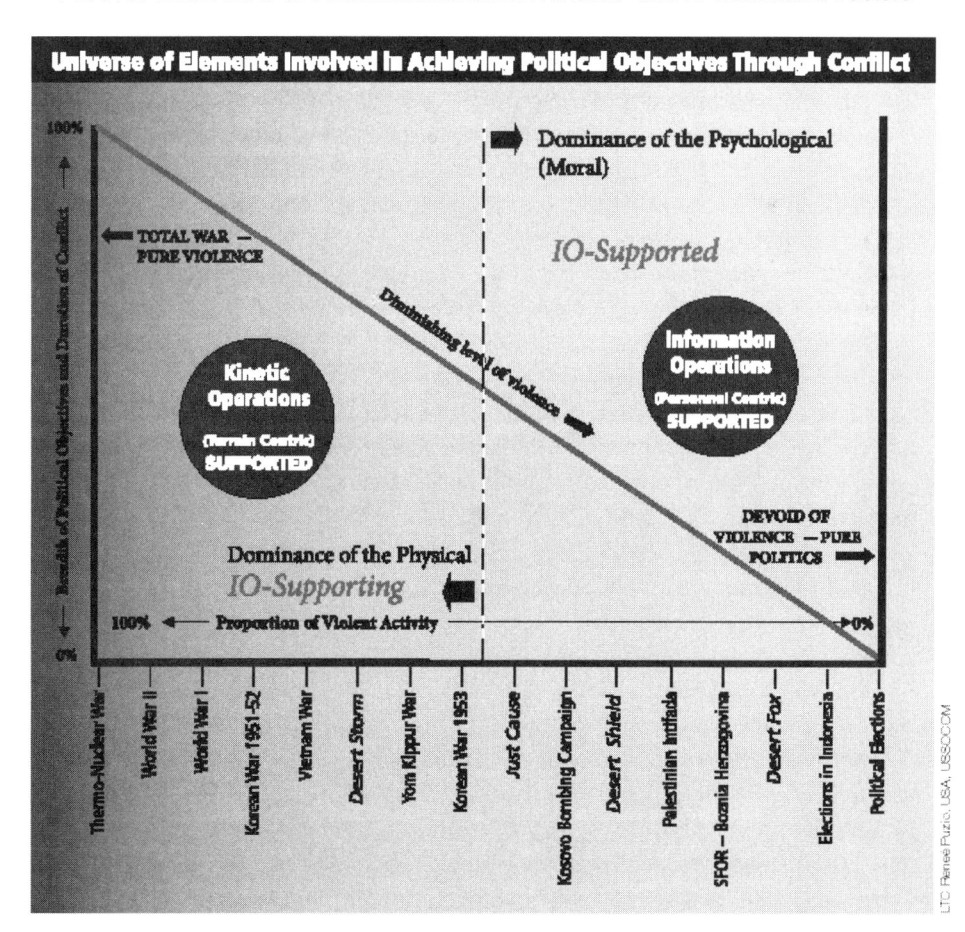

FIGURE 13.3: A Line of Demarcation between Kinetic- and IO-Dominated Factors

and destructive activity for the purpose of seizing terrain. As positioned on the spectrum, information operations stand in a supporting role.

As conflicts approach the other end of the spectrum, however, the model predicts an increasing requirement for significantly different kinds of leadership training and experience, different skill set requirements from the units involved, and different equipment and training. Moreover, as one considers the environment within which political conflicts aimed at influencing rather than destroying are likely to take place, the theory obliquely implies an increasing need for cultural and human intelligence as opposed to technical intelligence for operations to achieve political objectives through persuasion and influence of people and populations rather than violence. In addition, the pattern suggests that conflicts along this sector of the continuum would properly be conducted as IO supported by kinetic operations rather than the reverse.

Practical Utility of the Theoretical Model

What has been missing in the IO debate—and the root of confusion—is recognition that information operations are not artifices of military culture; rather, they comprise necessary answers to natural dynamics of war that exist in some proportion side by side with the dynamics of violence that are generated by political violence. Policymakers and military operators must understand this because, all too often, the dominant influence of kinetic thinking creates a tendency to dismiss the relevance of information operations even where the circumstances of conflict might make IO not only essential but also predominant.

The long-term effects of this attitude have been under-resourcing IO core capabilities and inculcating a tendency into the military culture that invariably causes it to underestimate the depth, resilience, and ferocity of the moral dimension of conflicts that would prudently be regarded as predominantly IO conflicts by nature, especially in unconventional or constabulary environments. Under such circumstances, policymakers and military operators who lack this understanding or appreciation can be counted on to make decisions that actually undermine the political objectives they are flailing to achieve.

The model in figure 13.3, extrapolated from Clausewitz's theory, provides an intellectual framework in which the military community can consider an appropriate mix of kinetic operations and IO tools for contemplated military campaigns as envisioned along the spectrum of political violence. It demonstrates that IO is an intrinsic element of political policy formulation that will permeate the environment in which conflict is occurring—at times becoming more dominant in influence than kinetic operations, which are better understood as primarily tools of destruction directed by policy. It further suggests that IO and kinetic operations are inseparably linked, like strands of a DNA molecule in a gene, and in the same way have a dominant-recessive relationship. For example, one exercises dominance over the other depending on where the conflict falls on the continuum relative to the polar extremes. Thus, among the important issues it highlights, the theory shows the absolute need to refine both the specific political objectives of a campaign as well as their nature in order to determine whether the campaign is predominantly kinetic or informational. This suggests that neglecting consideration of the role of IO and its integration with kinetic operations imperils the entire campaign plan.

Consequently, information operations cannot be prudently conceived as merely added value to an operation, but rather as essential activities that address specific needs associated with the nature of political conflict itself. Perhaps most important, the theory points out the potential for defining IO as the main effort of a campaign, suggesting the absolute imperative of a refined commander's intent that identifies from the outset the main effort of the operation as either kinetic or IO, as well as describing how one should support and complement the other. This may urge, for example, introducing such previously inconceivable measures as subsuming the functions of a J–3/C–3 entirely beneath an IO-oriented staff element headed by a general officer uniquely trained and experienced with IO, or the establishment of linguistically capable and culturally experienced staff elements of political advisers at much lower levels of command than has previously been regarded as appropriate—perhaps to brigade or even battalion level. It also highlights a theoretical basis for increasing reliance on policing skills as opposed to maneuver combat skills the closer one approaches the devoid-of-violence end of the spectrum.

Additionally, the model implies that the political dimension of conflict is so essential that commanders must be prepared to establish their own local operational or even tactical political objectives in the absence of specific policy guidance for which information operations may be the key instrument. Clausewitz appears to allude to these predicted needs:

> Political considerations do not determine the posting of guards or the employment of patrols. But they are the more influential in the planning of war, of the campaign, and often even of the battle. . . . The only question, therefore, is whether, when war is being planned, the political point of view should give way to the purely military . . . or should the political point of view remain dominant and the military [military force and violence] be subordinated to it?[18]

The political nature of war as reflected along a continuum, which graduates in intensity of violence from one extreme to another depending on political objectives, makes Clausewitz's theory valuable for understanding information operations and their relationship to kinetic operations. What would the role of IO be at various points? The pattern that emerges confirms that IO-related factors are infused throughout the universe of political conflict and along the entire spectrum of violence associated with it.

14

Information (in) Operations: More Than Technology

—LtCol James P. West, USMC

Information has been a critical element in warfare since the time of Sun Tzu. "Know the enemy" and "know yourself" are not new ideas. In relatively recent times, compared to Sun Tzu's warring states, we have launched into the "information age," with Internet access widely available, twenty-four-hour news coverage from several news agencies, wireless cellular network access in most areas of the world, and numerous other advances in communications technologies. People even in impoverished areas have access to exponentially more information sources, which have provided more volume and differing views than ever before, and they have grown accustomed to and expect unfettered access. Therefore, many government and military organizations throughout the world have been developing and adopting methodologies for employing the information element of power in conjunction with the diplomatic and military elements. However, prior to the advent of the information age, some militaries employed the information element of power more effectively than we do today. The British in Malaya were able to defeat an insurgency and achieve their objective of installing an indigenous government that was in control of the country because they understood the information element of power. By examining the definitions and current mind-set of information operations (IO), reviewing the British employment in Malaya, and identifying the IO shortcomings in Iraq, we can refine our approach to effectively use the information element of power.

The U.S. military definitions associated with information operations, some written more than ten years ago, have driven the tactics and techniques that have been developed throughout most of the Western world today. According to the February 13, 2006, edition of Joint Publication 3-13 *Information Operations*, the U.S. military's most recent definition of information operations is the "integrated employment of the core capabilities of electronic warfare, computer network operations, psychological operations (PSYOPS), military deception (MILDEC), and operation security (OPSEC) . . . to influence, disrupt, corrupt, or usurp adversarial human or automated decision making while protecting our own." Many military commanders and planners are executing this definition by primarily targeting the information systems that aid decision makers. This focus on systems and communications technologies has been derived from at least three existing thought processes:

1. Original IO definitions concentrated on affecting adversary information and information systems while protecting one's own
2. We live in the "information age," which is a term that was coined to describe advances in communications technologies and the exponential increase in information to which individuals have access
3. We in the Western world tend to rely on our technological dominance over most adversaries in any conflict.

Keeping with the IO definition's objective of influencing or disrupting an adversary's decision-making process while protecting our own, we approach the IO core capabilities to jam or exploit communications through electronic warfare means, attack or exploit networks by computer network operations, or protect our command and control capabilities with frequency-hopping radios and encryption devices for operation security. Additionally, PSYOPS methods, which are dependent on means to drop leaflets, propagate messages over radio or television, or utilize public address systems, are focused on general populations with an objective of removing support from adversarial leaders or causing a group of people to move from a specific area.

A technologically advanced, engineering-focused society is compelled to measure the effectiveness of specific actions to determine their contribution to achieving the desired goal or end state. Therefore, military planners required to calculate the measure of effectiveness (MOE) for different types of kinetic operations tend to gravitate toward separating the core capabilities of IO to measure their individual MOEs. Recording the number of leaflets dropped per person in a given area, determining the number of radio frequencies jammed versus the number of known frequencies used by the adversary, and reporting the number of hours a U.S. message is broadcast per twenty-four-hour period are some of the most common MOE reported for information operations conducted today. These measures are easily quantifiable, and the staff officers determining the kinetic (a term usually identified with traditional fire and maneuver) MOE—determining what percentage of a building or depot is unusable, how many aircraft are no longer operational after a strike on a flight line, etc.—can combine these measurable results. However, IO is fundamentally different from kinetic operations (KO) and the generally accepted MOEs for IO as depicted above are truly more measures of effort vice effectiveness. Because we measure the effectiveness of KO and level of effort of information operations, IO becomes just a check in the box that it is being conducted and a level of effort exists.

The British in Malaya

Long before the advent of the "information age," the British effectively employed information to achieve their end state. Though they did not identify any actions as IO, they did realize that every military activity sends a message. Therefore, they shaped their concept of operations to ensure a consistent message was delivered to their enemy, the indigenous people, and their own population at home.

Still recovering from the almost unimaginable loss of men and cost of matériel from World War II, in 1948 the British were in the process of relinquishing most of their colonial possessions when the Communists rebelled in Malaya. The British were far from completing the transition to Malayan self-rule, so they could not leave the infant Malayan government to fend off the insurgency alone. Leaders in London, like those in most Western nations, saw Communism as their primary threat and were focused on stemming the rising Communist tide. Many governments throughout the world had a heightened sensitivity to terrorist-type attacks, since they had just witnessed a train derailment in France in December 1947 that killed twenty and injured twice that number, Mohandas Gandhi's assassination in India in January 1948, and two American diplomats murdered in Vietnam in March that same year. Therefore, when a Communist-instigated insurgency replete with similar acts of terrorism began in Malaya, the British had to respond. In June 1948, the government of Malaya, still very much dominated by the British, declared a state of emergency. This was for all practical purposes a war to combat terrorism and restore government control.

The British in Malaya knew that everything they did had to support their desired end state of the indigenous government in control. GEN Sir Gerald Templer was aware that every military operation, policy, public statement, and so on had to support that objective. He had to get the message to the Malayan people, the Communist-backed insurgents, and, just as important, the British population thousands of miles away, whose tolerance of military action had not recovered from World War II. General Templer shaped his concept of operations to deliver a consistent message to each of those target audiences. First he designated areas within Malaya as being "white" or "black." The black areas were where the insurgents still operated freely. He established curfews, travel restrictions, and food rationing (to deny support for the insurgents) and allowed no one to possess firearms. He told the locals, who reeled from these tight controls, that they were being protected from being forced or coerced into supporting the insurgents. Once their area was stabilized, they would be free to govern themselves locally. Small unit patrols frequently went through populated areas and became acquainted with the locals, and Special Forces units operated in the jungles to maintain constant pressure on the insurgents. Indigenous males were trained to become police for that area. As their training progressed and loyalty was gained, they were allowed to carry weapons. Gradually the area residents became the policing force, and the military became a security force to protect the police officers. A village government was established, with the British assuming more of an advisory role the more stable that area became. Once the sector was free from attack and no longer supported the insurgents, it changed to white on the map and in the minds of the locals. A white area was free from curfews and restrictions, had indigenous police providing the security, and saw the local government establish the laws. Templer ensured that all military, including the British, were equally subject to the local laws. The Malays interpreted those actions to mean the British did want to protect them, truly sought Malayan self-governance, and did not place themselves above the law. Once that information was promulgated, using their word-of-mouth networks, other population centers became fully engaged in making themselves insurgent-free as well. Additionally, the British public at home could track the progress of the war in Malaya by watching the number and size of white areas grow on the map. As the map depicted more white areas, local village and city governments merged into regional and, eventually, a national Malayan government. These British actions and policies all supported the overall objective of secure self-rule for the Malays. Though the policy of restrictions and curfews in the black areas was extreme, it was applied fairly across the country, and it motivated the people to help change the color labeling of their area, with each step in that direction providing more autonomy and loosening of restrictions. The message was consistent and clear, and it did not depend on advanced technology to get promulgated. Templer and his planners acknowledged that every action generates a message, so they focused on how it would be interpreted by each target audience. They did not get mired by the way information was passed. They concentrated on how each group would interpret action and if that supported their overall objective. They altered operations to invoke the desired information flow and thus performed IO well before the term was in vogue.

The United States in Iraq

Five decades after the Malayan insurgency, the Western world was thrust into another war against people willing to conduct terrorist attacks to support their cause. This conflict was occurring well into the information age. The focus of IO shifted from the target's interpretation of information to the message transmitted to him and the means of transmission. Coupling this change in approach with a lack of understanding of the local culture has made information operations less effective in supporting the overall military objective because it fails to concentrate on the end state: favorable perceptions in the population.

In early 2003, prior to Operation Iraqi Freedom I and the march up to Baghdad, several senior Department of Defense (DOD) leaders claimed that the Iraqis would welcome the U.S.-led Coalition with open arms. A Western mind could not comprehend, or senior leaders would not accept, that a people who had been oppressed and abused for so long would not welcome their rescuers. A few intelligence analysts warned of the Mohammad Farrah Aideed Model, but these analysts were quickly discounted, because in the minds of some, the Iraqi people would logically be grateful for a release from the bondage of Saddam and his henchmen. What these DOD leaders did not understand or take into account was the proliferation of the Aideed Model in the Middle East. General Aideed's actions caused most Middle Easterners to believe that the most powerful and technologically advanced military in the world could be forced to withdraw by making the U.S. servicemen bleed on international television. Though very few in the United States have heard of this model, most in the Middle East have heard of it. To accentuate the validity of the model, it had been relayed to Iraqis accompanied with the story of how the United States encouraged the Kurds to rebel against Saddam's regime in March 1991 and then turned its back on those Kurds shortly after the rebellion was suppressed. When Saddam's forces quashed the rebellion and started committing atrocities against the Kurds and Shi'a, the United States did nothing in their defense. True or not, that is what most Iraqis believed when the U.S.-led Coalition started the march to Baghdad. The Iraqis reacted exactly as expected, given an understanding of their perceptions. They were overjoyed and relieved but, most important, guarded in their overt actions. Saddam and most of his leaders were still alive and free. The Iraqis did not understand what type of government would follow Saddam's regime. Too many Iraqis were surviving day-to-day since the Coalition had moved the food and medical supplies designated to support the Iraqis far back in the flow of matériel to the theater. They were afraid of starving. The Iraqi population as a whole did not oppose the Coalition forces, but the Coalition did nothing to assuage the misperceptions of the people or build a level of confidence that the Coalition governments and forces were interested in the well-being of all Iraqis. The Iraqi people, even today, fully expect to be left alone before a stable government is developed in Iraq. The Aideed Model and tales about the Kurds were information victories for Saddam's regime. The DOD's failure to understand this and claim that Iraqis would welcome the United States with open arms also backfired with the U.S. population. This was a compound IO loss for U.S. leadership.

After four Blackwater Security Consulting contractors were murdered in Fallujah, Iraq, in late March 2004, the U.S. military was ordered into the city to quell the violence. Fallujah, a known hotbed of anti-American sentiment, had already been identified as an area of concern. After seeing American bodies hung from a bridge on international television, which reminded too many of the vivid pictures out of Somalia eleven years earlier, the city became a problem that Department of Defense leaders were determined to solve immediately. Soon after the U.S. forces attacked to the city, they were told to stop and pull out of Fallujah. The timing of the attack and the reason for the pullout were politically driven and went against the advice of military commanders in theater. These events turned the information element of the conflict over to the adversarial forces in Fallujah. Terrorists and criminals in the city could make any claim of U.S. atrocity during the attack, stage scenes of destruction and civilian deaths, and tout victory over the U.S. forces when they pulled out. The IO initiative had been handed to the adversaries, and U.S. and Coalition forces were not allowed into the city to disprove false claims or show the world they had not been defeated. Additionally, the withdrawal gave terrorists and their sympathizers throughout the Middle East more proof that the Aideed Model was still valid. Throughout the summer and into late fall of 2004, the Coalition forces around Fallujah were not allowed into the city. They could only watch from the perimeter as crimes and atrocities were committed against local residents by the terrorists flowing into the area. Fallujah became a safe zone, rallying point, and training area for insurgents, criminals, and terrorists. This was another IO loss for the Coalition, and with the U.S. military's hands still tied, the only possible operation that could reverse this loss was an information operation.

Local commanders turned to their IO planners to affect the frustrating and debilitating situation in Fallujah. Most of these planners, with the exception of the PSYOPS battalion Soldiers, were relatively new to IO. Several of the most senior had just completed an IO course a couple of weeks prior to deploying. They were newly schooled on the definitions and policies associated with IO. These planners were taught that all the elements of IO are functionally unique, as described in Marine Corps Combat Development Command's War-fighting Concepts, so the IO staff identified the core capabilities and assigned personnel to develop possible courses of actions for each. They quickly concluded there were no traditional communications nodes or computer networks to attack; military deception was not feasible, because the entire region knew that Coalition forces were not allowed in Fallujah; and operation security was automatic because of the radios the Coalition military forces used. As a result, planners focused on the PSYOPS element. There was a PSYOPS battalion assigned to the area of operation around Fallujah; however, its message approval process bypassed local commanders and went straight to the battalion's higher headquarters in Baghdad, where the request languished or the approved message did not support the area commander's objectives. This approval process was not responsive to the commanders' needs, so the local IO planners became a second set of PSYOPS developers and executioners, sometimes in concert with the PSYOPS battalion.

One of the first PSYOPS efforts after the Coalition forces were told to leave Fallujah was to establish a radio station that would broadcast into Fallujah an appeal to the people not to support the terrorists in their city. The Arabic speaker the U.S.

forces hired as the radio announcer was a Kurdish woman. Feedback from some intelligence sources indicates that many Fallujah residents were put off with their culturally based gender bias and reluctance to trust non-Arabs. Some apparently did tune in to the station, because as soon as the terrorists identified the station, they persecuted all those caught listening to it. To those in the city, the Kurdish woman's voice stood out as much as a child's voice does in an adult office setting. Therefore, those who did choose to listen could only do so within the privacy of their homes when they knew they could not be overheard. Additionally, when the U.S. forces identified the degree of attacks the terrorists were committing against the general population to get money or scare the people into complicity, the radio station set up a hotline for Fallujah residents to call to identify the terrorist and the threat or abuses. However, it only took a couple of phone calls for the residents to realize that calling was not worth the risk of exposure, since Coalition forces were not allowed in the city to respond to the hotline calls. The terrorists claimed this was further proof that the U.S.-led Coalition truly did not care about the people. The radio station was a tremendous effort to appeal to the Fallujah residents, but the results were, at best, ineffective due to operational constraints. At worst, it became another IO victory for the adversaries in the city.

In addition to the radio station, the IO efforts included leaflet drops. The sheer volume of leaflets became problematic for the Fallujah residents, because if terrorists saw anyone handling them, they would be punished. The paper also became a huge trash burden for the city. Last, the messages on the leaflets depicted a lack of understanding of the Iraqi mind-set. While some effectively directed the population away from impending battle areas just prior to when the Iraqi and U.S. forces were allowed to enter and liberate the city, several others gave the wrong impression altogether. IO planners did not have an overarching strategy, and too few understood the existing perceptions of the people in the city. One PSYOPS message showed a picture of a skull in the sand with a boot print by the skull. The intent was to show the adversaries in the city that they would die if they resisted the Iraqi and U.S. forces entering the city. However, most of the previous messages that had been delivered were designed to appeal to the general population, and there was nothing on these to indicate the intended audience was anyone different. The population already believed Coalition forces had very little regard for the people in Fallujah. Since the boot print was identifiably American and nothing identified the skull as terrorist, the general population took the message to mean that all in the town were in jeopardy of being killed when the Americans entered the city. As another example of delivering a message other than what was intended, a leaflet was designed to show the Coalition forces feeding and caring for Iraqis. U.S. forces had developed special prepackaged meals, called *halal* meals, that took Muslim dietary restrictions into consideration. The leaflet meant to illustrate that the Coalition was looking out for residents' basic needs and moreover was cognizant of and respected their religious customs and traditions. The information that was delivered, however, had a picture of U.S. and Iraqi forces handing out special prepackaged meals marked "kosher" not "halal." The message gleaned from that leaflet was U.S. forces were feeding Jewish food to the Iraqis. Consistently, U.S. forces sent the wrong message to the target audience.

A Better Approach

Information can be portrayed in many more ways than just radio broadcasts and leaflets. Every action or inaction from very small units, even individual Soldiers, to theater-wide operations and policies sends a message to the adversary, the indigenous population, and even your own population. A smile from a Soldier on a walking patrol can tell a few locals that the patrol means no harm, while a fully armored Soldier carrying his weapon in the horizontal position ready to fire sends an entirely different message to the same group. Both messages are necessary, and they are beneficial as long as they are sent at the right time to the right people. Likewise, theater-wide rules of engagement and detention policies relay to a much broader group whether you are lenient on criminal behavior, are serious about protecting the population, or view yourself as a conqueror who is above the law. All of these messages can and will be received and promulgated to a wider audience, and most of them will be analyzed, commented on, and redistributed by many sources with divergent views.

We have become enamored with the seemingly limitless volume of information available and the technological advances that have made it accessible to a majority of the world's population. Too often we lose the ultimate message in the sea of information. The main difference in the message promulgated by military forces prior to the information age and by forces today is the speed with which audiences have access to the information, to include all its resultant divergent views and interpretations. Information was disseminated in yesterday's operations as well as today's. Audiences received and processed that information with preconceived ideas and perceptions, just as they do today. They believed some sources of information more than others based on their own cultural and personal biases. As an example, it was common knowledge that GEN George Patton was censured for slapping a Soldier during World War II. The U.S. military leaders and American public demanded it, because that behavior was not tolerated. However, the German military and public could not believe the censure was legitimate. They determined it was a ruse to take attention away from General Patton, because their ideas of military protocol would not allow them to interpret the information any other way. The United States was not trying to send a message to the Germans, but one was sent, and the Germans became more convinced than before that General Patton would lead the Allied landing in Europe.

The Chinese, who happened to have backed the insurgency in Malaya, have a more holistic approach to information operations. According to Timothy L. Thomas in *Cyber Silhouettes: Shadows over Information Operations*, the Chinese teach that in the military, attacking minds is the primary mission and attacking fortifications is the secondary mission. Thomas describes the Chinese approach to IO as a more humanistic-oriented view that focuses on manipulation and cultural aspects of knowledge while the U.S. focus is on network attacks and communications systems degradation. The U.S. approach to IO during operations in Iraq support that conclusion.

The objective of this chapter is not to denigrate the importance of electronic warfare, computer network operations, psychological operations, military decep-tion, and operations security. Using these critical tools, along with our kinetic actions and operations, military commanders and planners can and must shape their message. A message is being sent whether it is intended or not. This message will be disseminated to our adversaries, their supporters, those we are trying to help, our own population, and those outside the conflict. The message will be refined or misshaped by divergent views and interpreted according to the preconceived ideas and perceptions of the audience. No doubt detractors said the British restrictions were excessive for the people in the black areas of Malaya. However, the message sent remained constant, never wavering to chase or respond to the headlines, and the detractors were proven wrong as soon as the white areas grew. Information operations must be viewed as operations and individual actions conducted to promulgate a message. To ensure the message is properly received, IO planners must have a thorough understanding of the culture, the perceptions, and the most trusted information sources of the target audience. These planners must also know how others will receive the message outside the target audience, or there could be "collateral damage." We must stop overly focusing on the means by which information is passed prior to determining what message we want to send. The Chinese focus on the effectiveness of information operations, and the United States remains fixated on measuring the effort of the information operation. In Frank Hoffman's article "Assessing the Long War," he notes a strategic thinking deficiency. He states that this "deficiency lies at the root of the current challenges in Iraq" and that "it limits our ability to measure what is important from what is merely expedient."

The same can be said about IO. We have a holistic thinking deficiency. We limit our ability to achieve what is important because our efforts remain on the IO elements that are expedient. We must take a holistic approach to IO and take into account cultural and societal biases that will determine what message a target will receive from the information we provide. The objective of IO is to shape the minds of the targets by understanding the way information is processed and interpreted; what they hear or see is secondary.

15

Winning on the Information Battlefield: Is the Story Getting Out?*

—LtCol Roger S. Galbraith, USMCR

The traditional dimensions of warfare are known and taught to us as land, sea, air, and space. In their book *Endgame: The Blueprint for Victory in the War on Terror*, LtGen Thomas McInerney, USAF (Ret.), and MG Paul Vallely, USA (Ret.), introduce a fifth dimension that is applicable to the Global War on Terrorism (GWOT)—the dimension of information. Many Department of Defense personnel and senior officials say we are losing the information war in the GWOT, using as evidence the discrepancy between actual conditions and successes on the ground in Iraq and the reporting of news in Iraq by national-level U.S. media.

The military public affairs (PA) community is the primary conduit between military operational forces and media representatives. Measuring PA effectiveness in getting the military's story to the American public and others is crucial to the commander's decisions as to how he can effectively do battle in the dimension of information.

The Marine Corps Forces Command PA Office conducted an analysis of U.S. media reporting on Operation Iraqi Freedom (OIF) from August 2004 to August 2006 in an effort to determine if there really is a media bias and to determine effective PA techniques to get the Marine Corps' story more widely reported. The sample chosen for the study included mostly print media reports with an Iraqi dateline attributed to a certain author. (Many Associated Press or other wire service

---

* *This essay appeared in the* Marine Corps Gazette *in January 2007 and is reproduced by permission of the Marine Corps Association. Copyright is retained by the* Marine Corps Gazette.

reports are not attributed to an author, so they were excluded from the sample.) Marine expeditionary force PA officers deal directly with media representatives in Iraq and not with Washington-based reporters or editorial page columnists, so the latter were not included in the study. The study focused primarily on reporting of large-circulation newspapers because those articles are easily retrievable for free and can be easily categorized for trends. A comparison of print to television reporting was performed on a small sample of TV reports aired in August and September 2005 to determine any differences or similarities from the print media study results. The sample eventually included more than 1,500 print and TV reports from Iraq. Reports were graded with a standardized scoring system for the presence of military PA products to help military PAs determine which products are reported by the civilian media and which are not. For the purpose of the study, a military PA product may be quotes from named military sources from interviews or press conferences, information from military press releases or statements, or reporting from embedded reporters.

Bias in Reporting

The study showed conclusively that the print and TV media reporting from Iraq is not biased. Not a single report was found to purposefully paint a military spokesperson or service member in a bad light, to try to twist his words in an interview, or even misrepresent his statements by creative editing. When the U.S. media travels to Iraq the journalists are there to report the story they observe. The choice to engage them and support their reporting is a choice between getting coverage of our Marines and other service members or getting no coverage at all. Getting bad or distorted coverage should not be a concern that keeps us from engaging the civilian media and supporting their reporting of Marines.

Effective PA Techniques

Getting the U.S. media correspondents out of Baghdad and into the provinces is the single largest factor in getting U.S. military visibility into their reports. It sounds easy, but in reality, the coordination of airlift, ground transportation, and media escorts, and the availability of correspondents and events to report on, is difficult.

If we cannot put a civilian correspondent on the ground outside of Baghdad to report on a military operation, then the next most effective technique is to provide timely PA products to the media. For example, a timely press release describing an operation in November 2005 was widely published in U.S. print, network news, and cable news outlets within twenty-four hours of its release. However, photos and excellent combat correspondent reports from the operation sat on a senior officer's desk waiting to be cleared for more than two weeks, losing all news value in the delay and thus were never published. What military PA staffs do is effective and will be used in civilian media but only if their products are timely and newsworthy.

TV and other video images are the most popular and most preferred means by which Americans receive their information. In fact, nearly 80 percent of Americans get their news from TV. This study addressed broadcast reporting from Iraq and compared it to print media reporting. TV is a visual medium, and video from Iraq, particularly from the front, is very difficult to get. It takes a much larger footprint to embed TV media, and where a national newspaper will have three or more correspondents in Baghdad, a TV network will have only one crew, so it may not be able to send that one team outside the city. Without video to support a TV story, the typical TV story from Iraq only includes a few words about the Marines killed or injured that day. TV news producers will not spend more than a few seconds of a broadcast on a story that has no video, so TV coverage of Marines in Iraq is very limited. In the absence of civilian videographers, the PA community must work toward providing nearly real-time (within the news cycle) video imagery to support TV media and increase the presence of the U.S. military in a typical nightly news broadcast.

What Will Work Tomorrow

The exponential growth of the Internet and the development of twenty-four-hour news networks have radically expanded the media space available for information on combat operations, most notably OIF. The growth of information mediums has led the transfer of information to become consumer controlled instead of source and medium controlled. All organizations, even the very disciplined Marine Corps, should not think that all information on an actual physical operation that involves large combat formations can be controlled. For example, if you want to see videos of Marines blowing up or shooting things in Iraq, go to an Internet site that is not controlled by the Marine Corps but is a direct outlet for Marines (and others) to get videos to consumers. Marine Corps commands and PA staffs can use the explosion of information mediums to their advantage. Such techniques as creating interesting, relevant websites with information of interest to the consumer and then publishing the existence of those websites on other media (roadside billboards, communications and interviews in the mainstream media, etc.) can help make more consumers aware of our PA-controlled communications efforts. It is easy to imagine a day when instead of the MCNews page of the Headquarters Marine Corps website being populated by text and photo articles (ready to print in a base newspaper), it will be populated by video-based reports, aided by computer graphics, scans of maps, and so forth, to help the consumer understand and stay interested in the report.

In conclusion, winning the GWOT will demand that the world, particularly the American public, knows its military is winning the war on the battlefield. In the span of this study, when the U.S. media reports from the front or uses our PA products, the outcome is positive, and the story of our Marines is told. The choice is to support the U.S. media and get our story widely published or have no story published. If we want to win on the information battlefield, we need to be engaged, which means we need to support mass media efforts to tell the Marine Corps' story. In the absence of civilian media, we need to document that story in newsworthy formats for the civilian media to use. The future of the information battlefield will see an increase in video-based reporting, with the Internet taking the place of more traditional media as an outlet for those reports. We can win in the information dimension of GWOT, but just like the land, sea, air, and space dimensions, we need to recognize that the information battlefield exists and be engaged in that dimension with the same tenacity that Marines take to every other battlefield.

16

In Defense of Military Public Affairs Doctrine*

—*CDR J. D. Scanlon, Canadian Forces*

The simultaneous expansion of information operations (IO) and the effects-based approach to operations is challenging traditional notions of military public affairs (PA).[1] Politicians looking for more support in waging an ideological war against extremism, and military commanders seeking more precise effects on the battlefield through the coherent application of all elements of alliance and national power, are blurring the boundaries between IO and PA.[2]

The Pentagon's short-lived Office of Strategic Influence (OSI) is an example of the move toward a more propagandistic information model. According to one news report, the aim of this Orwellian organization was to "influence public opinion abroad," a mandate that some U.S. generals felt would "undermine the Pentagon's credibility and America's attempts to portray herself as the beacon of liberty and democratic values."[3]

Although OSI was dismantled (at least in name), the U.S. military and many other armed forces are continuing to invest in IO capabilities. At the same time, commanders are pressing PA to contribute more tangibly to achieving effects or gaining influence on the battlefield and elsewhere. Public affairs doctrine, however, traditionally seeks to inform audiences, not influence them. NATO policy, for example, specifically states that while PA's "overall aim is ultimately to promote public understanding and support of the alliance and its activities, information is

---

* *This essay appeared in the* Military Review, *May–June 2007, and is reprinted by permission.*

provided in such a way that media representatives and the citizens of the countries concerned are able to make their own judgment as independently as possible."[4]

Similarly, as cited in a Department of Defense (DOD) directive, U.S. doctrine states, "Propaganda has no place in DOD public affairs programs."[5] Some might suggest that this statement only applies within America's borders, but the same directive says, "Open and independent reporting shall be the principle means of coverage of U.S. military operations."[6]

At a glance, these lofty principles seem to offer politicians and military commanders little hope that PA can bring any tangible capabilities to the battlefield or anywhere else. Where are its measurable effects? In contrast, the effects of enemy propaganda seem evident, from decreasing support for U.S. interventions to increasing numbers of suicide bombers.

It may be true that PA "effects" are not always immediately evident, but this is a consequence of Western political ideology, which calls for transparent government, freedom of speech, freedom of the press, and other such principles that militate against shaping public opinion. Therefore, before discarding current doctrine because of a desire to see immediate effects, its origins in the democratic tradition should be carefully considered.

Modern democracies find their roots in the seventeenth-century Age of Reason and the eighteenth-century Enlightenment. The philosophers of those ages nurtured the radical notion that all men and women are created equal. This belief began to erode the long-accepted view that kings, queens, and other nobles were somehow superior and better suited to rule. Early liberal democracies like France and the United States entrenched these notions in their constitutions.

The American Declaration of Independence, written in 1776, reflects this new political outlook: "We hold these truths to be self-evident, that all men are created equal, that they are endowed by their Creator with certain inalienable Rights, that among these are life, liberty and the pursuit of happiness. That to secure these rights, Governments are instituted among men, deriving their just powers from the consent of the governed."[7]

Central to the new outlook were the notions of freedom of speech and freedom of the press. One of the most influential arguments in favor of such rights can be attributed to the English poet John Milton, whose pamphlet *Areopagitica* assailed the British government's licensing of books. Milton wrote, "This I know, that errors in a good government and in a bad are equally almost incident; for what magistrate may not be misinformed, and much the sooner, if liberty of printing be reduced into the power of a few?"[8]

The First Amendment of the 1789 U.S. Bill of Rights adopted Milton's arguments: "Congress shall make no law respecting an establishment of religion, or prohibiting the free exercise thereof; or abridging the freedom of speech, or of the press; or the right of the people peaceably to assemble, and to petition the government for a redress of grievances."[9]

Two centuries later, the constitutions of most democratic nations include similar provisions, including freedom of speech and freedom of the press, as fundamental human rights. The constitution of one of NATO's newer member nations, Romania, states, "Freedom of expression of thoughts, opinions, or beliefs, and freedom of any creation, by words, in writing, in pictures, by sounds or other means of communication in public are inviolable."[10]

Of course, such rights do have limits. The Canadian Charter of Rights and Freedoms, for one, "guarantees the rights and freedoms set out in it subject only to such reasonable limits prescribed by law as can be demonstrably justified in a free and democratic society."[11]

Although limited, these rights extend far beyond national borders. They are found enshrined in international treaties and conventions. Article 55 of the United Nations Charter says that the UN shall promote "universal respect for, and observance of, human rights and fundamental freedoms for all without distinction as to race, sex, language, or religion."[12] These rights are more broadly delineated in a separate document, the Universal Declaration of Human Rights, which the UN adopted in 1948. Article 9 of the declaration reads, "Everyone has the right to freedom of opinion and expression; this right includes freedom to hold opinions without interference and to seek, receive and impart information and ideas through any media and regardless of frontiers."[13]

Freedom of speech and freedom of the press are not the only democratic rights stipulated in the UN's declaration. According to Article 21, "everyone has the right to take part in the government of his country, directly or through freely chosen representatives . . . the will of the people shall be the basis of the authority of government; this shall be expressed in periodic and genuine elections which shall be by universal and equal suffrage and shall be held by secret vote or by equivalent free voting procedures."[14]

NATO nations are doubly bound to honor these human rights by virtue of their simultaneous membership in the UN and the alliance. The NATO Treaty proclaims, "The parties to this treaty reaffirm their faith in the purposes and principles of the Charter of the United Nations and their desire to live in peace with all peoples and all governments."[15]

The NATO alliance also adopted the principles of democracy as part of its 1994 Partnership for Peace program, an initiative designed to help former Warsaw Pact countries with post–Cold War transition. The framework document states,"Protection and promotion of fundamental freedoms and human rights, and safeguarding of freedom, justice, and peace through democracy are shared values fundamental to the Partnership. In joining the Partnership, the member States of the North Atlantic Alliance and the other states subscribing to this Document recall that they are committed to the preservation of democratic societies, their freedom from coercion and intimidation, and the maintenance of the principles of international law."[16]

That a political-military alliance like NATO committed itself so unequivocally to the principles of democracy is significant, for it implies that such principles are not limited to the national borders of the member nations or the boundaries of the Euro-Atlantic region; they also extend to the battlefields where alliance troops are sent. The Geneva Conventions, also ratified by all NATO nations, offer specific protections of human rights on these fields of battle, including the rights of journalists.

Article 4 of the 1949 Geneva Convention "Relative to the Treatment of Prisoners of War" states, "Persons who accompany the armed forces without actually being members thereof, such as civilian members of military aircraft crews, *war correspondents,* supply contractors" shall be treated as prisoners of war [italics added].[17] The term "war correspondent" was found somewhat restrictive, however, and additional provisions for journalists were added to the Geneva Conventions in 1977 under Protocol I, "relating to the Protection of Victims of International Armed Conflicts."[18]

Article 79 of Protocol I specifically addresses "measures or protection for journalists," stating that "journalists engaged in dangerous professional missions in areas of armed conflict shall be considered as civilians [and] shall be protected as such . . . provided that they take no action adversely affecting their status as civilians."[19] (Interestingly, embedded journalists could therefore be imprisoned if captured while journalists not accompanying armed forces should be accorded the same rights as civilians.)

If any conclusions are to be drawn from the above legacy, foremost would be that the international community views the trampling of fundamental human rights, including freedom of the press, as one of the underlying causes and consequences of war. It was by trampling such rights that the Third Reich rose to power and committed some of the most horrendous atrocities in history. Codifying such rights was one way by which the international community hoped to avoid "the scourge of war" in the future.[20]

At the Tehran Conference in 1943, Winston Churchill told Joseph Stalin, "In wartime, truth deserves a bodyguard of lies."[21] The British prime minister was speaking of Allied efforts to deceive the Germans in advance of the Normandy invasions. When directed at an enemy, such deceit is justifiable; however, the notion that in wartime the truth should "always" be protected by lies is precisely what the international community was trying to circumvent. Notions like freedom of speech and freedom of the press are the safeguards.

The tension between today's PA and IO doctrines reflects the historical struggle between truth and deceit. U.S. joint PA doctrine explicitly states in bold letters, "Tell the truth. PA personnel will only release truthful information. The long-term success of [PA] operations depends on maintaining the integrity and credibility of officially released information."[22] British joint media operations doctrine also cites the importance of truthfulness: "All communication with the media must be honest, transparent and accurate."[23]

Romania's military public affairs policy states, "No information will be classified nor will it be prevented from release in order to protect the military institution against criticism or other unpleasant situations."[24] According to British policy, "information should be withheld only when disclosure would adversely affect [operational security], force safety or individual privacy."[25]

On the other hand, NATO's IO policy holds that influencing or deceiving one's adversaries is, at times, justifiable: "The primary focus of [information operations] is on adversaries, potential adversaries and other [North Atlantic Council–] approved parties."[26] While "approved parties" is a vague term, it is understood not to include the alliance's own citizenry.

Still, many governments do in fact routinely seek to influence domestic public opinion through such things as recruiting advertising or health promotions. Likewise, government communicators routinely develop "messages" designed for target audiences. Such practices differ from IO, however, because they are normally transparent and follow policy decisions openly taken by elected governments. They are also subject to democratic checks and balances, including the scrutiny of the free press, attacks by elected opponents, and legal challenges. Finally, the news media resist being repeaters of government messages and strive for balance by questioning government policy and seeking alternative viewpoints.

Notwithstanding the existing doctrinal divisions between PA and IO, many commanders still desire the more tangible effects promised by information, deception, and psychological operations; thus, they lean toward integrating PA into IO. Concern that some of these commanders were blurring the lines between the "inform" doctrine of PA and the "influence" doctrine of IO led the former Chairman of the U.S. Joint Chiefs of Staff GEN Richard B. Myers to issue a letter directing the military's top brass to keep PA distinct from deception and influence functions.[27]

Can PA deliver the effects commanders desire without violating current doctrine and all of its attendant liberal-democratic baggage? Like other military disciplines, PA has to adapt to a changing world with asymmetric threats and a ubiquitous media environment that showers the entire planet with streaming multimedia. In this new information world, terrorists can propagate their information faster than Western militaries can respond.

NATO doctrine calls for the "timely and accurate" release of information. Despite this, the alliance and its member nations have had difficulty getting inside the enemy's so-called OODA-loop (observe, orient, decide, act).[28] In the OODA-loop theory of decision cycles, time is the critical element, but Western forces tend to be hindered by time-consuming processes or decision-making loops that often require approvals from multiple national capitals across a spectrum of time zones.[29] The challenge, then, is not necessarily a doctrinal one for PA; rather, it is predominantly a process issue that requires political will and trust to be resolved.

In terms of tangible effects from PA, many nations are already taking steps to push the doctrine of "informing" to a new, proactive level. Since the 1990s, Canada has been routinely sending its several Combat Camera teams off to cover Canadian Forces operations around the globe. The videos and stills the teams bring or transmit home are then pushed to national and international media.

In 2004, the U.S. military invested more than $6 million in the Digital Video and Imagery Distribution system (DVIDS) hub at Atlanta that collects and distributes raw video to U.S. and international broadcasters on a daily basis. Additionally, U.S. Central Command (CENTCOM), which oversees U.S. operations in Iraq and Afghanistan, has made the move from reactive media relations to a robust proactive program by standing up a full-time team of PA specialists who suggest story ideas to the media.

While some nations are moving to invest in more proactive PA capabilities, the current trend is to invest robustly in IO and PSYOPS. Once IO and PSYOPS are activated on operations, there is also a trend to continue applying them on audiences that are no longer adversarial. The term "IO" is even being used to define communication activities where there is no defined adversary.

Given that the majority of what nations and coalitions are communicating is factual information, these trends are counterintuitive. Meantime, PA offices continue to be understaffed, under-trained, and under-resourced. If more resources were invested in simply informing the media and the public, the results could be impressive. The power of the truth, presented factually, should not be underestimated.

Moreover, if target audiences understood they were not the targets of IO or PSYOPS, they might find conveyed information more credible. America's black propaganda program in Iraq—where the Lincoln Group (initially contracted through a military PA office) surreptitiously placed articles in newspapers—damaged U.S. credibility.[30] It aided and abetted the enemy's portrayal of America as a hypocritical interloper.

In the face of IO, the obvious questions an adversary might pose are: If Western nations are so confident in democracy, why do they resort to propaganda? If they are so confident in the truth as a moral force, why lie?

It might be justifiable to deceive an adversary for the sake of saving lives and winning battles, but in accordance with national and international laws and conventions, it is not acceptable to violate the human rights of those who have done no wrong. Telling the truth is not a simple proposition in today's complex media environment, where information targeted at an adversary in a remote location will inevitably bleed into media and reach friends and allies in every corner of the globe.

As with kinetic weapons, there will be collateral damage in the information war. So long as the military PA arm of government remains true to its doctrine, friendly publics will be told the facts, and the free press will be accorded its place. If the West is so confident that this works at home, then this confidence should be projected into the regions where the West sends its fighting troops. In the meantime, those seeking immediate effects must be reminded that it takes time to build democracy and that although it can be painful at times, the truth will ensure democracy's survival.

17

Waging an Effective Strategic Communications Campaign in the War on Terror
—CAPT Timothy J. Doorey, USN

> How can a man who lives in a cave out-communicate the world's leading communications society?
>
> —Richard Holbrooke,
> Former U.S. Ambassador to the United Nations[1]

Of all the U.S. government's actions since 9/11 to counter the threat of global militant Islamism, its weakest response by far has been its strategic communications and public diplomacy efforts. While there are many and varied reasons for this hapless effort, the consequences are just now coming into focus. Failure to recognize the pivotal role information plays in this ideological struggle will condemn our military and law enforcement forces to an unsustainable and unwinnable defensive strategy involving a perpetual war of attrition. Five years into this fight, we must find an alternative to simply killing or capturing Islamist terrorists and insurgents coming from a potential bottomless recruitment pool of more than one billion frustrated and disillusioned Muslims dispersed around the world.

Since 9/11, despite the expenditure of hundreds of billions of dollars—not to mention several thousands of lives and tens of thousands of wounded—there is little evidence to indicate that the United States is winning the ideological struggle against radical militant Islam. Yet winning this struggle is essential if we are to starve radical Islamist terrorist and insurgent movements of new recruits, funding, and sympathetic populations throughout the Muslim world and in the West. Why can't America and its moderate allies, with all of their combined resources, foreign assistance, and historic ties to the Middle East and Muslim world, compete against shadowy adversaries with little to offer beyond violence masquerading in religious garb? This chapter will attempt to answer that question and will offer recommendations on how the United States can restructure and revitalize its failing strategic communications and public diplomacy efforts in order to make them efficient and imaginative weapons in the war on terror.

Facing Reality

In April 2006—nearly five years after 9/11—the U.S. Intelligence Community (IC) released its first National Intelligence Estimate (NIE) on the global strength of radical Islam since the invasion of Iraq in March 2003. Titled "Trends in Global Terrorism: Implications for the United States," the NIE's declassified key judgments stated, "... that the global jihadist movement—which includes Al Qaeda, affiliated and independent terrorist groups, and emerging networks and cells—is spreading and adapting to counterterrorism efforts."[2] The NIE also stated, "The Iraq conflict has become a cause célèbre for jihadists, breeding a deep resentment of US involvement in the Muslim world and cultivating supporters for the global jihadist movement."[3] The *Washington Post*'s Karen DeYoung claimed the NIE warned "the war in Iraq has become a primary recruitment vehicle for violent Islamic extremists, motivating a new generation of potential terrorists around the world whose numbers may be increasing faster than the United States and its allies can reduce the threat."[4] Such a disturbing finding is not surprising given the torrent of gruesome images coming out of Iraq via the Western media, numerous Arabic-language satellite television stations, and thousands of clandestine Internet websites. In addition to the NIE's stark findings, there were other "indicators" that America's Global War on Terrorism was not going well. State Department statistics show the numbers of terrorist attacks worldwide steadily increasing since 2001, with Iraq becoming the major venue. In 2005 alone, there was nearly a fourfold increase in attacks worldwide from the previous year.[5]

Public opinion polls conducted since 9/11 by well-respected polling organizations such as the Pew Research Center, Zogby International, and Dr. Shibley Telhami's Saban Center for Middle East Policy at the University of Maryland show a consistent downward trend in support for America and its counterterrorism policies, with the steepest declines in the Arab and Muslim world.[6] Most disturbing, recent polling indicates that many Arabs, including citizens of America's staunchest allies in the Middle East, no longer make a distinction between their dislike of U.S. policies and dislike of the American people.[7]

The preponderance of data shows the United States losing the ideological struggle to wean mainstream Muslims, especially the huge demographic of young, alienated Muslim men around the world, from radical Islamist movements that advocate violence. Why is the United States failing the ideological information war? What advantages do radical Islamist competitors have in the information struggle for the youth of the Muslim world? How can America and its allies reverse these disturbing and dangerous trends?

The Centrality of the Information War

Unlike our state and non-state adversaries in the Middle East, the U.S. government still fails to comprehend or appreciate the centrality of the information domain in this ideological conflict. The strategic advantage will always go to the side that manages to field the most credible and compelling message, not to the side with the most firepower. Our adversaries have long understood this key point while we still tend to view information more as an enabler or adjunct to traditional military, intelligence, or diplomatic power rather than a core competency that must be mastered and fully supported. To borrow a Clauswitzian term, we have failed to appreciate that information is the enemy's "center of gravity." By failing to do so, we have made it America's Achilles' heel or critical vulnerability.

The battle for information dominance in the Middle East has a long and rich history. Since the early twentieth century, various governments and opposition movements ranging from colonial powers to post-colonial authoritarian regimes, insurgencies, terrorists groups, and religious fundamentalists have battled to either dominate or wrestle control of the information environment from their opponents. All of these various actors recognized that by controlling the media—and the message—they could also control the population. Those in power who unwittingly lost sight of this fact, such as Egypt's King Faruk in the early 1950s or the Shah of Iran in the late 1970s, unintentionally ceded the information domain to their adversaries and were often swept from power by either military coups or revolutions.

Ayatollah Khomeini's 1979 overthrow of the Shah of Iran—who at the time possessed the most powerful military and security services in the region—set the standard for subversive information warfare in the Middle East. While still in exile, Khomeini adroitly and ingeniously circumvented the Shah's ruthless intelligence service, the SAVAK, and Iranian state-controlled radio and television. His secret weapon? The simple cassette tape. From his home in France, Khomeini's fiery sermons were relayed into Iran by phone where they were taped, copied, and distributed to Iran's 80,000 mosques. The disembodied cleric's sermons were then played for millions of literate and illiterate Iranians alike, giving Khomeini a supernatural quality that he exploited to great effect.[8] By the time Ayatollah Khomeini returned to his homeland in April 1979, after fourteen years in exile in Iraq and France, his message and voice were very familiar to all Iranians.

Khomeni's successful example of subversive propaganda terrified autocratic regimes and inspired various opposition movements. Since then, many radical Shiite and Sunni Islamist movements throughout the region, such as Hezbollah and Hamas in the 1980s, Al Qaeda in the 1990s, and such various spin-off groups as Abu Musab al-Zarqawi's network in Iraq following the U.S. invasion in 2003, adopted Khomeni's strategy and simple tactics. Instead of using the cassette tape, however, these militant Islamist movements have skillfully leveraged many of the tools of the information revolution to outmaneuver both authoritarian governments and the Western media alike.

America has neither fully understood nor appreciated the power of these state and non-state information warriors or their tactics. Enamored with our "shock and awe" kinetic weapons and capabilities, as well as our media dominance during the Cold War and in Desert Shield and Desert Storm in 1991, we abandoned the government-sponsored information environment after the fall of the Berlin Wall in 1989. Ironically, just as the United States and its allies were dismantling their government-sponsored overseas broadcasting and other public diplomacy programs in the Middle East, an information revolution consisting of Arabic-language satellite television stations, the World Wide Web, and cell phones was spreading across the region like wildfire. Unlike the Western media and many state-controlled stations, these new sources filled the information void with graphic images and messages critical of U.S. policies in the Middle East and the rest of the Muslim world. This uncensored information revolution immediately found a large and receptive local audience starved for alternate sources of information.

The Al Jazeera Effect

In the 1990s, following CNN's dramatic and influential role as the only major satellite television news channel covering the first Gulf War, many defense analysts and Pentagon officials began talking about "the CNN effect." The CNN effect referred to the station's ability to not only report news in real-time from remote areas of the world, but to also shape government policy by bringing dramatic images of suffering in unfolding crises directly into the homes of viewers. The emotional impact of these images often compelled American and European governments to take military or humanitarian action to relieve the suffering their constituents were witnessing on their television screens. The clearest example of the CNN effect in action was the U.S. intervention in Somalia in December 1992. The U.S. government was prodded to intervene to relieve widespread famine. Ironically, the CNN effect reappeared the following year in Somalia when images of the brutal deaths of eighteen Army Rangers in the infamous "Blackhawk Down" incident in October 1993 forced America's hasty departure.

The Middle Eastern version of the CNN effect became possible with the establishment and rapid growth of Al Jazeera and other Arabic-language satellite television stations in the mid- to late 1990s.[9] Before then, Arab and Muslim publics were forced to watch stale and uninspiring state-run television. S. Abdallah Schleifer, senior editor for the *Transnational Broadcasting Studies Journal*,[10] observes that until the introduction of satellite television, television journalism didn't exist in the Arab world. Until then, "TV was the most policed of all media."[11] The widespread access to Arab satellite television news organizations like Al Jazeera changed not only the way Arabs and Muslims received information, it changed who controlled what the "Arab street" saw and, thus, the Middle East's political dynamic. In 2001, 70 percent of those living in the Persian Gulf region received their news and information from satellite television broadcasts.[12] While Qatar's Al Jazeera television, which provides news and information twenty-four hours a day, is the most recognized Arabic-language television station in the West, it is only one of many such operations and faces stiff competition for viewers from other Arabic-language satellite television stations, including the Dubai-based Al Arabiya and the radical Lebanese Islamic group, Hezbollah's Al-Manar ("The Beacon" in Arabic).

The political impact of this wide selection of provocative television news is difficult to comprehend. In 1982, when *New York Times* correspondent Thomas L. Friedman covered the Israeli invasion of Lebanon, it took hours or days for file footage to get out of the country. This delay allowed Arab regimes to easily censor what was shown to their publics. Today, Israeli military actions in the Palestinian-occupied territories or Lebanon, or Coalition actions in Iraq, Afghanistan, or Somalia, are broadcast into Arab living rooms before the host government is even aware such provocative material has entered the country. Graphic footage of the Israeli operations in the West Bank is broadcast live by stations like Al-Manar, accompanied by an emotionally gripping soundtrack of terrified Palestinian mothers screaming blow-by-blow descriptions to the satellite stations from their cell phones. Such dramatic television is compelling for all Arabs and Muslims throughout the region. During the 2002 Israeli incursion into the West Bank, Al-Manar was the most popular television station in Jordan.[13] Since the U.S. attack on the Taliban in October 2001 and, more important, the 2003 invasion of Iraq, the Arab street has been fed a steady diet of the most gruesome images of collateral damage, brutality, and humiliation. This provocative media is the oxygen for radical militant Islamist terrorist and insurgent movements. Its messages serve as effective recruitment tools for young, angry Muslims unwilling to accept the status quo.

Some media and political analysts even compare the impact of satellite televised news coverage of Arab and Muslim crises to the role television news coverage had on American public opinion during the Vietnam War.[14] Indeed, the emotional power of such footage cannot be underestimated. One only needs to think back to the early 1990s, when a crude, soundless, black-and-white video of uniformed Los Angeles police officers beating an unarmed black man named Rodney King sparked days of rioting by some in the African American community after the officers were arrested, tried, and acquitted. If segments of the U.S. population, with decades of televised news coverage experience, can be incited by a media image, one can only imagine the impact a daily diet of even more emotional coverage would have on vast Arab and Muslim populations, untutored in the finer points of propaganda and spin.[15]

Along with satellite television, the Internet's rapid growth in the Middle East—and the rest of the Muslim world—has also opened many new opportunities for unconventional information warfare and propaganda. Professor Gabriel Weimann, a professor of communications at Haifa University and expert on Internet communications and terrorism, states in his recent book, *Terror on the Internet*:

> In 1998, fewer than half of the thirty organizations designated as foreign terrorist organizations by the U.S. Department of State maintained Web sites; by the end of 1999, nearly all thirty terrorist groups had established their presence on the Net. Today there are more than forty active terrorist groups, each with an established presence on the Internet. A thorough and extensive scan of the Internet in 2003–05 revealed more than 4,300 Web sites serving terrorists and their supporters.[16]

The explosion in communications technologies over the past decade has led not only to dramatic changes in the way Arabs and Muslims receive information, but also how they form opinions on the motives and intentions of the outside world. This makes propaganda not an adjunct to Islamist terrorism; it makes terrorism an adjunct to militant Islamist propaganda. According to Philip Taylor, the Director of the Institute of Communications Studies at the University of Leeds,

> The enemy really has only one weapon with which to fight—propaganda—although to this we should perhaps add terror, surprise and the generation of fear. Starving terrorists of the "oxygen of publicity"—by taking out Taliban radio stations, by pressuring Muslim governments to moderate their state-controlled media and western media outlets to "think carefully" about what they show—is only part of the strategy needed to wage propaganda war in the information age. The fact that western democracies are already on the defensive in the "war against terror" suggests a failure of their propaganda—but on a much longer timescale dating back to well before the twin tower attacks.[17]

Any U.S. or allied information strategy for the region must take all of these dynamic developments into consideration or its messages will unlikely have any impact on Muslim views of the West. The homegrown competition is constantly bombarding their audiences with dramatic images of Muslims being humiliated, brutalized, and killed in Iraq, Afghanistan, the Israeli-occupied territories, Chechnya, Kashmir, or the Balkans. How has the United States responded to this new reality?

A Feeble U.S. Response

America has always been, at best, ambivalent about waging information warfare. Today, we still have a hard time agreeing on definitions, let alone crafting or implementing a comprehensive strategy. We are naturally leery of all government-sponsored information efforts, overt or covert, since we see them as activities potentially at odds with our democratic heritage, especially support for freedom of speech and the press. Besides brief periods of patriotic fervor, such as the Spanish-American War and World War I, we have reluctantly embraced government-supported media twice in our history: during World War II and then the Cold War. Even then, our efforts lagged years behind our Axis and Communist adversaries. Only reluctantly, after the rapid fall of France to the Nazis in 1940 and Pearl Harbor, did the U.S. government overcome its aversion to government-supported information and implement robust overseas broadcasting to counter our enemies' massive propaganda advantages. Not surprising, once those conflicts concluded, Congress and various administrations scrambled to cut funding and either shrink or eliminate these efforts.

During the early days of the Cold War, when it became clear that the Cold War would last decades, not years, President Eisenhower established the United States Information Agency (USIA) in August 1953. The USIA operated under that name until April 1978, when its functions were consolidated with those of the Bureau of Educational and Cultural Affairs of the Department of State and the agency was called the International Communication Agency (USICA). However, in August 1982, as part of the Reagan administration's revitalized and robust strategic communications effort against the Soviet Union, the agency's name was restored as USIA. In the 1990s, after the end of the Cold War, the United States and its allies slowly abandoned many of their government-funded public diplomacy and information efforts around the world. What remained of the U.S. government's truncated public diplomacy efforts in the Middle East was often stale, antiquated, and unimaginative programming, catering to tiny, niche overseas audiences.

America's traditional method of reaching wide audiences in the Middle East and elsewhere was through government-sponsored international radio broadcasting, such as the Voice of America (VOA), Radio Free Europe/Radio Liberty (RFE/RL), Radio Free Asia, and so on. However, by September 11, 2001, U.S. government radio broadcasting to the Middle East, North Africa, and Central Asia had a very limited reach. The VOA's Arabic-service programming, with just a few hours a day of shortwave programming, had little, if any, impact on Middle Eastern attitudes.[18] By comparison, the VOA, along with Radio Free Europe and Radio Liberty, reached 50 percent of the Soviet population and 70 to 80 percent of the Eastern European population every week at the height of the Cold War.[19] Despite the dramatic changes in information technology over the previous two decades, such as satellite television and the Internet, the United States was still trying to reach critical audiences in the early twenty-first century with broadcasting techniques and technologies dating back to the 1940s.

Following 9/11, Congress and the U.S. government, led by former Broadcasting Board of Governors (BBG) member Norman J. Pattiz, attempted to rebuild U.S. overseas broadcasting with new satellite radio and television broadcasting technology specifically designed to reach the Muslim world. Radio Sawa ("Together" in Arabic) and Alhurra (Arabic for "The Free One"), its satellite television counterpart, were quickly fielded. However, by the time these new initiatives were finally up and running, the Arabic-language media field was already crowded, and the United States faced stiff competition from regional alternatives with established audiences. The United States was going to have to work very hard to reach skeptical Arab and Muslim ears and eyes.

Nor was the U.S. government's antiquated communications infrastructure the only major obstacle standing between U.S. broadcasters and varied audiences in the Muslim world. Content and methodology were also serious problems. What was available was limited in quantity and often deficient in quality. The U.S. government's track record for reporting unbiased regional news, or its policies, was seen by skeptical Muslim audiences as mixed at best. These messages became increasingly muddled after intensive bureaucratic infighting among power centers in the White House, Congress, the State Department, the Defense Department, and sometimes the overseas broadcasting organizations themselves. The result, from the intended audience's perspective, was often unconvincing messages at odds with independent news, Coalition partner positions, or eye-witness accounts from various nongovernmental and private volunteer organizations. Such fights further undermined the credibility of U.S. government reporting and served to push skeptical audiences into the arms of Al Jazeera and other Arab-owned satellite broadcasters seen as more sympathetic to the Arab and Muslim perspective.[20]

Even our specially designed strategic communications efforts in support of major U.S. and allied combat operations such as Operation Enduring Freedom (OEF) in Afghanistan or Operation Iraqi Freedom (OIF) have fallen short. Both strategic communications efforts were ad hoc, focused almost exclusively on domestic rather than international audiences, and heavily "outsourced" to contractors. During the Afghan campaign in the fall of 2001, the U.S. and British communications teams were slow to recognize or respond to false or exaggerated collateral damage and atrocity claims by the Taliban and their supporters. Yet, because of the time difference between Afghanistan, the United Kingdom, and the United States, there would often be an eight- to ten-hour delay before the American or British rebuttal of even the most outlandish Taliban atrocity claim in Pakistan. Washington and London, were finally forced to stand up three 24/7 Coalition Information Centers in Washington, London, and Islamabad to quickly refute these claims before they could spread and linger unchallenged in the Muslim world. However, soon after the fall of Kabul, these centers were disbanded and the mission of communicating Coalition intentions and actions to 25 million Afghans and 120 million Pakistanis fell to overworked or inexperienced tactical military forces in the field or embassy public affairs offices with limited resources for a robust strategic communications effort.

In March 2003, the U.S. Central Command set up an elaborate media operation in Doha, Qatar, called the "Coalition Information Center," to manage information during the invasion of Iraq. Under the direction of the White House's Director of

Strategic Communication, Jim Wilkinson, CENTCOM built a multimillion-dollar public affairs operation, complete with desert camouflage netting, a stage, and daily press briefings by U.S. Army BG Vincent Brooks. Following the fall of Baghdad, this too was also quickly disbanded, leaving the mission to the Combined Joint Task Force-7 (CJTF-7) and eventually the Coalition Provisional Authority (CPA).

These brief yet expensive strategic communications efforts reveal much about the biases and defects of U.S. public diplomacy efforts in the Middle East since 9/11, especially compared to efforts of Al Qaeda, Saddam's Ba'athists, and the Iranians. U.S. strategic communications campaigns were usually led by people with either political campaign or advertising experience and expertise. Like American political campaigns, they were short lived and, not surprising, focused more on the Western media than on either the Middle Eastern broadcasters or Muslim audiences. The strategy during the combat phase of Operation Iraqi Freedom appears to have been to marginalize Al Jazeera and the other Arabic media operations, since they were seen as non-supportive of U.S. goals for the region. For example, despite the fact that the Coalition Information Center in Doha, Qatar, was set up only twenty miles from Al Jazeera's headquarters and, by extension, Al Jazeera's forty million Arabic-speaking viewers, the Coalition Information Center made little effort to reach out to this station. CENTCOM assigned a young Marine public affairs officer, 1LT Josh Rushing, to be the liaison officer to Al Jazeera. The more seasoned DOD public affairs officers were sent to work with supportive U.S. and British media networks. Lieutenant Rushing, despite heroic efforts on his part, ran out of talking points on his first day when challenged by more experienced Arab journalists. Fortunately, he was rescued by Nabeel Khoury, a State Department spokesman with extensive Middle Eastern experience.[21]

American neglect of the Iraqi or Arab information environment continued into the thirteen-month period when the CPA was in charge of strategic communication. *Washington Post* reporter Thomas Ricks points out in his book, *Fiasco*,

> The CPA ceded the playing field in other, more important ways. Charles Krohn, a veteran of Army public affairs, was surprised when he served in Baghdad to see that the CPA early on lifted the ban on TV satellite receivers, but failed to begin satellite broadcasting until months later, in January 2004, leaving a gap in which Iraqis got all of their news from Arab stations essentially hostile to the U.S. presence. "What this means is that for the first nine months, we essentially forfeited the contest for hearts and minds to the competition," he wrote later.[22]

Compare this hapless U.S. information effort in Iraq with that of Iraq's key neighbor, Iran. While the U.S. strategic communications team in Iraq was still trying to decide which contractor to hire to fill the information void left by the collapse of Saddam's information apparatus, robust Iranian efforts were already well under way.[23] In March 2003, as U.S. forces were racing toward Baghdad, Iran began broadcasting Alalam, a new twenty-four-hour Arabic-language terrestrial television channel, into Iraq. The new station's anti-Coalition bias was soon shaping information-starved Iraqis' attitudes on the conflict and America's intentions. Alalam emphasized the war's impact on ordinary Iraqis and showed repeated images of dead and wounded Iraqi noncombatants under the slogan "war of domination." Also, in a sophisticated subliminal propaganda campaign, its broadcasts continually referred to Coalition troops as "occupiers." The station was also available on the Internet to reach a wider Arab audience.[24]

The Iranian government's aggressive information campaign in post-Saddam Iraq coincided with its continued determination to control its own information environment. In 2003, the same year Alalam began broadcasting into Iraq, the Islamic republic resorted to jamming a relay satellite signal from the United States to Iran from its embassy in Havana, Cuba. This provocative move was likely an attempt to prevent Iranian expatriate community satellite television programming from reaching Iranians inside the Islamic republic.[25] The Iranian government continues to censor information from abroad. In October 2006, Iran banned all high-speed Internet access (above 128 kilobits a second), and in December, it blocked access to several major international websites. These increasingly desperate moves show what the Iranian Islamic government really fears, and it is not American military power in the Persian Gulf.

U.S. Struggles with Target Recognition

As the Coalition Information Center examples clearly show, U.S. efforts ostensibly designed to influence Arab and Muslim audiences usually end up focusing instead on U.S. audiences. This is a problem of target recognition. Throughout modern history, the U.S. and other militaries have trained pilots and gun crews to recognize, at a distance, enemy and friendly aircraft as well as naval combatants to assist targeting and prevent or minimize fratricide. Unfortunately, no such training exists for U.S. officials involved in strategic communications strategies for American, Arab, and Muslim audiences. Since many of the senior officials chosen to lead strategic communications efforts developed their communications expertise managing U.S. political campaigns, the tendency is to believe "one-size-fits-all" and one must "keep on message." It was unrealistic to think Iraqis would embrace either Ambassador L. Paul Bremer or his chief Coalition Provisional Authority spokesman, Dan Senor, as "the face of the new Iraq." Yet for almost fourteen months, that is all they saw on their television sets, that is, when they had electricity to run them. An example of this "mirror imaging" was the CPA's Strategic Communications Center in the Green Zone, where an official remembers seeing all the television channels but one tuned to Fox News.[26] For them, the audience that really matter-ed was not the Iraqis but the American public. Iran and the insurgents never failed to make the distinction. The former and current Undersecretaries for Public Diplomacy and

Public Affairs have also struggled to connect with hostile and suspicious Muslims abroad. To be fair, none of these senior officials had robust and experienced staffs to lean on for continuity, experience, or area expertise. Following the demise of USIA in 1999, the task of reaching more than a billion Muslims fell on the shoulders of shrinking and demoralized staffs buried deep within the State and Defense departments' bureaucracies. In May 2006, the Government Accounting Office reported that despite the State Department spending $597 million on public diplomacy in 2005, it still lacks a strong central message and a strategic plan of communication to reach more than a billion Muslims in fifty-eight countries.[27] Many of the more ambitious efforts have been outsourced to contractors, such as the Rendon Group or the Lincoln Group, with little thought on how they should fit into an overall U.S. government communications strategy. When the U.S. media discovered the Lincoln Group was planting favorable stories in Iraqi newspapers, a Pentagon Inspector General's audit of the practice concluded that the taxpayer-funded propaganda campaign did not violate the law or Pentagon regulations but that military officials in Baghdad violated federal contraction guidelines by failing to keep adequate records. Sadly, like many of these efforts, there was no assessment of the program's effectiveness.[28]

Nor did the Lincoln Group embarrassment stop the U.S. military in Iraq from putting out a request for bids for a two-year, twenty-million-dollar public relations contract in August 2006. According to Walter Pincus of the *Washington Post*, the proposal called for extensive monitoring of Iraqi, Middle Eastern, and American media designed to help Coalition forces understand "the communications environment," and for monitoring "Iraqi, pan-Arabic, international and U.S national and regional markets media in both Arabic and English."[29] This broad contract proposal shows how unfocused our strategic communications efforts have become and how we continue to mix our target audiences. The contract comes dangerously close to violating the Smith-Mundt Act of 1948, which prevents U.S. government-funded propaganda from being directed at U.S. citizens. In addition, the vast scope of the contract shows disarray within the U.S. government's strategic communications effort. The fact that the Multinational Force-Iraq (MNF-I) commander and his temporary staff must contract out such support services speaks volumes about out inability to support our efforts in theater more than five years after 9/11. The contract is similar to asking GEN William Westmoreland to run a global, foreign broadcasting monitoring and communications effort for both the Communist and free world from his headquarters in Saigon during the Tet Offensive. One would think that such an effort would be well beyond the capabilities of any temporary military command or individual contractor.

Credibility and the Policy-Message Mismatch
As daunting as the U.S. strategic communications efforts' technological, content, and organizational challenges are, the most difficult obstacle facing U.S. public

diplomacy and strategic communications in the Arab and Muslim world is a lack of credibility. Credibility requires more than providing information that is factually correct—something the Lincoln Group fiasco has not helped. It also means a consistency between stated U.S. foreign policy goals and actions and what is said to domestic and international audiences. For this reason, crafting the U.S. public diplomacy and strategic communications cannot, and should not, be delegated below the National Security Council staff level. According to Professor R. S. Zaharna of American University,

> Credibility is the cornerstone of effective persuasion. America has a credibility problem. Technically, it is a source credibility problem ... Namely, America as a source is not believable. America's credibility problem stems from the perceived duplicity between American ideals and American policy. From the perspective of people in the region, what America says it stands for—justice, liberty, freedom, human rights, equality, fairness—is not reflected in its policies. One hears repeated reference to the Palestinian-Israeli conflict and Iraqi sanctions. The reason they haunt the U.S. message is because both resonate strongly with people's perceptions of American duplicity. What America does, through its policies and practices in Iraq and Palestine, speaks louder than all the official statements coming out of Washington. Until America addresses its policy in the region, American efforts to intensify its message are more likely to hurt than help.[30]

U.S. public diplomacy and strategic messages must agree with U.S. foreign policy actions, especially if these policies impact the Islamic world. Already battered, U.S. credibility could be further eroded by policy-message mismatches in the presidential elections as speeches and promises designed for domestic audiences are exploited by radical Islamist propagandists as additional examples of U.S. duplicity toward Muslims worldwide.

Militant Islamists are adept at exploiting U.S. support for repressive regimes in Central Asia, Russia, and the Middle East. They point out to potential supporters that the West is biased against Muslims, offering as proof the fact that Christian East Timor is allowed to gain independence from predominantly Muslim Indonesia while similar pleas from persecuted Muslims in Chechnya, Palestine, and Kashmir are ignored by the West. U.S. foreign policy and public diplomacy will need to provide plausible explanations to these legitimate concerns or risk that its message will ring hollow to Muslim ears.[31]

The Way Ahead

Clearly, the United States stumbled badly in its first five years of the infor-mation war with radical Islamist militants. It can no longer continue with its dysfunctional structure and information strategy if it intends to make progress and convey a credible and positive message to an increasingly hostile Muslim world. The administration and new Congress must recognize that the current approach is failing and that fixing the problem will require more than tinkering around the edges. It will require a fundamental strategic reassessment of the conflict we are facing. As Carl von Clausewitz wrote more than two hundred years ago:

> The first, the supreme, the most far-reaching act of judgment that the statesman and commander have to make is to establish by that test the kind of war on which they are embarking; neither mistaking it for, nor trying to turn it into, something that is alien to its nature. This is the first of all strategic questions and the most comprehensive.[32]

Such a strategic reassessment will likely show us that this war is multi-dimensional as both an information war and, more important, a number of civil wars within the Arab and Muslim world. Reaching a consensus on the nature of the enemy we face will serve as a guide for policy, much as George F. Kennan's famous "X" article on the "Sources of Soviet Conduct" did in July 1947 and allowed policymakers to draft *NSC 68: United States Objectives and Programs for National Security* in April 1950 before the outbreak of the Korean War.[33] Such an unvarnished reassessment will fundamentally change not only our structure and tactics, but could also reveal our adversaries' vulnerabilities and how we can best exploit them. Pakistani journalist Ahmed Rashid explains why radical Islam as an ideology is not ten feet tall and cannot provide Muslims with a better future:

> These new Islamic fundamentalists are not interested in transforming a corrupt society into a just one, nor do they care about providing jobs, education, or social benefits to their followers or creating harmony between the various ethnic groups that inhabit many Muslim countries. The new jihadi groups have no economic manifesto, no plan for better governance and the building of political institutions, and no blueprint for creating democratic participation in the decision-making process of their future Islamic states. They depend on a single charismatic leader, an amir, rather than a more democratically constituted organization or party for governance. They believe that the character, piety, and purity of their leader rather than his political abilities, education or experience will enable him to lead the new society.[34]

This shows why our radical Islamist adversaries, both state and non-state, are vulnerable to a well-thought-out and implemented information campaign. Yet, such vulnerabilities are unlikely to be exploited by uncoordinated, under-resourced, unimaginative, or incoherent U.S. and allied efforts in the information arena. To say the United States is far behind its adversaries today in the information war would be a gross understatement. Yet, we have been in a similarly weak position before in our history. Despite Kennan's brilliant "X" article and NSC 68, America was consumed for three years fighting the Korean War before it got around to building a permanent and robust information organization to fight Communism ideologically and not just kinetically. Like our efforts in Afghanistan and Iraq, the fighting in Korea was costly yet inconclusive. It is not a coincidence that the new President Eisenhower established the U.S. Information Agency in 1953; he knew that America could best compete with the Communist ideological threat in an information war and not in a protracted conflict. We need to realize, and quickly, that without a comprehensive overhaul of our strategic communications effort against this sophisticated ideological threat, we will continue to fight unconventional enemies on their terms. Failure to improve the non-kinetic dimension of the war on terror could prolong and intensify the conflict for decades. The administration and Congress must focus on five major areas as it overhauls U.S. information warfare capabilities. First, we must rebuild the strategic communications infrastructure by reestablishing the United States Information Agency. Second, we must better assess the information environment we are trying to influence. Third, we must reexamine U.S. policies to see which ones are providing grist for the militant Islamist propaganda mill and develop ways to mitigate these problems. Fourth, we need to work much closer with our allies around the world who have been struggling with the radical Islamist ideological threat much longer than the United States. Finally, the United States and its allies must attempt innovative approaches to influence the internal debate already under way in many Arab and Muslim countries on the future of Islam and on Muslim relations with the rest of the world.

Resurrect and Revitalize the United States Information Agency

The U.S. government's strategic communications effort can no longer rely on ad hoc structures and outside contractors as it has since 9/11. America needs a new U.S. Information Agency to coordinate and professionalize interagency efforts. The new USIA must be adequately staffed with both regional subject matter experts and career communications professionals, and it must be funded with appropriate resources to reach at least a quarter of the world's population. Since the demise of the USIA in 1999, U.S. efforts have frequently been led by individuals unfamiliar with the audiences whom they are trying to reach and influence. The Department of State should divest itself of most traditional public diplomacy functions, since such efforts will always be subordinated to their core mission of private diplomacy. However, as during the Cold War, State Department professionals could and should serve in rotational assignments at the new USIA.

The Department of Defense should limit its strategic communications to traditional public affairs—such as highlighting U.S. forces' involvement in Tsunami relief in Indonesia and earthquake relief in Pakistan—and focus its remaining efforts on tactical psychological operations (PSYOPS) and support to civil affairs. This has always been DOD's strength, and it is at this battlefield level where DOD efforts are most appropriate and effective.

Assess the Environment

Many U.S. strategic communications initiatives since 9/11 have been implemented without adequate research on the target audiences, such as how do more than a billion Muslims receive information and make judgments on credibility. Officials with extensive experience in U.S. political or commercial advertising assumed that they knew which media and messages would persuade target audiences in the Arab and Muslim world based on conjecture or "mirror imaging." Few had in-depth cultural or historical knowledge—or overseas experience—in the Muslim world on which to base their assessments. Insufficient effort has gone into researching which messages, both hostile and supportive, resonate with Arab and Muslim audiences. We must capture and analyze the growing body of evidence on Middle Eastern attitudes since 9/11, including extensive polling data, which can be used to help guide future information campaigns.

Reassess Policies

In order to reestablish America's credibility in the Arab and Muslim world, we must not turn a blind eye or deaf ear to the people's legitimate concerns. While it is unrealistic to think that the United States can make dramatic changes in its foreign policy to completely satisfy Arab and Muslim grievances, it can mitigate some of the concerns and therefore restore its credibility as an evenhanded participant in serious negotiations. There is tremendous suffering in the Arab and Muslim world, and America must not try to minimize or dismiss this reality in its statements to the world, especially the Muslim world.

Build a "Coalition of Persuasion"

The United States has watched its list of Coalition partners and, more important, their contributions in troops and other resources dwindle over the past few years. Many nations were opposed to the Iraq invasion from the beginning while others have become disillusioned by our overreliance on a kinetic strategy. However, nearly all of our current and former Coalition partners remain committed to the post-9/11 goal of confronting and defeating the extremist ideology that sustains Islamist-inspired terrorism at home and abroad. It would not take much effort to convince them to pool their resources for a non-kinetic approach to this problem, using NATO, United Nations, or other international organizations as possible venues.

We could also benefit from a healthy dose of humility. Many of our European and Asian allies have had many years of experience battling this enemy. They have an excellent understanding of what motivates this adversary. We must learn how to leverage their unique regional and functional capabilities in the fields of assessment and influence.

Attempt Imaginative Approaches

To date, many U.S. strategic communications initiatives in the twenty-first century have been either based on false assumptions or poorly implemented responses. For example, former State Department Undersecretary for Public Diplomacy Charlotte Beers implemented a "Shared Values" campaign after 9/11 until her departure in March 2003. Her effort to counteract growing anti-American sentiment in Arab countries was an ad campaign showing Muslims thriving in America. "However, several Arab nations refused to run the ads and they were discontinued after a focus group in Jordan said the ads left them cold."[35] DOD's and the Lincoln Group's effort to plant favorable stories in Iraqi newspapers was also ineffective—if not counterproductive—when it was leaked to the press.

Perhaps if we looked back into our history we could find examples that were innovative, factual, credible, pertinent to vast audiences, and effective. For example, in the early days of World War II, Army Chief of Staff George C. Marshall recruited legendary Hollywood film director Frank Capra to produce the *Why We Fight* series of seven films. Marshall's goal for the series was to explain to millions of young men who had been indoctrinated by years of isolationist propaganda why it was necessary for them to leave the comfort of their homes, join the Army, and fight Nazi Germany and Imperial Japan. After watching hours of sophisticated German and Japanese propaganda films, Major Capra told General Marshall that he could not duplicate the quality of the enemies' propaganda. However, he came up with a novel approach: use their propaganda against them. "Let the enemy prove to our Soldiers the enormity of his cause—and the justness of ours." He decided to "use the enemy's own films to expose their enslaving ends. Let our boys hear the Nazis and the Japs shout their own claims of master-race crud."[36]

While few Americans or Westerners need convincing of the evil of Islamist-inspired terrorism, many Arabs and other Muslims remain uncommitted to fighting the Islamist terrorists. They remain unconvinced of the harm terrorism has inflicted on Muslims and Islam. Perhaps they do not see radical Islamists as a threat to their own way of life in Pakistan, Saudi Arabia, Egypt, Morocco, or the Palestinian territories. Perhaps they are cowed by the Islamists. Yet, by magnifying the themes of Islamist propaganda, such as the words and deeds of the militant ideologues over the years, we can provide them with a glimpse of what life would be like if the Islamists came to power in their country. Let bin Laden and his lieutenants explain why thousands of innocent Muslims in Iraq, Africa, and New York must die for his ill-defined utopia. Footage of the aftermath of their terrorists' grizzly acts should be accompanied with segments of Osama bin Laden, Ayman al-Zawahiri, or Abu Musab al-Zarqawi callously gloating and showing their disregard for widespread Muslim suffering. There have been only three countries where radical Islamists have actually come to power: Iran, Sudan under the National Islamic Front (NIF), and Afghanistan under the Taliban. All have been brutally repressive regimes. We should allow Muslims who have suffered under the Taliban and other militant

Islamist regimes to tell their co-religionists their stories and why flirting with radical Islamist solutions to real political, economic, social, and cultural problems is playing with fire. If such factual documentaries are professionally produced, this accurate portrayal of the face of radical militant Islamism could, over time, discourage millions of Muslims from following such a nihilistic ideology.

In summary, as was true in our early World War II and Cold War information warfare experiences, we have been slow to respond to our enemies' sophisticated and effective propaganda efforts. Now is the time for the U.S. government to develop a multiyear informational strategy for what is likely to be a protracted ideological struggle against militant Islamism. The United States must rebuild its antiquated and under-resourced information capabilities and implement a strategy that will succeed in a dynamic mass media environment. Much of the research on what needs to be done has already been conducted by various committees and study groups such as the Defense Science Board.[37] America's challenge is to act on this research and confront our enemies where they are most vulnerable: the ideological and information environment.

18

Marketing: An Overlooked Aspect of Information Operations*
—*CPT Stoney Trent, USA, and CPT James L. Doty III, USA*

Defeating enemy formations on the field of battle is merely the first, and often the easiest, phase of a military operation. Ultimate success (accomplishing the political goals of the National Command Authority) hinges on a successful post-high-intensity conflict occupation in which the population comes to accept the new state of affairs. In all phases, understanding and influencing the people are critical to reducing the cost of victory in terms of lives, dollars, and time.

The U.S. Army has had varying degrees of success over the past hundred years in influencing the people of opposing nations. In Cuba, the Philippines, the Dominican Republic, Italy, Germany, Japan, Korea, Vietnam, Haiti, Grenada, Panama, Somalia, Bosnia, and Kosovo, we have run the gamut from success to failure. Recognizing the need to win over populations, the Army has begun to emphasize information operations (IO) in every deployment. Such operations are one part of the Army's campaign to achieve information superiority during a conflict. Information superiority is "the operational advantage derived from the ability to collect, process, and disseminate an uninterrupted flow of information while exploiting or denying an adversary's ability to do the same."[1] According to U.S. Army Field Manual 3-0 *Operations*, information operations are "actions taken to affect the adversary's and influence others' decision making processes, information and information systems while protecting one's own information and information systems."[2]

---

* *This essay appeared in the* Military Review, *July–August 2005, and is reprinted by permission.*

The concept of influencing an enemy force's or local population's decision-making process is not new. American psychological operations (PSYOPS) personnel have attempted to disseminate messages and influence enemy forces or local populations since World War II.[3] Propaganda, the attempt to influence threat forces and populations through directed messages, has been used by warring countries for centuries. Americans view propaganda negatively because past enemies such as Nazi Germany, North Vietnam, Imperial Japan, and the Soviet Union used it. Yet, propaganda, PSYOPS, and information operations seek to accomplish the same goal: to influence the target audience to make a decision beneficial to the user. What is new in information operations is the integration of the plan to influence threat forces and local populations into a larger effort to achieve an operational advantage by controlling the flow of information.

Recent challenges in Iraq highlight the difficulty of developing and sustaining an effective IO campaign. The U.S. military's failure to adequately integrate and successfully execute IO campaigns is ironic; after all, Americans live in a society dominated by marketing communications. From political lobbying to commercial advertising, organizations sway Americans' decisions. Information operations have the same goal as marketing communications: to influence a target audience to respond positively to a message. Because IO and marketing both attempt to elicit physical as well as psychological responses, both ought to utilize similar methods. The U.S. military should tap the abundance of creative marketing talent in America and implement a more complete approach to IO planning and execution.

In units such as the 1st Armored, 1st Infantry, and 3rd Infantry divisions, field artillery staff officers under the supervision of the S3/G3 are responsible for information operations.[4] This is because staffs approach IO planning from a targeting perspective. The decide, detect, deliver, and assess targeting cycle is, in fact, similar to the process many advertising agencies use: discover, define, design, and deliver. However, the Army provides no training for officers who must plan, coordinate, and execute its version of a successful marketing campaign. Even IO career field (FA 30) selectees are not required to possess marketing training, although FA 30 Reserve-component officers "with civilian experience in information technology and management, communications, marketing, organizational behavior or other IO-related fields are a valuable army resource."[5] While U.S. Army Training and Doctrine Pamphlet 525-69, *Concept for Information Operations*, recommends all officers receive "awareness training in IO" in officer training schools, it does not address the additional resources needed for IO training and emphasizes technology and computer skills rather than the complex skills of expert marketers—message development and tailored delivery.[6]

At the strategic level, the Army has established the 1st Information Operations Command (IOC) (Land [L]) to support combatant commands in an array of IO specialties, including operations security, PSYOPS, electronic warfare, military deception, civil affairs, and public affairs.[7] While casting its net over the entire span of information superiority, the 1st IOC (L) has neglected to integrate key specialties that would result in successful "mission-tailored, thoroughly developed, IO plans."[8] Officers wishing to specialize in information operations are afforded opportunities for advanced schooling but only in information systems and computer science. These areas provide technical skills necessary to link IO to the broader information superiority effort, but they are not particularly helpful in developing effective IO campaigns aimed at diverse populations. No mention of marketing skills or education can be found in the material describing the value of IO or its officers.[9]

Information operations are marketing communications. A review of marketing textbooks reveals the four key aspects of marketing are product, price, promotion, and place.[10] As conceived by the Army, IO starts and stops with a shallow promotion plan (talking points for Soldiers and leaders, and public relations and advertising venues) directed at a particular place (the neighborhood or civil leader). The plan fails to consider what "product" is being "sold" and at what "price to the consumer." Others have also noted the importance of considering the relative cost of supporting U.S. operations.[11] A good way to clarify the nature of the Army's "product" is to think of the U.S. mission as a "brand" that will bring certain benefits to the target audience if the audience chooses to buy it.

The U.S. Mission as a Brand with a Cost

In marketing terminology, a brand is the summary of all perceptions about products, employees, the organization, and so on that marketing creates. According to Professor Terry Paul, "A strong brand is more the result of good marketing, rather than the cause of good marketing."[12] A brand makes a promise to consumers, and companies must be obsessive about fulfilling such promises. The United States already has a strong brand name among people all over the world (who have strong perceptions about it, good and bad). The U.S. military must understand those perceptions and work to capitalize on its brand's strengths while marginalizing its weaknesses. In civilian marketing circles, this is viewed as "leveraging a brand."[13]

Leveraging the U.S. brand in a military operation can take many forms. We could extend the brand in the form of U.S.-sponsored organizations such as security forces or civil engineering firms that have their own identity but are consistently supportive of the promises of the U.S. mission. When doing this, though, we must keep in mind that just as corporate reputations can be damaged by their associates' actions, so too can the U.S. mission be jeopardized by affiliates that act in ways inconsistent with American promises.

When possible, U.S. forces should partner with civilian or government organizations that have already established their own credibility within the region, including nonlocal governments that have a better reputation than the United States does. And finally, the United States could license its brand to other organizations that support U.S. operations or ideals. For example, a store owner who allows minorities to shop in his store could be a licensee and receive a Coalition forces' (CF) storefront ad and a government supply contract for his cooperation.

In marketing, product price is an important consideration. The price associated with a particular brand indicates how the brand compares with competing brands in quality and status.[14] A skilled marketer is aware of the competing products a consumer might choose to support. While the U.S. brand might offer many benefits, its cost might be too high. In Iraq, for example, the cost of supporting the U.S. brand through its extensions, partners, and licensees is potentially death. Information operations, like marketing, must find a way to sell a product with such a high cost. An effective plan might include messages that point out the costs versus the benefits of supporting each product, that compare the relative cost of the U.S. brand to other brands (for instance, the terrorist brand), and that appeal to the consumers' desire for a prestigious product. In order to succeed in marketing the high-cost U.S. brand, one must understand the customer's perceptions and goals.

Understanding the "Customer"

An information operation can be viewed as selling a mission (such as the U.S. presence in Iraq) to the local population. Just as a sound marketing strategy must first comprehend the target market, or customers, successful IO must begin with understanding the people it is attempting to affect. For the military, civilians and business leaders are analogous to household consumers and business buyers. The household consumer is typically concerned with only his household and is significantly more emotional in his decision making. The business buyer or civil leader represents an organization and consults with experts and associates. Both buyers balance the benefits of cooperating with multiple entities. In pursuing their goals, leaders and locales might consort with both the United States and its enemies. However, they will do business with neither if it is not advantageous to them.

A significant shortfall in military operations continues to be insufficient knowledge about the local populace and how to influence it. Combat units and intelligence sections in the 1st Armored Division and 3rd Infantry Division deployed to Iraq with country studies printed before 1991 for Operation Desert Storm.[15] These studies included only general population information. Well-developed information about tribes, such as their motivation, leaders, interrelationships, or even general locations, simply did not exist.

Successful marketing campaigns begin with thorough research to identify consumer trends. Just as military intelligence spends much of its time assessing the many facets of threat organizations, we must make a greater effort to collect usable market data about the IO target population. At a minimum, this includes identifying market segments and their leaders, their goals, motivations, expectations, and daily rituals. While it would be time and manpower intensive, conducting surveys and cooperating with successful marketers in the region could make the difference between advertising successes and colossal backfires. Assessment of the consumer must also continue over time to track changes in the market.

Successful marketing campaigns draw on emotions, and strong brands have good stories. Psychological studies have shown people to have much better recall of details when they receive information in a story format.[16] The story provides a framework for learning and is easily transferable. Even in Western societies people rely more on their own personal networks of family and friends than on traditional media for acquiring information about ideals and purchases. In the United States, the average person shares a bad experience with at least twenty-five other people. This phenomenon is amplified in Muslim societies, which rely even more on story-telling traditions.[17] Unfortunately, stories and emotional appeals that apply to consumers in the United States are often obscure, confusing, or have the reverse effect in other cultures. Finding the right story and the right people to deliver it to is critical.

Touch Points and Consistency

Everything an organization does conveys a message, and to varying degrees, the message content depends on the source and the recipient. Thus, salesmen must prioritize their efforts so they communicate the right message to the right person. Key points where an organization interacts with its customers are known as "touch points."[18] By analyzing the needs of the local population, we can identify intrinsic touch points (interaction with patrols) and civilian-initiated touch points (public service complaints). While IO should maximize the effectiveness of planned, military-created touch points (ads, news releases, public announcements), only consistent communication and proper Soldier behavior will positively influence spontaneous touch points. The latter are particularly important, because in the eye of the public, they often define deployments.

Just as sound strategic thinking applied consistently from design to communications to sales is essential for strong branding, so consistency, sensitivity, and creativity are the keys to gaining and maintaining credibility in military operations. Consistency generates positive relationships; a unified outward image reflects an organization's internal stability. Consistency must be maintained at both tactical and strategic levels. At the tactical level, messages directed at the same target audience should have the same style and tone. For example, in two communications, one targeting potential insurgent recruits and one targeting active guerrillas, both should discourage resistance. The potential recruits might be shown a message of hope and prosperity while the active guerrillas receive a message about the futility of resistance, but both messages should still have a similar personality, positioning, and identification. They would be tactically tailored but strategically alike.

Information operations are not trivial undertakings for an Army operating across a large area populated by a diverse people. Even when higher echelons have personnel who can draft a strategically consistent plan, the separation between them and the marketplace where subordinate units' work often results in ineffective or out-of-synch messages. For example, a battalion in Kosovo was unexpectedly flooded with local nationals demanding construction aid that had been promised on television, but the battalion had not been funded or equipped to conduct the construction. Moreover, it first heard of the plan from the locals.[19] The higher echelon's failure to coordinate with the unit on the ground decreased the effectiveness of the IO campaign and reduced the legitimacy of that coalition's effort.

The challenge of achieving consistency makes some decentralized IO planning and execution necessary and requires higher skills at lower echelons. Adjacent units developing separate messages and operating procedures can confuse local citizens, who view all Soldiers as the same "U.S. brand." IO planners must consider the effects of their messages on many different consumers and ensure a message at one level or in one area conflicts as little as possible with messages at other levels in other areas. Sending contradictory messages or making promises that cannot be kept undermines credibility.[20] Such was the case when the international media promised Iraqis security and stability that local forces were not able to provide. The Iraqis' bad experiences with looting, shootings, and kidnappings were reinforced by anti-U.S. marketing messages that emphasized the illegitimacy of the CF campaign. The result was a lack of trust in Coalition messages. The Abu Ghraib prison scandal has also been skillfully exploited by opponents of the United States in many ways. One example was dressing hostages in orange jumpsuits to mimic U.S. treatment of detainees.

Media Planning and Execution

The Army has long employed mass media (radio, print, and limited television) in support of operations, but like commercial marketers, the Army should begin to move away from mass media to niche media. With technology, messages can be tailored and made interactive, which should reduce the risk of delivering conflicting messages to consumers. Information operations should use new forms of communication. A prevailing misperception is that Third World societies are ignorant of or have no access to multiple media sources. In fact, they have come to distrust mass media outlets because of their control by the state. Interactive Internet sites and free CDs or DVDs can carry messages to identifiable targets and allow two-way communication between the organization and the target.

An IO campaign must begin with understanding the target market. Most parts of the world perceive the United States as headstrong, pro-big business, dangerous to local cultures, and pro-Israel.[21] This reputation is not an insurmountable hurdle, but it must be taken into account. Recent history provides many examples of successful companies that had poor public images but still grew and succeeded (for example, Halliburton, R. J. Reynolds, and Wal-Mart).

Many believe the West can solve all problems with ease and efficiency. Such an expectation can undermine U.S. legitimacy. Trust rapidly deteriorates when the public does not see action and results. Iraqis see the failure to quickly solve local problems as proof America does not intend to solve them rather than evidence of their difficulty. What this reality demands is a quality IO or marketing communications plan that is integrated, introspective, interactive, and imaginative—a plan more expansive and complex than current military staffs can generate or supervise.

Insurgents Capitalize on IMC

To illustrate how successful integrated marketing communications (IMC) can be developed with much more thought than resources, consider the recent IO campaign waged by insurgents in Iraq. In July 2004, National Public Radio (NPR) reported on the use of DVDs and CDs by insurgent groups to increase public support, recruiting, and funding: "Intended to appeal directly to average Iraqis, insurgents are bypassing the mainstream media and using compelling forms of direct marketing. Videos depicting insurgents on the attack, wounded Iraqis (apparently collateral damage from U.S. aggression), and hooded Abu Ghraib prisoners are overlaid with patriotic and religiously motivating music and chants. Earlier versions of these products were very crude, but in recent months, the production quality has increased to that of a professional, broadcast level. Integrating combat cameramen into their operations, they demonstrate experienced use of cameras and listening devices. While a more experienced military observer would notice crude tactics and skill demonstrated (firing wildly, poor weapons maintenance, and small unit tactics) on the part of the armed insurgents, these are not readily apparent to the target market, which has been termed the 'Jihad Market.' Money and recruits from Iraq and abroad follow performance and success, and here it is apparent that success in the information campaign is much more important than real tactical combat success."[22]

Since the beginning of the occupation in Iraq, the United States has attempted to run its own IO campaign using traditional media (flyers and U.S.-funded television and radio networks). Unfortunately, the NPR report also illustrated the breadth of mistrust Iraqis have for traditional media outlets: "Because the truth has been denied to Iraqis for so long, they are now searching the Internet for truth. A taxi driver stated that he stays away from [news] websites that are sponsored by foreign governments, the news media, or insurgent groups. He states that it is simply 'hard to find [a] reliable source of news.'"[23]

With such skepticism running rampant in the Middle East, a large window of opportunity is open for a powerful marketing campaign using alternative media. It could have a tremendous effect.

Understanding marketing is critical to understanding the strengths and limitations of U.S. Army information operations. More important, the art and success of IO as a marketing application come from skilled, impassioned practitioners. The Army should acquire skilled marketing professionals by contracting with U.S. companies, by co-opting the best local national counterparts, or by providing marketing training for military IO practitioners.

While information operations have parallels to the business world practices of marketing, promotion, and sales, the military has much more at stake than quarterly earnings. The IO mission is so crucial and complex it deserves the most skilled marketers the United States has to offer. Selling the United States in current and future deployments is of paramount importance. Without proper planning and resourcing of the IO mission, much effort, and many lives, will be wasted on diminished successes, or even failures.

19

Religion in Information Operations: More Than a "War of Ideas"

—*Pauletta Otis, Ph.D.*

The subject of religion and how it "plays" in terrorism and warfare has been the single most problematic, complicated, sensitive, volatile, and debated subject in the current Global War on Terrorism. Anyone dealing with security and defense policies in the Middle East knows that religion plays a role at the tactical and strategic levels and that it cannot be ignored.[1]

Yet, the efforts to "deal with" religion (Islam, in particular) have often been inaccurate, inconsistent, and inadequate. This indictment has been leveled at the Defense Department, State Department, and even the American public. Some go so far as to say that "U.S. efforts are seen as naïve, lacking understanding of the Muslim world and [being] off target at best and dangerous at worst."[2]

Prior to the events of 9/11, religion was talked about in rather hushed, apologetic tones in the Department of State, the Department of Defense (DOD), and the Intelligence Community almost as if it were an embarrassment. The command and staff colleges did not have any courses that addressed the subject of religion and warfare, academics working for DOD were not focused on religion, and even the best of strategic analysis and intelligence professionals were not prepared to take on the topic. The information operations community was almost blindsided by the criticality of religion as it impacted national security.[3]

Although it was generally recognized that religion played a role in warfare, very few people studied that role in its contemporary context and were prepared for the events of the past decade. In the current strategic environment, religion is the topic du jour and has been elevated from playing a role to being a single-factor explanation of all violence—particularly as it concerns Islam. In fact, there seems to be a growing belief that in some way religion is responsible for the current strategic imbroglio around the world.

When the Defense Department had no choice but to take on the idea that religion played a role in warfare, it was unprepared to figure out whether and to what extent religion (i.e., Islam) contributed to terrorism and violence. Understandably, approaches to the subject defaulted to the tools and techniques used in fighting the last "war of ideas"—the Cold War conceptualized as a war against Marxist-Communist ideologies. For Cold War warriors who fought the "ideology of Communism," religion was simply another ideology to be fought in the same way.[4] This came with the assumption that there must be something inherently wrong with an ideology/theology that perpetuated and caused war and terrorism. (The naked, reductionist, simplistic statement was "Islam causes terrorism." Based on that assumption, conceived as "truth," the challenge was how to conduct a war against the idea/ideology of Islam.)

Framing "Islam" as an ideology rather than as a religion has three important consequences:

1. If there is a denial of a Supreme Being, God, or Ultimate Reality, religion loses its unique power.
2. The teleology of the "clash of civilizations" arguments and the "clash of culture" models, however reductionist, becomes the basis for strategic engagement.
3. Most important for the Department of Defense, the idea of predictive analysis becomes moot.

Ideology and theology speak to the meaning of life, ideals, rewards, and penalties, and serve as standards of evaluation of life events. The beliefs of cultural groups and the behaviors of those groups and of specific individuals cannot be predicted on the bases of that framing. Much is lost between the ideal and the actual.

The focus on Islam as ideology by the IO community relied on the assumption that "if we understand the ideology we will understand the behaviors" and that if we change the ideology we can change the behaviors. Ideology was assumed to be predictive—if a person was Muslim, he would act in certain predictable ways consistent with the thinking and teachings of Islam.[5] This implied that the subject matter experts, and the new studies, would be focused on the theology/ideology of Islam. The war of ideas would be based on "competitive theology" or "proving how Islam causes—or does not cause"—violence. The related derivative thinking was that since Islam is primarily based on the Koran and the Koran supports *Sharia* (law) and the law mandates jihad, then all Muslims must engage in jihad.

Therefore, all Muslims are jihadis. Very few people would agree with this raw and unsophisticated analysis, but it seems to be at the core of many current discussions in the IO community.

Other analysts and scholars maintained that Islam had been co-opted by political actors, and others held that individuals misunderstood Islam and its tenets and should be reeducated. Everyone had an opinion however informed or uninformed by fact and analysis. The cacophony of voices became almost overwhelming and remains so to some extent. The consequences of inadequate framing, conceptualization, and lack of precise vocabulary have impeded understanding the message of Islam as a religion.

How can the IO community best address the subjects of religion and terrorism, Islam and violence, and win a "war of ideas"? This chapter will discuss the current ways of dealing with the topic of religion and violence, the results of those efforts, and what religion is and will provide a "power analysis" that can be used in an area of operations to find out how religion factors in the violence and warfare on the ground—both as ideological framing and behavior. It will also provide a short list of suggestions for information operations that may be useful at both strategic and operational levels.

Understanding the message as well as the messenger is a critical, primary concern to IO methodology. Not everyone will agree, of course, as the conversations range from (a) "Islam is responsible" to (b) "Islam is being used by cynical and manipulative political actors" to (c) the violence is only perpetrated by a few "violent extremists" to (d) "Islam as a religion has nothing to do with terrorism—economic and political factors are more important."

Part I: Current Ways of Talking about Religion and Warfare

There have been five major ways of dealing with the topic of religion and violence in the Department of Defense, each with specific consequences:

- Ignore it, although this is tantamount to ignoring the "elephant in the corner" and is done at some risk to life and limb.
- Reframe religion as ideology, that is, as a war of ideas rather than a war against Islam or a war against violent extremism.
- Give it over to the theologians who focus on theology, although few theologians address religious violence and even fewer have suggestions about what to do about it.
- Marginalize religion as a factor used by cynical politicians to manipulate the citizenry—an elitist attitude that basically denies the spiritual and thereby may offend all major religious traditions.
- Engage in mirror imaging with words and concepts that, while familiar and of some use in the study of religion in the United States, are of dubious effectiveness when applied to comparative religion or comparative violence.[6]

This includes the assumption that the American way of handling the secular and sacred will be known and understood and replicated as the "best way."

Each of these reactions—or frameworks for conceptualizing religion and violence—has specific outcomes for information operations strategies. For those who wish to ignore them, IO campaigns will focus on other factors in the area of operations and conceptualize the religious leader as a political force and discount the spiritual dimension of the problem. Those who would frame religion as ideology with a transcendent aspect are stuck trying to construct information operations that are basically religious arguments about "whose truth" is superior. The focus on theology is grand thinking and interesting study but does little to provide specific ideas about how religion factors in contemporary violence. Denying and dismissing the independent power of religion in culture and warfare deprive the community of powerful intellectual tools that could be used to influence religious actors in war-fighting situations. Using content-empty vocabulary when trying to agree on a definition sends us off on tangents, which is a waste of time and energy. Good academic, useful, and systematic definitions have been around for a long time; just because IO planners don't know about them does not mean they do not exist.[7]

Religion Cannot Be Ignored

Religion, as it supports both war and peace, is a powerful force for societies around the globe. If the IO community wants to exert influence in the current operating environment in support of tactical, operational, and strategic interests of the United States, it is critical that the religious factor be understood, analyzed, and properly contextualized. Only then can appropriate measures and countermeasures be undertaken in ways that have measurable impact. This presupposes a sophisticated understanding of the religious factor in violence as well as how religion can contribute to peace and justice.

The information available suggests that religion is a salient factor in armed conflict in the contemporary global environment. This implicates all major religious traditions. Religion plays a specific role in differing types of violence and plays different roles in each stage or phase of armed conflict. There is evidence that the more religion is involved in a conflict the more lethal the conflict (lethality includes measurements of duration, scope, intensity, and severity).

For example, most acts of international terrorism in the 1990s have shown evidence of religious motivation and intent. The genocides of the past twenty years have had significant religious drivers. Groups involved in insurgency warfare are often supported by religious institutions and personages. Even criminal groups, drug runners, and human traffickers are often identified by some aspect of their ethnicity or religion. These facts seem pertinent and apparent in all corners of the globe and encompass all religious traditions to some extent.[8]

Each type of military mission or form of warfare has a religious dimension: conventional warfare and irregular warfare—terrorism, insurgency, ethnic conflict, suicide bombing, and genocide.[9] This implies that each phase and each mission needs a corresponding "religious impact" strategy integrated by the information operations community. This needs to include religious factors when they contribute to violence as well as the potential use of religious factors in supporting peace.

The idea that religion can and does play a role in violence is not a new idea, nor is it a single-factor explanation. What is missing in this era is a sophisticated understanding of how, when, where, and under what conditions religion plays a role in armed conflict and what can we do about it.[10]

Religion as Ideology

Theology is often conceptualized as simply an ideology with God as a default authority, the guiding principal, or the basic assumption on which all authority of the ideology is derived. Theology defined is the part of religion that explains man's relationship to God. This includes ideas about what life is about, reasons for living and dying, and for killing or offering one's life for the good of others, and basic rules for getting along with God and others. Theologians talk about theology, debating and discussing meanings and applications for everyday life. The debates are often long and heated—theology is not a static reified belief system.[11]

Differing social settings expose different theologies; for example, the theology of Christianity is played out in Africa and Germany and the United States in quite different ways. The theology of Islam is played out in Arab countries quite differently than in Indonesia or Morocco. Although the principles may be the same, the behaviors are socially constructed and vary across cultures as a part of local adaptation of theological principles as applied in everyday life. Time and technology also play a role: the early theologians did not have to address the questions inherent in web-based pornography or whether the nuclear bomb was religiously ethical. As times and technology change, the questions asked of theologians change, and different theologians, although subscribing to the same principles, will derive differing conclusions that make sense for their culture group.

Theology becomes belief—often as translated by theologians but always as applied by individuals and societies in behavioral terms. Whether individuals know, understand, and practice in relationship to any given theological system is quite another question. For individuals, beliefs and behaviors are often incongruent. It is obviously an understatement that if we all lived our theology, the world would be a different place. Mohandas Gandhi once made the statement that "[he] would be a Christian if he had ever met one." Hypocrisy is alive and well; most people do not live up to their own ideals, let alone those of a Supreme Being.

The conclusion is that theology is not predictive—i.e., it is not possible to predict either culturally specific adaptations to a theology or individual human behaviors on the basis of a known theological system.

Commonly, military personnel are given a briefing before deploying that explains the theology of Islam and jumps to guidance on how to respect local religious traditions and practices. The chasm between theology and local beliefs and individual behaviors is often ignored. This teaching strategy is arguably less than useful. If not done right, it can and does contribute to further misunderstanding by emphasizing the ideal as opposed to the actual, the reality of local cultural adaptations of theological principles, the changes in theology or emphasis in the message that related to war situations, as well as by producing mirror-image stereotypes.

Having a basic understanding of theology contributes both to a more sophisticated conversation among ourselves about our own religious traditions and to accurately portraying or conversing with those in other religious traditions.

On a side note, if religion is seen exclusively as an idea, as exemplified in the First Amendment to the U.S. Constitution, how can we not encourage the freedom of speech, religion, and the press? These are values that resonate with the American public, and it would be hypocritical if they were not applied on the global scene. Only when ideas or beliefs are acted on and in certain circumstances become violent or criminal do we prosecute in relationship to the behavior, not the idea. It is the violence—or the behaviors, not the beliefs or the free expression of those beliefs—that is at the core of "religious factors" in warfare.

The following chart is illustrative of the idea that ideology frames and informs, that core values from that ideology are drawn by theologians based on scripture and interpretation, and that the resulting beliefs and behaviors are derivative but not coterminous (see figure 19.1). It is not possible to "go in the other direction" and imply that all behaviors and beliefs mirror theology. Theology may provide a "mindset," but the resultant behaviors vary from (a) what individuals and theologians define as "ideal" and (b) how individuals choose to apply those ideas and "codes" in their daily lives. Theology as ideology sets the stage but is not "predictive."

FIGURE 19.1: Ideology to Behaviors

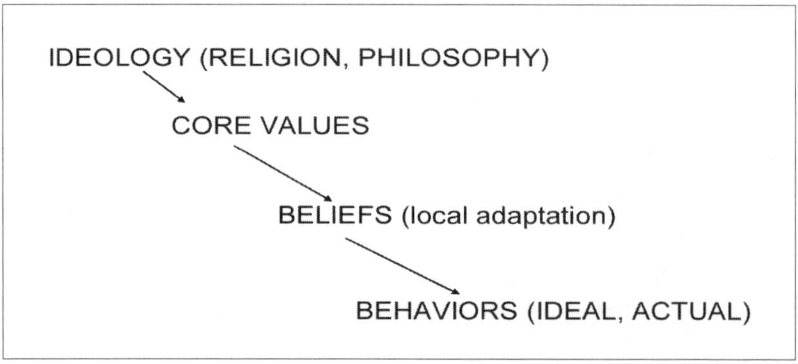

IDEOLOGY (RELIGION, PHILOSOPHY)
　↘
　　CORE VALUES
　　　↘
　　　　BELIEFS (local adaptation)
　　　　　↘
　　　　　　BEHAVIORS (IDEAL, ACTUAL)

THEOLOGY AND POLITICAL VIOLENCE

The emphasis in American theological writing and research as it deals with warfare has focused on specific topics either in relationship to just war theory, pacifism, and conscientious objector status and/or in relationship to a specific type of weapon. The theologians concerned with just war theory have a strong historical, academic, and sound tradition to rely on. Writers concerned with pacifism and conscientious objector status also build on a strong American tradition emanating from the Quaker and Mennonite communities. The writings of the 1960s and 1970s that were concerned with nuclear proliferation were informed and contributed enormously to the public dialogue.

Contemporarily, there are notably very few respected scholars who have taken on the task of writing about contemporary violence from a "religious" perspective. It must be noted that "many have written," but few have appropriate credentials or backgrounds, or at times their intellectual framing of these complex topics has been less than useful. There is a morass of literature about other religions either as apologetics or condemnations of the theology of Islam, but the works tend to be written by individuals with either an "ax to grind" or questionable credentials. Many times the perspective is simply mirror imaging and does little to inform either the public or the military community.[12]

POLITICAL MANIPULATION AND MARGINALIZATION

A statement made daily in the press and as a default when the power of religion is not understood is that "they are using religion for political purposes." This implies cynical manipulation of religion and focuses on the intent and motive of individuals with selfish agendas. There are several problems with this approach; the most basic is that the language of manipulation is inherently insulting. That sort of statement may be a mirror-imaging problem that reflects familiar American problems such as Jonestown massacre, the Oklahoma City bombing, and the financial and sexual malfeasance of well-known religious personages. The statement also reflects only a superficial understanding of the role of religion in culture and society. Religion is inherently a part of identity, language, territory, authority patterns, and economic values. Even assuming that one person could manipulate something somewhere to some effect does not explain why people would follow such a leader.

MIRROR IMAGING

The United States has had an idiosyncratic approach to religion and politics. The United States is a very religious country but one that separates the power of religious institutions from the powers of government. The religion of the U.S. public, the religious statements by political leaders, and the media's use of religious language are known to the entire world. When U.S. leaders advocate a nonreligious secular government for other countries (such as Iraq), it seems hypocritical, unrealistic, and as if we simply do not understand our own system, let alone theirs. In addition, the appropriate use of words is critical for the information operations community. The language used must reflect good hearing, good understanding, and effective response. There are two parts to this problem: how we use inherently incendiary language or carelessly use neutral language, and how they understand what we think of them as a result of that language.

The terms "adherent," "fundamentalist," "radical," "extremist," and "terrorists" are important in that they reflect a requirement to communicate yet also the absence of clarity and definition. An adherent is generally assumed to be a "check the box" kind of person who may identify with a religion or religious tradition by name but whose level of knowledge, information, or behavioral adherence to a given religion is not known. A fundamentalist is basically one who wants the beliefs and behaviors to correspond and is constantly searching for God's will for all daily activities. The terms "radical" and "extremist" could apply to Mother Theresa, Jesus Christ, or Buddha with equal accuracy. A violent extremist could include many fighting against the Inquisition of fourteenth-century Spain and France. The terms themselves are used as shorthand in the military community but are misleading, theoretically slim, and academically unsupportable (i.e., they are political terms). The problem is what word(s) will accurately pinpoint the problem? What is the problem? Is it religion? Is it violence? Is it a combination of the two? What conceptual definitions and analytical framework will lead to better answers?

Appropriate use of terms and categories is important for us and them. If we do not get it right, we can fall into the trap of thinking that we know something that we do not know. And perhaps more important, when we communicate with carelessly used terms, we communicate our ignorance and insult the very community we wish to influence.

An example may be helpful. If we assume that jihad is mandatory for all Muslims and means violence in the name of Islam, and communicate that notion using the term "jihad," we may insult the hearer by not knowing the range of definitions of jihad and assuming that the individual we are talking to is somehow implicated in violence. Either way, it has done nothing to solve a problem and possibly made further conversation useless.[13]

Part II: The Power of Religion—Framing the Issue of Religious Factors in Violence

Most people acknowledge that religion is a two-edged sword. Religion supports the most beautiful and idealistic of worldviews, yet it is often associated with the most tragic situations of maximum human suffering. The principles of faith, hope, and love can be denigrated to cynicism, despair, and hate. That which should support life can support death; that which supports peace can be used to perpetuate war. It is suggested that religion plays a role in all aspects of warfare. It is invariably linked to support for violence and support for peace. The balance between the two is the focus of any information operations campaign.

Instead of addressing religion as a mind-set divorced from the reality of daily life, it would be helpful to see religion as the beliefs and behaviors of a social-ethnic group. Where the strength of beliefs is hard to measure and the effects of beliefs and belief systems are inconsistent over time, the institutions, behaviors, and patterned ways of integrating religion into cultural systems are rather predictable and findable.

Although religious ideas provide a framework for individual relationships within the group, group adaptation to the social and physical environment and identification of threats to group survival also define that group's behaviors. These aspects are clearly seen in a cultural group and identified as identity, territory, language, economics, and authority (politics). Individual and group behaviors are knowable; that is, they can be subjected to examination using historical pattern analysis, variable analysis, and tests of reliability and validity. It brings "religion" down from the transcendent and gives it a human face.

A simple list of the power of religion as pertaining to particular religious communities is suggested. Religious factors are power resources in the sense that religious institutions and leaders control resources, define interpersonal relationships, establish and maintain group communication, and provide expertise.

RESOURCES

The resources of religious personages and institutions include control over goods and services, organizational capabilities, social networks that are community based but may also be global in scope, and various types of support for political personages, agendas, and programs. The resources of a particular religion are a direct result of their numbers, reputation, coherence, and willingness to mobilize for political/religious purposes.

Specifically, churches, mosques, synagogues, temples, and other places of worship may own land, control money and banking, provide a center for social services, supply medicine and health services, manage who is identified as a member by providing burial space for individuals and families, control inheritance through marriage and family law, provide sanctuary for travelers, possess communications technology, be historical repositories of information about individuals and the community, and have individuals who can be human resources deployed for any number of tasks. Resources will be used to support the religious institution itself and the social-cultural base of that religious community.

Two examples may suffice. The *vakif* system in northern Cyprus is grounded in religious tradition and authority. It influences or controls inheritance, ownership of property, social services, marriage, and burial and impacts the social and economic development of northern Cyprus. The Greek Orthodox Church does the same for the Republic of Cyprus. Both impact the population in very real ways—not at all reflective of theology and with only the practical power of religion in a social-cultural context.

In another example, one of the first signals of impending violence in the Croatia-Serbia conflict was the ethnic cleansing of cemeteries by church authorities. The use of the symbol of the Ustache cross in Croatia, a Christian symbol, is another example of the power of religious symbols quite divorced from theological principles.

INTERPERSONAL

Religion is an important power broker in human relationships. Religion helps define the attributes of a good and trustable person; prescribe rules concerning how individuals transact social, political, and economic business; and identify friend and enemy according to a set of traditional and legitimate factors. When states fail, or particular political personages are de-legitimized, religious personages often help define who, when, and under what conditions a new political leader will emerge. Most important, religious authorities are also assumed to be in touch with the power of a Supreme Being and therefore have special insight concerning social relations among God's children.

Religious leaders are often m*ore believable* in failed or fragile states than political leaders are and therefore have power above and beyond the sheer strength of numbers or observable resources. Religious leaders, as force multipliers, have significant social-cultural power and are able to affect war and peace more than is commonly recognized. Both on the U.S. side and the other side, religious leaders must engage the topic of peace and use their inherent power to move toward a more peaceful world in order to be constructive.

COMMUNICATION

Religion provides for common language and means of communication between members of a group. Religious leaders communicate with authority, generally have written and spoken expertise, have access to media, and know significant music, poetry, and art forms of nonverbal, symbolic communication. Historical languages often provide a sense of continuity and may be used to motivate or in symbolic communications. Religious personages and institutions are often deeply involved in the education of children and the training of future generations. Parents rely on religious educational and medical institutions when the state fails to provide those resources. Religious leaders are often accustomed to keeping confidences or secrets and are trusted for their discretion.

EXPERTISE

Religious authorities have expertise in many areas above and beyond that of the general population. They generally have an in-depth knowledge of people, places, and communities. They know the sensitivities of the community. They know the personal history of leaders and their families. They move easily in a community and have access to areas off-limits to others. Quite literally, they know where the bodies are buried. In a very real sense, religious personages and communities know more about food, water, and health than others in the community. They are the individuals people go to when all else fails. A leader is not a leader without followers: it is important to investigate who follows and why.

THE CHANGE DYNAMIC

In addition to this flat analytical framework, it is important to follow through with the questions of how religion factors into current warfare in the area of operations. One of the ways to analyze religious factors in conflict is to go directly to the form of violence and try to identify the specific religious content over the stages and phases of a particular conflict situation. In the preparation for war, religion contributes to the identify of friend and foe; in the heat of battle, religion contributes all of the power resources available as well as solace and sanctuary; and near the end of conflict, religious personages and ideas contribute practical social suggestions as well as theologically based peace-making strategies. These can be usefully fleshed out by the information operations professionals assigned to a particular zone of warfare.

Part III: Information Operations and Religious Factors of Warfare—The Contemporary Case of Islam and Christianity on the World Stage

Here is the problem: we have become so wrapped up in theology and endless disputations that we have forgotten the core and context—warfare. If the Department of Defense wants to be a Department of Theology, there will be something of a problem. Addressing the factors of religion that contribute to violence and warfare needs to be the primary focus.

If the information operations community wants to inform, influence, persuade, and change perceptions, a few tried and true measures are suggested.[14]

INFORMATION

The Positive: The first premise for the information operations community is that information is important. Information, as facts, as perception, and in context, provides the groundwork for any strategic influence campaign. The focus is on the usefulness of information. For the military community, it is always the "so what" factor.

With regard to religious information, it is important to understand both the theological big picture and the nitty-gritty, on the ground reality. Theology is useful, but the analysis of religious power at the ground level provides useful, actionable information about the role of religion in a specific place at a specific time.

The Negative: Do not assume that people know their theology any better than you know yours or that all Muslims know the theology behind the idea of jihad any more than all Christians know the theology of baptism.

Do not assume that they are more religious than we are or that religion permeates daily life in Islamic countries more than it does in the United States. That statement does not bear the scrutiny of facts or logic. The numbers alone would decry the statement: 1.3 billion Muslims and 1.5 billion Christians are enormously differentiated by their culture, society, religious practice, belief systems, and individual understanding and behaviors.

UNDERSTANDING

The Positive: We try to understand because it shows the ability to hear and to listen to the needs, wants, and articulated demands of others. It also shows good will and a desire to understand the other, reflects good intentions, and basically provides a basis for all other communication efforts.

The Negative: Understanding broad theoretical concepts is useless unless we know how to apply those concepts in policy and daily practice. Understanding can be shorthand for wanting information in order to manipulate, change, or otherwise demean the other. This is easily identified in conversation and is insulting and counterproductive.

Note that understanding can also contribute to not liking as much as accepting the other. Sometimes when we truly understand people we like them less. It is the same with religious personages and religious powers: the understanding may lead to revulsion and rejection. Nevertheless, understanding will provide a basis for communication and action agendas.

COMMUNICATION

The Positive: There is an old adage that "God gave you two ears and one mouth to be used in that proportion." Hearing *and* listening to the heart as well as the language is the basis of all good communication skills.

Hear meaning. Language alone does not provide communication, because in any language, words are meaning laden in both a linguistic sense and in a social context. For example, the word "friend" is easy to define and maybe to translate, but in a variety of settings for a variety of meanings, its use becomes a communication challenge.

Volume and tone are as important as the words. The same words spoken differently have different meaning. Volume generally implies importance or immediacy but may also just mean that the speaker does not believe he can be heard because of noise, deafness, or inattention. The tone of voice varies culturally and by gender, age, and status—all enormously complicated. When communicating with religious leaders (hearing and speaking), the volume and tone are as culturally significant as the words themselves as these aspects will add believability and credibility to the language capability. For example, a minister, priest, rabbi, or mullah may be in the habit of speaking loudly to reach the crowd or in the habit of speaking with low volume in order to have individuals move toward him or her both physically and emotionally.

Communication is integrated. Both listening and speaking happen at the same time. As we hear both words and meaning, we translate in the context of our own words and meanings within the range of our experience and learning. This is complex and annoyingly imprecise. When this is further complicated by a tendency for religious communities to teach by analogy or storytelling, it takes on an incredibly complex cultural context. The use of ancient poetry by Kurdish insurgents to indicate future targeting sites is an example of knowing language but needing to know analogy.

Communication includes relational posturing. This means that communication is never between equals. One will be speaking, implying an obligation on the part of the other to listen—a power dimension of communication that is often ignored. Just speaking itself is a power statement. Acknowledging this by the use of silence, or waiting for the other to speak and exert social relational power, is important to maintain at least the perception of status equality. An example is the length of sermons: the obligation of being and listening is controlled by the religious speaker. Americans tend to be time sensitive and will commit less time to sermons than people in many other cultures will—a clear indication of religious power or lack thereof.

Communication about religious ideas and behaviors is often place dependent. In the United States, we tend to talk about religion in private venues or religious structures but not in the professional workplace or in educational institutions. It is important to acknowledge that the place for talking about religion differs by religion and by country. It is not considered discreet, for example, to talk about Islamic religious theology in a social or political context wherein Muslims are persecuted minorities; neither is it appropriate to talk about Christian communities in places where to do so would put them at risk.

Communication that focuses exclusively on religious theology without acknowledging the other factors that concern people is narrow minded. For example, in an area of human insecurity, such as Darfur, to focus on the Islamic nature of the violence while ignoring government repression, economic injustice, environmental devastation, and human cupidity is heartless and inhumane.

Communication needs to focus on the good, positive, and contributing aspects of religion as well as the negative. Religious leaders, institutions, ideals, ideas, and related behaviors can be valued, reinforced, and used to support the good, the peaceful, and the well intended.

The Negative: As with understanding, communication can have serious negative consequences. When accurate communication takes place, it may lead to less, rather than more, helpful consequences. If an individual communicates the intent to destroy and ravage a village, we may understand why and the communication may be clear, but the consequent reaction is to immediately prevent the violence.

Specific Suggestions

- To engage the moderate, the middle, and the lukewarm in religious terms does no good. Logically, those in the middle does not want to be engaged for a variety of reasons or they already would be. In addition, the middle may not consider the machinations of international politics to be any of their business (i.e., they are not responsible for the few and those who would demean the "real Islam"). In the case of the 9/11 attacks, the Department of State reports that Muslims from countries all over the world (with the exception of Libya) went to U.S. embassies to sign books of condolence. There is a tendency for journalists to report news but not the middle's everyday occurrences. This contributes to a biased perception on our part. The idea that is if we did not see it, it must not have occurred.
- Remember that religious leaders operate differently from political leaders. They do not have authority separate from a Supreme Being. This means that individuals who do not believe that a religious leader represents God will defect. Religious authority emanates from the bottom and from the "God level"—not as political or military power. Charts that assume hierarchy are inherently flawed.
- In the same vein, religious decisions are community based through consensus type decision making regardless of the religion or the congregation. This reflects the idea that real authority and responsibility are between God and man.
- Do not assume that gender practices are religiously grounded; often the culture, history, tradition, and practical accommodations have more explanatory power. Ranked relationships between genders in public and private life are known in all societies.
- Engage at the tactical and operational level with the "positive" in mind. The religious communities desire survival and security. They will help, contribute, and cooperate without regard to theology as long as their interests are maintained.
- Show respect. The first of the commandments for Christians, Jews, and Muslims indicates a requirement to love God and keep His commandments, which include loving others as you love yourself. . . . This was not framed as a request.

The information operations community has few individuals with significant intellectual training and scholarship on religious factors as related to contemporary warfare. The scholarly community has not contributed significantly in this area until the past several years, and this research is important but insufficient for DOD. The theological community has, for the most part, assiduously avoided international relations and warfare and focused on the spiritual. The U.S. Chaplaincy, the only DOD element specifically charged with being knowledgeable about religion and warfare, is understaffed, underfunded, over tasked, and underutilized as a source of subject matter experts.

There is precious little research that probes religious violence on a global scale and tries to find commonalities and differences in types and forms of violence in relationship to religious ideology and power. Most of the work has addressed Islam specifically and as such is subject to the mirror-imaging problem of dichotomous studies. Since 2004, various scholars have contributed parts and pieces to the available body of literature. The community needs to fully exploit these resources to better understand and respond to the current challenge.

I suggest a focused effort on religion and warfare on the part of the information operations community. It is a subject that is poorly understood, under researched, and often handled rather clumsily in spite of the good intentions. The volatility and sensitivity of the subject should mandate that the subject be handled in the most sophisticated way possible and not by "flavor of the month" or "instant" experts, however smart, intelligent, and well positioned. Specifically, a group could be tasked to find or conduct research that would give the community a solid base of information, frameworks for analysis, a lexicon for discussing religion politely and usefully, and an outlet for additional research that would contribute to any strategic information campaign in a more sophisticated way.

20

Telling the Afghan Military Story . . . Their Way*

—LTC Charles W. Ricks, USA (Ret.)

Several times a week, a Soldier from the Afghan National Army (ANA) hops on a bicycle in downtown Kabul and delivers press releases to news media bureaus within the city. When the weather is bad, he accomplishes this mission on foot. For Americans and other outsiders, this rather primitive distribution system reinforces a perception of backwardness, but it is a mistaken perception.

The Afghan Ministry of Defense (MOD) Office of Parliamentary, Social Relations, and Public Affairs employs limited technology mostly when it is necessary to alert reporters to breaking news, to invite them to an unscheduled news conference, or to respond to questions.[1] In Afghan culture, face-to-face contact and the personal delivery of information are more consistent with social expectations.

By contrast, the military public affairs staffs of Combined Forces Command-Afghanistan (CFC-A) rely on e-mails, cell phones, faxes, or other high-tech communications devices that provide immediacy but, ultimately, limit the direct human contact central to Afghan culture.

Other important differences exist in the assumptions that drive the emerging Afghan public affairs (PA) system. For instance, Afghan military leaders are often more open to the news media than outsiders expect them to be or are themselves. Afghan officers have been known to organize internal video and still-photograph crews to follow them and document what they are doing.[2] Operational commanders

---

* *This essay appeared in the* Military Review, *March–April 2006, and is reprinted by permission.*

regularly interact comfortably with local news media to provide information.[3] Such openness is all the more unexpected knowing that in 2001 two Al Qaeda terrorists posing as reporters assassinated the prominent Afghan resistance leader Ahmad Shah Massoud.

American public affairs officers (PAOs) will also be surprised by the absence of any wall between MOD-generated news and the civilian media. In Afghanistan, the MOD controls news about the military; its stories move seamlessly between military-run media and Afghan National TV, radio, and newspapers. That does not happen in the United States.

The unaware PAO will be confounded, too, by some of the simple facts of life in Afghanistan: only about 20 percent of the population is literate; TV penetration is limited to major cities; radio is the primary mass communications medium; and tribal, village, and religious leaders are the most respected sources of information for the average citizen. Radio and community relations are the primary techniques for reaching the Afghan people. No credible nationwide public opinion surveys exist.[4] Such an unfamiliar environment demands tailored information policies and procedures, but too often we assume that modern PA techniques that work elsewhere will work with equal effectiveness in Afghanistan. They do not.

In Afghanistan, conducting stability operations is an adaptive experience. At least in public affairs, the complaint that Afghans "are not doing it right" usually means that they are not doing it our way. Our way is not necessarily or even usually the right way. Those who train Afghan PA personnel must understand this basic fact if they wish to lay the foundation for effective systems development and mentoring. Would-be mentors must resist the urge to interfere with the natural evolution of Afghan PA systems and avoid forcing Western information solutions into an unfamiliar Afghan environment. As we have begun to understand that, we have made substantial progress in helping to improve Afghan PA capabilities.

The Afghan PA System

In January 2004, the MOD PA office consisted of a single person: MG Mohammed Zahir Azimi, the official MOD spokesman. As of fall 2005, Azimi's staff numbered thirty-three PAOs, with an additional twenty-four in the five regional corps and the Kabul Military Training Center.

As with any PA structure, developing institutional credibility is essential. Azimi and his growing staff come from a variety of operational and information positions within earlier MOD structures. Some were mujahideen resistance fighters; all were well known and respected within the defense establishment. In fact, Azimi is often called on by President Hamid Karzai to help with specific projects.

Information accuracy and message consistency are particularly essential in Afghanistan, where public trust has been shattered in the past. Delivery is important too. To provide information to a population that lives primarily in rugged terrain and isolated villages, the MOD must use techniques that mix traditional social interaction with developing broadcast, print, and Internet technology. In such an environment, the bicycle messenger becomes understandable as a bridge between old and new.

Do Not Do It for Them

Afghan PA structures, policies, and procedures have evolved as a result of collaborative workgroup meetings involving Afghan PA leaders and a PA mentor from the Office of Security Cooperation-Afghanistan; however, the Afghans make final decisions about the way ahead. Their investment in systems development and their ability to adapt quickly contributed directly to PA successes.[5]

CFC-A must stand back and allow the Afghans to operate. If it does not, it risks getting in the way. In August 2004, provincial unrest forced Karzai to deploy ANA Soldiers to conduct stability operations. The MOD PA put together a media coverage plan and invited reporters to go along. When this initiative conflicted with CFC-A PA and information operation plans, Afghan PAOs were replaced and different media transported.

Confronted with a similar situation in Herat a month later, the MOD acquired its own aircraft from the national airlines and transported Afghan PAOs and news media to the scene. What had been negative reporting about the situation by reporters hundreds of miles away in Kabul improved dramatically once the MOD gave them direct access. The MOD's effective independent initiative noticeably affected the Afghan people's perception of events.

Another example of misdirected help involves writing styles. Afghan culture relies heavily on an oral tradition. Even the simplest tales take the form of epics told over and over. Those who can write frequently adopt the complexity of oral communication, which is referred to as flowery or literary language.[6] Western advisers, however, often encourage the Afghans to abandon their writing style in favor of the compact techniques Americans favor. Such a change would have no value.[7]

During the presidential election process, PAOs from CFC-A and the NATO-led International Security Assistance Force (ISAF) translated English talking points into Dari words and handed them to Azimi to read to reporters. The problem is that English words translated directly into Dari do not automatically form Dari thoughts. Azimi, his interpreter, and the reporters were confused by what he was trying to read. Azimi abandoned the effort and returned to developing his own messages to support the operational information available to him from Afghan, CFC-A, and ISAF sources. From then on, his presentations were prepared in Dari from the beginning and were consistent with familiar Afghan language structures. As a result, they were credible.

As these anecdotes reveal, one of the strongest temptations advisers face is the urge to step in and accomplish PA tasks for the Afghans using Western techniques. Generally, if outsiders try to help, the Afghans will step aside and allow others to do it, thus learning nothing. Such an outcome limits their ability to take over

PA responsibilities, undermines the reform process, and requires continued outside intervention to sustain artificial performance levels. The question becomes, How long do you want to be here? The longer outsiders perform the tasks Afghans should be doing, the longer outsiders will have to remain to perform those tasks and the Afghans will learn fewer skills. It is at once logical yet difficult to accept that Afghans will conduct PA operations in ways unique to their culture. For instance, their news conferences are typically fluid events with reporters continuously moving about, shifting microphones, and ganging up on questioners for pictures. The apparent chaos is comfortable for them. We, on the other hand, try to organize and control the news media—a practice that runs counter to Afghan culture.

Except for special situations (most often involving security for the President), the MOD usually does not participate in media control efforts, although it will allow outsiders to herd reporters around during an event. But control efforts can backfire. The most disturbing example involving outside media control took place at the presidential inauguration on December 7, 2004. Except for a few photographers organized into pools, reporters were locked inside a cage consisting of a large tent surrounded by a ten-foot-tall fence draped with flags and banners to prevent media observation. Armed guards at a narrow gate further prevented free media access and coverage of the event. These were not Afghan decisions. Imagine how the Afghans perceived this approach, which was completely inconsistent with even the strictest security precautions they employ.

Gauging Success

One of the toughest PA challenges is to measure the success of the operation. In an environment as unfamiliar as Afghanistan's, this is even truer. An immediate goal of the Afghan PA effort has been to develop an information system that will cause the Afghan people to trust the ANA and its international allies more than they fear the Taliban. But how does one credibly measure progress in such an endeavor?[8] One of the first ways to measure progress is to develop a series of unconventional metrics based on an awareness of Afghan culture and recent history. For example, children flying kites, young girls going to school, music playing openly on the streets, and burkhas replaced by scarves reflect a strong confidence in the prevailing security environment. Under Taliban rule, all such activities were banned, and violators were severely punished. If the public lacked confidence in the ability of the Afghan government and its allies to maintain security, such activities would not occur as often as they do.

Commercial districts in Kabul are going through a dramatic upgrade; modern storefronts are replacing openings in mud walls. Such investment is an encouraging sign. Sidewalk and street repairs, though still rare, also demonstrate a sense of optimism brought about by an evolving confidence in the security environment. Admittedly, these indicators are subtle and rather inconclusive and are nowhere near as dramatic as battlefield victories, but they can help decision makers and the public measure success.

To these subtler measurements, public affairs officers can add more quantifiable, somewhat less equivocal metrics to assess operational performance. An example of this is the number of references to MOD information cited in news stories. Information given to news media is meaningless if it is not published in a story. Today, even the most superficial reading of in-country news clippings and Internet search engines reveals an increasing number of direct references to the MOD, especially after the weekly news conference. Of course, the numbers are situation dependent, but generally, if the MOD is involved in an event, its information and messages receive a strong hearing in the national and international news media.[9]

The number and quality of MOD-managed special events and special subject news briefings are other viable metrics. The MOD has been quite active in this area, running numerous events and briefings in which senior MOD officials discussed their achievements, such as:

- The ANA's improved status, featuring Chief of the General Staff GEN Bismullah Khan
- Legal reform, including implementation of a military nonjudicial punishment system
- New personnel accession and promotion systems, including the conduct of a mock promotion board
- MOD officer education
- The establishment of the National Military Academy of Afghanistan
- The completion of the militia disarmament program

VERIFIABLE OPERATIONAL SUCCESSES

The results of individual events and programs go some way toward helping assess the overall effectiveness of a PA operation. Not only was the MOD's aforementioned initiative to give PAOs and reporters direct access to Herat in September 2004 a clear victory on the ground at the time, it also suggested that the ministry had reached a particular level of competence and autonomy. In fact, Azimi's plane lift of PAOs and reporters is only part of the Herat story. The MOD also implemented a community relations program to help calm unrest in the province. The program set up meetings to introduce the new provincial governor to community and religious leaders province-wide.

Gaining the support of local leaders to help restore order was one measure of success; another was the extensive coverage given the meetings by regional radio, TV, and newspapers—coverage that reflected a broad PA effort to inform the Afghan people about the state of security within the province. Azimi's personal management of this effort benefited from his Herat roots and his experience as a resistance fighter in the region.

The Presidential Election

The first-ever Afghan presidential election, in late 2004, offered a great opportunity to evaluate the effectiveness of MOD's PA team. On August 29, 2004, then-Minister of Defense Fahim Khan issued a proclamation through Azimi at the weekly news conference affirming the ANA's neutrality in the upcoming election and pledging to secure all aspects of the election process, including polling sites. This democratic theme was pursued during subsequent news conferences and public statements. The MOD also conducted a six-week presidential election information program that focused on those weekly news conferences, and Azimi presented sixteen security briefings to the national and international news media covering the election.

Ultimately, Azimi was able to assert the effectiveness of the MOD's election security efforts (shared with the Ministry of Interior, CFC-A, and ISAF) during his briefings to reporters at the UN's Media Results Center, where he assumed the role as the only briefer for those organizations. Perhaps the best indicator of the MOD's information reach came from UN spokesman Manuel de Silva, who announced on October 21, 2004, that 1,245 members of the news media had registered to cover the election. Seven hundred of those were Afghan; the balance represented eleven other countries.

Voter Turnout

With the Taliban promising to kill voters at polling stations throughout the country, the MOD's PA office instituted an information program to emphasize the ANA's commitment and ability to secure the election. The message obviously got through, as some 70 percent of registered voters participated.[10] As an additional benefit, in the days before the election the Afghan people reported suspected terrorists to security officials, who made important arrests and averted major attacks.[11]

Unplugging the "Taliban Spokesman"

Several individuals regularly contact the news media claiming to speak for the Taliban. They take credit for any mishap that occurs and often concoct tales of battles never fought and casualties never inflicted. Their comments used to go unchallenged and were printed verbatim. Not any longer. Now, Azimi regularly reminds the news media on the record to contact him before printing Taliban claims. He also collects examples of what he considers to be inaccurate or irresponsible reporting and periodically goes over those stories during weekly news conferences to set the record straight. Western public relations practices frown on Azimi's very public corrective measures, the conventional wisdom being that such corrections call attention to stories best ignored.[12] In most cases, however, that is nonsense. It has been a long process, but by the spring of 2005, the Afghan news media had, for the first time, begun to include comments about the unreliability of reports from the Taliban spokesman. That is a clear success.[13]

After the February 2005 Kam Air crash, the worst aviation disaster in Afghan history, in which one hundred people died, a Taliban spokesman launched a series of false messages, including the odd claim that many, if not all, passengers had survived the crash on the mountain peak but that the government was ignoring their cell phone calls for help. Sadly, many believed this. But, as weather allowed, Azimi transported reporters and photographers to the crash site to establish conclusively that no one could have survived the violent impact. He also reminded the public that the crash site was on an 11,000-foot-plus mountain, that snow depths reached five feet and more, that Soviet land mines littered the area, and that the snowstorm that led to the crash had continued for many days. Once the bodies were recovered, MOD-initiated coverage of their return to their families confirmed the care taken during the entire operation.

Tsunami Relief

The tsunami that struck Southeast Asia in December 2004 gave the MOD an opportunity to help that further enhanced its standing. Karzai deployed a twenty-person planning and medical response team with relief supplies. GEN Suhaila Siddiq, an ANA surgeon, led the team, which also included a MOD journalist. The team received a lot of positive publicity, including a ceremony at the main ANA hospital in Kabul that marked its departure and two well-attended news conferences. The team also received extensive news coverage that found its way back home. Although its return was overshadowed by the air-crash recovery efforts, a recognition luncheon hosted by Karzai once again brought the team's effort to the attention of the Afghan people. This operation boosted the MOD's and ANA's credibility both nationally and regionally.

The Newsweek Riots

In May 2005, rioting ignited by *Newsweek*'s allegations (later retracted) of U.S. military desecration of the Koran presented a major challenge for the Afghan government.[14] Many people were killed or injured, Korans and other cultural treasures were desecrated, and mosques, libraries, and other public buildings were destroyed. Azimi responded decisively with three central messages:

- Blame those directly responsible for the mayhem: the rioters themselves and their organizers
- Support the U.S. military by affirming that the behavior portrayed by *Newsweek* was inconsistent with Afghan experience of U.S. troops
- Criticize *Newsweek* for irresponsible reporting.

The riots also marked the first time that Azimi allowed members of his staff to speak on the record for the MOD during a crisis. Azimi is gaining confidence, and the MOD PA's effort is gaining depth.

Life Is Not (Always) a Good News Story

In Afghanistan, ignoring bad news is not possible as it recovers from a quarter century of warfare and 2.5 million deaths. Afghanistan is a rugged place in which to survive.[15] Fortunately, Afghan PA systems have not succumbed to the "good news story" obsession. Instead, the fledgling MOD PA system has successfully managed many difficult issues and situations, including disarmament of the militias; public sparring with Pakistan and Russia; civil unrest in Herat, Jalalabad, and elsewhere; the air crash; daily combat operations; and the presidential and parliamentary elections.

As with any democracy, the effective, responsible practice of public affairs is essential to building public awareness, understanding, credibility, and support. Afghanistan is a young and vulnerable democracy whose leaders are attempting to apply useful communications models learned from others to their own situation. Do they sometimes adopt Western PA practices? Yes, but not so often as to make outsiders comfortable; thus, there is the temptation to interfere. The words of T. E. Lawrence about his experiences in Arabia, adapted to Afghanistan, provide a friendly reminder to outsiders seeking to help: "Do not try to do too much with your own hands. Better the [Afghans] do it tolerably than that you do it perfectly. It is their war, and you are to help them, not to win it for them. Actually, also, under the very odd con-ditions of [Afghanistan], your practical work will not be as good as, perhaps, you think it is."[16]

The practice of using an ANA Soldier to deliver news releases on a bicycle will surely not long survive the reliable performance of emerging technology, but that change, like introducing PA policies and procedures, should come at a pace comfortable to the Afghans themselves. And although many difficulties remain, indications are that establishing a democratic Afghan defense organization is on course. That story, with all of its components, must be told loudly and clearly—by Afghans. That will continue to be the most effective way for keeping the people informed about the progress of their military and government.

21

Army IO Is PSYOPS: Influencing More with Less*

—*COL Curtis D. Boyd, USA*

The purpose of this chapter is to briefly examine some of the root causes of the ongoing fracture of Army information operations (IO) in general and the dysfunctional friction between IO and the various Army agents of influence, in particular, psychological operations (PSYOPS) and public affairs (PA). The chapter will provide an overview of Army PSYOPS today and possible constructs for tomorrow, suggest steps to mitigate friction or fracture between the subelements of IO to assure a greater unity of effort, and recommend the development of a strategic communications framework built on media and broadcast expertise secured by a culturally attuned and regionally aware cadre of professionals.

In both war and peace, success in the battle for hearts and minds hinges primarily on one side's ability to operate comfortably in the other side's human terrain. In such an emotionally charged, competitive communications environment, the ability to affect the psychological and informational battle space of the adversary and the local population depends on the credibility of both the message and the messenger. Historically, the Army's PSYOPS branch has been the U.S. military's principal foreign communications agent of influence. Using words and symbols, Army PSYOPS has coordinated and executed influential actions and information programs specifically aimed at affecting foreign perceptions, behavior, and thought processes for longer than half a century. As a result, Army PSYOPS as an institution

---

* *This essay appeared in the* Military Review, *May–June 2007, and is reprinted by permission.*

has long consisted of a career force specially trained and equipped to formulate and conduct operations to inform and influence while using ideas and images to shape an adversary's attitudes and perceptions.

PSYOPS has subscribed to the rule that words alone are not the only motivator of changes in perception, attitude, or behavior. Moreover, psychological operations are coordinated to synchronize with the influence potential of kinetic actions or the intended effects of the more deliberate and obvious military activities. Apart from PSYOPS, the U.S. military has, over time, developed an array of agents of influence with (non-kinetic) niche capabilities that also shape the perception and decision making of foreign neutral, friendly, and adversarial target audiences. These agents include specialists in deception operations, computer network operations (CNO), operations security (OPSEC), and electronic warfare (EW), as well as other related activities, such as civil affairs (or civil-military operations) and PA.

In the 1990s, the Army introduced a new functional specialty, IO. Ostensibly, the IO career field was created to better organize and integrate the aforementioned disparate agents of influence, which were widely perceived to be operating more or less independently and without sufficient integration and synchronization into an overall operational planning and execution scheme. Regardless of good intentions, IO has struggled to establish a legitimate presence in the Army and is still in the process of defining its mission and role within the context of planning, organizing, and conducting coordinated military information operations. Additionally, during this difficult developmental period, IO has generated a great deal of friction between itself and the various agents of influence that have well-established, clearly defined, and fully integrated roles in force protection, information management, public communications, and so-called influence operations.[1]

Distinguishing between IO and PSYOPS Roles

Army IO doctrine, as defined by the Combined Arms Center (CAC), Fort Leavenworth, which is currently rewriting it, and joint doctrine describe IO as the integrated employment of the core capabilities of EW, CNO, PSYOPS, military deception, and OPSEC in concert with other specified supporting and related activities (such as civil affairs, PA, Combat Camera, and, when appropriate, combat operations).[2] The collective purpose of IO synchronization is to inform, influence, deter, degrade, deny, or disrupt adversarial human and automated decision making while protecting our own.[3] Under the current paradigm, PSYOPS is a subelement of IO on a par with the other subelements noted above. Under the Army IO doctrine rewrite, CAC proposes to reassimilate four subelements of IO into the core staff (deception to G3, operations; EW to fires; CNO to G2, intelligence, and G6, information management; OPSEC to G2), leaving PSYOPS and the related activity PA (with Combat Camera) as the only subelement(s) to be coordinated and integrated by the IO staff officer.

The apparent intent of the new IO construct is to redefine Army IO not as a collection of actual operational capabilities (as in joint IO doctrine), but as a "niche-knowledgeable" staff integrator responsible for reconciling only the differences between PSYOPS and PA targets of information or influence. Unfortunately, with this move the Army has accidentally created unnecessary and potentially dysfunctional overhead at the coordinating staff level. The Army IO staff officer might only plan, organize, and direct how PSYOPS will create psychological effects against an enemy or targeted foreign population—tasks that were formerly done by the PSYOPS staff officer or supporting tactical PSYOPS unit. Likewise, the Army IO staff officer will coordinate PA activities, both foreign and domestic—here again an assignment Army PA officers and noncommissioned officers (NCOs) have been performing without issue until now.

The proposed changes to Army IO doctrine would eliminate any hope of maintaining a clear distinction between IO and PSYOPS (and now possibly PA). Army IO will become a simple, single-niche integration activity of only one agent of influence—PSYOPS. Fundamentally, Army IO will become an extension of PSYOPS and possibly PA. While PA (like civil affairs) is doctrinally considered an IO-related activity, PA has serious concerns about associating itself directly with IO. Operational and policy restrictions complicate PA integration by IO staff officers, most of whom lack the expertise to perform PA-specialized tasks and functions. Additionally, the association of PA with activities known to employ deception or to use selective information or images to influence perceptions (i.e., PSYOPS) is generally forbidden. In the event that the association between PA and IO becomes common knowledge, PA will risk damaging the integrity, truthfulness, and credibility of the sources and content of its messages. For years, long before the advent of IO, the integrity of the PA message was protected by unofficial coordination between PA and PSYOPS professionals without incident or ill intent. So where or what is Army IO's niche, regardless of doctrinal change? And is it smart to dismantle the current Army IO doctrinal model when military operations are becoming more joint and full spectrum?

Potentially, IO could ensure more potent and precise use of the elements of information operations in support of PSYOPS themes and objectives. Army IO might also serve as a functional area or the next step in a more sophisticated and coherent Army career-force approach for former PSYOPS and PA staff officers. Moreover, IO could be categorized as a military operation (like urban operations, Military Operations on Urban Terrain), planned, synchronized, and directed by the PSYOPS branch officer. In the end, CAC's proposed doctrinal concept has oversimplified IO to such an extent that IO is de facto or fundamentally PSYOPS, at least at the tactical level. While our war fighters at corps and below require a greater ability to inform and influence audiences in their areas of operations than they do the means to degrade adversary communications or computer networks, Army IO still requires an ability to remain fully capable and interoperable in a joint, interagency, or multinational construct.

The Roots of Confusion between IO and PSYOPS

Confusion over the IO coordination scheme is not just a product of the current doctrinal oversimplification of Army IO at CAC; it is likely symptomatic of self-defeating PSYOPS tendencies as well. Unfortunately, in the current sociopolitical environment, PSYOPS has devolved into a pejorative term both inside and outside our military. This is evident in the careful avoidance of its use by senior military and defense officials when publicly discussing activities aimed at influencing or informing enemies or foreign audiences. IO has been widely adopted as a euphemism for PSYOPS. Consequently, the term "IO" is now commonly and erroneously used to discuss activities that are, by doctrine, PSYOPS. For example, unified combatant command theater security cooperation plans now routinely use IO synonymously for PSYOPS to describe regional security information programs, activities, and exercises with other nations, thereby wrongfully categorizing what should be PSYOPS capabilities, themes, messages, and actions in the theater plans as IO.

The practice of mistakenly describing PSYOPS activities as IO now permeates the Army's institutional lexicon. So thoroughly inculcated is this misuse of terms that it is now common to hear the military's most prominent leaders, including most flag officers, senior Pentagon officials, and others, routinely and improperly use "IO" and "PSYOPS" interchangeably. For example, retired MG David Grange, former commander of the 1st Infantry Division, has written that in Bosnia he used IO and PSYOPS interchangeably.[4] Similarly, in his recent book *Plan of Attack*, Bob Woodward points out how then-Defense Secretary Donald Rumsfeld referred repeatedly to PSYOPS as IO while describing leaflet drops and Commando Solo broadcasts as IO preparation weapons against Saddam and his cronies.[5] In another example, Nathaniel Fick, author of *One Bullet Away*, the story of his experiences as a Marine platoon leader in Iraq, stated that as he and his recon platoon crossed into the southern portion of the country, nine out of ten Iraqis surrendered without fighting. He contends it was the result of an "intense *IO* campaign that dropped leaflets and broadcasted surrender appeals from HMMWV mounted loudspeakers."[6]

Such misuse of terms is prevalent in the IO community itself. For example, in an article published by 1st IO Command, the author argues that everything the Army does that fails to fit neatly or categorically elsewhere—which includes PSYOPS—is information operations.[7] Unfortunately, this misuse of terminology masks the fact that IO planners cannot actually do PSYOPS—they do not have the training, or the operational experience, or the authorities, or the organic capability. If IO staff officers want to plan employment of PSYOPS capabilities for an operation, they must requisition the services of personnel assigned to one of the Army's three PSYOPS groups. How then can PSYOPS continue to be referred to as IO?

In contrast, a case could be made that the Army's PSYOPS branch—which possesses organized units from team to brigade composed of branch officers, NCOs, and junior enlisted specialists with appropriate equipment, linguistic ability, regional expertise, and experience in the art and science of foreign influence—could easily and readily assume most, if not all, of the so-called IO coordinating functions. As a subelement of the traditional C3/J3/G3, the PSYOPS officer and/or NCO could logically assume the principal duty of staff coordinator for the other elements of IO tasked with achieving a desired influential effect using the other elements of IO to informational and psychological advantage. We would spare ourselves the involvement of another intermediate staff element—in this case, one with minimal practical experience, specialized training, education, and understanding of the influence mission—that degrades the speed and accuracy required to deliver a timely and relevant message to a foreign target audience.

In any case, the unfortunate consequence of using PSYOPS and IO interchangeably is confusion about the proper role of each specialty. The near-universal misinterpretation that IO is PSYOPS has also had the unfortunate tendency to raise expectations among commanders about the capability IO practitioners (i.e., staff officers) can actually deliver. For supported commanders and their staffs who envision the robust operational capabilities described by their newly anointed IO staffers, IO's inability to deliver credible and timely messages to audiences in the supported commander's area of responsibility has perpetuated frustration and disappointment.

To mitigate such perceptions, PSYOPS and IO must form a single, unified capability to maximize the Army's potential to speak with one voice. The status quo cannot prevail, for in the near term, PSYOPS and IO tensions will not be reconciled, nor will the potential for PSYOPS, PA, or strategic communications scoordination be maximized. It is inevitable that under the current construct, the Army might begin to view IO as duplicative, an unnecessary redundancy that increases neither the speed nor the accuracy of our military message. Moreover, an additional tactical staff coordinator adds little value to PSYOPS, PA, or the other IO tools and techniques that might add potency and precision to the psychological-influence message or method.

Efforts to raise concerns about the operational utility of IO (i.e., questioning what value another layer of staff supervision and management actually adds) have not been well received. Somehow, all seem content to potentially establish another staff layer in an already robust "transformational" headquarters—despite PSYOPS/IO comparisons and analyses of staff actions and critical tasks that clearly point to redundancies and inefficiencies. A strong contributing factor to the apparent intransigence is the fact that PSYOPS expertise is not well represented at Headquarters, Department of the Army. Additionally, there is an ongoing shortage of company-grade PSYOPS officers at the tactical and institutional levels; the combined active and Reserve force fill for captains is less than 30 percent. The result has been misrepresentation and a lack of understanding about a capability critical to our Army today and in the future. A strong case can be made to reexamine the number of authorizations for IO and PSYOPS staff officers and NCOs across our Army to fully appreciate the redundancies and inefficiencies of two career forces competing for similar assignments and performing many of the same functions (e.g., at what level do we need a specialist in PSYOPS or a generalist in IO?).

Given its limited resources, PSYOPS actually can and does accomplish a lot. PSYOPS assets habitually task organize to give commanders the maximum capability possible in terms of media development skills, analytical talent, foreign language expertise, cultural knowledge, linguistic skills, marketing techniques, and broadcast means. These capabilities can serve as the core component of an Army IO career force and an information campaign to introduce U.S. ideas and images into the hearts and minds of foreign enemy, friendly, and neutral audiences.

Currently, such is the general satisfaction with PSYOPS' performance and contributions to the Global War on Terrorism that, despite known limitations, PSYOPS has become DOD's recognized single-source "one-stop shop" for analysis, media development, production, and dissemination of tactical- and operational-level information intended to engage, inform, and influence foreign audiences.[8] Lessons learned from operations in Iraq and Afghanistan repeatedly echo the need for more PSYOPS forces, as well as a greater ability to culturally and linguistically influence the local populace with ideas, images, and information consistent with U.S. political and military goals and objectives.[9] Likewise, Defense Science Board studies (2000, 2001, 2004, 2005), PSYOPS master plans (1985, 1990), and a National Defense University study (2004) mirror the same point: we lack sufficient force, capabilities, and authorities to inform and influence to an adequate degree foreign populations when and where we desire.[10]

PSYOPS by Necessity

Despite concerns by some regarding the appropriateness or legitimacy of military involvement in global PSYOPS or strategic communication efforts, others see such as a necessity, essential given the lack of capability or willingness by other departments of government to fill the communication void. PSYOPS expertise is regionally, culturally, and experientially based; it has skills and knowledge uncommon among the other agents of influence. Jerrold M. Post, a highly regarded scholar of the psychology of terrorism, contends, "There has been little attention to the potential of strategic PSYOPS in undermining the enemy to prepare the battlefield. . . . PSYOPS should be the primary weapon in the war against terrorism." According to Post, if terrorism is an inherently psychological phenomenon, then it should stand to reason that psychological operations would and should be a primary method of attack or defense at the global planning level.[11] Since the Global War on Terrorism is less a shooting war involving guns, boats, or planes than a psychological war involving ideas, images, ideologies, information, and intentions, the first and most essential condition is to shape or prepare the psychological battle space in a manner favorable to our intentions, an effort to which PSYOPS is integral. To this end, the

U.S. Army must regain the psychological advantage, retain the informational edge, and keep its message straight.

Owing to the sheer magnitude and scope of the information and influence effort, PSYOPS units can no longer be trained and equipped in a one-size-fits-all proposition. The PSYOPS force has only recently undergone a major realignment, the result being that the two Reserve PSYOPS groups formerly under U.S. Army Special Operations Command (USASOC) have been reassigned to Army Reserve Command (USARC). (The Army's only active group, the 4th, remains under USASOC). The PSYOPS branch must now differentiate between active- and Reserve-component tactical, operational, and strategic levels of foreign media operations and public communications; and between conventional, special, and interagency operations.

The active-duty PSYOPS force is uniquely suited to support special operations and sensitive operational- and strategic-level foreign information and communication programs. Reserve-component forces should assume the other mission of predominantly providing support to the conventional Army (from brigade to corps level) and reinforcing active-duty PSYOPS efforts consistent with mission and intent. Although the pairing of active-duty PSYOPS with special operations and Reserve PSYOPS with conventional forces should vastly increase the capabilities, scope, impact, and effectiveness of foreign-aimed communications programs and dissemination potential, the new paradigm prompts a reexamination of PSYOPS doctrine, organization, training and education, leadership development, matériel and equipment, personnel management and force development, and facilities (DOTLMPF) authorizations to ensure full operational effectiveness. Additionally, the distinction between PSYOPS and PA operations at different levels must also be reassessed, keeping in mind that:

- The specialties of PSYOPS and PA are mutually supportive in today's information environment, with policy and law in place that sufficiently protect the rights of American citizens.
- PSYOPS and PA have complementary talents and techniques similar to foreign relations, media operations, public communications, mass communications, marketing, advertising, sales, and public relations directed toward a foreign target audience.
- Tactical PSYOPS engages in media production, development, and dissemination in partnership with foreign PA detachments (active and Reserve).
- Operational-level psychological operations leverage IO and interagency tools and techniques to engage early, often, and accurately.
- Defense and interagency information programs must coordinate without friction.
- Strategic-level communications expertise must be harnessed to engage and influence states and macro cultures.

Given that two-thirds of the PSYOPS force (and PA expertise as well) now resides in the Army Reserve, we must also consider rebalancing the force, creating active-duty brigade-level authorizations, and reviewing proponent-led accessions, training, and retention strategies. Inevitably, a future strategic communication framework must account for tactical PSYOPS and/or PA as the basis for "information for effect" that assimilates the skills of foreign journalists, videographers, and broadcasters with the talents of regionally experienced PSYOPS specialists into foreign media operational constructs. These constructs would be supported by more specialized PSYOPS regional and operational support sufficient to bridge the cultural gaps between U.S. and foreign target audiences and work the information seams between potentially neutral and friendly target audiences.

Finally, PSYOPS' image must be rendered more acceptable so that it can be employed effectively in current and future information environments and strategic communication frameworks. The branch must lose its pejorative connotations both inside and outside the Army. References to it must simply roll off the tongue; it should be easy to mention and talk about. To rehabilitate PSYOPS will require "total Army" participation.[12] The active-Reserve realignment of the PSYOPS force cannot be allowed to widen the gap between message developers and disseminators.

More generally, partnership among organizations responsible for strategic information development and dissemination has become a necessity rather than a good thing to do if convenient. If information is central to our ability to shape the future battlefield or geopolitical landscape, then unity of informational effort and purpose is vital. Moreover, doctrinal concepts of unconventional warfare and counterinsurgency, which critically rely on the ability of PSYOPS and PA to inform and influence audiences across the globe where we have a presence and where we have none, are notably central to our ability to succeed in the Global War on Terrorism. Therefore, PSYOPS, PA, and public diplomacy stovepipes or firewalls must come down, and collaborative bridges must be built. PSYOPS must leverage the full potential of IO tools (information applications), tactics, and techniques to maximize the influence necessary to isolate and eliminate aggressive non-state actors and transnational threats. We can no longer afford mistaken identities or dysfunctional relationships among PSYOPS, DOD public affairs, State Department public diplomacy, and IO.

While some useful initiatives (e.g., realignment) are already under way, the realities of the foreign communication challenges we face demand even greater Army structural and organizational change. Such change should place at the center of campaign planning the integration of nonstandard special and conventional PSYOPS-like forces able to operate across the continuum of warfare (peace to combat and back to peace). These forces must be precisely designed and efficiently echeloned to function and integrate informative multimedia operations at all levels of war. To achieve such capabilities, an amalgam of PSYOPS and PA professionals would provide the required depth. Such a team would comprise a more transformational, better-focused "inform and influence" investment; would ensure greater assimilation of pertinent skills (PSYOPS, IO, and PA); and would enable increased collaboration with both public and private sectors.

Information Mania: The Army's Persuasive Partnerships

Given the recent realignment of Army Reserve PSYOPS forces from USASOC to USARC and their re-designation as conventional forces, the timing is ideal for a formal reevaluation of the relationship between IO and PSYOPS. Now that two-thirds of the PSYOPS force works for the conventional Army, PSYOPS should be more fully integrated into Army-wide planning, programming, exercises, and operations. Likewise, the increased presence of PSYOPS in Army formations should greatly facilitate its effective synchronization with the Army's other key agents of influence, public affairs and civil affairs. This can only be good for the Army in both the short and long term. In contrast, the suppression and/or complication of the use of PSYOPS and other information activities caused by the redundant IO staff proposed by future Army IO doctrine would be detrimental to the Army in part and to the credibility of the PSYOPS and PA message as a whole.

The proper, untrammeled employment of PSYOPS and its supporting agents of influence can provide the Army greater effects across the entire continuum of conflict and add greater full-spectrum potential to the Army's brigade combat teams. It can influence the psychological and physical aspects of the battle and information space in a manner that could lead to success in the Global War on Terrorism. There is no reason to consign ourselves to a less responsive, less efficient capability.

PSYOPS Merger

As they are currently configured, the IO and PSYOPS forces are improperly balanced. PSYOPS has greater tactical potential than the other four subelements combined (EW, CNO, deception, OPSEC). The other subelements of IO—minus PSYOPS—tend toward greater operational- and strategic-level presence and potential. Not surprisingly, PSYOPS has the fewest assignments on staffs and in agencies at corps and above that are critical to the Army's effort to communicate consistently with foreign audiences anywhere, anytime.

Inevitably, there is a disparity between the planners (IO) and operators (PSYOPS). If the operational environment changes and our threat becomes more or less symmetric, so too must the IO force adapt, rebalance, or assimilate into the tactical war fighter structure to ensure operator-level confidence and responsiveness consistent with the scheme of maneuver. Understandably, the Army would want more operators than specialty planners; however, the way the IO force is configured, the ratio of planners to operators is skewed. There are simply too many planners and perhaps not enough operators.

Another problem caused by the IO force configuration is that it almost works against the creation of expertise in the IO ranks. Commanders and their primary staffs must engage in capabilities-based planning, in the course of which subject matter experts or branch officers must accurately represent the capabilities they bring to the table. This accuracy is crucial to ensuring that intended effects and outcomes can be achieved. But functional-area-designated IO staff officers (planners) responsible for planning and integrating IO capabilities (operators) at all levels are not necessarily well qualified in any one of the IO subcomponents. Thus, PSYOPS, EW, and CNO practitioners are often subordinate to planners or IO generalists less knowledgeable, experienced, or qualified in the capability (or capabilities) they are employing.

This imbalance is a feature unique to IO; tactically, our Army employs "fully qualified" branch officers and senior NCOs who are specialists in the field (subject matter experts) capable of planning, organizing, and directing the execution of capabilities they are uniquely familiar with and knowledgeable about. The Combined Arms Center's proposed changes to IO doctrine seem to address this inequity by returning the responsibilities for planning and integrating the capabilities of the IO subelements (minus PSYOPS) to experts elsewhere on the staff.

Under the proposed doctrinal revision, the minority IO staff officer will be the integrator for PSYOPS and possibly PA. Accordingly, we must have a more practical and pertinent framework from which to launch a professional career force dedicated to the tactics, tools, and techniques used to inform and influence. The underlying rationale for reformulating the IO construct has everything to do with doing more and planning less, the intent being to provide the war fighter a ready, responsive, and reliable IO capability that has the capacity to inform and influence combatants and noncombatants in the commander's area of operations. A more appropriate model would show that PSYOPS might be more useful tactically (at the brigade combat team level) than are the other elements of IO. It would also show that there is no great intellectual leap required to add the other elements of IO, as supporting efforts, to a more potent and persuasive PSYOPS effort.

Accordingly, figure 21.1 reorients the IO model and sets PSYOPS as the base for Army IO, forming the tactical "foreign media operations" center of attention and main effort at corps and below. The other IO subelements offer greater effectiveness if employed as supporting efforts along the PA and PSYOPS axes of inform and influence. Furthermore, the figure portrays the more practical and precise method of employing PSYOPS and PA as the Army's agents of inform and influence both today and tomorrow. IO practitioners or generalists, absent education and experience in either of the two disciplines, will lack sufficient credentials to contribute effectively and credibly to this mission.

These officers without credentials might find themselves assimilating into a future Army career force that encompasses the talents and techniques of PSYOPS and PA, which could conceivably engage in unencumbered foreign media operations. PA and PSYOPS are converging as the means and methods of informing and influencing foreign media and populations become remarkably similar and necessarily mutually supportive. Thus, the more pristine PA aimed at

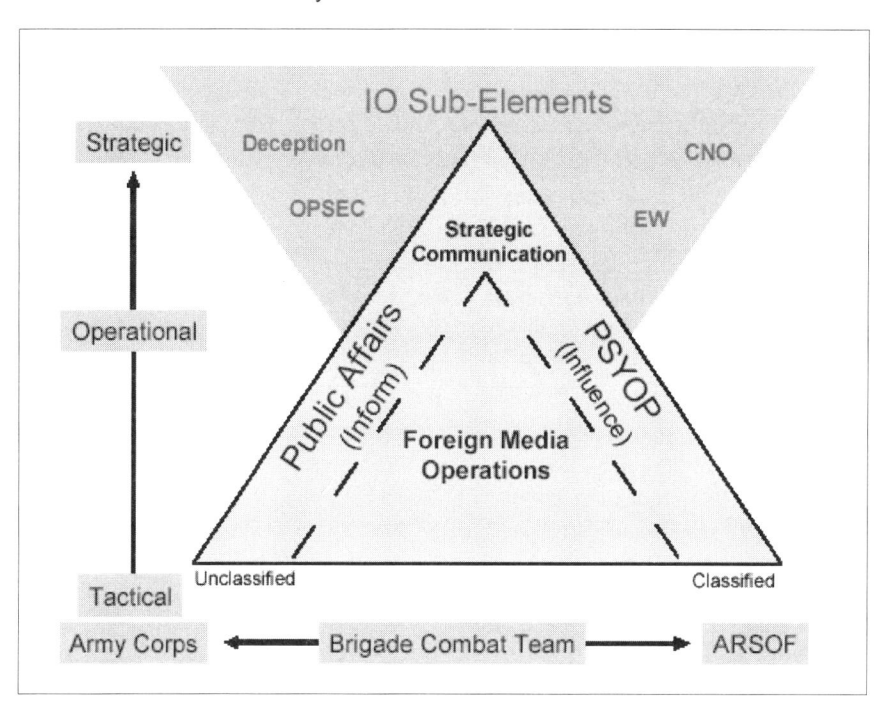

FIGURE 21.1: A Better Way to Do IO Business: PSYOPS and PAO in the Lead

domestic audiences is delineated on the left (to inform) and the more sensitive, more compartmented PSYOPS is at the right (to influence).

Meanwhile, both PA and PSYOPS professionals find themselves specialists in a career force committed to speaking with one voice in a manner that is consistent with the commander and national interest and intent. In the figure, the two career fields converge at the triangle's pinnacle, "strategic communication." There, each field's "most qualified" officers will compete for service at the highest level as our Army's preeminent communication professionals.

Last Word

Going forward, we will need to reevaluate the IO and PSYOPS assignments in every brigade combat team and maneuver headquarters, as well as in the Department of the Army, Training and Doctrine Command, Strategic Command, Joint Forces Command, Forces Command, the several combat training centers, and elsewhere. We must ensure that Army PSYOPS has a fully sufficient structural, cultural, organizational, and institutional presence to be a successful combat multiplier and peacetime contributor now and in the future.

To achieve such influential capabilities, we need to secure a strategic communication framework from the bottom up based on the policies, processes, principles, and practices of psychological operations and public affairs. We must also incorporate into this framework the skills, talents, and tradecraft of public relations and marketing and advertising specialists with foreign culture and language expertise to complement the analysis, planning, and integrating talents of seasoned veterans from a career field that understands and can communicate our nation's interests and objectives. The focus of this DOD "strategic communication framework" would be foreign audiences only.

Ultimately, to better employ PSYOPS and PA in the future means we must invest now in an "IO" career force, one that is an easily recognizable and dominant feature on an operational road map that employs all the military's information weapons. This force must have a strong, active psychological and analytical base capable of operational preparation of the psychological, informational, and multimedia battle space. It should be reinforced by a similarly well-educated, knowledgeable, experienced, and expert Reserve force. PSYOPS, in support of the maneuver commander, disseminates information that appeals to the masses, generally to inform rather than influence. Meanwhile, PSYOPS in special operations performs discreet and potentially classified missions. Designed to influence with potency for personal effect, special operations PSYOPS purveys more sensitive, more protected, and precise information to affect foreign target audiences of operational and strategic significance.

From tactical to strategic, one active-component group and two Reserve-component groups proudly identifying themselves as PSYOPS will continue to deploy to inform and influence target populations in support of U.S. operations. In OEF, OIF, and elsewhere in the Global War on Terrorism, as well as on hundreds of foreign deployments supporting unified combatant commanders elsewhere around the world, PSYOPS teams, companies, battalions, and groups will be present to make an informative and influential difference.

Current and pending doctrinal and structural problems aside, DOD has recognized the importance of PSYOPS to the Army of the future. PSYOPS, the ability to favorably influence foreign audiences with information at the right time, place, and intensity in the "war of ideas," is perceived favorably within our military. Approved manpower increases that will double the active-duty PSYOPS force and increase the Reserve component by one-third indicate DOD's confidence in PSYOPS' ability to play a critical role in the Global War on Terrorism. Furthermore, the establishment of PSYOPS as an official Army branch is a clear signal that we understand the importance of being able to influence foreign audiences with information and actions—two means that will promote U.S. interests and reduce the risk to American Soldiers well into the future. With so much at stake, we should be sure not to squander this considerable investment of the Army's resources in dysfunctional and redundant staff practices. PSYOPS is the Army's IO force of choice—an expeditionary, full-spectrum, interagency-capable, joint interoperable, and proven competitor in today's complex information environment.

22

Estimates, Execution, and Error: Losing the War of Perception in Vietnam, 1960–1973

—*Col Eric M. Walters, USMC*

> The campaign plan and strategy must be adapted to the character of the people encountered. National policy and the precepts of civilized procedure demand that our dealings with other peoples be maintained on a high-moral plan. However, the military strategy of the campaign and the tactics employed by the commander in the field must be adapted to the situation in order to accomplish the mission without delay.
>
> —*U.S. Marine Corps,* Small Wars Manual[1]

Perception management and the war of ideas have long been recognized as common currency in conducting effective insurgency and, for the challenged government, counterinsurgency warfare. Additional problems surface within alliances involved in counterinsurgency as the clash of social, political, economic, and cultural goals conspire against unity of effort. Certainly such difficulties plagued combined American and Republic of Vietnam (RVN) efforts against the National Liberation Front (NLF) insurgency and the external interventions and support from the Democratic Republic of Vietnam (DRV), particularly in the years 1960 to 1973.

While there were many target audiences that Washington and Saigon sought to influence, the crux of the war lay the with South Vietnamese people, particularly the rural component. While the eventual outcome was not decided by an NLF "massive uprising" in the South but by a DRV conventional offensive, nevertheless the only way for the allies to win was for the South Vietnamese populace to successfully defend themselves. International public and political opinion certainly mattered in the war, but the central battleground was in the rural villages south of the seventeenth parallel. The Communist goal was to win just enough loyalty to ensure an effective shadow government to rival the Saigon bureaucracy. The objective of the allies was to maintain the political sovereignty and territorial integrity of the Republic of Vietnam against any Communist depredations, whether mounted internally by the NLF (labeled the "Viet Cong" [VC] within South Vietnam) guerrillas or by People's Army of Vietnam (PAVN) regulars of the DRV.

Major allied strategic errors in estimating the causes of the conflict, in executing pacification programs within South Vietnam, and—most important—in ignoring contradictions within the social nature, political/economic structure, and agendas of the ruling Saigon body politic subverted attempts to successfully influence populations that the NLF contested. This chapter briefly examines the causes and effects of such allied dissonance, best exemplified in the policies and programs in the war of perception.

Errors in Strategic Estimates

> In accepting [an intelligence] assignment in Saigon [in 1964], I had mistakenly assumed that from that vantage point my analysis of the situation might be more effectively heard in policy deliberations than if I remained in Washington. For years I had been told that my views were not as credible as those expressed by authorities in the field. . . . As it turned out, being in Saigon had no effect on the credence given to my analysis. It seems that message itself was the problem, not the messenger. . . . Some people I met with suggested that in Saigon I was probably "too close to the trees to be able to see the forest." Only in Washington, I was told, could one see the big picture.
>
> —*George W. Allen,* None So Blind [2]

Fatal to success was the failure of both Washington and Saigon to either form or act on accurate strategic estimates. Given flawed understandings of the causes of the conflict and the nature of the war itself, it is no wonder that execution of RVN and U.S. strategy against the Communists left much to be desired.

The Saigon ruling clique never recognized the indigenous Communist movement in South Vietnam as anything other than Hanoi's partisan arm. It could not accept that there were disaffected segments of the RVN population, genuinely fed up with the blatant inefficiency and rampant corruption of the Saigon government.[3] Saigon leaders could not attempt to solve problems in the countryside that they did not believe existed and—given the class and religious differences between the rulers and the ruled—there was never any motivation to seriously investigate the matter.

Regarding the United States, the Kennedy, Johnson, and Nixon administrations were continuously judging the situation in Vietnam as part of a larger geostrategic international Cold War equation. They viewed the Vietnam problem purely as part of a global effort led by the Soviet Union to undermine the free world. Containing such aggression was the key tenet of U.S. foreign policy and it is within this premise that the U.S. government always judged the Indochina situation. There was also the failure to act on available knowledge concerning the true nature of America's ally against Communism—the RVN government. Even before the anti-Diem coup in November 1963, the need to reform the Saigon government was apparent to U.S. observers.[4] After Ngo Dinh Diem's murder, this view continued in a number of channels both inside the RVN and the United States.[5]

As early as 1965, General Westmoreland composed an analysis for Secretary of Defense Robert McNamara, saying that final victory would not be through American effort but achieved through a strong government of Vietnam (GVN). His initial diagnosis, however, argued that the war would not be over quickly and that the GVN was too weak to win the counterinsurgency without major assistance.[6] Secretary McNamara would make a similar assessment in the summer of 1966:

> By and large, the people in rural areas believe that the GVN when it comes will not stay but that the VC will; that cooperation with the GVN will be punished by the VC; that the GVN is really indifferent to the people's welfare; that the low-level GVN are tools of the local rich; and that the GVN is ridden with corruption.
>
> The U.S. cannot do this pacification security job for the Vietnamese. All we can do is "massage the heart." For one reason, it is known that we do not intend to stay; if our efforts worked at all, it would merely postpone the eventual confrontation of the VC and GVN infrastructure. The GVN must do the job, and I'm convinced that drastic reform is needed if the GVN is going to be able to do it.[7]

Despite this clear-eyed assessment of the problem by senior defense and military leaders, the implications were too difficult to grapple with while executing the counterinsurgency strategy at the highest levels within the national capitals to the lowest levels in the field.[8]

Errors in Execution: U.S. Policy toward Saigon
Despite acknowledging the need for GVN reform at nearly every level with the U.S. governmental bureaucracy—both inside and outside the military—the machinery of American political diplomacy was unable to effectively encourage or even coerce

it.[9] On occasions where corruption was brought to light, the political tendency at the highest levels was to ignore it.[10] And while Secretary McNamara provided an accurate estimate of the GVN's systemic problems, he could only recommend in 1966 that better management and more efficient allocation of resources were the answer![11]

Even President Nixon, who should have been freed of such concerns given his "Vietnamization" program, was caught in the same dilemma of maintaining global credibility in helping a sovereign nation allied with the United States and, in the process, continuing to prop up unpleasant political realities within Nguyen Van Thieu's South Vietnam regime. Ousting Thieu as the United States had done to Diem was not seen as helpful to an RVN government faced with taking charge of the war and in portraying it as a U.S. partner—not a U.S. "puppet"—in the international community.[12]

Errors in Execution: Training the RVN in Conventional Warfare

> In Western terms Vietnamese peasants have always identified with the fox rather than with the lion. Believing that ruse and cunning will (and should) prevail over brute force, they disdain the displays of prowess so much admired by the hunter.
> — *Frances Fitzgerald,* Fire in the Lake [13]

Jeffrey Record notes the "supreme irony" that South Vietnam was eventually conquered though a DRV conventional attack, despite many previous defeats the allies had inflicted on main force PAVN units in the field.[14] U.S. senior military leadership, field commanders, and advisers had been molding the Republic of Vietnam Armed Forces (RVNAF) for longer than a decade, aiming to create a credible and capable conventional force to defend the country against just this kind of aggressive threat mounted by the "real" enemy.

U.S. officials did not often understand that Saigon saw the RVNAF as its praetorian guard to secure the regime against coup attempts, expected to originate from within its own ranks. The 1963 anti-Diem coup led to more governmental instability; between January 1964 and June 1965 there were six successful and two unsuccessful attempts at military takeovers within the GVN. Thus, unit dispositions and missions were usually made to counterbalance rival political factions within the armed forces. This rationale typically was lost on American observers in the mid-1960s while the resulting sluggishness of RVNAF responses to American-initiated operations was not.[15] Given so much frustration over the RVNAF's inability to get the job done, senior commanders and minor U.S. officials forged ahead on their own to accomplish the missions set out for them, with or without their ally's help.[16] Not surprisingly, the RVNAF stood aside to let the Americans fight the war for them after mid-1965.

U.S. military support focused on what the American field forces did best: conduct conventional military operations following the World War II and Korean War pattern, which featured high-technology firepower and logistics. One Army of the Republic of Vietnam (ARVN) general characterized American support as "founded on American doctrine, American equipment, and American money."[17] This led to profligate ARVN uses of firepower as the rule—typically problematic in insurgency situations—and equally excessive expenditures of ammunition, equipment, spare parts, and other costly supplies. The American way of war was expensive and so the RVNAF attached itself permanently to U.S. technical know-how and logistical prowess. Thus, the RVNAF was eventually unprepared for any kind of warfare—conventional or otherwise, defensive as well as offensive—without a heavy infusion of U.S. leadership, firepower, and logistical support.[18]

The RVNAF devolved into a static defense with little provision for mobility or taking the initiative since either could be seen as the means to challenge the Saigon leadership. RVNAF senior officers focused on internal politics and building personal fortunes through corruption and favoritism. Until 1968, there was no discontinuity between the U.S. senior leadership and the RVNAF commanders; both eventually settled into their respective roles as master and subordinate when it came to field operations.

A major break came in 1969 when the Nixon administration implemented the "Vietnamization" concept, designed to eventually withdraw American military forces and turn the war over to the South Vietnamese. It would take much time for an effective RVNAF conventional capability to be built—and time was a resource the GVN did not have much of between Nixon's decision to "Vietnamize" the war and the eventual 1975 DRV offensive. This discontinuity in American policy toward the war and its concept for assisting Saigon was so abrupt the South Vietnamese military could not cope with the immense and immediate task of reshaping its doctrine, force structures, and capabilities to successfully fend off a large-scale conventional attack alone.

Errors in Execution: The Pacification Campaign

When the NLF was created in 1960, it was designed to carry out the Communists' new program of "armed struggle" in the rural countryside. Termed "tru gian" by the party (translated as "extermination of traitors"), NLF combatants killed RVN government officials and agents hindering Communist political progress. Usually, these were security officials who were successful in hunting down party members, but they also were often influential anti-Communist teachers, Civic Action personnel, and RVN local officials who were actually efficient, dedicated, honest, and effective.[19] While Communist cadres used violent sanction in the past, it was selective and secretive; in 1960, the NLF broadened this effort across South Vietnam as a response to the Diem regime's equally violent pressures.[20] The NLF would continue this until the end of the war.

For Saigon, the way to control the rural population was to leverage the idea of "nationalism"—that is, to create links of loyalty between individuals and the centralized government directly, limiting delegation and decentralization that could threaten the ruling elite. Local leadership was tightly controlled and initiative discouraged. Of course, this "nationalism" idea had little relevance to peasants whose loyalties lay completely within the village confines. What was worse, Saigon's nationalism translated into controls on movement and forced labor, with people giving up cherished ancestral lands as part of forced relocation programs to establish strategic hamlets or to clear free-fire zones. Centrally appointed officials, who hailed from nonlocal areas and gained their positions through personal connections and favoritism, ensured compliance.[21]

If the senior officials of the U.S. government were not going to pressure the GVN to reform, then the American advisers and trainers assigned to South Vietnamese field forces would do what they could in working around it. Because the GVN's problems were not going to be officially recognized, much less dealt with, there was considerable variation in the means and methods applied.

U.S. Air Force Gen Edward Lansdale, dubbed "the Clausewitz of Counterinsurgency" for his role in suppressing the Huk Rebellion in the Philippines in the early 1950s, argued well before the 1965 U.S. intervention for relying on U.S. advisers to create a strong RVN capability against the NLF. Advisers would develop rapport with Vietnamese counterparts, eventually energizing the RVN counterinsurgency campaign through role model examples that advisers would set for their RVN counterpart officials.[22] What is important, and what put the advisers in a most delicate situation, was that these U.S. officers were not going to run rural South Vietnam on their own authority. The principal goal was developing a responsible RVN rural administration through their proper example; coercive controls over funding pacification projects were not granted to the advisers.[23] Adviser duty was difficult, and many grew disillusioned with the high level of corruption and inefficiency they witnessed on a daily basis.[24]

Once the massive influx of U.S. ground forces into South Vietnam occurred in mid-1965, it was natural that many expected conventional forces to be the primary means of victory, and adviser training of the RVNAF took a backseat until "Vietnamization" began.[25] Introduction of major U.S. forces took the wind out of the NLF's sails, which was clearly on the verge of victory.[26] Saigon was slow to take advantage of such a "breathing space" the surge of U.S. military forces provided. For their part, American conventional ground forces had their own unique way of communicating with the rural populace and the Regional Forces/Popular Forces (RF/PF) "protectors"; they focused on U.S. unit combat power and engineering capabilities supporting short-term humanitarian assistance projects and not on the long-term problems the rural population faced.[27]

If the U.S. conventional military was taking the war to the Communist main force units in the field and the RVNAF manned static defenses, one could expect the latter would concentrate on pacification. Unfortunately, nothing could be further from reality. The ARVN effort in this area was primarily mounted by the Regional Forces and local Popular Forces, formations not recruited from local area natives and manned by "less than desirable" personnel. While there were occasional leaders and Soldiers who were well-regarded by the U.S. advisers who worked with them, the vast majority were regarded as "next to worthless."[28]

Social discontinuities were the problem; the RVNAF officers were urban elites with little love for rural life. Their drafted troops merely took advantage of opportunities to suppress their fellows living in other provinces. Those few RF/PF members who were drawn from the local area often had relatives in the NLF and therefore actively hindered the RVN cause.[29] The prospect of an NLF assassin's bullet or bomb usually deterred any RF/PF leaders from showing any dedication. This, in addition to the fact that most had no kinship or other bonds of obligation to the peasants they were supposed to protect, meant that RF/PF units remained generally ineffective.[30]

We have already seen that the regular ARVN forces did not operate without extensive supporting firepower and that they were very loose with restrictions in the field. ARVN forces routinely did not exercise due caution when applying air- and artillery-delivered firepower in villages, astounding U.S. advisers who observed it.[31] Such misdeeds perpetrated by ARVN and RF/PF units on the very peasants they were supposed to protect communicated to the latter that these agents of the Saigon government were not their friends. It was a reality that the NLF never failed to capitalize on.

So-called Revolutionary Development Cadre (RDC) efforts, conducted by the RVN government with material assistance from the United States, were to leverage the security provided by these forces. In practice these proved completely ineffective. Success in these efforts required delegation of authority to locally elected officials, not outsiders appointed through cronyism. Any instability in Saigon also trickled down into rural areas as new favorites were appointed, creating personnel turbulence among administrators.[32] On top of that, RVN government officials with grudges against vocal local villagers often forced them to work on special construction and other "self-help" projects. Such measures did great harm to the RVN cause in the countryside, despite the infrequent successes that were achieved.[33]

American adviser frustration with this situation led to many agreeing with the NLF that the GVN was structurally unsound, regardless of official U.S. policy statements to the contrary. Yet these Americans never saw this as meaning the war was lost; instead, these same officials attempted to find other ways of energizing and even remolding rural society without Saigon's help.[34] Veteran U.S. adviser John Paul Vann, the subject of Neil Sheehan's biography *A Bright and Shining Lie*, wanted the United States to subsume the RVN government and take over the social development of the RVN itself; he and his supporters did not care how this was perceived in international circles.[35]

In December 1965, it was this same realization that led LtGen Victor "Brute" Krulak, USMC, the Fleet Marine Forces Pacific commander, to advocate a pacification plan that eliminated the influence of the GVN in the rural countryside and implemented a U.S. strategy offering land reform and other social and economic benefits that Saigon could never provide. To Krulak, a veteran of prior "small wars" in Central America and the Caribbean, such an approach was the only path to success against the NLF.[36] While Krulak never saw his strategy adopted, he was able to make limited progress at the tactical level. The most significant measures were the Marine Combined Action Program (CAP) and the Army's Mobile Advisory Team (MAT) concept. Both were generally similar in that a squad or team of uniformed men was assigned to reinforce and live with a unit of Popular Forces within a village. The concept was that the Americans would train these forces and set the proper example. For Krulak, the CAP would go even beyond this—the PF Soldiers knew who was VC, and if they were reluctant to kill them, then the Marines certainly would not hesitate.[37]

The statistical record appeared encouraging. CAPs and MATs appeared more effective in winning hamlets away from NLF control and contributed more on a per capita basis to the attrition of NLF strength yet with lower costs in friendly casualties. Despite this, many CAP participants had mixed feelings about the program's effectiveness. While all felt it was a positive action compared to the conventional force operation, the cultural differences, difficulties in acquiring capable infantry in numbers large enough to make a difference, and a sense that they were poorly equipped to offer any real solutions to the political ills that plagued the peasants caused them to downplay the program's success.[38]

The real problem with the CAP was that it nevertheless compromised the strategic situation vis-à-vis the counterinsurgency. Other than the local PF forces, no other RVN officials or pacification organizations were involved. The end result was that villagers—in the best of cases—saw the United States and not the RVN government as providing for them. Thus, the NLF strategy of discrediting the Saigon regime was actually assisted through this effort. While the CAP concept was originally supposed to create enough security so that local RVN officials could apply meaningful programs to solve local village problems, in reality this never occurred. Local infantrymen improvised solutions on their own to help out villagers, regularly bypassing the entire U.S. embassy/U.S. Agency for International Development (USAID) network. Of course, that was one way to sidestep the corrup-tion and diversions that American aid suffered at the hands of RVN officials involved, but this virtually ensured systemic problems would remain unresolved.[39] The success of the CAP and MAT efforts manifested the weaknesses and inefficiencies of the GVN administration, further preventing formation of any ties between Saigon and the villagers, playing into the hands of the information-savvy NLF.[40]

What the allies said in their propaganda to the rural areas aiming to win "hearts and minds" was one thing—what they did in actual practice was quite another.

Eventually, even the pretense of making positive contributions was effectively dropped, particularly in the wake of Tet, through the implementation of the Accelerated Pacification Campaign (APC).[41] After all, the NLF suffered horrendous casualties in Tet and appeared not to be so much of a threat after that offensive. So, more allied resources were layered onto the same old ideas, particularly regarding establishing security forces in villages.[42]

U.S. advisers in December 1968 characterized the APC program as occupation, not pacification, of previously held NLF areas. There was enough NLF cadre left to conduct selective attacks, causing local villagers to doubt the security effectiveness of the RVNAF.[43] By this time, the slogan "Grab them by the balls and their hearts and minds will follow" became something more than merely an American in-country joke. Given the discontinuity between the publicly stated theory of social and economic assistance to the South Vietnamese rural peasantry and the practice of applying solely military solutions, the GVN and United States handed the NLF an incredible information coup. It was indeed this practice—how the pacification elements behaved, or what they actually did—that the NLF pointed to and what the peasants remembered. The differences between allied words and deeds never yawned wider.

In summary, if pacification was of decisive importance to eventual victory—if only in U.S. eyes—then the allocation of effort, resources, and support to it was disproportionately minor. But perhaps even more problematic was that the Americans themselves could not achieve unity on the approach to take in training the RVNAF in pacification. The major disconnects between the relative importance of conventional operations compared to advisory ones and the basically negligible CAP and MAT training effort provide sufficient evidence of that.

Such disconnects between the messengers—as well as the messages—did little to create a unity of effort in pacification progress. But these problems paled in comparison to the larger issue regarding the true nature of the Saigon regime—a reality that no amount of Madison Avenue advertising could hide.

Social Contradictions within the RVN and the Correlation of Coercion

> The application of purely military measures may not by itself restore peace and orderly government because the fundamental causes of the condition of unrest may be economic, political, or social. These conditions may have originated years ago and in many cases have been permitted to develop freely without any attempt to apply corrective measures. An acute situation finally develops when conditions have reached a stage that is beyond control of the civil authorities and it is too late for diplomatic adjustment. The solution of such problems being basically a political adjustment, the military measures

to be applied must be of secondary importance and should be applied only to such extent as to permit the continuation of peaceful corrective measures.
—*U.S. Marine Corps,* Small Wars Manual [44]

We come now to the fundamental nature and character of the GVN that Saigon's political and military machinery—as well as that of the United States—claimed provided a better life than the Communists could offer to the South Vietnamese rural poor. The Communist Party held a view far different than that of the allies:

> Party cadres believed that the GVN never had nor ever could obtain legitimacy because of structural factors that could not be changed. The Party viewed the inefficiency and wholesale corruption that characterized the GVN at every level as the inevitable result of social contradictions. An urban, Westernized, and largely Catholic elite, the Party maintained, could never create a just society—or one viewed as such by the peasantry—in a poor, rural Asian country. The Party argued, with considerable justification, that Diem and his successors had kept intact the French colonial apparatus, with the Americans assuming the role of protector.[45]

A number of modern historians would seem to agree. As one example, Jeffrey Record concludes that the U.S. government knew full well the true nature of the Saigon regime at least ten years before the final collapse of the RVN in 1975 but could not admit to itself that the ultimate outcome was necessarily inevitable. It is not hard to come to this conclusion, given General Westmoreland's and Secretary of Defense McNamara's analyses early in the Americanization phase of the war. Indeed, Mark Moyar and Record agree that U.S. actions generally undermined whatever thin veneer of legitimacy the RVN possessed, even as American officials claimed to be acting in its interests.

In the aftermath of the Tet Offensive, the primary means the allies relied upon of achieving rural security was through coercion—and only coercion—at the local level. While the NLF also practiced violent sanction, its political cadres also promised a better life and ensured that local grievances were incorporated into local NLF agendas—this did not change, even after Tet. In contrast, the GVN and their U.S. assistants could effectively promise the peasantry nothing they wanted. By 1969 and onward, the South Vietnamese rural poor were caught between two competing political entities, both applying the threat of violence to win neutrals over to their respective sides.[46]

All things being equal in the balance of fear, it was quite natural for those who would take on personal risks to choose that side that offered the most hope, the entity with which it held something socially and/or culturally in common, and the organization that attracted others of similar talent and ability because they were valued and gainfully employed. For the more intelligent and politically aware in the rural south who could provide the best local leadership and were willing to risk their lives, the choice remained—as it always had been—to side with the NLF.[47]

> An undetermined but substantial number of peasants always either supported the Front or were sympathetic towards it. An even larger number of people were in doubt over the eventual outcome of the struggle, an attitude that encouraged neutrality. To be sure, the GVN did have its supporters. . . . There were good commanders, good soldiers, good officials, and even a few good policemen, but never enough of them. . . . Popular Forces, the units most responsible for hamlet security, were next to worthless; a very good indication that a great many people felt little reason to take major risks to protect the state. In this regard, Americans usually missed the point. When they constructed a political equation for Vietnam, it always resembled a hypothetical public opinion poll that asked whether most people supported the GVN or the Front. The question they should have asked was which side were more people willing to die for. Had they asked the second question, they would not have liked the answer.[48]

In short, it didn't matter how good the tactics, techniques, and procedures for fighting the war of perception were, the problem remained with the kind of government the counterinsurgency campaign supported. No amount of "message packaging," no matter what the qualifications of the "messengers," nor any action—unified or otherwise—other than that needed to resolve the causes of the conflict could remedy the GVN's deficiencies in the eyes of a significant portion of its citizens. Indeed, the peasants would not have recognized any political clique in Saigon as their master; such groups showed little loyalty to them and it was only natural that they would reciprocate.

While the defeat of the RVN in 1975 was not directly at the hands of the NLF, there was indeed no uniformly enduring will of South Vietnamese society to defend itself against any threat—external or internal. The government in Saigon was incapable of creating legitimacy in the minds of its people and, indeed, proved time and again unworthy of trust. The party understood this to be true and effectively acted upon this knowledge. No amount of military or political finessing by the allies could alter this fundamental fact even when it was acknowledged. Better estimates and fewer mistakes in their execution of the war of perception inevitably led the Communists to decisive victory.

Part III: Operational

23

Iraq and a Singular, Enduring Information Failure

—Bing West

In order to improve, we must be willing to look at our record and acknowledge mistakes. As I write this in February 2006, President Bush has adopted a "new strategy" for Iraq—essentially, for Baghdad—and is sending 21,000 more troops into the conflict. The strategic concept is that the troops will operate from about thirty combat outposts in the city's dozen districts, interacting with the people and bringing security 24/7.

But how to bring security? Our military is organized to fight wars, and it designs strategies and procures equipment within that frame of reference. That's the rub. Iraq is not a military battlefield; it is a series of intense police actions, centered in Baghdad and a dozen key cities to the west and north, where Sunni insurgents and Shi'a militiamen, both sides dressed as civilians, control the streets.

American and Iraqi Soldiers have no idea who their enemies are. In the rare instances when insurgents are actually captured, American rules and a corrupt Iraqi judicial system have converged to ensure that most are released. Our military did not adapt its procedures and information techniques to the war it was fighting, a police war.

In October 2006, I accompanied Marine squads on patrols in the violent Fallujah-Ramadi area. Of forty grunts on their second tour, over the course of seven months they estimated they had cumulatively shot about seven insurgents. These experienced riflemen described the insurgents as "ghosts" who emplaced improvised explosive devices (IEDs) or fired a few shots and fled. American firepower was not eroding the ranks of the Sunni insurgents because the insurgents chose not to engage. Nor were American units engaging the Shiite militias. Put simply, we were not killing the enemy.

By the military measures of killing or capturing the insurgents, the return on investment for 140,000 American Soldiers was unacceptably low. We had entered the phase where police methods and attitudes were key to success. Our counterinsurgency manuals stressed civic action and respect for the people. These norms were laudable but of little help in the arrest of insurgents. Acting decently toward Iraqi civilians was a moral imperative. In itself, it did not significantly improve counterinsurgency effectiveness. The role of the policeman is to apprehend the criminal, not to rehabilitate him.

Yes, military force can be used to identify and imprison the insurgents and death squads. But in Iraq, we don't have a program for identifying the military-age population. The police have no detective equipment; no reliable identification system has been widely fielded. As a result, American Soldiers on patrol futilely call in the phonetic spelling of Iraqi names on whatever ID card they are handed. Between 1966 and 1968, by contrast, the South Vietnamese government implemented a labor-intensive census program to register every military-age male in every hamlet. That broke the back of the Viet Cong guerrilla movement; they had nowhere to hide in the villages. They had to operate as companies, living in what we then called the "bush."

A few enterprising American rifle companies have conducted their own independent censuses, employing rudimentary spreadsheets and personal digital cameras. But no central information system exists.

For all of our efforts, we have ignored one of the most fundamental axioms of counterinsurgency warfare: an insurgency cannot be defeated if the enemy cannot be identified. In Chicago and elsewhere, the police carry palmtop devices that take fingerprints, send them over the radio, and in two minutes have a reply. If the suspect is not in the database, he is automatically entered. While our border police routinely use this system, we have not provided such a simple system for the Iraqis. Yet an insurgency cannot be quelled if the insurgents hiding among the civilians cannot be identified. The lack of an identification system, such as American police have in every patrol car, is the greatest technical failure of the war.

Handheld, unclassified devices to fingerprint and enter location data are available and proven at a cost of about $1,000 each. The military bureaucracy fought successfully from 2003 through 2006 to prohibit their introduction into Iraq because the bureaucracy had settled on a secret identification system called "BAT." The result was that the military-age male population in Baghdad and the Sunni Triangle escaped identification year after year.

U.S. and Iraqi battalions make arrests at a rate about one-eighth that of U.S. law enforcement agencies. Iraqi police make even fewer arrests. The police in Baghdad are among the most wretched in the world. New York City cops send some 26,000 criminals to prison every year; in Baghdad, with twenty times the murder rate, that number is at best 2,000. New York City's population is eight million; Baghdad's is about six million.

If Iraqi police had the same arrest and imprisonment rate for violent crime as does the United States, there would be 85,000 in Iraqi jails, instead of 14,000. Texas, with a population less than Iraq, has 168,000 in jail. The Iraqi court system in Baghdad imprisons ten to twenty-four criminals and insurgents each week—twenty times fewer than in New York City. It is unlikely that a resident of Baghdad believes his neighbors are twenty times more law-abiding than those in Dallas or New York City.

To justify that so few are kept in prison, some senior officers assert that the recidivism rate is about 6 percent versus 60 percent in the United States. This is a goofy rationalization for a system that is broken. In a misplaced gesture of reconciliation, the United States and Iraq released several thousand prisoners last summer. In Fallujah alone, three Marines were killed shortly after the release. Recidivism is low because rearrests are absurdly low.

The other excuse offered for imprisoning so few is that the United States lacks interrogators. Yet tens of thousands are available in the Arab American communities in the States. By offering a decent wage—a contractor truck driver in Iraq earns $100,000—and a televideo hookup, extensive interrogations of every detainee could easily be done.

In Iraq, the "rule of law" is aiding the insurgency. An enemy Soldier in uniform is imprisoned for the duration of the hostilities. An insurgent in civilian clothes can kill an American Soldier and, unless the evidence is airtight, walk free in a few days to kill again. Michael Frank, an experienced lawyer, spent a year analyzing the problem and wrote about it extensively in law reviews. "The acquittals and paltry sentences," Franks wrote, "exposed U.S. military to contempt and frustrated the soldiers who risked their lives daily to destroy the insurgency."

Iraqi and American forces have been in the same locations for four years. They know the usual suspects. But to make more arrests, they would have to overcome their cynicism about the system, and we would have to stop releasing so many detainees.

That will be hard for the United States to do. Currently, the U.S. military processes every detainee through four layers of review and releases eight out of every ten. Everyone knows why this persists. This "catch and release program" is driven by a hyperbolic overreaction to the abuses at Abu Ghraib in 2003 and frustrates both American and Iraqi Soldiers. If Americans imprison more Iraqis or if Iraqis imprison more Iraqis, the odds of prisoner abuse will increase. The press will shine a bright spotlight that will be followed by a torrent of political castigations. Ironically, it is easier for the President of the United States to send more Americans into combat than it is to convince the U.S. Senate to endorse harsh prison terms for those trying to kill those Soldiers, our Soldiers.

The Iraqi Security Forces cannot win if the insurgents cannot be identified, arrested, and imprisoned for the long haul. In combating an insurgency, the police are a crucial force. Throughout the Sunni Triangle, the police hid in their stations and refused to get involved, casting a blind eye to the insurgents burrowed in like ticks among the population. Police forces in major Sunni cities like Fallujah and Ramadi made as few as ten arrests a month. "No police chief in the U.S. could keep his job with such performance," Ralph Morten, a senior detective in the Los Angeles Police Department on his sixth visit to Iraq, told me.

Last May in south Baghdad, an American battalion proudly showed me photos of six Shiites captured with blood on their hands, weapons and shell casings in their car, and a dead Sunni a few blocks away. In September, a judge released all six.

Iraqi police do not make arrests that stick. More than 80 percent of the Sunni insurgents and Shi'a militiamen detained by American and Iraqi forces are set free. Some senior American officers told me that the rearrest rate of released prisoners was only 6 percent, compared with a recidivism rate of 65 percent in the United States. So either the Iraqi insurgents were ten times as likely as American ex-convicts to see the error of their ways, or they found it all too easy to evade justice.

The Sunni insurgents are under insufficient pressure to give up violence because, if captured, they are usually set free. If the insurgents wore military uniforms as required of combatants, the war would be over in a month. Instead, insurgents kill Americans by dressing as civilians. Because they are not wearing uniforms, they are not treated as prisoners of war and detained until the war ends. Instead, they are accorded rights exceeding those given to a criminal suspect in a liberal democracy.

Let's look at the data reported in one month from one American battalion in Ramadi. The battalion detained 178 suspects—35 percent for possession of explosive devices that kill Americans, 45 percent for illegal weapons or inciting to riot, and 20 percent had arrest warrants outstanding. Each was questioned by an experienced team of seven Iraqi and Arabic-speaking American interrogators, supervised by a military lawyer who had been an assistant district attorney in the States. Within eighteen hours, one hundred were warned and released. Most had been illegally carrying weapons in their cars.

The remaining eighty were charged with serious offenses. Most refused to answer questions. The American Soldiers filed two sworn statements for each arrest together with photos from the crime scene. The detainees were sent to the brigade level. The brigade released fifty and sent thirty to Abu Ghraib prison to await an Iraqi hearing.

Once at Abu Ghraib, still more were released by a Combined Review and Release Board consisting of American and Iraqi officials. The battalion was notified of each release via a convoluted Internet system. To protest any release, the battalion had to secure the signature of a colonel.

The twenty prisoners still being held at Abu Ghraib were scheduled to appear individually before an Iraqi judge, usually four to six months later. The American Soldiers who had made the arrest were required to appear at each trial. In the majority of cases, this has not been possible. Iraqi judges, openly suspicious of written testimony from American Soldiers, tend to free the accused.

The net result is more than 80 percent of all those detained are released within six months and usually in less than one month.

The senior American headquarters level believed the battalions were indiscriminate in making arrests; the battalions believed the seniors were under political pressure to release hard-core killers who knew how to lie. In the United States, 1 in 32 adults is in jail, according to the U.S. Department of Justice in late 2006; in Iraq, the number is 1 in 112. Iraqis, apparently, are more law abiding than Americnas are. Our senior officers believe the recidivism rate in Iraq is low, perhaps 6 percent; in the United States, it is over 60 percent. Again, Iraq appears to be far more law-abiding. Our Soldiers mock the arrest of insurgents as a "catch and release" fishing tournament.

Our military chose to do this. Iraq is the first in thirteen occupations in the past 132 years where the U.S. military classified all insurgents as common criminals, to be tried not by a U.S. military tribunal, but by a corrupt and essentially non-existent Iraqi judiciary system that had fatal flaws in its prosecution legislation. As for identifying the male population, the U.S. military simply chose not to do so.

The essential technical problem was an institutional inability to adapt information systems to a police war. Overall, however, the U.S. ground forces did adapt remarkably, altering from a kinetic maneuver warfare doctrine to counterinsurgency and forbearance.

24

Between War and Peace: Low-Intensity Conflict Doctrine and the Iraqi Scenario

—*Jose L. Delgado*

"To engage in any activity the Warrior needs to know what to expect, how to achieve the objective, and whether or not he is capable of carrying out the proposed task."

—*Paulo Coelho,* Warrior of the Light

Introduction

Since 1945, the collusion of three major developments has reshaped the international arena: nuclear weaponry, modern revolutionary doctrine, and the development of the Third World. The aforementioned, combined with the American experience related to the terrorist incidents in Washington, D.C., and New York, in Afghanistan, and more recently in Iraq, has had a significant impact on American national will, political resolve, and perceptions of international security.[1]

The United States has lost a significant number of service members in postwar combat in Iraq, underscoring the hardships the United States faces quashing Iraqi resentment as the fledgling government continues work on the stabilization and democratization process. Although U.S. officers largely blame Saddam loyalists and imported Muslim extremists for attacks on their Soldiers, many ordinary Iraqis have expressed frustration at what they say has been the slow pace of returning the government to Iraqis and rebuilding the country. This chapter is an attempt to try to understand the evolving scenario in Iraq using the institutional understanding available from past conflicts on the lower end of the violence spectrum.

U.S. policymakers seem to have forgotten about the incredible volume of intellectual capital and knowledge that were invested in comprehending the nightmare scenarios that were predicted for American forces in the 1980s and 1990s—the threat of low-intensity conflict (LIC). Even with all the accumulated knowledge and experience at our disposal, LIC is particularly difficult to understand because the term does not describe anything that can be visualized instantly. It was a catchall phrase that came to describe a constellation of military, economic, and political activities taking place within a broad environment that was also difficult to characterize. This environment was frequently described as an "unstable peace"— peaceful to those who are geographically removed from the problem, but unstable and often violent to those who are directly involved.[2]

The term is not a satisfactory one, but it gained general acceptance through usage prior to the inception of an even more ambiguous term, "asymmetric warfare." For our purposes we will continue to use the less ambiguous of the two terms (i.e., LIC). During the early 1990s, the Department of Defense defined LIC as:

> a limited political-military struggle to achieve political, social, economic, and psychological objectives. It is often protracted and ranges from diplomatic, economic, and psycho-social pressures through terrorism and insurgency. LIC is generally confined to a geographic area and is often characterized by constraints on weaponry, tactics and levels of violence.[3]

Clearly, the definition seems to fit the current situation in Iraq.

During the last decade, most military scholars generally accepted there were two basic dimensions in the LIC environment: the participants and the means that they use.[4]

Background Terms

Participants
In the case of postwar Iraq, the primary participant is the United States, which took the leadership role with other allies as an intervening power. Although there is usually a secondary participant—a supported government or entity—in the case of Iraq, the situation is a bit more convoluted as the government was toppled by the military actions undertaken by the U.S. military and its Coalition partners. This notwithstanding, it has inadvertently created another set of participants: the emerging government and the opposition to the nation-reconstruction and democratization of Iraq.

Authority
The second term consists of the four major elements of power that convey the authority necessary to oversee an effective government entity: coercive elements,

economic elements, psychological and opinion-forming elements, and political elements. Examples include:

- Coercive elements—police, the military, regional peace-keeping forces, paramilitary forces, terrorists, and insurgents
- Economic elements—banks; the agricultural, manufacturing, and service sectors; multinational corporations; and trade unions
- Psychological and opinion-forming elements—news media; international, regional, and local associations; lobbyists; and religious groups
- Political elements—laws, political parties, and coalitions of parties.[5]

LEGITIMACY

The environment of LIC is one in which psychological and political considerations prevail; therefore, a key to understanding the political aspect of LIC is the concept of legitimacy. Legitimacy, taken in this concept, can be defined as the moral authority underpinning the right to act, and it can be derived from law, international and regional relationships, societal values, religion, and political or public perceptions.[6]

We can think of legitimacy as a tug-of-war between two teams. By using the elements of power and supporting actors, either one team or the other gets more of the rope on its side. The rope allows the force of one team to be effective against the other. Victory is usually a result of superior strength and a sound strategy. Defeat results from poorly executing the strategy, misjudging the strength of the opponent, or losing legitimacy. Gaining legitimacy is a long-term effort that depends on a thoughtful and consistent strategy, the trend of which must be maintained in one's favor.[7] The United States is currently in an ongoing struggle to create and maintain the legitimacy necessary to stabilize the ever-morphing situation in Iraq.

Fertile Ground

Traditionally, the U.S. government has been functionally organized to manage its diplomatic efforts and to undertake more conventional wars. It was neither organized nor prepared to undertake the LIC scenario that evolved in postwar Iraq. The ad hoc committees with representatives from a variety of federal agencies (each with separate agendas) that were sent into Iraq to stabilize the situation created a veritable chaos that is still being sorted out. If these agencies had done their homework, they would have learned from the plethora of documentation generated during the LIC "craze" of the 1980s and 1990s that LIC required the coordinated efforts of a wide range of government agencies.[8]

The realities of geography, history, politics, and economics have created the necessary conditions for instability, terrorism, and ultimately insurgency in Iraq. Today, more than ever, U.S. national interests are directly tied to the successful resolution of the regime change and democratization of Iraq. The issues, however, are complex and not always resolved by conventional military means or conventional thinking.

The inability of the U.S. administrators and the fledgling government agencies to satisfy the basic needs of the people of Iraq reflects on the viability and legitimacy of the developing government and is a factor that the increasingly organized opponents of that government may be more than willing to exploit. Even the perception that the administration and occupying force are not doing enough to protect it can give credibility to the claims of a terrorist or insurgent movement. More often than not, a government faced with serious economic, social, and political problems is not able to effectively meet all the needs of its people, especially if those problems are compounded by the security requirements of dealing with a terrorist threat against public officials and infrastructure.

With resources restricted; a limited pool of professional, technical, and managerial talent; and an often inadequate public security structure, a government's ability to successfully attack its more pressing issues is severely hampered. Under these circumstances, an insurgent movement may have fertile ground to grow and prosper.

Despite the instability of the current security environment in Iraq, the center of gravity is not on the battlefield but in the political-social system of the state. Thus, the main battle lines are political and psychological rather than between opposing armed units. The nature of this conflict is likely to continue to include a variety of tactics ranging from ambushes, assassinations, hit-and-run raids, sabotage, and terror. Actions will most likely follow a pattern of nibbling away at the U.S. forces in order to achieve a political-psychological victory over the long haul.[9]

In a country in which the government is threatened by subversive terrorism, every military act must be designed to accomplish a political end: to establish, maintain, and preserve a government that can operate effectively, under law, to meet the needs and aspirations of the people of that country. Military operations that cause unnecessary civilian casualties and property damage may create sympathy for the terrorists and their cause and add to popular grievances against the government. This type of conflict may be seen as basically a contest for public support. The "hearts and minds" theory affirms that if support can be gained, people will withhold information and material support from terrorists, refuse to do their bidding, give information about the terrorists to government functionaries, support public programs, and volunteer assistance so that the conflict can be won.[10]

The long-range goal of all action in Iraq should be oriented toward reestablishment of a viable government and the reconstruction of the nation. The occupying military establishment has a great capability to nurture national development and, particularly in this case, has a relative monopoly over the leadership, technical skills, administrative experience, and mobility. All of these attributes are essential to the development and recuperation of transitional societies.[11]

Successful Strategies

Four factors can be used to measure the success or failure of U.S. policy initiatives in Iraq. As presented here, these trends apply to U.S. efforts to stabilize the situation in Iraq. These four broad trends help form an impression of overall tendencies toward successful or failing U.S. strategies. Each trend is a major category that may be augmented with as many factors as desired to permit more detailed analysis. For example, the second trend could be measured more specifically with data on the number of military engagements, number of arrests, and amount of property destroyed. Taken over time, these augmenting factors could give detailed insight into positive and negative trends.[12]

CONFLICT TERMINATION STRATEGY

Intelligent terrorists and insurgents do not expose their forces willingly or chance their destruction. They use hit-and-run tactics that avoid major military confrontations, and the conflict is unlikely to be resolved by a decisive military engagement. Thus, the strategy of the military forces must be aimed at incremental changes, not a grand, final battle. Controlled use of coercive elements may actually increase in frequency during the conflict, but eventually—through small-unit engagements, security patrols, identification checks, and arrests—the conflict begins to fade away. If the strategic objectives, as indicated by preference for set-piece battles, appear to dominate, then the trend is toward failure.[13]

COERCIVE FORCE LEVELS

In Iraq, the goal should be to reduce and eventually eliminate the use of force by using nonmilitary alternatives. An increase in the use of force by either side indicates that the opposition is gaining strength and is challenging the legitimacy of the emerging government. Force levels may need to be increased for a time to counteract the opposition. Sustained high levels of violence, however, are usually counterproductive to success. High levels of violence disrupt the developing economy, the governmental infrastructure, and the population. If the force level is unabated, much of the effort needed for national recovery will be diverted to the coercive element. Indicators of a trend toward failure are an escalation in the use of force or a prolonged, high level of coercive force.[14]

DOMINANT POWER ELEMENTS

When the stability of a nation is threatened by an unstable security environment, a controlled amount of coercive force is necessary to reestablish order. Establishing security gives the population confidence and provides a chance for the other power elements to work unimpeded by the opposition.[15]

Eventually, the frequency of violent action decreases, and the remaining problems of the opposition are addressed by political and civilian means. Thus, social, economic, and political elements must balance the coercive element and eventually dominate because they lead to the defeat of the opponent's political agenda. When there appears to be an imbalance of coercive acts in relation to political, economic, and psychological elements, then the trend is toward failure.[16]

POLITICAL LEGITIMACY

Legitimacy determines when and with whom people take sides. Support from the population and assistance from supporting powers depend as much on the ideology, morality, and righteousness of a national cause as on its ability to further that cause by force. Recalling the tug-of-war metaphor, the balance of legitimacy is a give-and-take situation. If one side takes it away or loses it, the other side will gain it.[17]

Loss of legitimacy can also occur when coercive aspects of a stabilization effort are allowed to dominate and result in massive human rights violations. When the motives—honor or means of accomplishing objectives—are challenged and found wanting, there is a loss of legitimacy. When the government loses legitimacy, the trend is toward failure.[18]

Conclusion

Those who wish to challenge the resolve of the United States, and those who are determined to pursue interests that are counter to the establishment of a democratic and free society in Iraq, will do so indirectly—by threatening American lives and efforts and undermining the fledgling institutions and values that promote democracy and civil liberties. They now clearly understand that the only means available to them will be the various forms of indirect aggression such as terrorism, subversion, sabotage, and proxy warfare. Adding fuel to the fire is the fact that these activities can also provide them with a low-cost, low-risk, and high-visibility geostrategic payoff: the embarrassment and defeat of U.S. interests in the Middle East.[19]

Violence is less an instrument of destruction than a psychological tool to influence the attitudes of specific sectors of the population. Unchecked, this will become a form of political education that forces a reluctant, basically neutral civilian populace wanting only to be left alone to take a stand in support of the terrorist. Such a strategy is not easily pursued. It takes time. But the terrorists retain the initiative and push relentlessly to gain support by discrediting the evolving institutions of power.[20]

The United States and the evolving Iraqi government must first recognize what is happening and then be willing to acknowledge that the civic support in Iraq is fragile and the control over the populace is being contested. To reestablish political legitimacy, both parties must address contentious, long-ignored, but popular issues tied to key facets of national life—sociopolitical, economic, educational, juridical—as well as engage the increasingly coordinated attacks against them. The resulting burden on the security forces is large. Not only must they subdue an armed adversary while attempting to provide security to the civilian population, they must also avoid inadvertently furthering the terrorists' cause.[21]

To counter these threats, political, economic, and informational instruments of power must all be brought to bear. The main point is that this particular type of situation is not just a lesser degree of conventional conflict or a "mop-up" operation.

Interestingly, in 1962, President John F. Kennedy described this challenge—specifically the low-intensity conflict challenge—and what was required to confront it. He said,

> This is another type of war, new in its intensity, ancient in its origin—war by guerrillas, subversives, insurgents, assassins; war by ambush instead of by combat; by infiltration instead of aggression, seeking victory by eroding and exhausting the enemy instead of engaging him . . . and these are the challenges that will be before us in the next decade if freedom is to be saved, a whole new kind of strategy, a wholly different kind of force, and therefore a new and wholly different kind of military training.[22]

An ordered, interagency response will be needed that demonstrates a long-term, multifaceted commitment of support and resources rather than direct military actions. Clearly, military options in this scenario must be limited. The multidimensional nature of these threats requires an equally multidimensional and unconventional approach.[23] Within this context a detailed and extensive study of past LIC scenarios and responses may prove valuable in offering a menu of actions that can subsequently be tailored to the challenge posed.

25

Are We Outsmarting Ourselves?

—Col Keith Oliver, USMC (Ret.)

Comprehensive, coordinated "Information Operations" is the new kid on the battlefield. But beware: Americans still like their independence, and they prefer their news unfiltered ("Give it to me straight, Doc") with a side of hometown hero.

It's clever, but is it art?

—Rudyard Kipling

Information operations (IO), strategic communications, and the information battlefield are part of the wave of the present. Arrayed in abundance are the buzzwords, the organizational realignments, the merging of various info-related functions, and the minimizing or outright jettisoning of others.[1] But we need to be careful: absent the immediate application of some common sense and historical perspective, this glorious, new wave might just turn out to be a self-generated tsunami.

Others like William Darley[2] and Tadd Sholtis[3] have helped frame the debate on how we might look at this new information landscape and how its component parts should or should not work together. But what about good, old-fashioned public affairs itself? Is anybody paying serious attention to "brilliance in the basics"—the blocking and tackling of information war?[4]

One of the problems is that we've fallen in love with the technology. In much the same way that PowerPoint presentations can brief an audience into a coma (while sacrificing substance for bullets and bumper stickers), I've seen cases where organizations spend inordinate resources on blogging or predictable, often sycophantic, electronic roll-ups of "today's news," designed to show "the heavies" that their message is getting out. Is it?

Television is great, but it made me heartsick to talk to a public affairs officer in Beirut in 1984 and to a Baghdad-based operational spokesman more recently and hear each of whom express great concern over their physical appearance on camera. The latter, oblivious to the eyeball rolling all around him, shared with a post-deployment audience his careful attention to, literally, presenting (his) best side.

IO sounds new and sexy, but it's no stand-alone magic bullet, any more than air power was before it. It's a function of command and just as with intelligence, security, and data systems, IO is far too important to be left to the IO geeks to plan and execute. And because it's new, there's a lot of snake oil out there.

As this beast grows and evolves, at least four trends give cause for concern.

An Appetite for Bureaucracy

My old gunny used to call it "throwing rank at the problem"—and information operations are eaten up with it. Remember the furry little Ewoks in the *Star Wars* movies? They used spunk, ingenuity, and a little decentralization to defeat the giant, lumbering robots that had invaded their forest. We used to be those Ewoks. Now, I fear, we have become the big Erector set–looking dinosaurs, tromping around in the information battle space with all the grace of a pachyderm and sacrificing speed and nimbleness for over-tight, internal "message control" and an ever-increasing punch list of required reports to feed a hungry, self-propagating hierarchy of staff officers and contractors.

The prep work for the internationally televised briefings in Qatar during major combat operations in Iraq in 2003 is a case in point. The U.S. Central Command enthusiastically contacted retired Marine Gen Butch Neal for advice; he had been chosen as the key briefer during Operation Desert Storm in 1991. The general explained the daily drill in Riyadh, which was essentially to work his day job in operations and swing by public affairs for an hour of prep work before going on camera. Apparently, that was judged to be too easy. The well-meaning 2003 version tied up a dozen key staffers for two meetings a day in addition to a steady stream of conference calls and e-mail traffic aimed at perfect orchestration.

Fat headquarters are one thing, but down the line if we give away the American military tradition of trust tactics, with their inherent emphasis on independent thought and action when required, we're in trouble. Gen Walt Boomer's take on having the media in his area of operations during Desert Storm puts it succinctly:

> If you're going to (invite the media in), you better have faith in your troops. If you don't trust them, if you don't have faith in them, you can't turn the media loose. But I would submit that if you don't have faith and don't trust them, you're not a very good leader and you shouldn't be there either.[5]

Being Too Slick

Regardless of how history judges Operation Iraqi Freedom, the embedded media program was a resounding success. It covered a multitude of sins, committed mostly at higher headquarters. Take the media operations center at Camp As-Saliyah in Qatar. Already-cynical reporters walked into a million-dollar-plus, Hollywood-designed studio decorated with four redundant plasma screens and a richly appointed greenroom that would've made David Letterman blush.

Much more galling than the surreal wartime digs, though, was a consistent pattern of overpromising and under delivering. Qatar-based media members were led to believe they'd be treated to a steady diet of substantive information and that they'd have almost unfettered access to senior leaders. There was to be a media embed assigned to the headquarters itself.

Instead, reporters were told they couldn't even remain overnight at the cavernous press facility even though the building was staffed with public affairs and security personnel around the clock. Meantime, temporarily assigned civilian public relations flacks dreamed of an ever-cheering liberated populace and the discovery of those pesky weapons of mass destruction.

But the lowlight of the experience was a Washington-directed, four-day "news blackout" imposed during the "shock and awe" phase of the operation. But the blackout morphed into a tense period of zero official contact with Central Command media officers, exacerbated by live video of fellow journalists' easy access to commanders in the field and, in too many cases, a stark absence of rudimentary professional courtesy. Even the "hotel warriors" of Operation Desert Storm more than a decade earlier had it better than this.

But we got by because the embeds—soda straw perspective notwithstanding—accurately reported what they saw up close and personal: the horrific chaos of combat and the selfless bravery of young American Soldiers. The legitimate complaints by reporters assigned to cover the war from Central Command's theater headquarters were easily discounted.

It's not just the physical surroundings or other Madison Avenue trappings that come off as being too slick, it's also the way we sometimes do business. News leaks. Late Friday afternoon release of information to minimize impact. Overdependence on off-the-record interviews. Leave the trick plays to the politicos. Uniformed military leaders and their spokesmen have an ethos of honor to protect. No perceived short-term gain is worth besmirching the Soldier's reputation for straight talk.

Forgetting What Got Us Here

All the strategic communications plans and officer staffing in the world will not replace the goodness of having in the field trained, innovative enlisted storytellers: active-duty writers, photographers, broadcasters, and videographers. Like the vast majority of their civilian war correspondent counterparts, the best of these young men and women embody a colorful mixture of intellect, guts, and improvisation—just the kind of warrior-scribe you need on the ground to crank out timely information.[6]

Sgt Neil Gillespie, a World War II combat photographer, exhibited these traits when famed U.S. aviation pioneer CPT Eddie Rickenbacker and six companions were lost in the South Pacific, surviving in an open raft for twenty-four days. The enterprising NCO (he sometimes souped his film in a discarded Corsair fuel tank) snapped the first photos of Rickenbacker when he was rescued, nabbing a big spread in *Life* magazine. Short on photographic equipment, Gillespie improvised. He rigged a flash from the refractor of a Seabee bulldozer headlight and placed the film canister in the hands of a Navy pilot for delivery to Samoa.[7]

That kind of savvy is still in our ranks today, as evidenced by the cover photography of many of our junior enlisted shooters in Iraq and chronicled by Gunnery Sgt Keith Milks in his fine *Marine Corps Gazette* article, "22d MEU Public Affairs in the Forgotten War."[8] During World War II, many of Neil Gillespie's counterparts entered the service from America's newsrooms, some with a decade of experience under their belts. Today, we mostly grow our own at Ft. Meade's Defense Information School where entry-level students from all services receive college credit for training in the various communication arts.

Policymakers would do well to carefully consider this critical, muddy-boots resource. Without it, any aspect of information operations is just fantasy football.

Bizarre Funding Priorities

There seems to be a lot of money available for some aspects of information operations—but what about our bread and butter? Not only has the Defense Information School not been substantially increased since 9/11, the institution does not enjoy meaningful visibility in the budget cycle. A little demoralizing, given the dollars being sown into information operations curricula elsewhere, not to mention the fortune that has been spent on civilian public relations agencies in Baghdad and Washington.

In light of an increased, largely unfunded demand for training, why have we established and maintained the resource-eating Pentagon Channel? As a taxpayer, I'm glad to throw money at the Defense Department's own television operation only after DOD organizations have fully exploited the civilian broadcast opportunities that already exist. I'm talking about the smaller-market TV stations in "flyover country" that welcome hometown-flavored, military-produced pieces.

Then there's radio. There are drive-time shows all over the country, in a wide variety of music or talk formats, that would relish the opportunity to host a daily or weekly "base report." Even better are ships' namesakes and units' home stations, with a special emphasis on the Guard and Reserve. Cost to the taxpayer? Negligible.

I paid a call on the Coalition Provisional Authority in Baghdad not long after the capital was secured in the spring of 2003. It seemed the palace was teeming with strategic communications counselors, consultants, and contractors. There was substantial planning and advising—but not so much doing. That was left largely to a beleaguered, Chicago-based Army Reserve public affairs detachment that did the best they could with what they had.

Col Mark Brikalis, a Marine artilleryman and selected brigadier general, wrote a wonderful piece in the January 2006 *Proceedings* that struck at the heart of our funding priorities in terms of high-tech weaponry, but his argument can be extended to information operations as well. "On one hand," he wrote, "these big-ticket airplanes, ships, satellites, etc., are the things we dream of—bigger, faster, smarter, and deadlier. On the other hand, there are so many little things we lack day to day—radios, batteries, field gear, even buildings with heat."[9]

Before we get all starry eyed about new strategic information concepts, it might be useful to take inventory of the rudiments at the tactical level. Are we training and equipping our young specialists in adequate numbers to win the information war? Are we still paying attention to the basics? Are we turning out folks who can write good copy, take striking photographs, and work with the civilian news media to get those products placed?

Have we become too sophisticated and CNN-centric to serve the hometown media outlets of America—the newspapers and broadcast stations that can't afford to embed but would welcome words and images with a local tie?

Our armed forces, resourced with tax dollars and, more significantly, our nation's treasured sons and daughters, are properly subject to public accountability. Mom and Dad are not looking for fancy briefings or packaged messages that smack of spin. They want to know what the U.S. military is doing and whether their son or daughter is well trained, well led, and reasonably protected from harm.

When it comes to information operations, certainly we should heed the biblical injunction to be "wise as serpents and harmless as doves." Planning and coordination among and between the functional areas is nonnegotiable. But our fellow citizens will not tolerate any effort that is even perceived as methodically packaging or, especially, politicizing the performance of American troops in the field. Nor should they.

Typical is the attitude of Professor Eliot A. Cohen, posted in March as counselor to Secretary of State Condoleezza Rice. Having a son who served an Army tour in Iraq, Cohen told the *Washington Post* that "what the father in me expects is, simply, the truth—an end to happy talk and denials of error, and a seriousness equal to that of the men and women our country sends into the fight."[10]

We can best foster and preserve those ideals Cohen expresses with the robust care and feeding of two uniquely American assets: an independent, civilian news media and a properly trained and equipped corps of enlisted storytellers.

26

Marines Are from Mars, Iraqis Are from Venus

—*Maj Ben Connable, USMC*

Marines find themselves regularly frustrated by the behavior and reactions of the Iraqi people. There are very fundamental cultural differences between Americans and Arabs, but for a variety of reasons these differences are exaggerated between the Marine tribe and the Iraqi tribe. Our fundamental differences lead to fundamental misunderstandings. As we enter a period of ambiguity leading up to the transition, it may be helpful to look at how we deal with our Iraqi counterparts from a fresh perspective. American Marines and Iraqis are hardwired at far ends of a cultural void not by genetics but by social conditioning.

These descriptions are necessarily simplified, skewed, and hyperbolic to make a point. No two people are the same, and I have used very sweeping generalizations that may not match preconceived notions or reflect common wisdom on the nature of our two cultures. Both the Iraqi and the American people share the same human spark. My purpose is to help Marines in the Al Anbar Province find the patience and understanding to help an embattled people.

American Marines

People are hardwired to see obstacles or problems, find solutions for those problems, and execute those solutions. The American culture reinforces this natural instinct in what most other cultures consider an extreme manner. Americans focus on winning, achieving, succeeding, and producing. Our children learn and play aggressive, competitive sports from a very early age.

For example, football, arguably the most popular and widely played American sport, is a linear, aggressive, goal-oriented endeavor that usually ends with concrete results. This is a simple construct that satisfies our basic needs. We see a problem (the other team, the goal line), we see a solution (drive forward, score more points), and we can easily envision an end state—unambiguous victory. Ties are a disappointment, not a means to an end. In professional football we have done away with ties entirely because they don't satisfy our Manichean need for a concrete solution.

As children, most of us are taught that lying and cheating are wrong and that honesty is always the best policy. You might say that honor in the American ideal means never quitting, never betraying your word, and living up to a high standard of performance and behavior. Honor on the athletic field means playing by the rules and giving your best performance no matter what the conditions. People who give excuses for poor performance are deemed weak and are shunned.

When we are presented with challenges, we are expected to overcome them with personal initiative. People who overcome personal disaster are held up as examples to the rest of us. The worse the disaster faced, the greater the comeback, the better the story. The skier who breaks both legs in a fall and drags himself five miles for help is a hero, but it's even better if he crawls all the way back to save his dog from an avalanche. Most Americans are generous, but we tend to lack respect for those who don't help themselves. Most of us can still relate to such statements as, "Pull yourself up by your bootstraps," "self-made man," "I don't take handouts."

We see ourselves as separate and distinct individuals. Choosing our own relationships, memberships, associations, and paths in life, we see it as standard practice to move 3,000 miles across the country, away from family and friends, to "start over." If we don't like our families, we simply dissociate ourselves from them and seek other relationships. We marry and divorce with impunity and often without input from friends or family. We decide what is best for ourselves. If we fail, we're generally expected to view it as our own fault. We have a responsibility to take care of our parents in their old age, but we often pay someone else to take this burden off our hands.

Most Americans are lucky enough to have a fairly high standard of living compared to the rest of the world. More than 90 percent of families can afford three full meals a day for their children, and nearly everyone has an opportunity to go to school. Our safety is buffered by regulatory agencies that protect us from dirty water, dirty air, and even noise pollution. Although we have many bad neighborhoods, there is little threat from brutal torture, state-sponsored mass murder, oppressive martial law, or enemy invasion across our borders. Our health care isn't perfect, but our life expectancy is high and most of us feel good about our futures.

In fact, our ability to envision our future is one of our greatest strengths. Because most of our basic survival needs are met, we have the luxury of a long-term view. Retirement planning is a normal part of life. Most Americans envision their children going on to college and have no reason to expect they won't be able to fulfill this expectation even if they have to take out student loans. We save money and plan our careers.

Our system of government gives us the perception that we also have a greater role in our collective future. Although many Americans say they feel disenfranchised, our ability to vote elected officials in and out of office gives us an avenue of participation. Our anger and frustration can be vented with the pull of a lever or a letter to our congressman. The fact that the congressman writes back and will probably look into each individual case would shock most people from the developing world.

The respect for the rule of law is the foundation of our way of life. We modify our daily behavior based on the belief that it's our responsibility to follow laws, that we will be punished if we don't follow laws, and that most other people will follow laws. Law gives order and protects us from each other, from the government, and oftentimes from ourselves. Our faith in this system of laws is reflected in the amount of time we dedicate to following the creation of law in Congress and the adjudication of law in the courts. Publicly, corruption is unacceptable, and when discovered it is usually rooted out.

We take great pride in being a free people. Our unquestioning belief in our rights to life, liberty, and the pursuit of happiness make us uniquely American. Unencumbered by the shackles of tyranny, our hearts host the seeds of generosity and altruism. Most of us have an unfailing belief that we make the most of our freedom, living good lives, helping others, and trying to live up to our personal standards.

Our altruism and earnestness often make us somewhat naive. We expect that everyone else can see that our hearts are pure, and we expect them to play by the Marquis of Queensbury rules that we imagine we ourselves live by. When we find out that people in the rest of the world necessarily live by a more survival-oriented set of rules, we're often overly disappointed. We have trouble adjusting to other people's way of life because we think our way of life is the ideal. We have trouble seeing things from other people's eyes because we think they should always see things from our perspective.

Our sense of moral superiority comes from a real desire to help others and do the right thing, but it also gets in our way when we have to deal with those who live by more nebulous rules. Our earnest overtures are seen as false and naive instead of moral and brave. If they have a hidden angle, we must have one too. Sometimes our lack of street smarts catches up to us. When we don't live up to our own expectations on the national stage, we are our own worst enemies. The embarrassment over Abu Ghraib is a case study in American guilt.

Our national character is built on high moral concepts that not many of us live up to, but most of us aspire to. Our nature is to be strong, moral, and productive. We set the bar high.

American Marines take these characteristics and drive them to a new level. With notable exceptions, we tend to be exceptionally aggressive, mission focused, and strong believers in the American ideal. We do not accept weakness, indecision, laziness, or incompetence because we know that these things lead to death in combat. We drive ourselves past normal points of endurance, often damaging our own bodies just to reach a finish line or save a buddy. We expect no less from anyone else, a point that often leads to friction with our old high school friends, our families, and especially other Marines. We have been called "extremists," and in many ways we are. Marines can best be described as "extreme Americans."

Iraqis of Al Anbar

Although we don't like to call ourselves "Arabs," the Iraqi culture is an Arab culture. We are a communal people, and our lives revolve around our family—close, extended, and tribal. The paths of our lives are less lineal than the Americans', less "A to B," more nebulous. Our sport of choice is also football but not the American variety.

We play the sport played extensively everywhere in the world except America. Soccer isn't a direct, aggressive kind of sport like the game you play. In fact, we spend a lot of time kicking the ball backwards instead of toward the goal. Much time is spent on the field lining up shots and less time on shooting. The goal is to win, but a tie is okay as long as it was a good tie. We often view a tie as a victory if it is against a better team.

Our perception of victory and success is often malleable to the circumstances. Our honor demands victory; we have trouble accepting anything less. We're not lying to ourselves; we just adjust the standards to fit the situation. The Gulf War was a victory for Saddam because we prevented you from driving into Baghdad. Despite the fact that we were losing on the field, Fallujah I was a victory because you could not finish the attack. Our will to hold out defeated your will to crush our forces. If you push us into a position where we have obviously lost, we become distraught and angry, and our honor demands that we seek a victory to balance things out. This is no different from you—Americans hate losing as well—but it is dif-ferent from you because to us it is all that matters.

This sense of honor permeates everything we do. This isn't the Western definition of honor; it's more like Hispanic honor. Perception of manhood is vital and can be a matter of life and death. A man without honor gets no wife and often no work, and in Iraq he may be shunned or killed by his family depending on the gravity of the offense. Defending one's honor is part of our cultural heritage, and it is a focal point for our behavior. We protect the virtue of our women and the pride of our family. We are disgusted that American men allow their women to act and dress like *sharmuta,* or "whores." If our wives dressed in public like Britney Spears we would kill them or burn them with cooking oil.

An Iraqi man unable to support his family has no honor and must take action to counterbalance this loss. It doesn't necessarily matter how we support our families as long as we provide. In many cases, we are pushed out the door by our wives to conduct attacks against the Coalition to regain our honor and to make money. An Iraqi woman knows that a husband without honor is worthless to her and her children.

Saddam was a terrible father, but many of us loved him as an abused child loves the parents who beat him. We still act like abused children, playing one side against the other and looking for an advantage, support, and acceptance. We will play you against your boss, against the CPA, and against the government to get what we want. Don't expect loyalty from us; we are survivors. When we give loyalty to a cause it is to God's cause. When we give loyalty to people it is to our family.

When we are presented with challenges, we accept the fate prescribed by God. Acceptance of fate is an Islamic trait and it guides almost everything we do. If we are poor, then it is God's will that we are poor. If there is a task to be completed, then by the will of God it will be completed—*Insh Allah*. In many cases, except for those of us educated in Baghdad or the West, we see no reason to put extra effort into succeeding beyond the norm. Getting by is good enough because that is our lot in life. We have basic expectations, and these are tied to our hono: we need food, shelter, water, electricity, and medical help just as everyone else.

Don't expect any miraculous stories of hardship overcome, "personal best" in the marathon, or an "I can make it on my own" attitude. These concepts are luxuries for people who live in pampered societies like America. Even when we are poor we have our families and that is enough to keep us happy. When you ask us to do something, we rarely think to ourselves, "Gee, how can I do a great job?" We are answering the call of our stomachs and our screaming wives. Some of us seek much more; many of us seek what we call a normal life.

Our families make us who we are. The family is everything, and only those on the margins of society live without family support. Because we live in a developing country and our needs are more survival oriented than yours, we have to rely on common survival techniques. People group together to survive, to protect each other, to look out for each others' interests. The closer the grouping, the closer the interest of the group. Our immediate families are most important to us, then our larger families, then subtribe, then tribe, then tribal confederation (see figure 26.1).

Our loyalty expands and contracts based on our survival needs, but we almost always work within this construct. If you kill or imprison one of us, you have taken some of our pooled resources and reduced our chance of survival. Because we survive as a group, an attack on one is an attack on all. This is why we demand blood money for death, injury, and damage. You must replace the resource you have taken from our pool to balance things out. As long as you recognize that need, we can work together. Here's a real-life example of how seriously we take our tribal resources:

FIGURE 26.1: Iraqi Loyalty Range Fan

Iraqi Loyalty Range Fan

- Immediate Family
- Greater Family
- Sub-Tribe
- Tribe
- Tribal Confederation

More Loyal ← → Less Loyal

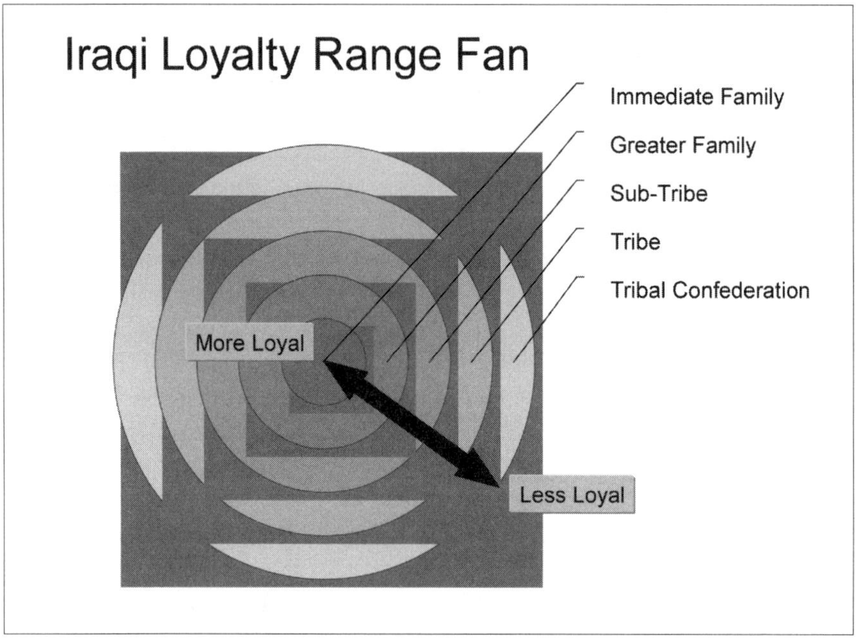

The tribal feud started when three members of one tribe borrowed some money from a sheikh of another tribe. They had borrowed the money because they could not find jobs to support their families. After allowing sufficient time for repayment of the loan, the sheikh attempted to collect the money he was owed by taking possession of a vehicle that the three borrowers had purchased in an attempt to start a small business carting groceries from the market to surrounding towns. An argument ensued between the two groups, and the sheikh threatened to harm members of the three men's families if they didn't repay the money. Upon hearing this, the three men shot and killed the sheikh. The sheikh's tribe immediately vowed revenge. Soon, all three of the borrowers had also been killed by a member of the sheikh's tribe. The feud will continue until blood money is paid, balancing out the losses on each side. Very much like your Hatfields and McCoys, no?

Pooling resources and interest within a family means that there is little room for individualism. We rarely choose our own path in life. If a father owns a business, the son will almost certainly work for his father. If marriage to another tribe solves an intertribal conflict, we marry whom we are told. Our parents pick our spouses, and we often have little or no input in whom we marry. Only the rich and the elite choose their own life. This lack of individuality further reduces our sense individual responsibility. Again, don't expect us to act like independent Americans.

Our tribalism is tightly bound to our sense of honor. Just as honor is vital to each one of us, it is also vital to the tribe. A dishonored tribe loses *wasta*, or "influence." Less influence means less money, less power, less ability to support the members of the tribe. Therefore, a tribe's honor is jealously guarded as a group resource. Mistreating a sheikh of our tribe makes him less powerful, making all of us less powerful. Less power means fewer contracts, less money, less food, angrier families. We must regain this honor any way we can. Because Iraqi tradition is violent, we often choose violence to regain our honor. If you dishonor our tribe, we have to negotiate with you . . . or attack you until our honor is restored.

We don't ask for much. Our standard of living is low compared to the Western world. If you put us in the United States, most of us would fall well below your poverty level. Since the collapse of our economy, many of us cannot afford to feed our families without finding odd jobs, begging money from family members, or supporting the Anti-Coalition forces. Look around—most of us live in humble homes, farming small plots with a few animals and a broken-down car. If we have a big home, we may have had a good job before the war, and now we have nothing and are twice as angry as our poor neighbors.

There are certainly rich people among us, but they don't represent the majority. When you tell us you can improve our lives and make us rich, you have an image of your own homes in mind. Most of us cannot even imagine what your lives must be like in America, and we do not necessarily value what you value. We don't dream of Outback Steakhouse. We are proud of our lives even if they don't meet your expectations.

Unlike you, we do not enjoy the protection of concerned government leaders. Nobody cares if there is lead in our water or pollution in the air. Sometimes our leaders feign concern about our health care system, but that's only because our harried tribal leaders take up our cry. Your system is so refined that every little whimper draws the ire of a champion congressman. Our system is so broken our raging screams are barely heard. We must use the power of our tribes and our religious groups to effect any change; so again, if you weaken our affiliations you weaken our only hope of being heard.

Where you have been protected from invasion, martial law, and torture for nearly two centuries, we have experienced nothing but for our entire lives. We have been in a state of almost constant warfare with either the United States or with Iran. When we weren't fighting you, we were fighting ourselves in the north and the south. Our sons and brothers were killed fighting to keep Saddam in power, and our lives seemed painfully short. At any time, a government official, police officer, or secret policeman could decide that we had done something wrong and have us killed. They might have to pay off some blood money, but so what?

Just as many of you have become callous about death in combat, we have grown up to be callous about death in everyday life. We are not the Baghdad elite.

All of us have seen animals slaughtered and have helped pull their guts from their bodies, so blood is nothing new to us. Beatings are a part of life, pain is a part of life, and death is an ever-present part of life. If pain and death are our lot in life, we accept that as part of God's plan. This is how we are able to accept money for a relative you have killed—we accept God's will, and you have balanced out our resources. What can we complain about?

Because our lives are so brutal, we have almost no capacity to view the long term. Our inability to envision our own futures is our greatest weakness. We are faced with a simple hierarchy of needs. One must breathe before he can think about shelter and security, shelter and security before water, water before food, and so on. It is only by building a normal, healthy society that you can extend that focus into the long range, to think about things like education, leisure time, investment, and retirement. You have heard our complaints. We want shelter, security, water, and food. Your talk about democracy and culture and prosperity mean little to people who are simply surviving.

With this short-term view, if you give us money we spend it. If you give money to one of our public officials, he'll steal as much as he can because he doesn't even know if he'll have a job next week. He has to get more, now, to fulfill basic needs. He can't see into the long term, to see the effect his corruption will have on the future of his community. He may even be a good person, but he has to look out for his family first.

What you see as corruption we see as part of the normal process of doing business. Because most jobs underpay, we always take a cut. This is built into the price of the job. Iraq follows the trend of many other Arab countries; there aren't enough jobs for the expanding population so the government hires everyone. The government can't afford high salaries for so many people, so the pay is low. Because the pay is low, it's expected that you accept bribes and cheat to get by. Everyone knows the rules, even the government.

Typically, we'll take a slice of 10 percent to 15 percent off the top of a contract or a work order. Nobody will really get too upset if we keep things in this "normal" range. If we go too far and take 30 percent or higher, then we know we are stepping over the line. However, unless you catch on we'll take what we can get. If you're too stupid to figure out what we're doing, it's your fault, not ours. There is no real shame in corruption; after all, we're looking out for our families, as expected.

Corruption is natural in a country without the rule of law. We do not respect law the way you do because for us law comes from the end of a gun. In the absence of the gun, we try to respect our families and friends and live by God's will. If the government passes laws, or you give us a transitional law, we don't respect it because we don't respect the government. Government to us means corruption, violence, dictatorship, and rule by fear. In the absence of fear, there is no rule.

We know that Saddam lied to us often. We feel that he did this to protect us, but also to protect himself. We have never trusted our social institutions as much as we trust our families and our friends. It all comes back to the family and tribe. If the government tells us that the Americans are going to enter our town in peace, but our cousin tells us they are coming to murder everyone and rape our women, we will almost always believe our cousin. You have made many promises to us but kept so few. Why should we believe you? In the absence of trusted institutions, our lives are ruled by rumor, and rumor is spread by word of mouth.

In such a nebulous society, where life is a tenuous prospect, we rarely take responsibility for our own actions. "Owning up" for our poor performance or behavior would be a stupid thing to do if it reduces our chance of survival and success. If we can put off our mistakes on others, we'll do it in a heartbeat, not because we're lazy or incompetent but to avoid damaging our honor and possibly losing our jobs. Remember, without honor and a job, we are nothing. So we break a few rules and lie about our mistakes. We don't care about rules anyway; we do things to achieve an effect not because they're right or wrong.

We're masters of achieving effect. Everything we do is designed to coax, cajole, trick, or steer you into doing what we want you to do. This is a standard survival skill, one that you obviously haven't mastered. Your naiveté never ceases to amaze us. You either take us at face value or you get mad when we "lie." It's not lying if you get what you want, and we almost always get what we want from you. We are in a constant state of negotiation, and there are no permanent solutions to any problem. You pretend to be so honest, but we see you as the biggest liars of all. You promised us security, jobs, and peace. All we have is crime, unemployment, and war. Who's the liar?

You may have noticed we have a very emotional nature. There's no imperative to control our emotions, and in fact we're encouraged to express ourselves. We wear everything on our sleeves and we change our minds at will. We can be furious at you one minute when you offend us and truly love you the next minute. Every death is a massacre, every accident a murder, every threat an impending disaster.

Iraqis are complicated people. We can be kind, generous, and forgiving in the worst circumstances. If you are a visitor in our homes, we will feed you our last morsel of food. If you become a true friend, we will die for you. But we see no future for ourselves or for our families.

We are stuck in a rut, and we need someone who has the capacity to see a better future to guide us onto the right path. We may take your hand, or we may bite your hand because we do not trust you. It is on your head to be patient and forgiving, not ours. Do not expect us to be American Marines. If you expect too much from us, you will be disappointed. There is nothing worse than unmet expectations, my friend.

Conclusion

Iraqis will never live up to the Marines' expectations because they are Iraqis, not American Marines. We haven't lived up to their expectations either. We freed the Iraqis from the dictatorship of Saddam Hussein, and by that action we have assumed responsibility for helping them along the road to recovery. This is a sacred duty, and we cannot allow our personal frustrations to overcome our patience and dedication to their well-being. Understanding both the Marine culture and the Iraqi culture is the first step to envisioning a day when they are strong and healthy, and we can return to our friends and families knowing we've followed through on our inherent promise.

27

Clouding the Issue: Intelligence Collection, Analysis, and Dissemination during Operation Iraqi Freedom

—*LTC George J. Stroumpos, USA*

Counterinsurgency is a difficult business for intelligence officers. The knowledge required for such a venture is both vast and deep if one is to glean meaningful, actionable intelligence for counterinsurgency forces to use. Such is the case with Iraq—a counterinsurgency problem compounded by depth, size, and complexity.

Yet, despite this complexity, Coalition forces have greatly narrowed the odds and are relatively successful at the margins, but we lack a solid understanding of the heart of the matter. This lack of understanding has chased us since our haphazard beginnings of the war to the fitful, reactive, and stodgy manner that we prosecute the war today. Ultimately, but for our skillful application of force, it may well be our undoing.

Our intelligence apparatus has been our Achilles' heel. While we do not lack in competence, the lack of organization and general lack of understanding or preparation for the challenges that we face cause this disparity. The Coalition intelligence apparatus is a hodgepodge pick-up team, conflicting in its organization and lost in a sea of data. This, coupled with the sheer volume and complexity of the environment, is the primary problem. A secondary problem with our intelligence apparatus is poor information management and the resulting syntheses that follow from poor technique.

In the following pages, I hope to explain these weak points in the Iraqi intelligence effort and their manifest effects. In this search, we will examine intelligence analytical technique as well, since part of our difficulties lies in outmoded thinking in terms of analysis. Moreover, I hope to suggest a method that may fix these issues both in the short and longer term. The issues Coalition intelligence faces are not insurmountable, nor are they permanent. Indeed, some of these issues are slowly being acknowledged and addressed.

To parse this examination logically, we will examine our current intelligence structure, our current methods of collection and analysis, and our methods of dissemination. Then we will examine the outmoded methodologies. Finally, we will examine a possible method to solve these problems.

It's All How You Look at It: A View of the Iraqi Insurgency

To understand the intelligence problems the Coalition has to deal with, one must first understand the scope of the Iraqi insurgency itself. The nation, approximately the landmass of California, has a population of approximately 25 million. Of that population, an estimated 1 percent is actively involved in the insurgency—about 14,000 to 25,000 persons.

The insurgency itself is nonhomogeneous and comprised of four main groups: Sunni nationalists (former Ba'athists), Sunni extremists (primarily the groups Ansar al Sunnah and Al Qaeda in Iraqi [AQI]), Shiite militias, and criminal organizations. Foreigners and outside national actors are also involved to varying degrees throughout these groups, but their involvement and level of active participation are in dispute. Most current assessments deem this activity to be low. Ultimately, it are a safe analytical viewpoint to say the insurgency is primarily a homegrown problem with limited external involvement. The resources, matériel, and manpower are primarily domestic; tactics, organizational constructs, and techniques are generally thought to be imported.

Within the insurgency, no group in and of itself is homogenous either. For example, the Sunni nationalists comprise some twenty-seven separate and distinct insurgent groups with about a hundred (best guess) subgroups, no names, and independent operators. Extremists have two major and numerous subelements, or franchises (subgroups and independents), which operate in concert with the main groups. Shi'a militias comprise three primary and multiple subelements, or splinter groups (this organization changes constantly, so it is really difficult to categorize). The country is also rife with criminal gang activity at both the national and local levels with an as yet indeterminate number of groups and population.

There are few common characteristics shared by all groups and subgroups. Each group uses a different command and control method. Each group has differing levels of popular support and different agendas and displays a wide disparity between group capabilities, reach, and footprint. Within different regions there is a distinct balance of power and distinct grievances fuel the insurgency. Two similarities are shared by all groups: no group is terrain focused and strategic ends are perpetrated solely by pedestrian tactical means. To insurgents, all activities are tactical in nature; each activity by itself has the potential for strategic implications.

Coalition forces are fully aware of some elements, partly aware of others, and dimly aware of emerging threats and elements within this tapestry. The problem lies not in capability but in the organization, understanding, and volume of data that must be processed. The first two issues can be addressed in time. The latter issue can be mitigated but not entirely solved.

Welcome to the Jungle:
Intelligence Organization for Combat

It's a jungle out there—throughout the country and throughout the Coalition forces' intelligence apparatus. The Coalition's intelligence infrastructure is vast and complex. In a sense, it is more complex than the insurgency itself. From the outside, this monolith stands seemingly all knowing. From within it is a Rube Goldberg machine of mammoth proportions. Within this contraption, intelligence is processed and analyzed; but little is discerned for a variety of reasons, not least of which is the structure itself.

Within the intelligence structure, there are no fewer than twenty-six distinct organizations that are designed or modified to supposedly work together in Iraq. The Multinational Division (MND) and Multinational Corps (MNC) elements create the preponderance of intelligence collection, dissemination, and analysis. Within the MND and MNC construct there are at least five bureaucratic layers, or gatekeepers, to raw intelligence, analysis, and disseminated product: battalion, brigade, division, corps, and force. The layers are structured as an inverted pyramid, with the majority of analysis and collection capability husbanded at the upper-most echelons and dealing primarily with "strategic" analysis. Supporting this core construct are six functional intelligence support organizations and four special task forces that add to the confusion.

Other organizations outside the Iraqi Theater of Operations suffering from the "me too" disease also have their own Iraq section or division. These add-ons often damage the already cloudy intelligence picture further by creating an even greater necessity for coordination and, at times, debate within the intelligence community with little end. Often these debates result in less clarity than before. Quite simply, your viewpoint on the theater activities depends on where in the mess you sit. Moreover, as a rule, you never agree with anyone else.

Predictably, coordination for collection, analysis, and dissemination is unwieldy, if not downright impossible. At one coordination meeting alone, no fewer than sixteen separate organizations attempt weekly to synchronize their work. Theater-wide duplication and contravention of existing work were and still are commonplace. Coordination for other agencies' information, if done correctly, can easily consume your entire workforce.

Special task forces, the resultant symptom of this dysfunctional organization, numbered four at my last count, each of which hoarded a tremendous share of the collection, analysis, and fusion assets within the theater. Finally, outside agencies, more or less independent of the military command structure, also contribute to the effort but on their own time line and with their own agendas. Hypothetically crowning this list of current agencies and organizations that collect in theater is the Coalition Intelligence Operations Center (CIOC), providing the MNF commander with a bird's-eye view of the theater-wide intelligence effort.

How We Describe the Elephant: Outdated Methods and Techniques of Intelligence Collection, Analysis, and All Their Fleas

Within intelligence organizations in theater, there is no specific, codified division of effort in the collection and analysis of intelligence except a geographical focus by each MND in addition to the interrogation of prisoners. Within the intelligence apparatus there is a massive amount of overlap, the exception being British collection and analysis, which was primarily focused on MND-South (where U.S. forces and agencies had few collection assets present). Because of an inverted pyramid personnel design, lower elements never have enough time or resources to work complex intelligence issues in their respective areas. This issue arises as a result of information flowing up, not down. Each brigade- and battalion-level unit has the responsibility to collect and target in its area of operation, plus feed higher echelons with whatever data they require. As a result, all units have the implied responsibility to analyze and understand the intricacies of all groups in their operational environment—an essentially impossible feat.

The lack of centralized, apportioned collection and fusion efforts causes limited unit understanding of the various groups in their local environment. While lower echelons know what they are facing, they rarely clearly understand who their adversaries are or, more important, why they act as they do. Consequently, many tactical units find themselves relegated to a day-to-day, "see target, service target" type analysis. Little predictive intelligence occurs, except in areas where commanders forcibly break the reactive intelligence cycle with organizational changes, method retooling, and painstaking, time-intensive intelligence analysis.

Higher echelons attempt to provide limited intelligence support on the more global aspect of group associations and structures. But this support comes at the expense of collection and analysis support at the tactical level. Thus, major limitations exist in the Coalition's understanding of group dynamics, resulting from poor intelligence resource utilization and distribution of those resources. However, some of the issues with intelligence collection and analysis reside with outdated methods and procedures. The way we are trained to approach intelligence tradecraft and the inherent limitations in the analysis tools we use create many analysis gaps regardless of whether the organization is structured effectively or not.

Intelligence professionals have a series of tools to work their trade, each of which was designed and validated during the Cold War. Such tools, both automated and procedural, are fantastic at fighting other armies but have limited value when applied against an asymmetric threat. This is owing to the sheer volume of data synthesis that must be performed to even recognize an insurgent element, let alone understand it. Because of the volume of data that must be analyzed, most tools that are at a unit's disposal are limited to useless. Additionally, these process limitations canalize commanders into thinking that an insurgent group's higher-level leadership is the primary source of organizational vulnerability. Such thinking is not the result of a group's real dynamic, but rather the throughput limitations of analysis tools. Three examples of such processes and methods are the human intelligence (HUMINT) analysis tools, intelligence preparation of the battlefield (IPB), and the priority information requirement (PIR) process.

HUMINT analysis tools, such as the association matrix and the currently taught link diagramming technique, are adequate tools if you have a small group of fewer than thirty members to analyze. Though these tools are effective in a micro sense, they do not scale to the size required for the current situation in Iraq without extensive automation and prework performed by analysts. By its nature, insurgency is asymmetric and requires a different approach in collection and analysis. You need a wider net to catch the smaller fish. Existing HUMINT tools fail to provide that net.

For example, if I have thirty members in my local insurgent group and each of those members has four to six supporters, an analyst must track up to 180 individuals and the strong and weak associations of each member to get a meaningful look at group dynamics in order to determine vulnerabilities. Also, keep in mind that this example would be one of multiple groups and independent operations occurring within a particular environment. HUMINT processes are not structured to handle such a volume of data nor do they operate in such a fashion. In an insurgent-rich environment, the throughput of effort for one company's area is enough to overwhelm a brigade's level of intelligence analysis capability using school-taught methods.

The need to meaningfully modify traditional methods of intelligence analysis is also apparent in IPB. A process of battlefield visualization, IPB is a very complex, Byzantine process that requires the intelligence analyst to go through a sequence of steps to fully describe a battlefield and its effects to the commander. It is a living process, requiring constant refinement, and is extremely time and manpower intensive. But it is inadequate to the task of counterinsurgency operations. Rather than abandon the process or meaningfully modify it, contracted think tanks and schoolhouse instructors have simply added steps to the process, requiring even more intensive, time-consuming effort to be expended. If such a process could be accomplished in its current state, IPB could prove very useful. But presently, with the analysis limitations inherent in the model, it becomes eyewash and a poor descriptor of the enemy that commanders actually face.

Since much of IPB work is simple yeoman's work, it is easily accomplished by outside sources. But bureaucratic reluctance to abandon procedure and the prevalent "not invented here" mentality predominate. To date, no solution to the volume of work has been proposed, tested, or even attempted. Thus, IPB, a useful tool, is rendered useless by the process itself.

Another procedural issue to be overcome is focus. The intelligence lens must be constantly guided and focused to be effective. Moreover, yesterday's intelligence gold mine quickly becomes today's dry hole. To focus intelligence the commander uses questions to guide the intelligence effort. The quality of questions invariably determines the validity of the answers. Correct questions beget hard, useful analysis. Poor questions beget a lack of actionable intelligence. Priority Information Requirements is the procedural vehicle that keeps the intelligence lens in focus. The PIR process remains a great method to obtain the appropriate questions for intelligence collection. Unfortunately, the manner in which these requirements are created, revised, and propagated is seriously flawed.

In short, PIRs are recommended by intelligence officers to their respective commander based on gaps in intelligence collection and analysis methods. Then these questions are approved at that echelon and propagated down to the subordinate levels. The subordinate units adopt the higher echelon's questions and rephrase them, often adding other questions to reflect the unique conditions present in that area of operation. And therein is the problem. Often PIRs are poorly formed at the top echelons and too vague to reflect requirements to deal with the current local conditions. Additionally, if these questions that serve as the rally point for collection and analysis atrophy over time, which they do frequently, the unit collection, analysis, and targeting effort atrophies as well, leading to unpleasant surprises. The relative suddenness and surprise of the militia problem today are an examples of poor PIRs.

A PIR that no longer fits the situation should be discarded, but often it is not. The process of updating these core questions is easily done; the approval process, however, can often be nightmarish, especially at the higher echelon. Let's examine this further. Suppose the Multinational Force PIR is "What threats are there to good governance?" Such a question would likely focus intelligence collection on two areas: government and threats. The question is very broad and vague and does not give the lower-echelon commander a good focal point on which to base his questions. This problem of question precision is part of what ails the collection effort.

If a PIR question is too broad, it cannot be refined and executed meaningfully at lower levels. If it is too specific, the question myopically prevents other relevant data from being collected. If the question becomes irrelevant, as they often do over time, or does not represent the appropriate focus on the ground then it must change. If it is not changed in a timely fashion, precious assets are wasted by allocation to a useless endeavor. Specifically, an opportunity to predict an event or outcome is missed.

The process of PIR revision at higher levels is a committee process, reflected by both senior-level intelligence officer involvement and committees of commanders as well. Too often, by the time a PIR is amended, it is already irrelevant. As PIRs expire and fail to acquire information relevant to the immediate tactical interest, commanders and intelligence officers often bypass or override existing collection efforts (standing PIRs), then haphazardly throw effort into the crisis of the moment. This sort of activity is commonplace in the Coalition and often results in siphoning away vital assets at inappropriate times. But, again the revision process and the vagueness of requirements prevent PIRs from adapting to the ever-changing environmental circumstances, often rendering intelligence analysis useless.

Information Management: Lack of a Common Language and Confusion Regarding the Difference between Data and Information

Another problem plaguing intelligence efforts is a lack of standardization and common language to describe insurgency and the social networks that they inhabit. Without such common standards, the Intelligence Community is often lost in endless negotiations, attempting to codify a set of common, universally understood descriptors of the networks studied and nodes targeted. This common lexicon must also be ubiquitous throughout all agencies that assist in the effort to ensure interchangeable analysis and analysts. Otherwise, needless coordination ensues to ensure correct understanding and interpretation of different analysis products. Presently, such a lexicon does not exist. Analytical descriptors that do exist are under constant revision, causing even more analytical confusion. In fact, the lexicon is so convoluted no single analyst will be able to explain the same situation or insurgent group to another analyst from another organization in a manner that is clear to both parties.

Now, let us compound this problem. Every day, thousands of messages and tens of gigabytes are received, processed, and warehoused in the emerging intelligence database being created on Iraq. This database is fed by specific documents, legacy programs, and old analysis reports of various sorts, all dealing with the Iraqi insurgency. It is monstrous and can be quite effective when used properly; however, this database has lead to sloppy analysis and analytical laziness.

The contemporary attitude of intelligence professionals toward this database is that it relieves them of the obligation to constantly cull it to refine standing analysis. Their view is that this data, which can be recalled in an instant, plotted, analyzed, and compared to other points of time, can determine all sorts of accurate and useful bits of information on the fly, with little or no prior preparation. Therefore, to many, the painstaking daily accumulation and synthesis of data into information does not have to be done until deemed necessary. To an extent, this attitude is correct. However, there are four problems with this train of thought: accessibility, normalization, time decay, and the difference between data and information.

Since the Iraqi information database is compiled from different sources, much of the data is not normalized and therefore is inaccessible to the average analyst owing to this deficiency. By normalization, I mean that all of the data is not in similar formats to speed integration. So, instead of a search leading to a series of cross-correlated pieces of data, often an analyst gets disparate pieces of data, some current and some old, some normalized and some not. Some portion of the database search is simply indecipherable due to poor data normalization within the database. A time-pressed analyst simply snatches the most accessible pieces of data and dumps the rest without further contemplation. This creates large gaps in our enemy knowledge base and in our information. Most of these gaps aren't even realized. I would also venture to say that some of these gaps are crucially important.

Another issue is the active filtering for time decay within information management and database technique in theater. In the beginning of the Iraq War, much of the information was spottily acquired and hastily input. As such, its usefulness is limited at best. If an analyst is new or sloppy, this nuance is missed, causing analysis gaps in addition to prediction errors. Some of the data pulled in a search is of dubious value because of this fact. Some pieces of data collected from a database search are too old to be of any value, except for historical reference. The problem with such simple data searches is the analyst is incapable of telling the difference between time-decayed and relevant data because of his lack of familiarity with the subject he is researching. The analyst must consequently accept all of the data pulled in a search as correct, which leads again to analysis errors.

The final problem that the Intelligence Community wrestles with is the misperception of data. Many confuse data with information, which it is not. Data, by itself, is of limited use and is far too vast with regards to any particular subject to be of any specific value. Information, or the synthesizing of disparate pieces of data, is of value. The difficulty is the analytical understanding of the value of information versus data. Too often, analysts become overconfident, misunderstanding that a database, while beneficial, is useless to the analytical effort unless there is a conscientious effort to extract necessary pieces of information into a cohesive picture of the enemy. Let's examine this further since, at times, the distinction between data and information in intelligence analysis can be too subtle to discern.

A piece of data that indicates that an insurgent group member makes twice-weekly trips to a town market for supplies is not in itself information. If later, intelligence collection comes to know the type of supplies and the quantity of the purchase and combines the two pieces of data so that we now have information. Specific-ally, analysts can now determine the relative effect of Coalition activities on the group's operation should the Coalition decide to act on the information. Moreover, they would likely have the leads necessary to track and eventually interdict the group's primary and secondary suppliers, or facilitators. Just one piece of data gives just one bit of a puzzle, an incomplete bit. Juxtaposed against other pieces of data, analysts come to know a key nodal vulnerability and an indicator of a group's possible future plans or state of lethality.

The most important conclusion to draw from this example is that a database must be regularly and unfailingly culled for information to maintain a semblance of advantage over the insurgent. Data cannot be readily or accurately pooled quickly enough with little or no prior preparation. Information, actionable intelligence, is lost this way. More important, a piece of data that may presage an enemy activity or rise to prominence is useless when trapped inside a database. I submit that that is exactly the problem that occurs repeatedly in Iraq today.

Taken together, process and organization present the majority of what ails the intelligence effort in Iraq today. In the speed at which the Coalition has adapted itself to changing conditions, Coalition intelligence leaders appear loath to destroy one element or process in the creation of another. In this sense, numerous task forces, processes, and organizations, having outlived their function, are allowed to linger and continue consuming resources, personnel, and time. In other words, the organization and process decisions do not allow for creative destruction: if you create one item, you must also destroy another to pay the bill. Too often, having outlived their usefulness, organizations and procedures perpetuate, inadequately adapted to a changed reality. The effect of this phenomenon is a dilution of intelligence collection and analysis focus.

Once created, new organizations and processes gain constituents, who in time become vested in the elements' perpetuation. As these constituencies grow and develop, rivalry ensues, resulting in additional bureaucracy, resource hoarding, gate keeping, and sand boxing to maintain relevance. Such behavior leads to bureaucratic, jaundiced, and inadequate intelligence collection, processing, and analysis. It also leads to inertia, creating a tremendous drag effect on the agility and accuracy of the Coalition's intelligence structure as a whole.

Pareto Rules: A 20 Percent Effort to Straighten out the Organization and You Fix Many Problems

I believe that we have sufficient collection and analysis capability to prevail in our current fight. This has been amply demonstrated in our continuously successful efforts at stifling insurgent and militia intentions. However, a reorganization of the intelligence operation is in order if we are to speedily adapt, anticipate, and ultimately defeat the insurgency. To do this, we must first analyze insurgent organizational structure for clues.

An insurgent organization is intent based, local, and operates in a flat, confederated manner. Because of this decentralized arrangement, an insurgent network is highly resistant to nodal reduction. Essentially, it functions like the Internet: no single path is solely responsible for command and control and any will do to varying degrees of effectiveness. This strength is also a weakness in that decisions and information propagation are slow and cumbersome. Tactical and operational decisions and planning are very time consuming and not necessarily effective because of the high degree of autonomy of each subelement. To counter this effect, subgroups use the Internet and other forms of communication to speed propagation of information and instructions. We should emulate aspects of this model to our advantage in creating our own intelligence organization. Namely, we should emulate the flattened, nodal structure of the insurgent and maintain a local, not regional, focus.

First and foremost, the majority of analysis must occur at the point of collection: brigade, battalion, and company level. To accomplish this, we must turn the intelligence pyramid on its head and eliminate the middle layer (division). Additionally, compartmentalizing and task forcing should cease. Those elements that already exist should be dissolved and distributed equally throughout the force. Finally, as in business, consolidation of function must occur at the top, absorbing higher-echelon layers and divisions' intelligence capabilities to reduce duplication of effort.

The primary function of the new intelligence apparatus must be to solely augment and complement the local effort in order to ensure the weight of our capability is properly leveraged downward. A primary intelligence node should be created to manage this function. Such a node must not only direct traffic, but must also attempt to plot the course of the conflict. Such a central intelligence node (CIN) must have a governing, or controlling, body distributing tasks to all elements to ensure synergistic, distributed collection across all facets of the intelligence apparatus. This control node would also direct participation by outside agencies to ensure a complementary, shared collection and analysis effort. In other words, all intelligence elements must fall under a central traffic control system to ensure that PIRs, both local and theater-wide, are being answered to meet the commanders' needs at all levels. Optimally, this node would also act as an elaborate query and research service, augmenting the local analysis effort.

The CIN would have four structures: coordination/tasking element, a liaison element, a functional analysis (close fight) element, and a theater awareness, or current intelligence section.

The coordination/tasking team would be the strong arm, orchestrating the parsing, tasking, and coordinating of all disparate efforts and assets to ensure a complete picture in congruence with the commander's PIR. This element would also have exclusive control of all outside agency participation in theater, coordinating these agencies' collection and analysis capabilities and ensuring a complementary theater-wide effort.

The functional analysis section would be the knowledge base of the organization, acting as a theater information service for lower echelons. The element would be segmented into a number of cross-functional teams responsible for analysis and the identification of collection gaps for each identified militia, criminal, and insurgent group. This section would also be in charge of creating the green, or Iraqi, intelligence picture (government, religious, and tribal) of the country and their ties.

Each of these functional teams would be cross disciplinary in terms of intelligence capability, representing all aspects of the intelligence discipline. Whatever functional gaps that were identified would be outsourced to the coordination/tasking team to ensure that the proper collection activities are identified and coordinated. These functional teams would act in an advisory capacity to tactical intelligence elements, providing specific analysis of different groups regarding their respective area of responsibility.

Within the CIN, a liaison element would also be present, representative of all brigade combat commands and participant agencies. These elements would be operationally controlled by their parent unit, fielding questions and requirements from each section. These liaisons would serve three functions: as a research librarian to get analytical answers to specific unit questions, as a transmission element for needed and disseminated product, and as a "surge" analytical reserve to meet unit or CIN analysis needs. These liaisons would be rotated through their respective units every ninety days to ensure CIN regional awareness. In this way, the brigade intelligence organization would have extensive knowledge of current long-term predictive analysis and developed unit-CIN relationships to ensure their local analysis needs are advocated and met.

The current intelligence section would issue theater-wide assessments and answer questions for higher agencies, writing the analytical reports and analysis that keep uninvolved military and civilian leadership aware of the Iraqi situation. Their assignments would be controlled and directed by the CIN coordination element, which would act as the filter.

Some of these elements described already exist in one form or another. Other parts would have to be formed from existing structures and all aspects of the change would necessarily be staged and, unfortunately, organizationally painful to live through. But they are necessary to properly leverage the existing resources to their maximum capability.

Be Smarter Than Your Equipment: Critically Rethink Standardization, Information Management, and Analytical Procedure

As discussed before, the current analytical procedure and tool integration are in need of revision. Because of the elemental differences in counterinsurgency versus a force-on-force conflict, a new and revolutionary, not evolutionary, series of procedures must be created to account for the peculiar needs of the Iraqi counter-insurgency effort. This reassessment must be a zero-based approach—that is, requirements must be derived and solutions must be designed based solely on need without using existing methods or technique as a basis. To do otherwise would simply reintroduce procedural bias and errors that we currently suffer from.

This procedural, analytical, and doctrinal revision must be scalable, flexible, and adaptable. It must leverage existing data-processing strengths to solve existing problems. Finally, analytical outsourcing must be considered as an option to ease throughput limitations on existing unit structures. The answer to a lack of manpower is not wishing for or growing the specific specialties on paper, but using what we have in a new way that is complementary and synergistic to the needs of the environment. To quote Theodore Roosevelt, we must do what we can, with what we have, where we are. Redesigning our collection and analysis tools would be a large step in that direction.

For example, this means reassessing compartmentalization of intelligence collection and streamlining or outright eliminating bureaucratic divisions of labor, be they procedural or administrative. Such revision would require leveraging existing automation equipment to maximize automation capability rather than procedural preference. Finally, such methods must imbue looking at data as a means and not an end to information.

All aspects of our operation must be examined, then streamlined, revised, or simply eliminated. We must push the theoretical limits of our art and derive analytical tools specific to a counterinsurgency. Everything must be questioned, assessed, and, if necessary, discarded. We must create the right tools for the environment. Nothing less will do.

Conclusion

To date, the intelligence collection and analysis apparatus has been directly responsible for some stunning Coalition successes. But currently, our organizational and procedural methods have succeeded in creating the perfect storm of lost opportunities and poor analysis and have lead us to reactive, instead of proactive, prosecution of the counterinsurgency. In our present state, these are problems we do not even realize are occurring. But although these current series of issues that face Coalition intelligence are daunting, they are still solvable.

Addressing these issues requires a serious reexamination and revision of how we organize to collect intelligence, process that intelligence, and analyze that intelligence to determine vulnerabilities and predict future trends. We need to design analytical procedures to fit the environment, not try to change the environment to fit the procedure. Such activity leaves us scratching our head when the leadership of the insurgency is eliminated yet there is no resulting collapse of the group he led. It also leaves us unprepared for the current militia threat, intense sectarian violence, and whatever else may lie ahead.

There is no question that we will eventually prevail and defeat our enemies. But unless there is an overhaul in the manner in which we research and study the weaknesses in the insurgent environment, we will be at the mercy of rude surprise, shock, and a very long fight. A reorganization of our intelligence apparatus and our method will go a long way to shortening the path to victory. Sun Tzu admonished, "In war, let your great object be victory, not lengthy campaigns." Perhaps we should heed his advice and reshape our intelligence tools with this maxim in mind.

28

Massing Effects in the Information Domain: A Case Study in Aggressive Information Operations*

—LTG Thomas F. Metz, USA, with LTC Mark W. Garrett, USA; LTC James E. Hutton, USA; and LTC Timothy W. Bush, USA

> I say to you: that we are in a battle, and that more than half of this battle is taking place in the battlefield of the media. And that we are in a media battle in a race for the hearts and minds of our Umma.
>
> —Ayman al-Zawahiri [1]

> If I were grading I would say we probably deserve a "D" or a "D-plus" as a country as to how well we're doing in the battle of ideas that's taking place in the world today.
>
> —Secretary of Defense Donald Rumsfeld, March 27, 2006 [2]

In 1995, the Department of the Army, Forces Command, and the Training and Doctrine Command began a joint venture called Force XXI, the focus of which was to understand how information-age technology could improve the U.S. Army's war-fighting capabilities. While many experiments with information technology and theory were conducted across the Army, the Task Force XXI (TFXXI) and Division XXI Advanced War-fighting Experiments (AWE) were the capstone events of this venture. More than seventy initiatives were reviewed in the TFXXI AWE, which culminated at Fort Irwin, California, in March 1997 with the 1st Brigade Combat Team, 4th Infantry Division's National Training Center rotation.

* This essay appeared in the Military Review, May–June 2006, and is reprinted by permission.

At the heart of this experiment was near-real-time location knowledge of friendly units down to individual vehicles and, in some cases, individual Soldiers. The experiment proved that "where I am and where my buddies are" is powerful information for combat leaders. Leaders at all echelons became convinced that information-age technology would help our Soldiers, leaders, and formations become much more capable.

Post-AWE, the Army decided to reduce its combat power in combat and combat support formations by a quarter to afford the coming technology. However, our Army has not fully exploited the available technology, especially in the domain of information and knowledge management operations.

Information Operations (IO) in the AWE

After graduating from the U.S. Army War College and serving as a division G3, brigade commander, and division chief of staff, I was assigned to the Training and Doctrine Command with duty at Fort Hood in the 4th Infantry Division to support the Force XXI Joint Venture. Although I had no background in information technology or acquisition experience, I was involved with the preparation, execution, and after-action reviews of the TFXXI AWE and preparation for the Division XXI AWE. In the summer of 1997, I was assigned as assistant division commander for support of the 4th Infantry Division. As I took on this assignment, I was optimistic that the results of the Division XXI AWE would support what we had learned with the TFXXI AWE, and that our Army would continue to aggressively pursue applying information-age technology to improve our war-fighting capabilities. Although I lacked a technical background in information technology, I was confident that we were only beginning to understand the potential improvements to war fighting. I believed that funding, developing, understanding, and maturing these capabilities were certainly going to be challenging. I was excited about their prospects. But I was not prepared for the management of information operations (IO).

Shortly before the Division XXI AWE, a decision was made to add an objective to the experiment, focusing attention on IO. Because the simulation that would drive the Division XXI AWE was not designed to train this new aspect of war-fighting, a "Green Cell" was established that would inject information operations events. MG William S. Wallace, commanding general of the 4th Infantry Division at that time, gave me the task to manage this new IO challenge.

I wasted no time gathering all I could find on the subject of IO and began to study it. At this stage of our preparations, our standard operating procedures, battle rhythm, and command post drills were well established. Adding IO at this late date seemed to be a good idea added too late. Nevertheless, in the short time available, I learned as much as I could about the five disciplines that make up our doctrinal IO: psychological operations (PSYOPS), deception, operational security (OPSEC), electronic warfare (EW), and computer network operations (CNO).

IO's Importance in Iraq

Although I don't think we enhanced the AWE by adding IO, the opportunity to focus on this new doctrine did pay dividends six years later when, as the commanding general of III Corps, I found myself preparing the corps' headquarters to deploy to Operation Iraqi Freedom. Although IO doctrine had not changed over those six years, its importance to a successful campaign in Iraq and to the Global War on Terrorism was clear to many in and out of uniform.

On February 1, 2004, III Corps relieved V Corps. LTG Ric Sanchez remained the commander of Combined Joint Task Force-7, and I became his deputy. Over the next thirteen months—five as Sanchez's deputy and eight as the commander of Multinational Corps-Iraq (MNC-I)—my staff, our subordinate units, and I gained a very healthy respect for IO and knowledge and perception management, primarily because our enemy was better than we were in operating in the information domain, certainly in perception management. Although little has formally changed in our IO doctrine, many leaders, both friend and foe, understand its awesome power. So why is it that we can't seem to be the best at IO as we are in so many other areas? Where is our initiative? Where is our offensive spirit?

In April 2006, with the help of the Battle Command Training Program (BCTP), III Corps conducted a constructive simulation to train the headquarters of the 1st Cavalry Division as it prepared for its potential return to Iraq. As the exercise director of this Warfighter, I was disappointed at what little progress we have made in IO. The capabilities to move information not only around the battlefield but also around the world have grown exponentially, IO's importance grows daily, and our enemy, who recognizes that victory can be secured in this domain alone, has seized the opportunity to be the best at operating in the information domain.

The Green Cell had matured over the eight years since the Division XXI AWE, and although its formal objective for 1st Cav's BCTP Warfighter was to drive IO, it spent little time in the five disciplines of our doctrinal IO. It did, however, spend very important time in helping division headquarters prepare for the perception of a war it might face in Iraq—regretfully by being reactive instead of proactive.

I am absolutely convinced that we must approach IO in a different way and turn it from a passive war-fighting discipline to an active one. We must learn to employ aggressive IO. We cannot leave this domain for the enemy; we must fight him on this battlefield and defeat him there just as we've proven we can on conventional battlefields.

The Current Information Situation

In an open letter to President George W. Bush published in the January 2006 issue of the *Armed Forces Journal*, Joseph Collins, a former Deputy Assistant Secretary of Defense for Stability Operations in Bush's administration, predicted that "[i]f our strategic communications on Iraq don't improve, the strategy for victory will fail and disastrous consequences will follow."[3] We are not consistently achieving synergy and mass in our strategic communications (consisting of IO, public affairs [PA], public diplomacy, and military diplomacy) from the strategic to the tactical level, but blaming the IO component for the overall situation is too convenient and too narrow. The perception that IO should shoulder the blame is based on expectations that are beyond the doctrinal charter or operational capabilities of IO as currently resourced. The collective belief is that we lack the necessary skills, resources, and guidance to synchronize IO in order to achieve tangible effects on the battlefield.

Further complicating our efforts in the information domain is the fact that we are facing an adaptive, relentless, and technologically savvy foe who recognizes that the global information network is his most effective tool for attacking what he perceives to be our center of gravity: public opinion, both domestic and international. And the truth of the matter is that our enemy is better at integrating information-based operations, primarily through mass media, into his operations than we are. In some respects, we seem tied to our legacy doctrine and less than completely resolved to cope with the benefits and challenges of information globalization. We are too wedded to procedures that are anchored in the Cold War–industrial age.

Nevertheless, there appears to be an emerging recognition among war fighters that a broader, more aggressive, comprehensive, and holistic approach to IO—an approach that recognizes the challenges of the global information environment and seamlessly integrates the functions of traditional IO and PA—is required to succeed on the information age battlefield. Furthermore, a clear need exists for strategic and operational commanders to become as aggressive and as offensive minded with information operations as they have always been with other elements of combat power and war-fighting functions—movement and maneuver, fire support, intelligence, and so on. Given the follow-on successes of XVIII Airborne Corps and the current success of V Corps, we are clearly making progress, but we still have much to do to ingrain these advances into the institutional structure.

Examples abound where we have failed to mass effects and leverage all of the available tools in the information domain; likewise, we have examples where we have effectively bridged the gap between IO and PA to achieve integrated full-spectrum effects. Comparing Operation Vigilant Resolve and Operation Al Fajr clearly illustrates the power of an aggressive, holistic approach to integrating IO into the battle plan. A careful study of IO in support of Operation Al Fajr suggests three imperatives for the future of full-spectrum operations:

- The successful massing of information effects requires the commander to clearly articulate his intent for the integration of all the available elements of operations in the information domain into the battle plan.
- The successful massing of information effects requires precise and disciplined execution from shaping operations through exploitation.

- Commanders at all echelons must, at present, serve as the bridge across the doctrinal gap between IO and PA in order to synchronize efforts in the information domain. Only in this way will the intended effect be achieved.

Information Power

In April 2004, in response to the murder and desecration of Blackwater contractors in Fallujah, Coalition forces led by the I Marine Expeditionary Force (I MEF) launched Operation Vigilant Resolve, an assault to restore control of Fallujah. In spite of the superior combat power of I MEF—in leadership, movement and maneuver, and fire support—the operation failed because operations in the information domain were not integrated into the battle plan. In effect, we failed to give the war fighter on the ground the best opportunity to achieve a decisive victory. Steps to prepare the information battlefield, including engaging numerous and varied Iraqi leaders, removing enemy information centers, and rapidly disseminating information from the battlefield to worldwide media, were not woven into the plan.

U.S. forces unilaterally halted combat operations after a few days because of a lack of support from the Iraqi Interim Government and international pressures amid media focus on unsubstantiated enemy reports of collateral damage and excessive force. Marines won virtually every combat engagement throughout the battle and did so within the established rules of engagement. The missing element was an overall integrated information component to gain widespread support of significant influencers and to prepare key publics for the realities of the battle plan. Without such advance support, the finest combat plan executed by competent and brave Soldiers and Marines proved limited in effectiveness. The insurgent forces established links with regional and global media outlets that had agendas of their own. Our failure to mass effects in the global information sphere proved decisive on the battleground in Fallujah.[4]

Raising the IO Threshold

As the summer of 2004 passed and the Fallujah brigade experiment failed, it became imperative that the city's festering insurgent safe haven had to be removed. Planning for Operation Al Fajr—an assault to decisively clear Fallujah of insurgent activity—was initiated. A key task for MNC-I planners was to ensure that the information defeat of Vigilant Resolve was not repeated in Operation Al Fajr. Accordingly, we focused our planning to avoid replication of Vigilant Resolve and to prevent the worldwide media clamor and international public condemnation that would negatively impact operations.

To articulate a clear intent in the information domain, we developed what we called "the IO threshold." Its purpose was to enable the MNC-I commander to visualize a point at which enemy information-based operations (aimed at international, regional, and local media coverage) began to undermine the Coalition forces' ability to conduct unconstrained combat operations. As Operation Vigilant

Resolve proved, the enemy understands the idea of an IO threshold. He is capable of effectively using the global media to impede our operations by creating the perception that our combat operations are indiscriminate, disproportionate, and in violation of the rules of war.

Using the commander's intent for massed effects in the information domain as expressed in terms of the IO threshold, we illustrated to our subordinate commanders that kinetic shaping operations had to be conducted underneath the IO threshold; that is, we couldn't remove a city block to prepare the battlefield because such an act could create negative effects in the information domain. Any resulting negative international and local media coverage could impair the conduct of the overall campaign, as had happened during Operation Vigilant Resolve.

We used the same concept to brief the operation to Multinational Force-Iraq (MNF-I) commander GEN George Casey and to convince him that when I MEF executed the decisive operation, crossing the IO threshold could not distract us from our tactical and operational objectives. Once across the threshold, we planned for success to be achieved in days and hours.

Using this intent as a guideline, MNF-I, MNC-I, and Multinational Force-West (MNF-W) developed courses of action to mass effects in the information domain, thereby raising the IO threshold and creating additional "maneuver" room for combat operations in Fallujah. We deliberately countered enemy information campaigning, planned and executed IO shaping operations, and executed carefully planned senior leader engagements, military diplomacy, and public diplomacy activities. As a result of these synchronized, integrated, and complementary actions, we were able to mass information effects and build a strong base of support for combat operations in advance of the operation. In other words, we were able to raise the IO threshold by preparing key influencers and agencies for the impending operation.

This offensive mind-set and aggressive massing of effects resulted in two additional complementary effects. First, MNC-I placed additional pressure on the enemy throughout Iraq through the elimination of widespread support for his activities. Second, decision makers were prepared for the pending operation and given the necessary information to prepare their constituencies for the operation.

IO in Operation Al Fajr

As with other operations, massing effects in the information domain requires disciplined execution by leaders, Soldiers, and staffs at all echelons. In Operation Al Fajr, this meant precise, painstaking execution of all the core elements of traditional IO as well as other elements of combat power that had information implications. Doctrinal IO—deception, OPSEC, PSYOPS, EW, and CNO—played a significant role in our shaping operations. Fallujah became a textbook case for the coordination and use of the core elements of IO capabilities in support of the tactical fight.

Deception and OPSEC—MNF-I, MNC-I, and MNF-W used deception and OPSEC to conceal our buildup of forces north of Fallujah. We attempted to focus the enemy's attention on the south by constant and aggressive patrolling and feints from the south while simultaneously executing precision strikes in the southern parts of the city. Movement by the British Black Watch Battle Group and employment of a very maneuverable brigade combat team in a dynamic cordon also aided in this effort.

PSYOPS—MNC-I conducted very effective PSYOPS encouraging noncombatants to leave the city and persuading insurgents to surrender. These doctrinal psychological operations might have been the most important aspect of our operations to defeat the enemy in Fallujah, as some estimates showed that 90 percent of the noncombatants departed the city.

Electronic warfare—MNC-I and MNF-W also controlled the enemy's communications capabilities by restricting his access to select communications. They not only denied the enemy a means to communicate but also directed him to a means that we could monitor.

Computer network operations—Although we cannot discuss operations in this realm here, we must not allow the enemy to win the battle in cyberspace.

The massing of information effects in Al Fajr was also apparent in the incorporation of information considerations into the application of other elements of combat power. The seizure of the Fallujah Hospital by Iraqi commandos during the early stages of the battle provides an excellent example of the integration of full-spectrum planning, rehearsing, and execution of IO in support of overall campaign objectives. During the military decision-making process, MNF-W identified a piece of key IO terrain that it believed had to be secured early in the operation to begin eliminating the enemy's ability to disseminate misinformation and propaganda. The Fallujah Hospital had long been used as a propaganda organ by insurgent forces and had been one of the most significant sources of enemy information during Operation Vigilant Resolve. By securing this key IO terrain, MNF-W could significantly disrupt the enemy's access point to disseminate information.

The Iraqi 36th Commando Battalion captured the Fallujah Hospital in the first major combat operation of Al Fajr. Documented by CBS reporter Kirk Spitzer, this operation established Coalition control of the enemy propaganda platform while building the legitimacy of the Iraqi Security Forces as well as the Iraqi Interim Government. Although this small attack garnered only a footnote in history, it was decisive to winning the IO battle. Without this portal, the enemy had a much weaker voice.

Bridging the IO-PA Firewall

In order to mass effects in the information domain and effectively integrate IO into the battle plan, the war fighter must find a way to bridge the doctrinal firewall separating IO and PA without violating the rules governing both. This firewall is essential to ensuring PSYOPS, deception operations, EW, and CNO do not migrate into PA and discredit the PA effort. We need to be proud of our values and be prepared to underwrite the risk that we will expose too much in the service of transparency; this is counterbalanced with an implicit trust that our values and the truth will eventually prevail. Truth and transparency are strengths and not hindrances. Truth and transparency in PA are the military's legal obligation, and they also reinforce the effectiveness of our IO by providing a trusted source of information to domestic and international media. Providing information is only effective in the long run if the information is truthful and squares with the realities faced by its recipients.

The challenge is getting the truth out in an appealing package before the enemy does. Timing is critical. Furthermore, we must recognize that the current global media gravitates toward information that is packaged for ease of dissemination and consumption; the media will favor a timely, complete story. The enemy knows this, but he is not encumbered by the truth or regulations, making our challenge that much harder.

As our main force entered Fallujah from the north (which the enemy did not expect until 2,000-pound precision weapons breached the railway berm and the main attack launched), they did so with guidance:

- To be prepared to execute actions specifically tailored to capture photographic documentation of insurgent activities (see figure 28.1).
- To pass that information quickly up the chain to MNC-I, which would then turn that documentation into products that could be disseminated by the Iraqi government and our PA elements.

Specific guidance was handed down to key elements to develop bite-sized vignettes with graphics and clear story lines.[5] An example of massing effects, this small component of the battle enabled the Coalition to get its story out first and thereby dominate the information domain. Figure 28.2 is an example of this type of product. MNC-I used information from combat forces to construct a document that illustrated insurgent atrocities discovered in Fallujah. To borrow a football analogy, MNC-I flooded the zone with images and stories that the media could—and did—use.

The public affairs officer (PAO) and other staff sections can use information gathered from external sources. For example, the 1st Cavalry Division, operating as Task Force Baghdad, used information gained from multiple sources to create a product for public distribution. On the eve of the January 2005 election, insurgents attacked the U.S. embassy with rockets and killed embassy personnel. Media outlets fixated on the event. Some media coverage initially focused on the Coalition's inability to stop the insurgents even in the most secure areas. Even though the truth

Massing Effects in the Information Domain — 271

FIGURE 28.1: Operation Al-Fajr—Fallujah Insurgent Activities Map

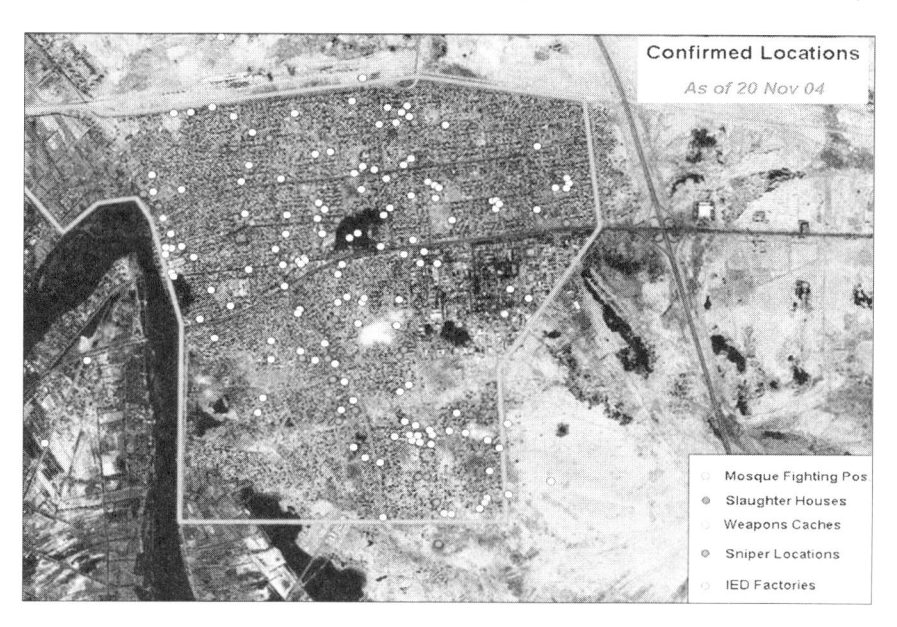

Confirmed Locations
As of 20 Nov 04

- Mosque Fighting Pos
- Slaughter Houses
- Weapons Caches
- Sniper Locations
- IED Factories

FIGURE 28.2: Fallujah Vignette #3, National Islamic Resistance Operations Center (NIROC) Atrocities

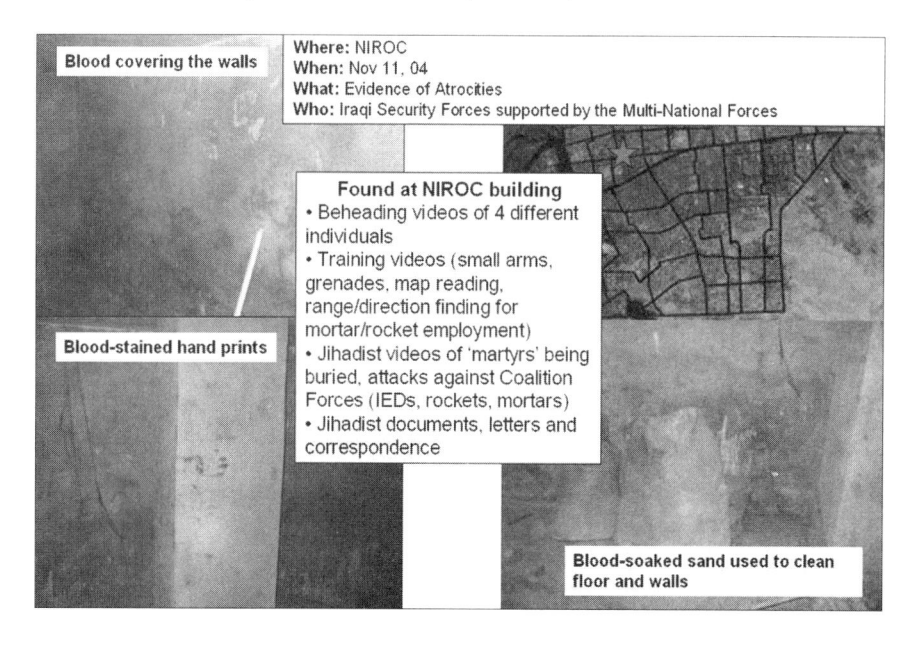

Blood covering the walls

Where: NIROC
When: Nov 11, 04
What: Evidence of Atrocities
Who: Iraqi Security Forces supported by the Multi-National Forces

Found at NIROC building
- Beheading videos of 4 different individuals
- Training videos (small arms, grenades, map reading, range/direction finding for mortar/rocket employment)
- Jihadist videos of 'martyrs' being buried, attacks against Coalition Forces (IEDs, rockets, mortars)
- Jihadist documents, letters and correspondence

Blood-stained hand prints

Blood-soaked sand used to clean floor and walls

of the matter was that the insurgents had no targeting capability and had merely struck the building through luck, the story line still had resonance.

What the insurgents did not know was that the image of the rocket firing was captured by an unmanned aerial vehicle (UAV). Through the UAV, analysts saw the group assemble and fire the weapon and then tracked their movement. Coalition forces moved to a house where the insurgents reassembled following the firing and detained most of those who had participated.

The 1st Cavalry Division simultaneously recorded the event, and the recording was quickly taken to the public affairs officer and edited for delivery to media. The product showed the rocket firing, the attempted escape from the area by the insurgents, and their capture. Using the relatively new capability for posting such items to a publicly accessible Web page via the Digital Video and Imagery Distribution System (DVIDS), the division alerted the media to its availability.[6] Media outlets downloaded the product, and the story line in the media shifted from the Coalition's inability to stop insurgent activity to how successful the Coalition was in detaining the insurgents.

Was this PA or IO? Developing a packaged product for dissemination might appear more like IO than PA, but it was clearly a PA action to utilize the DVIDS' capability. No media outlet could have collected this information independently. The PAO is charged by the commander to determine how best to provide information about the conduct of operations within the construct of doctrine and law. Surely, close cooperation with IO officers fits within doctrinal and legal parameters. Of course, such work should be done in conjunction with standard embedding of reporters and the provision of senior-leader access to the media as often as possible. Firsthand reporting by reporters from commercial outlets is indispensable to commanders seeking transparency. In fact, embedded reporters were critically important in the media coverage of Operation Al Fajr. More than eighty embedded reporters worked with MNF-W during combat operations.

In reality, these two vignettes (Al Fajr and the embassy attack) are clear examples of how we can mass effects in the information domain by leveraging all available tools. The 1st Cavalry PAO decided to use available technology to deliver a clearer public message about the course of events. Why shouldn't we use our situational awareness technology and network-centric warfare to give us an asymmetric advantage over our enemies? In Fallujah, when enemy forces used a mosque, a minaret, or some other protected site as a sniper position, the rules of engagement rightfully—and legally—enabled our Soldiers and leaders to engage with lethal force. We must have the agility to use our technological advantage, too, so that as a main gun round moves downrange to destroy a sniper position, simultaneously the digital image of the sniper violating the rules of war, plus the necessary information to create the packaged product, can be transmitted for dissemination to the news media.

Implications for the Future

> The big issue in our world is whether our doctrine and our policy are up to date. We owe more thinking to the combatant commanders. What are the things that should be balanced when you look at information and communications issues?
>
> *—Lawrence Di Rita[7]*

MNF-I, MNC-I, and MNF-W were successful in massing effects in the information domain in Operation Al Fajr for three reasons: we articulated an achievable end state; we took pains to integrate, synchronize, and execute with discipline all of the elements of combat power (leadership, movement and maneuver, intelligence) and all of the tools available in the information domain (traditional IO, PA, engagement, and political actions); and we were able to effectively bridge the firewall between IO and PA to achieve our desired end state without violating the rules of either discipline.

This integration has broader implications. We must consider how tactical actions will influence the operational and strategic levels. Because of its failure to influence important audiences, Operation Vigilant Resolve offers a cautionary tale for anyone who would downplay the significance of information in modern warfare.

If general expectations are that we should be able to compete and win the information battle in the global media environment—and this appears to be the general perception within our Army—then we must reshape our doctrine and develop ways to train in the new domains, ways that will evolve as the information age evolves. We should restructure the definitions of IO and PA and the relationship between them and develop a considerable global mass-marketing and public relations capability. There is no other option because "winning modern wars is as much dependent on carrying domestic and international public opinion as it is on defeating the enemy on the battlefield."[8]

This idea is not without controversy. The recent debate in the media concerning the use of the Lincoln Group to push written op-eds to Iraqi news outlets by paying for their placement illustrates that there are no clean lines in this discussion. Despite this situation, innovation and the use of new techniques will help us win future campaigns. The new reality simply will not enable Cold War methods to figuratively outgun technologically able enemies unfettered by cumbersome processes for dissemination of information.

In an article published in the *New York Times* on March 22, 2006, Lawrence Di Rita, co-director of a Pentagon panel studying communications questions for the Quadrennial Defense Review, said Rumsfeld and other senior officials were considering new policies for regional combatant commanders. Di Rita noted that "[t]he big issue in our world is whether our doctrine and our policy are up to date. We owe more thinking to the combatant commanders."[9]

Massing of effects in the information domain can be achieved, as evidenced by Operation Al Fajr. Functional progress within the realms of the communications professions (IO and PA) requires that we accommodate to the globalization of information. After III Corps departed and XVIII Airborne Corps took over as the new MNC-I in early 2005, it remained (and remains) clear that in Iraq our U.S. and Coalition partners have inculcated the lessons of Vigilant Resolve and Al Fajr.

We must address the challenges an interconnected global media/communications environment and its processes pose to our information-related operations, an environment in which timely and fully packaged stories are far more valuable than mere imagery. While acknowledging continued greater levels of globalization, we must be able to harness all of the elements of national power in an integrated manner. Doing so is absolutely critical if the United States is to successfully defend itself. Failure to do so could be ruinous.

29

Getting Inside the Cultural Context and Achieving Intelligence Success: Strategic Debriefing in the Iraq Survey Group

—*Col John A. Wahlquist, USAF (Ret.)*

Consequences of Intelligence Failure

On March 31, 2005, President George W. Bush formally received the report of his Commission on the Intelligence Capabilities of the United States Regarding Weapons of Mass Destruction (hereafter referred to as the President's WMD Commission). In a scathing indictment, the commission concluded "that the Intelligence Community was dead wrong in almost all of its pre-war judgments about Iraq's weapons of mass destruction."[1] It continued, "While the intelligence services of many other nations also thought that Iraq had weapons of mass destruction, in the end it was the United States that put its credibility on the line, making this one of the most public—and most damaging—intelligence failures in recent American history."[2]

The report of the President's WMD Commission, the eleventh examining failures of one sort or another in the Intelligence Community since 9/11,[3] immediately generated a certain wariness and fatigue on the part of beleaguered intelligence officials. One commented anonymously that "we've been spending so much time reorganizing, we haven't had time to see if the changes we've already made have worked."[4]

Since the report's release, the effects of the intelligence failure it documented continue to reverberate as the United States identifies and confronts new threats from Iran and North Korea. National security professionals, members of Congress, as well as the public at large remain skeptical of Intelligence Community assessments.

In the case of Iran, some individuals, such as Harvard professor and former U.S. government official Graham Allison, question the Intelligence Community's unanimous estimate that Iran will not be able to assemble a nuclear weapon until "early to mid next decade."[5] Noting more pessimistic estimates by Israeli intelligence, Allison asks, "Could the unanimity of American intelligence be 'déjà vu all over again,' only the reverse of the Iraq WMD fiasco?" Others suggest the Intelligence Community is erroneously inflating the threat with regard to Iran. In a February 23, 2007, article in *The Guardian*, a diplomat from the International Atomic Energy Agency, knowledgeable about his agency's inspections in Iran, stated that most of the intelligence on secret nuclear sites provided by U.S. intelligence "turned out to be incorrect."[6] Similar doubts about the accuracy of previous assessments of North Korea's nuclear capabilities reportedly are being raised within the Intelligence Community itself.[7] In this atmosphere of second-guessing from both inside and outside the Intelligence Community, what can be done to address the causes of these perceived failures and restore the confidence of military commanders, policymakers, the Congress, and, most important, the American people in the Intelligence Community's capabilities and professionalism?

Getting Inside the Cultural Context

The answer to this question could take a variety of paths; however, a constant theme emerging from publicly released reports confirms the late Markus Wolf's broad assessment of how to measure the effectiveness of any state's foreign intelligence service. Wolf, who spent thirty-four years as Chief of the Foreign Intelligence Service for the German Democratic Republic's Ministry of State Security and was one of the West's most effective Cold War adversaries, asserted that "it is the human factor that makes an espionage service successful, not its high-tech bells and whistles."[8]

While Wolf makes an important point, upgrading "the human factor" requires more than just a renewed emphasis on what we traditionally call HUMINT. To reverse the course of the Intelligence Community's public embarrassments, the community should adopt the broader concept of getting inside the cultural context. In an October 2004 article in *Proceedings*, Robert H. Scales, Jr., U.S. Army (Ret.), noted that Soldiers returning from Iraq have expressed concerns that the initial "conflict was fought brilliantly at the technological level but inadequately at the human level. The human element seems to underlie virtually all the functional shortcomings . . . most glaringly, intelligence, from national to tactical." Refining what that meant to the commander on the ground, General Scales quoted an officer from the 3d Infantry Division: "I had perfect situational awareness. What I lacked was cultural awareness."[9] No matter what intelligence collection discipline or combination of disciplines provides the sources of our information, if we do not get inside the cultural context of friends and allies, as well as enemies and adversaries, our efforts will be less effective or may fail. On the other hand, when we do get inside the cultural context, our capabilities to collect, analyze, understand, and advise will be magnified. It is, in effect, a force multiplier.

When I speak of the value of getting inside the cultural context, however, I am not confining it merely to studying and learning foreign languages or comprehending unfamiliar cultural, ethnic, and religious characteristics, as important as they may be.[10] Applying this concept is equally significant in our dealings with our joint, interagency, and Coalition intelligence and operational partners. Anyone who has worked in a joint or Coalition military headquarters, in an embassy, or has attempted to establish liaison relationships with any of the other members of the U.S. Intelligence Community or a foreign intelligence service, understands what I am talking about regarding the importance of cultural context in operating effectively with these organizations.

What follows is a case study of how getting inside the cultural context contributed to the success of our strategic debriefing program in the Iraq Survey Group (ISG). I will conclude by summarizing some ongoing initiatives that I believe will help the Intelligence Community expand this vital capacity.

Detainee Strategic Debriefing in the Iraq Survey Group

The mission of ISG was to find, exploit, and eliminate. The ISG was a presidentially mandated joint, interagency, and combined organization created in the wake of the Coalition invasion of Iraq and tasked with finding the truth about Iraq's weapons of mass destruction (WMD). Secretary of Defense Donald Rumsfeld established ISG on June 3, 2003, at Camp Slayer, a former Ba'ath Party recreation site near Baghdad International Airport. Early on, the Defense Intelligence Agency (DIA) became the ISG's executive agent, with operational leadership provided by Army MG Keith Dayton for the first year of ISG's existence, then Marine Corps BGen Joseph McMenamin, and last by Air Force Col Lloyd Summers, who formally closed ISG in late April 2005. The Special Adviser to the Director of Central Intelligence (DCI) on Iraq's WMD provided overall analytical leadership for ISG and oversaw the writing of ISG status reports, including the publicly released, three-volume *Comprehensive Report of the Special Adviser to the DCI on Iraq's WMD with Addendums* (hereafter referred to as the *Comprehensive Report*), finalized in March 2005. Dr. David Kay, a former official of the International Atomic Energy Agency who previously led compliance inspections in Iraq, held this post until February 2004. He was replaced by Charles Duelfer, a former Deputy Executive Secretary of the United Nations Special Commission (UNSCOM), an international body set up by the UN Security Council to find and dismantle Iraq's WMD capability after the first Gulf War.

The motto on ISG's crest was "Find, Exploit, Eliminate," but it should have included "Explain" when it became clear after months of looking that the alleged WMD stockpiles—the primary threat Operation Iraqi Freedom was launched to suppress—were not there. Responding to this development, Charles Duelfer's solution to framing his proposed formal explanation to the DCI was to focus less on the presence or absence of WMD stockpiles and more on what Mr. Duelfer called the former Iraqi regime's (strategic) "intent."[11] In other words, what would Saddam and his henchmen likely have done had they been able to pursue their strategic designs unhindered by UN sanctions and unchecked by the Coalition invasion.

To support this new approach, Mr. Duelfer created within the ISG Survey Analysis Center a Regime Strategic Intent (RSI) team whose role was to understand and explain Saddam's decisions to acquire, retain, and conceal Iraq's WMD and missile delivery capabilities, at the risk of regime destruction. The RSI team provided an overarching contextual and conceptual umbrella for the ISG's other functional analytical teams—nuclear, chemical-biological, delivery systems, regime finance and procurement, and political-military—to ensure "dynamic analysis rather than simple static accounting" of Iraq's WMD programs.[12] The information sources available to support RSI research were captured Iraqi documents and electronic media and former senior Iraqi officials in U.S. custody—so-called high-value detainees (HVDs). It was the testimony of this latter group, Saddam's most trusted agents as well as Saddam himself, that constituted the RSI team's primary references for shaping the content of Mr. Duelfer's *Comprehensive Report*.

To facilitate comprehensive HVD debriefing, certain members of the RSI team were designated to lead ad hoc, cross-functional teams focused on specific HVDs. On my arrival at Camp Slayer in April 2004, I was assigned to the RSI team and shortly thereafter to lead Team Huwaysh, the cross-functional team overseeing the debriefing of 'Abd-al-Tawab Al Mullah Huwaysh—the ten of hearts in the deck of cards identifying Iraq's most wanted former senior officials. Huwaysh was Saddam's fourth-ranking Deputy Prime Minister and Minister of Military Industrialization. From 1997 to 2003, he headed Iraq's mainly state-owned military-industrial complex, the Military Industrialization Commission. The assignment to lead Team Huwaysh prompted my serious contemplation of how to get inside the cultural context, first of my cross-functional team and, second, of Huwaysh himself.

Getting Inside the Cultural Context: Team Huwaysh

In its original formulation, Team Huwaysh consisted of representatives from all the functional analytical teams, including U.S. and allied military and civilian personnel. The military folks, fewer in number, were a mixture of active-duty and Reservists from the Air Force, Army, and Navy. The civilians, both U.S. and allied, were even more diverse in terms of affiliation and background. Among the American civilians, most represented national or military intelligence agencies, but agents from the Department of the Treasury and the Federal Bureau of Investigation participated sporadically based on their specific mission requirements. Several of the civilians were DIA contractors, most with prior military service. The allied civilians were active participants and contributors, equal partners in the debriefing and analytical process. A key member of Team Huwaysh was an assigned interrogator-debriefer from the Joint Interrogation and Debriefing Center (JIDC), an autonomous element within ISG's Survey Operations Center. Only a very few members of Team Huwaysh had prior service in Iraq, most as former UNSCOM inspectors. Only two, including the first JIDC interrogator-debriefer assigned to Team Huwaysh, spoke Arabic and only one or two had lived for any considerable time in the Middle East. The majority were subject matter experts (SMEs) in specific WMD-related technical fields or intelligence analysts detailed to Iraq by their respective agencies or governments.

Participation by a JIDC interrogator-debriefer on a cross-functional analytical team—in what might be considered a subordinate role—was a new and not particularly welcome arrangement for many old-school interrogators. The core mantra of an interrogator-debriefer is control: he or she develops the interrogation-debriefing strategy, directs everything that goes on in the interrogation booth, and is the primary authority figure in the lives of the individuals being interrogated. Traditionally, interrogator-debriefers have formal and impersonal relationships with intelligence analysts—receiving requirements, generally in the form of questions, from anonymous analysts and in return addressing those questions based on information acquired through interrogation or debriefing of human sources. Occasionally, analysts provide formal feedback to interrogator-debriefers on the value of the information, as well as pose more questions. While interrogator-debriefers seek this feedback, they also sometimes feel that analysts' expectations are unrealistic. To improve feedback, the intelligence agencies periodically apply pressure to increase the number of reports analysts evaluate. Generally this approach is counterproductive. The resulting fluctuations in the quantity and quality of analyst feedback confirm to some interrogator-debriefers what they already believe—that analysts are "clueless" about the real world.

Analysts, on the other hand, are inclined to view collectors, especially interrogator-debriefers, as "Neanderthals." They are convinced it is the intellectual discipline of analyzing and reconciling disparate and often contradictory information that actually creates intelligence, not merely extracting it from witting and unwitting sources. Analysts' notions of interrogation, formed from exposure to the popular media and the vivid images associated with the Abu Ghraib scandal, suggest its practitioners are focused primarily on intimidation. Analysts view the reports written by interrogators as too often semiliterate and unimaginative. In fact, analysts tend to see the entire intelligence collection and reporting system as another triumph of form over substance—form that serves primarily to lengthen the turnaround between collection and analysis in the intelligence cycle.

This clash of cultural stereotypes came to a head when JIDC agreed to assign an interrogator-debriefer to Team Huwaysh, with a senior RSI analyst overseeing the team. The initial instantiation of the concept, which occurred before I arrived, did not immediately alter the traditional expectations of analysts and collectors. But as their relationship evolved, it quickly lost its previous anonymity, roles began to blur, and a dynamic interactive process replaced the stereotypes. Most important, the collection-analysis loop tightened. While JIDC still required analysts to draft formal requirements before scheduling debriefings, often they were generic umbrella documents that allowed interrogator-debriefers maximum flexibility in their questioning. Because of the technical nature of WMD subject matter and the nontechnical backgrounds of most interrogator-debriefers, some analysts felt the HVDs were misleading their debriefers or were just misunderstanding their debriefers' questions. The answer was to put analysts in the interrogation booth as a resource directly available to the interrogator-debriefers. Seeing the actual debriefing was helpful to analysts in determining how their expertise could best be applied; little by little they became more involved in developing the debriefing strategy and their association with the interrogator-debriefers became a partnership. This turn of events was anathema to some old-school JIDC interrogators, who were accustomed to working solo in the booth and resisted having "outsiders," especially analysts, invade their space. But such reactions were the exception. Most interrogators saw the analysts as useful and even vital adjuncts in setting the conditions for successful debriefings.

Having previously been a HUMINT collector, I immediately recognized the importance of getting inside the cultural context of my JIDC interrogator-debriefers. Although I headed Team Huwaysh, I recognized and respected their ultimate authority in the booth. They bore overall responsibility for the success or failure of each debriefing, controlled its atmospherics (such as how we approached Huwaysh on different subjects), and were answerable for Huwaysh's health and welfare, including how he was treated by the guards. Fulfilling this responsibility required a host of administrative documentation in addition to the most important task—reporting the substance of the debriefing. Since interrogator-debriefers were consistently in short supply, those assigned to Team Huwaysh generally also covered several other HVDs. Sensitive to my interrogator-debriefers' demanding schedules, from my first day in the booth I took thorough notes during each debriefing. Two scribes are better than one, and my interrogator-debriefers always appreciated having another narrative of each debriefing that they could quickly check against their own notes, edit, and then push forward for publication.

Ascertaining cultural context was equally important in my relationship with the other members of Team Huwaysh. Each team member brought his or her own set of priorities, equities, talents, and bureaucratic perspectives to the team. Most team members represented one of the WMD functional-analytical teams: nuclear, chemical-biological, delivery systems, regime finance and procurement, and political-military. Except for the political-military team, each was under considerable pressure to produce a draft chapter for Mr. Duelfer's forthcoming *Comprehensive Report*. Some members of Team Huwaysh, because of the government agencies they represented, had separate requirements they were seeking to fulfill. Similarly, investigators assigned to the Regime Crimes Liaison Office, an independent organization set up by the President to gather evidence for prosecuting Saddam and former senior Iraqi officials,[13] coordinated their interviews with Team Huwaysh.

Each week Team Huwaysh would meet to discuss the results of the previous week's debriefings, review existing requirements, consider new requirements, and look for potential overlaps in order to maximize the efficiency of our debriefings. As team leader, my job was to orchestrate this process, primarily by serving as a liaison between the analysts and the interrogator-debriefer to help us prepare a tailored strategy for each session in the booth. Most analyst team members were simply looking for an opportunity to ask a set of "burning questions" that had been missed altogether, handled incompletely in previous debriefings, or had only recently arisen based on newly available evidence. Although I also had a list of "burning questions" relating to regime strategic intent, I opted to give priority to my fellow team members in the debriefing schedule. I did this for two reasons. First, it set a standard of cooperation that reassured everyone on the team that they would have an equal opportunity to address their list of debriefing priorities. Just because Team Huwaysh was an RSI-led enterprise did not mean that I would give automatic preference to my own requirements. This dispelled any lingering doubts among team members about fairness. Second, evidence of regime strategic intent was embedded in the debriefing results of all the functional-analytical teams, besides being a discrete subject in its own right. Recognizing my unique role, the interrogator-debriefer endorsed my presence at all of Huwaysh's debriefing sessions. As a result, I developed a unique rapport with both Huwaysh and the interrogator-debriefer that served our mission well.

Getting Inside the Cultural Context: 'Abd-al-Tawab Al Mullah Huwaysh

Most important for the success of Team Huwaysh was to understand its namesake, 'Abd-al-Tawab Al Mullah Huwaysh. Who was Huwaysh, what motivated him, and why did he serve Saddam with such loyalty? Answers to these questions were central to how we approached Huwaysh in seeking answers to the larger questions of regime strategic intent. The key was getting inside Huwaysh's cultural context, a unique blend of traditional and modern Arab influences. Born in the Sunni Muslim heartland of Fallujah and the son of a wealthy businessman and property owner whose family roots were in Tadmur, Syria (ancient Palmyra), Huwaysh grew up in Baghdad and attended primary and secondary school there. In the late 1950s he won a government scholarship to study petroleum engineering in Romania. After a one-year matriculation, he abruptly moved to the Federal Republic of Germany (because of his claimed dislike for Communism) and convinced the Iraqi government to reinstate his scholarship if he learned enough German to pass university entrance exams there. He accomplished this remarkable feat in one year and eventually completed a bachelor's degree in mechanical engineering and a master's in industrial engineering. In the meantime, he married a German woman and started a family that eventually produced three children. Interestingly, his language at home with his family was German, not Arabic, and he also spoke English (learned in secondary school) and Romanian. Although proud of his Sunni Muslim heritage, throughout most of his professional career, Huwaysh was not a devout Muslim.

Rising rapidly within the Iraqi government bureaucracy, Huwaysh joined the Ba'ath Party and gained a reputation as a competent engineer and an innovative, aggressive, and rather impetuous technocrat. In 1987, Saddam Hussein appointed him Minister of Industry only to fire him less than a year later after an altercation in a cabinet meeting between Huwaysh and Saddam's son-in-law, Husayn Kamil. Huwaysh barely avoided jail and was relegated to the role of presidential adviser, where Saddam retained him on the government payroll and assigned him a few tasks but did not talk to him for the next nine years. During this period, Huwaysh received Saddam's permission to seek opportunities in the private sector. His frozen foods business and other pursuits flourished despite Iraq's unrelenting economic tragedy, incurred as a result of UN sanctions. In March 1997, Saddam unexpectedly rehabilitated Huwaysh, appointed him Director of the Military Industrialization Commission (MIC), and tasked him to rebuild Iraq's shattered state-run military-industrial complex, the previous home of Iraq's WMD research, development, and production programs. Although never a member of Saddam's political inner circle, Huwaysh nevertheless established a close association with Saddam that continued uninterrupted over the next six years until the Iraqi government disintegrated, in March 2003, under the onslaught of Operation Iraqi Freedom. Saddam promoted Huwaysh to Minister of Military Industrialization in late 1997 and then appointed him a Deputy Prime Minister in July 2001. During his tenure, "the MIC budget increased over forty-fold from Iraqi dinar (ID) 15.5 billion to ID 700 billion, despite ongoing UN sanctions and Coalition attacks on its facilities.... MIC's reemergence provided the research, technological, and industrial foundation on which Saddam hoped to rebuild and modernize Iraq's military-industrial capabilities" once UN sanctions were lifted.[14]

Perhaps Huwaysh's defining characteristic was his status as an engineer. Among his generation of talented young Arab men who were sent abroad to study, almost all returned as either medical doctors or engineers, commanding respect beyond their years for having risen early to this pinnacle of professional achievement within the Middle East. As engineers, even when they received other political titles or military ranks, "engineer" was nearly always attached. Justifiably, Huwaysh took great pride in being an engineer and regarded other engineers as his only true intellectual equals. His highest accolade was to describe someone as "accurate." While he considered himself an enlightened manager, he freely acknowledged dealing harshly with dishonest and lazy employees and had a reputation as a bully among some of his subordinates.[15] Competence, performance, and accountability are what counted with Huwaysh, not family connections or sectarian affiliation. Among the leadership of the massive 65,000-employee MIC bureaucracy he headed, seven of his nine Directors General were Shi'a Muslims (Iraq's generally distrusted majority Muslim sect), prompting Saddam Hussein himself to take note and express reservations. Huwaysh pulled individuals of talent and skill for his various weapons programs from wherever he could find them, including Saddam's jails. He was not, however, entirely egalitarian when it came to his perception of where the Shi'a fit in Iraqi society. Although Huwaysh believed that Shi'a made very good and even brilliant technicians and administrators, he considered them ill suited for Iraqi political or military leadership because of what he felt were inherent conflicts in their loyalty between the Iraqi state and their coreligionists in Iran.

Huwaysh had no military experience, but he relished wearing his green Ba'ath Party military-style uniform and a pistol, which subordinates reported seeing him fire in the air enthusiastically at pro-Saddam rallies.[16] Despite his apparent zeal for military trappings, Huwaysh was not in awe of the military as an institution or of its leadership, believing that most of Saddam's officers, except for the engineers, were sycophants who advanced their careers based on party or family connections rather than competence. A workaholic who regularly worked every night until 11:00 and only rarely took a day off, Huwaysh was motivated not only by his fear of displeasing Saddam, but also by his love of Iraq. It was very important to Huwaysh to be seen as a loyal Iraqi who loved his country and who provided service to it out of affection rather than self-aggrandizement. By all credible accounts, he was free of financial impropriety. He was dedicated to expending his best efforts as well as MIC's resources to see Iraq take its place on its own terms as an equal with the West. And while he took great pains to keep his personal affairs separate from affairs of state, he managed almost every day to have lunch at home with his wife.

With these basic personality and character traits in mind, I worked with each of my interrogator-debriefers to devise a strategy that would get us inside Huwaysh's cultural context. A primary focus was his pride in being an engineer. By assiduously preparing for each session, including studying unclassified UNSCOM and other United Nations technical reports, reviewing available Iraqi documents, and being tutored by SMEs from other ISG teams, I was determined to appear technically competent. The effort paid off. Based on our interactions, Huwaysh believed me to be an engineer and responded accordingly. He viewed our sessions as deliberations among colleagues, not as an interrogation. Often in the midst of a technical discussion Huwaysh would confide to me *muhandis illa muhandis* (engineer to engineer) some specific piece of information that he had intentionally withheld during earlier debriefings because his interlocutors were not engineers. In particular, he seemed to derive great satisfaction from demonstrating his command of the wide variety of technical projects and issues associated with MIC. He was eager to convince us that he was not just some Ba'ath Party hack or Tikriti family member, as were so many of Saddam's other senior people, but a skilled engineer and hands-on senior manager whose work measurably enhanced Iraqi military-industrial capability. We used his professional zeal to our advantage by giving him unclassified technical papers and UNSCOM reports on Iraqi WMD and other issues and then discussing their conclusions. He professed to enjoy the stimulation of this give-and-take, and it opened opportunities for him to share detailed information with us that had not surfaced in earlier debriefings. Additionally, the discussions provided an occasion for him to alter his thinking on certain issues when the facts so persuaded him. In the process, he admitted he learned new things and began to see the former UN inspection regime and the Coalition position vis-à-vis Iraq in a different light, even if he didn't agree with it.

In stature, Huwaysh was not an imposing figure, but his self-confidence enhanced his physical presence. As self-assured as Huwaysh normally appeared, he did suffer from debilitating ailments—early symptoms of Parkinson's disease and congenital deafness in both ears requiring hearing aids. The latter defect gained him some notoriety with Saddam, who accused Huwaysh, only half in jest, of turning down the volume on his hearing aids in cabinet meetings when he got bored with the proceedings. As his internment lengthened, Huwaysh's physical and emotional reserves continued to wane. Physically, we ensured he had adequate medication to counteract the effects of his worsening Parkinson's symptoms and even purchased batteries from the United States to keep his hearing aids operational when the right batteries were not available in Iraq. Emotionally, we spent time talking with him about his family and arranging periodic phone calls to them in Jordan to buoy his spirits. My age also was a positive factor. He favored debriefing with individuals closer to his generation. He often would talk about his grandchildren and his aspirations for their future. Being a grandparent myself worked to my advantage. On one occasion he brought a picture of his family to show me, including his two sons and all his grandchildren. I commented that their combined Iraqi and German heritage was clearly evident. For our next debriefing session, I brought a picture of one of my granddaughters and my daughter-in-law, who is Lebanese American and has very strong Lebanese features. Looking at the picture and then at me, Huwaysh remarked, "They are part of us!" Besides these personal connections, my years spent living and working in the Middle East, my knowledge of Middle East and Iraqi history, and my appreciation for Islam (I recounted to Huwaysh that I had once fasted throughout the holy month of Ramadan) provided several breakthrough, rapport-building opportunities with Huwaysh that we used to good advantage in our debriefings.

Huwaysh accepted our invitation to conduct our debriefings in English, but on occasion he would resort to German or Arabic to more precisely express the meaning of certain concepts. Fortunately, my first interrogator-debriefer spoke both fluent German and Arabic, and since I also understand and read Arabic (but am far short of being fluent), we could move smoothly from one language to another without missing anything substantive. Even when discussing various individuals and programs in English, it was helpful to have Huwaysh write names and key words in Arabic, to ensure we were hearing and transcribing them correctly. Our knowledge of Arabic also helped us identify some key documents among the multitude of captured documents the ISG had acquired. These were especially valuable in prompting Huwaysh's memory about various events or personalities that during earlier questioning he had overlooked or conveniently forgotten. It always focused his attention when we were able to produce a copy of a potentially controversial document that he had either signed or initialed, or one that showed his name on a list of senior government officials who had their phones tapped by Iraqi internal security. Additionally, we gave Huwaysh "homework" assignments that he chose to answer in detailed, handwritten Arabic, with one draft totaling almost thirty pages. ISG linguists translated his drafts into typed English transcripts that we returned to Huwaysh for discussion and further editing in English. Given his penchant for accuracy, Huwaysh was very meticulous in these reviews to ensure details were not lost in translation. Whether in English, Arabic, or German, he remained the consummate engineer throughout this process.

Results

So what results did we achieve by getting inside Huwaysh's cultural context? Our debriefing sessions with Huwaysh, and those conducted by earlier interrogator-debriefers, provided reports covering a multitude of technical, political, and organizational issues. The depth and breadth of the information he supplied, much of which was incorporated in Mr. Duelfer's *Comprehensive Report*, was essential to discerning and documenting Saddam's strategic intent. All of the following topics (and more) are included in the more than 150 reports drawn from Huwaysh's debriefings:

- Iraqi WMD and missile delivery system research and development programs during the 1990s
- History, organization, and functioning of the MIC, including detailed information on research, development, and production of specific weapons systems
- Former Iraqi regime's high-level decision-making processes
- Iraq's interaction with the UN Special Commission and UN Monitoring, Verification, and Inspection Commission, and their inspectors and leaders
- Saddam's personality, character, leadership, and decision-making style
- Biographical information on key Iraqi scientists and government officials
- Significant Iraqi industrialization efforts in the government as well as private sector
- Development of sophisticated Iraqi government procurement channels with complicit international parties to circumvent UN sanctions

- Iraq's use of the UN Oil for Food program to earn additional hard currency for funding weapons programs
- Iraq's political and economic relations with regional and international partners
- Iraqi government's use of academics to further research and development of WMD and other weapon systems, including scams perpetrated by unscrupulous entrepreneurs.

The Way Ahead

While the intelligence activity I have recounted is anecdotal, it is also suggestive of the decisive advantages to be gained by improving our ability to get inside the cultural context of friends and foes alike. So what is the Intelligence Community doing to increase its capacity in this vital area?

Getting inside the cultural context, as I have defined it, figures prominently in former Director of National Intelligence (DNI) John D. Negroponte's bold reform agenda for the Intelligence Community as published in his October 2005 *National Intelligence Strategy of the United States of America*. First of all, it emphasizes that "transformation of the Intelligence Community will be driven by the doctrinal principal of integration."[17] The community must "tap expertise wherever it resides . . . leveraging the unique capabilities of each component" as well as making use of outside expertise.[18] This principle is especially important in our collaborative efforts at home and abroad to "identify, disrupt, and destroy terrorist organizations" wherever they exist.[19] Additionally, the *National Intelligence Strategy* stresses the value to the Intelligence Community of achieving greater insight into the "intentions of hard targets . . . improving human intelligence capabilities," and "develop[ing], sustain[ing], and hav[ing] access to expertise on every region, every transnational security issue, and every threat to the American people."[20] To meet these ambitious requirements the Intelligence Community must "coordinate closely with foreign intelligence services" and "promote deeper cultural understanding [and] better language proficiency . . . among personnel at all levels."[21]

A primary means of inculcating cultural awareness across the board within the military, according to General Scales, is to focus on professional and cultural education, instilling learning as a lifelong process.[22] The U.S. Marine Corps, in particular, has taken this concept to heart. The corps' forward-looking Center for Advanced Operational Cultural Learning (CAOCL) was formally chartered in January 2006 to ensure "Marines are equipped with operationally relevant regional, culture, and language knowledge to allow them to plan and operate successfully in the joint and combined expeditionary environment in any region of the world." The CAOCL's tailored approach uses short- and long-term training and professional education programs throughout a Marine's career to develop cultural awareness as a force multiplier.[23] Focusing more specifically on such reforms within the Intelligence Community, former Speaker of the House of Representatives Newt Gingrich recommended to Congress a continuing regimen of intellectual development for intelligence professionals throughout their careers. Gingrich asserts that the

> National Intelligence University (NIU) System proposed by the DNI should be formally chartered to not only train the next generation of intelligence leaders but to use the best of its faculty and students to . . . develop and reshape the intellectual framework of the Intelligence Community. . . . NIU should develop, nurture, and build leaders with community-wide vision and culture.[24]

The "crown jewel" of such an NIU System already exists. "The Joint Military Intelligence College [now the National Defense Intelligence College]," noted the President's WMD Commission, "currently operates a very successful program—a structured intermediate/advanced curriculum for Intelligence Community officers across the Community."[25] A fully accredited institution of higher learning, the Intelligence College is unique in its emphasis on all-source intelligence education and research, offering degrees at both the bachelor's and master's levels. Under the leadership of President A. Denis Clift, the college is expanding and diversifying its faculty and refocusing it programs to meet the demands of today's and tomorrow's intelligence missions. In a June 2005 commencement address, Mr. Clift explained to graduates the eclectic nature of those missions:

> In a strategic environment where U.S. forces with their allied and coalition partners are called upon to provide forward deterrence, produce forward stability, and ward off threats to the U.S. homeland, there is virtually no geography, no political, cultural, ideological or religious presence anywhere that is not of potential relevance to you in the professional conduct of your future responsibilities.[26]

As a key player within the emerging NIU, the college is rising to the occasion to produce intelligence professionals who are prepared to get inside the cultural context.

In the *National Intelligence Strategy* President Bush describes "intelligence [as] America's first line of defense, in service to our people, our interests, our values, and our Constitution." To adequately perform that role, according to the *National Intelligence Strategy*, "U.S. national intelligence must be tailored to the threats of the 21st century" and "the time for change is now. . . . To preserve our security in a dangerous century, vigilance is not enough. U.S. national intelligence must do more."[27] A critical aspect of doing more and thereby achieving intelligence success is getting inside the cultural context.

30

Insights from Colombia's "Prolonged War"*
—GEN Carlos Alberto Ospina Ovalle, Colombian Army

Colombia is the second oldest democracy in the Western Hemisphere after the United States, but political violence has plagued its history since independence. The causes lie in the unique geography, demographics, and history of the nation.

Since the end of World War II, Colombian violence has been dominated by insurgencies. Though the insurgents have used terror, that has only been one of the tactics employed in pursuit of their larger aims.

Colombia faced fairly small insurgencies before the 1980s. At that point, unable to mobilize popular support, the insurgents began funding their revolutions through criminal enterprises such as drug trafficking, extortion, and kidnapping. These activities proved lucrative beyond all expectations. As a consequence, the insurgents began to ignore popular mobilization completely, relying increasingly on terror to force the people to obey their will.

The combination of these factors led one of the insurgent groups, the Revolutionary Armed Forces of Colombia (Fuerzas Armadas Revolucionarias de Colombia, or FARC), to develop a strategy to take power—with several distinct phases and a number of supporting tasks to be accomplished within each phase. The war grew worse year after year, despite increases in defense spending and in the growth of the public security forces. It was only after the military understood the insurgent strategy and designed its own strategy to defeat this plan that the war began to turn in the government's favor.

* *Reprinted by permission from* Joint Forces Quarterly, *3rd Quarter 2006.*

In the end, then, no matter what the enemy is called—"insurgent," "terrorist," "narco-trafficker," or "narco-terrorist"—successful counterinsurgency depends on a thorough understanding of the enemy and his real intentions. The government's response must be shaped by this understanding.

Early Lessons Learned

To counter insurgents, one must remember that they have doctrine. When captured, they have often been carrying the works of Mao Tse-Tung and Truong Chinh (the Vietnamese theorist of people's war) translated into Spanish.

These insurgents were Colombians, fellow citizens, a point that should never be forgotten in internal war. After their capture, they were induced to discuss the process by which they became insurgents. Several points emerged:

- All internal wars have their deepest roots in grievances and aspirations that create a pool of individuals who can be recruited, after which the organization takes extraordinary measures to shape their worldview and keep them in the organization.
- Thus, leaders of a subversive group are the most dangerous members. Followers may be dangerous tactically, but leaders read, find ideology, and come up with "big picture" solutions to the ills of society. They will then commit any crime tactically to gain their strategic end.
- Insurgents are organized, which helps them develop plans and approaches, much as the military does. They have procedures and rules. They attend schools and strive to learn. They have a set of core beliefs that one can combat once he understands them.
- Combating insurgent beliefs is not simply a military task; it is a struggle for legitimacy. If all members of a society accept that the government is just, none will allow themselves to be won over by insurgents. So all elements of national power must be mobilized, and all parties must participate in the battle for the survival and prosperity of society.

Colombia's Internal War

There have been three main illegal armed actors in Colombia in recent history. FARC emerged by the mid-1980s as the primary threat to the state. Marxist-Leninist in its ideology, funded by criminal activity, and manned by combatants recruited from the margins of society, it has followed people's war doctrine for waging its struggle. The organization has a precise strategy for taking national power that it follows to this day.

FARC's rival, the National Liberation Army (Ejército de Liberación Nacional, or ELN), also developed a strategy and was ascendant in the late 1980s and early 1990s, but it was never able to achieve the cohesion, power, and strength of FARC. After subsequent military losses and waning of political support, the power of ELN was much diminished.

Finally, the vast areas of ungoverned territory in Colombia and the terror actions of FARC and ELN generated public mobilization against them in self-defense *autodefensas* (often called "paramilitaries" by the media, which is not the best translation). These groups gained power through an alliance with drug-trafficking organizations that did not like being taxed by the guerrillas. By 1996, many of these organizations merged to form the United Autodefensas of Colombia (Autodefensas Unidas de Colombia, or AUC). These combined forces grew quickly, became as strong as FARC, and perpetrated a dirty war against the insurgents, fighting terror with terror.

In addition to these three main threats were a number of minor groups and the drug traffickers. The resources and ambition of the Medellin and Cali cartels made them national threats because they fielded armies of their own, carried out acts of terror and violence, and had varying relationships with FARC, ELN, and AUC. The threat these groups posed eclipsed that of the three enemies mentioned above through much of the 1980s until the death of Pablo Escobar and the arrest of the leadership of the Cali cartel in 1993.

Meanwhile, FARC had been steadily building its power. In 1996, things became critical as the organization transitioned from guerrilla war to mobile war—what the Vietnamese defined as "main force warfare"—while the Colombian Army remained in a counterguerrilla posture. Mobile war employs large units to fight government forces but, unlike conventional war, does not seek to defend positions.

While the Army had spread its forces to conduct saturation patrols to fight small bands, FARC now operated in large columns, complete with crew-served weapons and artillery (improvised gas tank mortars). Predictably, the result was a series of engagements in which FARC surrounded and annihilated isolated Army units. It was only when the military recognized that FARC was employing mobile warfare techniques as practiced in Vietnam and El Salvador that measures were taken to stabilize the situation. Three important lessons emerged from these realizations:

- The Western concept of a continuum with "war" on one end and "other than war" on the other was irrelevant. The enemy did not conceptualize war that way. There was only war, with different combinations of the forms of struggle depending on the circumstances.
- Military forces had been so focused on the contingencies of the moment, especially the drug war and the actions of the Movimiento de Abril 19 (M–19), that they failed to see the larger strategic picture. This left the military open to strategic surprise when main force units (guerrilla columns in battalion or larger strength) appeared, operating in combination with terror and guerrilla warfare, much as Western armies use combinations of regular operations and special operations.

- There was a disconnect between the political establishment and the military. The political establishment regarded the problem as solely one of violence: the insurgents were using violence, so the violence of the security forces had to be deployed against them. Moreover, the war was the problem of the military, not of the political establishment. There was no concept of a multifaceted, integrated response by the state.

The learning curve was steep, and as the military was regaining its balance, it suffered a series of reverses, one of which can be compared to Custer's Last Stand at the Little Bighorn in circumstances and casualties. In March 1998, at El Billar in southern Caquetá, the FARC annihilated an elite army unit, the 52nd Counterguerrilla Battalion of the Army's 3rd Mobile Brigade. By the time reinforcements could land on March 4, the battalion had been destroyed as an effective fighting force, with a loss of 107 of its 154 men.

Regaining Strategic Initiative

Ironically, it was when Andres Pastrana assumed office that regaining the strategic initiative began. The irony lay was that President Pastrana was elected on a peace platform. Recognizing that the conflict was political, he opened peace negotiations with FARC and attempted similar discussions with ELN to end the violence. This included ceding a demilitarized zone (DMZ) twice the size of El Salvador to FARC in which the negotiations could take place free of conflict.

At FARC's insistence, however, there was no cease-fire outside the DMZ. While Pastrana took on the political responsibility of negotiating peace with FARC, he left the conduct of the war outside the zone to the military. The negotiations were critical because they demonstrated conclusively that FARC was not really interested in ending the violence, but rather in using the peace process to advance its revolutionary agenda. This bad faith on the part of the rebels opened the door for a more aggressive approach, which, in turn, helped the military to regain the strategic initiative.

The success of this effort stemmed from both new leadership and a new method. The chain of command that was set in place in December 1998 remained throughout the Pastrana administration: GEN Fernando Tapias as joint force commander and GEN Jorge Mora as army commander. General Tapias was able to interact with the political establishment and represent military interests to the civilian leadership while General Mora was a good military leader, mobilizing the Army to make the necessary internal reforms to regain the initiative.

In eastern and southern Colombia, IV Division faced FARC's strongest operational unit, called the "Eastern Bloc," which had inflicted the worst defeats on the military, and it abutted the DMZ on two sides. FARC was using the DMZ to mass its main force units for new offensives.

Instead of negotiating peace, FARC launched five major offensives out of the DMZ, some even employing homemade but formidable armor. Assessing the success of IV Division against these attacks, the following factors are prominent:

- The division operated as a part of a reinvigorated and reorganized military. There was scarcely an element that was not reformed and improved, and the division worked closely with true professionals.
- The enemy's strengths and weaknesses, but especially their strategy, operations, and tactics, were assessed correctly. That meant operations took place within a correct strategy. There was great pressure, especially from the American allies, to focus on narcotics as the center of gravity, but the real strategic center of gravity was legitimacy.

FARC had three operational centers of gravity: its units, territorial domination, and funding. The first is self-explanatory. The second resulted from the government's traditional neglect and abandonment of large rural swaths. The final one resulted from FARC's perversion of the people's war. The organization had little popular support, so attacking its bases, mobility corridors, and units had the same impact as in major combat. Finally, FARC's domination of the narcotics industry was possible owing to its control of large areas of rural space.

Thus, to elevate counternarcotics to the main strategic effort would have been a critical mistake—one that was never made. Despite this success story, however, neither the personnel nor the resources were available to provide security for the populace. A variety of techniques were used, such as offensives to clear out areas, then rotating units constantly in and out of the reclaimed locations, but these were poor substitutes for a permanent, long-term presence. That had to wait for the next administration.

An Integrated National Approach

When Colombia's next President, Alvaro Uribe, took office, the missing pieces fell into place. Strategically, a national plan, Democratic Security, was formulated, which made security of the individual its foundation. This plan involved all components of the state and used the public forces, under Plan Patriot (Plan Patriota), as the security element for a democratic society. Legitimacy was a given, but the population needed to be mobilized, and that was the central element of what took place operationally. The people were involved in better governance and in "neighborhood watch," and a portion of the annual draft was ultimately allocated to local forces.

A revived economy provided funding for additional strike and specialized units as well as a substantial increase in manpower (Plan Choque). Volunteer manpower was greatly augmented and became a third of total army strength (which now exceeds 200,000). The changes were relentless and extensive.

During this period, the public forces worked closely with civilian authorities in a national approach to national problems. Contrary to the inaccurate and vindictive criticisms leveled against the armed forces in some quarters, Colombia's military did not violate its oath to serve democracy during the era of military rule in Latin America.

It is noteworthy that there has been only one poll in recent years that has not identified the military as the most respected institution in the country, and the single exception placed it second. That says a great deal about its relationship with the Colombian people. Still, the military has worked hard to improve its already good record on human rights and its respect for international humanitarian law. At times the criticisms from international organizations are truly astonishing. Colombian military personnel are subject to law in much the same way as their U.S. counterparts, and this is critical in the war against bandits.

Shifting Ground

The military's goal during the Pastrana administration (1998–2002) was to regain the strategic initiative. It did so by attacking enemy strategy, operations, and tactics. The goal during the first Uribe administration (2002–2006) was to move to the strategic offensive by strengthening normal pacification activities throughout the country, using local forces and specialized units to reincorporate areas. In addition, the military employed joint task forces to attack FARC strategic base areas, as was done in Operations Libertad 1 around Bogotá and Omega in Caquetá, the latter designed to eliminate the "strategic rearguard" FARC's used to launch its main forces.

The results so far are that FARC can no longer function in large units, so it must engage in operations similar to what the United States faces in Iraq. Improvised explosive devices are the major cause of casualties. While these devices kill and mutilate, the focus on them is evidence of FARC strategic and operational weakness.

Both ELN and AUC have been addressed principally through negotiations. Demobilization has its own difficulties and critics, but it is preferable to combat operations. Even some FARC units have begun to surrender, although the organization has resisted this trend and is determined to use terror and guerrilla warfare in an effort to repeat the cycle of past years.

Yet the ground has shifted beneath FARC's feet. Minefields and murder can disrupt life in local areas, but the relentless maturation of the democratic state makes the rebels' defeat inevitable if things continue as they are going. Mobilization of the eyes and ears of the neighborhood watch, linked to local forces, area domination forces, and strike forces, all within a grid of specialized forces and the actions of a democratic state, guarantees that FARC combatants will eventually be found and invited to return to their place within the state.

FARC's massive resources from the drug trade and increasing reliance on external bases slow progress in our campaign because they allow an insurgency to engage in unpopular conduct, to include the use of terror, and not suffer the same consequences that would result if a mass base was essential. Hence, light should not be sought at the end of the tunnel too soon. Instead, Colombian metrics will be similar to U.S. metrics in the war on terror—measures of the perception that citizens are secure, the economy prospers, and society allows the fulfillment of individual desires.

In Colombia, every indicator that can be measured is proceeding in a positive direction, from the decline in murder and kidnapping rates to the growth of the economy and freedom of movement. These factors can be quantified, but there is no way to tell when a magic line is crossed where one less murder suddenly makes all the difference in the way Colombians see their country. What is known is that the citizens will show their feelings through the ballot. That is why the military defends and serves a democratic state, and that is as it should ever be.

31

Winning in the Pacific: The Special Operations Forces' Indirect Approach*

—MG David P. Fridovich, USA, and LTC Fred T. Krawchuk, USA

Combat operations in Iraq and Afghanistan dominate the headlines, but Southeast Asia has emerged as a quiet yet increasingly crucial front in the Long War. Given the suicide bombings in Bali, the presence of the terrorist groups Jemaah Islamiyah and Abu Sayyaf, and increased anti-Americanism,[1] the need for a continued and comprehensive approach to combating terror in the Pacific is clear. The U.S. Special Operations Command, Pacific (SOCPAC) has been improving ties with regional allies and increasingly applying an *indirect approach* to address the threat posed by militant groups with connections to Al Qaeda.

The Indirect Approach

Addressing threats requires a sophisticated and indirect approach. The nation cannot simply enter sovereign countries unilaterally and conduct kill-or-capture missions. It must blend host nation capacity-building with other long-term efforts to address root causes, dissuade future terrorists, and reduce recruiting. *The 9/11 Commission Report* states that the United States must "help defeat an ideology, not just a group of people."[2]

To address the underlying conditions that foster terrorism, SOCPAC works with host nation partners to help provide security and stability. This method promotes economic development and shapes conditions for good governance and

---

* *Reprinted by permission from* Joint Forces Quarterly, *1st quarter 2007.*

rule of law. Much of the command's effort consists of foreign internal defense and unconventional warfare.[3] The primary contribution of Special Operations Forces (SOF) in this interagency activity is to organize, train, and assist local security forces. The indirect approach relies heavily on the SOF capability to build host nation defense capacity, provide civil affairs forces to give humanitarian and civic assistance, and offer information operations assets to aid the partner.

The indirect approach demands diplomacy and respect for political sensitivities. SOCPAC focuses on working in close coordination with host nation military and political leadership, law enforcement, and U.S. country teams in the region (to include the U.S. Agency for International Development and Department of State's Public Diplomacy officials). These stakeholders share the responsibility of capacity-building and leverage each other's strengths and synchronize efforts. To produce institutional change, host nation partners have to be willing to reform as required. Interagency and multinational will and capacity-building must go hand in hand for the indirect approach to succeed.

Success is measured in terms of accomplishments through, by, and with host nation partners. Over time, these partners are building a long-lasting, self-sustaining capability to provide security, develop good governance, attract foreign direct investment, and counter violent ideology. This process is slow, but it achieves lasting results. Part of our commitment is to remain patient and focus on a long-term indirect method that results in self-sustaining host nation partners.

Relationships

Besides their long-term benefits, relationships also play a vital role in combating terrorism. SOCPAC members have significant regional experience as well as constructive relationships with other nations' SOF and conventional force leadership. Frequent deployments, exercises, and exchanges allow U.S. personnel to immerse themselves in the region, build a socio-cultural knowledge base, and sustain relationships over an extended period.

Through experience, we know we can succeed only through bilateral or multilateral cooperation. Unilateral actions are neither necessary nor welcome. Partner nations willingly accept the lead in their own countries. Additionally, many nations prefer that the United States maintain a low-visibility presence on their soil. SOF can do this with little external support and low overhead from higher headquarters, which supports the Department of Defense's concept of small footprints in the region. This method respects local populaces, increases legitimacy, and improves the American image among host populations.

By working with host nation partners and the country team, SOCPAC creates trust and credibility. Serving in the "advise and assist" role, participants have to be open with each other about the training needs of the security forces as well as which capabilities they bring that can help build capacity. Developing competent forces on both sides requires candid assessments and dedication as well as clear communication. Participants must not ignore feedback or overreact to training setbacks. Instead, they must continue to assess and adapt training programs and be aware of which capacities are improving.

Such a focused training cycle produces quantifiable and observable results. Typically, the host nation's force performs a capabilities demonstration during a closing ceremony. Host nation government and senior military officials, as well as the ambassador for the United States, often attend. The demonstration is visible proof of what the host military gained from U.S. participation. Tangible improvements and demonstrated abilities enhance American credibility with host nation officials and the ambassador alike.

Indirect Approach Elements

Three elements constitute SOCPAC's indirect approach in the Pacific region: institution-building, capacity-building, and outside factors. These elements influence whom we partner with and the breadth and depth of those relationships. Integrating the parts provides a comprehensive method of helping host nation partners become self-sufficient in defense capabilities:

- *Institution-building*—The broader populations that support terrorist groups are often economically and educationally deprived. The groups use this deprivation in a *quid pro quo* way (for example, the terrorist group gives a child an education along with radical indoctrination). Finding out how to get there first to give the people a leg up without creating resentment is an important aspect of institution-building. SOF supports these efforts to help countries build healthy institutions of security, governance, rule of law, infrastructure, and economic stability.
- *Capacity-building*—U.S. Special Operations Command, Pacific, works closely with host nation forces to assess training needs and assist in building a more professional and modernized force that respects human rights. The command ensures that it is operating within the political and legal constraints of the United States and the partner nation before committing to a training program. A comprehensive capacity-building program requires assessments of unit capabilities, cultural awareness of political-military sensitivities, appropriate training programs, expert SOF trainers, and validation of efforts.
- *Outside factors*—The war on terror extends beyond the Pacific region. Today, the majority of SOF is deployed in support of Operations Iraqi Freedom and Enduring Freedom. This deployment requires that SOCPAC must do more with less. The command must prioritize where personnel go and what they do and ensure that they can manage expectations. Outside factors also include external support of terrorist organizations in the form of finance, logistics,

equipment, communication networks, and ideology. Close cooperation between host nation forces and U.S. country team officials to help eliminate the lifelines of transnational threats is vital.

For more than five years, SOCPAC involvement in the war on terror in the Pacific region has been consistent and ongoing. The command now partners with ten countries and participates in more than fifty military-to-military events a year. This indirect approach has been a slow and deliberate process that requires commitment to building trust and confidence throughout the region and knowing that the results will not be immediate. This effort is especially well along in key areas.

The Philippines

SOCPAC's continued contribution to its counterparts in the Philippines exemplifies a successful interagency, multinational, indirect approach to combating terror. In the aftermath of 9/11, SOCPAC deployed to the Muslim south of the Philippines for the first time since World War II to assist the military and civilian population in light of the security challenges in Basilan. The rest of Southeast Asia was watching to see if the U.S. military would honor its words with action.

SOCPAC personnel arrived on Basilan Island in January 2002 with the mission of advising and assisting the Armed Forces of the Philippines (AFP), which would then conduct operations against Abu Sayyaf. At the time, Basilan Island was known to the AFP and local population as a terrorist safe haven. The command operated under strict rules of engagement and stayed in the background to ensure that the AFP was up front.

On hitting the ground, SOCPAC personnel assessed the units they would work with and conducted a series of population surveys to learn what the people of Basilan needed to sever their ties with Abu Sayyaf. The islanders' greatest concerns were roads, water, security, medical care, and education. Addressing those needs meant digging wells and building roads. SOCPAC also worked with its Philippine counterparts to construct piers and an airstrip for AFP operations. The plan was for this infrastructure to be left for the Philippine military and civilian population.

This collaboration helped the command gain the confidence of our counterparts and the population through a variety of engineering, medical, and community outreach projects. The AFP led in setting security conditions that enabled capacity-building efforts. Within months, SOCPAC received additional forces that extended its humanitarian assistance program. Units, working side by side with the Filipinos, began improving schools, hospitals, and mosques. The local population became supportive of the SOCPAC and national military presence, and the AFP increasingly developed trust in the U.S. advise-and-assist role.

After two years, the environment no longer fostered terrorist activities on Basilan Island, and Abu Sayyaf left. With U.S. assistance the AFP had effectively drained the swamp of the underlying conditions favorable to terrorists. With the

Basilan people now living in a safer environment, the AFP downsized its presence from fifteen infantry battalions to two. By guaranteeing security, the Philippine military allowed teachers and doctors to return while business and nongovernmental organizations could operate in areas they once shunned. The AFP won back the support of the population and government, producing a long-lasting effect.

Another indicator of success came from the Basilan people, who chose to support the government rather than Abu Sayyaf. The populace saw that the AFP was more powerful and legitimate than the terrorists were. The indirect approach of the Basilan model enabled the AFP to provide locals with a stable environment that enabled commerce and quality of life improvements.

Archipelago Region

Because of the transnational nature of terrorist organizations, the archipelago of the Philippines, Malaysia, and Indonesia is a key focus of SOCPAC's indirect efforts. The approach is similar to that taken in Basilan and has been adapted to the socioeconomic and geographic characteristics of the archipelago region. Once stability and good governance are established in the outer islands, nongovernmental and private organizations will more likely operate and commerce will more likely expand.

Initial steps in this region have included slowly and steadily reestablishing ties with the Indonesian military. The command initially engaged with its military through a series of two-week subject matter expert exchanges (SMEEs) and post-tsunami civic action projects. After conducting five SMEEs and several humanitarian assistance initiatives in eight months, the Indonesian military approached SOCPAC regarding expanding its role to advise and assist the forces. The SMEEs and civil-military operations set the conditions for continuing the partnership. We have now completed six combined events and several construction projects with the Indonesian military that have increased the trust between the forces. More events are planned.

SOCPAC has also started achieving stronger military-to-military relationships in Malaysia. Success with Malaysian forces focuses largely on partnering during multinational naval exercises. The world-class training events and professionalism of U.S. forces impressed the Malaysian military, and we gained immensely from their state-of-the-art training facilities, which assisted SOCPAC's efforts to execute realistic training scenarios. Strengthening ties with the three archipelago nations builds a solid foundation for a multilateral indirect approach to transnational security.

Thailand

In addition to the archipelago nations, SOCPAC counts on Thailand as an important regional partner. The command has enjoyed a rich relationship with the Thai military for many years. It consistently participates in a variety of combined training and exercises, maintaining extended relationships with some units. This military partnership demonstrates the importance of building on the trust already established with host nations.

The Thai military gives SOCPAC solid, quiet support. Its leaders have asked for advice and assistance in areas of concern and provide constructive feedback on the indirect approach. Because the relationship is strong, the Thai officers reveal when a specific approach does not work for them and how we might improve, all with complete candor. They are also open to our comments, a sure indicator of a firm relationship formed over time.

Effects-Based Measurement

In the end, the only meaningful criteria for judging SOF strategy and operations in the war on terror in Southeast Asia are the results and changes that ensue. SOCPAC has established an effects-based assessment system that looks closely at its return on investment regarding activities with host nation partners, measuring the effects quarterly.

This effects-based system assesses how we are doing in building strong relationships and improving capacity—not simply counting the number of activities. The intent is to measure how *effectively* SOCPAC assists host nation partners in winning over populations and developing institutions of stability. The system has shown that we are making lasting progress even though the results are not instant. The effects-based approach helps the command prioritize efforts, shift resources, and ensure that the indirect approach remains focused and balanced.

Given its success in the southern Philippines, the command plans to partner with other countries to achieve similar effects, with host nation forces in the lead. Every situation is different and requires a program that is appropriate to the local context and needs of the stakeholders. The approach in other Asian nations will be methodical, assessing underlying conditions and host nation units, improving the socioeconomic and security situation at hand, enhancing the legitimacy of local government, and severing ties with terrorists.

In five to ten years, the command will be working with new partner nations while sustaining existing partnerships. We have anchored relationships in the Philippines and Thailand and will continue growing partnerships in Malaysia and Indonesia. SOCPAC will most likely broaden indirect efforts to include working by, through, and with forces in Bangladesh, Sri Lanka, and India. The U.S. approach will continue to develop trusting relationships, with host nation partners in the lead. The command will engage these nations in a purposeful manner to ensure that it can build relationships as successfully as it did in Southeast Asia.

As it creates partnerships, the command looks forward to establishing strong links with U.S. embassies and Asian multilateral security organizations. Diffusing terrorist organizations requires working together to offer alternative ideologies, economic opportunity, safety, different channels for political influence to travel, and ways to strengthen family and cultural ties outside of terrorist movements.

A better understanding of the concerns of stakeholders will aid the search for alternatives to political violence. This requires leveraging the knowledge and capabilities of U.S. and host nation diplomatic, informational, military, economic, and law enforcement instruments of power in a coordinated and focused effort.

U.S. Special Operations Forces are uniquely organized and equipped to win the warfare of the twenty-first century. Through its actions and tangible results, Special Operations Command, Pacific, has demonstrated that the indirect approach is an effective model for addressing asymmetric threats. By actively implementing an indirect approach, the command has shaped conditions so that commerce, rule of law, and education can flourish and provide alternatives to violence and despair. Relationships with host nation counterparts have provided a robust exchange of actionable recommendations that promote measurable results. This innovative approach is relevant in an increasingly complex security environment. Working by, through, and with multinational and interagency partners will be critical to continued success in combating terror in the Pacific.

Part IV: Tactical

32

Tactical Information Operations in West Rashid: An Iraqi National Police Battalion and Its Assigned U.S. Transition Team

—*Maj E. Lawson Quinn, USMC*

Tactical information operations (IO) on the part of United States forces in West Rashid, or southwest Baghdad, from December 2005 to November 2006 amounted to little more than a whisper. The Iraqi National Police (INP) IO campaign, however, rang clearly throughout the *mulhalla*s,[1] sending messages, often sectarian, that subverted U.S. efforts to establish security in coordination with the INP as a "national" police force. To some extent, U.S. transition teams, or advisers, assigned to the INP were able to reform the INP messages through the course of their year deployments with the INP. However, the teams had neither the physical capacity nor the opportunity within the scope of their mission to conduct a focused IO effort.

Information operations at the tactical level in West Rashid during the aforementioned period were almost exclusively perception management through action, primarily on the part of the INP and Iraqi police (IP) but to some extent on their U.S. transition teams.[2] Other IO activities conducted by the U.S. maneuver unit assigned to the area, such as the distribution of leaflets or flyers and the hanging of posters, had an extremely limited effect in themselves but to some degree on occasion reinforced positive perceptions created through physical operations.

The Situation in West Rashid

West Rashid was and still is a mixed Shi'a and Sunni area that was permeated with sectarian tension and violence, domestic insurgent and foreign fighter violence, and criminal activity that was itself interwoven with sectarian and insurgent violence

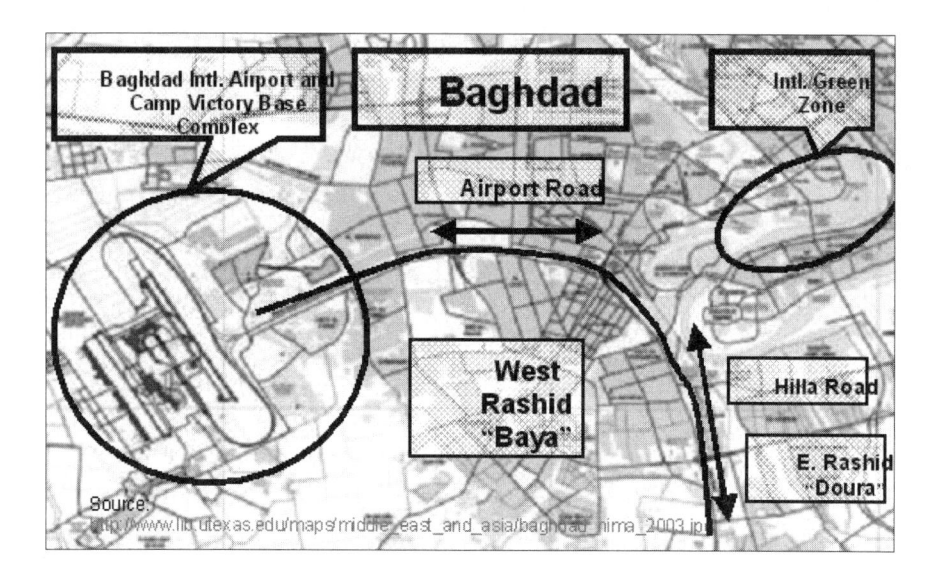

FIGURE 32.1: Situation in West Rashid. *Author's collection*

(see figure 32.1). Whereas Sunni and Shi'a used to live in relative peace with each other, Sunni extremists throughout 2006 forced Shi'a out of their homes and businesses in certain neighborhoods through intimidation and violence, and Shi'a extremists did the same to Sunnis. It was the INP's job to stop the insurgent and sectarian intimidation and violence.

One of the principal problems was that the INP was almost exclusively Shi'a and a relatively fledgling organization, particularly among its rank-and-file members. As such, the Sunnis perceived the INPs as partisan and ineffective, whereas many Shi'a, although supportive of the INP from a sectarian point of view, questioned its practical efficacy. To overcome these perceptions, establish itself as the legitimate legal authority, and establish security in the area, the INP had to convince the Sunnis that it was nonsectarian and demonstrate to all that it was competent to establish and maintain law and order. Only then could the INP become a truly "national" police that protects and serves, not an extension of politico-religious militias.

Essentially, three INP battalions of the Seventh INP Brigade operated throughout the West Rashid Area of Operations (AO)[3] from December 2005 through November 2006.[4] Although their specific missions, whether to conduct cordons and searches, conduct raids, or operate checkpoints, changed often, their overall purpose was to establish security in their respective AOs with a focus on counterinsurgency as opposed to one on crimes. Simple assault and theft that were to be handled by the Iraqi police.[5]

The lowest tactical level in West Rashid was an INP battalion of between 250 to 450 personnel along with its assigned National Police Transition Team (NPTT) of eleven Marines or Soldiers.[6] An INP battalion's AO in West Rashid was typically four to eight square kilometers that consisted of one or two *Hayys*, which are named neighborhoods. A *Hayy* is composed of several mulhallas, which are smaller numbered neighborhoods consisting of several city blocks. A NPTT was assigned to each INP battalion, brigade, and division. The NPTT's mission was to advise, mentor, and train its assigned INP unit. As such, a NPTT, in a sense, assumed the AO and mission of its partnered INP unit. In the case of this author, it was the 2nd Battalion, 7th Brigade, 2nd Division (2/7/2) INP.[7] The U.S. maneuver battalion assigned to West Rashid and surrounding area also supported and operated with the INP and coordinated with the NPTTs.

The public image, in terms of sectarianism and competency, that the INP battalions portrayed in West Rashid was at the very heart of the fight for security there in 2006. Furthermore, within the context of this uniquely combined relationship, the U.S. application of IO at the tactical level in the fight for West Rashid was inextricably linked to the image of its partnered Iraqi unit.

The Problem: Sectarianism and Competency

In order to achieve the desired end state in West Rashid, relative security sufficient to establish legitimate governmental institutions responsive to all the people and enable the rebuilding of critical infrastructure, the INP had to gain the trust, acceptance, and recognition as the legitimate legal authority of the people of West Rashid. This was first and foremost a matter of perception and, therefore, essentially an IO campaign that had to be conducted mulhalla by mulhalla. Security was local. What the prime minister or other national-level officials said inside the fortified International or Green Zone meant little to the local Iraqi citizen in the mulhalla if bombs continued to explode and bullets continued to fly outside his or her door.

Furthermore, security and peace cannot be imposed by the sword alone within an emerging democratic or otherwise representative community if it is to continue to develop. Rather, it must be achieved through agreement among all the residents and groups within the community to live in peace and settle disputes in a peaceful manner through a civil process recognized as legitimate by all said residents, albeit supported by the sword, or police force. And that force must be perceived as serving and in fact must serve the entire community, resulting in a genuine partnership for security and peace between the citizens and the police. In West Rashid, it needed to be a trust and partnership between Sunnis, Shi'a, and the Shi'a-dominated Iraqi National Police.

Therein lay the first problem: overcoming the perception among Sunnis that the INP was a Shi'a sectarian organization that served the interests solely of the Shi'a and supported or condoned the activities of Shi'a extremist militias and their attendant political parties. Exacerbating the problem was that the INP had to overcome this sectarian perception problem with troops that had little to no training while fully engaged in counterinsurgency operations, such as conducting cordons, searches, and raids and operating checkpoints.

So, at the lowest tactical level, how does an almost exclusively Shi'a INP battalion, namely 2/7/2, convince both Sunni and Shi'a residents in its AO within West Rashid to trust and rely on 2/7/2 instead of militias for protection and to invest their future with the INP and the Iraqi government? First and foremost, 2/7/2 at least had to be perceived as nonsectarian and representing the interests of all residents. Second, it had to be perceived as—and actually be—competent and able to establish and maintain security and peace. Consequently, 2/7/2's tactical fight for security and peace in Rashid was primarily a war of perception, as discussed above, though one waged almost exclusively through the character of physical operations, but reinforced with more traditional IO activities such as the distribution of flyers or leaflets.[8]

Our INP battalion, 2/7/2, had no intention of conducting such an IO campaign, at least not the kind that our team or the Coalition envisioned. Our NPTT was not in a position to wage such a war of perception either. NPTTs, being such small teams of eleven Marines or Soldiers, were not structured to conduct IO.[9] Rather, they were structured and focused on building their partnered INP units almost from scratch, primarily in the areas of life support and infrastructure, pay, the most fundamental tactical capabilities, and other aspects of maintaining the existence of the unit and its viability, however limited. Our 2/7/2 NPTT spent most of its time with its battalion engaged in such activities. Moreover, the team, and NPTTs in general, had little to no IO training. Consequently, any IO in the traditional sense was conducted by the U.S. maneuver unit assigned to the area and higher echelons with virtually no coordination with the team. Nevertheless, although neither staffed nor trained to conduct a focused, coordinated IO effort, the team was cognizant of many of the IO implications of its work with 2/7/2.

The Sectarian Perception

The Sunni population in West Rashid unquestionably viewed 2/7/2 as a sectarian organization that served the interests of the Shi'a majority at the expense of the Sunnis, if not an instrument of or in collusion with the Shi'a militias. The very demographic makeup of 2/7/2, less than ten Sunnis among the four hundred or so Shi'a members of the battalion,[10] precluded overcoming that sectarian perception even if the Shi'a majority and leadership wanted to do so, but their actions clearly did not evince the slightest proclivity toward it.

Symbology

In fact, it was quite clear that at least the battalion leadership understood the value of information operations in reinforcing that perception. Even the casual Western observer who was only somewhat familiar with Iraqi history and culture on his first visit to the 2/7/2 compound would have understood the message trumpeted by the large Shi'a flag posted at the front of the compound high atop the tallest building.

Although the sentiment may not have been held by all Shi'a in West Rashid, 2/7/2 made it clear to all that the once oppressed Shi'a were now the authority. And this certainly was the message the Sunnis received (see figure 32.2).

The NPTT's effort to not only remove the Shi'a flag but replace it with an Iraqi flag was one of the first IO battles that the team waged. The INP battalion commander, a brigadier general at the time, reluctantly, over the course of about two to three months and under continuous pressure from the team, transferred the flag from the building at the front of the compound to one in the middle of the compound and then back again until he removed it altogether. The struggle was almost comical, almost as much a test of the team's resolve as part of his IO campaign. Permanently hoisting an Iraqi flag above the 2/7/2 compound occurred a couple of months and battalion commanders later. Such was also the case with the Shi'a emblazoned marquise at the compound entrance, which was eventually replaced with a less sectarian Seventh Brigade National Police symbol that included a white dove of peace, as well as Shi'a stickers on INP trucks replaced with Iraqi flag stickers and other similar cases. Perhaps by posting an Iraqi flag alongside the Marine Corps flag on one of our NPTT HUMVEEs, we at least shamed or otherwise encouraged 2/7/2 into at least putting on a public face of nationalism as opposed to sectarianism (see figure 32.3).

Inasmuch as the Shi'a flag and other symbology were 2/7/2 messages, by association they were unintended messages from our team and thus the Americans. By training, supplying, supporting, and otherwise working intimately with a "Shi'a"

FIGURE 32.2: Symbology. *Author's collection*

312 — Ideas as Weapons

FIGURES 32.3: Signs and Their Meanings.
Author's collection

INP battalion, the team, and the United States in general, appeared to the Sunni population to be aligned with the Shi'a, thus producing at least two unfortunate effects. It bolstered the confidence of the local Shi'a as deserving of the privileges of the majority, if not reparations for Sunni oppression, and not unlikely emboldened the Shi'a militias. The second effect was that the Sunnis perceived the Marines and the United States as supporting the Shi'a over the Sunnis. And although the Marines and the United States publicly condemned militia murder and intimidation, their support of the Shi'a 2/7/2 meant to much of the Sunni population support (even if indirectly) for Shi'a extremist activity and alienation of the Sunni community.

The Character of the Conduct of Operations Sends Messages

The character of physical operations was itself information operations. Character includes, but is not limited to, the types of targets or target sets, the manner in which an operation is conducted, and the makeup of the force conducting the operation. Each of these characteristics in itself sends a message as well as the operation as a whole. Choosing which operations to execute and how they were to be executed, as well as the conduct of every other aspect of 2/7/2 activities, thus had to be considered from an IO perspective. The effects of the conduct of operations on gaining trust and confidence within the community it was supposed to have served should have been considered as much as the physical effects (detentions, weapons cache discovery) against sectarian extremists, insurgents, foreign terrorists, and criminals. One cannot occur without the other. And achieving the former effect, arguably, is a condition precedent to creating the latter effects as desired. Unfortunately, such was not typically the case with 2/7/2.

The overwhelming majority of 2/7/2 detainees during 2006, regardless of how they were apprehended, were Sunni. This occurred despite the fact that the *Hayys* of West Rashid were all fairly mixed Sunni and Shi'a, although with some notable sectarian enclaves, and that violence was perpetrated against Sunnis as well as against Shi'as throughout the area. Even if every detainee was a legitimate insurgent or criminal, and regardless of what flag flew over the 2/7/2 compound or what nationalist, nonsectarian rhetoric was preached from the International Zone, this sent a clear message to the local Sunni community: the likes of "insurgents" and the criminal element in West Rashid reside within the Sunni community, and the Shi'a-dominated 2/7/2, INP, and Ministry of the Interior will cleanse West Rashid of the Sunni-supported cancer. Furthermore, the national dialogue, including speeches from the International Zone and the Prime Minister, referred to Sunni groups as "insurgents" or "terrorists" and to Shi'a only as "militias"; this can can have nostalgic and semi-positive modern news media associations in Arabic akin to the New England militia of the American Revolution.

The manner in which 2/7/2 conducted operations early in the NPTT's relationship with the battalion demonstrated how keenly attuned one battalion commander was to perception management and local community atmospherics in the execution of his operations. The fact that the majority of 2/7/2's men was Shi'a was juxtaposed against the somewhat respectful manner in which this battalion commander treated the local residents, even those living in the homes of targets. Instead of breaking down doors, he often personally knocked on the doors of homes in which he expected to find his target.[11] Of course he was prepared to break down the door and rough up someone if necessary. Relatively speaking, these operations at times seemed to be a gentlemanly roundup of suspected Sunni insurgents. Perhaps to some degree this was influenced by the NPTT's presence, particularly during the early stages of the NPTT-2/7/2 relationship as the Iraqi commander was not yet sure what to expect from the team.

Nevertheless, the commander had a mission to eliminate the Sunni insurgency in his AO. He no doubt understood that apprehending suspected Sunni insurgents alone would continue to fuel the insurgency to some degree. However, the wholesale breaking down of doors and the destroying of property in search of insurgents would enrage the entire Sunni community to a point that would result in uncontrolled, widespread, vindictive violence throughout West Rashid. The cordon and knock method, although leaving a household of wailing family members, told the local community that he had a job to do, but as long as people behaved and accepted that some of their sons would have to be taken away, there was no need to destroy neighborhoods and spill more blood than was necessary. The message was clear that the Shi'a and 2/7/2 were the authority now, and it was time for the Sunnis to subject themselves to that authority, thus reinforcing the symbolic message transmitted by the large Shi'a flag that initially flew over the 2/7/2 compound.

Throughout the NPTT's deployment, the aggressiveness of the character of 2/7/2's operations waxed and waned. This often depended on the revolving Iraqi leadership of the battalion (six in less than a year), the level and scale of violence (not only in West Rashid but throughout the Baghdad area and at important religious sites like the al-Askari mosque in Samara), direction from Iraqi higher headquarters, and the pressure put on 2/7/2 by the team, among many other factors.

As discussed above, the makeup of the force, almost exclusively Shi'a INP together with its American NPTT, sent the message of Shi'a dominance supported by the Americans to the local community. This was not lost on 2/7/2. It was not uncommon for 2/7/2 patrols, particularly during periods of heightened sectarian tension, to pass by Sunni mosques or other buildings that they were reasonably certain would precipitate Sunni armed responses. Of course, this would necessitate an immediate response by the entire 2/7/2 battalion. Inevitably, the NPTT would receive a call from 2/7/2 that a hundred heavily armed insurgents had engaged the battalion and that it needed the NPTT and maneuver unit to support with heavy firepower. Actually, this kind of engagement typically involved six or ten mosque guards armed with AK-47 assault rifles and a rocket-propelled grenade launcher. These were classic deception operations designed to leverage overwhelming American military support for arguably sectarian operations, or at the very least sectarian as perceived by the Sunni community, and legitimate 2/7/2's actions under the auspices of combined U.S.-Iraqi operations

Projecting a Perception of Professionalism and Tactical Competency

Aside from developing professionalism and tactical competency to effectively conduct physical operations, simply projecting such a perception to engender trust in the community and deter insurgent violence, if only to present a hard target for force protection, was difficult at best. The overwhelming majority of 2/7/2 had no police or military training. They were often recruited straight off the street, provided an AK-47 assault rifle with minimal instruction on its employment, and joined to a platoon for immediate service without so much as a standard uniform. Only the officers, and not all of them, had any real training and a standard uniform.

Usually, one's first impression of a person is one's appearance. A police force that presents a collage of multiple uniforms does little to paint a picture of professionalism for the community it serves, the threat it is supposed to address, or among the individuals within the organization itself. Old U.S. Army tricolor desert BDUs were available to provide to the INP, although probably not enough for the entire force.[12] However, the Army initially was reluctant to authorize their distribution as not all U.S. Soldiers in theater had transitioned to the new digital ACUs.[13] Many of the BDUs undoubtedly would have ended up in the hands of insurgents, who would have used them to gain entrance to Coalition bases; but the uniforms had been available to insurgents for years on the open market. In fact, even the new digital uniforms, both U.S. Army and Marine Corps patterns, were for sale in the Baghdad markets.

Once the BDUs were authorized for distribution, some NPTTs immediately outfitted their respective INP units, while our team and others used them as rewards to leverage compliance with NPTT training requirements and to develop discipline in individuals and small units. This was a mistake as there were other means of leverage to those ends. Immediately outfitting 2/7/2 with uniforms without strings attached would have gone far in hastening the establishment of goodwill with the battalion, instilling a measure of pride and professionalism within its members, strengthening unity within the command, and presenting the image of professionalism to the local community (Sunni and Shi'a alike) while garnering its respect and support.

The INP uniform situation, or lack thereof, also complicated the IO effort at the operational level. It proved to be an almost insurmountable hurdle to the psychological operations company in Baghdad, which was eventually charged with developing products to instill in the Iraqi population a sense of national pride, respect, and support for its INP. How could the psychological operations company produce a poster or television advertisement depicting a professional-looking INP with each of the policemen wearing a different outfit and looking much like the insurgents the INP were supposed to be fighting? Even when a single INP uniform design was adopted in the fall of 2006, a poster depicting INP wearing it could not be disseminated as no units yet had the uniform or were likely to have it in the foreseeable future. The poster would have been recognized immediately as false propaganda, thus having the opposite effect of that desired. The problem of an "un-uniformed" INP at the end of 2005 and throughout 2006 certainly was a lost IO opportunity from the tactical to the operational level.

Relationships

One of the most effective weapons against the insurgents and militias in Iraq is mutual understanding of one another—that is, the Iraqi people and Americans and the Coalition in general. This should have been the heart of the tactical IO effort, and the overall U.S. effort, in West Rashid. Unfortunately, this was not as much the case as could have been.

The most important relationship was between 2/7/2 and the community it was charged to serve. Unfortunately, no such relationship could be developed effectively because the battalion's AO changed every four to six weeks for many, usually not good or appropriate, reasons.

The Iraqis of West Rashid had relatively little personal contact with U.S. forces during much of 2006 other than watching the maneuver unit drive by or conduct raids, other operations, and the occasional meeting between community leaders and the U.S. maneuver unit leadership. Force protection concerns often resulted in U.S. forces perceived not as people, but walking body armor with sunglasses and goggles instead of eyes. This certainly did not go far in putting a human face on the Coalition mission; instead, it fostered more of an uneasy tension, if not an antagonistic distrust of U.S. forces.

The NPTT's intimate relationship with 2/7/2 helped immensely in this regard. Although the NPPT's relationship with 2/7/2 certainly fueled Sunni suspicions as discussed above, the yang to that unfortunate yin is that the team's daily contact throughout the year with 2/7/2 enabled the individuals of the Iraqi battalion to get to know us on an individual and personal level and take that understanding back to their families and friends. In Iraq, the most trusted and believed message, and thus most effective message, is that conveyed by a family member or friend as opposed to a poster or radio broadcast. As we broke bread with 2/7/2 and shared many of the same risks, we became people—sons, husbands, and fathers with children—to the Iraqis instead of warriors and representatives of a foreign government whom many saw as occupiers of their country instead of as welcomed guests there to help. Additionally, establishing strong, personal relationships with our Iraqi counterparts enabled the team members to convince some of them of the sincerity of the U.S. mission to help them establish a secure and prosperous Iraq and leave as soon as possible to rejoin our own families, or at least the team's desire to that end.

It also provided the opportunity to soften the negative IO effects of unfortunate events, such as when our Soldiers and Marines were suspected of or found to have committed crimes against Iraqis. As our INP counterparts had come to know us as people with families and concerns similar to theirs, it was more difficult for them to condemn the U.S. military and the United States in general. Additionally, our relationships with the Iraqis provided opportunities to explain how such circumstances could be resolved in a civil manner that did not inevitably lead to uncontrolled vengeful sectarian violence fueled by emotion and sectarian ties. Instead, a quest for the facts guided by logic and unbiased law could result in an appropriate final outcome that served the interests of all involved and that all could accept.

By no means was the team under the illusion that we would or could change the Iraqi culture and institute our American system of justice. However, we believed that we certainly could plant the seeds of such notions that might someday, with continued nurturing, develop into something better than the current violent situation.

Although the NPTT spent nearly every day and many nights with 2/7/2, we were severely handicapped in that we were not permitted to move in and reside with

2/7/2 at its compound. One of the ideas central and critical to the transition team concept was that of teams embedding with the Iraqi units. Teams at all echelons lived with their respective Iraqi units throughout Iraq. However, none of the NPTTs in West Rashid were permitted to embed with their Iraqi counterparts. Regardless of how many safe house designs our NPTT developed in which to live on the 2/7/2 compound, it was continuously deemed too risky by higher headquarters. Aside from the constraints on conducting training and operations with our Iraqi battalion that this placed on our team, not living with our unit severely hindered our relationship. What kind of message did we send to our Iraqi counterparts when after a thirty-hour operation with them, we returned to the security, air-conditioning, and Pizza Hut of Camp Victory, leaving them in their compound recently cleared of standing sewage, six hours of electricity, and myriad other problems? The message was at best American hypocrisy; at worst it said our mission was a lie.

Again, the relationships we worked so hard to create and maintain despite such constraints greatly mitigated the negative IO effect created by not embedding with the Iraqis. Moreover, our relationships helped to begin bridging the relational gap between the Iraqis of West Rashid and the U.S. maneuver unit assigned to the area, leading to the conduct of combined operations. Nevertheless, even as our team turned over with our NPTT relief, both our teams, without body armor and sunglasses, enjoying chai with our Iraqi counterparts inside the 2/7/2 compound stood in stark contrast to the U.S. military police platoon socializing with us in full battle dress. This was nothing less than an insulting slap in the face to the Iraqis and clear evidence that a sizable portion of U.S. forces in Iraq simply do not understand the war we are waging. It was absolutely amazing how U.S. forces could send such diametrically opposed and competing messages. Unfortunately, the Iraqis perceived the NPTTs as the exception rather than the rule. Some U.S. units quickly came around, some took a while, and a few continued to keep the Iraqis at arm's length. Is this unity of effort?

U.S.-Iraqi Combined Operations

U.S. maneuver unit and INP combined operations began to occur and grow in the latter half of 2006 as the Iraqis were supposed to be taking the lead and responsibility for security. Unquestionably, combined operations with the INP taking the lead sent a great message and one that was preached at the highest levels of government. How these operations were executed and the actual message they often sent were something else.

As was discussed earlier, the manner in which operations are conducted sends a tremendous message. During the latter half of 2006 as part of one of the iterations of the Baghdad security plans, the U.S. maneuver unit began conducting combined cordon and sweep-search-hold operations. A U.S. maneuver company together with an element of an INP battalion would cordon a mulhalla or two while search teams would search ostensibly every structure and room therein, thus removing the insurgent and militia and their tools from the mulhalla and disrupting their operations. The mulhalla then would be declared clear.

The first point is that all the locals would tell the NPTT and the U.S. maneuver unit time after time that the insurgents and militia had removed all their weapons and left the night before the operation. The insurgents' and militias' perception was that the United States and the government of Iraq do not have the capability to clear and hold West Rashid, were not serious about it, and that the insurgents and militias just have to remain flexible and patient until the Americans give up or declare victory and leave.

The second issue was the makeup of the search teams. Search teams typically were composed of four to six U.S. Soldiers and one, on occasion two, 2/7/2 policeman. This could hardly be seen as a combined operation with Iraqis beginning to take the lead for security. The local Iraqi's perception was that of an unwelcome occupying U.S. force invading and searching his home with a token INP policeman to legitimize the U.S. propaganda of U.S. and Iraqi forces working hand in hand to create a secure and stable Iraq with Iraqis securing Iraqis. Neither 2/7/2 nor any other single INP battalion could muster the number of troops under their force structure, leave policy, and other operational commitments to amend this situation.[14]

The obvious solution would have been to attach forces from two or more INP battalions for the search operation so that the majority of each search team would be Iraqi and to have the Iraqis actually conduct the search with U.S. Soldiers only supervising and assisting as necessary. Although this would have presented planning problems, command and control problems, and lengthen the time required to effectively complete a mulhalla-wide search, the IO effect likely would have been the opposite of that experienced; Iraqis would have seen Iraqi forces conducting security operations with U.S. forces supporting and relinquishing authority as opposed to U.S. forces intruding into Iraqi homes with token Iraqi forces in tow. Additionally, Iraqis searching Iraqi homes is less intrusive than U.S. forces searching Iraqi homes, arguably even if it is a Shi'a INP searching a Sunni home. Furthermore, it would have bolstered the confidence of the INP members in themselves individually and in their leadership.

However, there were positive IO aspects of these operations. Although the degree of Iraqi participation was not optimal, that there was Iraqi participation at all was a step in the right direction. It certainly softened the impact of the intrusions. Additionally, the searches were conducted respectfully with as little disruption to the local population as possible under the circumstances. While many residents were clearly displeased with the invasion of their homes, some appreciated that at least something was being done to improve the security situation regardless of the effectiveness of these cordon and search operations.

More direct or traditional IO activities such as the distribution of flyers and the hanging of posters were incorporated into the cordon and search operations.

The tactical psychological operations team assigned to the maneuver battalion developed posters and flyers in support of these operations to encourage cooperation and patience with the cordon and search operations, discourage sectarian violence, and persuade local citizens to turn in terrorists and criminals (see figure 32.4). Of course the definition of a terrorist and criminal often differs depending on family and sect. At the tactical level, these activities had some positive impact, but only insofar as they reinforced operations that were conducted in a non-sectarian, restrained, respectful manner that disrupted life as little as possible. Had operations been conducted in a heavy handed way, any such products would have been dismissed out of hand as lies, serving more to fuel anger against the United States and support for insurgents and militias than foster cooperation with the United States.

FIGURE 32.4: Safety Announcements. *Author's collection*

[Poster: "Safety will not come from sectarian killings / Report terrorists and criminals to 130" shown in English and Arabic versions]

The NPTT attempted to further reinforce the theme that these operations were for the safety and security of the citizens of the mulhallas and to put a human face on the operations. With smiles and without sunglasses the team did this through engaging the people in casual conversation about family, soccer, and business and presenting children with toys. This seemed to work relatively well in a few mulhallas, particularly in northern Hayy al-Bayaa in the northwest section of West Rashid. Here, the confluence of all the efforts of combined operations, operational restraint, the hanging of posters, and NPTT "public relations" came together within a relatively mixed population that was doing better economically than most. However, the team was in no way under the illusion that the Hayy had bought into the nationalistic rhetoric and had put their faith in the INP, or that information about insurgents, militias, and criminals would be pouring in over the hotline. On the contrary, the operation, although somewhat successful from an IO perspective relative to most operations in planting the seeds of nonsectarian nationalism, was but a small and fleeting inroad toward such an outcome.

Assuming this type of operation was the correct tactic to reduce violence in West Rashid, it should have been the baseline in terms of IO, with an ever-increasing involvement of Iraqi forces. More important, every such operation should have been followed immediately by a tangible economic benefit to reward mulhallas for cooperation, namely, a measure of good faith and taste of what the future could hold without sectarian and insurgent violence. And that economic benefit needed to be tied to the INP and, more important, to key local leaders who might be susceptible to being co-opted into the notion of peaceful cohabitation of Shi'a and Sunni under a representative form of government. Iraqi-led security operations immediately followed by improvement to quality of life would have stood in stark contrast to the chaos created by insurgent and sectarian violence. However, this would have taken more Iraqi and U.S. forces than existed in West Rashid and a focused IO effort coordinated with civil affairs that included a great deal of targeted funding with significant oversight to ensure that the money went where it was supposed to go.

Conclusion

Information operations at the tactical level are all about the message, mostly sent through physical action, whether through symbols, establishing personal relationships; the character of physical operations; or civil affairs. Combined operations conducted properly in a restrained and nonsectarian manner simultaneously infused with a blitzkrieg of economic engagement that results in immediate improvement in quality of life within the individual mulhallas are the acumen of tactical IO.

During 2006 progress was made with 2/7/2 in the areas of tactical competency, operational restraint, and the conduct of combined operations, although not as much as could have been made. Unfortunately, the fundamental and overarching problem of the Sunni perception of 2/7/2 as a Shi'a sectarian organization continued to loom large and taint everything that 2/7/2 and U.S. forces did in West Rashid. Unless that perception can be changed significantly through a focused, coordinated information operations effort, neither 2/7/2 nor any Iraqi National Police unit will ever become a "national" police force trusted and relied upon for security by the community it is supposed to serve.

33

"But How Do I Do It?" Tactical Information Operations and the Planning Process

—*Maj Phillip M. Bragg, USMC*

Information operations (IO), as a field of military expertise, is in a state of growth and evolution. It seems as if every interview of a general officer or prominent civilian defense official includes reference to the importance of information operations and how much better the enemy is than the United States is. Fortunately, with the publication of Joint Publication 3-13 *Information Operations* in 2006, the U.S. military finally has a coherent doctrine that can guide it in learning and teaching the fundamentals of information operations.[1] However, the doctrine only goes so far; it lacks the detail necessary to guide individual IO officers in the development of an effective IO plan. At the lower tactical level, ideas and concepts have to be translated into executable orders. This is perhaps the greatest challenge and one for which there are few doctrinal guiding lights.

This chapter will first address the question of what constitutes a complete and sufficient plan. In other words, after all the planning, what documents need to be produced so that subordinate units and staff members can continue their planning and can, ultimately, execute the IO plan? Next, the chapter will walk through the Marine Corps Planning Process (MCPP) step-by-step and explain the actions, outputs, recommendations, and potential challenges faced by the IO officer. The reader will then be able to understand how to use the planning process to develop the specific elements of the plan as originally outlined.

A few cautions are in order. First, this chapter is directed strictly at the lower tactical level, where an IO plan must result in tangible products and tasks for subordinate units, not "pie-in-the-sky" theorizing but actual tools to move from commander's guidance to an actionable plan. Consequently, these tools and techniques may not be applicable at the operational and strategic level. Second, throughout the paper, the MCPP is used as the planning model, but these techniques can be easily adapted to the military decision-making process (MDMP).[2] Finally, most of the planning methodologies used are modifications of fire support planning methods. This statement is valid for two reasons. The most basic requirement for fire support planning is the necessity to be tied to maneuver actions; therefore, all of its processes are directed to this end. Information operations planning has the same requirement and, thus, should use similar processes. Additionally, it is always easier to use an old tool in a new way than to learn an entirely new tool. Anyone familiar with fire support planning will quickly adapt to the proposed IO planning methodologies.

The IO Plan

Before any planning begins IO planners need to understand what constitutes a complete and sufficient plan. What is the end state? This is no small question. Most officers have seen or prepared enough maneuver plans to identify their key elements, but how many of those same officers can say the same about an IO plan? Probably not many. The average officer simply does not have enough experience to identify, much less develop, the key elements of an IO plan.

A complete and sufficient IO plan needs the following six elements:

- Commander's guidance for IO
- Concept of IO
- Themes and messages (usually)
- IO synchronization matrix
- Consequence management plan
- IO products or tabs as required by the plan.

Naturally, more can be added to a plan, but if the plan does not consist of these six parts, it probably does not contain enough information to be executable. The six parts are defined below and an example is provided using planning products that have been proven to work. Each of these planning products is designed to serve three different functions with the ultimate purpose of gaining speed and tempo in the planning process. First, each helps the planner through the process by providing a framework for the required information. Second, each product can be used for briefing. Finally, each can be put directly into the order for execution.

Commander's Guidance for IO

As in any other part of the plan, the commander's guidance is the most important part. It provides focus for the IO staff and helps them visualize the battlefield and what the commander wants to achieve. Ideally, the commander will express his intent using the *task* and *purpose* terminology, leaving the details of execution to his staff. Additionally, he should establish any constraints and restraints. Recognize, however, that this process is iterative. As the commander and his staff begin to understand the problem in greater detail, the initial guidance will evolve into the final, published commander's guidance for IO. Below is an example of a commander's IO guidance that would be applicable for a battalion operation.

> While this operation will be primarily a kinetic one, there are four things that IO will need to do to support our operations. These four IO objectives cut across the spectrum from the tactical to the strategic level. Marines at all levels must understand how these actions have strategic implications.
>
> First, we need to ensure that the local civilians in our AO [area of operations] do not interfere with our operations IOT [in order to] prevent the unnecessary deaths of BLUE civilians and facilitate the MEBs' [Marine Expeditionary Brigades] freedom of movement. Ensure we not only use our own capabilities but also those of the host nation to achieve this objective. Second, I want to attack the will of the enemy's forces IOT reduce his combat capability. Third, I want to degrade the enemy's ability to understand our CoA [course of action] by a systematic use OPSEC [operations security], limited deception operations, and attacks on his RSTA [reconnaissance, surveillance, and target acquisition] capabilities IOT reduce his ability to respond to our chosen CoA. Finally, IO will promote the legitimacy of our mission and our support to the BLUE government IOT prevent the RED government from achieving its strategic objectives. This needs to be accomplished using an aggressive PA [public affairs] plan, talking points for our Marines, and a solid consequence management plan.

Concept of IO

The concept of IO represents the "meat" of the order. Similar to the concept of operations or the concept of fires, it provides the details of how the plan will be executed. Unfortunately, doctrine is extremely vague on the elements and construction of this part of the order. What follows is a methodology for developing the concept of IO that is simple and ensures a positive link between maneuver and IO.

In the simplest terms, the concept of IO is the combination of the IO tasks that have been derived from the commander's guidance. Whereas the commander uses only the task and purpose to express his guidance, in the concept for IO, the IO planners will add the method of execution and the desired effects. Therefore, each IO task will ultimately be expressed using the task, purpose, method, and effects (TPME). Logically it follows that the concept of IO will then be a combination of the

FIGURE 33.1: Concept of IO: The Combination of All the IO Tasks

IO Concept		1	2	3
TASK	Objective			
	Target Audience			
	Capability			
Purpose - Describes maneuver purpose				
Method	EW			
	Psyops			
	CMO			
	PA			
	COM CAM			
	MilDec			
Effects				

IO tasks expressed using TPME (see figure 33.1). This is often best communicated using the example of a commander's guidance for IO above.

Since the IO task is the most critical aspect of the plan, each element must be fully understood and clearly articulated. Refer to figure 33.2, a completed IO task, as the remainder of this section is read. As stated above there are four elements to each IO task:

$$\text{IO TASK} = \text{TASK, PURPOSE, METHOD, AND EFFECTS}$$

Each of these four elements will be evaluated in turn. First and most important is the task. The task has three subelements:

$$\text{TASK} = \text{OBJECTIVE} + \text{TARGET AUDIENCE} + \text{CAPABILITY}$$

The objective is the word that best describes what the planner wants to do to the target audience. It is a verb. The key is to find the correct word and not be constrained. Any verb will work if it helps explain what to do.

- Inform: Provide purpose, goals, objectives, and/or instructions.

- Warn: Provide notice of intent in order to prevent a specific action.
- Influence: Curtail or cause a specific action.
- Disorganize: Reduce effectiveness/ability.
- Isolate: Minimize power/influence.
- Co-opt: Gain cooperation.
- Promote: Positively reinforce a desired behavior or attitude.
- Deceive: Cause a person to believe what is not true.
- Gain information: Acquire new facts, details or information.
- Deny: Withhold information about friendly force capabilities, status, or intentions that adversaries need for effective and timely decision making.
- Enhance: Add to an already positive situation.
- Demonstrate: Provide information on capabilities or intent through convincing actions and appearances.
- Deter: Curtail a specific action.
- Disrupt: Reduce effectiveness/ability by preventing synchronization of effects.
- Limit: Reduce effectiveness by denying options or by portraying adversary tactics in such a way that their use causes unintended negative effects for the adversary.
- Influence: Cause adversaries or others to behave in a manner favorable to friendly forces.
- Mitigate: Reduce or negate the impact of misinformation, a problem, or a concern.

FIGURE 33.2: Example of a Completed IO Task

TASK		
IO Objective	**Target**	**Function**
Influence	local population	Depart Regt AO
PURPOSE		
Limit civilian deaths during combat operations and enable freedom of action		
METHOD		
• Psyops: Use TPTs to contact all houses located in engagement areas. • PA: Disseminate message via local radio and TV stations. • CA: Contact law enforcement and local leaders to organize displacement operations. • S4: Establish evacuation routes within AO.		
EFFECTS		
Immediate: No civilians in Regt AO except essential government workers		
2nd Order: • Simplified target identification and ROE • Reduction of civilians using military medical facilities • Reduced road traffic		
3rd Order: Will increase difficulty of acquiring civilian property for military use Limit negative reaction by local population		

The second subelement is the target audience. Since IO is ultimately about attacking or protecting the command and control (C2) system, the target audience will normally be some component of the C2 system. The target audience can be a leader, a group, a system, and so on. It does not necessarily have to be an enemy. It can be friendly, neutral, or nonhostile. The key is to be as specific as possible when identifying the target.

Finally, the third subelement is the capability of the target audience that will be affected. What is it that the target audience should do or not do? Again, the key is to be as specific as possible. If this subelement is vague, it will result in wasted effort.

The next main element, the purpose, explains why the task needs to be achieved. The key to writing a good purpose statement is ensuring that it is clearly linked to some maneuver objective. The purpose is the main link between the IO plan and the maneuver plan. A poorly written purpose will inevitably lead to disconnects between the two.

The method portion of the IO task provides the detail on how the task and purpose will be accomplished. This is the "meat" of the task. Ultimately, the method will evolve into the missions that will be sent to the executers of the plan. It will list the core, supported, and related capabilities of IO but might also include maneuver units or other staff sections if applicable. Initially, the method portion of the task will be conceptual. As the plan evolves the method should be very detailed. In fact, by the time "war-gaming" is complete, the method portion should include all necessary details to permit the plan to be executed.

The last element of the IO task is the effects. Defining good effects is probably the most difficult but essential part because it enables the staff to assess the impact of a particular IO task. Done correctly, planners will analyze first-, second-, and third-order effects of the IO actions. In many cases, the second- and third-order effects may be easier to observe and measure than the desired first-order effects. A word of caution, in some cases there may be insufficient time or assets to assess the results of an IO task. In these cases the IO officer needs to be prepared to articulate these constraints and to evaluate the risk for the commander.

It is essential to understand the evolution of an IO task as the planning process proceeds. When conceptual planning takes place, the IO tasks will most likely be defined by only the task and purpose. The method and effects may not be complete. As the plan progresses thorough the process, the method and effects will be determined when conducting functional and detailed planning. Figure 33.2 shows a fully developed IO task. Once all of these tasks have been fully developed and refined during war-gaming, the concept of IO can be completed. It is important to understand this evolution so that the appropriate level of detail is maintained throughout the process. Doing too much too early is almost as bad as not doing enough.

Themes and Messages

Most IO plans will include themes and messages. It is possible that a plan might not include them, particularly if it is heavily kinetic. If the plan uses public affairs, psychological operations (PSYOPS), civil-military operations (CMO), or deception, then themes and messages will undoubtedly be needed.

Themes are those overarching ideas that must be sent to the target audiences. Within each theme supporting messages will be derived. These are more detailed ideas that reinforce the theme. For example, in a noncombatant evacuation operation (NEO), the theme may be "We are coming to evacuate American citizens and are not involved in the current conflict." This theme could have three to five messages:

- American citizens will be evacuated because of the current security situation.
- The helicopters are not hostile and are being used for the evacuation only.
- American forces will defend themselves if needed.

Themes and messages serve two purposes. First, they provide unity of effort. All subordinate units have to operate within the bounds of the published themes. Everyone stays on message, and the message is the same for everyone. Second, themes and messages provide tempo. A subordinate unit can tailor IO products within its AO as long as it stays within the left and right lateral limits provided. The unit does not need to seek higher approval on every new item.

IO Synchronization Matrix

The IO synchronization matrix is, perhaps, the easiest part of the plan. All military members, regardless of specialty, have built or used synchronization matrices. The IO matrix is very similar. The time or event is listed along the horizontal axis. All elements involved in the plan are listed along the vertical axis. An example is provided in figure 33.3.

This document serves several purposes. First, by combining all IO events, it will ensure that there are no redundancies or gaps. Second, using the matrix will assist each supporting element in ensuring it has accounted for all of its tasks and knows when they are to be executed. Finally, the matrix is an excellent tool to help the IO officer or the battle captain track execution of the plan.

Consequence Management Plan

The IO consequence management plan (CMP) can be conceptualized as the branches and sequels to the basic IO plan. The CMP is used to anticipate future events and increase IO tempo. Speed is as important in the information domain as it is in the physical domain. A solid consequence management plan will go a long way in increasing a unit's tempo.

During execution both friendly and enemy units will take actions that have IO implications. Planners need to be prepared to either exploit or mitigate these actions.

FIGURE 33.3: IO Synchronization Matrix*

Time					
Phase					
MilDec					
OPSEC					
PSYOP					
EW					
CNO					
Fires					
PA					
CMO					

* This can be expanded as needed.

Figure 33.4 explains the four different possible actions and the appropriate response. When visualizing the operation, the IO planner should identify these events and plan for an IO response. Figures 33.5 and 33.6 are examples of documents that can be used to communicate this plan.

IO Products or Tabs as Required by the Plan

Every IO plan is different, but each will undoubtedly require additional tabs or IO products. Experience will help the IO planner decide what is needed in each case.

Planning IO

Once an IO planner has a firm understanding of where to go, the officer needs to figure out how to get there. The Marine Corps Planning Process can be tailored by the IO officer to meet his ends and stay integrated with the rest of the staff. The next section describes what needs to take place during each step of the process and some common pitfalls.

STEP 1: MISSION ANALYSIS

As with any other area, the key to a successful plan begins with mission analysis. It is in this step that the problem is defined, an understanding of the capabilities and limitations is developed, and solutions begin to be formulated.

Of course, mission analysis begins with intelligence preparation of the battlefield (IPB). Good IPB provides understanding of the environment and the enemy. The IPB process for IO is out of the scope of this chapter; however, this is the first

"But How Do I Do It?" Tactical Information Operations — 331

FIGURE 33.4: Consequence Management: Gaining and Maintaining the Initiative in the Information Environment

		Force	
		Friendly	Enemy
Action	Good	Exploit	Mitigate
	Bad	Mitigate	Exploit

FIGURE 33.5: Planning Template for an Enemy Action That Has Informational Effects

Consequence Management Event - Enemy		
Enemy Action:		
Effects: Immediate-		
2nd Order-		
3rd Order-		
TASK		
Obj	Target	Function
PURPOSE		
METHOD		
• Psyops:		
• PA:		
• CMO:		
Messages and Themes		
EFFECTS		

FIGURE 33.6: Planning Template for a Friendly Action That Has Informational Effects

Consequence Management Event - Friendly		
Friendly Action:		
Effects: Immediate-		
2nd Order-		
3rd Order-		
TASK		
Obj	Target	
PURPOSE		
METHOD		
• Psyops:		
• PA:		
• CMO:		
Messages and Themes		
EFFECTS		

place the IO officer is warned of potential problems. Intelligence preparation of the battlefield has proven to be an essential and effective tool. Unfortunately, Field Manual 34-130 *Intelligence Preparation of the Battlefield* lacks instruction about how to modify the process for IO. Field Manual 3-13 *Information Operation TTPs* provides only the most rudimentary guidance. The bottom line is that the IO officer must begin early to confer with the intelligence officer to determine which IPB products and information will need to be developed. In many cases the requests for information and expected formats may be new to the average intelligence officer. The IO officer needs to be a mentor and trainer for the intelligence officer, not just a consumer.

Once the IO officer has collected his IPB, read the higher IO order (assuming one exists), and conducted his staff estimate, he is ready to begin mission analysis. The IO officer follows a process that is identical to the standard planning process except he views everything from the information perspective. He needs to evaluate several areas:

- Higher specified and implied IO tasks
- Higher IO themes and messages
- Higher IO products
- Resource shortfalls
- SME shortfalls

- IO information requirements
- Recommended commander's critical information requirements (CCIRs) that are related to IO.

At the end of the process, the IO officer should have a good understanding of the military problem and will likely begin formulating some solutions. In fact, it is not unusual to have a few IO tasks developed at this juncture. In most plans, many of the same IO tasks will need to be accomplished regardless of the final course of action selected. At this time, only the task and purpose will be identified; they will be further fleshed out in the course of action development.

Step 2: Course of Action Development (CoA Dev)

During CoA Dev, the bulk of the IO plan is developed. When complete, the IO concept, synchronization matrix, themes and messages, and consequence management plan for each maneuver CoA will have been developed. This appears to be a lot of work. However, due to the nature of IO, there is usually significant overlap between CoAs. It is normal and acceptable for the IO concept for each CoA to identify the same task and purpose for a given IO task and vary only in the method portion.

These planning products are usually developed in two steps. The IO officer completes the first step while working in the operational planning team (OPT). Working in conjunction with the other staff planners, he establishes the task and purpose of each IO task required to support the CoAs. The first step is conceptual planning. The second step is done in the IO working group. The IO working group takes the results from the OPT and develops the method and effects. The second step is functional and detailed planning. Once the tasks are complete, they are combined into a synchronization matrix. Next the IO working group will make any refinements or additions to the themes and messages provided by higher. Last, they will develop the consequence management plan. When all this is complete for each CoA, the plan is ready to proceed to war-gaming.

Step 3: War-gaming

War-gaming the IO plan is no different than war-gaming any other aspect of the plan. The primary objective is to improve the CoA by testing it against the thinking enemy. The IO officer will need to ensure that the "red cell" includes IO in its actions and that it is prepared to brief the informational effects of all friendly actions. Additionally, the IO officer needs to be prepared to act as the "white cell" by determining the effects of friendly and enemy actions on nonhostile target audiences. By the end of war-gaming, the IO concept should be refined for each CoA, the synchronization matrix finalized, and all reasonable branch plans analyzed and incorporated into the consequence management plan.

Step 4: CoA Comparison and Decision

Step four is the most intuitive step in the process. The IO officer needs to be able to communicate to the commander which of the CoAs is preferred and why. Additionally, he needs to be able to quantify the risk involved in each CoA with regard to the informational domain. In many cases, it is wise to invite subject matter experts to answer the commander's questions, particularly when they involve areas that are out of most officers' normal expertise as are many of the technical aspects of some IO capabilities.

Step 5: Orders' Development

The key to this step is to quickly create and rapidly disseminate the IO order and products necessary for execution. If done correctly, many of the planning and briefing products already developed can be used as elements of the order. As stated previously, the formats used as examples in this chapter can serve double duty and increase staff tempo.

A second crucial element to the IO plan is the many information products that are required for execution. This is always an issue, mainly because of the paucity of production capability at the lower tactical level. IO officers need to consider not only the time to develop, translate, and reproduce products, but also the logistics of getting them to the user. Clearly the logistics officer should be involved in the IO working group.

Step 6: Transition

The IO officer needs to consider three key events when executing step 6. First, transitioning the plan from the OPT to the staff. The mechanics of this action will vary from staff to staff, but the key is establishing an effective mechanism to articulate the plan to the staff as a whole. Effectively communicating the plan requires balancing conceptual understanding with sufficient detail, never a simple task. Second, the IO officer needs to establish procedures to allow bottom up refinement. Every effort should be made to provide the time and resources to allow the subordinate units to adjust the plan to fit their needs. However, the IO officer needs to include a "good idea cut off point" to prevent wasted efforts. Finally, the IO officer needs to include a rehearsal. This may include execution and reporting the actual IO task and also conducting dry runs of specific consequence management issues to test staff action and information management. If these three items are addressed, the plan will be well on its way to execution.

Conclusion

The enemy's dominance of the information spectrum is not inevitable. He is winning now because the U.S. military has not developed effective techniques to defeat him. The enemy can act more quickly and more effectively. One of the primary reasons that the U.S. military has been unable to adapt is that it has lacked the processes that turn ideas into action. This chapter outlines the methodologies that can be used to translate a commander's ideas into an actionable plan. An IO planner must first understand what needs to be done. At the tactical level, a good plan includes six key elements as described in the first section of the chapter. Once planning begins, the IO officer must use both the OPT and the IO working group to develop the IO concept and then refine the necessary details. The entire process must be done while considering speed, the need for detail, and the inherent constraints at the tactical level. As stated in Marine Corps Doctrinal Publication MCDP5 *Planning*, "The ultimate measure of effective planning is the answer to the following question: Can we act faster and more effective than the enemy?"[3]

34

Operation Iraqi Freedom II: Information and Influence in South-Central Iraq

—*Maj Clint Nussberger, USMC*

Gen A. A. Vandegrift, Commanding General of the 1st Marine Division at Guadalcanal in 1942, asserted that positions in a conventional battle are often lost because an adversary *perceives* that his position is no longer tenable. The perceptions of combatants in battle may be what drive their actions regardless of actual conditions or the state of their adversary. This psychological aspect of armed conflict takes on an even greater dimension in irregular warfare because the objective includes concerned populations as well as combatant adversaries.

This chapter will explore the psychological impact of 24th Marine Expeditionary Unit (MEU) counterinsurgency operations in south-central Iraq from July 2004 to February 2005. This work is not intended to be a doctrinal review of 24th MEU information operations, but rather a discussion of how 24th MEU—particularly its commanding officer—incorporated psychological considerations into routine, everyday decisions. Moreover, the recurring theme throughout this essay is that psychological effects are shaped more by the actions of tactical units in the local area than by their words.

The 24th MEU assumed responsibility for the northern one-third of Babil Province and the southern district of Baghdad Province in late July 2004, one month after the transfer of sovereignty from the Coalition Provisional Authority (CPA) to the Iraqi Interim Government (IIG). During the first few weeks of the deployment, Col Ron Johnson, Commanding Officer of the 24th MEU, and his staff learned a key lesson about the value of actions, even small courtesies. The U.S. embassy's regional coordinator in Hillah, the capitol of Babil Province, explained to Colonel Johnson that he would garner the trust and respect of local and provincial Iraqi leaders by meeting with them in their offices rather than by meeting at the U.S. embassy office.

Colonel Johnson met with the governor of Babil Province on a biweekly basis, with virtually every meeting taking place at the governor's office in downtown Hillah. Every time Colonel Johnson arrived at the governor's office with his personal security detail, he was communicating to the Iraqi citizens that he and their governor were partners. During each meeting, the colonel would emphasize that he "worked for the governor," further solidifying the cooperative nature of the relationship. Whether a local citizen watched the arrival of this procession from afar or a prominent tribal leader or businessman participated in one of these meetings, each received a clear message about the U.S.-Iraqi partnership that they passed on to family and friends. In Iraqi culture, genuine displays of friendship and respect such as these provide effective images that reinforce the messages conveyed via billboards, posters, and other media.

Colonel Johnson's emphasis on treating the Iraqis with respect and fostering positive relationships was not limited to high-profile meetings with Iraqi leaders. On countless occasions at the MEU's forward operating base (FOB), one could observe Colonel Johnson chatting with an Iraqi contractor visiting the civil-military operations center or with junior officers and Soldiers of the Iraqi National Guard. He would seldom miss an opportunity to ask about their families or thank them for their service. Without a doubt, Colonel Johnson's personal example set the tone for the entire 24th MEU.

Colonel Johnson understood the value of information operations in an irregular warfare environment. His integration of information operations—psychological operations in particular—extended well beyond the efforts of 24th MEU's information operations cell. Instead, he emphasized the psychological impact of the MEU's actions as a whole, not just the actions of the psychological operations teams, and he required his staff to integrate psychological considerations into their routine.

One example of this holistic focus was Colonel Johnson's policy that wherever an Iraqi citizen saw a U.S. Marine, he or she would see at least two Iraqi Security Force members. As 24th MEU Marines dispersed from battalion-sized forward operating bases to company and platoon firm bases during the summer and fall of 2004, they met the commander's intent by assigning a platoon of Iraqi Soldiers (Iraqi National Guard, at that time) and a platoon of Iraqi police to a U.S. Marine rifle platoon. In a short period of time, 24th MEU intelligence sources revealed that the local populace overwhelmingly approved of the increased ratio of Iraqi Security Forces to U.S. Marines. Without saying a word, 24th MEU had ensured that the Iraqi citizens of North Babil and South Baghdad had tangible evidence of the transfer of sovereignty to the IIG. The pairing of U.S. and Iraqi forces, and tacit recognition of the Iraqi forces as equal partners, enhanced the Iraqi Security Forces' credibility among the local populace. Enhanced credibility fostered greater confidence in themselves and led to increased legitimacy for the local Iraqi government, both of which are critical components of any successful counterinsurgency. All of these efforts built trust and contributed to greater acceptance of Marines as a temporary occupation force.

Counterinsurgency operations are inherently more political than military in nature, and as is the case in any form of government, all politics is "local." In Arab culture in general and Iraqi culture in particular, personal relationships are paramount in business as well as government matters. In contrast to the American culture of law wherein personal feelings and relationships are subordinated to achieve fair and objective professional decisions without prior formalities, harmonious working relationships cannot be reached in Arab cultures until a personal relationship is established. Personal relationships build trust and mutual respect; without such a foundation, there is little incentive to work together to achieve military or government agreements in the absence of the rule of law.

The examples provided thus far are clear demonstrations of the 1st Marine Division's emphasis on serving as "no better friend" to the Iraqi people. However, Colonel Johnson understood that he would also need to ensure that those who opposed peace in Iraq would meet with "no worse enemy," and he understood that he could not achieve this objective with U.S. Marines alone. In June and July 2004, 24th MEU's Battalion Landing Team—1st Battalion, 2nd Marines—relieved the Soldiers of the 1st Battalion, 32nd Infantry Brigade, 10th Mountain Division in northern Babil province. During that turnover, the intelligence officer for the "1st of the 32nd" concluded that the Iraqi youth had few positive role models. The Iraqi Security Forces were in a critical rebuilding phase following extensive clashes during the Arba'een Offensive of April 2004, and the most prominent role models appeared to be the insurgents.

Colonel Johnson vowed to remedy this perception deficit. He determined that the Hillah Special Weapons and Tactics (SWAT) team was the Iraqi Security Force unit most capable of providing a positive role model for young Iraqi men. BG Qais Hamza, the provincial police chief, organized the Hillah SWAT team to be the Babil Province police force's chief counterterrorism and counterinsurgency unit. Colonel Johnson met General Qais within days of arriving in Iraq and determined that 24th MEU could provide valuable assistance to the Hillah SWAT team. The colonel capitalized on the cohesion and esprit de corps already developing within the SWAT team, and the 24th MEU's Force Reconnaissance Platoon provided small unit training to further hone the SWAT team's skills.

Colonel Johnson realized that the Hillah SWAT team needed to build a reputation of competence and military prowess in order to earn the respect of the Iraqi youth and the general public. He accomplished this in two ways. First, the colonel determined that the Hillah SWAT team needed to wear uniforms that distinguished them from the Iraqi police and National Guard. Tan flight suits were acquired to replace their khaki trousers and blue polo shirts and added prestige to the unit.

The next step was to engage in a public relations effort to enhance the reputation of Hillah SWAT, boost recruiting efforts, and elicit information regarding insurgent activity. Colonel Johnson tasked the 24th MEU information operations cell to design and produce hundreds of Hillah SWAT information cards. A picture of Hillah SWAT members in formation wearing their distinctive uniforms was printed on one side of the card. The opposite side of the card provided a phone number for Iraqi citizens to call to provide information on criminal or insurgent activity or to request information about joining the SWAT team. All text was printed in Arabic.

Colonel Johnson understood that success breeds success and that the exploits of Hillah SWAT would quickly spread by word of mouth. The Hillah SWAT team ultimately conducted more than sixty combined raids with 24th MEU's Force Reconnaissance Platoon, gaining a reputation of success throughout Babil Province and beyond. Over a seven-month period, Hillah SWAT's ranks swelled from a little more than 50 personnel to nearly 500. The people of the region finally had role models to compete with the insurgents.

Information operations play a principal role in irregular warfare. The efforts of the U.S Army's psychological operations teams are indispensable and must be given the same consideration as kinetic supporting arms during mission planning and execution. The information operations effort, however, must not stop there. Each tactical unit must consider the psychological effects of every interaction with the local populace. Just as operational security is the responsibility of every Marine, so too information operations must be the responsibility of every Marine in the theater. Every Marine must weigh the psychological impact of his actions and those of his or her unit. Col Ron Johnson understood this and achieved noteworthy tactical counterinsurgency successes in south-central Iraq.

35

The Massacre That Wasn't

—*Maj Ben Connable, USMC*

During the fighting in Fallujah in April 2004, the Associated Press reported that the U.S. Marines had bombed a mosque in the city, killing forty civilians gathered innocently for prayer. The story was picked up by the major international news networks and rebroadcast around the world. This report became the focal point for the intensive media backlash against the Fallujah assault that eventually forced a Marine withdrawal. Over the summer, Fallujah became a safe haven for the worst of the criminal gangs, insurgents, and terrorists, including Abu Musab al-Zarqawi. The problem was the Marines did not kill forty innocent people at that mosque.

I was working with the 1st Marine Division staff in Ramadi on April 7, 2004, at the height of the first Fallujah campaign. As the fight for the streets of the city developed, we watched a company of Marines in a firefight via the transmitted picture from an unmanned aerial vehicle (UAV). We were seeing everything unfold on the streets of Fallujah in a surreal but very clear, live, televised shot. The Marines were in a tough spot, pinned by insurgents laying down accurate fire from the minaret of the large Abdul-Aziz al-Samarai mosque that dominated the surrounding terrain. Other insurgents moved in and out of the ground floor during the fight, but if the Marines were unable to eliminate the snipers the advance in that sector would be stalled.

For several hours, the two sides traded shots, during which five Marines were wounded.[1] Tightly restricted by rules of engagement from using anything heavier than a light machine gun against the mosque, the Marines struggled unsuccessfully to put a "golden round" into the narrow slit at the top of the tower. After careful consideration and a clear discussion with the staff lawyers, the Marine commander eventually approved the launch of a single Hellfire missile into the tower to kill the snipers while minimizing damage to the mosque.[2]

We watched as the helicopter-launched missile streaked an errant path along one side of the tower, harmlessly slamming into the ground below and leaving the snipers unscathed. The minaret was too small a target, and the Marines were loath to take a second shot for fear of another missile going astray.

Pressure to advance increased as units on their flanks became exposed by the lack of progress around the mosque. The Marines on the ground asked to drop two bombs along the retaining wall around the mosque so they could rush the insurgents without becoming easy targets as they tried to break through. There was another heated debate, a command decision, and a fixed-wing jet aircraft[3] dropped two 500-pound bombs along the wall at 3:53 PM.[4]

The camera caught the explosion of the bombs on film (figure 35.1).[5] A huge cloud of black smoke flew up, and then settled, as the Marines rushed forward and cleared the mosque. The bombs had smashed a gap in the wall but clearly left the building completely intact (see figure 35.2). We saw no bodies live or otherwise near the wall before or after the impact of the bombs. As the unmanned aircraft slowly circled the compound, it became clear that the insurgents had fled. Some young infantry Marines climbed those steps and made sure the snipers were gone. They radioed back their report: mosque secured. They found no other personnel, weapons, or equipment, just empty shell casings on the ground floor. There were no bodies inside or outside the building.

Acutely aware that our entry into the mosque might make for negative media headlines, I began to monitor the news websites. It didn't take long for an AP reporter, Abdul-Qader Saadi, to relay "eyewitness accounts" of the incident to his bureau:

> *Associated Press* (3:01 PM UK Time)—A U.S. helicopter fired three missiles at a mosque compound in the city of Fallujah on Wednesday, killing about forty people as American forces batted Sunni insurgents, witnesses said. Cars ferried bodies from the scene, though there was no immediate confirmation of casualties. The strike came as worshippers gathered for afternoon prayers, witnesses said. They said the dead were taken to private homes in the area where temporary hospitals had been set up.[6]

Alarmed by what appeared to be an impending and wholly unwarranted public relations disaster, we scrambled to gather the facts so we could work a release through our public affairs officer, then-Lieutenant Eric Knapp. Our first task was

FIGURE 35.1: Impact

to confirm that we were all talking about the same mosque (we were). We then interviewed the Marines in charge of the video feed, and they confirmed that no unarmed people were seen anywhere near the fighting or the bomb impact site.

We ran the feed of the bomb drops again, taking video snapshots of the undamaged and completely intact mosque, the two craters, and the broken wall. We reviewed the facts as we knew them from our constant observation and the reporting from the Marines on the ground. There were no indications of any casualties, civilian or other. If anyone had been gathering in that mosque for prayers, they were long gone after the half-day intensive firefight in broad daylight.

In order to give the press an accurate and convincing rebuttal to the AP headline, we wanted to issue a copy of the video frames showing the intact mosque along with our version of events. Unfortunately, because the image was taken from a classified video system, the photo was considered classified and the word "Secret" was clearly visible inside the margins. It took us more than eight hours to get the

344 — Ideas as Weapons

FIGURE 35.2: Aftermath

image cropped and prepared for release; by that time the story had taken on a life of its own. The BBC picked up the lead from the AP:

> *BBC* (April 7, 2004)—A US air strike has killed up to forty people inside a mosque compound during heavy fighting in the Sunni Muslim Iraqi town of Fallujah, witnesses say. Forty Iraqis were reportedly killed when a US helicopter struck a mosque with three missiles today in the central Iraqi city of Fallujah. Cars ferried bodies of the dead from the scene and part of the wall surrounding the Abdul-Aziz al-Samarrai mosque was demolished, said an AP reporter, Abdul-Qader Saadi, who added that the mosque building itself was not damaged. The strike came as worshippers gathered for afternoon prayers, witnesses said. An angry crowd gathered as the wounded were taken to makeshift hospitals.[7]

Our frustration grew as we watched what we knew to be fictions develop into reported fact—the Americans bombed a mosque and killed forty innocent people in the midst of peaceful prayer. Things quickly got worse as the official AP report hit the Internet.[8] In a story entitled "U.S. Bombs Fallujah Mosque; More than 40 Worshippers Killed," by Bassem Mroue and Abdul-Qader Saadi, the AP reported the following:

An Associated Press reporter in Fallujah saw cars ferrying the dead and wounded from the Abdul-Aziz al-Samarrai mosque. Witnesses said a helicopter fired three missiles into the compound, destroying part of a wall surrounding the mosque but not damaging the main building. The strike came as worshippers had gathered for afternoon prayers, witnesses said. Temporary hospitals were set up in private homes to treat the wounded and prepare the dead for burial.

Most important, the inset picture AP story's by Agence France-Presse photographer Cris Bouroncle depicted three Marines on the streets of Fallujah. It was accompanied by this caption:

US Marines from the 1st Marine Expeditionary Force move into Fallujah. US Marines pressing an offensive in this Iraqi town west of Baghdad bombed a central mosque filled with worshippers and killed up to 40, a Marine officer said.

Now the AP was attributing the story of the massacre to an official, although unnamed, Marine source. We ran a request for information down the chain of command and quickly ascertained that nobody had confirmed this version of events. Reporters and editors were passing along the original AP report as if they were playing a bad game of "telephone." Every report seemed to loop back on the original story by Saadi. Later that day, Gwen Ifill interviewed Tony Perry, a reporter for the *Los Angeles Times* who spent a considerable amount of time in Al Anbar Province. He depicted a different version of events from the AP story:

IFILL: . . . We did hear today about an attack on a mosque that killed anywhere from forty to sixty people. Were you with that unit and can you describe what happened? (*Note: Now Ifill has introduced the number "sixty" into the story.*)

PERRY: Yeah, I'm with the unit right now. The first reports are a little misleading. What happened here . . . there are several mosques that have been used by the insurgents as places to either gather or strategize or even fire at Marines. One particular mosque had thirty to forty insurgents in it. They had snipers. They wounded five Marines. There were ambulances that drove up and the Marines let them come in to take the insurgent wounded away. But instead, people with RPGs . . . jumped out of the ambulances and started fighting with the Marines. Ultimately, what the Marines did is call in airpower. A helicopter dropped a Hellfire missile and then an F-16 dropped a laser-guided bomb on the outside of the mosque, put a huge crater outside the mosque. There's sort of a plaza outside the mosque. And suddenly, the firing inside stopped. But when the Marines examined the mosque and went in and went door-to-door in the mosque and floor-to-floor, they found no bodies, nor did they find the kind of blood and guts one would presume if people had died. Now one of two things must have happened: either the people died inside and were carted off somehow—and there is a tradition of the insurgents carting off their dead very quickly; or two, frankly, they escaped before the bomb was dropped. We cannot confirm that anybody actually died in that mosque. The Marines were quite willing to kill everybody in the mosque because they were insurgents. They had been firing at people, at Marines. And as the lieutenant colonel who ordered the strikes said, this was no longer a house of worship; this was a military target.[9]

Tony Perry had developed a reputation with the Marines for both professionalism and objectivity. Admittedly fearful of combat and death, he gained tremendous respect with his willingness to travel into hot spots alongside the Marines. However, he was never afraid to point out our failures or shortcomings on the front page of the *Los Angeles Times*.

If Perry, who was right on the scene, couldn't find evidence of any massacre, how did Saadi get the chain of events so confused?[10] I hesitate to question the fact that he personally witnessed carloads of casualties. There does not seem to be any evidence, however, that he confirmed the wounded and dead were actually removed from the compound, had been innocently gathering for prayer, had been hit by an air strike, or were not just insurgent fighters being evacuated from the ongoing fight down the street.

Even assuming Saadi's first-person account of casualties coming from the area around the mosque is accurate, the rest of the story relies entirely on second-hand accounts from Fallujah residents or, possibly, savvy insurgent fighters who regularly dropped their weapons to blend in with the civilian population. Reporting these secondhand stories as nearly unquestioned fact seems to be where truth separated from the fiction in the confusion of battle.

If "eyewitness" reports are to be taken at face value, the preponderance of Marine attacks on insurgent targets in Fallujah between April and November 2004 resulted in the deaths of women and children. Reporters regularly overlooked the fact that most of these accounts came from a spokesman in the insurgent-controlled hospital on the southwestern peninsula of the city or from other questionable sources.[11] Few media outlets seemed to take into account the power of Fallujan xenophobia or the active insurgent propaganda campaign aimed at the American and international media. The "truth" in Fallujah often wallowed helplessly somewhere between frantic street rumor and outright lie.

No matter whether the people reporting the story to Saadi were actual witnesses, insurgents, or simply Fallujans angered at the fighting around the mosque, some logical questions regarding the AP story remain:

- Why were Fallujah Muslims gathering for prayer at 3:53 PM when the closest prayer times for April 7, 2004, were 1:08 PM and 4:43 PM?[12]
- Why were forty people gathering for prayer at the mosque on a Wednesday afternoon when this kind of communal prayer gathering is usually reserved for Friday mornings?
- Why were forty people gathering peacefully for prayer at a mosque that had become the focal point for a broad daylight, raging firefight?
- If the Marine bombs killed up to forty innocent people, why were there no signs of any blood or bodies in or around the mosque compound?

Despite the doubts raised by Tony Perry, a CNN online article that seemed to dismiss the casualties as rumor,[13] protestations of the Marine battalion commander on site, and lengthy denials by military spokesman Brigadier General Kimmet, the story of the massacre at the Abdul-Aziz al-Samarrai mosque is now part of official history of Iraq. The website for the group "Iraq Body Count" (IBC), lists the incident not once but twice, accounting for forty deaths "confirmed" by the Associated Press and Middle East Online.[14] Antiwar bloggers made haste to turn the AP version of the incident into political fodder. An April 8 article by Anthony Gregory on antiwar.com entitled, "Fallujah Revenge and the War Disease" leads with the following paragraph:

> The recent bombing of a mosque in Fallujah meant fiery deaths for about forty Iraqis, but if the hawks get their way, it will be only the beginning of the deadly reprisals waged by the U.S. against that town in retaliation for the massacre of Americans there last week.[15]

The New World Blogger adds:

> This isn't good—an understatement. If even during the Middle Ages someone could call for sanctuary within a church, shouldn't mosques, churches and synagogues be off limits for bombing as well? Not only do they represent relentless revenge, but they also plant further seeds for anti-US hatred among those who feel their religion has been disrespected. I think we have seen enough of what blind retaliation has to offer us.[16]

The bloggers aren't the only ones to capitalize on the massacre-that-wasn't in Fallujah. Al Jazeera added a new twist to the story in its April 7 English-online Internet reporting:

> The bomb hit the minaret of the mosque and ploughed a hole through the building, shattering windows and leaving the mosque badly damaged.[17]

With the Associated Press and BBC stories to back up its claims, nobody bothered to question the Al Jazeera version of events. It should be noted that then-Prime Minister Ayad Allawi banned Al Jazeera from reporting in Iraq prior to the second Fallujah campaign because of ongoing collusion with the insurgents and blatant propagandizing.

There is no indication that the Associated Press or any other agency made any effort to confirm or deny the original story by Saadi. None of the post-incident interviews seems to indicate that the AP reporter actually entered the mosque compound to check his facts. Tony Perry's on-scene reporting was simply ignored.

What impact, if any, did this false report have on the conduct of the war? According to in-depth interviews and research done by Bing West, the author of *No True Glory*, stories like the one about the mosque "massacre" beamed across the BBC airwaves led in large part to a dramatic shift in British public opinion against the Fallujah assault.[18] The resulting pressure and public outcry over the reports of civilian deaths and images of dead babies repeatedly broadcast by Al Jazeera forced Prime Minister Tony Blair to pressure President Bush to cease offensive combat operations. Although not strictly causal by itself, the AP report was certainly a central factor in the media disaster that led to the withdrawal from Fallujah in the spring.

This withdrawal left the city in the hands of men like Abu Musab al-Zarqawi, Abdullah Janabi, and Omar Hadid. They turned it into a safe haven for criminals, terrorists, and murderers of every stripe. These men cut off Nick Berg's head and brutally slaughtered other Western hostages. They kidnapped, tortured, and murdered innocent Iraqi civilians who happened to get in their way. The Fallujah haven allowed them to conduct hundreds of operations that killed and maimed our Marines and Soldiers across the Al Anbar and northern Babil provinces in mid-2004.

We were eventually able to respond with Operation Al Fajr, the intensive Marine and Army assault to retake the city in November.[19] The six-month interval between Operations Vigilant Resolve and Al Fajr allowed the insurgents to dig tunnels, prepare defenses, and stock weapons and ammunition. We suffered more than 500 U.S. and Iraqi military casualties in this battle. Learning their lesson from the propaganda victory in April, the insurgents turned almost every mosque in Fallujah into a fortress and weapons depot in the hope they would take return fire during the fighting. Unfortunately, the fighting did indeed cause some damage, and the AP was there to point out American culpability.[20]

The reported events at the Abdul-Aziz al-Samarrai mosque continue to provide ammunition to the antiwar crowd and contribute to the outrage in the greater Arab world. The story seems to be handcrafted for extremist religious leaders trying to coerce young Muslim men to travel to Iraq and kill Americans. The Iraq Body Count casualty list that includes the numbers of dead reported by the

AP is regularly quoted as fact. The official BBC Iraq time line figures the mosque incident prominently, reminding its readers of this supposed atrocity and continuing to erode support for the war.[21]

Many reporters working stories in Iraq are professional, relatively unbiased, and willing to risk their lives to get first-person accounts. However, military and diplomatic officers also regularly complain about shallow, inaccurate reporting that exaggerates violence, ignores incremental success, and undermines American popular support. Some of the most vociferous critics of military cultural training display a stunning ignorance of post-Saddam culture when quoting the Iraqi street.

Spend enough time on the ground and one finds reporters content to re-report wire stories from the Green Zone (with a suitably dramatic backdrop) or rely wholly on Iraqi stringers who may or may not be working with insurgents, exaggerating events, or simply creating stories to turn a buck in the face of high unemployment. There are even a few mainstream reporters with dedicated antiwar agendas. One prominent wire service correspondent is well known for going on "hunting missions," looking for that one disgruntled Marine or Soldier who will give him a gripe or a pithy, antiwar comment, while ignoring positive or upbeat interviews.

It is unlikely that Mr. Abdul-Qader Saadi was hunting for a negative story. He was obviously brave and willing to risk his life on the streets of Fallujah, and his report was very straightforward and seemingly professional. It was technically accurate: some people told him that the Americans had bombed a mosque and killed forty innocent people. He says he saw people carting away casualties. He never says that he followed through with an investigation and did not confirm the details of the incident in any meaningful way. This is typical of AP "up-to-the-minute" coverage.

It took the assumptions and circular reporting of the BBC, Iraq Body Count, the Agence France-Presse photographer, Al Jazeera, and the bloggers to cement "the massacre that wasn't" into the history of the Iraq War. Some of them wanted the story to be true and will never question the facts. Those with a professional reputation for objectivity to uphold may want to take a second look. The Marines learned their lesson; it will never again take eight hours to release critical evidence to the media in the heat of battle. Perhaps if the truth had been told we could have avoided the murder and mayhem that emanated from the "city of mosques" throughout the long, hot summer of 2004. We may never know how many more reports like this one are woven into the narrative of the war in Iraq.

Other sources of information used for this story:
http://news.independent.co.uk/world/middle_east/story.jsp?story=509467
http://en.wikipedia.org/wiki/Abdul-Aziz_al-Samarrai_mosque
http://www.countercurrents.org/iraq-mccarthy240404.htm
http://www.uncensoredpress.com/

http://rense.com/general53/dde.htm
http://www.pbs.org/newshour/updates/iraq_04-07-04.html
http://www.guardian.co.uk/Iraq/Story/0,2763,1202163,00.html
http://www.ctv.ca/servlet/ArticleNews/story/CTVNews/20040407/fallujah_casualties_040407?s_name=&no_ads=

Keiler, Jonathan F., "Who Won the Battle for Fallujah?" *Naval Proceedings*, January 2005.

36

"Census Operations" and Information Management*
—Maj Morgan G. Mann, USMCR

Company F, 2nd Battalion, 24th Marines (2/24) was tasked with seizing the town of Al Yusufiyah, Iraq. The town, and the 200-square kilometers of area we became responsible for, was situated southwest of Baghdad in a semirural environment along the Euphrates River. Other than the town of Yusufiyah itself, the area was farmland, canals, small villages, and road network. The area was about 60 percent Sunni and 40 percent Shi'ite.

Shifting Gears

Our first two months in the zone were very busy. With frequent contact and a large target list, the company was primarily reacting to the existing conditions. However, by December 13, 2004, we had seen our last indirect fire attack until elections on January 30, 2005, and direct fire contests dropped to nil. We had detained more than a hundred personnel by this time. As the zone matured and stabilized we needed to become more proactive to develop the situation and seek out the enemy. To accomplish these goals we conducted "census operations." In conjunction with improved command post (CP) technology and work flow processes, our aggressive pursuit of the enemy achieved excellent results.

---

* *This essay appeared in the* Marine Corps Gazette *in April 2006 and is reproduced by permission of the Marine Corps Association. Copyright is retained by the* Marine Corps Gazette.

Census Operations

Company-developed targets and top-down targeting based on various intelligence sources were dwindling. We were killing or capturing the first echelon of enemy in the zone. The low-hanging fruit had been picked. To maintain the offensive we started to conduct census operations. The concept of operations was quite simple: identify a village, create platoon sectors, and catalog the full name, tribe, and ten-digit grid of every male in the town. A digital picture would be taken of each male as well. In conjunction with collecting this information we conducted a courteous house call and performed hasty searches for illegal weapons or possible cache sites.

Census operations are different than standard house calls or cordon and knocks because the unit conducts a systematic census of the entire village or area. In addition, the primary purpose is not to find something or someone but rather to learn about the village and collect information about the individuals who live there.

The company collected census information in more than 80 percent of the towns and villages in its zone. Towns like Yusufiyah, with more than 2,000 homes, took the company a week to search; however, smaller villages might take only one or two days. Areas where there was not an organized village but rather homes surrounded by farmland were cataloged by the platoon currently assigned to "offensive operations" as part of a security patrol, checkpoint operation, or other activity.

In most of these operations we conducted the operation without cordoning off the village unless it was known to be hostile. We maintained force protection by getting all Marines and vehicles off of the main roads instead of blocking traffic for hours at a time. We often set up one or two ambush vehicle checkpoints several kilometers away along parallel routes in an attempt to catch any enemy either traversing the zone or fleeing the area of the census operation.

There were several results of these types of operations:

- They facilitated daily interaction with the Iraqi population. We collected additional information, asked questions about enemy movement, and came to understand the level of morale in the zone.
- They denied the enemy safe harbor. We patrolled every village; we knocked on the door of every house.
- The enemy's attempt to "hide in plain sight" resulted in us being able to detain suspected enemy insurgents during census operations. Several times, the enemy tried to play it cool when we came into a village instead of attempting to flee. Oftentimes, in casual questioning, an insurgent would provide us with his real name. Thus, when we checked it against our growing database of

known or suspected insurgents we would find a positive match and detain the individual.
- In the event of having to conduct a cordon and search on a point target in the village at a later date, we had much better intelligence on the terrain, route selection, and target location.
- The ambush vehicle checkpoints we established as part of the census operation were successful in capturing enemy insurgents, as well as denying the enemy the benefit of surprise. The checkpoints reduced the enemy's ability to set up improvised explosive devices (IEDs) along our probable routes of egress and provided a defense in depth to possible vehicle-borne IEDs (VBIEDs).

CP Processes and Intelligence

The key to a census operation's success, however, was not the actual operation itself but the follow-up database work flow processes. When the platoon or company returned from a census operation, a designated platoon clerk would enter all the pertinent information into a Microsoft Excel spreadsheet on one of the laptop computers several Marines had brought with them. These spreadsheets would then be saved onto a memory stick. The information then was imported into a master company intelligence database in the company CP. Over time we had cataloged close to 17,000 Iraqi males, with all the critical information, including pictures, needed to build accurate target packages for future use.

In addition to entering names into the database from census operations, we also entered all names that came from top-down intelligence reports. The company was located approximately fourteen miles away from the battalion combat operations center. In addition to standard very-high-frequency radio connectivity, we also had an enhanced position location reporting system antenna and chat connectivity back to battalion. Through the chat application we were able to send and receive small files. The overnight watch officer in the company CP was responsible for ensuring that all of the relevant intelligence reports that were sent to battalion by higher or adjacent, and those reports created by battalion, were downloaded to the company CP's intelligence computer. Come morning the executive officer (XO), my intelligence cell leader, would print and read through all of the reports. These oftentimes consisted of draft information intelligence reports (DIIRs), Central Intelligence Agency (CIA) reports, Army intelligence reports, and battalion intelligence summaries. He would highlight names, tribes, and grid coordinates. He would then put these reports in a "to be filed binder." Our company clerk/intelligence chief was responsible for the next step.

The clerk would run each name of every report against our database. As the database grew to thousands of names, we started getting hits on these searches. The search would bring up a page with the full name, picture, and ten-digit grid of the person identified in an intelligence report as an enemy fighter, coordinator, financier, or sympathizer. Now, instead of having an intelligence report with no target location or vague information, we had the ability to hit a point target. The database allowed us to search on any variable and incorporate "fuzzy logic" so it would return best guesses to our queries. When we had positive matches, the senior man would notify the XO or me, and one of us would subsequently build a target package for use in a future mission. Depending on operational priorities, we would task a platoon to conduct a cordon and search on the target house, detain the individual target, and question the remainder of the household.

For those names that did not match any names in our database, the clerk promptly entered all of the relevant information available. Once the report was sifted through it would be placed in a "filed binder." I would read the binder once a day. It was available to the watch officers, who were platoon commanders or platoon sergeants, to read while on shift. Thus, all unit leaders developed a common intelligence picture from the reporting available. This information facilitated a better orientation and more efficient enemy situation briefings during nightly task meetings. As part of the data entry process the clerk would be sure to enter the specific report type and number. Thus, we could also search by CIA report or DIIR and so on. In addition, we could provide feedback to higher headquarters regarding potential conflicts or errors in reporting based on the information we had collected.

The success of these operations and processes required daily discipline from the squad up to the company CP to ensure that names, pictures, and grid locations were properly collected and entered in a timely manner. The use of the information became vital in the company. All units took advantage of the data. Local security patrols around the town of Al Yusufiyah would frequently call back to the CP and ask for a "name check" on an individual the patrol had stopped. Platoons would print lists of suspected insurgents from a specific village before they conducted a security patrol in the area. The quick embrace of this process was because of the rapid results we all saw. All of our units were capturing more enemies because of these operations and the information we now had available. Because Marines saw results, they were all for putting in the hard work to build our store of information.

Some might ask, why not use existing systems? Why would an infantry unit create its own database? The primary reason was because existing intelligence applications were not available at the company level, especially when conducting distributed operations. Because these systems stayed at a higher level, the information for local areas tended to be stale or nonexistent. In addition, many of the reports provided by higher headquarters contained incomplete information. Items such as grid locations, full names, or tribe names could be missing from individual targets. Our system was able to complete that picture on numerous occasions, thus allowing us to prosecute a target. Last, the database was simple to use, manage, and scale for a company-sized unit with no specialized information technology resources.

The net result of the censuses we took and the information we collected led to more than 300 enemy insurgents detained and 100,000 pounds of explosives located. The processes incorporated once units' missions were completed made future operations far more efficient and effective in a large zone with limited resources.

37

Frustration

—LtCol James McNeive, USMC (Ret.)

If there was one word to describe those officers and people who are working information operations (IO) in the war against terror, that word would be "frustration." Frustration at not being able to completely leverage information to defeat a ruthless and hateful enemy, at having commanders not understand the importance of information and the impact it can have, and at having rules and regulations that needlessly restrict and hamper the performance of their duties—this frustration is felt at all levels, especially at the tactical level. Despite the theory that IO is driven from the top down, success in the information war will be achieved from the bottom up.

The current war against radical fundamentalist Muslims will not end when peace is declared in either Iraq or Afghanistan but will continue in one form or another for generations. How information in the future is used to combat and nullify this threat will be based on what lessons are learned today. The IO lessons learned in the current conflicts will guide how IO is conducted and debated for the next twenty years. The question is, has the leadership and those frustrated IO warriors learned the right lessons?

IO has many definitions, both official and unofficial. Though it can be many things, there are several it is not:

- It is not a public relations campaign on steroids.
- It is not an effort to win the hearts and minds of a local population.

- It is not designed to show how friendly and compassionate Americans can be.
- It is not focused on systems and technology.
- It is not solely nonlethal.

What then is IO? For the purpose of this discussion, it is actions taken to protect, corrupt, or block that information a person, or target, needs in order to make a decision. The goal is to provide the right combination of information so the target acts in a predetermined manner, for in the long run, all that matters is that the target makes a decision that results in actions favorable to American interests. Nowhere is this more important than at the tactical level.

The tactical level is the point of contact where those actions designed to influence the decisions of the target are put into effect. Though the results can have strategic consequences, many will never be noticed outside the immediate area of operations (AO). Yet, the overall success or failure of an operation at the tactical level is the building block for success or failure at the operational and strategic levels. A key ingredient of success is the leveraging of information to influence the decisions of not only those noncombatants, but of the enemy as well. Attacking that decision cycle is paramount in the duties of the Marines and Soldiers serving as IO officers. It is these officers who have the highest degree of frustration.

Frustration stems from several different sources. One source is mechanical, or the actual staff work needed to execute a plan. For IO one of the most problematic sources is the approval process for such tools as PSYOPS products, combat camera footage, and press releases. This process is lengthy, slow, and too centralized, all of which gives a decisive advantage to an adversary. Another source is the command philosophy on how information should be leveraged. Too often, a lack of understanding or resistance by commanders, their primary staff, and planning team leaders create a command climate of in-the-box thinking. Experience from the last several years in dealing with information in Iraq can provide some lessons learned that, if enacted, could change such a weak command climate.

In the current campaigns in Iraq and Afghanistan, many complain that the military establishment spends too much time focused on the enemy and not enough time on the civilian population. The argument is that the real battle rests on which side the civilian population accepts and rejects. In these types of insurgencies the civilian population is the center of gravity. U.S. armed forces compete for their acceptance against an enemy that uses brutality, intimidation, cultural bias, and disinformation as extremely effective tools of persuasion. At some point the U.S. military must use its ability to leverage information and drive the enemy from the civilian population by attacking the enemy's mind-set. Understanding these four lessons can help make that happen.

It Is a New Type of Battlefield

The information environment presents a new type of battlefield with challenges and opportunities not previously seen. Commanders need to accept this fact and strive to understand it. The February 13, 2006, version of Joint Publication (JP) 3-13 *Information Operations* describes the information environment as the "aggregate of individuals, organizations, and systems that collect, process, disseminate, or act on information." It then breaks the information environment into the physical, informational, and cognitive dimensions. In this new battlefield, information flows in new and nontraditional ways throughout these dimensions that do not always neatly fit into the current staff planning process. There is new technology readily available to any adversary and culture norms that will have major impacts. In this new battlefield, the enemy may have information interior lines, meaning they speak the language, have an intimate knowledge of the society and culture, easily blend into the populace, and are not restricted by the same ethos. This allows them to have a faster tempo when it comes to controlling the information environment. Can the United States ever have information interior lines? Probably not, but if this is understood up front, plans and policies can be developed to mitigate it.

Part of this new battlefield will involve different conduits for information. Actions in Iraq give an insight into two examples, one historical and one modern. The historical conduit is the mosque, which in Islamic cultures is a central part of the society. By default, the mosque is a communication node and one radical fundamentalist Muslims take full advantage of. Face-to-face meetings, telephonic and Internet communications, sermons to large audiences, and financial dealings are just some of the types of information that flow in and out of mosques. Though destruction is always an option, it is not always practical, leaving actions against such a node as very challenging. It requires a special understanding of the environment if such a node is to be effectively neutralized.

The modern example is the cell phone. The cell phone is probably one of the most powerful weapons on the new battlefield of today. An adversary can use it to command and control, transmit messages, take photos, intimidate locals, and arm explosives. It can also be a source to gain information by listening to the cell phone conversations of American servicemembers and their local supporters. The importance of the cell phone has not been lost to radical fundamentalists. Its uses, to include security procedures that must be followed, are often discussed in their Internet forums.

It Is OK to Kill Someone or Break Something

Information operations has a lethal side. A person may need to be killed or equipment may need to be destroyed because of the impact it will have on the decision-making ability of the target. If the target relies on information from a certain source, whether a living being or man-made system, and that source is removed, it will impact the decisions that are made. There may also be times when the target needs to be eliminated in order to prevent his decisions from impacting others or from being carried out. This is as much a part of the information fight as putting out press releases or PSYOPS products. Many may see such actions as normal combat operations, but their impacts on the information environment cannot be overstated. The IO officer should be fully involved in the planning. Physical destruction was an original primary capability of IO, but in the rewrite of the JP 3-13 it became a supporting capability. It is still part of the equation when looking to leverage information. The problem is that in many commands IO is considered strictly nonlethal and completely separated from "fires" (the U.S. military's term for ordnance directed at the enemy from artillery, airplanes, etc.) or the direction by the staff of all lethal weapons systems besides troops in contact. This separation causes a lack of synergy that often results in poor staff coordination. It also helps build the false perception that IO is only concerned with noncombatant audiences and not an enemy. This poor thinking removes information as a major weapon when dealing with the types of enemies found on today's battlefield.

It Is OK to Lie
Truth is not the responsibility or concern of the IO officer. He is only concerned with what his enemy *believes* is the truth and how that perception can be modified and used to his advantage. Granted the different pillars of IO demand that different levels of truth be employed, but when command philosophy wants nothing but the truth to be told then the IO officer is greatly restricted in how he addresses the enemy's mind-set. The role of ensuring the real truth is told belongs to the public affairs officer (PAO), whose credibility should not be compromised. The problem is too many think that information operations only entails the press release the PAO puts out and that victory in the information environment is won or lost on the type of press coverage they receive. There is no argument that portrayal in the press is important, but the press is not the only conduit through which information can be leveraged. The art of lying to deceive an enemy has been a proven military tactic since the dawn of time, and lying so that it impacts the perception of an enemy should always be an option. The primary targets are the enemy combatant and those who support him. This adversary exists in a world of rumors and paranoia. Sometimes the truth is the best weapon; other times something less than the truth will be most effective. It is up to the IO officer to coordinate the approach, but he can only do that if the command accepts lying as a viable option. Many PAOs shy away from IO because they feel it will endanger their creditability. If lying is accepted as a viable option, it certainly will give credence to such an argument. This can be migrated if the PAO is fully integrated into the planning and coordinates with the IO officer. This way he will fully understand what is being done, will know when to talk to the press, and will prevent his comments from contradicting other efforts. Unfortunately, too often commands do not consider lying an option, preferring instead to fight the war only via press releases.

Listen to What the Enemy Says
The enemy will tell us everything we want to know about him. All we have to do is listen. The problem is that we don't.

Radical fundamentalist Muslims across the Middle East will use everything from flyers and sermons at the local level to the Internet to project their message. Common Internet methods include posting communiqués, audio speeches, or videos. Videos are particularly popular as their quality and sophistication have greatly improved over the last couple of years. Once posted, the message is passed across the Internet by supporters and sometimes picked up by mainstream media, reaching a potentially huge audience. In Iraq, all the major insurgent groups use the Internet to speak not only to their supporters and would-be supporters, but to the West as well. Though parts of their messages will contain religious quotes and poetic insults, they can include goals, main complaints, the rules they claim to live by, and the major themes they are using to try influence their audience. Often they will pepper these with the names of past Islamic scholars or quotes from Western newspapers as part of their effort to legitimize their actions. By actively listening to what they say, plans on how to counter them can be effectively developed. If done right, their own words can be used against them. Their main theme or complaints can be nullified. Their positions they rely on for motivation—recruitment and local support—can be countered.

These are just four of the lessons that should be learned from the present conflicts. As the junior officers and enlisted personnel of today grow into senior officers and enlisted of tomorrow, the lessons they learn today will impact their actions of tomorrow. The enemy they face today, they will face tomorrow. The way IO is conducted today cannot be conducted that way tomorrow. Changing attitudes as well as command guidance, staff actions, and rules and regulations will focus and bring synergy to how information can be effectively used. This change will also give those IO warriors a better ability to support their commanders and relieve much of their frustration.

38

Getting Out the Word: Information Operations on the Ground in Iraq

—*CPT Kyle Norton, USA*

Effective information operations (IO) are a necessity for the Coalition's success in Iraq. While the majority of the country was elated with the fall of Saddam's regime in 2003, much has transgressed since to diminish that elation. Iraqi society continues to face the emotions and struggles associated with a country undergoing a major transformation while simultaneously facing the fear of death from sectarian violence. Iraqis expected order and public services to be quickly restored after Saddam's fall. Lacking tangible improvements, they are emotionally tiring more and more each day. Consequently, Iraqis quickly look to religious leaders for help and distrust the government owing to perceived corruption. These factors, combined with the pervading sense of fear that has plagued Iraq for decades, make it imperative for commanders and Soldiers alike to understand the importance of IO.

My opinions and views result from two tours in Iraq. I am currently serving as an intelligence adviser and trainer to 2nd Battalion, 2nd Brigade, 8th Iraqi Army Division. Spending each day with the Iraqi Soldiers in my assigned battalion has only strengthened my belief in the importance of positive IO. At no time during my career have I undergone any training that I would consider solely focused on IO; however, I do believe that classroom training, without a basis for understanding, would be of marginal value. On-the-ground situational needs are more easily understood after having operated "outside the wire" and in frequent conversation with local sheiks and town council members. Effective training in IO could be accomplished by focusing on Soldiers within units who have been deployed and who have experienced both effective and ineffective IO methods in theater. Ultimately, a field training exercise or a National Training Center (NTC) rotation that focuses on a full spectrum of combat operations with civilians on the battlefield speaking Arabic would be most beneficial. This training would put Soldiers in realistic situations and force them to use an interpreter to convey a message. Soldiers need to see firsthand the positive effects IO can have in influencing or shaping a battlefield.

Operation Iraqi Freedom has most definitely become a war of perception. Our everyday actions continually mold and solidify these perceptions. Perceptions are often influenced by word of mouth and rumor instead of firsthand accounts of events. The organization or group that is able to get its message out quickest is often the one heard the loudest. The bombing of the Golden Mosque in Samarra was a prime example. Immediately after the bombing, an anti-Coalition message circulated that put the blame for the bombing on Coalition forces. This message, at least in part, was believed by a large number of individuals in my Iraqi battalion. It took intensive conversations on my part with several individuals to convince them that we had no part or involvement in the bombing and were not responsible in any way. These were individuals who personally knew me and spent every day with me but yet were still moved by the false anti-Coalition message.

Anti-Coalition groups in Iraq perform IO at extremely high levels of sophistication, continuously hampering Coalition efforts. They are operating in their own neighborhoods with an understanding of the area that we will never be able to achieve. Their networks have been built over several decades and are much stronger than we can hope to build in year-long rotations. They understand how to turn even the smallest of infractions into powerful messages against Coalition efforts. Iraqi militia and political party networks also use IO to build their organization and promote their causes. The enemy we face is not wearing a uniform and is not distinguishable by any visible characteristics. With the constant long lines at gas stations, common power outages, and reoccurring violence it is easy for anti-Coalition groups to implant IO messages in everyday conversations with fellow Iraqis. These conversations may play off the desires of Iraqis to lead a better, safer life but are not likely to definitively sway an individual. However, simple messages coupled with incidents such as the 2006 rape and slaying case in Mahmoudiya and the killing of civilians in Haditha make it easy for our enemy to convert individuals. All of these factors likewise make it difficult for us to win a war of perception. The enemy has a definite sociopolitical advantage while operating in their respective neighborhoods and tribal regions with a distinct understanding of the forces at work behind the scenes. Constant political struggles and easy criticism of unfortunate events are added bonuses to their ongoing IO efforts.

These factors put a great deal of pressure on ground units to quickly change people's perceptions. The use of IO is instrumental in creating this change, and units have a variety of methods to choose from in creating IO campaigns. News broadcasts, leader engagements, psychological operations (PSYOPS) products and messages, and news bulletins are all effective means, but the quickest and most effective often seems to be word of mouth. Units must quickly identify local leaders and major influences during the beginning stages of their deployments. They must understand the populace's concerns and needs and convey a sympathetic feeling to their plights. Creating alliances with these individuals can greatly impact the full spectrum of stability operations. Having positive relationships with sheiks in the units' respective areas of operations can lead to increased cooperation, targetable intelligence, and decreased levels of violence.

Units often place the majority of their efforts on human interaction but cannot neglect the impact of television. Iraqi citizens regularly watch television, often watching news broadcasts. Positive stories on the successes of Coalition and Iraqi Security Forces therefore can be critical to success. This is something I have witnessed several times within the Iraqi Army battalion I am integrated into. They do an excellent job of promoting their efforts in local news broadcasts. Another technique effectively used in my area of operations has been post-operation IO campaigns. These can be as simple as returning to the area of a recent operation with food, water, or other basic necessity items and publishing a message stating the purpose and results of the recent operation. Most people respond well to positive results and reinforcement, and Iraqis are no different. Ultimately, no one method alone will create an effective campaign. Units must study their area of operations to see what techniques have been successful in the past and look for ways to build on previous IO foundations. Once the plan is in place, units must relentlessly push their messages and counter those of their adversaries.

I feel using money, as we do with intelligence tips, for IO purposes could be an effective alternative IO method. Low-level insurgent operatives often cite the lack of money and employment as a reason for their activities. A fund system to promote our efforts and/or distract from enemy efforts may provide an advantage to reach individuals whom we are not otherwise able to reach. The difficulty with such a program, however, would be measuring tangible results. While it is easy to identify results with intelligence tips money, paying sources to spread positive messages could also be a useful tactic in areas where there is little cooperation or high tensions between civilians and Coalition forces. With the amount of money being spent on projects around the country, I believe testing this method in a difficult area of operations would be well worth the money spent given the potential payoff. Another IO technique that can be employed is partnering with Iraqi forces to jointly deliver messages. This puts an "Iraqi face" with the message and serves two purposes. It helps promote Coalition messages and helps build civilian faith in Iraqi Security Forces. This is already being done to an extent but has greater potential than is currently being utilized.

Our present pace of military operations seeking to detain anti-Coalition suspects could continue for years without significantly altering the status quo. I do believe these operations serve a vital importance in creating safer streets and do serve to build trust with local citizens. However, given the lack of employment opportunities and low levels of education in many parts of Iraq, insurgent groups are able to replenish their ranks and build support networks with their IO and recruitment techniques. The fluctuating periods of violence and the constant struggle to achieve our rebuilding goals illuminate the difficulty of quickly turning Iraq into a stable democracy with a solid infrastructure. The struggles will likely continue into the foreseeable future, but it may be possible to more easily achieve our desired end goal through shaping the local populace's perception of Coalition forces. IO campaigns allow commanders to build networks of supporters in local communities and can lead to positive effects on all areas of their missions. We will never be able to completely win over Iraqis or stop the violence, but with enough support and cooperation we will be able to successfully hand over a nation with a solid foundation for the future.

39

Fighting for Perceptions: Tactical IO in 2004 Iraq

— *Maj Jennifer Morris Mayne, USMCR*

Information operations (IO), as an adjunct to actions on the ground, can be a powerful supporting arm if properly performed, given appropriate resources, and employed in a timely and responsive manner. IO in Iraq has met with varying degrees of success dependent on the manner and situation in which it was used. This chapter presents a narration of my experiences as an IO planner in Iraq from 2004 to 2005.

I deployed with I MEF as an IO planner and watch officer. My duties included participation in planning as well as assessing our efforts by monitoring atmospherics. We defined atmospherics as the attitudes encountered by our troops on the ground in a particular town, neighborhood, or city. We monitored atmospherics by reading human intelligence (HUMINT) and signals intelligence (SIGINT) reports, as well as situation reports (SITREPS) from psychological operations (PSYOPS) units, civil affairs (CA) teams, and the maneuver battalions. What was being broadcast from the mosques at Friday prayers? Did the citizens welcome our patrols? Were people cooperating and offering information; were they elusive, hiding behind closed doors; or were they hostile, throwing stones and assisting the terrorists? Attitudes in towns changed from time to time, and we tried to see whether the shift correlated with a particular event. We also monitored news media to gauge how we were perceived by the world and in particular by the Arab world. Since satellite television was becoming more prominent throughout Iraq, it was important to monitor what the Iraqi people were receiving from this new source of information.

When I arrived at I MEF in the fall of 2004, the attitude among the Coalition personnel present was that we were losing the war of information and perception. In April 2004, Coalition forces (CF) had been pulled out of Fallujah after fighting to take more than half the city. The CF were pulled out because there was a perception in the press that we were killing too many civilians. The perception of the press influenced the opinions of the Iraqi Interim Government and the Iraqi and American public. In fact there were not many civilian casualties, but as the saying goes, perception is reality. Iraqi government officials demanded that our forces withdraw from Fallujah. In general, news coverage of Operation Iraqi Freedom (OIF) was very negative, with concurrent incidents such as Abu Ghraib and an air strike on an alleged wedding party fresh in everyone's mind. Al Jazeera and other Arab news sources claimed that Coalition forces were killing innocent civilians. They often had "eyewitnesses" and pictures to show of our "indiscriminate" attacks. Daily, we tried to counter these false allegations, but to no avail; even Western media was beginning to run these stories. The truth was that Al Jazeera had media stringers working with insurgents, and the insurgents paid other stringers to portray the Americans and the Coalition forces in a negative light. They often staged photographs and fabricated stories.

We needed to be proactive with the media instead of continuing to react to negative news stories. It was obvious that once a story hit the wires it was useless to try to counter the story or offer a response after the initial reports. We needed to get our message out first. I MEF public affairs worked to do that. Whenever there was a preplanned strike or operation, we prepared our story concurrent with the mission planning. As bombs hit the target, our press release would hit the wires. Our method was to tell the truth about what insurgents were doing. They were using schools, mosques, hospitals, and homes as weapons storage facilities. They used the Fallujah Hospital as a main base of operations and communications center. They used ambulances and police vehicles to transport weapons and fighters. They had intimidated or enlisted doctors to talk to the press and offer eyewitness accounts on how many civilians and children the Coalition had killed.

Our new proactive approach with the press prevented a great deal of misinformation from making the news and out cycled the enemy's IO. We described what we were fighting, telling the world about the insurgents' use of schools, mosques, and hospitals to conduct attacks. We explained that once a site had been used for military purposes it lost its protected status. PSYOPS and IO produced products to also drive this point across to the Iraqi population as well as to warn the terrorists. I MEF IO monitored the Arab media, and over the course of a few months we noticed a significant decrease in negative reporting. In fact, all the Arab news sources except Al Jazeera began to have more neutral reporting toward CF, a tremendous change.

In preparation for Operation Al Fajr, the second battle for Fallujah in November 2004, we prepared for the worst. We anticipated more negative news stories and dreaded the possibility that we would be forced to withdraw because of public perception. There was a great need to minimize civilian deaths while also encouraging the insurgents to come to the big fight. We developed a number of products warning the citizens of Fallujah to leave, that a battle was imminent. We said that they had allowed their city to be overrun by insurgents and the coming battle was the price to pay for their cowardice. Additionally, we developed other products encouraging the terrorists to stay and fight, telling them that if they were men they would come to Fallujah to fight.

By the time the battle of Fallujah began, the majority of the population of 250,000 people had evacuated. The people left behind were for the most part there to fight. The IO messages were successful in getting civilians off the battlefield and reducing the number of innocent deaths. The news agencies had no opportunity to spin stories about CF killing civilians indiscriminately. As the battle unfolded, we were surprised to see that the majority of Iraqis supported our actions. As it turned out, the citizens of Fallujah had been held hostage by the insurgents. Beheadings and intimidation had the civilians of the city living in terror. We found a large number of torture chambers. These were rooms literally covered in blood and filled with television and recording equipment. According to the survivors these rooms were used to film the torture and beheadings of prisoners. The films were sold as DVDs on the street corners in Fallujah and other cities across Iraq. We used Combat Camera extensively to provide footage and pictures of what we were encountering. They were embedded with our forces during the attack, taking pictures of the torture chambers and weapons caches stockpiled in schools, mosques, hospitals, and graveyards. We provided these photos to the media as proof of the atrocities being committed by the terrorists. As these stories spread both by word of mouth from the refugees and from news coverage, the world and the Iraqi people were shocked. The "Battle of Fallujah" quickly became the "Liberation of Fallujah."

To capture that theme and take advantage of our momentum, we produced a number of messages and products using Fallujah as a lesson to other cities and towns across Iraq—"Don't let your town be the next Fallujah." We conveyed that the citizens of Fallujah had allowed the insurgents to takeover their city. CF had removed the insurgents and was going to spend a lot of money rebuilding the city, but this was only going to happen once. We stated that if the citizens of Fallujah allowed the insurgents back in we would not be so generous next time. We saw that citizens in other towns and cities began cooperating with Coalition forces more, and in some towns the citizens forced the insurgents to leave. Iraqis really did not want their town to share Fallujah's fate.

Reconstruction followed Operation Al Fajr. For this phase of operations messages informed the locals about the money being spent to rebuild the city. Security was another important IO theme. Once major combat operations had concluded the city was cordoned off and a number of checkpoints were established. Only

Fallujah citizens were allowed back into the city following a thorough inspection of their person and vehicle. Additionally, identification cards were made for returning citizens. The information on the cards included the person's name, photograph, and fingerprints. The entire process of returning to the city took hours. Long lines of people and vehicles sat in the hot sun, each waiting to be processed through checkpoints and allowed back into the city. We developed messages to describe the process and explain the purpose behind it. We explained that by checking everyone returning to the city, we were preventing weapons and insurgents from entering and were providing security to the people. To our surprise we found that these citizens were not unhappy or frustrated with the long wait, nor were they angry that their city had been destroyed. The majority of people were happy and thankful that the insurgents had been removed from their city. They also wanted to have an identification card made; they felt that having one of these cards legitimized them and differentiated them from an insurgent.

The first Iraqi national elections took place in January 2005. A successful national election could be a turning point in the war. Everything since the beginning of the war was building toward this event. It was essential to get the citizenry out to vote without the appearance that CF was influencing the election. It was a very stressful time because we were told to remain "hands off" when it came to the elections. The U.S. armed forces were not to produce IO products or speak about elections on patrol. In Al Anbar Province, however, no members of the Independent Election Commission of Iraq (IECI) were present. There was absolutely no one in the entire province willing to come and promote elections; Al Anbar was considered too dangerous. There had already been numerous beheadings of Iraqis who had promoted the election. It was therefore left up to I MEF to do the job. We developed products to encourage people to vote without promoting any particular party or candidate. We also tried to reassure the Iraqis that they would be safe on election day; CF would provide security at the polling sites. There was a particular concern with publicizing the locations of the polling sites. We knew that the insurgents would destroy the polling sites if they knew their locations ahead of time. We decided to disseminate this information at the last minute. The day before the election, we dropped leaflets and broadcast over radio the locations of the polling sites. Still, many of polling sites were mortared before and during the election. Though we expected a low turnout, many Iraqis came out to vote, even amid mortar fire and all the intimidation that had taken place. The turnout in Sunni-dominated Al Anbar Province wasn't as impressive as throughout the rest of Iraq, but we felt we had achieved an important victory. More than half of the people who voted throughout the province were in Fallujah. Fallujah, which had previously been the most dangerous city in Iraq, was now a model of what other cities could become. We drew two conclusions from this. First, the citizens of Fallujah had a reason to believe in the government; it had promised to rid the city of insurgents and to rebuild, both of which had come to pass. Additionally, Fallujah had become the most secure city in the province following Operation Al Fajr. The cordon around the city provided such tight security that the population felt safe enough to come out and vote.

Information and messages are useless unless they are reinforcing action. We promised that we would rid the city of Fallujah of insurgents, and we delivered. We also promised to rebuild the city and to provide security. By the time the elections came the citizens of Fallujah were our biggest fans in Al Anbar. Promised security must be backed up with actual improvements. The citizens of these towns may not have been pro-insurgency as much as they were just plain intimidated. The insurgents would murder anyone who helped CF or was even suspected to have helped the Coalition. CF needed to eliminate that threat in order to build the confidence of the population. After CF secured an area, a transition to Iraqi-led security could begin.

Another target audience that I MEF tried to address was women. The role of women in Iraqi families has been downplayed to a great extent. Iraqi women have a huge influence on the family, especially in raising their sons and the future generations of Iraq. We produced magazines specifically for women, with articles written specifically to address women's concerns and to encourage them to support the new democratic Iraq. We also distributed handbills and leaflets. On one handbill were two pictures of young children, one child with weapons and the other child with books and toys. The caption asked Iraqi mothers which future they preferred for their sons, more violence or new opportunities. Anytime an insurgent attack killed Iraqi children we would quickly produce handbills and posters to capitalize on the event, driving home to the populace that the insurgents were killing innocents indiscriminately while the Coalition was working to provide new schools and opportunities. Our approach succeeded; more than half the callers to our tips line were women.

Every service member should have some degree of IO training. Although messages and themes are developed at the higher levels and pushed down, the Marines and Soldiers on patrol are in daily contact with the target audience. The actions of one lance corporal or one fireteam can have strategic implications. Troops at all levels need to understand the importance of information and perceptions. They need to understand that their actions can reinforce or counter our efforts to influence. Today's warrior is more technical than ever before, with the means to disseminate information almost immediately. Everyone has a digital camera and the ability to transmit images and information over the Internet via e-mails and personal blogs. Now, every person in the combat zone is an information officer regardless of training or Military Occupational Specialty (MOS).

In conclusion, while we always knew that our message must be true, we learned that IO products must be well timed and significant to the audience. IO objectives must be clearly defined, proactive, and quickly accomplished, often spontaneously. Since IO success often cannot be immediately assessed, prior knowledge, anticipation of possible outcomes, and concurrent planning are crucial to success. Last, in order to succeed IO teams must be well organized and familiar with the local customs, behaviors, expectations, and desired outcomes.

40

By Other Means*

— Capt Zachary D. Martin, USMC

"You can't win a game of poker if your opponent insists on playing spades."

—*U.S. Marine Corps,* Small Wars

We must not let our performance in the heavy fighting in Fallujah lead us to believe that we have broken the back of the insurgency. The insurgency is not the force that we destroyed in Fallujah. It is not a formation at all. It is a phenomenon, a disease that thrives in the chaotic matrix of Iraq. The center of gravity of the insurgency is not its massed combat power but its distributed forces that can attack us asymmetrically. The enemy's critical requirement is his ability to operate in the environment of Iraq—avoiding detection and choosing the time and place he will give battle. The enemy's critical vulnerability is the support he enjoys from the populace.[1]

We are at an important crux in the war. In the 1980s Lebanon was just such a collection of numerous ragtag factions and associated militias. With outside guidance (that Syria and Iran may again be providing in Iraq), elements of this unprofessional and disorganized mob became Hezbollah, a highly competent and

---

* *This essay appeared in the* Marine Corps Gazette *in September 2005 and is reproduced by permission of the Marine Corps Association. Copyright is retained by the* Marine Corps Gazette.

extremely dangerous terrorist organization, arguably a far more formidable enemy than Al Qaeda. The sophistication of the insurgency in Iraq is increasing. We cannot afford to give it space.

The ultimate political question in this kind of complex conflict is this: what will be the power structure—who will be in control—when the United States leaves? While this is a question for policymakers, it must inform every operational decision the military makes. We tend to focus on the negative aspects of the primacy of political goals in complex conflicts. When we speak of the "strategic corporal" it is generally in terms of his decisions having a potentially negative implication, particularly with regard to the international media. Perhaps this is the case on the tactical level, although nowhere is the overlap between the strategic and tactical levels of war as great as in "small" wars. On the operational level, we must ask ourselves how every action advances the political objective.

Cognitive Dissonance

Why are we mistaking the nature of the fight? Part of the problem relates to our training. The Marine Corps is at the forefront of thinking on insurgency and has been so for some time. We train our leaders and Marines in counterinsurgency and complex conflicts but only as the exception; our classes on small wars come after our classes on conventional offense and defense. Our Marines train to fight large, organized enemy formations, with insurgency treated as a "lesser included case." As a result, we apply the mental models of large-scale conflict where it is not appropriate. For example, we failed to secure our supply lines of communications on the Fallujah peninsula and had our logistics convoys ambushed repeatedly because we conceptualized them as the "rear area." This strategy might have worked in the fight against Saddam's army when we could have been confident that we had not bypassed an enemy formation. It does not work in an insurgency for there is no rear area.

We equate tempo with speed. Insurgencies are defeated not by lightning, focused actions but instead by persistent, comprehensive actions. All of this is not to say that we should neglect our traditional mission essential tasks. On the contrary, a decision not to prematurely focus on stability and support operations at the expense of conventional training ensured that our battalion had the balanced skill set required in this conflict. But looking to the future, we need to do more than talk about the Three Block War. We need to train for it in the same evolution. We need to integrate small wars as the rule rather than the exception.

A more fundamental problem is that complex situations are difficult to assess. On a psychological level, the mind shies away from a vague situation that cannot be developed in the traditional sense. We strive for an intuition-recognition-based comprehension of the enemy situation and critical vulnerability on the battlefield. From the intelligence perspective, insurgencies defy easy, quantitative analysis.

Our measures of effectiveness are only meaningful contextually and relative to the enemy's own situation.[2] While physical geography remains important, it is the human geography that is the key to our analysis.[3] Judgment is called for, both in intelligence products and the commander's estimate. Such judgment requires a lot more sophistication than the body count from Fallujah. It requires cultural sophistication that takes a serious investment of time and education to develop and retain.[4]

Operational Dislocation

Destroying the insurgents in Iraq is not the same thing as defeating the insurgency. Our cordon and search operations (what would, in an earlier time, have been called "search and destroy") have had some success in the former area, when we have had good intelligence to drive them. They have accomplished little toward the latter goal. For all of our forward thinking on the nature of complex contingencies, we continue to treat the insurgency as an enemy to be defeated by force of arms instead of as a Hydra that is generated by the political and structural conditions in Iraq.

The center of gravity of the insurgency is the support it enjoys from the populace. The Iraqi people provide the insurgent his cover and concealment. They are, as Mao Tse-Tung said, the sea the guerrilla swims in. They provide his intelligence network. They provide his logistics support, supply, and transportation. Most important, the people are his pool of recruits. The Iraqi people are the strength that enables the insurgency to fight.

There is a difference between this center of gravity that enables the insurgency and the conditions that give rise to the insurgency in the first place. The roots of the insurgency are deep and multifaceted. Some, such as economic conditions, may be ameliorated by U.S. initiatives. Others, such as the religious and tribal demographics, are less subject to our actions. While our unified campaign plan must address these factors, the critical vulnerability—the support of the populace—remains the key to undoing the insurgency. An insurgency deprived of support is incapable of effective action.

The populace provides support to the insurgency for a number of reasons, but all can be reduced to this fundamental political question: Who is in control? The answer is that the insurgents are in control. Unless an American patrol happens to be in the area, the insurgents are the only real authority and are free to enjoy (or compel) the support they require.

Gaining and Maintaining Contact

The Marine Corps has already developed an approach to counterinsurgency that is applicable to the complex situation in Iraq—the combined action program (CAP).[5] This program, which in Vietnam combined Marine rifle squads with local Vietnamese militia platoons, was extremely successful in spite of the lack of integration into any coherent campaign plan and misunderstanding and disinterest in the highest echelons of command. The Marines in CAP platoons lived among the people they were protecting, maintaining constant security, providing positive contact, and developing relationships that offered both a positive image and the opportunity for gathering the human intelligence that is the key to winning small wars—all while denying the insurgents their vital base of support.

A CAP for Iraq would pair Marine rifle squads with local forces, either local police or a "neighborhood watch." Our present efforts at training and conducting joint patrols with Iraqi Security Forces (ISF), as important as they are, do not begin to qualify as a CAP. The key to these operations is getting Marines out of our bases and into the towns and villages among the Iraqi people, who are, as LtGen Victor H. Krulak, USMC (Ret.), observed of the Vietnamese people, "the battlefield on which the war must be fought." CAP squads should come from a single unit that is assigned a geographic zone (rather than the haphazard process of Vietnam), which will ensure unity of effort, mutual support, effective supervision, and access to higher assets, such as air support.[6]

A constant Marine presence in Iraq's towns and villages (phased in by starting with daylight familiarization patrols and developing with Marines living among the populace) will answer the question of control for the local populace. Insurgents will be unable to conduct operations or enjoy support under the ever-present threat of a CAP platoon. Furthermore, it will empower the local ISF, which can begin to take responsibility for its own security, as well as co-opt recalcitrant ISF into taking a firm stance against the insurgency.

One of the greatest benefits of an Iraqi CAP will be increased intelligence; the amount of information gathered by the Vietnam CAP was so great as to overwhelm the CAP platoons' abilities to process it. Human intelligence is hard to generate without opportunities for contact with locals. The CAP concept provides this contact and gives the Marines a positive image that will encourage locals to volunteer information—information that enables their own operations (and their own security) and provides targets for raids and, often overlooked, intelligence in support of civil affairs efforts.

The ability for an Iraqi CAP to facilitate and leverage our information operations (IO) and psychological operations efforts is obvious, since the CAP presence represents an ongoing opportunity to spread our message while suppressing the insurgency's own IO efforts. (At present, the insurgents are able to propagandize freely with great effect in a society that does not have a well-developed discrimination between fact and conspiracy theory.) This ability will not only undermine their support but will substantially undermine their recruiting effort. It should go without saying that IO must be integrated into and tailored for all aspects of the CAP, rather than the generic afterthought it often is today. The consistent security provided by CAP will also enable longer-term civil affairs projects to improve the conditions that breed insurgency in the first place.

In Vietnam, the CAP was so effective at denying the insurgents their base of support that the Viet Cong were forced to take offensive action in an attempt to win back the center of gravity. These actions had a noted effect on the perceptions of the local populace; the guerrillas were now the ones bringing violence to the village rather than the Marines. In this area, as in others, the CAP forestalled the insurgency on its own terms.

The insurgents have the initiative in this conflict; disturbingly, we have subconsciously conceded the initiative to them. We have become reactive. Security has gradually become a greater concern than defeating the enemy; it is the first thing we think of when we venture out from our bases. This is not to say that we do not aggressively attack the enemy when we can locate him, but we have subtly begun to despair of locating him in the first place. And, in truth, the enemy does control the battle space and is thus able to choose the time and place he will give battle and to avoid our overwhelming combat power. Recent attacks on our bases confirm what we have known doctrinally all along—that there is no possibility of victory in the defense. We must gain contact with the enemy.

Security will be the greatest objection to a CAP in Iraq. This is ironic given that the Marine rifle squad has far more combat power today than during the Vietnam era. Our Marines have communications, fire support, and mounted and airborne reinforcement assets unheard of in earlier times. Our Marines are led by noncommissioned officers who are smarter, more strategic, better trained, and more schooled in leadership than ever before. Outside of a few pitched battles (that we initiated), we have not been faced with an insurgent force that is capable of withstanding the fire and maneuver of a single rifle squad. Interestingly, apropos of the conflict in Iraq, the CAP platoons in Vietnam had negligible casualties from improvised explosive devices (IEDs), even though IEDs accounted for 30 percent of American casualties overall. Intelligence gathered from villagers by the CAP Marines gave them advance warning of attacks.[7] An Iraqi CAP must be part of a larger, comprehensive program that includes civil affairs projects that target the underlying structural causes of discontent as well as direct action against identified enemy infrastructure. Neither a long-term campaign for the hearts and minds nor a search and destroy mentality focused solely on killing insurgent fighters can defeat the insurgency. As the centerpiece of this campaign, the CAP will allow civil operations to work toward permanent stability and growth and generate intelligence that will enable us to locate, close with, and destroy those who threaten that stability.

History Repeats Itself—Unless We Learn from It

The CAP might have turned Vietnam from defeat to victory. Modified and applied as the centerpiece of a unified campaign plan in Iraq, it offers the key to defeating the insurgency and accomplishing our nation's political goals. It is not sufficient to do some joint patrols with ISF without daily contact with the Iraqi people and an ongoing, positive presence in their lives. If the only time the populace sees Marines is as they blow through town in an armored vehicle on the way to a cordon and search, we will fail to answer the ultimate political questions. The insurgency will be in control and free to keep the initiative. We will win the battles but lose the war—again.

41

Patrolling Ar Ramadi*

—*Cpl Tom Sloan, USMC*

Leathernecks of 1st Battalion, 5th Marine Regiment are back for another combat tour in Iraq, and lessons learned from previous deployments are used daily as they challenge insurgents on several fronts.

On April 11, the Marines of Company A engaged insurgents in a different way during a patrol through the city of Ar Ramadi. It wasn't a firefight. This time, during a three-hour patrol, Marines used words instead of M16s to fight their enemy.

"Our mission is to find and identify all anti-Coalition and pro-insurgency propaganda painted on the walls along the streets that we're patrolling here," said Navy LT Mike A. Quaresimo, the information officer with Headquarters and Service Company. "We're replacing it with positive propaganda by spray-painting our message over it."

Quaresimo explained that insurgents are writing graffiti messages promoting terrorism on walls throughout the city. "Insurgents are trying to influence the local Iraqis with their propaganda," he added.

With help from LCpl Manuel Valle, Jr., a team leader with 2nd Squad, and other Marines with 1st Platoon providing security, Quaresimo walked the streets armed with aerosol cans and stencils, searching and destroying the insurgents' messages.

---

* *This essay appeared in* Leatherneck *magazine in June 2005 and is reproduced by permission of the Marine Corps Association. Copyright is retained by the* Marine Corps Gazette.

Valle, who is in Iraq for a third time supporting Operation Iraqi Freedom, and his fellow Marines went ahead of Quaresimo to ensure his route was clear of threats so he could safely accomplish his mission of countering insurgent propaganda.

An interpreter accompanied Quaresimo to help him determine what writings were from the insurgency. Quaresimo also posted pro-Iraqi Security Force flyers on light poles and walls during the war on words.

"We want the Iraqi people to know there is a viable alternative to the terrorists," he said while stenciling 1st Battalion, 5th Marines' motto "Peace brings prosperity" in green paint on a wall. "We're informing the Iraqis that we're offering peace and prosperity. We want them to have stability and security; the insurgents are promoting instability and destruction. The Iraqi people have a choice, and they need to know they do. That's what we're hoping to accomplish."

During that short patrol, Quaresimo posted more than twenty pro-ISF flyers and stenciled numerous positive and anti-insurgent messages on walls in a section of the city. With its mission accomplished, the patrol returned safely to its base at Camp Hurricane Point.

"The Iraqi people can become more prosperous," Quaresimo said. "We are here to help them, and that's the message we want to get across."

The lack of hostile contact did not last long. Later in the week leathernecks of "Alpha" Company's 2nd Platoon were engaged by insurgents while conducting a combat patrol in the southern part of Ar Ramadi.

On April 14, "we were sitting in a blocking position on the road, and a black car kept driving back and forth on the street in front of us," recalled Sgt Jacob W. Fox, a motor transportation operator with 2nd Platoon. "He slammed on the brakes and stopped about 300 meters away, fired and took off."

According to Fox, who was driving a Marine seven-ton truck, the shooter stopped and fired a single round before taking off in his car. "It made me mad because we didn't have time to engage back," he said.

The Marines weren't surprised when they took fire from an insurgent. Making contact was the primary focus for that particular patrol.

"We're looking for a fight, and there's a good chance we'll get in one down here," said Cpl Matt I. Bremer, the squad leader for the platoon's 2nd Squad, while posting security on a street corner. "We've had contact down here before. One of our guys was shot in the arm during a patrol through here recently."

The corporal said that insurgents are actively engaging Coalition forces in the sparsely populated southern part of the city.

"It's not like the marketplace, where there are lots of women and children walking around," explained Bremer.

However, the busy marketplace has certainly drawn the insurgents' attention. It is in Company A's area of operations, and while patrols there have been relatively uneventful, there have been a few improvised explosive device (IED) detonations.

In fact, on April 8, leathernecks of the company's 4th Platoon were near the market when terrorists detonated two IEDs closer to the market. Fortunately, no Marines were injured.

"The patrols are fast," said Bremer, who is on his third deployment to Iraq. "We run a lot of the time because moving constantly keeps us from getting hit and makes a hard target. When we stop and stay in one place for a while, that's when we run the risk of getting shot."

The discovery of a potential IED on the side of a road was the only thing that slowed the patrol. The leathernecks left the street and took to the nearest building, which was an Iraqi family's home, suitable for setting up an overwatch. From the building's rooftop, they provided patrol security as the members of the patrol checked out the IED threat.

"It looks like just a pile of rocks, but it's worth the time and sweat to verify it and destroy it if it is an IED," explained Bremer as he tipped his Kevlar helmet back and wiped his forehead. "IEDs are a big problem in Ramadi. They hurt a lot of people. My vehicle was just hit by one yesterday. The more we find and destroy, the less damage they can do to convoys driving around out here."

Bremer and the rest of the squad remained in the house and on its rooftop for half an hour. The residents of the home received their weapon-wielding guests with smiling faces and thumbs-up greetings. One young Iraqi boy gave Bremer a high five in exchange for candy.

After receiving word that the potential IED wasn't a threat and they were clear to continue their patrol, they left the Iraqi family and hit the streets. The patrol was completed without further incident as the leathernecks returned to their base at Camp Hurricane Point.

"I thought we would've seen a lot more action than what we did today," said Sgt Fidel A. Alcoces, 2nd Platoon's platoon sergeant. "We've taken lots of fire in that area before. We've had RPGs (rocket-propelled grenades) shot at us there too.

"We're now in the offensive after we had two Marines go down," he continued. "We're still watching all our rules of engagement, but if we feel threatened, we will engage."

Editor's note: This article was compiled from three releases prepared by Marine combat correspondent Cpl Tom Sloan, USMC, based on his patrols with elements of 1/5.

42

The Privatization of Victory*

—*Sgt Roger D. Huffstetler, Jr., USMC*

What causes terrorism? An excellent question, but one best answered by someone like Aristotle. A more interesting, and perhaps answerable, question is what causes terrorism to be used?

Disintermediation, the process of cutting out the middleman, is typically used in reference to the removal of intermediaries in a supply chain. Its application in other contexts is less clear. In terms of information, this principle allows parents to look up symptoms of their child's illness at WebMD without directly consulting the doctor. It allows shoppers at Bizrate.com to compare prices on digital cameras. Starting with newspapers and evolving into the Internet, disintermediation continually puts us closer to the information we seek. As a society, we welcome disintermediation. Unfortunately, the ancillary consequences of disintermediation are almost entirely overlooked, many of which play directly into terrorists' hands.

Flat World Complicates the Battlefield

My grandfather landed at Normandy. To my knowledge, he never even spoke of it in his lifetime. In contrast, Senator John Kerry thought he would be assured victory in his 2004 presidential bid because of his combat experience. He had the pictures and videos to prove it. This rapid rise of discussing, or outright exploiting, military service corresponds to the rise in disintermediation—i.e., bringing the

---

* *This chapter appeared in the* Marine Corps Gazette *in January 2007 and is reproduced by permission of the Marine Corps Association. Copyright is retained by the* Marine Corps Gazette.

front lines of war to everyday lives of Americans in real time. As the images of conflict became more readily available and distributed, it was only natural that more service members felt comfortable, or perhaps felt the necessity, to speak about what they had seen. The rise of the strategic corporal, shifting metric for victory, and perceived information transparency in all situations have all contributed to disintermediation's creep into national defense policy.

In the current conflicts in Afghanistan and Iraq, some service members have set up personal Web logs to comment daily on the progress of the war. If one of them says, "I don't have body armor," this might be interpreted as "no Soldier has body armor." Thus, some service members have the ability to jump the media and, more important, their chain of command to comment on national defense policy. This concept is called the "strategic corporal"—a service member at the bottom of the Marine Corps who is forced to serve as an ambassador for the entire Marine Corps or even all Americans. This principle gives undue influence and responsibility to those at the bottom. The problem is that this principle is not in good keeping with military discipline and thus allows certain service members, via the Internet or a Cable News Network reporter, to seem more important than their fellow service members. In addition, it makes the actions of a few represent the actions of everyone.

The permanence of the mission and its accomplishment should be the basis for victory; however, limiting the number of casualties now supplants mission accomplishment as the metric for victory. Limiting the number of casualties would never be seen as a bad thing; however, when used as the primary metric for victory, limiting the number of casualties threatens the sense of permanence that service members feel from their role in something so noble.

GEN Wesley Clark, USA (Ret.), is often cited as winning the Kosovo conflict "without a single casualty." That phrase is meaningless, but the fact that it is repeated every time General Clark is on television indicates the importance of limiting casualties in modern conflicts. Why is that a metric for victory? Simply put, it is not. However, disintermediation makes it seem so by constraining military commanders to subjective criteria rather than objective criteria like mission accomplishment. The number of acceptable casualties will change continuously based on the length of the conflict and whom you are asking. Forget politics and for a moment put yourself in the place of the junior Marine. All he knows is that he has to follow orders and accomplish the mission because his mission, like the Marine Corps' mission, is permanent. His government owes him the knowledge that, even if he dies, the cause will go on because it is immutable, noble, and clear. Missions cannot remain permanent if we allow outside, shifting criteria to determine their importance, and disintermediation has played a role in doing just that.

The greatest threat to our national security today is the perceived information transparency that exists in a flat world. I have access to all manner of information concerning flash functions on digital cameras, drug interactions between medicines, and the satellite image of my home through Google Earth. In a system where disintermediation grants us unprecedented access to information concerning everything else, why would we assume it is not true on issues of national defense? Knowing 90 percent of the information but thinking I know 100 percent of the information is a very dangerous thing. The argument goes something like this. The Internet brings all information to me. When I have all of the information, I know best. Therefore, I know best. What happens to this argument when I perceive that I have all of the information but actually don't?

I am quite certain that my grandfather had his own personal feeling on D-Day; however, I don't think he felt the necessity to share it with GEN Dwight D. Eisenhower or the general public. Contrast that with our current culture, where everyone feels the need to comment on national security, including Geraldo Rivera, who announced sensitive information on live television and endangered service members. Jeffrey B. Jones, in his chapter, "Strategic Communication," argues that one of the factors impacting the information environment is that the "traditional lines between public affairs, public diplomacy, and military information operations are blurred because of immediate access to information."[1] Many Americans, present company included, feel that their opinions on national security are at least as well informed as the President's. While I think I have access to all of the information, certain aspects will always be classified to safeguard service members' lives. This is the greatest danger that disintermediation has brought us—the feeling that I (or anyone else) am qualified to comment on matters of national security because I feel total transparency in the process. This new culture has an important and irrevocable impact on the political debate. Political enemies of any administration can hold hostage the political debate, knowing that classified information might exonerate an administration from wrongdoing but all the while let the public assume that they have all of the information.

The information trickle concerning the war in Iraq has greatly threatened whether the war can be won. This is a direct result of people becoming accustomed to having access to any and all information at the drop of a hat. Thus, the perceived information transparency has undermined the administration's effort to use a shifting rationale for war rather than a permanent one. Any single reason for going to war with Iraq—be it oil, terrorism, democracy, or liberation—might be reasonable, but taken as a whole, trickling them out gives the impression that the administration has withheld the real cause until it was forced to reveal it. The rise of the strategic corporal, the shifting metric for victory, and the perceived information transparency have all contributed to the challenges we have faced in this war—the first war in the information age.

Where to from Here?

Former President Jimmy Carter, in an interview with the Public Broadcasting Service, had this to say about the poor living in a time of globalization: "They become more aware of the difference between their life and the life of the outside world. So they tend to lash out at the affluent and fortunate world." That he can make this comment, having grown up on a peanut farm, is a tribute to disintermediation.

Many have argued that it is the gap between rich and poor countries that has caused modern terrorism to be employed; however, perhaps it is not the gap itself but the fact that the poor are aware that the disparity exists because of disintermediation. Certainly, there are many factors, but the portions of the Koran so often quoted in defense of killing civilians haven't changed in hundreds of years. The ability to deliver that terror has changed, and that has made the difference.

Disintermediation has not caused modern terrorism; it has empowered it. Consider how the terrorist wields disintermediation as his weapon of opportunity. Without it, he is not able to terrorize. Bringing terror to rural Georgia via New York City is right out of Osama bin Laden's playbook. I am quite certain that serfs were aware that their masters lived better than they did. However, couple the knowledge of that disparity with a weapon to exploit it and that is a lethal combination for a terrorist.

Even these results of disintermediation do not entirely aid terrorists. For example, poor people having more information on our standard of living may help empower them to hold their elected leaders accountable. As yet, this statement is at the very least unproven if not disproved by elections in Egypt, Iraq, and the Palestinian National Authority, where terrorists made significant gains. In addition, while terrorists can and have used disintermediation to spread fear and build support for their cause, their tactics can backfire as when they bomb mosques. These examples, however, pale in comparison to their usual exploitation of the media to sell their cause. In fact, terrorists are counting on us to rely solely on traditional operations, meaning we need to do more to turn the table on the terrorists.

Disintermediation is here to stay. Mark Leonard describes the vulnerabilities that superpowers will face down the road as the "privatisation of destruction,"[2] whether that is from a computer hacker or a rogue terrorist. In many people's eyes, the war on terror has one face—Osama bin Laden. Realizing before the Iraq War that disintermediation is the weapon of choice for our enemy would have given us a leg up. For example, not ensuring that every corporal was a strategic corporal caused the Abu Ghraib prison incident to set us back in the war on terrorism. Under this context, several concepts need immediate consideration, as follows:

- From the day they reach boot camp until the day they again become civilians, all Marines should receive two types of training to augment their basic warrior training—cultural training in a regional context and strategic communications training. It would not be hard to envision each squad in boot camp assigned to a different region (on a rotating basis), with one Marine serving as the squad's translator (squad to environment) and another as the squad's communicator (squad to homeland).

- The Marine Corps should coordinate and solicit, perhaps through its public affairs officers, stories from junior Marines reflecting operations on the ground. When Marines understand that part of their job in stopping terrorism is to outmaneuver their enemy in the court of public opinion, they will happily contribute with stories to their hometown papers.
- Placing Marines in different job fields should be contingent upon two factors—can they do the job, and can they do the job well? The second question cannot be answered by an Armed Services Vocational Aptitude Battery (ASVAB). For example, a Marine who scores 85 percent on the ASVAB may qualify for jobs ranging from air traffic controller to rifleman; however, there is certainly one job the Marine would perform most proficiently. More detailed information from secondary tests, such as a Myers-Briggs type indicator, and interviews with junior officers are part of the solution.
- Recruiting quotas should not only be based on numbers but also on job fields. We cannot afford to misallocate valuable resources—e.g., language aptitude—because a recruiter needs to find bodies rather than skill sets. Ensuring that the first Marine most of us meet—our recruiter—understands that job placement is as important as quotas is essential to fighting conflicts during the information age.

A media-savvy, culturally attuned lance corporal must be the rule, not the exception. Former Commandant Gen Michael W. Hagee, USMC (Ret.), has commented on the importance of the individual Marine within the broader context of war. We can talk about aircraft. We can talk about howitzers. We can talk about tanks, but the individual Marine is the most important part of the Marine Corps.[3] The war on terrorism will eventually be won by Marines. In pursuit of that goal, we are most vulnerable to setbacks by the acts of a single Marine. The selection, screening, and training of each individual Marine have never been more important to mission accomplishment. To counter the "privatization of destruction," the Marine Corps must embrace and implement the privatization of victory to win this and future conflicts in the information age.

43

"Twenty-Eight Articles": Fundamentals of Company-Level Counterinsurgency*

—*LTC David Kilcullen, Australian Army (Ret.)*

Your company has just been warned about possible deployment for counterinsurgency operations in Iraq or Afghanistan. You have read David Galula, T. E. Lawrence, and Robert Thompson. You have studied Field Manual 3-24 *Counterinsurgency Operations* and now understand the history, philosophy, and theory of counterinsurgency.[1] You have watched *Black Hawk Down* and *The Battle of Algiers*, and you know this will be the most difficult challenge of your life.[2]

But what does all that theory mean, at the company level? How do the principles translate into action at night, with the global positioning system (GPS) down, the media criticizing you, the locals complaining in a language you don't understand, and an unseen enemy killing your people by ones and twos? How does counterinsurgency actually happen?

There are no universal answers, and insurgents are among the most adaptive opponents you will ever face. Countering them will demand every ounce of your intellect. But be comforted: you are not the first to feel this way. There are tactical fundamentals you can apply to link the theory with the techniques and procedures you already know.

What Is Counterinsurgency?

If you have not studied counterinsurgency theory, here it is in a nutshell: counterinsurgency is a competition with the insurgent for the right to win the hearts, minds,

---

* This chapter appeared in the Military Review, *May–June 2006, and is reprinted by permission.*

and acquiescence of the population. You are being sent in because the insurgents, at their strongest, can defeat anything with less strength than you have. But you have more combat power than you can or should use in most situations. Injudicious use of firepower creates blood feuds, homeless people, and societal disruption that fuel and perpetuate the insurgency. The most beneficial actions are often local politics, civic action, and beat cop behaviors. For your side to win, the people don't have to like you, but they must respect you, accept that your actions benefit them, and trust your integrity and ability to deliver on promises, particularly regarding their security. In this battlefield, popular perceptions and rumor are more influential than the facts and more powerful than a hundred tanks.

Within this context, what follows are observations from collective experience, the distilled essence of what those who went before you learned. They are expressed as commandments, for clarity, but are really more like folklore. Apply them judiciously and skeptically.

Preparation

Time is short during pre-deployment, but you will never have more time to think than you have now. Now is your chance to prepare yourself and your command.

1. Know Your Turf

Know the people, the topography, economy, history, religion, and culture. Know every village, road, field, population group, tribal leader, and ancient grievance. Your task is to become the world expert on your district. If you don't know precisely where you will be operating, study the general area. Read the map like a book. Study it every night before sleeping and redraw it from memory every morning until you understand its patterns intuitively. Develop a mental model of your area, a framework in which to fit every new piece of knowledge you acquire. Study handover notes from predecessors; better still, get in touch with the unit in theater and pick their leaders' brains. In an ideal world, intelligence officers and area experts would brief you; however, this rarely happens, and even if it does, there is no substitute for personal mastery. Understand the broader area of influence, which can be a wide area, particularly when insurgents draw on global grievances. Share aspects of the operational area among platoon leaders and noncommissioned officers; have each individual develop a personal specialization and brief the others. Neglect this knowledge and it will kill you.

2. Diagnose the Problem

Once you know your area and its people, you can begin to diagnose the problem. Who are the insurgents? What drives them? What makes local leaders tick? Counterinsurgency is fundamentally a competition between each side to mobilize the population in support of its agenda, so you must understand what motivates the people and how to mobilize them. You need to know why and how the insurgents are getting followers. This means you need to know your real enemy, not a cardboard cutout. The enemy is adaptive, resourceful, and probably grew up in the region where you will be operating. The locals have known him since he was a boy; how long have they known you? Your worst opponent is not the psychopathic terrorist of Hollywood; it is the charismatic warrior who would make your best platoon leader. His followers are not misled or naive; much of his success may come from bad government policies or security forces that alienate the population. Work this problem collectively with your platoon and squad leaders. Discuss ideas, explore the problem, understand what you are facing, and seek a consensus. If this sounds unmilitary, get over it. Once you are in theater, situations will arise too quickly for orders or even commander's intent. Corporals and privates will have to make snap judgments with strategic impact. The only way to help them is to give them a shared understanding, then trust them to think for themselves.

3. ORGANIZE FOR INTELLIGENCE

In counterinsurgency, killing the enemy is easy. Finding him is often nearly impossible. Intelligence and operations are complementary. Your operations will be intelligence driven, but intelligence will come mostly from your own operations, not as a product prepared and served up by higher headquarters. So you must organize for intelligence. You will need a company S2 and an intelligence section (including analysts). You might need platoon S2s and S3s, and you will need a reconnaissance and surveillance (R&S) element. You will not have enough linguists—you never do—but carefully consider where best to use them. Linguists are battle-winning assets, but just as any other scarce resource, you must have a prioritized "bump plan" in case you lose them. Often during pre-deployment the best use of linguists is to train your command in basic language. You will probably not get augmentation for all this, but you must still do it. Put the smartest Soldiers in the S2 section and the R&S squad. You will have one less rifle squad, but the intelligence section will pay for itself in lives and effort saved.

4. ORGANIZE FOR INTERAGENCY OPERATIONS

Almost everything in counterinsurgency is interagency. And everything important, from policing to intelligence to civil-military operations to trash collection, will involve your company working with civilian actors and local indigenous partners you cannot control but whose success is essential for yours. Train the company in interagency operations: get a briefing from the U.S. Department of State, aid agencies, and the local police or fire brigade. Train point men in each squad to deal with the interagency people. Realize that rifles, helmets, and body armor intimidate civilians. Learn how not to scare them. Ask others who come from that country or culture about your ideas. See it through the eyes of a civilian who knows nothing about the military. How would you react if foreigners came to your neighborhood and conducted the operations you planned? What if somebody came to your mother's house and did that? Most important, know that your operations will create a temporary breathing space, but long-term development and stabilization by civilian agencies will ultimately win the war.

5. Travel Light and Harden Your Combat Service Support (CSS)
You will be weighed down with body armor, rations, extra ammunition, communications gear, and a thousand other things. The enemy will carry a rifle or rocket-propelled grenade launcher, a *shemagh* (head scarf), and a water bottle if he is lucky. Unless you ruthlessly lighten your load and enforce a culture of speed and mobility, the insurgents will consistently outrun and outmaneuver you. But in lightening your load, make sure you can always reach back to call for firepower or heavy support if needed. Also, remember to harden your CSS. The enemy will attack your weakest points. Most attacks on Coalition forces in Iraq in 2004 and 2005, outside preplanned combat actions such as the two battles of Fallujah or Operation Iron Horse, were against CSS installations and convoys. You do the math. Ensure your CSS assets are hardened, have communications, and are trained in combat operations. They may do more fighting than your rifle squads will.

6. Find a Political-Cultural Adviser
In a force optimized for counterinsurgency, you might receive a political-cultural adviser at company level, either a diplomat or military foreign area officer able to speak the language and navigate the intricacies of local politics. Back on planet Earth, the corps and division commanders will get a political adviser; you will not, so you must improvise. Find a political-cultural adviser (POLAD) from among your people—perhaps an officer, perhaps not (see article 8). Someone with people skills and a feel for the environment will do better than a political science graduate. Don't try to be your own cultural adviser. You must be fully aware of the political and cultural dimension, but this is a different task. Also, don't give one of your intelligence people this role. They can help, but their task is to understand the environment. The POLAD's job is to help shape it.

7. Train the Squad Leaders, Then Trust Them
Counterinsurgency is a squad and platoon leaders' war, and often a private Soldier's war. Battles are won or lost in moments; whoever can bring combat power to bear in seconds on a street corner will win. The commander on the spot controls the fight. You must train the squad leaders to act intelligently and independently without orders. If your squad leaders are competent, you can get away with average company or platoon staffs. The reverse is not the case. Training should focus on basic skills: marksmanship, patrolling, security on the move and at the halt, and basic drills. When in doubt, spend less time on company and platoon training and more time on squads. Ruthlessly replace leaders who do not make the grade. But once people are trained and you have a shared operational diagnosis, you must

trust them. We talk about this, but few company or platoon leaders really trust their people. In counterinsurgency, you have no choice.

8. Rank Is Nothing; Talent Is Everything

Not everyone is good at counterinsurgency. Many people don't understand the concept, and some can't execute it. It is difficult, and in a conventional force only a few people will master it. Anyone can learn the basics, but few naturals exist. Learn how to spot these people, and put them in positions where they can make a difference. Rank matters far less than talent. A few good men led by a smart junior noncommissioned officer can succeed in counterinsurgency, whereas hundreds of well-armed Soldiers under a mediocre senior officer will fail.

9. Have a Game Plan

The final preparation task is to develop a game plan, a mental picture of how you see the operation developing. You will be tempted to try and do this too early. But wait, as your knowledge improves, you will get a better idea of what needs to be done and a fuller understanding of your own limitations. Like any plan, this plan will change once you hit the ground, and it may need to be scrapped if there is a major shift in the environment. But you still need a plan, and the process of planning will give you a simple, robust idea of what to achieve, even if the methods change. This is sometimes called "operational design." One approach is to identify basic stages in your operation—for example, "establish dominance, build local networks, and marginalize the enemy." Make sure you can easily transition between phases, forward and backward, in case of setbacks. Just as the insurgent can adapt his activity to yours, so you must have a simple enough plan to survive setbacks without collapsing. This plan is the solution that matches the shared diagnosis you developed earlier. It must be simple and known to everyone.

The Golden Hour

You have deployed, completed reception and staging, and (if you are lucky) attended the in-country counterinsurgency school. Now it is time to enter your sector and start your tour. This is the golden hour. Mistakes made now will haunt you for the rest of your tour while early successes will set the tone for victory. You will look back on your early actions and cringe at your clumsiness. So be it. But you must act.

10. Be There

The most fundamental rule of counterinsurgency is to be there. You can almost never outrun the enemy. If you are not present when an incident happens, there is usually little you can do about it. So your first order of business is to establish presence. If you can't do this throughout your sector, then do it wherever you can. This demands a residential approach: living in your sector, in close proximity to the population rather than raiding into the area from remote, secure bases. Moving on foot, sleeping in local villages, night patrolling—all these seem more dangerous than they are. They establish links with the locals, who will see you as real people they can trust and do business with, not as aliens who descend from an armored box. Driving around in an armored convoy, day-tripping like a tourist in hell, degrades situational awareness, makes you a target, and is ultimately more dangerous.

11. Avoid Knee-Jerk Responses to First Impressions

Don't act rashly; get the facts first. The violence you see may be part of the insurgent strategy; it may be various interest groups fighting it out with each other or settling personal vendettas. Normality in Kandahar is not the same as in Seattle—you need time to learn what normality looks like. The insurgent commander wants to goad you into lashing out at the population or making a mistake. Unless you happen to be on the spot when an incident occurs, you will have only secondhand reports and may misunderstand the local context or interpretation. This fragmentation and "disaggregation" of the battlefield, particularly in urban areas, mean that first impressions are often highly misleading. Of course, you can't avoid making judgments, but if possible, check them with an older hand or a trusted local. If you can, keep one or two officers from your predecessor unit for the first part of the tour. Try to avoid a rush to judgment.

12. Prepare for Handover from Day One

Believe it or not, you will not resolve the insurgency on your watch. Your tour will end, and your successors will need your corporate knowledge. Start handover folders in every platoon and specialist squad from day one. Ideally, you would have inherited these from your predecessors, but if not you must start them. The folders should include lessons learned, details about the population, village and patrol reports, updated maps, and photographs—anything that will help newcomers master the environment. Computerized databases are fine, but keep good backups and ensure you have hard copy of key artifacts and documents. This work is boring and tedious but essential. Over time, you will create a corporate memory that keeps your people alive.

13. Build Trusted Networks

Once you have settled into your sector, your key task is to build trusted networks. This is the true meaning of the phrase "hearts and minds," which comprises two separate components. "Hearts" means persuading people their best interests are served by your success; "minds" means convincing them that you can protect them and that resisting you is pointless. Note that neither concept has anything to do with whether people like you. Calculated self-interest, not emotion, is what counts. Over time, if you successfully build networks of trust, these will grow like roots into the population, displacing the enemy's networks, bringing him out into the open to fight you, and letting you seize the initiative. These networks include local allies, community leaders, local security forces, nongovernmental organizations (NGOs) and other friendly or neutral non-state actors in your area, and the media. Conduct village and neighborhood surveys to identify needs in the community, then follow through to meet them. Build common interests and mobilize popular support. This is your true main effort; everything else is secondary. Actions that help build trusted networks serve your cause. Actions—even killing high-profile targets—that undermine trust or disrupt your networks help the enemy.

14. Start Easy

If you were trained in maneuver warfare you know about surfaces and gaps. This applies to counterinsurgency as much as any other form of maneuver. Don't try to crack the hardest nut first. Don't go straight for the main insurgent stronghold, try to provoke a decisive showdown, or focus efforts on villages that support the insurgents. Instead, start from secure areas and work gradually outward. Do this by extending your influence through the locals' own networks. Go with, not against, the grain of local society. First win the confidence of a few villages and see who they trade, intermarry, or do business with. Now win these people over. Soon enough the showdown with the insurgents will come, but now you have to have local allies, a mobilized population, and a trusted network at your back. Do it the other way around and no one will mourn your failure.

15. Seek Early Victories

In this early phase, your aim is to stamp your dominance in your sector. Do this by seeking an early victory. This will probably not translate into a combat victory over the enemy. Looking for such a victory can be overly aggressive and create collateral damage, especially since you really do not yet understand your sector. Also, such a combat victory depends on the enemy being stupid enough to present you with a clear-cut target, which is a rare windfall in counterinsurgency. Instead, you may achieve a victory by resolving long-standing issues your predecessors have failed to address or by co-opting a key local leader who has resisted cooperation with our forces. Like any other form of armed propaganda, achieving even a small victory early in the tour sets the tone for what comes later and helps seize the initiative, which you have probably lost during the inevitable hiatus entailed by the handover-takeover with your predecessor.

16. Practice Deterrent Patrolling

Establish patrolling methods that deter the enemy from attacking you. Often our patrolling approach seems designed to provoke, then defeat, enemy attacks. This is counterproductive; it leads to a raiding, day-tripping mind-set or, worse, a bunker mentality. Instead, practice deterrent patrolling. There are many methods for this, including multiple patrolling in which you flood an area with numerous small patrols working together. Each is too small to be a worthwhile target, and the insurgents never know where all the patrols are, making an attack on any one patrol extremely risky. Other methods include so-called blue-green patrolling, where you mount daylight, overt humanitarian patrols, which go covert at night and hunt specific targets. Again, the aim is to keep the enemy off balance and the population reassured through constant and unpredictable activity that, over time, deters attacks and creates a more permissive environment. A reasonable rule of thumb is that one- to two-thirds of your force should be on patrol at any time, day or night.

17. BE PREPARED FOR SETBACKS

Setbacks are normal in counterinsurgency, as in every other form of war. You will make mistakes, lose people, or occasionally kill or detain the wrong person. You may fail in building or expanding networks. If this happens, don't lose heart; simply drop back to the previous phase of your game plan and recover your balance. It is normal in company counterinsurgency operations for some platoons to be doing well while others do badly. This is not necessarily evidence of failure. Give local commanders the freedom to adjust their posture to local conditions. This creates elasticity that helps you survive setbacks.

18. REMEMBER THE GLOBAL AUDIENCE

One of the biggest differences between the counterinsurgencies our fathers fought and those we face today is the omnipresence of globalized media. Most houses in Iraq have one or more satellite dishes. Web bloggers; print, radio, and television reporters; and others are monitoring and reporting your every move. When the insurgents ambush your patrols or set off a car bomb, they do so not to destroy one more track, but because they want graphic images of a burning vehicle and dead bodies for the evening news. Beware of the scripted enemy who plays to a global audience and seeks to defeat you in the court of global public opinion. You counter this by training people to always bear in mind the global audience, to assume that everything they say or do will be publicized, and to befriend the media. Get the press on your side, help them get their story, and trade information with them. Good relationships with non-embedded media, especially indigenous media, dramatically increase your situational awareness and help get your message across to the global and local audience.

19. ENGAGE THE WOMEN, BEWARE OF THE CHILDREN

Most insurgent fighters are men. But in traditional societies, women are hugely influential in forming the social networks that insurgents use for support. Co-opting neutral or friendly women, through targeted social and economic programs, builds networks of enlightened self-interest that eventually undermine the insurgents. You need your own female counterinsurgents, including interagency people, to do this effectively. Win the women, and you own the family unit. Own the family, and you take a big step forward in mobilizing the population. Conversely, though, stop your people from fraternizing with the local children. Your troops are homesick; they want to drop their guard with the kids, but children are sharp-eyed, lacking in empathy, and willing to commit atrocities their elders would shrink from. The insurgents are watching. They will notice a growing friendship between one of your people and a local child, and either harm the child as punishment or use them against you. Similarly, stop people from throwing candies or presents to children. It attracts them to our vehicles, creates crowds the enemy can exploit, and leads to children being run over. Harden your heart and keep the children at arm's length.

20. TAKE STOCK REGULARLY
You probably already know that a body count tells you little, because you usually can't know how many insurgents there were to start with, how many moved into the area, how many transferred from supporter to combatant status, or how many new fighters the conflict has created. But you still need to develop metrics early in the tour and refine them as the operation progresses. They should cover a range of social, informational, military, and economic issues. Use metrics intelligently to form an overall impression of progress, not in a mechanistic traffic light fashion. Typical metrics include percentage of engagements initiated by our forces versus those initiated by insurgents, longevity of friendly local leaders in positions of authority, number and quality of tip-offs on insurgent activity that originate spontaneously from the population, and economic activity at markets and shops. These mean virtually nothing as a snapshot; it is trends over time that help you track progress in your sector.

Groundhog Day
Now you are in "steady state." You are established in your sector, and people are settling into that "groundhog day" mentality that hits every unit at some stage during every tour. It will probably take you at least the first third of your tour to become effective in your new environment, if not longer. Then in the last period you will struggle against the short-timer mentality. So this middle part of the tour is the most productive, but keeping the flame alive, and bringing the local population along with you, takes immense leadership.

21. EXPLOIT A "SINGLE NARRATIVE"
Since counterinsurgency is a competition to mobilize popular support, it pays to know how people are mobilized. In most societies there are opinion makers—local leaders, pillars of the community, religious figures, media personalities, and others—who set trends and influence public perceptions. This influence, including the pernicious influence of the insurgents, often takes the form of a "single narrative": a simple, unifying, easily expressed story or explanation that organizes people's

experience and provides a framework for understanding events. Nationalist and ethnic historical myths, or sectarian creeds, provide such a narrative. The Iraqi insurgents have one, as do Al Qaeda and the Taliban. To undercut their influence you must exploit an alternative narrative or, better yet, tap into an existing narrative that excludes the insurgents. This narrative is often worked out for you by higher headquarters, but only you have the detailed knowledge to tailor the narrative to local conditions and generate leverage from it. For example, you might use a nationalist narrative to marginalize foreign fighters in your area or a narrative of national redemption to undermine former regime elements that have been terrorizing the population. At the company level, you do this in baby steps by getting to know local opinion makers, winning their trust, learning what motivates them, and building on this to find a single narrative that emphasizes the inevitability and rightness of your ultimate success. This is art, not science.

22. LOCAL FORCES SHOULD MIRROR THE ENEMY, NOT THE AMERICANS

By this stage, you will be working closely with local forces, training or supporting them and building indigenous capability. The natural tendency is to build forces in the U.S. image, with the aim of eventually handing our role over to them. This is a mistake. Instead, local indigenous forces need to mirror the enemy's capabilities and seek to supplant the insurgent's role. This does not mean they should be irregular in the sense of being brutal or outside proper control. Rather, they should move, equip, and organize like the insurgents, but have access to your support and be under the firm control of their parent societies. Combined with a mobilized population and trusted networks, this allows local forces to hard wire the enemy out of the environment, under top cover from you. At the company level, this means that raising, training, and employing local indigenous auxiliary forces (police and military) are valid tasks. This requires high-level clearance, of course, but if support is given, you should establish a company training cell. Platoons should aim to train one local squad, then use that squad as a nucleus for a partner platoon. Company headquarters should train an indigenous leadership team. This mirrors the growth process of other trusted networks and tends to emerge naturally as you win local allies who want to take up arms in their own defense.

23. PRACTICE ARMED CIVIL AFFAIRS

Counterinsurgency is armed social work, an attempt to redress basic social and political problems while being shot at. This makes civil affairs a central counterinsurgency activity, not an afterthought. It is how you restructure the environment to displace the enemy from it. In your company sector, civil affairs must focus on meeting basic needs first, then progress up Maslow's hierarchy as each successive need is met. You need intimate cooperation with interagency partners here—national, international, and local groups. You will not be able to control these partners—many NGOs, for example, do not want to be too closely associated with you because they need to preserve their perceived neutrality. Instead, you need to work on a shared diagnosis of the problem and build a consensus that helps you self-synchronize. Your role is to provide protection, identify needs, facilitate civil affairs, and use improvements in social conditions as leverage to build networks and mobilize the population. Thus, there is no such thing as impartial humanitarian assistance or civil affairs in counterinsurgency. Every time you help someone, you hurt someone else—not least the insurgents—so civil and humanitarian assistance personnel will be targeted. Protecting them is a matter not only of close-in defense, but also of creating a permissive operating environment by co-opting the beneficiaries of aid (local communities and leaders) to help you help them.

24. SMALL IS BEAUTIFUL

Another natural tendency is to go for large-scale, mass programs. In particular, we have a tendency to template ideas that succeed in one area and transplant them into another, and we tend to take small programs that work and try to replicate them on a larger scale. Again, this is usually a mistake. Often programs succeed because of specific local conditions of which we are unaware or because their very smallness kept them below the enemy's radar and helped them flourish unmolested. At the company level, programs that succeed in one district often also succeed in another (because the overall company sector is small), but small-scale projects rarely proceed smoothly into large programs. Keep programs small; this makes them cheap, sustainable, low key, and (more important) recoverable if they fail. You can add new programs—also small, cheap, and tailored to local conditions—as the situation allows.

25. FIGHT THE ENEMY'S STRATEGY, NOT HIS FORCES

At this stage, if things are proceeding well, the insurgents will go over to the offensive. Yes, the offensive, because you have created a situation so dangerous to the insurgents (by threatening to displace them from the environment) that they have to attack you and the population to get back into the game. Thus, it is normal, even in the most successful operations, to have spikes of offensive insurgent activity late in the campaign. This does not necessarily mean you have done something wrong (though it may; it depends on whether you have successfully mobilized the population). At this point the tendency is to go for the jugular and seek to destroy the enemy's forces in open battle. This is rarely the best choice at company level, because provoking major combat usually plays into the enemy's hands by undermining the population's confidence. Instead, attack the enemy's strategy. If he is seeking to recapture the allegiance of a segment of the local population, then co-opt them against him. If he is trying to provoke a sectarian conflict, go over to peace enforcement mode. The permutations are endless, but the principle is the same: fight the enemy's strategy, not his forces.

26. Build Your Own Solution—Only Attack the Enemy When He Gets in the Way

Try not to be distracted or forced into a series of reactive moves by a desire to kill or capture the insurgents. Your aim should be to implement your own solution, or the game plan you developed early in the campaign and then refined through interaction with local partners. Your approach must be environment-centric (based on dominating the whole district and implementing a solution to its systemic problems) rather than enemy-centric. This means that particularly late in the campaign you may need to learn to negotiate with the enemy. Members of the population that support you also know the enemy's leaders. They may have grown up together in the small district that is now your company sector, and valid negotiating partners sometimes emerge as the campaign progresses. Again, you need close interagency relationships to exploit opportunities to co-opt segments of the enemy. This helps you wind down the insurgency without alienating potential local allies who have relatives or friends in the insurgent movement. At this stage, defection is better than surrender, surrender is better than capture, and capture is better than a kill.

Getting Short

Time is short, and the tour is drawing to a close. The key problem now is keeping your people focused; maintaining the passion on all the multifarious programs, projects, and operations that you have started; and preventing your people from dropping their guard. In this final phase, the previous articles still stand, but there is an important new one.

27. Keep Your Extraction Plan a Secret

The temptation to talk about home becomes almost unbearable toward the end of a tour. The locals know you are leaving and probably have a better idea than you do of the generic extraction plan. Remember, they have seen units come and go. But you must protect the specific details of the extraction plan, or the enemy will use this as an opportunity to score a high-profile hit, recapture the population's allegiance with scare tactics that convince them they will not be protected once you leave, or persuade them that your successor unit will be oppressive or incompetent. Keep the details secret within a tightly controlled compartment in your headquarters.

Four "What-ifs"

The articles above describe what should happen, but we all know that things go wrong. Here are some what-ifs to consider:

- What if you get moved to a different area? You prepared for Ar Ramadi and studied Dulaim tribal structures and Sunni beliefs. Now you are going to Najaf and will be surrounded by al-Hassani tribes and Shi'a communities. But that work was not wasted. In mastering your first area, you learned techniques you can still apply: how to "case" an operational area and how to decide what matters in the local societal structure. Do the same again, and this time the process is easier and faster since you have an existing mental structure and can focus on what is different. The same applies if you get moved frequently within a battalion or brigade area.

- What if higher headquarters doesn't "get" counterinsurgency? Higher headquarters is telling you the mission is to "kill terrorists" or is pushing for high-speed armored patrols and a base camp mentality. They just don't seem to understand counterinsurgency. This is not uncommon, since company-grade officers today often have more combat experience than senior officers do. In this case, just do what you can. Try not to create expectations that higher headquarters will not let you meet. Apply the adage "first do no harm." Over time, you will find ways to do what you have to do. But never lie to higher headquarters about your locations or activities—they own the indirect fires.
- What if you have no resources? You have no linguists, the aid agencies have no money for projects in your area, and you have a low priority for civil affairs. You can still get things done, but you need to focus on self-reliance: keep things small and sustainable and ruthlessly prioritize effort. The members of the local population are your allies in this. They know what matters to them more than you do. Be honest with them, discuss possible projects and options with community leaders, and get them to choose what their priorities are. Often they will find the translators, building supplies, or expertise that you need, and they will only expect your support and protection in making their projects work. And the process of negotiation and consultation will help mobilize their support and strengthen their social cohesion. If you set your sights on what is achievable, the situation can still work.
- What if the theater situation shifts under your feet? It is your worst nightmare: everything has gone well in your sector, but the whole theater situation has changed and invalidates your efforts. Think of the first battle of Fallujah, the Al-Askariya shrine bombing, or the Sadr uprising. What do you do? Here is where having a flexible, adaptive game plan comes in. Just as the insurgents drop down to a lower posture when things go wrong, now is the time for you to drop back a stage, consolidate, regain your balance, and prepare to expand again when the situation allows. But see article 28. If you cede the initiative, you must regain it as soon as the situation allows, or you will eventually lose.

This, then, is the tribal wisdom, the folklore that those who went before you have learned. Like any folklore it needs interpretation and contains seemingly contradictory advice. Over time, as you apply unremitting intellectual effort to study your sector, you will learn to apply these ideas in your own way and will add to this store of wisdom from your own observations and experience. So only one article remains, and if you remember nothing else, remember this:

28. Whatever Else You Do, Keep the Initiative

In counterinsurgency, the initiative is everything. If the enemy is reacting to you, you control the environment. Provided you mobilize the population, you will win. If you are reacting to the enemy, even if you are killing or capturing him in large numbers, then he is controlling the environment and you will eventually lose. In counterinsurgency, the enemy initiates most attacks, targets you unexpectedly, and withdraws too fast for you to react. Do not be drawn into purely reactive operations. Focus on the population, build your own solution, further your game plan, and fight the enemy only when he gets in the way. This gains and keeps the initiative.

CONCLUSION: INFORMATION IN CONFLICT

—Maj G. J. David, Jr., USMC, and LtCol T. R. McKeldin III, USMCR

This anthology presents a wide range of views with varying opinions on how information has been, and might be, used in international conflict. Whether the authors chose to observe through the eyes of so-called information operations, strategic communications, public affairs, psychological operations, or simply the moral impact of operations on the ground, all presented some aspect of the utility of information. This diversity of opinion reflects the extent to which representative governments grapple with the issue today, uncertain of precisely how to proceed. While these opinions do not provide a final answer, they do shed light on the scope of the challenge.

The diversity of opinion on whether or not such focus on information as a primary weapon of conflict is an innovation reflects also in these works. The chapters that purport to focus on other subjects, such as insurgency, often present the uses of information as a natural line of objective approach in the conflict. For this reason, we included many such chapters. The perspective that claims that information conflict is entirely new seems to be fading in recent years; few authors chose to present it that way today. Instead, they discuss the novelty and potency of today's means of disseminating the message. One part of the problem, therefore, appears to be drawing toward a resolution: divergent opinions on the novelty of information war. In the minds of practitioners of political, strategic, and military art, use of directed information appears to be a timeless part of adversarial endeavor, but modernity has upgraded the means of using information radically.

By extension, those timeless aspects of warfare and the application of violence between nations or groups have not changed, but the tactics of information certainly have. The ability to project powerful images at will with the simplest of communications equipment has served well the side that cares little for honesty. Conversely, the nation-state, bounded by its own rules and seemingly fearful of the impact of such images, texts, and messages, has responded slowly. Part of this diffidence must be attributed to the universal application of a moral code acceptable to the public consumers and voters of representative governments. The standards applied to formal soldiery in the heat of tactical fighting have never been higher. The merest assertion of a possible infraction of rules applied to nations draws inquiry, whereas the insurgent or terrorist commits atrocities with such frequency that the public is practically immune to them. Almost immune, but not quite; the message of terror is the terrorist's main effort and must not lose its impact to be effective. Despite the unquestionable power of destruction that would certainly bring any environment under sway, the representative republic has refused to accept its own wanton use of force because it would be antithetical to its values. It has, however, failed to capitalize on any moral advantage that this restraint confers. Meanwhile, in the space provided by this restraint, the adversary thrives, rapidly projecting messages of horror.

When Ghengis Khan attacked Bukhara in 1219, he made a deliberate choice not to first launch his main effort against the most important city of the Sultanate of Khwarizm at Samarkand. Instead, he chose targets whose defenses were less robust both to test their strength and to send his initial messages to the leaders of the sultanate and their people in a strategy that included the conquest of Bukhara. Crushing the outer defenses, he slew all those who did not surrender, sent the civilian population fleeing in a panic, and used the forced labor of the captured to construct his siege works against the main fortifications. Ghengis then filled the defensive ditches outside the walls with these captives' still-living bodies to provide a level approach for his siege engines. No one who fought was left alive, though enough who fled were left alive to spread a tale of terror along with a tide of refugees more numerous than the public infrastructure of the sultanate could manage. The Mongol method has repulsed many historians down the centuries, in part because the sheer ferocity of the message of the Mongol armies was so totally effective in its absolute lack of regard for life. It was a message opposite of that which the armies of representative government are attempting to project—the benevolent actor using violence only as a last resort and valuing above all the individual human life. The latter message is not just opposite the former, it is also much more difficult to project convincingly. We will see neither our leaders nor our Soldiers do things that we would not do.

There are, however, messages coming from representative republics that their adversaries both abhor and fear. The adversary consistently and continuously points to the social values portrayed in the media of representative republics from the

West, South, and East Asia as amoral and contrary to their views or to the laws of God. To some extent, the sensitivity displayed by others when interacting with the Islamic world and also the world visions of legacy leftist terror movements, such as the Revolutionary Armed Forces of Columbia (FARC), seem to encourage their cultural criticisms of these values. As representative republics themselves engage in extensive internal dialogue about the direction of cultural and social values, it seems natural to them to attempt to be sensitive to those who disagree. Domestically, this sensitivity makes sense. Internationally, it becomes an acknowledgment of the validity of the criticism and a capitulation to ideas opposed to those portrayed in the social messages emanating from those representative republics. Whether or not the social system of these republics is flawed, most citizens would agree that they prefer it to alternatives their adversaries, such as terrorist organizations like Al Qaeda or movements like the Taliban, propose in violent confrontations.

In the context of adversarial conflict involving violence, it makes far more sense to project self-confidence in one's values, social morals, and cultural norms than to exhibit uncertainty. Whether the individual concurs with the positions put forward by each program on a given channel or each comment on a given blog matters less than the overall sense of social confidence that the dialogue itself is valid. This perspective returns to the notion that the introduction of the voluminous communications of representative republics has a role itself during confrontations involving ideological differences. While standard cultural communications, such as publicly available programming, printing, and network activity should be encouraged, if not subsidized, in a projection of confidence in our social system, this level of communication is not enough. This cultural confidence provides the defensive screen that must not be relinquished because of the sensibilities of our enemies—those who would destroy our culture as a whole, given the opportunity—but this confidence is only a *defensive* screen.

Clearly, against the directed messages of the adversary, representative government must join the fight with both defensive and offensive information resources. The information age has not brought better understanding across humanity; instead, it has brought the ability to coalesce groups of individuals around points of ideology, however extreme, because of their novel ability to find others who agree and to manage the flood of available knowledge by focusing on that with which they concur. Offensive uses of information should therefore involve intervening in those communications links to interdict that circle of extremism and supplant it. The challenge has been to do so within the legal, moral, and social codes established for society as a whole and while maintaining the freedom of internal self-examination.

As some of our authors demonstrate, however, to win the bulk of the populations devoted to a cause, a nation sometimes has little but its actions by which to enunciate its message. In an insurgency environment, a steady stream of commentary throughout the twentieth and into the twenty-first centuries provides guidance on how to approach the problem in order to send the correct message to the people concerned; whether this guidance has been heeded remains a problem. Small actions—a single building project in Baghdad, for example—cannot by them-selves counter the spectacular effect of a high-casualty car bomb. But large-scale trends in public attitudes can, and generally these trends respond to the actions of the nations involved.

These assembled works on the uses of information in conflict provide a framework, a foundation on which to build thinking on the subject. They do not provide a template or checklist for how to proceed. As with any military endeavor, planning depends on assumptions, and as the military saying goes, "no plan survives the first shot." In the end, leaders, and those who must act at the forefront of policy, must adapt their foundation of knowledge to the situation at hand to find a way to proceed. Today, their assumptions need to include the reality that the battle they fight for information may, in fact, be the primary field of conflict, even if their only weapons are their actions. Whether the paramount principles of violent clashes remain the same, the ultimate objective of all that they do may be their message—the message of war.

NOTES

Chapter 1: Exploiting Structural Weaknesses in Terrorist Networks
1. See, for example, Bruce Hoffman, "Al Qaeda, Trends in Terrorism, and Future Potentialities: An Assessment" (Santa Monica: RAND, 2003); Rohan Gunaratna, *Inside Al Qaeda: Global Network of Terror* (New York: Berkley Books, 2002); and Karen DeYoung, "Terrorist Attacks Rose Sharply in 2005, State Dept Says," *Washington Post*, April 29, 2006.
2. For an overview of this school of thinking, see John Arquilla and David Ronfeldt, *Networks and Netwars* (Santa Monica: RAND, 2001).
3. Jean Lave and Etienne Wenger, *Situated Learning: Legitimate Peripheral Participation* (New York: Cambridge University Press, 1991).
4. For a more detailed application of this model to networked terrorism, see Calvert Jones, "Al Qaeda's Innovative Improvisers: Learning in a Diffuse Transnational Network," *Cambridge Review of International Affairs* (June 2006).
5. Information operations are defined in the Defense Department's Joint Publication 3-13 *Information Operations* (Washington, DC: Department of Defense, February 13, 2006). Aimed at achieving information superiority, information operations refer to the "integrated employment of electronic warfare (EW), computer network operations (CNO), psychological operations (PSYOPS), military deception (MILDEC), and operations security (OPSEC), in concert with specified supporting and related capabilities, to influence, disrupt, corrupt or usurp adversarial human and automated decision making while protecting our own" (I-1).
6. For more information on training offered in the Afghanistan camps, see Gunaratna, *Inside Al Qaeda*, 93–101.
7. Douglas Frantz, Josh Meyer, Sebastian Rotella, and Megan K. Stack, "The New Face of Al Qaeda," *Los Angeles Times*, September 26, 2004.
8. Marc Sageman, *Understanding Terror Networks* (Philadelphia: University of Pennsylvania Press, 2004), 53.

9. Elaine Sciolino, "Casablanca Bombers Were Probably Lost," *International Herald Tribune*, May 20, 2003.
10. Jerry Seper, "Miami Terrorism Suspects Planned 'War' against U.S.," *Washington Times*, June 29, 2006.
11. See, for example, Audrey Kurth Cronin, "Cyber-Mobilization: The New Levée en Masse," *Parameters* (2006): 77–87; Jarret M. Brachman, "High-Tech Terror: Al-Qaeda's Use of New Technology," *Fletcher Forum of World Affairs* 30, no. 2 (2006): 150–164; and Gabriel Weimann, "How Modern Terrorism Uses the Internet," *Journal of International Security Affairs* 8 (2005): 91–105.
12. Calvert Jones and Sarai Mitnick, "Open Source Disaster Recovery: Case Studies of Networked Collaboration," *First Monday* 11, no. 5 (2006).
13. Matthew Forney, "China's Web Watchers," *TIME Asia Magazine*, October 3, 2005.
14. Philip Pan, "A Trip through China's Twilight Zone: One Woman's Quest for Truth in the Authoritarian Maze," *Washington Post*, December 18, 2004.
15. For example, Daniel Benjamin and Steven Simons, NSC counterterrorism directors under the Clinton administration, describe jihadist networks as "supple, malleable, and invisible" foes in the *Age of Sacred Terror: Radical Islam's War against America* (New York: Random House Trade Paperbacks, 2003), 170.
16. Bill Keller, "Self-Portrait of an Informer: An Innocent," *New York Times*, February 21, 1995.
17. See, for example, "Harmony and Disharmony: Exploiting al-Qa'ida's Organizational Vulnerabilities," Combating Terrorism Center, Department of Social Sciences, U.S. Military Academy, February 14, 2006; Audrey Kurth Cronin, "How Al Qaeda Ends: The Decline and Demise of Terrorist Groups," *International Security* 31, no. 1 (2006): 7–48; and Fawaz A. Gerges, *Journey of the Jihadist: Inside Muslim Militancy* (Orlando: Harcourt, 2006).
18. David Kilcullen, "Countering Global Insurgency: A Strategy for the War on Terrorism," *Journal of Strategic Studies* 28, no. 4 (August 2005): 597–617.

Chapter 3: Defining the War on Terror
1. Carl von Clausewitz, *On War*, trans. and ed. Michael Howard and Peter Paret (Princeton, NJ: Princeton University Press, 1976), 87–88.
2. Ibid., 88.
3. Department of Defense, Joint Publication 1–02, *DOD Dictionary of Military and Associated Terms* (Washington, DC: Department of Defense, November 30, 2004).
4. Henry Yule and Henri Cordier, eds., *The Travels of Marco Polo*, vol. 1 (New York: Dover Publications, 1993), 143.
5. Barbara Tuchman, *The Proud Tower: A Portrait of the World before the War, 1890–1914* (New York: Ballantine Books, 1962), 64.
6. Ibid., 63–113.
7. Jessica Stern, *Terror in the Name of God: Why Religious Militants Kill* (New York: HarperCollins, 2003), 165.
8. Ibid., 269–270.
9. Michael Scheuer, *Through Our Enemies' Eyes: Osama bin Laden, Radical Islam, and the Future of America* (Washington, DC: Brassey's, Inc., 2002), xvii.
10. Bernard Lewis, *What Went Wrong? Western Impact and Middle Eastern Response* (Oxford: Oxford University Press, 2002), 151.
11. Christopher Henzel, "The Origins of Al Qaeda's Ideology: Implications for U.S. Strategy," *Parameters* 35 (Spring 2005), 70.
12. Marc Sageman, *Understanding Terror Networks* (Philadelphia: University of Pennsylvania Press, 2004), 4.

13. Albert Hourani, *Arabic Thought in the Liberal Age, 1798–1939* (Cambridge: Cambridge University Press, 1983), 115–117; quoted in Henzel, "Origins of Al Qaeda's Ideo-logy," 72.
14. Gilles Kepel, *The War for Muslim Minds: Islam and the West*, trans. Pascale Ghazaleh (Cambridge, MA: Harvard University Press, 2004), 92.
15. Sageman, *Understanding Terror Networks*, 97.
16. Graham Fuller, *The Future of Political Islam* (New York: Palgrave Macmillan, 2004), 85–86.
17. *The National Defense Strategy of the United States of America* (Washington, DC: The Pentagon, March 2005).
18. T. E. Lawrence, Twenty-Seven Articles, from Public Broadcasting System website "Arab Warfare," available at www.pbs.org/lawrenceo-farabia/revolt/warfare4.html.

Chapter 4: Information Warfare
1. "Fourth Generation Warfare Presented by the Global Islamic Media Front" (Washington, DC: SITE Institute, July 11, 2006).

Chapter 6: Strategic Communication
1. Jeffrey B. Jones, "The Third Wave and the Fourth Dimension," in *Special Operations Forces: Roles and Missions in the Aftermath of the Cold War*, ed. Richard H. Schultz, Robert L. Pfaltzgraff, and W. Bradley Stock (Collingdale, PA: Diane Publishing, 1996).
2. Joseph S. Nye, *Soft Power* (New York: Public Affairs, 2004).
3. Alvin Toffler and Heidi Toffler, *War and Anti-War* (Boston, MA: Little, Brown, 1993).

Chapter 8: New Tools, New Rules
1. *See* Michael N. Schmitt, "Computer Network Attack and the Use of Force in International Law: Thoughts on a Normative Framework," *Columbia Journal of Transnational Law* 37 (1999): 885, 890. A companion version of this chapter, written for an international legal audience, appears as "Why States Need an International Law for Information Operations," *Lewis & Clark Law Review* 11 (2007): 1023.
2. Chairman of the Joint Chiefs of Staff, U.S. Department of Defense, Joint Publication 3-13 *Information Operations* (Washington, DC: Department of Defense, February 13, 2006), ix.
3. See Ibid., at II-1. I regard psychological operations not involving information networks to fall outside the IO definition and subject to regulation by existing international law.
4. See, e.g., Ibid., at II-4–II-5; Michael Schmitt, "Wired Warfare: Computer Network Attack and Jus in Bello," *International Review of the Red Cross* 846 (2002): 365, 367.
5. See Max Boot, *War Made New* (New York: Gotham, 2006); Eric Talbot Jensen, "Computer Attacks on Critical National Infrastructure: A Use of Force Invoking the Right of Self-Defense," *Stanford Journal of International Law* 22 (2002): 207, 212.
6. *Declaration Renouncing the Use, in Time of War, of Explosive Projectiles under 400 Grammes Weight*, Saint Petersburg, Russia, November 29–December 11, 1868.
7. Thucydides, *History of the Peloponnesian War* V, trans. Rex Warner (New York: Penguin, 1972), 95–97, 402–403. The Melians argued Athenian conquest would send a different message: "Is it not certain that you will make enemies of all states who are at present neutral, when they see what is happening here and naturally conclude that in course of time you will attack them too?"
8. Sun Tzu, *The Art of War*, trans. Roger Ames (New York: Ballantine Books, 1993), 111.

9. Carl von Clausewitz, *On War*, trans. and ed. Michael Howard and Peter Paret (Princeton, NJ: Princeton University Press, 1984).
10. See "The S.S. *Lotus* (France v. Turkey)," *Permanent Court of International Justice* (1927): 18–19.
11. Named after Russia's Friedrich Martens, the clause first appeared in "Hague Convention II with Respect to the Laws and Customs of War on Land of 1899." It has continued to appear in subsequent law of war agreements, including the 1949 Geneva Conventions.
12. "Protocol Additional to the Geneva Conventions of August 12, 1949, and relating to the Protection of Victims of Armed Conflict (Protocol I)," June 8, 1977, art.1(2) (AP I); see also Ibid., art. 35(1). Although not a party, the United States considers many of AP I's provisions declaratory of customary international law. See, e.g., Michael J. Matheson, "The United States Position on the Relation of Customary International Law to the 1977 Protocols Additional to the 1949 Geneva Conventions," *American University Journal of International Law & Public Policy* 2 (1987): 419.
13. "Legality of the Threat or Use of Nuclear Weapons (Advisory Opinion)," *Report of the International Court of Justice, 1996*, 226, 105(2)(D).
14. AP I, Article 36.
15. See Louise Doswald-Beck, "Some Thoughts on Computer Network Attack and the International Law of Armed Conflict," *International Law Studies* 76 (2002): 163, 164.
16. See "Protocol for the Prohibition of the Use of Asphyxiating, Poisonous or Other Gases, and of Bacteriological Methods of Warfare, June 17, 1925," *U.S. Treaties and Other International Agreements* 26:571; "Convention on the Prohibition of the Development, Production and Stockpiling of Bacteriological (Biological) and Toxin Weapons and on Their Destruction, April 10, 1972," *U.S. Treaties and Other International Agreements* 26: 583; "Convention on the Prohibition of the Development, Production, Stockpiling and Use of Chemical Weapons and on Their Destruction, January 13, 1993," *International Legal Materials* 32 (1993): 800.
17. See AP I; "Protocol Additional to the Geneva Conventions of August 12, 1949, and Relating to the Protection of Victims of Non-International Armed Conflicts (Protocol II), June 8, 1977" (AP II).
18. See "Letter Dated September 23, 1998, from the Permanent Representative of the Russian Federation to the United Nations to the Secretary General Concerning Agenda Item 63," U.N. Doc. A/C.1/53/3 (1998); *Report of the Secretary General on Developments in the Field of Information and Telecommunications in the Context of Information Security*, U.N. Doc. A/54/213 (1999).
19. Office of the General Counsel, Department of Defense, "An Assessment of International Legal Issues in Information Operations (Nov. 1999)," *International Law Studies* 76 (2002): 459, 475, 520 ("DOD GC Memo").
20. See International Committee of the Red Cross, *Report, International Humanitarian Law and the Challenges of Contemporary Armed Conflicts* (September 2003), 4; Sean Watts, *Civilian Participation in Computer Network Attacks*, 32 (on file with author).
21. See, e.g., Eric Talbot Jensen, "Unexpected Consequences from Knock-On Effects: A Different Standard for Computer Network Operations," *American University International Law Review* 18 (2003): 1145, 1149; Schmitt, "Wired Warfare," 396. A 1999 Naval War College conference disfavored CNA-specific rules with respect to information warfare. Philip A. Johnson, "Is It Time for a Treaty on Information Warfare?" *International Law Studies* 76 (2002): 439. Many there argued that the law of war could operate by analogy. See, e.g., Yoram Dinstein, "Computer Network Attacks and Self-Defense," *International Law Studies* 76 (2002): 99, 114–115; Daniel B. Silver, "Computer Network Attack as a Use of Force under Article 2(4) of the United Nations Charter," *International Law Studies* 76 (2002): 73, 75; Douglas S. Anderson

and Christopher R. Dooley, "Information Operations in the Space Law Arena: Science Fiction Becomes Reality," *International Law Studies* 76 (2002): 265, 298. Others characterized the idea as premature or unrealistic. See, e.g., Charles J. Dunlap, "Meeting the Challenge of Cyberterrorism: Defining the Military Role in a Democracy," *International Law Studies* 76 (2002): 353, 362–363; David Tubbs, Perry G. Luzwick, and Walter Gary Sharp, Sr., "Technology and Law: The Evolution of Digital Warfare," *International Law Studies* 76 (2002): 7, 17.

22. UN Charter, arts. 2(4), 42, 51.
23. Schmitt, "Computer Network Attack," 905; Horace B. Robertson, "Self-Defense against Computer Network Attacks," *International Law Studies* 76 (2002): 121, 134.
24. Silver, "Computer Network Attack," 75; see also Emily Haslam, "Information Warfare: Technological Changes and International Law," *Journal of Conflict and Security Law* (2000): §4.2; DOD GC Memo, 491. But see Davis Brown, "A Proposal for an International Convention to Regulate the Use of Information Systems in Armed Conflict," *Harvard International Law Journal* 47 (2006): 179, 181, n. 12 ("*jus ad bellum* of information warfare can be derived with little difficulty").
25. Sean P. Kanuck, "Information Warfare: New Challenges for Public International Law," *Harvard International Law Journal* 37 (1996): 272, 288–289; David DiCenso, "Information Operations: An Act of War," *Air & Space Power Chronicles*, July 2000.
26. See, e.g., Walter Gary Sharp, Sr., *Cyberspace and the Use of Force* (Falls Church, VA: Aegis Research Corp., 1999), 129–132; Jensen, "Computer Attacks on Critical National Infrastructure," 229.
27. DOD GC Memo, 483; Schmitt, "Computer Network Attack," 913, 919; Silver, "Computer Network Attack," 85; Dinstein, "Computer Network Attacks," 105; Robertson, "Self-Defense against Computer Network Attacks," 133. Not all uses of force will constitute an "armed attack"; bullets fired across a border may be a use of force but not an armed attack for purposes of triggering self-defense. Dinstein, "Computer Network Attacks," 100.
28. AP I, art. 48. Other jus in bello principles may also require translation into the IO context—e.g., rules on indiscriminate weapons and proportionality. See Ibid., art. 51(4)–(5); Knut Dormann, "Applicability of the Additional Protocols to Computer Network Attacks," *International Committee of the Red Cross*, November 19, 2004, 5, http://www.icrc.org/Web/Eng/siteeng0.nsf/html/68LG92; Doswald-Beck, "Some Thoughts on Computer Network Attack," 168–169; Jensen, "Unexpected Consequences," 1177–1179; Schmitt, "Wired Warfare," 389–390.
29. AP I, art. 52(2).
30. Ibid., arts. 51(2), 52(1). The law of war also provides special protection to certain objects—e.g., medical facilities and objects indispensable to the civilian population's survival such as drinking water.
31. See DOD GC Memo, 471–472; Schmitt, "Wired Warfare," 381–382; Haslam, "Information Warfare," §4.3.2.
32. The status of civilians whom militaries employ to conduct IO raises its own set of translation questions. See, e.g., Dormann, "Applicability of Additional Protocols," 8–9; DOD GC Memo, 470–471; Schmitt, "Wired Warfare," 383–384.
33. AP I, art. 49(1). However, all "[a]cts or threats of violence the primary purpose of which is to spread terror among the civilian population are prohibited." Ibid., art. 51(2).
34. See Schmitt, "Wired Warfare," 378–379; Haslam, "Information Warfare," §4.3.2. On the other hand, even if it has more civilian effects, by having more humane effects than traditional kinetic weapons, we might want IO to expand traditional targeting rules. See Jensen, "Unexpected Consequences," 1166.
35. AP I, art. 58.
36. Arnaud de Brochgrave and Frank J. Cilluffo, "Cyber Threats and Information Security:

Meeting the 21st Century Challenge," *Center for Strategic and International Studies Report*, May 2001, 7; Dormann, "Applicability of Additional Protocols," 10; DOD GC Memo, 472.
37. Doswald-Beck, "Some Thoughts on Computer Network Attack," 167. Of course, as military objectives, they would remain subject to the rules on discrimination and proportionality that might limit how an adversary's military could attack them. *See* Schmitt, "Wired Warfare," 385.
38. See AP I, art. 37(1).
39. Dunlap, "Meeting the Challenge of Cyberterrorism," 363.
40. Silver, "Computer Network Attack," 74.
41. See, e.g., Sharp, *Cyberspace and the Use of Force*; Anderson and Dooley, "Information Operations in the Space Law Arena," 268; Brown, "Proposal for an International Convention"; Dormann, "Applicability of Additional Protocols," 1; Jensen, "Unexpected Consequences," 1150–1151; Christopher C. Joyner and Catherine Lotrionte, "Information Warfare as International Coercion: Elements of a Legal Framework," *European Journal of International Law* 12 (2001): 825, 828; Brian T. O'Donnell and James C. Kraska, "Humanitarian Law: Developing International Rules for the Battlefield," *Journal of Conflict & Security Law* 8 (2003): 133, 139; Schmitt, "Wired Warfare," *Journal of Transnational Law* 37 (1999): 939, 942. A smaller body of work has considered IO in a broader context. See, e.g., DOD GC Memo; Jason Barkham, "Information Warfare and International Law on the Use of Force," *New York University Journal of International Law & Policy* 34 (2001–2002): 57; Haslam, "Information Warfare," §4.
42. The U.S. Supreme Court recently answered that question in the negative. See *Hamdan v. Rumsfeld*, 548 U.S. 557 (2006).
43. AP II, arts. 11–13.
44. Jean-Marie Henckaerts, "Study on Customary International Humanitarian Law: A Contribution to the Understanding and Respect for the Rule of Law in Armed Conflict," *International Review of the Red Cross* 87 (2005): 175, 189. For U.S. views critical of the ICRC study, see John Bellinger, "Wrap Up Discussion I," *Opinio Juris*, January 20, 2007, http://opiniojuris.org/2007/01/20/wrap-up-discussion-i/.
45. See, e.g., "Legal Consequences of the Construction of a Wall in the Occupied Palestinian Territory, International Court of Justice, Advisory Opinion," *International Legal Materials* 43 (July 9, 2004): 1009, 1050; Silver, "Computer Network Attack," 93; Barkham, "Information Warfare and International Law," 72.
46. See, e.g., Emerich de Vattel, *The Laws of Nations, or the Principles of the Law of Nature*, ed. J. Chitty (Philadelphia: T. & J. W. Johnson, 1855), bk. 1, ch. 3; "Military and Paramilitary Activities in and against Nicaragua (*Nicaragua v. United States*)," *Report of the International Court of Justice 1986*, 4, 106.
47. DOD GC Memo, 487–488; Dinstein, "Computer Network Attacks," 103.
48. See, e.g., "Corfu Channel (*United Kingdom v. Albania*)," *Report of the International Court of Justice 1949*, 4, 22 (merits); *Responsibility of States for Internationally Wrongful Acts*, art. 49, UN General Assembly Resolution 56/83, *Annex*, December 12, 2001; DOD GC Memo, 488.
49. DOD GC Memo, 516; Tubbs and others, "Technology and Law," 16; Simon Chesterman, "The Spy Who Came in from the Cold War: Intelligence and International Law," *Michigan Journal of International Law* 27 (2006).
50. See, e.g., "Treaty on Principles Governing the Activities of States in the Exploration and Use of Outer Space, Including the Moon and Other Celestial Bodies, Jan. 27, 1967," art. IV(2), *U.S. Treaties and Other International Agreements* 18:2410 (Outer Space Treaty).
51. Ibid., art. IX; Anderson and Dooley, "Information Operations in the Space Law Arena," 281–282.

52. "Constitution of the International Telecommunications Union, July 1, 1994," art. 45(1), *Annex*, 1003.
53. Ibid., art. 48.
54. See, e.g., "U.N. Convention on the Law of the Sea, December 10, 1982," *United Nations Treaty Series* 1833:396, arts. 19, 109 (UNCLOS). The United States regards UNCLOS as generally codifying customary international law. Other regimes (e.g., cyber crime) that might otherwise appear applicable do not govern IO because the negotiating states excluded their own conduct from regulation. See *Council of Europe Convention on Cybercrime*, Treaty Document 108-11, art. 2 (November 8, 2001); *Explanatory Report*, Cyber-Crime Convention, ¶38 (November 8, 2001).
55. See, generally, David Kaye, "Complexity in the Law of War," in *Progress in International Organization* (Chicago: Fred B. Rotham & Co., 2007).
56. Dormann, "Applicability of Additional Protocols," 3.
57. See, e.g., *Agreement between the Government of the United States of America and the Government of Jamaica Concerning Cooperation in Suppressing Illicit Maritime Drug Trafficking*, Kingston, May 6, 1997, as amended. Of course, such cooperative efforts would need to be calibrated to protect legitimate privacy interests even as they facilitate the fight against terror. See John F. Murphy, "Computer Network Attacks by Terrorists: Some Legal Dimensions," *International Law Studies* 76 (2002): 324, 344.
58. Louise Doswald-Beck, ed., *San Remo Manual on International Law Applicable to Armed Conflicts at Sea* (Cambridge: Cambridge University Press, 1995).

Chapter 9: Learning Counterinsurgency
1. The Center for Army Lessons Learned website was retrieved from http://call.Army.mil/.
2. T. E. Lawrence, "Twenty-Seven Articles," *Arab Bulletin*, August 20, 1917. Known popularly as "Lawrence of Arabia," T. E. Lawrence developed an incomparable degree of what we now call "cultural awareness" during his time working with Arab tribes and armies, and many of his twenty-seven articles ring as true today as they did in his day. A website with the articles can be found at www.pbs.org/lawrenceofarabia/revolt/warfare4.html. A good overview of Lawrence's thinking, including his six fundamental principles of insurgency, can be found in "T. E. Lawrence and the Mind of an Insurgent," *Army* (July 2005): 31–37.
3. I should note that this has been much less the case in Afghanistan, where, because the expectations of the people were so low and the abhorrence of the Taliban and further civil war was so great, the Afghan people remained grateful to Coalition forces and other organizations for all that was done for them. Needless to say, the relative permissiveness of the security situation in Afghanistan also helped a great deal and made it possible for nongovernmental organizations to operate on a much wider and freer basis than was possible in Iraq. In short, the different context in Afghanistan meant that the half-life of the Army of liberation there was considerably longer than that in Iraq.
4. In fact, we often contended with what came to be known as the "Man on the Moon Challenge"—i.e., the expectation of ordinary Iraqis that Soldiers from a country that could put a man on the moon and overthrow Saddam in a matter of weeks should also be able, with considerable ease, to provide each Iraqi a job, twenty-four-hour electrical service, and so on.
5. The military units on the ground in Iraq have generally had considerable capability to carry out reconstruction and nation-building tasks. During its time in northern Iraq, for example, the 101st Airborne Division had four engineer battalions (including, for a period, even a well-drilling detachment), an engineer group headquarters (which is designed to carry out assessment, design, contracting, and quality assurance tasks), two civil affairs battalions, nine infantry battalions, four artillery battalions (most of which were "out of battery" and performed reconstruction tasks), a sizable logistical

support command (generally about six battalions, including transportation, fuel storage, supply, maintenance, food service, movement control, warehousing, and even water purification units), a military police battalion (with attached police and corrections training detachments), a signal battalion, an air defense battalion (which helped train Iraqi forces), a field hospital, a number of contracting officers and officers authorized to carry large sums of money, an air traffic control element, some nine aviation battalions (with approximately 250 helicopters), a number of chaplain teams, and more than twenty-five military lawyers (who can be of enormous assistance in resolving a host of problems when conducting nation-building). Except in the area of aviation assets, the 4th Infantry Division and the 1st Armored Division, the two other major Army units in Iraq in the summer of 2003, had even more assets than the 101st.

6. The FY 2005 Defense Budget and Supplemental Funding Measures approved by Congress provided some $5.2 billion for the Iraqi Security Force's train, equip, advise, and rebuild effort. Just as significant, it was appropriated in just three categories—Ministry of Defense, Ministry of Interior, and Quick Reaction Funds—thereby minimizing substantially the need for reprogramming actions.

7. GEN John R. Galvin, "Uncomfortable Wars: Toward a New Paradigm," *Parameters* 16, no. 4 (Winter 1986): 6.

8. As soon as the "kinetic" part of that operation was complete, we moved into the neighborhood with engineers, civil affairs teams, lawyers, officers with money, and security elements. We subsequently repaired any damage that might conceivably have been caused by the operation and completely removed all traces of the house in which Uday and Qusay were located, as the missiles had rendered it structurally unsound and we didn't want any reminders left of the two brothers.

9. Over time, and as the effort to train and equip Iraqi combat units gathered momentum, the Multinational Security Transition Command–Iraq placed greater and greater emphasis on helping with the development of the Ministries of Defense and Interior, especially after the mission to advise the ministries' leaders was shifted to the command from the embassy's Iraq Reconstruction Management Office in the fall of 2005. It is now one of the command's top priorities.

10. The Army, for example, has incorporated scenarios that place a premium on cultural awareness into its major exercises at the National Training Center and Joint Readiness Training Center. It has stressed the importance of cultural awareness throughout the process of preparing units for deployments to Iraq and Afghanistan and in a comprehensive approach adopted by the U.S. Army Training and Doctrine Command. As part of this effort, language tools have been developed—e.g., the Rosetta Stone program available through Army Knowledge Online—and language training will be required of Command and General Staff College students during their second and third semesters. Doctrinal manuals are being modified to recognize the importance of cultural awareness, and instruction in various commissioned and noncommissioned officers' courses has been added as well. The Center for Army Lessons Learned has published a number of documents to assist also. The U.S. Marine Corps has pursued similar initiatives and is, in fact, partnering with the Army in the development of a new counterinsurgency field manual.

11. David Galula's classic work, *Counterinsurgency Warfare: Theory and Practice* (St. Petersburg, FL: Hailer Publishing, 2005), is particularly instructive on this point. See, for example, his discussion on pages 88–89.

12. As I noted in a previous endnote, preparation of leaders and units for deployment to Iraq or Afghanistan now typically includes extensive preparation for the kind of "non-kinetic" operations our leaders are called on to perform, with the preparation period culminating in a brigade combat team's mission rehearsal exercise at either the National Training Center or the Joint Readiness Training Center. At each center, units conduct

missions similar to those they'll perform when deployed and do so in an environment that includes villages, Iraqi American role players, "suicide bombers," "insurgents," the need to work with local leaders and local security forces, etc. At the next higher level, the preparation of division and corps headquarters culminates in the conduct of a mission rehearsal exercise conducted jointly by the Battle Command Training Program and Joint Warfighting Center. This exercise also strives to replicate—in a command post exercise format driven by a computer simulation—the missions, challenges, and context the unit will find once deployed.

13. A great piece that highlights the work being done by young leaders in Iraq is Robert Kaplan's "The Future of America—in Iraq," *latimes.com,* December 24, 2005. Another is the video presentation used by Army Chief of Staff GEN Peter J. Schoomaker, "Pentathlete Leader: 1LT Ted Wiley," which recounts Lieutenant Wiley's fascinating experiences in the first Stryker unit to operate in Iraq as they fought and conducted nation-building operations throughout much of the country, often transitioning from one to the other very rapidly, changing missions and reorganizing while on the move, and covering considerable distances in short periods of time.

14. In fact, the U.S. Army is currently in the final stages of an important study of the education and training of leaders, one objective of which is to identify additional programs and initiatives that can help produce the kind of flexible, adaptable leaders who have done well in Iraq and Afghanistan. Among the issues being examined is how to provide experiences for our leaders that take them out of their "comfort zone." For many of us, attending a civilian graduate school provided such an experience, and the Army's recent decision to expand graduate school opportunities for officers is thus a great initiative. For a provocative assessment of the challenges the U.S. Army faces, see the article by UK Brigadier Nigel Aylwin-Foster, "Changing the Army for Counterinsurgency Operations," *Military Review*, November–December 2005, 2–15.

15. The Department of Defense formally recognized the implications of current operations as well, issuing on November 28, 2005, DOD Directive 3000.05 "Military Support for Stability, Security, Transition, and Reconstruction Operations," which establishes DOD policy and assigns responsibilities within DOD for planning, training, and preparing to conduct and support stability operations. This is a significant order that is already spurring action in a host of different areas. A copy was retrieved from www.dtic.mil/whs/directives/corres/html/300005.htm.

16. A brief assessment of the current situation and the strategy for the way ahead is in Ambassador Zalmay Khalilzad's "The Challenge before Us," *Wall Street Journal*, January 9, 2006, 12.

17. Galvin, "Uncomfortable Wars," 7. One of the Army's true Soldier-statesman-scholars, General Galvin was serving as the Commander in Chief of U.S. Southern Command at the time he wrote this article. In that position, he oversaw the conduct of a number of operations in El Salvador and elsewhere in Central and South America, and it was in that context that he wrote this enduring piece. He subsequently served as the Supreme Allied Commander, Europe, and following retirement, was the Dean of the Fletcher School of Law and Diplomacy at Tufts University, Medford, Massachusetts.

18. Ibid.

Chapter 11: Strategic Innovation

1. David Galula, *Counterinsurgency Warfare: Theory and Practice* (St. Petersburg, FL: Hailer Publishing, 2005), 89.
2. See David J. Kilcullen, "Countering Global Insurgency," *Journal of Strategic Studies* 28, no. 4 (August 2005): 597–617, for an important description of a strategy to win the Long War.

3. National Security Council, *National Strategy for Victory in Iraq*, November 2005, retrieved from http://www.whitehouse.gov/infocus/iraq/iraq_national_strategy_20051130.pdf.
4. Donald Rumsfeld, cited in Ann Scott Tyson, "Rumsfeld Urges Using Media to Fight Terror," *Washington Post*, February 18, 2006, A7.
5. Peter Schoomaker in "Foreword" to John A. Nagl, *Learning to Eat Soup with a Knife: Counterinsurgency Lessons from Malaya and Vietnam* (Chicago: University of Chicago, 2005), x.
6. The best summary of historical best and worst practices in counterinsurgency is Kalev I. "Gunner" Sepp, "Best Practices in Counterinsurgency," *Military Review*, May–June 2005, 8–12.
7. Sir Michael Howard, "Military Science in the Age of Peace," *RUSI Journal* (March 1974): 3–4.

Chapter 12: Maneuvering against the Mind
1. T. E. Lawrence, *Seven Pillars of Wisdom: A Triumph* (New York: Anchor Books, 1991), 192.
2. Bruce Hoffman, *Inside Terrorism*, rev. ed. (New York: Columbia University Press, 2006), 198.
3. Gabriel Weimann, "How Modern Terrorism Uses the Internet," *Journal of International Security Affairs* (Spring 2005): 91–105. See also the series by Susan B. Glasser and Steve Coll, "The Web as Weapon," *Washington Post*, August 7–9, 2005, A1.
4. John Mackinlay, "Defeating Complex Insurgency: Beyond Iraq and Afghanistan," *Whitehall Papers* 64 (London: RUSI, 2005): 9.
5. See Bing West, *No True Glory* (New York: Random House, 2005).
6. U.S. Marine Corps, *Small Wars Manual* (Washington, DC: GPO, 1940), 1–13.
7. I am indebted to Dr. Steve Metz and Dr. John Mackinlay of King's College London for these terms. See Steven Metz, *Learning from Iraq: Counterinsurgency in American Strategy* (Carlisle, PA: Strategic Studies Institute, 2007).
8. Robert Thompson, *Defeating Communist Insurgency* (Saint Petersburg, FL: Hailer Publishing, 2005), 141–149.
9. Paul Staniland, "Defeating Transnational Insurgencies: The Best Offense Is a Good Fence," *The Washington Quarterly*, Winter 2005–2006, 21–40.
10. Steven Metz and Raymond Millen, *Insurgency and Counterinsurgency in the 21st Century* (Carlilse, PA: Army War College, Strategic Studies Group, 2004), 21.
11. David Galula, *Pacification in Algeria, 1956–1958* (Santa Monica, CA: RAND, 1964; repr. 2006), ix. Citations are to the 2006 edition.
12. Frank. G. Hoffman, "Small Wars Revisited: The United States and Nontraditional Warfare," *Journal of Strategic Studies*, December 2005, 913–940.
13. Secretary of Defense Donald Rumsfeld, Speech at Army War College (Carlisle Barracks, PA, March 27, 2006).
14. Rick Brennan and others, *Future Insurgency Threats* (Santa Monica, CA: RAND, 2005).
15. Lawrence E. Cline, *Pseudo Operations and Counterinsurgency: Lessons from Other Countries* (Carlisle, PA: Strategic Studies Institute, 2005).
16. For additional insights into Al Qaeda's cellular networks and their group dynamics, see Marc Sageman, *Understanding Terror Networks* (Philadelphia: University of Pennsylvania Press, 2004).
17. On net wars see John Arguilla and David P. Ronfeldt, "Netwar Revisited: The Fight for the Future Continues," in *Networks, Terrorism and Global Insurgency*, ed. Robert J. Bunker (London: Routledge, 2005), 8–19.

18. Joint Publication, *Information Operations: A Strategy for Peace—the Decisive Edge in War* (Washington, DC: The Joint Chiefs of Staff, March 1999), 3.
19. T. E. Lawrence, "The Evolution of a Revolt," *The Army Quarterly and Defence Journal*, October 1920.
20. Audrey Kurth Cronin, "Cyber-Mobilization: The New *Levée en Masse*," *Parameters* 36 (Summer 2006): 77–87.
21. Ibid., 87.
22. Lawrence, *Seven Pillars of Wisdom*, 195.
23. Elaine Grossman, "Mattis, U.S. Has Barely Begun War vs. Jihadis for Global Hearts and Minds," *Inside the Pentagon*, August 25, 2005, 1.
24. U.S. Marine Corps, MCDP 3-42, *Information Operations* (September 2003).
25. Maj Andy Dietz, USMC, interview transcript, February 21, 2006, Operational Leadership Experiences Project, Combined Army Research Library, Combat Studies Institute, Leavenworth, Kansas.
26. Reinforced by e-mail by the Division Information Officer, LtCol D. Olsen, to the author, October 20, 2004.
27. Colonel Conlin interview with author and e-mail of March 14, 2006.
28. Maj Joseph Paschall, "Tactical Information Operations in OIF," *Marine Corps Gazette*, March 2004, 56–59.
29. Dietz interview.
30. James N. Mattis and F. G. Hoffman, "The Rise of Hybrid Warfare," *Proceedings*, November 2005.
31. Cited in John Ballard, *Fighting for Fallujah: A New Dawn for Iraq* (Westport, CT: Praeger, 2005), 101.
32. Lawrence, *Seven Pillars of Wisdom*, 195.
33. David Kilcullen, "Counterinsurgency Redux," *Survival*, Winter 2006–2007, 123.
34. Suggested by Lawrence Freedman, *The Transformation of Strategic Affairs* (Abingdon, NY: Routledge for the International Institute for Strategic Studies, 2006), 71.

Chapter 13: Clausewitz's Theory of War and Information Operations
1. Carl von Clausewitz, *On War*, trans. and ed. Michael Howard and Peter Paret (Princeton, NJ: Princeton University Press, 1976), 89.
2. Ibid., 141.
3. Ibid., 88.
4. Ibid., 75, 87.
5. Ibid., 86–88.
6. Ibid., 77.
7. Ibid., 87.
8. Ibid., 605.
9. Ibid., 87–88.
10. Ibid., 86–87.
11. Harry G. Summers, Jr., *On Strategy: A Critical Analysis of the Vietnam War* (Carlisle Barracks, PA: Strategic Studies Institute, 1982), 8.
12. Clausewitz, *On War*, 645.
13. Ibid., 80–81.
14. O. Gene Clanton, *Kansas Populism: Ideas and Men* (Lawrence: University of Kansas Press, 1969), 57.
15. Clausewitz, *On War*, 88.
16. Ibid., 81.
17. Ibid., 184–185.
18. Ibid., 606–607.

Chapter 16: In Defense of Military Public Affairs Doctrine

1. "Effects-based approach to operations" is a term NATO uses, but it is synonymous with similar effects-based terminology employed by U.S. forces. The glossary on the U.S. Joint Forces Command website offers this definition: "the coherent application of national and alliance elements of power through effects-based processes to accomplish strategic objectives."
2. The White House's September 2006 *National Strategy for Combating Terrorism* refers to both "a battle of arms and a battle of ideas," stating, "We will attack terrorism and its ideology," and cites the need to neutralize terrorist propaganda.
3. Tom Carver, "Pentagon Plans Propaganda War," *BBC News*, February 20, 2002, http://news.bbc.co.uk/1/hi/world/americas/1830500.stm. This is only one example of the many articles and editorials attacking the Office of Strategic Influence.
4. "Final Decision on Military Committee 457," *NATO Military Policy on Public Information*, June 14, 2001. For more information, see www.nato.int/ims/docu/nmpi.htm.
5. "Assistant Secretary of Defense for Public Affairs and Enclosures," *U.S. Department of Defense Directive 5122.5*, September 27, 2000, http://www.dtic.mil/whs/directives/corres/html/51225.htm. The latest version of joint U.S. public affairs doctrine cites the same principles.
6. Ibid.
7. U.S. Declaration of Independence, July 4, 1776, http://www.ushistory.org/declaration/document/index.htm.
8. John Milton, *Areopagitica: A Speech for the Liberty of Unlicenced Printing to the Parliament of England*, November 23, 1644, http://www.econlib.org/library/essays/mila1.html.
9. U.S. Bill of Rights, Amendment I, September 25, 1789, ratified December 15, 1791, http://www.cs.indiana.edu/statecraft/cons.bill.html.
10. Constitution of Romania, Article 30, "Freedom of Expression," http://www.oefre.unibe.ch/law/icl/ ro_indx.html.
11. Constitution Act, 1982, Article 1, Part 1, "Canadian Charter of Rights and Freedoms," http://thecanadianencyclopedia.com/index.cfm?PgNm=TCE&Params=A1ARTA0001270.
12. Charter of the United Nations, San Francisco, California, June 1945, http://www.un.org/aboutun/carter/.
13. UN, Universal Declaration of Human rights, adopted and proclaimed by the UN General Assembly, December 10, 1948, http://ccnmtl.columbia.edu/projects/mmt/udhr/.
14. Ibid.
15. North Atlantic Treaty, Washington, DC, April 4, 1949.
16. NATO, Ministerial Communiqué Annex to M-1(94)2: "Partnership for Peace: Framework Document," Brussels, January 10, 1994, http://hq.natio.int/docu/comm/49-95/c940110b.htm. This document also commits NATO partners to "reaffirm their commitment to fulfill in good faith the obligations of the Charter of the United Nations and the principles of the Universal Declaration on Human rights [para. 2]."
17. Ratified by all NATO nations, the Geneva Conventions were adopted on August 12, 1949, by the Diplomatic Conference for the Establishment of International Conventions for the Protection of Victims of War. They entered into force on October 21, 1950.
18. "Protocol Additional to the Geneva Conventions of August 12, 1949, and relating to the Protection of Victims of International Armed Conflicts (Protocol 1)," adopted June 8, 1977, by the Diplomatic Conference on the Reaffirmation and Development of International Humanitarian Law applicable in Armed Conflicts, and entered into force December 7, 1979.
19. Ibid.
20. Charter of the United Nations.

21. Library of Congress, *Churchill and the Great Republic*, http://www.loc.gov/exhibits/churchill/wc-unity.html.
22. Joint Chiefs of Staff, Joint Publication (JP) 3-61 *Doctrine for Public Affairs in Joint Operations* (Washington, DC: U.S. Government Printing Office, May 9, 2005), http://www.au.af.mil/au/awcgate/awmedia.htm.
23. British Army, JSP 512, *Joint Services Media Handling Guide* (nc: March 2006), http://www.army.mod.uk/atgl_service_pubs/_agais/jsp/index.htm.
24. From documents provided to the author by the Directorate of Public Affairs, Romanian Ministry of Defense.
25. British Army, *Joint Services Media Handling Guide*.
26. NATO Policy, MC 422/1, NATO Military Policy on Information Operations, 2002.
27. Joint Chiefs of Staff, *Doctrine for Public Affairs*.
28. Ibid. The doctrine states, "The first side that presents the information sets the context and frames the public debate. It is extremely important to get factual, complete, truthful information out first [chap. 1, 1–4]."
29. For a discussion of the OODA-loop by its originator, see John R. Boyd, *A Discourse on Winning and Losing* (Maxwell AFB, AL: Air University, 1987).
30. Willem Marx, "Misinformation Intern: My Summer as a Military Propagandist in Iraq," *Harper's*, September 2006, 51–59.

Chapter 17: Waging an Effective Strategic Communications Campaign in the War on Terror

1. R. S. Zaharna, "American Public Diplomacy in the Arab and Muslim World: A Strategic Communication Analysis," *Foreign Policy in Focus Policy Report* (November 2001), http://www.foreignpolicyinfocus.org/papers/communciation_body.html.
2. The Office of the Director of National Intelligence, "Trends in Global Terrorism: Implications for the United States," *National Intelligence Estimate* (April 2006), http://www.dni.gov/press_releases/Declassified_NIE_Key_Judgments.pdf.
3. Ibid.
4. Karen DeYoung, "Spy Agencies Say Iraq War Hurting U.S. Terror Fight," *Washington Post*, September, 24, 2006, http://www.washingtonpost.com/wp-dyn/content/article/2006/09/23/AR2006092301130_pf.html.
5. Karen DeYoung, "Spy Agencies Say Iraq War Hurting U.S. Terror Fight," *Washington Post*, September 24, 2006.
6. Carl Conetta, "Losing Hearts and Minds: World Public Opinion and Post-9/11 U.S. Security Policy," *Project on Defense Alternatives Briefing Memo* 37, September 14, 2006, http://www.comw.org/pda/fulltext/0609bm37.pdf.
7. Eric Pfeiffer, "U.S. Standing Sinks in the Mideast," *Washington Times*, December 15, 2006, 3.
8. For a detailed account of how Ayatollah Khomeini's "small" media eventually undermined the Shah's "big" media, see Annabelle Sreberny-Mohammadi and Ali Mohammadi, *Small Media, Big Revolution: Communication, Culture, and the Iranian Revolution* (Minneapolis: University of Minnesota Press, 1994).
9. Mohammed El-Nawawy and Adel Iskandar, *Al-Jazeera: The Story of the Network That Is Rattling Governments and Redefining Modern Journalism* (Boulder, Co: Westview Press, 2003).
10. The *Transnational Broadcasting Studies Journal* is published by the American University in Cairo's Adham Center for Television Journalism. It provides excellent insight into media developments in the Middle East and assesses U.S. public diplomacy efforts in the region. See *Transnational Broadcasting Studies Journal*, http://www.tbsjournal.com/jazeera_sas.html.

11. See S. Abdallah Schleifer, "The Sweet and Sour Success of Al Jazeera," *Transnational Broadcasting Studies Journal* 7 (Fall 2001), http://www.tbsjournal.com/jazeera_sas.html.
12. William B. Reinckens, "Satellite Television Floods the Middle East with Information," *Washington File Staff Writer*, August 27, 2001, http://usinfo.state.gov.
13. Thomas L. Friedman, "The Hidden Victims," *New York Times*, May 1, 2002.
14. Tim Golden, "Crisis Deepens Impact of Arab TV News," *New York Times*, April 16, 2002, A12.
15. During the Israeli incursion into the West Bank in April 2002, many Arabs abandoned normal routines to follow events on Arab television. A neighborhood lawyer, Essam al-Sayed, claims, "Every Arab is watching this closely. . . . It may be worse for us than even September 11 was for you—because it goes on and on. Every time you turn on the television, it's as though you were watching someone beat you." Tim Golden, "Crisis Deepens Impact of Arab TV News," *New York Times*, April 16, 2002, A12.
16. Gabriel Weimann, *Terror on the Internet: The New Arena, the New Challenges* (Washington, DC: U.S. Institute of Peace Press, 2006), 15.
17. Philip Taylor, "Spin Laden," *The World Today*, December 2001, 8.
18. Testimony by Norman J. Pattiz, *The Message Is America: Rethinking U.S. Public Diplomacy*, November 14, 2001, http://commdocs.house.gov/committees/intlrel/hfa76189.000/hfa76189_0.HTM.
19. Kurt M. Campbell and Michèle A. Flournoy, *To Prevail: An American Strategy for the Campaign against Terrorism* (Washington, DC: Center for Strategic and International Studies, 2001), 144.
20. See Sanford J. Ungar, "Pitch Imperfect," *Foreign Affairs*, May–June 2005, http://www.foreignaffairs.org/20050501facomment84302/sanford-j-ungar/pitch-imperfect.html?mode=print.
21. This disconnect between U.S. public affairs and the Arab audiences it claims it was trying to reach during OIF is best illustrated in Jehane Noujaim's documentary *Control Room*, which was filmed inside Al Jazeera headquarters in Doha, Qatar, during March and April 2003. See *Control Room*, DVD, directed by Jehane Noujaim (Santa Monica, CA: Lions Gate, 2004).
22. Thomas E. Ricks, *Fiasco: The American Military Adventure in Iraq* (New York: Penguin, 2006), 209.
23. Those of us tasked to monitor Saddam's state-controlled television and radio during the invasion were stunned by the tenacity Saddam's regime took to keep their radio and television propaganda on the air. It should be studied since it provides an important lesson and unique insight into the critical role this instrument of national power plays on Iraqi and Arab psychology. Despite repeated bombing and other Coalition efforts to knock Iraqi television and radio off the air, the Ba'athists propaganda machine kept broadcasting. Saddam's lieutenants even resorted to using mobile broadcast vans when their fixed facilities could no longer transmit. Saddam's efforts to hold on to his television and radio capabilities could be best summed up in an updated version of the National Rifle Association bumper sticker: "You will get my transmitter when you pry it from my cold, dead fingers!" In July 2006, Hezbollah's Al-Manar displayed similar tenacity, maintaining its propaganda broadcast arm during its war with Israel. Al-Manar defiantly remained on the air throughout the Israeli bombardment and was even disseminated over the Internet.
24. BBC News, "Iran TV Channel Targets Iraq," April 3, 2003, http://news.bbc.co.uk/2/hi/middle_east/2913593.stm
25. Safa Haeri, "Cuba Blows the Whistle on Iranian Jamming," *Arab Times*, August 22, 2003, http://www.atimes.com/atimes/Middle_East/EH22Ak03.html
26. Ricks, *Fiasco*, 206.

27. Associated Press, "GAO Faults Pro-U.S. Effort with Muslims," *Washington Post*, May 3, 2006.
28. Mark Mazzetti, "Pentagon Audit Clears Propaganda Effort," *New York Times*, October 20, 2006, A12.
29. Walter Pincus, "Positive Press on Iraq Is Aim of U.S. Government Contract," *Washington Post*, August 31, 2006.
30. Zaharna, "American Public Diplomacy in the Arab and Muslim World."
31. This theme of a U.S. double standard for Muslims and non-Muslims is pervasive in the Islamic world. For a detailed assessment on how the U.S. policy-message mismatch impacts U.S. public diplomacy in the Islamic world, see Lamis Andoni, "Deeds Speak Louder Than Words," *The Washington Quarterly*, Spring 2002, 85–100; and Jihad Fakhreddine, "The U.S.-Arab Cross-Communication Exchange: A Dialogue amongst Mutes," *Transnational Broadcasting Studies Journal*, Spring 2002, http://www.tbsjournal.com/fakhreddine.html.
32. Carl von Clausewitz, *On War*, trans. and ed. Michael Howard and Peter Paret (Princeton, NJ: Princeton University Press, 1984), 88–89.
33. George F. Kennan, "Sources of Soviet Conduct," *Foreign Affairs*, July 1947, http://www.cnn.com/SPECIALS/cold.war/episodes/04/documents/x.html; National Security Council, *Report 68: U.S. Objectives and Programs for National Security*, April 14, 1950, http://www.fas.org/irp/offdocs/nsc-hst/nsc-68.htm.
34. Ahmed Rashid, *Jihad: The Rise of Militant Islam in Central Asia* (New Haven, CT: Yale University Press, 2002), 3.
35. "Charlotte Beers," *Source Watch: A Project of the Center for Media and Democracy*, http://www.sourcewatch.org/index.php?title=Charlotte_Beers.
36. Frank Capra, *The Name above the Title* (New York: MacMillian, 1971), 331–332.
37. In September 2004, the Defense Science Board released a report on Strategic Communications stating, "Since the Defense Science Board's October 2001 Task Force Study, more than fifteen private sector and Congressional reports have examined Public Diplomacy.... There is a consensus in these reports that U.S. Public Diplomacy is in crisis. Missing are strong leadership, strategic direction, adequate coordination, sufficient resources, and a culture of measurement and evaluation." See Defense Science Board, *Report of the Defense Science Board Task Force on Strategic Communication* (Washington, DC: Office of the Undersecretary of Defense for Acquisition, Technology, and Logistics, September 2004), http://www.acq.osd.mil/dsb/reports/2004-09-Strategic_Communication.pdf.

Chapter 18: Marketing
1. Field Manual (FM) 3-0, *Operations* (Washington, DC: U.S. Government Printing Office, 2001).
2. Ibid.
3. For recent work on PSYOPS in the Pacific Theater, see Alison Gilmore, *You Can't Fight Tanks with Bayonets: Psychological Warfare against the Japanese Army in the Southwest Pacific* (Lincoln: University of Nebraska Press, 1998). For a discussion of American use of propaganda at the strategic level, see Alan M. Winkler, *The Politics of Propaganda: The Office of War Information, 1942–1945* (New Haven, CT: Yale University Press, 1978).
4. The observation about field artillery officers in IO planning reflects the authors' personal experience with officers assigned to IO positions in training and deployments to Kosovo and Iraq. See also Marc Romanych and Kenneth Krumm, "Tactical Information Operations in Kosovo," *Military Review*, September–October 2004, 56–61.
5. Department of the Army, Pamphlet 600-3 *Commissioned Officer Development and*

Career Management (Washington, DC: U.S. Government Printing Office, 1998): 226–229. Currently under revision.
6. U.S. Army Training and Doctrine Command Pamphlet 525-69 *Concept for Information Operations* (Washington, DC: U.S. Government Printing Office, 1995).
7. The 1st Information Operations Command website can be found at www.1stiocmd.army.mil. This particular reference was retrieved from www.1stiocmd.army.mil/aboutLIWA.html.
8. Ibid.
9. Department of Army Pamphlet 600-3 and the 1st IO Command website do not mention marketing skills or training as elements of IO training, although Department of Army Pamphlet 600-3 does refer to Reserve-component IO officers with marketing skills as "a valuable asset."
10. Tom Duncan, *Principles of Advertising and IMC*, 2nd ed. (New York: McGraw-Hill Irwin, 2004), 7.
11. Norman Emery, "Information Operations in Iraq," *Military Review*, September–October 2004, 11–14. Emery refers to an "Insurgent Payoff Function" that provides a simplified relationship between the cost and value of supporting a particular course of action. While oversimplifying the nonlinear interactions of the two, it does attempt to illustrate the need to evaluate, and thus communicate, the utility of supporting U.S. operations among the population.
12. Terry Paul, "Promotional Strategy," class and lecture notes, Ohio State University, Columbus, Ohio, Summer 2004.
13. Duncan, *Principles of Advertising and IMC*, 94–96.
14. Ibid., 111.
15. The example is based on personal experiences of the authors in 1st Armored Division and of CPT Steve Barry in the 3rd Infantry Division.
16. Nancy Pennington and Reid Hastie, "Explaining the Evidence: Tests of the Story Model for Juror Decision Making," *Journal of Personality and Social Psychology* 62, no. 2 (Winter 1992): 189–206.
17. Paul, "Promotional Strategy."
18. Duncan, *Principles of Advertising and IMC*, 117–125.
19. The example is based on the authors' personal experiences in the 1st Armored Division.
20. George E. Anderson, "Winning the Nationbuilding War," *Military Review*, September–October 2004, 48. The authors witnessed similar experiences in the Balkans and Iraq.
21. Duncan, *Principles of Advertising and IMC*, 54–55.
22. National Public Radio News, *All Things Considered*, July 12, 2004.
23. Ibid.

Chapter 19: Religion in Information Operations
1. Or for that matter, anywhere else on the globe as all religions are involved with the issues of life and death and therefore contribute to our understanding of warfare.
2. Critics cited in "From Uncle Ben's to Uncle Sam," *The Economist*, February 2002, 70.
3. It is also important to note that there was a belief that individuals could not and would not be "objective," but would bring personal beliefs into the analysis inappropriately.
4. There were countering arguments that the ideology did not fail, but rather that the economy failed for Communist states.
5. If I behaved the way my Christian theology teaches, assuming I had a clear understanding of that theology, I would probably be a far different person. It may be natural to assume that many Muslims do not understand the theology of Islam and that even if they do, they may not practice it "perfectly."
6. Writers trying to "explain" the nature of contemporary religion as it relates to armed

conflict tend toward three explanations: (1) religious exceptionalism; (2) comparative fundamentalisms, i.e., religion as a social movement trying to return to the idealized past with the help of God and use of modern technology; and (3) a political movement based on class analysis—the poor trying to make up the difference through violence.
7. A particularly good example of this is the word "fundamentalist," which has been defined coherently, cogently, and accurately by such experts as Scott Appleby in the Fundamentalism Project from Harvard University. Scott Appleby, *Ambivalence of the Sacred: Religion, Violence, and Reconciliation* (Lanham, MD: Rowman & Littlefield, 2000).
8. Note religious factors in Christianity, Judaism, Islam, Hinduism, Buddhism, and other traditions as found in Croatia-Serbia-Bosnia, Ireland, Israel, Palestine, Kashmir, Nepal, Chechnya, Tibet, Somalia, Rwanda, Haiti, and, of course, Iraq, Iran, and Afghanistan.
9. There is a paucity of good research data and analysis possibly because scholars tend not to agree simply on how to define and tabulate statistics on (a) when religion is the primary factor, and/ or (b) when religion plays a role in the escalation and maintenance of conflict. Current research tends to be politically or religiously motivated and thus inherently biased. In the recent volume by Mark Juergensmeyer, *Terror in the Mind of God: The Global Rise of Religious Violence* (Berkeley: University of California Press, 2002), Juergensmeyer provides information and analysis of six terrorist groups. His work provides clear evidence of both the global nature of the violence and the fact that all major "global" religions are somehow implicated.
10. See Jonathan Fox, *Ethnoreligious Conflict in the Late Twentieth Century* (Lanham, MD: Lexington Books, 2002); or Jonathan Fox, "Do Religious Institutions Support Violence or the Status Quo?" *Studies in Conflict and Terrorism* 22 (April 1999): 119–139.
11. Even the Apostle Paul warned against endless disputations or arguing incessantly over genealogies in the epistle of First Timothy.
12. The works of Scott Appleby, Douglas Johnston, Michael Walzer, and Marc Gopin are unusual in regard to their comprehensiveness, timeliness, and focus on global applications of theological concerns.
13. I have personally witnessed a number of attempts to solve a problem that were stopped at the first sentence. A U.S. representative used a word such as "jihad" incorrectly or inappropriately, and the Muslim found it necessary to "correct" and went into endless explanations of the definitions of "jihad." Nothing was accomplished except to raise the frustration level of all concerned.
14. These are a combination of the author's understanding of information operations and the brilliant work of Marc Gopin, *Healing the Heart of Conflict* (New York: Rodale Press, 2004).

Chapter 20: Telling the Afghan Military Story . . . Their Way
1. At the time this chapter was written, the Ministry of Defence public affairs staff of thirty-three was supported by two "hard" phone lines and fewer than ten cell phones. The office maintained two computers with intermittent Internet access and a single commercial e-mail account. The MOD established a computer network on December 20, 2004.
2. MOD or personal video crews usually accompany Minister of Defense Abdul Rahim Wardak, Chief of Staff to the Commander in Chief GEN Abdul Rashid Dostum, and other senior leaders to document their daily activities, which are often broadcast on Afghan television.
3. The four regional corps—Kandahar, Gardez, Mazar-e-Sharif, and Herat—were established in September 2004 but had no PA staffs until June 2005. In the interim, field commanders worked willingly with local news media, many of whom they had known during the decades of conflict.

4. The cited literacy rate represents a midpoint of various estimates; its accuracy is compromised by the fact that girls and women did not attend school from 1996 to 2002. Commercial competition for government radio and television is beginning to appear, but its penetration is limited by the same factors limiting government broadcasts. Afghan National Army and Combined Forces Command-Afghanistan recruiting efforts have produced a few useful localized opinion surveys, but no credible nationwide database is available.
5. As of mid-July 2005, MG Mohammed Zahir Azimi and his staff were operating with final drafts of the MOD directive that established the Office of Parliamentary, Social Relations, and Public Affairs; the Afghan MOD "Public Affairs Systems Guide"; the "Guide to News Media Center Procedures," which included "News Media Facilitation and Ground Rules," the "Guide to Conducting News Briefings and Press Conferences," and the "Crisis Communications Guide"; a "Glossary of Public Affairs Terms" to establish a common language for operations and training; "MOD Public Affairs Directive 1," establishing the MOD public affairs system; "MOD Public Affairs Directive 2," outlining MOD PA planning; and PA doctrine discussing PA fundamentals, functions, and responsibilities. Also, seven final draft parliamentary affairs directives were in place to guide communications with the National Assembly. Azimi and his staff participated in the work-group process that developed each of these documents.
6. The opening lines of a news conference statement dated December 12, 2004, give us an example of the literary language Afghans prefer: "The Beautiful State of Afghanistan, with a long history of evolving civilizations, is now entering a new stage of its history, one that it has never experienced before. After three decades of war, the Afghan Nation has now decided to head towards Peace and Freedom. Freedom, which is the right of humankind, is exercised by electing the new president by free and fair elections."
7. Western PA training took place in February 2004 and August 2005, the first provided by in-country PA assets and the second by a mobile training team (MTT). Both sessions provided high-quality instruction to Afghanistan's new PA officers. However, trainers in the first session spent considerable time focusing on the development and repetition of messages and slogans. As most of the Afghans are former political officers who worked under the Soviet model, they are skilled in messaging and sloganeering. The important new skills they need concern collecting, processing, and communicating information. The MTT also spent the better part of two days training the Afghans on Western writing styles, including the inverted pyramid structure, for communicating with Western reporters and audiences. As a rule, however, Western reporters do not attend MOD news conferences or events; moreover, it is reasonable to assume that today's limited Western media interest in Afghan affairs will only decrease as stability increases. Thus, Afghan MOD PAOs must learn to communicate with Afghan and regional news media and audiences, not with those of Western countries.
8. Ironically, modern technology that brings events to us in real time does not automatically breed understanding of what success and victory look like. The public needs to be regularly reminded of the goals of any conflict and how each day's events contribute to achieving those goals.
9. CFC-A publishes an excellent daily summary of articles covering issues of interest within Afghanistan and around the region. Of particular interest is the section that tracks Afghan news reporting. The MOD also operates a media monitoring section that closely tracks coverage of issues within Afghanistan, especially those dealing with the defense establishment.
10. For more information, see UN General Assembly Security Council, Report A/59/58 5/2004/925, 59th sess., http://www.unamaafg.org/docs/_UNDocs/_repots-SG/2004/2004/-925.pdf. On November 4, 2004, the Joint Election Management Board

and the UN announced a final voter turnout of 70 percent. More than eight million Afghans went to the polls, including refugee voters in Iran and Pakistan.
11. Perhaps the most dramatic prevention of an attack came when authorities, acting on a tip, were able to stop fuel trucks trying to enter Kandahar just before the presidential election. The trucks were to be detonated inside the city. Azimi reported this success during his briefings on election day, October 9, 2004.
12. The usual Western practice is to contact reporters privately and attempt to correct the record quietly. Azimi's approach proved successful within the Afghan environment.
13. Beginning in April 2005, daily CFC-A news summaries contained stories referring to the Taliban spokesman, usually Mullah Abdul Latifi Hakimi, as the "purported Taliban spokesman" and noted the "uncertain credibility" of his reports. On October 5, 2005, Pakistan reported that two days earlier it had captured Hakimi in the border region between Afghanistan's Zabul Province and Pakistan.
14. Azimi's primary forum for delivering his messages was his weekly news conference, *Newsweek,* May 15, 2005. He imparted the same messages to individual reporters when queried.
15. Ascertaining the accuracy of this figure is difficult in a country whose population size is open to conjecture. However, Azimi regularly uses 2.5 million in his public statements and President Hamid Karzai cited the same number in public remarks at the National Day Parade, April 28, 2005.
16. T. E. Lawrence, "The Twenty-Seven Articles of T. E. Lawrence," *The Arab Bulletin*, August 1917, http://www.lawrenceofarabia.info.

Chapter 21: Army IO Is PSYOPS
1. For more on this topic see Susan L. Gough, "The Evolution of Strategic Influence," U.S. Army War College Strategic Research Paper (Carlisle, PA: U.S. Army War College, 2003), http://fas.org/irp/eprint/gough.pdf. See also Kim Cragin and Scott Gerwehr, *Dissuading Terror: Strategic Influence and the Struggle against Terrorism* (Santa Monica, Ca: RAND, 2005).
2. Joint Publication 3-13, *Information Operations: Doctrine, Tactics, Techniques, Procedures* (Washington, DC: U.S. Government Printing Office, 2003); *Information Operations* (Washington, DC: U.S. Government Printing Office, 2005), ix. For a discussion of the evolution of Army IO doctrine, see Richard H. Wright, "Information Operations: Doctrine, Tactics, Techniques and Procedures," *Military Review*, March–April 2001, 30–32.
3. Joint Publication 3-13, 132.
4. David l. Grange and James A. Kelly, "Victory through Information Dominance," *Army*, March 1997, 33–37.
5. Bob Woodward, *Plan of Attack* (New York: Simon & Schuster, 2004), 57, 77, 108, 110–111, 126.
6. Nathaniel Fick, *Economics of National Security* (Cambridge, MA: Harvard University National Bureau for Economic Research, March 7, 2006).
7. Hampton Stephens, "It's All Info Ops to Me," *Defense Tech*, April 6, 2006.
8. Department of Defense, *Psychological Operations Master Plan* (Washington, DC: Department of Defense, March 1990).
9. See Center for Army Lessons Learned, "Information Operations at Brigade Combat Team and Division," Call Newsletter 04–13, Operation Iraqi Freedom (OIF). Impressions Report (IIR), Topics E and F, http://www.globalsecurity.org/military/library/report/call/call 04-13 chap01-e.htm; and http://www.globalsecurity.org/military/library/report/call/call 04-13 chap01-f.htm. For lessons learned from Desert Shield/Storm, see the *Conduct of the Persian Gulf War*, Final Report to Congress (Washington, DC: National Defense University, April 1992), www.ndu.edu/library/epubs/cpgw.pdf, 623.

10. See Defense Science Board, *Managed Information Dissemination* (Washington, DC: Office of Undersecretary of Defense for Acquisition, Technology, and Logistics, October 2001), 5; Defense Science Board, *The Creation and Dissemination of All Forms of Information in Support of Psychological Operations (PSYOPS) in Time of Military Conflict* (Washington, DC: Office of Undersecretary of Defense for Acquisition, Technology, and Logistics, May 2000), 1.3, 2.1, http://cryptome.org/dsb-psyop.htm#chapter%202; Defense Science Board, *Strategic Communication* (Washington, DC: Office of Undersecretary of Defense for Acquisition, Technology, and Logistics, September 2004), http://www.fas.org/irp/agency/dod/dsb/commun.pdf; National Defense University, "Review of Psychological Operations Lessons Learned from Recent Operational Experiences," *Institute for National Strategic Studies* 30 (October 2004).
11. Jerrold M. Post, "Psychological Operations and Counterterrorism," *Joint Forces Quarterly* 37 (April 2005): 105–110.
12. For more discussion on the term "PSYOPS," see Lynne Duke, "The World at War," *Washington Post*, March 26, 2006, D1; Thomas H. Taylor, "By Any Other Name," *Perspectives* 5 (Spring 1989): 9; and Fred W. Walker, "PSYOPS Is a Nasty Term—Too Bad," *Air University Review* 28 (September–October 1977).

Chapter 22: Estimates, Execution, and Error
1. U.S. Marine Corps, *Small Wars Manual* (Washington, DC: U.S. Government Printing Office, 1940), 13.
2. George W. Allen, *None So Blind: A Personal Account of the Intelligence Failure in Vietnam* (Chigaco: Ivan R. Dee, 2001), 194–195.
3. This is not to say the NLF received no assistance and guidance from the DRV; it certainly did to some extent prior to the Tet Offensive and did to a far greater degree afterward.
4. Two schools of thought emerged that would collide with each other time and time again throughout the period of major U.S. military intervention. The first was articulated in the early 1960s by Ambassador Frederick E. "Fritz" Nolting Jr., then the senior State Department official in Saigon, and Gen Edward Lansale, USAF, a recognized counterinsurgency expert. This particular perspective argued that the war was fought and had to be won by the indigenous RVN government first and foremost. U.S. efforts should be seen primarily as aiding a sovereign nation. Any attempts at reforming RVN domestic policy would be confined to political persuasion and setting the example. A crucial element in Nolting's and Landale's assessment was that the inefficiency of Saigon was not systemic but instead resulted from NLF actions to make it so. The other concept was held by the Central Intelligence Agency and a number of Special Forces operatives; it saw the Saigon regime as much as the cause of the insurgency problem as the NLF. Eric Bergerud, *The Dynamics of Defeat: The Vietnam War in Hau Nghia Province* (Boulder, CO: Westview Press, 1991), 32.
5. "I had seen nothing during my tour to even remotely suggest that the South Vietnamese government could or would purge itself of the corruption that so hindered its cause and assisted the Communists. I know all too well from conversations with countless Vietnamese that any attack against corruption would have to be initiated from Saigon. 'The roof leaks from the top on down . . .' was the favorite Vietnamese aphorism my friends were fond of quoting each time we discussed the subject of corruption." Stuart A. Herrington, *Silence Was a Weapon: The Vietnam War in the Villages* (Novato, CA: Presidio Press, 1982), 201.
  "The South Vietnamese government was corrupt. . . . There were some dedicated people driven by feeling nationalistic pride, but most of the field grade officers under General Lam at I Corps were just a bunch of fat cats. I feel very strongly that the South Vietnamese government was destroyed from within by the self-serving attitude of those

entrusted to save their country." Capt Thomas Moore, USMC (Ret.), in Al Hemingway, *Our War Was Different: Marine Combined Action Platoons in Vietnam* (Annapolis, MD: Naval Institute Press, 1994), 151.

Not only was the inability of the RVN apparent in the field, but also to CIA analysts writing intelligence for the President of the United States. See Center for the Study of Intelligence, *CIA and the Vietnam Policymakers: Three Episodes, 1962–1968* (Washington, DC: CSI Publications, 1998), particularly the chapter entitled "Three Episodes in Perspective," https://www.cia.gov/library/center-for-the-study-of-intelligence/csi-publications/books-and-monographs/cia-and-the-vietnam-policymakers-three-episodes-1962-1968/epis3a.html.

6. Mark Moyar, *Triumph Forsaken: The Vietnam War, 1954–1965* (Cambridge: Cambridge University Press, 2006), 407.

7. Secretary McNamara also laid out the specific faults of the GVN and ARVN: "The first essential reform is in the attitude of GVN officials. They are generally apathetic, and there is corruption high and low. Often appointments, promotions, and draft determents must be bought; and kickbacks on salaries are common. Cadre at the bottom can be no better than the system above them.

"The second needed reform is in the attitudes and conduct of the ARVN. The image of the government cannot improve unless and until the ARVN improve markedly. They do not understand the importance (or respectability) of pacification nor the importance to pacification of proper, disciplined conduct. Promotions, assignments, and awards are often not made on merit, but rather on the basis of having a diploma, friends, or relatives, or because of bribery. The ARVN is weak in dedication, direction, and discipline." James William Gibson, *The Perfect War: TechnoWar in Vietnam* (Boston: Atlantic Monthly Press, 1986), 274–275.

8. "From Washington, far from the frustrations of the village struggle, the war was viewed within the context of overall U.S. foreign and domestic policy. . . . A policy based on the assumption that the GVN was corrupt, rotten, and basically responsible for the conditions of the insurgency would have been extremely difficult to defend." Bergerud, *Dynamics of Defeat*, 112.

9. The problem dated back to the Kennedy days in dealing with Diem and his brother Nhu prior to the 1963 coup that ousted them. Despite calls from Washington to change the RVN government's domestic policies, Pentagon military advisers would argue that Diem was not going to be persuaded as he had to appear not to be a U.S. puppet. So U.S. assistance was eventually provided when requested—any withholding of resources was perceived as weakening the war effort against the common Communist enemy. Ibid., 30.

10. In the summer of 1965 when Saigon was tottering on the brink of defeat, the United States Operations Mission (USOM) accused the Binh Tuy province chief of misusing a quarter million dollars of USAID funds, yet the RVN government took no action. USOM stopped all resourcing to the Binh Tuy province and even withdrew its liaison personnel. The GVN relented and fired the province chief, but as it had lost face in the press because of this, GVN officials complained to Ambassador Henry Cabot Lodge. Lodge ensured that USOM understood in no uncertain terms that this would not happen again. It never did, despite further misappropriations elsewhere. Ibid., 107.

11. Gibson, *Perfect War*, 275–278.

12. Jeffrey Kimball, *Nixon's Vietnam War* (Lawrence: University of Kansas Press, 1998), 337.

13. Frances Fitzgerald, *Fire in the Lake: The Vietnamese and the Americans in Vietnam* (Boston: Little, Brown, 1972), 196.

14. Jeffrey Record, *The Wrong War: Why We Lost in Vietnam* (Annapolis, MD: Naval Institute Press, 1998), 73.

15. Instead, U.S. planners at the Military Advisory/Assistance Group (MAAG)—and subsequently in 1965 within the Military Assistance Command-Vietnam (MACV)—continuously focused on conventional operations to engage the Communist enemy in the field. They drew up plans for RVNAF operations, translated them into Vietnamese, and issued orders to the units. The Vietnamese did not often comply with the spirit, if they even understood the letter, of these instructions. Senior RVNAF military leaders were content not to argue with the Americans but yet still follow their own agendas when push came to shove. See discussions of the Hop Tac ARVN operations around Saigon in Bergerud, *Dynamics of Defeat*, 41–42, and assessed by Gibson, *Perfect War*, 270–271. Also see Gabriel Kolko, *Anatomy of a War: Vietnam, the United States, and the Modern Historical Experience* (New York: Pantheon Books, 1985), 242.

16. "[The] military can hardly be faulted for correctly concluding that the RVNAF was simply not up to the task of defeating its communist opponents. Indeed, it was perhaps the very combination of self-confidence and disdain for the RVNAF as a military ally that accounted for the MACV's relative disinterest before the Tet Offensive in preparing the South Vietnamese military for the day when U.S. forces would depart Vietnam. MACV, CINCPAC, and the JCS all seemed to assume that U.S. forces could finish the job once and for all, and that there would be a postwar residual U.S. presence in South Vietnam as there was in Korea, to stand guard against a re-eruption of communist aggression." Record, *Wrong War*, 72.

17. Kolko, *Anatomy of a War*, 234. Jack Radey, contributor to the VHS video series *Vietnam Combat*, makes yet another insight: "What do they [the RVNAF] gain by being aggressive and taking the initiative? OK, take an ARVN unit out into the field, and get aggressive. Are the troops well motivated? Trained? What are the possible outcomes? Worst case, of course, is you get your clock cleaned. The NLF probably has ears in your own HQ, or if not, will be unlikely to be surprised. Maybe you just get to Search and get booby trapped for days, either way, you lose people. Which means you have less men on the payroll, so less you can skim, are less valuable a political piece in internal politics, maybe lose equipment which may be expensive to get replaced, etc. In either case you make it clear to everyone in the area that you are weak and vulnerable. Get too aggressive, and maybe get killed. If you succeed, say, and roll up some small NLF units, maybe you look good, get a promotion, the good will [of the Americans], etc. Just as likely you cause jealousy, your boss claims the credit, and you get in trouble for doing something without permission. So where is your incentive? If the cash flow is good, what is so bad about go along and get along by a puppet officer? He has no cause to motivate him, and no reason to stick his neck out." Radey, e-mail to the author, May 30, 2007.

18. Kolko, *Anatomy of a War*, 232.

19. The NLF was conscientious in leaving corrupt and inefficient officials in place, propagandizing against them as examples of all that was wrong with the Saigon regime.

20. Bergerud, *Dynamics of Defeat*, 18–19.

21. Jeffrey Race, *War Comes to Long An: Revolutionary Conflict in a Vietnamese Province* (Berkeley: University of California Press, 1972), 180.

22. Just how "rapport" was to be established across cultural, social, and political lines—particularly when "counterparts" had far different personal and professional goals that "setting the example" would not often influence—was not definitely explained. Bergerud, *Dynamics of Defeat*, 105.

23. While Lansdale sought autonomy and protection from Saigon and Washington for his advisers, this did not happen. Whatever coercive controls the advisers originally had through disbursing of funds to their Vietnamese counterparts were eventually halted. Ibid.,106.

24. GVN officials—members of the South Vietnamese urban elite—often used unwitting

advisers to pursue their own schemes. More frequently, U.S. advisers were kept at a distance, perceived as "untutored and uncultured" troops who "had to be tolerated." Advisers were paradoxically cautioned to let "the Vietnamese way" be practiced yet to report and stop corruption in order to "energize" the Vietnamese war effort. As we have seen at the strategic political level, there was little will within U.S. decision-making circles—even at the tactical level—to pay heed to or act positively upon adviser reports of corruption. Ibid., 156. See also CPT David Harrington's comments (page 232) about the distance between advisers and ARVN counterparts enforced by one province chief even after Tet.

25. During the conventional "Americanization" of the Vietnam War, the adviser effort was a distant second place to the main force "search and destroy" operations mounted in the countryside. Assignment to these adviser elements was not as prestigious or career enhancing as the U.S. troop command billets, particularly given that the focus of MACV was on the larger conventional campaigns and that the natural tendency of U.S. military bureaucracy to reinforce more traditional (i.e., recognizable) career paths and patterns. For more on this "Army Concept," see Andrew F. Krepinevich, Jr., *The Army and Vietnam* (Baltimore: Johns Hopkins University Press, 1986).

26. Eric Bergerud describes the role and influence of the American intervention forces thusly: "Although the goal of comprehensive security for the population . . . continually eluded allied forces, American ground troops were indispensable. They were used to guard installations, open roads, make difficult or impossible enemy main force operations, impede insurgent political activities during daylight, and occupy hamlets controlled by the NLF for years. Most importantly, [their] presence . . . promised a breathing space for Saigon during which it would have the opportunity to create forces appropriate to a renewal of the political struggle." Bergerud, *Dynamics of Defeat*, 105.

27. Consider this leaflet disseminated by the 25th Infantry Division—and note the coercive elements in the tone of the translation: "[English Translation: Side1] The U.S. soldiers of the 25th Infantry Division have been in your area making it safe by clearing the area of VC. You have only seen a small part of our mission strength. This mighty force, known the world over, stands ready to make your life safe. [Side 2] Your friends, the U.S. soldiers of the 25th Infantry Division, are here to help you. We will give you medical assistance when you need it. We can build schools, bridges, roads to make life easier for you. Help us together to defeat the VC forever." *25th Operational Reports, Lessoned Learned* (May 1 –July 31, 1966), 25, cited in Bergerud, *Dynamics of Defeat*, 155.

28. Bergerud calls the "ruff-puff" forces "next to worthless." Ibid., 327. Study after U.S. study articulated low opinions of the effectiveness of these troops in the rural villages of South Vietnam. National Security Council and RAND Corporation papers noted widespread criminal behavior of these troops, including murder, rape, extortion, and theft. South Vietnamese villagers had no confidence that these military units—supposedly charged to defend them from Communist depredations—could actually be relied upon for their security. Gibson, *Perfect War*, 279–280.

29. When RF/PF units performed well, it was usually because they were teamed with U.S. forces since they then received better logistical and medical support than what would otherwise be the case. Some simply did not want to lose face in front of the Americans. Bergerud, *Dynamics of Defeat*, 269.

30. In late 1967, 25th Infantry Division observers lamented: "In recent advisor/training missions with RF/PF forces, D Troop Aero Rifles have found that RF/PF shortcomings are attributable more to lack of RF/PF command and leadership than lack of training. They appeared reluctant to disrupt the local balance of power and have explicitly voiced fear of retribution if Viet Cong are aggressively pursued. This is partially understandable in view of their lack of appropriate weapons and low ammunition supply. . . . However,

they are capable of sound tactical maneuvers at squad, platoon, and company levels. They lack only the will to kill VC." *25th ID Operational Reports, Lessoned Learned* (November 1, 1967–January 31, 1968), 29, cited in Bergerud, *Dynamics of Defeat*, 167.

31. While the troops might have been recruited from the farms, their leaders generally were not and thus held little regard for the poor rural peasants whose land they traversed and whose lives they so often disrupted or ended. Kolko, *Anatomy of a War*, 235.
32. George W. Allen, an Indochina hand at CIA, relates, "After the Diem coup, however, wholesale changes occurred in most positions at almost every level. Following the second coup—just ten weeks after Diem was overthrown—when General 'Big Minh' was displaced by General Khanh, a second set of sweeping changes occurred, and this pattern of wholesale 'purges' continued after each of the successive changes of government that erupted during the turbulent period that ended in June 1965 when Generals Nguyen Cao Ky and Nguyen Van Thieu finally stabilized the military hierarchy. Each new head of government in his turn had purged key military police, and civilian officials whom he trusted (and who were willing to meet his 'price' for the job). And each of these subordinates then brought in his 'loyal' friends and relatives into key staff and command positions under his control, and so on down the line. The city of Da Nang had five mayors and five police intelligence chiefs during the year following the Diem coup but that was far from unique." Allen, *None So Blind*, 178.
33. The results were not hard to predict, as a hamlet chief from Thu Thua pointed out: "You want to know how the communists got into our strategic hamlet? All of us in the Combat Youth were poor people. We asked ourselves, why should we be carrying rifles and risking our lives when Xoai's son doesn't have to? His family is rich and has used its power to get him out of it. When the communists come in, they never bother us—they go to the homes of those who got rich by taking from others. Are we so stupid to protect them?" Race, *War Comes to Long An*, 181.
34. Bergerud, *Dynamics of Defeat*, 33. John Paul Vann himself was extremely vocal in his criticism of the government, saying in his 1965 thesis, "Harnessing the Revolution in South Vietnam": "The existing government is oriented toward the exploitation of the rural and lower class urban population. It is, in fact, a continuation of the French colonial system of government with upper-class Vietnamese replacing the French. Although the wealth of the country lies in its agricultural production, it is the agrarian population which is realizing the least out of either the technological advancements of the twentieth century or the massive assistance provided by the U.S." John Vann, *Harnessing the Revolution in South Vietnam* (CMH Publications, 1965), 7, cited in Bergerud, *Dynamics of Defeat*, 108.
35. Vann had no qualms about having the label of "U.S. imperialists" applied to the Americans by either the South Vietnamese or anyone else. Any characterization of the RVN as a U.S. "puppet" did not bother him either, particularly as he thought the Communists and other adversaries of the allies already were using that terminology. Ibid., 113.
36. Neil Sheehan, *A Bright and Shining Lie: John Paul Vann and America in Vietnam* (New York: Random House, 1988), 631.
37. Hemingway, *Our War Was Different*, x.
38. Tom Harvey in ibid., 83; Maj Edward Palm in ibid., 39; and Michael E. Peterson, *The Combined Action Platoons: The U.S. Marines' Other War in Vietnam* (New York: Praeger Publishers, 1989), 123.
39. Local RVN officials were only too happy to let the Marines do the hard work, as any show of effectiveness on their part would often entail violent NLF retribution.
40. Record, *Wrong War*, 94.
41. While the U.S.-sponsored efforts such as the "Civil Operations and Revolutionary

Development Support" and RVN pacification programs continued to espouse reformist rhetoric in senior decision-making circles, after Tet the United States and the RVN had even less reason to "sell" their ideas to the peasants given that their competitor for "hearts and minds"—the NLF—had impaled itself on allied firepower and suffered catastrophic casualties.

42. Eric Bergerud explains how this occurred in one particular province in the vicinity of Saigon: "The central position of force and coercion for the political struggle in Hau Nghia [Province] was rarely, if ever, more clear than during the APC. . . . In contrast to earlier pacification initiatives, the APC involved virtually no talk about 'revolutionary development' or any sort of social transformation. Rather, the goal was very simply to establish an armed Government of Vietnam presence in contested or Front-controlled hamlets." Bergerud, *Dynamics of Defeat*, 224.
43. Ibid., 234–235.
44. U.S. Marine Corps, *Small Wars Manual*, 15.
45. Bergerud, *Dynamics of Defeat*, 326.
46. "The need to cope with daily pressures of existence now began to create a cleavage between the peasant and the NLF, to an extent which greatly encouraged Americans to continue these relentless pressures, but its terror did not strengthen its political alternative. On the contrary, such violence began to alienate and depoliticize, for practical purposes, an increasingly important section of the south's population—and to create an insolvable political crisis for its RVN dependents from which only the NLF could benefit." Kolko, *Anatomy of a War*, 143.
47. Mark Moyar attributed the strength of the early NLF on its ability to field better overall leaders than what the Diem government could provide, citing this as the result of "political and cultural differences." See Moyar, *Triumph Forsaken,* xv. Bergerud also offers his penetrating analysis: "So it really did not matter whether or not the Front had the support of the majority of the peasantry. . . . The Party had what it needed, the support of the most politically aware and most determined segment of the peasantry. There can be no doubt that, in Hau Nghia [Province] and several other provinces, the Front has a virtual lock on the 'best and brightest' of rural youth. The revolutionary movement that had demolished the RVN in Hau Nghia by 1965, although controlled by outsiders, was locally recruited and self-sustaining." Bergerud, *Dynamics of Defeat*, 326.
48. Bergerud, *Dynamics of Defeat*, 327–328.

Chapter 24: Between War and Peace
1. Sam C. Sarkesian, "Low Intensity Conflict: Concepts, Principles, and Policy Guidelines," *Air University Review* 36, no. 3 (May–June 1985): 4–23.
2. Barry D. Crane, Joel Leson, Robert A. Plebanek, Paul Shemella, Ronald Smith, and Richard Williams, "Between Peace and War: Comprehending Low-Intensity Conflict," *Special Warfare*, Summer 1989.
3. Department of Defense, *Department of Defense Dictionary of Military and Associated Terms*, Joint Chiefs of Staff Publication 1 (Washington, DC: U.S. Government Printing Office, 1986).
4. Crane and others, "Between Peace and War."
5. Ibid.
6. Ibid.
7. Ibid.
8. Ibid.
9. Sarkesian, "Low-Intensity Conflict."
10. Wesley A. Groesbeck, "Training to Win Hearts and Minds," *Army*, April 1998.
11. Ibid.

12. Crane and others, "Between Peace and War."
13. Ibid.
14. Ibid.
15. Ibid.
16. Ibid.
17. Ibid.
18. Ibid.
19. James R. Locher III, "Low-Intensity Conflict and the Changing Nature of Warfare," *Infantry*, September–October 1991.
20. John R. Galvin, "Uncomfortable Wars: Toward a New Paradigm," *Parameters* 16, no. 4 (1986).
21. Ibid.
22. John F. Kennedy, speech at U.S. Military Academy graduation, West Point, NY, June 6, 1962.
23. John F. Stewart, "Military Intelligence Operations in Low-Intensity Conflict: An Organizational Model," *Military Review*, January 1988.

Chapter 25: Are We Outsmarting Ourselves?
1. Among recent organizational changes is the Navy's new enlisted mass communications specialty, which merges print and broadcast journalism with photography, videography, and graphic production. The Air Force has placed public affairs within a directorate of strategic communications scheme and is integrating its public affairs and visual information capabilities. The Air Force also abandoned hard-copy command newspapers in favor of exclusively Web products.
2. William M. Darley, "Why Public Affairs Is Not Information Operations," *Army*, January 2005, 9–10.
3. Todd Sholtis, "Public Affairs and Information Operations: A Strategy for Success," *Air & Space Power Journal*, Fall 2005, 97–106.
4. Mark A. Brilakis, "Martian Alert!" *Proceedings*, January 2006, 37–40. Here, Colonel Brilakis quotes former Marine Commandant Gen Michael Hagee. While the thrust of Brilakis's discussion is a criticism of expensive (and perhaps unnecessary) military hardware, his points apply to the information debate—i.e., bigger, costlier, and more sophisticated are not necessarily better.
5. Walter Boomer, "Stop Whining," *Proceedings*, July 1997, 2.
6. Often lost in information policy debates is the nation's small but talented population of military journalists. See, for example, Keith Oliver, "Combat Correspondents: Reporters in Uniform," *Proceedings*, August 2005, 74–75.
7. Keith Oliver, "Back to the Future in Public Affairs," *Marine Corps Gazette*, March 2003, 42.
8. Keith A. Milks, "22d MEU Public Affairs in the Forgotten War," *Marine Corps Gazette*, August 2004, 50–51.
9. Brilakis, "Martian Alert!"
10. Glenn Kessler, "Rice Names Critic of Iraq Policy to Counselor's Post," *Washington Post*, March 2, 2007, A5.

Chapter 28: Massing Effects in the Information Domain
1. Ayman al-Zawahiri, intercepted letter to Abu Musab al-Zarqawi, July 9, 2005, www.dni.gov/letter_in_english.pdf.
2. Secretary of Defense Donald Rumsfeld, in response to a question after a speech at the Army War College (Carlisle Barracks, PA, March 27, 2006).
3. Joseph J. Collins, "An Open Letter to President Bush," *Armed Forces Journal* 143, no. 6 (January 2006): 28, http://www.armedforcesjournal.com/story.php?F=1403423_0106.

4. Ralph Peters, "The Counterrevolution in Military Affairs: Fashionable Thinking about Defense Ignores the Great Threats of Our Time," *The Weekly Standard* 11, no. 2 (February 6, 2006).
5. Thomas F. Metz, "The Battle of Fallujah: A Case Study for Warfare in the Information Age," briefing to the Capitol Bohemian Club, Washington, DC, October 26, 2005.
6. The Digital Video and Imagery Distribution System (DVIDS) feeds a signal from a portable machine to a satellite. News stations can pull the signal from the DVIDS's website either live or from stored data on the site. It was first used in Iraq in 2004.
7. Thom Shanker, "No Breach Seen in Work in Iraq on Propaganda," *New York Times* (March 22, 2006).
8. Kenneth Payne, "The Media as an Instrument of War," *Parameters* 35, no. 1 (Spring 2005): 81. Retrieved from http://www.carlisle.army.mil/usawc/Parameters/05spring/payne.htm.
9. Shanker, "No Breach Seen."

Chapter 29: Getting Inside the Cultural Context and Achieving Intelligence Success
1. The Commission on the Intelligence Capabilities of the United States Regarding Weapons of Mass Destruction, *Report to the President of the United States* (Washington, DC: Government Printing Office, March 31, 2005), transmittal letter.
2. Ibid., 3.
3. Associated Press, "Report Joins 10 Others on Intelligence Failures," MSNBC, March 31, 2005, http://www.msnbc.msn.com/id/7345568/.
4. David Johnston and Scott Shane, "Study Faults Response to Outlawed Arms," *New York Times*, March 31, 2005, A10.
5. Thomas Fingar, then-head of the National Intelligence Council and now deputy director of National Intelligence for Analysis, quoted in Graham Allison, "How Good Is America's Intelligence on Iran's Bomb?" *YaleGlobal Online*, June 2006, http://yaleglobal.yale.edu/display.article? id=7553 (accessed March 3, 2007). This estimate was reiterated by newly confirmed Director of National Intelligence ADM John M. "Mike" McConnell in testimony before the Senate Armed Services Committee ("While our information is incomplete, we estimate Iran could produce a nuclear weapon by early to mid next decade"), as quoted in Jim Garamone, "Terror, Iran, North Korea Top List of Threats," *American Forces Press Service*, February 2007, http://www.defenselink.mil/News/NewsArticle.aspx?id=3214 (accessed March 3, 2007).
6. Julian Borger, "US Intelligence on Iran Does Not Stand Up, Say Vienna Sources," *The Guardian Unlimited*, February 23, 2007, http://www.guardian.co.uk/frontpage/story/0,,2019666,00.html (accessed March 3, 2007).
7. David E. Sanger and William J. Broad, "U.S. Had Doubts on North Korean Uranium Drive," *New York Times*, March 2007, http://www.nytimes.com/2007/03/01/washington/01korea.html?em&ex=1172984400&en= b948b78063 e4fd7d&ei=5087%0A (accessed March 3, 2007).
8. Markus Wolf, *Man without a Face: The Autobiography of Communism's Greatest Spymaster*, with Anne McElvoy (New York: Times Books, 1997), 285.
9. MG Robert H. Scales, Jr., U.S. Army, "Culture-Centric Warfare," *Proceedings*, October 2004, 32.
10. Regarding the importance of foreign languages see Newt Gingrich, "Status of the Office of the Director of National Intelligence," testimony before the House Permanent Select Committee on Intelligence, Subcommittee on Oversight, 109th Cong., 1st sess., October 19, 2005 (transcript provided by the American Enterprise Institute for Public Policy Research, http://www.aei.org/publications/filter.all,pubID.23345/pub_detail.asp [accessed October 27, 2005]). In appendix 2 of Gingrich's testimony he addresses in greater detail one of the reasons for the Intelligence Community's failure to penetrate

North Korea. He notes, "We have been involved in Korea in one way or another since 1945. We have been committed to the active defense of South Korea since 1950. Yet only 35% of our Korean analysts speak any Korean. Only 10% of our analysts are fluent in Korean. So that means that 90% of Korean analysts are unable to read the newspapers or only marginally understand the newscasts from the country that they are responsible for briefing the rest of the government about. Sixty-five percent of the analysts are unable to order food in a Korean restaurant or ask for directions to the restroom. Yet these are the people we depend on to plumb the depths of North Korean psychology. Admittedly, Korean is a hard language to master. It takes up to sixty-three weeks of dedicated study to learn the language at an elementary level. However, one would think that after fifty-five years of involvement, we might have more than 10% of the analysts actually able to speak the language of the country that they study. In fact, speaking a foreign language fluently is often considered a liability in some intelligence agencies because the individual is considered too specialized."

11. Charles Duelfer, Director of Central Intelligence Special Adviser for Strategy, regarding Iraqi Weapons of Mass Destruction (WMD) Programs, Testimony to the U.S. Congress, 108th Cong., 2nd sess., March 30, 2004, http://www.cia.gov/cia/public_affairs/speech/2004/tenet_testimony_03302004.html (accessed August 31, 2005).
12. Charles Duelfer, "Transmittal Message, September 23, 2004," 1.
13. "Attorney General Gonzales Travels to Baghdad to Visit DOJ Personnel, Military Troops, and Iraqi Officials," Department of Justice Online News Release, July 3, 2005, http://www.usdoj.gov/opa/pr/2005/July/05_ag_360.htm (accessed May 5, 2006).
14. Charles Duelfer, "Iraq's Military Industrial Capability—Evolution of the Military Industrialization Commission," *Addendums to the Comprehensive Report of the Special Advisor to the DCI on Iraq's WMD* (Washington, DC: U.S. Government Printing Office, 2005), 11–12.
15. Mahdi Obeidi and Kurt Pitzer, *The Bomb in My Garden: The Secrets of Saddam's Nuclear Mastermind* (Hoboken, NJ: Wiley, 2004), 9–10.
16. Ibid., 9.
17. John Negroponte, *The National Intelligence Strategy of the United States of America* (Washington, DC: Office of the Director of National Intelligence, October 2005), 4.
18. Ibid., 12.
19. Ibid., 6.
20. Ibid., 9–10.
21. Ibid., 15, 10.
22. Scales, "Culture-Centric Warfare," 35.
23. See "CAOCL Charter" and "CAOCL Brochure," USMC Center for Advanced Operational Culture Learning (CAOCL), http://www.tecom.usmc.mil/caocl/ (accessed May 4, 2007).
24. Gingrich, "Status of the Office of the Director of National Intelligence," appendix 3.
25. The Commission on the Intelligence Capabilities, *Report to the President of the United States*, 428.
26. A. Denis Clift, "Commencement Address," unpublished transcript, Joint Military Intelligence College, Washington, DC, May 27, 2005, 5.
27. Negroponte, *National Intelligence Strategy*, 1–2.

Chapter 31: Winning in the Pacific
1. Pew Global Attitudes Project, *America's Image Slips, but Allies Share U.S. Concerns over Iran, Hamas*, June 13, 2006, http://pewglobal.org/reports/display.php?ReportID=252.
2. National Commission on Terrorist Attacks, *The 9/11 Commission Report: Final Report of the National Commission on Terrorist Attacks upon the United States* (New York: Norton, 2004), 376.

3. According to Joint Publication 3–07.1, *Joint Tactics, Techniques and Procedures for Foreign Internal Defense*, foreign internal defense "is the participation by civilian and military agencies of a government or other designated organization to free and protect its society from subversion, lawlessness, and insurgency." Unconventional warfare builds on the foundation of working by, through, and with indigenous or surrogate forces. Although the military and law enforcement agencies kill, capture, and detain terrorists, these direct action missions should not be at the expense of the "advise and assist" approach that foreign internal defense and unconventional warfare offer as their centerpiece.

Chapter 32: Tactical Information Operations in West Rashid
1. A *mulhalla* is a numbered small neighborhood roughly the size of one to three city blocks. Several mulhallas make up a *Hayy*, which is a named larger neighborhood. Several Hayys make up a Beladi, which is a district or municipality.
2. The Beladi West Rashid is also called Bayaa, not to be confused with Hayy al-Bayaa, a neighborhood within West Rashid. It encompasses the area south of the Airport Road that leads from Baghdad International Airport to the International Zone and west of Hilla Road, which leads south out of Baghdad.
3. The concept of an INP battalion AO is a very fluid one. Battalion AOs changed often within a brigade AO, and it was not uncommon for battalions from other brigades to assume AOs within another brigade's AO with little to no notice or subordination to the brigade whose AO in which the "interloper" battalion was operating.
4. This author's team was assigned to and operated with 2nd Battalion, 7th Brigade, 2nd Division (2/7/2) from December 2005 through November 2006 until relieved by a follow-on Marine team.
5. The Iraqi National Police (INP) is a sort of paramilitary organization and falls under the Ministry of the Interior (MOI). It consists of two INP divisions (formerly the Commandos and the Public Order Brigades [POB] and a mechanized battalion. The Iraqi police also fall within the MOI but fill more of a local constabulary role focusing on crime of a more traditional nature such as theft and simple assault.
6. NPTT is pronounced "nipit." NPTTs were formerly called "Special Police Transition Teams" (SPTTs—pronounced "spits") when the INPs were called "Special Police Commandos" and "Public Order Brigades" (POBs).
7. The 7/2 INP was a commando brigade prior to renaming the commandos and POBs the INP.
8. The military prefers to use the term "kinetic" to describe activities or operations that involve the use of bullets and explosives that cause physical damage to persons or things through the movement of mass.
9. Our 2/7/2 NPTT was a U.S. Marine team of eleven members: the team leader (major), assistant team leader (first lieutenant), operations officer (captain), intelligence officer (major), supply/logistics officer (first lieutenant), team chief (master sergeant), operations noncommissioned officer (NCO) (gunnery sergeant), supply NCO (gunnery sergeant), training NCO (staff sergeant), communications chief (staff sergeant), and a Navy corpsman (hospitalman second class). Some NPTTs were not as senior. Additionally, the team that relieved us was junior in all ranks except team leader.
10. The battalion's concept of an accurate accounting of all its members of 2/7/2, at least an accounting to the NPTT, was a very fluid one, with a weekly, and sometimes daily, deviation of between 50 and 150 individuals, even taking into account personnel on leave.
11. Iraqi general officers proliferated in Baghdad. An Iraqi National Police Battalion could as likely be commanded by a brigadier general as a lieutenant colonel. During the team's relationship with 2/7/2, the battalion had six commanding officers of which two were brigadier generals.

436 — Notes

12. A BDU is the battle dress uniform, the tricolor pattern uniform worn for the last decade.
13. The Army combat uniform was the digital pattern uniform that replaced the BDU.
14. The 2/7/2 was composed of 350 to 450 personnel in four line companies and one headquarters company. Other battalions often had fewer personnel. Typically, one-third or more of the personnel of each company were on leave pursuant to a leave policy of roughly ten to fourteen days on, ten days off. The typical operational tempo for the latter half of 2006 was the operation of three to four checkpoints twenty-four-hours per day and twenty-four-hour patrols as well as day-to-day command post operations and security. This left few troops to conduct combined cordon and search operations of an entire mulhalla or two with a U.S. maneuver company. Furthermore, as each of the line companies rarely had more than two-thirds of its force available because of leave, troops from each of the companies had to be cobbled together for any such operation, thus presenting obvious command and control issues.

Chapter 33: "But How Do I Do It?"
1. Joint Chiefs of Staff, Joint Publication 3-13 *Information Operations* (Washington, DC: Department of Defense, February 13, 2006).
2. For more information on the Marine Corps Planning Process, refer to Marine Corps Warfighting Publication 5-1 *Marine Corps Planning Process*, January 5, 2000. For additional information on the military decision-making process, refer to U.S Army Field Manual 5-0 *Army Planning and Orders Production*, January 20, 2005.
3. Marine Corps Doctrinal Publication 5 *Planning* (July 21, 1997), 92.

Chapter 35: The Massacre That Wasn't
1. All five were wounded in the initial contact when a rocket-propelled grenade (RPG) fired from the mosque compound struck a Marine vehicle. According to press reports one later died, although this has not been confirmed by the Marine Corps.
2. The AGM-114 series Hellfire is a laser-guided antitank missile with a small, shaped-charge warhead typically used to destroy armored vehicles.
3. "Eyewitness" accounts would later incorrectly identify a Marine helicopter as the source of all three strikes: the missile and the two bombs. Marine helicopters do not carry or employ 500-pound aerial bombs.
4. This time is taken from the original time stamp on the uncleared, classified imagery.
5. Images sanitized and cleared for release by the appropriate Marine Corps units and public affairs officials.
6. "IBC Falluja April 2004 News Digest," *Iraq Body Count*, http://www.iraqbodycount.net/resources/falluja/ibc_falluja_apr_07.php#bna1.
7. BBC News, "U.S. Bombards Iraq Mosque Complex," April 7, 2004, http://news.bbc.co.uk/1/hi/middle_east/3609665.stm.
8. Bassem Mroue and Abdul-Qader Saadi, "US Bombs Fallujah Mosque; More Than 40 Worshippers Killed," CommonDreams.org News Center, April 7, 2004, http://www.commondreams.org/headlines04/0407-06.htm.
9. "IBC Falluja April 2004 News Digest."
10. Perry himself later filed a joint report with Edmund Sanders (Tony Perry and Edmund Sanders, "U.S. Bombs Mosque in Fallouja: Military Says Site Was Used to Launch Strikes; Troops' Tours May Be Extended," *Los Angeles Times*, April 8, 2004) that repeated both the eyewitness claims and the Marine denials. This version did not point out that there had been no confirmation of deaths in or around the mosque and did not go into the level of detail presented in the Ifill interview.
11. See http://www.fair.org/activisim/nyt-fallujah.html; http://english.aljazeera.net/NR/exeres/6890A8DA-AF79-45AD-BB4F-42C060978A07.htm; Brian Dominick, "In

Fallujah, U.S. Declares War on Hospitals, Ambulances," *The New Standard*, November 9, 2004, http://newstandardnews.net/content/index.cfm/items/1208; Iraq Body Count website, http://www.iraqbodycount.org. (All websites accessed November 30, 2006.)
12. Exact prayer times for April 7, 2004, in Fallujah can be found at http://www.islamicfinder.org.
13. CNN.com, "Marines: U.S. Bombed Iraqi Mosque Wall," April 7, 2004, http://www.cnn.com/2004/WORLD/meast/04/07/fallujah.strike/index.html.
14. Iraq Body Count typically (and commendably) lists only incidents confirmed by two sources. However, in this case they refer to the original AP story and a website that references the AP story in an obvious case of circular reporting.
15. Anthony Gregory, "Fallujah Revenge and the War Disease," Anti-War.com, April 8, 2004, http://www.antiwar.com/orig/gregory.php?articleid=2274.
16. New World Blogger.com, "New Additions," April 10, 2004, http://new-world-blogger.blogspot.com/2004_04_04_new-world-blogger_archive.html.
17. Al Jazeera English website: http://english.aljazeera.net/NR/exeres/A73529F1-1554-4C68-8774-BA478D565B02.htm (accessed November 30, 2006).
18. Bing West, *No True Glory: A Frontline Account of the Battle for Fallujah* (New York: Bantam, 2005). West refers to the incident at the mosque from two separate vantage points.
19. "Phantom Fury" is the other name for Al Fajr. "Vigilant Resolve" was the code name for the first Marine assault on Fallujah.
20. AP Photo/Bilal Hussein, "An Iraqi Man Inspects Damage," November 8, 2004, http://www.commondreams.org/headlines04/1108-08.htm.
21. BBC News, "Timeline: Iraq," October 14, 2005, http://news.bbc.co.uk/2/hi/middle_east/4343078.stm.

Chapter 40: By Other Means
1. On the center of gravity, critical capability, critical requirement, critical vulnerability model, see Joe Strange and Richard Iron, "Center of Gravity: What Clausewitz Really Meant," *Joint Forces Quarterly* 35 (October 2004): 20.
2. Thomas A. Marks, "Evaluating Insurgent/Counterinsurgent Performance," *Small Wars and Insurgencies* 11, no. 3 (Winter 2000): 21. See also V. I. Kurochkin, "Objectives and Effectiveness Criteria in Counterinsurgency Warfare," *Military Thought*, January 2002, 119–120.
3. We also need to be aware that higher political media imperatives—such as the national security adviser's subscription to neorealist theory, with its assumption of the primacy of state actors, or the overemphasis of the role of foreign fighters—may misdirect or color our thinking on the ground.
4. Here we are taking appropriately aggressive steps, such as offering in-depth language training as a reenlistment incentive and developing a spectrum of cultural training. We should take care not to focus solely on Iraq. There is a vast "fracture zone" that may see complex conflict in the near future, and it would be unwise to train for the present war and not a future one. While expanding the ranks of true cultural experts, such as foreign area officers, we need to create a broader spectrum of cultural and linguistic competence by bridging the gap between the expert advisers and the "boots on the deck" through tiered training programs and a means of identifying and exploiting preexisting cultural and linguistic expertise.
5. See Curtis L. Williamson, *The U.S. Marine Corps Combined Action Program (CAP): A Proposed Alternative Strategy for the Vietnam War*, Marine Corps Command and Staff College Paper (2002). Williamson suggests convincingly that the CAP, properly implemented, could have changed the course of the Vietnam War.

6. Williamson suggests that this strategy would have alleviated many of the problems of the Vietnam CAP.
7. Francis J. West, *An Area Security System for Vietnam Incorporating Combined Action* (Santa Monica, CA: RAND, 1969), 64, cited in Williamson, *U.S. Marine Corps Combined Action Program*.

Chapter 42: The Privatization of Victory
1. Jeffrey B. Jones, "Strategic Communications," *Joint Forces Quarterly* 39 (October 2005): 109.
2. Mark Leonard, "The Geopolitics of 2026," *The Economist*, November 18, 2005, 24.
3. Cindy Fisher, "Commandant's Vision Focuses on Marines, Extends Corps' Capabilities for Future Conflicts," *Pass in Review* 24, no. 2 (July 2005), http://www.marines.mil/marinelink/mcn2000.nsf/0/AB48512EB3B7B57585256FFC00523746?opendocument.

Chapter 43: "Twenty-Eight Articles"
1. Field Manual 3-24 *Counterinsurgency* (Washington, DC: U.S. Government Printing Office, 2006).
2. *Black Hawk Down*, DVD (Los Angeles: Scott Free Productions, 2002); *The Battle of Algiers*, DVD (Rome: Casbah Film and Igor Film, 1967).

INDEX

I Marine Expeditionary Force, 367–68
1st Armored Division, U.S. Army, 164, 166
1st Infantry Division, U.S. Army, 164
1st Information Operations (IO) Command, 164, 198
3rd Infantry Division, U.S. Army, 164, 166
24th Marine Expeditionary Unit, 337
101st Airbone Division, in Iraq, 80, 85

Abdel Aziz al-Samarai Mosque, 341
Abizaid, John, 86
Abu Ghraib, 14, 45, 168–69, 223, 225, 243
academia, 4
Accelerated Pacification Campaign (ACP), 215
Afghan Ministry of Defense (MOD), 187–91, 193–94
Afghan National Army (ANA), 187, 190, 192
Afghan public affairs, 187, 188–89
Afghani, Jamal ad-Din Al-, 21
Afghanistan, xi, 1; as Al Qaeda sanctuary, 7–8, 15; Al Qaeda's new base in, 23–24; insurgents in, 27, 76, 32, 37, 41; journalists in, 88, 142, 150, 152, 158; popular support in, 56; Soviet invasion of, 22; state defense against IO, 67; under the Taliban, 160, 187–94; U.S. message to, 57
Africa, 160, 175
Aideed Model, 127–28
Al Arabiya, 149
Al Jazeera, 107, 148–49, 152–53, 347–48
Al Qaeda, xi; attacks from Pakistan bases, 70; evolution of, 7, 11; expulsion from Afghanistan, 8, 11; link to Batiste, 9; organizational dynamics of, 20; psychology of, 23–24; review of, 17; use of propaganda, 41, 91, 146–61, 188; use of new technologies, 28, 31–32; waging war against, 14, 24–26
Alalam, 154
Al-Fajr, Operation, 269
Alhurra, 16, 152
Al-Manar, 149
Americans, and the media, 135, 171, 176, 241
anarchism, 18
Anbar Province (Iraq), 108, 241, 244
Arab Americans, 223, 241, 244
Arab League, 47
Arabic: speakers of, in Fallujah, 128, 148; -speaking Americans, 224, 244; survival Arabic, 83, 95; VOA's programming in, 151, 152
Arabs, 14, 16; Lawrence on, 77, 91, 149, 175, 194
Areopagitica (Milton), 138
Army, U.S., 95; Forces Command, 205; headquarters, 199, 205; IO, 163, 195–206, 168; IO in Iraq, 107; policing Iraq, 222; Reserve Command, 201–3; Special Operations Command, 201, 203; Training and Doctrine Command, 205
As-Saliyah, Camp, 237
Associated Press (AP), 133, 342, 345
asymmetric warfare, 13, 62, 76, 141, 227
atrocities, alleged U.S., 128
Azimi, Mohammed Zaher, 188–89, 192
Azzam, Sheik Abdullah, 22–23

B-52 (bomber), 112
Ba'athists, 1, 153

439

Babil Province (Iraq), 338
Baghdad, 1, 14, 77; advance on, 89; initial victory in, 90–91, 134–35, 153–55, 221–23, 235, 244, 248; U.S. embassy in, 86
Bana, Hassan Al-, 20
Balkans, 150
BAT, 222
Batiste, Narseal, 9
BBC, 344
Beers, Charlotte, 160
Beirut, 135
Berlin Wall, 148
Bill of Rights, 138
Bin Laden, Osama, 3, 14, 20; alienation from house of Saud, 23, 32, 160; early days of, 22
Blackhawk Down, 148
Blackwater contracting, in Iraq, 127
blitzkrieg, 7, 9–11, 36
blogs, 10
Bolsheviks, 1
Boomer, Walter, 236
Bosnia, 117, 163
Boyd, John: OODA Loop, 27; three levels of war, 35, 37
Bremer, L. Paul, 154
Bright and Shining Lie, A (Sheehan), 213
Brikalis, Mark, 239
British: government, 137; joint media operations doctrine, 140, 141; in Malaya, 123, 131; use of IO, 125–26
Brooks, Vincent, 153
Buddha, 178
Bush, George W., 221
Bush Doctrine, 14

Canada, 142
Capra, Frank, 160
CBS News, 88
cell phones, 148
censorship, 88
census operations, 351, 352–53
Center for Army Lessons Learned (CALL), 76
center of gravity, 102, 105, 147, 230
Central Asia, 156
Central Command (CENTCOM), U.S., 142, 152–53, 236–37
Central Intelligence Agency (CIA): attack on employees of (1993), 19; and Mossad, 15
Chaplaincy, U.S., 184–85
Chechnya, 150, 156

Chicago, police methods in, 222
China: government suppression, 10, 59; support of insurgents, 130
Christ, Jesus, 178
Christianity, 181, 183
Churchill, Winston, 140
CIA. *See* Central Intelligence Agency (CIA)
Civil Affairs (CA), 42; and IO, 164, 196–97; in Iraq, 81, 85, 107–8, 159
Civil Operations and Revolutionary Development Support (CORDS) program, 52
clandestine operations, 108
Clausewitz, Carl von, 25, 60, 111–12, 114–15, 118, 120–21, 147, 157
CNN factor, 66, 148, 239
Coalition forces, in Iraq, 51, 166, 168
Coalition Information Center (Doha), 152–54
Coalition Provisional Authority (CPA), 78, 153, 154, 238, 245
Cohen, Eliot A., 239
Cold War, 88, 94, 151, 158, 161, 172
Cole, USS, bombing of (2000), 23
Colombia, 289–95
Combat Camera teams: American, in World War II, 238; Canadian, 142, 196
combatant commands, 42–44
Combined Action Program (CAP), 214, 214, 375
Combined Arms Center (CAC), 196–98, 204
Combined Forces Command–Afghanistan (CFC-A), 187, 189, 192
Combined Joint Task Force 7 (CJTF-7), 153
Combined Review and Release Board, 224
command post (CP), processes and intelligence, 353–55
Commander's Emergency Reconstruction Program (CERP), 78–79
commander's guidance for IO, 325–26
Commando Solo, 198
Communism, 1, 208; in Malaya, 135, 172
Computer Network Attack (CNA), 59, 67, 104–5, 114, 128
Computer Network Defense, 104
Computer Network Operations (CNO), 29, 112, 124, 131, 196, 203–4, 269
Congress, U.S., 151–52, 158, 243
Constitution, U.S., 176
conventional warfare, 103
counterinsurgency, xi, 17, 24, 389;

complexity of, 86, 93–95; in El Salvador, 80; and intelligence, 251–53; in Iraq, 222, 225; leadership of, 84; theories of, 101–2, 105–6, 108; in Vietnam, 212
"Counterinsurgency Redux" (Kilcullen), 50
counterterrorism, 11
covert action, 17
criminals: in Fallujah, 128; groups of, 174
Croatia, 180
Cronin, Audrey, 104–5
Cronkite, Walter, 88
Cuba, 163
cyber operations, 103

Darfur, 15, 183
Dari, 189
Darley, William, 235
deception operations, military (MILDEC), 104; as a component of IO, 112, 114, 124, 128, 131, 164, 196; as distinctive from IO, 141, 203
Declaration of Independence, 138
de-escalation, 37
Defense Information School (Ft. Meade), 238
Defense Intelligence Agency (DIA), 44
Defense Science Board, 161, 200
Democratic Republic of Vietnam (DRV), 207–17. *See also* Vietnam
Department of Defense (DOD): addiction to technology, 29; definition of terrorism, 18, 26; on Iraq War, 127–28, 133, 152, 155, 160, 171–73, 184, 200, 227; support of the State Department, 44; transformational efforts of, 101
Department of International Development (UK), 47
Department of Justice, 225
Department of State, 32, 39, 41–42, 44, 146, 152, 155, 158, 171, 184, 202
Desert Shield/Desert Storm, 148, 236
Diem, Ngo Dinh, 209, 210, 211, 216, 427, 430, 431
Digital Video and Imagery Distribution System (DVIDS), 142
diplomacy, 4
DiRita, Lawrence, 273
disintermediation, 383
distributed operations, 354–55
Doha Coalition Briefing Center, 89
Dominican Republic, 163

Dubai, 149

East Timor, 156
effects-based operations, 302–3
Egypt, 160
Eisenhower, Dwight, 151; and USIA, 158
El Salvador, 50, 55–56, 57, 80
elections, as a form of war, 115
electronic warfare (EW), 29, 104–5, 112, 124, 131, 164, 203–4
embedded reporters, 272
Enlightenment, Age of, 138

Fallujah, 127–29, 221, 223–24, 244, 266–67, 341, 368, 374
Farabundo Martí National Liberation Front (FMLN), 55–56
Faruk, King, 147
Fatah, 91
fatwa, 47
Federal Bureau of Investigation (FBI), 9
Fiasco (Ricks), 153
Fick, Nathaniel, 198
Field Manual 3-13 *Information Operations*, 332
Field Manual 3-24 *Counterinsurgency Operations*, xi, 389
Fitna, 21
Fitzgerald, Frances, 210
FMLN, 55–56
football, American, 242
foreign policy, 14
Foreign Service, 4
Fourth Generation Warfare (4GW), 28, 35, 38, 103, 106
Fox News, 154
France, 125, 138, 151, 178
Frank, Michael, 223
Franks, Tommy, 89
French Revolution, 104
Friedman, Thomas L., 149
Fuerzas Armadas Revolucionarias de Colombia (FARC), 289
fundamentalists, 147, 178

Galula, David, 93, 102
Gandhi, Mahatma, 125, 175
Geneva Conventions (1949), 61–62, 66, 140
genocide, 175
Germany, 140, 163, 175
Giap, Vo Nguyen, 3
Gillespie, Neil, 238

Global War on Terrorism (GWOT), 14, 16, 17, 29, 133, 135–36, 146, 158, 200, 202–3, 206
globalization, 7
Grand Armée, 104
Grange, David, 198
Greek Orthodox Church, 179
Grenada, U.S. action on (1983), 88, 163
Guantanamo Bay, 14
Guard forces (U.S.), 38, 238
guerrilla warfare, 35, 50, 233; in El Salvador, 55; and isolation, 101
Gulf War (1990–91), 88, 244

Hadrian, Emperor, 101
Hagee, Michael W., 387
Haifa University, 150
Haiti, 163
halal meals, 129
Hamas, 15, 91, 147
hard power, 14
hearts and minds, 15
Herat, 189, 191–92, 194
Hezbollah, 147
Hillah (Iraq), 77, 338
Hoffman, Frank, 131
Holbrooke, Richard, 16
Howard, Michael, 97
Hughes, Karen, 30
Huk Rebellion. *See* Hukbalahap Rebellion
Hukbalahap Rebellion, 53, 212
human intelligence (HUMINT), 80–81, 107, 276
humanitarian operations, 43, 212
Hussein, Qusay, 80
Hussein, Saddam, 16, 78, 127, 227, 244–45, 248–49
Hussein, Uday, 80

ideology, 1
improvised explosive devices (IEDs), 57, 91, 221
Independent Electoral Commission of Iraq (IECI), 370
India, 59, 125
Indochina, 209
Indonesia, 117, 175; Muslims of, 156; tsunami relief in, 158
influence operations, xii, 13
information battlefield, 1, 13, 16, 104, 158, 169, 235
information defeat, 266–67

information management, 88, 257–59
information operations (IO), xii, 47, 103–8, 126, 142, 178, 180–81, 235–36, 238; Chinese approach to, 131; debate, 111; explanation of, 112–15, 118–20; in Fallujah, 128–29; and international law, 59–72; in Iraq, 265, 363; Joint Publication 3-13, 27–28; as main effort, 121; in Malayan Emergency, 123; and manipulation of jihadists, 11; and marketing, 163–70; and media operations, 140; methodology of, 173–74; NATO's policy on, 141; and PA, 137, 141, 269–70; tactical, 307, 323, 357, 367; as threat to terrorist networks, 8–9; and U.S. Army, 195–206; U.S. military efforts with, 29, 37–38; U.S. need for, 3, 264
insurgency, 30, 50, 93, 145–46, 233; in Afghanistan, 27; complex networks of, 103; evolution into 4GW, 28; IO campaigns against, 33; in Iraq, 27, 32, 86, 91, 221–24, 230, 252–53; in Malaya, 125–26; in the media, 149; and morality, 57; and religion, 174–75; and U.S. target recognition, 154; war of ideas in, 207. *See also* counterinsurgency
integrated marketing communications (IMC), 169
intelligence, 9; actionable, 50; analysts, 96, 127, 254–57; collection of, 103; derived from a supportive population, 95–96; failure of, 275; as key to success, 80; and Marine Corps, 106–7; Preparation of the Battlefield (IPB), 44, 255–56, 330–32; structures, 253–54; and Western militaries, 103
Intelligence Community, U.S. (IC), 146, 171, 236
International Committee for the Red Cross (ICRC), 62, 67, 69
International Court of Justice, 61
International Criminal Court, 66
international law for information operations (ILIO), 60–72
International Security and Assistance Force (ISAF), 189, 192
Internet, 39, 123, 148; impact on the information cycle, 76; in the Middle East, 149, 151; in OIF, 135–36; in PSYOPS, 108; and strategic communication, 45, 47; and U.S.

reputation, 16; use of, by insurgents, 94; use of, by Iraq justice system, 224; use of, by terrorists, 9–11, 13, 91
interpreters, 96
interrogators, U.S., in Iraq, 223
Iran, 91, 147, 153–54, 160
Iraq, xi; empowering people of, 77–78; 4GW in, 37; IMC in, 169; insurgents in, 27, 32, 86, 91, 221–24, 230, 252–53; IO in, 123, 127, 142; IO vs. PSYOPS in, 198; justice system of, 221–25; leaders of, 84; lessons from operations in, 200; local combatants in, 51; low-intensity conflict in, 227–34; and the media, 88, 90, 101, 107, 133–35; people of, 241–50; possibility of uniting, 53–54; strategic communications in, 146–61; support for U.S.-backed governments in, 56–58. *See also* Iraq War
Iraq Survey Group, 275
Iraq War, 75–86, 93–98, 146–61, 198, 200, 227–34, 241–50, 251–62, 275–88, 307–22, 337–40, 363–66, 367–72, 379–82. *See also* Iraq
Iraqi National Police, 307–16
Iraqi Security Forces (ISF), 85–86
Irish Republican Army (IRA), 18, 103
irregular warfare, 101–2, 106, 108, 175, 289
Islam, 14–16, 23–26, 47, 91, 94, 227; and cyber mobilization, 104; importance of, in world politics, 171–72; and IO, 107; jihad, 9; return to early form of, 22; struggle against, 14, 145–61; theology of, 175, 177–78; and the West, 20; on the world stage, 181–85. *See also* Sh'ia Islam; Sunni Islam
Islamabad, 152
Israel, 15, 18, 91, 148
Italy, 163

Jalalabad, 194
Japan, 1, 19, 160, 163–64
jihad, 173, 178, 181; in Afghanistan, 7–8; structure of, 10
"Jihad Market," 169
Johnson, Lyndon B., 88, 209
Joint Chiefs of Staff (JCS), 41–42, 105
joint direct attack munition, 112
Joint Forces Command (JFCOM), 76, 205
Joint Publication 3-13 *Information Operations*, 124, 359–60

Jomini, Baron Antoine-Henri, 99, 108
Jordan, 149
journalists, 87, 90
Judaism, 184
just war theory, 177

Kabul, 152, 189–90
Kam Air crash (2005), 193
Karzai, Hamid, 188–89, 193
Kashmir, 150, 156
Kennan, George F., 157–58
Kennedy, John F., 209, 233
Kenya, 3, 18, 23, 103
Khalilzad, Zalmay, 85
Khan, Bismullah, 191
Khan, Fahim, 192
Khomeini, Ayatollah, 147–48
Khoury, Nabeel, 153
Kilcullen, David, 11, 50
kinetic operations, 14; definition of, 124–25; and IO, 67, 111, 113–14, 118, 120, 131; vs. non-kinetic, 85, 108
Koran, 172, 193
Korea, 157. *See also* Korean War
Korean War, 88, 158, 163
Kosovo, 65, 87, 117, 163
Krulak, Victor, 214
Kurds, 33, 96, 127, 129, 183
Kuwait, 16, 23

Lansdale, Edward, 212
law of war, 61–62
Lawrence, T. E., 26, 77, 102, 104–5, 108, 194
Lebanon, 149
Lenin, 18
levée en masse, 104
Lewis, Bernard, 20
Libya, 184
Life, 238
Lincoln Group, 142, 155, 160
London, 125, 152
Lotus principle, 61
low-intensity conflict, 227, 228–29, 233

MACV-SOG, 103
Madrid subway attack (2003), 3, 11
Mafia, in U.S., 103
Malaya, 3, 123, 125, 126, 130–31. *See also* Malayan Emergency
Malayan Emergency, 53, 123, 130
Mao Tse-tung, 1, 50, 102
Marine Corps, U.S., 95, 105–8; Combat

Development Command, 128;
    Expeditionary Force (MEF), 134;
    Forces Command (MARFORCOM),
    133; *Gazette*, 238; in Iraq, 135–36,
    198, 221–23, 241–50
marketing, 164, 166
Marshall, George C., 160
mass media, 107, 133
massing effects, 263, 266, 268
Massoud, Ahmad Shah, 188
Mattis, James, 105
Mau Mau, 103
McInerney, Thomas, 133
McNamara, Robert, 209–10, 216
measure of effectiveness (MOE), 124
media, 88; Arabic, 92, 153; British joint
    operations doctrine, 140–41; in the
    Cold War, 148; as counterbalance to
    government messages, 141; foreign
    media operations, 202, 204; planning
    and execution of, 168; U.S., in Iraq,
    134–36
Melian Dialogue, 60
Middle East, 85, 91, 101, 232; IO in, 107;
    misperceptions of people of, 127–28;
    strategic communications in, 145–61;
    U.S. record in, 92
military deception. *See* deception
    operations, military (MILDEC)
military operations in urban terrain
    (MOUT), 197
Milks, Keith, 238
Milosevic, Slobodan, 65
Milton, John, 138
Minh, Ho Chi, 30
Mobile Advisory Team (MAT), 214
Mohammed, Prophet, 20–21
Morocco, 160, 175
Morton, Ralph, 224
Mosul University, 79, 80, 81, 82
Mother Theresa, 178
Mubarak, Hasni, 22–23
Multinational Force-Iraq (MNF-I), 83, 155,
    265
Murrow, Edward R., 88
Muslims. *See* Islam
Myers, Richard, 141

Nasser, Gamal Abdel, 20
National Command Authority (NCA), 163
national communications strategy, 42–43
National Defense Intelligence College
    (NDIC), 286

National Defense University (NDU), 43,
    200
National Intelligence Estimate (NIE), 146
National Intelligence Strategy, 286
National Liberation Front (NLF), 207
National Public Radio (NPR), 169
National Security Council (NSC), 155
National Training Center (NTC), 364
nation-building, 81
Nazis, 1, 151, 160, 163
neo-conservatives, 15
network-centric warfare, xi
New York City, 160, 222–23, 227
New York Times, 149
Newsweek, 193
Ninevah Province (Iraq), 81
Nixon, Richard M., 209–11
nongovernmental organization (NGO), 44
non-kinetic operations, 108, 158, 196. *See
    also* kinetic operations
non-state actor, 17
Normandy invasion (1944), 140
North Atlantic Treaty Organization
    (NATO), 43, 137, 139–41, 159
North Vietnamese Army (NVA), 52–54
nuclear weapons, 61, 114–15, 227
Nye, Joseph, 40

Office of Strategic Influence (OSI), 137
oil, 15
On War, 112
One Bullet Away (Fick), 198
OODA-loop, 141
open source requirements, 44
operational security (OPSEC), 29, 112,
    131, 164, 196, 128, 203
operations: Al-Fajr, 266–74, 348, 369;
    Desert Storm, 112, 166; Enduring
    Freedom, 117, 152, 206; Iraqi
    Freedom (OIF), 14, 105, 107, 127,
    133, 135, 152, 206, 237, 337; Just
    Cause, 117; Uphold Democracy, 42;
    Vigilant Resolve, 266–69, 273, 274,
    348
Outer Space Treaty, 68

Pakistan, 19, 152, 160, 194; Al Qaeda
    bases in, 70; earthquake relief in, 158;
    radicals in Peshawar, 22–24; U.S. aid
    to, 91
Palestine, 15–16, 18, 91, 156, 160
Panama, 163
Pastrana, Andrés, 292

Patton, George S., 130
Paul, Terry, 165
Pearl Harbor, attack on, 151
penetration, as a tactic, 103
Pentagon, 15, 148, 155, 198; censorship, 91; efficiency of, 102; embedding journalists (2003), 88; failure to use information, 29; spin, 89–90; TV channel, 238
People's Army of Vietnam (PAVN), 208
perceptions, of the populace, 78
Persian Gulf, 149
Pew Research Center, 146
Philippines, 53, 163, 212, 299–301. *See also* Hukbalahap Rebellion
phishing, 10
"Phoenix" program, 53
Phuong Hoang program, 53
Pincus, Walter, 155
Plan of Attack (Woodward), 198
police, 121, 126; in Iraq, 222, 224
political will, as aspect of warfare, 28
politics, and IO, 117
Post, Jerrold M., 200
Proceedings, 239
propaganda, xi, 13, 15; anti-, 3; distribution of, 64; in enemy campaigns, 106; "of the deed," 101; use of, by radical Islamists, 156, 158; use of, by terrorists, 9; use of, by the U.S., 137, 150–51, 163
pseudo operations, 103
psychological operations (PSYOPS), xii, 13, 40, 42, 104, 114, 128–29, 142, 159, 164, 358; alternatives to, 57–58; and IO, 29, 59, 112, 123, 164; in Iraq, 51; in support of 4GW, 106–8; by U.S. Army, 195–206; U.S. need for, 3; U.S. practices, 49
public affairs (PA), 40, 87, 94, 105–6, 107–8, 146, 155, 190–91, 236, 238; Afghan government, 187; doctrine, 137; and IO, 140–42, 164, 196, 360; in Iraq, 135, 342, 368; military, 133, 326; U.S. Army, 195–206; U.S. Marine Corps, 134
public diplomacy, xii, 40–41, 44, 105, 114, 151; in GWOT, 202; U.S. efforts, 153–56
public opinion, U.S., 91

Qatr, 89, 149, 152–53, 236–37
Qutb, Sayyid, 21

Radio Free Asia, 151
Radio Free Europe/Radio Liberty (RFE/RL), 151
Radio Sawa, 151
Ramadi, 221, 224, 341, 379
Rangers, U.S. Army, 148
Rashid, Ahmed, 157
Reagan, Ronald, 151
recidivism, in Iraq, 223
reconstruction, in Iraq, 77–78, 85
Record, Jeffrey, 210, 216
Red Brigade, 19
Regime Strategic Intent, 278
religion, 1, 171, 175, 180, 181
Rendon Group, 155
Republic of Vietnam, 207–8; armed forces of, 211–17; army of, 211–17; government of, 209–17, 222; National Liberation Front in, 207; popular support for, 50; Regional Forces/Popular Forces (RF/PF), 213–17; Revolutionary Development Cadre (RDC), 213–17. *See also* Vietnam War
Reserve forces (U.S.), 38, 164, 238
revolution in military affairs (RMA), xi
Rice, Condoleezza, 239
Rickenbacker, Eddie, 238
Ricks, Thomas, 153
Riyadh, 236
Romania, 139, 141
Rumsfeld, Donald, 16, 117, 198
Rushing, Josh, 153
Russia, 18, 59, 156, 194
Rwanda, 44

Saban Center, 146
Sadat, Anwar, 21
Saigon, 207–17
Salafism, 20–21, 24
satellite TV, 151
Saudi Arabia, 23, 160
SAVAK, 147
Schleifer, S. Abdullah, 148
Schoomaker, Peter, 96
Seabees, 238
Second Generation Warfare, 35
secretary of defense, 39, 42, 102, 105
Selous Scouts (Rhodesia), 103
September 11 terrorist attacks, xi, 17, 24, 145–61, 171, 238
"Shared Values" campaign, 160
sharia, 172
Shat-al-Arab river, 89

Sheehan, Neil, 213
Sh'ia Islam, 33, 94, 96, 127, 147, 221–24
"shock and awe," 237
Sholtis, Tadd, 235
Siddiq, Suhaila, 193
signals intelligence (SIGINT), 114
Silva, Manuel de, 192
Simon, Bob, 88
Six Days' War (1967), 89
Small Wars Manual (USMC), 101, 216
Smith-Mundt Act (1948), 155
social networks, 8
soft power, 14, 16
Soldiers, U.S., 128, 130, 206
Somalia, 128, 148, 163
Soviet Union, 3, 151, 157, 164, 193, 209
Spain, 178
Spanish-American War, 151
Special Operations Command, Pacific (SOCPAC), 297
Staff Judge Advocates (SJA), 42
Stalin, Joseph, 140
State Department. *See* Department of State
status of forces agreements (SOFAs), 68
Strategic Command (STRATCOM), 205
strategic communications, xii, 13, 30, 32–33, 44, 105, 146, 153–54, 158, 199–200, 235, 238–39; components of, 48; definition of, 40, 42
strategic debriefing, 277
strategic message, 32, 155
strategy, 4, 13, 17, 39
subversion, 102
Sudan, 23, 160
suicide bombers, 57, 94, 175
Sun Tzu, 60, 123
Sunni Islam, 33, 94, 96, 147, 221–22; extremism, 17; insurgents, 224; in Iraq, 83; split with Sh'ia, 20; Sunni Triangle, 224

Taliban, 26, 149, 152, 160, 190, 192–93
targeting, 45, 154, 164
Taylor, Phillip, 150
Tehran Conference (1943), 140
Telhami, Shibley, 146
Templer, Gerald, 125
terrorism, 2, 24, 141, 145–61, 172, 174–75, 230–32; DOD definition of, 18; in Fallujah, 128–29; history of, 18–19; in Malaya, 125; networks of, 7,11; overview of, 17; psychology of, 200; use of Internet for, 10

terrorist attacks on U.S., 227
Tet Offensive (1968), 215
Texas, 223
Thailand, 302
theology, 175. *See also* Islam
Third Generation Warfare, 35
Third Reich, 140
Third World, 168, 227
Thomas, Timothy L., 130
Three Block War, 108
Thucydides, 60
Toffler, Alvin, 40–41
Toffler, Heidi, 40–41
touch points, 167
Transnational Broadcasting Studies Journal, 148
tsunami, in Indonesia (2004), 193
Turkey, 20

United Kingdom (UK), 3, 152
United Nations, 41, 47, 139, 192
Uribe, Alvaro, 292
U.S. Agency for International Development (USAID), 40, 42, 46–47, 214
U.S. government, 15; failure of IO strategy, 106; foreign policy, 209; message in Iraq and Afghanistan, 57–58; and religion, 177; and strategic communications, 145–61; and U.S. brand, 165–69; and U.S. public, 107; use of media, 92. *See also specific government agencies*
U.S. Information Agency, 16, 40–41, 94, 151; demise of, 155, 158
U.S. International Communication Agency (USICA), 151–52
U.S. military, 137; in El Salvador, 55; failure to adapt, 28; in Fallujah, 127, 129; lessons from Afghanistan, 200, 227; and media in Iraq, 134; and religion, 181–85, 193; and strategic communications, 145–61; and technology, 101; and U.S. brand, 165–69. *See also specific branches of service*
U.S. Senate, 223

vakif system, 179
Vallely, Paul, 133
van Creveld, Martin, 35
Vann, John Paul, 213
Viet Cong (VC), 52, 208, 222

Vietnam. *See* Democratic Republic of Vietnam; Republic of Vietnam
Vietnam War, 88, 92, 149, 163–64; CORDS in, 52–54; MACV-SOG in, 103. *See also* Democratic Republic of Vietnam; People's Army of Vietnam; Republic of Vietnam; Viet Cong
Vietnamization, 210–11
Voice of America (VOA), 151

war correspondents, 88
war crimes, 66
Warsaw Pact, 139
Washington, D.C., 15, 152, 207–8, 227
Washington Post, 146, 153, 155, 207, 239
wasta, 247
Waziristan, 26
weapons of mass destruction (WMD), 48, 277–78

Weimann, Gabriel, 150
West Bank, 149
Westmorland, William, 155, 209, 216
White House, 30, 89–90, 152
Wilkerson, Jim, 153
women, 371, 412
Woodward, Bob, 198
World Trade Center, 15, 91
World War I, 117, 151
World War II, 2, 16, 18, 88, 114, 117, 125, 130, 151, 160–61, 164

Yousef, Ramzi, 11

Zaharna, R. S., 155
Zarqawi, Abu Musab al-, 41, 148, 160
Zawahiri, Ayman al-, 22–23, 160
Zimbabwe, 15
Zogby International, 146

ABOUT THE EDITORS AND CONTRIBUTORS

Editors

Maj G. J. David, Jr., is an active-duty major in the U.S. Marine Corps with field experience in the operating forces, with the Joint Staff, and with the national intelligence agencies and military services of the United States and other nations. He has also worked as a congressional staffer. He is a resident of Arlington, Virginia.

LtCol T. R. McKeldin III is a Marine Reserve lieutenant colonel who began his service as a Marine combat engineer officer. He is now an intelligence officer. He has served in operations in Cuba, Iraq, Afghanistan, Kuwait, Somalia, South Korea, and Kosovo, among other countries. A native of Baltimore, Maryland, he now teaches intelligence strategy, policy, and collections in Washington, D.C.

Contributors

COL Curtis Boyd, USA, is currently assigned as the assistant chief of staff, G-3, at the United States Army Civil Affairs and Psychological Operations Command. He earned a BA from Norwich University and holds an MA in national security affairs from the Special Operations and Low-Intensity Conflict Curriculum at the Naval Postgraduate School. A former fellow at the John F. Kennedy School of Government at Harvard University and a graduate of the Joint Forces Staff College, he has served in various command and staff positions in the infantry, information operations, and psychological operations.

Maj Phillip M. Bragg, USMC, is an artillery officer currently serving as an instructor at the Expeditionary Warfare School in Quantico, Virginia. He has served combat tours as a battery commander and as a planner in the 1st Marine Division fires and information operations section.

LTC Timothy W. Bush, USA, is the executive officer to the Commanding General, III Corps, at Fort Hood, Texas. He received a BS from Bowling Green State University and an MA from the University of Cincinnati. He has held various command and staff positions in the continental United States (CONUS), Iraq, Korea, and Panama.

Maj Ben Connable, USMC, is an Arabic-speaking Marine Corps intelligence officer and foreign area officer with three tours in Iraq. He has also served overseas tours in Saudi Arabia, Japan, and Egypt. Ben holds a BA in political science and MA degrees in national security affairs and strategic intelligence. Prior to assuming his current position as the U.S. Marine and naval attaché in Amman, Jordan, he was the program lead for the Marine Corps Cultural Intelligence Program in Quantico, Virginia.

COL William M. Darley, USA, is a public affairs officer and editor in chief of *Military Review*, a part of the Combined Arms Center in Fort Leavenworth, Kansas.

Jose L. Delgado is a career federal government employee who has spent the majority of his career as a military intelligence officer in various military and civilian assignments stateside and overseas. He is currently employed as a counterintelligence operations specialist for the U.S. Army at Fort George G. Meade, Maryland.

CAPT Timothy J. Doorey, USN, is a career Navy intelligence officer who has served twenty-six years in various tactical, theater, and national-level intelligence assignments. He is currently the senior intelligence officer at the Naval Postgraduate School in Monterey, California. From June 2002 to June 2005, he served as vice deputy director for Intelligence for Crisis Management on the Joint Staff and as deputy commander of the Iraq Intelligence Task Force from February to May 2003. During his career, Captain Doorey has supported U.S. and Coalition military operations in Beirut, Lebanon (1982–1984), Grenada (1983), El Salvador and Panama (1987–1989), and Iraq (1990–1994). From 1995 to 1998, he served as special assistant to NATO's Supreme Allied Commander Atlantic and Commander-in-Chief, U.S. Atlantic Command, in Norfolk, Virginia. He was the senior intelligence officer on the aircraft carrier USS *Carl Vinson* (CVN-70) from 1999 to 2001. He earned MA degrees in national security affairs and strategic studies from the Naval Postgraduate School in 1986 and the Naval War College in 2002. He also was a Navy Federal Executive Fellow at Harvard University's John M. Olin Institute for Strategic Studies from 1998 to 1999.

CPT James L. Doty III, USA, is an instructor in the Department of History at the U.S. Military Academy. He received a BS from the U.S. Military Academy and an MS from Ohio State University. He has served in various command and staff positions in CONUS, Germany, and Kosovo.

About the Editors and Contributors — 451

Tom Fenton has been a foreign correspondent for CBS News since 1970. Prior to that he had worked as a surface warfare officer in the U.S. Navy and then for the *Baltimore Sun*. In his career with CBS he has covered nearly every major European and Middle Eastern story of the day—from the 1967 Six Days' War to the wars in Afghanistan and Iraq. He has covered hundreds of international summits, natural disasters, riots, the civil war in Northern Ireland, famine in Africa, the *intifada* in Palestine, the assassination of Indira Gandhi, the death of Princess Diana, the end of Communism in the Soviet Union, the collapse of the Soviet empire, and now the new American crusade against terror. Fenton is the recipient of four Emmy awards, a Columbia University Alfred I. duPont Award, a Georgetown University Edward Weintal Prize for Diplomatic Reporting, and numerous Overseas Press Club awards for his reporting. A native of Baltimore, Maryland, Fenton earned a BA in English from Dartmouth College. He and his wife have two children, both of whom have followed him into the television news business. He is currently based in London, England.

MG David P. Fridovich, USA, is commander for the U.S. Special Operations Command, Pacific. He and Lt. Col. Fred Krawchuk, USA, wrote their piece for the *Joint Forces Quarterly*.

LtCol Roger S. Galbraith, USMCR, is the public affairs officer for the Marine Forces Command Individual Mobilization Augmentee Detachment. He is an engineer at a nuclear power station in his civilian life.

LTC Mark W. Garrett, USA, is the information operations chief, III Corps, at Fort Hood, Texas. He received a BS from Texas Tech University and an MS in information operations from the Naval Postgraduate School. Lieutenant Colonel Garrett has served in various command and staff positions in CONUS, Germany, the Balkans, and the Middle East.

Col Thomas X. Hammes, USMC (Ret.), over a span of thirty years, has served at all levels in the Marine Corps' operating forces, including command of a rifle company, weapons company, intelligence company, infantry battalion, and the Chemical/Biological Incident Response Force. He participated in stabilization operations in Somalia and Iraq as well as training insurgents in various places. He is currently reading for a PhD at Oxford University. He is the author of *The Sling and the Stone: On War in the Twenty-First Century* and has published more than eighty articles in the *Washington Post*, the *New York Times*, *Jane's Defence Weekly*, and professional journals.

LtCol Frank G. Hoffman, USMCR (Ret.), is a research fellow at the Marine Corps Center for Threats and Opportunities as well as a nonresident senior fellow at the Foreign Policy Research Institute. His career includes twenty-four years as a Marine infantry officer and several tours at the Pentagon. He has served on the staff of the Commission on Roles and Missions of the Armed Services and of the U.S. National Security Commission/21st Century. He also served on three defense science boards. He is a frequent contributor to professional military journals. His recent contributions include "Complex Irregular Warfare: The Next RMA" in the summer 2006 issue of *Orbis*. A graduate of the University of Pennsylvania, Mr. Hoffman holds graduate degrees from George Mason University and the Naval War College.

Duncan B. Hollis is an assistant professor of law at the Temple University Beasley School of Law and from 1998 to 2004 was attorney adviser, Office of the Legal Adviser, U.S. Department of State. He would like to thank Jeffrey Dunoff, Craig Green, David Hoffman, David Kaye, Jaya Ramji-Nogales, and Peter Spiro for valuable comments on earlier versions of his chapter, and George Deeney and Maria Murphy for invaluable research assistance.

Sgt Roger D. Huffstetler, Jr., USMC, is currently assigned as the operations chief, VMAQ-3, and is deployed to Al Asad, Iraq. He is a native of Newnan, Georgia.

LTC James E. Hutton, USA, is the public affairs officer, III Corps, at Fort Hood, Texas. He received a BS from Oklahoma State University and an MA from Webster University. He has served in various command and staff positions in CONUS, Germany, Bosnia, Kosovo, and Iraq.

Calvert W. Jones, of Maryland, earned her BA from Columbia University and graduate degrees from the University of California at Berkeley and Emmanuel College, University of Cambridge. She is now at Yale University.

Jeffrey B. Jones is a senior associate with Booz Allen Hamilton and was the director for Strategic Communications and Information on the National Security Council.

LTC David Kilcullen (Ret.), PhD, served twenty-one years in the Australian Army. He commanded an infantry company during counterinsurgency operations in East Timor, taught counterinsurgency tactics as an exchange instructor at the British School of Infantry, and served as a military adviser to Indonesian Special Forces. He has worked in several Middle Eastern countries with regular and irregular police and military forces since 9/11 and was a special adviser for irregular warfare during the 2005 U.S. Quadrennial Defense Review. He is currently seconded to the U.S. State Department as chief strategist in the Office of the Coordinator for Counterterrorism and remains a Reserve lieutenant colonel in the Australian Army. His doctoral dissertation is a study of Indonesian insurgent and terrorist groups and counterinsurgency methods.

LTC Fred T. Krawchuk, USA, is a staff officer with the U.S. Special Operations Command, Pacific.

William S. Lind, director of the Center for Cultural Conservatism at the Free Congress Foundation, Washington, D.C., is a native of Cleveland, Ohio. He graduated magna cum laude and Phi Beta Kappa from Dartmouth College in 1969 and received an MA in history from Princeton University in 1971. He worked as a legislative aide for armed services for Senator Robert Taft, Jr., of Ohio from 1973 to 1976 and held a similar position with Senator Gary Hart of Colorado, from 1977 to 1986. He joined the Free Congress Foundation in 1987. Mr. Lind is the author of the *Maneuver Warfare Handbook*; coauthor, with Gary Hart, of *America Can Win: The Case for Military Reform*; and coauthor, with William H. Marshner, of *Cultural Conservatism: Toward a New National Agenda*. Mr. Lind coauthored the prescient article "The Changing Face of War: Into the Fourth Generation," which was published in *The Marine Corps Gazette* in October 1989 and first propounded the concept of "Fourth Generation War."

Maj Morgan G. Mann, USMCR, was the company officer for Company F of the 2nd Battalion, 24th Marine Regiment, during the actions described in chapter 36.

Capt Zachary D. Martin, USMCR, is serving with the 3rd Light Armored Reconnaissance Battalion currently deployed to Iraq. Chapter 40 was his 2004 Chase Prize Essay Contest entry.

Maj Jennifer Morris Mayne, USMCR, was commissioned as a communications officer (0602) in 1997. She worked as a data platoon commander, a radio platoon commander, and the assistant communications officer for the 31st Marine Expeditionary Unit (Special Operations Capable). After completing the Expeditionary Warfare School, she was assigned to the Navy's Fleet Information Warfare Center, now called the Navy Information Operations Command. While there, she worked for the Navy's Red Team protecting Navy networks from cyber attack. Major Mayne later attained the additional MOS 9934 as an information operations (IO) planner. She participated as an IO planner in a number of large exercises with II Marine Expeditionary Force (MEF), XVIII Airborne Corps, and with the Second Fleet. She deployed with I MEF as an IO planner for Operation Iraqi Freedom from September 2004 until March 2005. In the summer of 2005, she resigned from active duty and worked as an information operations analyst for the 1st Information Operations Command at Fort Belvoir, Virginia.

LtCol James McNeive, USMC (Ret.), served twenty-four years in the Marine Corps from 1980 to 2004. During his last five years he served in the II Marine Expeditionary Force, G-3, where he had an additional duty as the II MEF information operations officer. During Operation Iraqi Freedom I, he served as the 2nd MEB/TF Tarawa IO officer. After retirement he went to work as a defense contractor for the U.S. Army 1st Information Operations Command. There he has worked as a lead planner for its Iraqi Reach Back Team. In this capacity he has worked with and supported Army and Marine officers working in support of information operations in Iraq.

LTG Thomas F. Metz, USA, is the deputy commanding general, Training and Doctrine Command. He commanded III Corps from February 2003 to May 2006, including thirteen months in Operation Iraqi Freedom. From January to May 2004, he served as the deputy commanding general, Coalition Joint Task Force-7, and from May 2004 to February 2005 commanded the Multinational Corps-Iraq. He has commanded at every echelon, from company to corps, in CONUS and multiple theaters overseas.

LTC John A. Nagl, USA, commands the 1st Battalion, 34th Armor, at Fort Riley, Kansas. He led a tank platoon in Operation Desert Storm, taught national security studies at West Point's Department of Social Sciences, and was the operations officer of Task Force 1-34 Armor in Khalidiyah, Iraq, from September 2003 through September 2004. Nagl served as a military assistant to Deputy Secretaries of Defense Paul Wolfowitz and Gordon England. He is a West Point graduate who holds an MMAS from the U.S. Army Command and General Staff College and the MPhil and DPhil in international relations from Oxford University. Nagl is the author of *Learning to Eat Soup with a Knife: Counterinsurgency Lessons from Malaya and Vietnam* and was on the writing team that produced Field Manual 3-24 *Counterinsurgency* in 2006.

CPT Kyle Norton, USA, is a military intelligence officer and a 2002 graduate of the U.S. Military Academy. Captain Norton has served two tours in Iraq. As a platoon leader in the 1st Cavalry Division, he wrote weekly atmospheric reports for the division's commanding general concerning Baghdad citizens' views on key topics as well as their opinions on daily events. Most recently, Captain Norton served as an embedded adviser to 2nd Battalion, 2nd Brigade, 8th Iraqi Army Division, where he regularly interacted with Iraqi Soldiers and citizens in a multitude of roles. He is a two-time recipient of the Bronze Star Medal.

Maj Clint Nussberger, USMC, enlisted in the Marine Corps in 1986, was commissioned upon graduation from the University of Wisconsin–Madison in 1993, and has served as a signals intelligence officer, a platoon commander, company executive officer, and battalion adjutant, on the Defense Language Institute staff. Major Nussberger has served with the 24th Marine Expeditionary Unit during deployments to Kosovo for Operation Dynamic Response, the Horn of Africa for

Operation Enduring Freedom, and Iraq for Operation Iraqi Freedom I and Operation Iraqi Freedom II. Major Nussberger holds an MS in international relations from Troy University and is a graduate of the Marine Amphibious Warfare School and the Marine Air-Ground Task Force Intelligence Officer Course. He served as a faculty adviser at the USMC Expeditionary Warfare School in Quantico, Virginia, and retired from the armed forces in 2008.

Col Keith Oliver, USMC (Ret.), served in mostly public affairs billets during a twenty-eight-year career that included deployments to Lebanon, Panama, Somalia, and both Gulf Wars. He retired from the Marines in 2004 and chairs the Public Affairs Leadership Department at Defense Information School, Fort George G. Meade, Maryland. His academic credentials include an MA in communications from Oklahoma University and an MS in national resource strategy with a concentration in information strategies from the Industrial College of the Armed Forces. He is national president of the U.S. Marine Corps Combat Correspondents Association.

Dr. Pauletta Otis is a professor of strategic studies at the Marine Corps University and teaches at the Marine Corps Command and Staff College and the Marine Corps War College in Quantico, Virginia.

Gen Carlos Alberto Ospina Ovalle was chief of the Colombian Armed Forces until 2006 and was coming to the end of his term of service at the time of this writing.

Ambassador David Passage is a thirty-three-year veteran of the State Department. He served with CORDS in Vietnam, was deputy chief of mission and chargé d'affaires in El Salvador at the height of that country's civil war in the 1980s, helped negotiate the removal of Soviet and Cuban forces from Angola at the end of the 1980s, and ended his career as coordinator of the policy shift in the late 1990s that allowed the United States to help Colombia combat its internal insurgencies and narcotics trafficking.

GEN David H. Petraeus, USA, wrote this piece just after taking command of the Combined Arms Center and Fort Leavenworth, Kansas, in October 2005. He also served as the commandant of the U.S. Army Command and General Staff College and as deputy commander for the Combined Arms of the U.S. Army Training and Doctrine Command. General Petraeus commanded the 101st Airborne Division (Air Assault) in Iraq during the first year of Operation Iraqi Freedom, returning to the United States with the division in mid-February 2004. He returned to Iraq for several weeks in April and May 2004 to assess the Iraqi Security Forces, and he subsequently returned in early June 2004 to serve as the first commander of the Multinational Security Transition Command-Iraq, the position he held until September 2005. In late 2004, he also became the first commander of the NATO Training Mission-Iraq. Prior to his tour with the 101st, he served for a year as the assistant chief of staff for operations of the NATO Stabilization Force in Bosnia. A graduate of the U.S. Military Academy, General Petraeus earned MPA and PhD degrees from the Woodrow Wilson School of Public and International Affairs at Princeton University. General Petraeus served as commanding general, Multinational Forces-Iraq from 2007 to 2008 and is currently the commanding general of U.S. Central Command.

Maj E. Lawson Quinn, USMC, served as the intelligence trainer for the Marine transition team assigned to the 2nd Battalion, 7th Brigade, 2nd Division, Iraqi National Police in Baghdad from December 2005 through November 2006. In 2004 he served in the civil affairs and information operations section of the 1st Marine Division in Ar-Ramadi, Iraq. He is currently serving as the operations officer, G-2, in the I Marine Expeditionary Force "Forward" preparing for deployment to Al Anbar Province, Iraq.

LTC Charles W. Ricks, USA (Ret.), recently served as a contract public affairs systems developer, mentor, and trainer with the Office of Security Cooperation in Afghanistan. He received a BA from the University of Wisconsin–Madison and an MA from the University of Kentucky, and is a graduate of the U.S. Army Command and General Staff College and the Army Advanced Public Affairs Course. He has served in various command and staff positions in CONUS, Belgium, Germany, Korea, and Afghanistan.

CDR J. D. Scanlon, Canadian Armed Forces, has practiced military public affairs for eighteen years. He is an honors graduate of the U.S. Defense Information School and has studied journalism at the graduate and postgraduate levels. Commander Scanlon has served in military public affairs at all levels of command in Canada, and he has worked with NATO as a spokesperson in Bosnia (1999) and as the alliance's head of public affairs education and training at the time he wrote this essay.

Cpl Tom Sloan, USMC, is a Marine combat correspondent who patrolled with elements of 1st Battalion, 5th Marines in Ar Ramadi.

LTC George J. Stroumpos, USA, served as an intelligence officer for the Multinational Forces-Iraq, Coalition Intelligence Operations Center from February 2005 through February 2006 in Baghdad, Iraq. During his tour he acted as the Sunni nationalist insurgent team chief, extensively studying Ba'athist insurgent operations, organizational structures, and group dynamics. He also served as a member of the MNF-I Counterinsurgency Survey Team (conducted in late 2005), assessing Coalition unit capabilities and documenting counterinsurgency best practices throughout theater. Currently, Lieutenant Colonel Stroumpos serves as an operational environment analyst for the Threats Division, TRADOC Intelligence Support Activity, Fort Leavenworth, Kansas.

Dr. Philip M. Taylor is a professor of international communications at the University of Leeds in Britain. In 2006 he was also distinguished visiting professor in the new Centre for Media and Information Warfare Studies at UiTM, Shah Alam, Malaysia. He is also a fellow of the Royal Historical Society (UK) and of the Center for Public Diplomacy at the University of Southern California. He has written more than ten books, including *Munitions of the Mind: A History of Propaganda from the Ancient World to the Present Era*, and nearly a hundred scholarly journal articles and book chapters. He lectures all over the world, especially to military educational establishments, including the Defence Intelligence and Security School and the Joint Services Command Staff College in the United Kingdom, the Supreme Headquarters Allied Powers Europe (SHAPE) in Belgium, the Swedish National Defence College, the Department of National Defence in Canada, and the U.S. Army War College.

CPT Stoney Trent, USA, is an instructor in the Department of Behavioral Sciences and Leadership at the U.S. Military Academy. He received a BS from the University of Notre Dame and an MS from Ohio State University. He has served in various command and staff positions in CONUS, Germany, Kosovo, and Iraq.

Col John A. Wahlquist, USAF (Ret.), is a faculty member at the National Defense Intelligence College and a member of the Government Experts Committee for the Intelligence Science Board Study on Educing Information. As a member of the Iraq Survey Group in Baghdad (2004–2005), he headed Team Huwaysh, consisting of interrogator-debriefers and international WMD experts dedicated to debriefing Iraqi detainee 'Abd-al-Tawab Al Mullah Huwaysh, Saddam Hussein's former fourth-ranking deputy prime minister and minister of military industrialization. Drawing on the results of those debriefings, he was a primary contributor to the Comprehensive Report of the Special Adviser to the DCI on Iraq's WMD that was published in 2005. Previously, Colonel Wahlquist served as defense attaché to Oman and deputy director of intelligence at U.S. Central Command.

Col Eric Walters, USMC, is a Marine Corps intelligence officer with service at the strategic, operational, and tactical level with experience in the Middle East, Latin America, and extensive tours in Asia. He is a staff blogger for the *Small Wars Journal* website and taught military intelligence, military history, and military science for American Military University in 2000–2002. His writings on tactics, command and control, war-gaming, and military history have been published in military professional and commercial publications.

Col Philip G. Wasielewski, USMCR, is a Foreign Service Officer currently serving as a political officer at the U.S. embassy in Ashgabat, Turkmenistan.

Francis "Bing" West is a former Marine and former Assistant Secretary of Defense. Mr. West has spent over fourteen months in Iraq, accompanying more than thirty U.S. and Iraqi battalions. He is the author of several books on Iraq and insurgencies.

LtCol James P. West, USMC, is serving at the Joint Information Operation Warfare Command in the Joint Electronic Warfare Center. He is also head of the Intelligence Plans & Policy/TENCAP Branch, Headquarters, U.S. Marine Corps. He enlisted in the Marine Corps in 1985 and was assigned as a cryptologic equipment technician. Sergeant West was then selected for the Marine Enlisted Commissioning Education Program in 1988 and was commissioned in 1990 after graduating from Rice University. He has commanded platoons and companies of Marines, made numerous deployments with the Marine Corps, and served with the National Security Agency. He is a graduate of the Amphibious Warfare School, holds an MA in military studies from the Marine Corps Command and Staff College, and has recently served in Operation Iraqi Freedom as the intelligence plans officer.